D1823901

"This manuscript is written in accordance with the changing times and environment for the conduct of business operations. The authors have presented the purpose of business to include both economic and social contributions of the business firm to society. Business is explained as a 'provider of goods, services, and benefits for people.' It may be the first 'Introduction to Business' text that is oriented around the social values as well as the economic rewards to a modern society."

JOHN F. MEE
Indiana University

UNDERSTANDING BUSINESS TODAY

Elwood S. Buffa, Ph.D.

Professor of Management
University of California, Los Angeles

Barbara A. Pletcher, D.B.A.

President
Creative Sales Careers, Incorporated

1980
RICHARD D. IRWIN, INC. Homewood, Illinois 60430
Irwin-Dorsey Limited Georgetown, Ontario L7G 4B3

ISBN 0-256-02257-7

Library of Congress Catalog Card No. 79–88779

Printed in the United States of America

1 2 3 4 5 6 7 8 9 0 K 7 6 5 4 3 2 1 0

PREFACE

Understanding Business Today has been written with one purpose in mind—to present in the most understandable and up-to-date manner the realities of our fascinating business and economic environment to students in the introduction to business course. Our basic philosophy is that business makes sense. There is an underlying logic. By revealing that logic rather than simply describing the surface activities, we can provide students with a meaningful and lasting understanding that will serve them as they move into their careers, continue their roles as consumers, and exercise their duties as citizens. This understanding will help them to work within the corporate structure or to function more effectively in the environment of small business.

If the business system is logical, then there must be a framework that will enhance the meaning and assure the most complete coverage of the material. We feel that we have that framework. The 20 chapters in this text are organized into seven parts, each of which answers one of the seven basic questions:

> *What* is the mission of any organization? As a part of the economic system, the individual firm is presented as the provider of goods and services to meet society's needs. This section deals with the objectives of the individual firm and how its mission is affected by the industry structure and degrees of competition. It discusses the needs of society and how well those needs are being satisfied. This involves both economic measures such as Gross National Product (GNP) and inflation, and social measures such as quality of life, health and safety, meaningful jobs, full participation of minorities and women, clean air and water, and the social responsibilities of both business and citizens.

Why do people participate and what benefits do they expect? There are both risks and opportunities in business. This section presents the idea of profit and discusses the various forms of business organization from sole proprietorships through corporations. Emphasis is on the rewards to all of the participants. Franchising, an increasingly important business arrangement, is covered in detail. Finally, accounting is introduced as the method for keeping score in business.

When do actions occur? How does the business community forecast and plan? As the pace of economic, social, and technological change quickens, so does the human and economic cost of error. Since timing is so important to business success, forecasting and planning are becoming much more important for both large and small firms.

Who are the targets of these actions? Which market is business trying to satisfy? Each firm strives to satisfy some group of customers. These may be consumers, other firms, government buyers, or multinational customers. The firm must find a group of potential customers which not only has unsatisfied needs, but has both the willingness and the ability to purchase goods and services which fulfill those needs.

With what support are these actions undertaken? The main activities of every firm are dependent on a number of support functions. Among these are the financial management, personnel management, and information management. Without these functional supports, the main activities would soon be halted.

How is value created? How are worthwhile goods and services actually produced? There is more to the productive process than driving nails or pouring molten steel. Production of either goods or services requires careful selection of location and design of facilities. Then the right raw materials must be ordered in the right quantities with delivery scheduled for the right time. Machinery and people must be assigned according to a well planned production schedule and then the entire process must be monitored and controlled so that any problems can be corrected rapidly.

Within what environments does the business system function? How do the actions of government and the history of our business and social systems impact on the present and future actions of the business firm? Business does not exist in a vacuum. Many of today's business practices are an outgrowth of business history. By examining the patterns of business and government regulation, support, and taxation, we are more able to gain insights to the future of the economic system.

A second guiding philosophy is that as instructors we can provide the learning materials and experiences, but we cannot force students to absorb any of it against their will. Therefore we have worked very hard to develop a text that is both substantive and interesting to read. We have included a wide range of real-life examples to highlight business concepts. We have presented special features such as the "Did You Ever Wonder" series, which provides surprising answers to questions which have bewildered many business students. And to be very practical about the intentions of most students, we have prepared a career guide to help students make use of the many resources available to them as they begin to make career plans.

Acknowledgments

No single person can be an expert in all of the areas of business. While as authors we have combined our divergent backgrounds to develop a balanced treatment of the material, we have also called upon a number of experts in specific fields to assure that the material is accurate and reflects the most current thinking in each field. The following persons reviewed the material related to their specific areas of expertise. We appreciate their contributions.

Campbell R. McConnell, University of Nebraska
Chapter 2—Economics

Gilbert A. Churchill, Jr., University of Wisconsin-Madison
Chapters 6, 7, and 10—Marketing

William W. Pyle
Chapter 6—Accounting

Ralph M. Stair, Jr., Florida State University
Chapter 15—Data Processing

John F. Mee, Indiana University
Management section

A. James Barnes, Beveridge, Fairbanks & Diamond
Chapter 19—Legal Environment

Herbert J. Chruden, California State University-Sacramento
Chapter 13—Personnel Management

We are indebted to the many well grounded and clear-thinking colleagues who have reviewed our total manuscript and added their helpful comments. These complete reviews have assisted us in developing a text that is both thorough and consistent. These reviewers are Kathryn W. Hegar, Mountain View College; Gary W. Falkenberg, Oakland Community College; Clair W. Fisher, Des Moines Area Community College; Paul James Londrigan, Charles Stewart Mott Community College; and John F. Mee, Indiana University.

December 1979   **Elwood S. Buffa**
                                                                        Barbara A. Pletcher

CONTENTS

INTRODUCTION:
WHY SHOULD YOU
STUDY BUSINESS?

There are a lot of reasons to study business. The first is because you are going to participate in the business system; you cannot avoid it. Business is the provider of our standard of living, so you must interact with the business system to survive. If you understand the system, you will be better off within it.

Second, there is a good chance that you will earn your living within the business system. Most people work for a business firm or even start their own businesses. Even if you don't go to work for a business firm, the organization for which you work will interact with the business system. Schools buy paper, computers, and new buildings from business firms. Churches buy flowers, printing, and landscape services. The government is the business system's biggest customer. You might even find an understanding of business practices to be useful in other ways. Churches, scout troops, professional and social organizations, government agencies, and other social and nonprofit groups are constantly faced with needs for business guidance in their activities.

Third, it is interesting. The business system involves human emotions, discovery, intrigue, risk, espionage, and all the thrills and spills you can imagine. In fact, most of the great events in history have had some tie-in to business. Queen Isabella financed the voyages of Columbus with a business objective in mind. She hoped that he would find new trade routes to India. Today we wouldn't even have national sports events such as the Indianapolis 500 or the Super Bowl without business backing. Business is an integral part of our society.

WHAT DO WE HOPE TO ACCOMPLISH?

We hope to help you to understand not only what business is like but also why it is that way. We have written this text with three purposes in mind. First, we hope to explain the business system so clearly that you will be better able to interact with that system to meet your needs and responsibilities as a consumer, an employee, and a citizen.

Second, at the end of the text you will find a special appendix with information on finding careers in business. This is included to give you a start on your investigation of the career choices in your future. And third, of course, we hope to make this subject extremely interesting.

One of the outstanding features of a system based on profits is that it adapts to meet a changing environment. We know that our environment is changing. Profits serve as a reward for those firms that are able to adapt quickly to meet changes in human needs or resource availability. On the other side, losses are a natural way of eliminating those firms whose goods or services are no longer needed. The business systems are always changing. While this text includes the most up-to-date information as of the moment it was written, the environment will continue to change. We hope to help you to understand the logic of the system so that you will be prepared to understand those changes.

AND HOW?

Just as a journalist follows a plan to make sure that all of the relevant elements are included in a news story, we have followed a plan to make sure that all of the major facets of business are covered in this text. The text is organized in seven sections, each dealing with an important issue:

WHAT?—WHAT is the purpose of the business system. What is the mission of an individual firm?

WHY?—WHY do people get involved in business? Why does an individual firm prosper? What kind of rewards does it expect?

WHEN?—Timing is very important. How does business attempt to forecast the future. To meet your needs, business must plan to be ready WHEN those needs arise.

WHO?—WHO is business trying to satisfy? Who are the customers and how do they behave?

WITH?—Business has many resources to work WITH while striving to meet your needs. How do marketing, finance, management, and information fit together and contribute to the firm's efforts?

HOW?—HOW does the productive system work? How are these systems designed, supplied, operated, and controlled?

WITHIN?—Business does not exist in a vacuum. How do the government and the social system provide opportunities and impose constraints on the business system?

These seven areas—What, why, when, who, with, how, and within—provide the framework for this introduction to the American business system. To give you the opportunity to add to your understanding of the ideas in this text, Kathryn Hegar has written a *Student Study Guide.* Not only will you find the guide useful in reviewing concepts and terms, it shows you all of the practical steps in starting a new business, investing in business, and using business concepts in your daily life.

part I

WHAT:

The mission of the organization

The business system and every large and small firm within that system exist for a purpose. Each firm has a mission. If the firm is efficient in accomplishing that mission, its owners are rewarded with profits. Inefficiency eventually will lead to its failure.

There are many different kinds of firms. There are manufacturing and distribution firms. Some firms specialize in physical products, while others offer services. But all firms must satisfy the needs of some group of customers. In Chapter 1 we take an overall look at the efforts of the business community to provide for the needs of the members of our society. How does our system differ from alternate economic systems? How do the parts of the system fit together?

In Chapter 2 we examine the factors of the business systems more closely, asking how the economic system controls the flow of society's resources. Here we introduce some standards by which firms, industries, and economies are measured.

We all know that there are standards other than the amount of goods and services produced. Many other factors enter into our evaluation of the quality of life. The focus of Chapter 3 is the social responsibility of business. How well is the business community meeting the challenges of converting our resources into satisfying goods and services without spoiling the environment or subjecting workers to health and safety hazards? Is it providing rewarding opportunities to all citizens?

chapter
1

SOCIETY'S NEEDS: BUSINESS AS A PROVIDER

By studying this chapter you should be able to find answers to these questions:

1 What is business?
2 What are your options for meeting your needs and wants?
3 What are the elements of utility?
4 What is the private enterprise system and what are the alternatives?
5 What is a system and how does that term apply to business?
6 Who really controls the system?

Terms you should know:

business	place utility
capital	possession utility
capitalist	production
communal system	socialism
division of labor	specialization
exchange	system
form utility	time utility
market mechanism	utility
need	want

Were you one of the people who waited in long lines for the chance to see the King Tut treasures? Some people think he had the ultimate lifestyle. But while the ancient Egyptian system enabled King Tut to live in splendor, his subjects were not so fortunate. Every society has to set up some system to meet the needs of all its members, and some systems work better than others.

You have needs. You want things. Our society is made up of a lot of people who have needs and wants just like you. How are these needs and wants satisfied? Most of them are satisfied through the business system. Business firms exist to satisfy the needs and wants of the society. Our business system developed into its current form and persists because it provides for those needs more efficiently than any other system we can imagine. It may not be perfect, but it is better than the alternatives.

As a group, we possess a wealth of resources. Imagine a huge pile of resources including raw materials, human energy, brain power, and money. First we must decide how to convert those resources into products and services that will best satisfy the needs of the members of our society. Then we must find some way to distribute those satisfactions fairly and efficiently.

This is a complex task. Society's needs are complex and hard to define and evaluate. We know that we are striving toward an improved standard of living—toward a higher quality of life. But what does that mean? Is it a longer life, more possessions, more fun, inner peace, better health, or what? If you can't have everything, which things are more important?

It is hard enough to make those decisions for yourself, but would you like to be responsible for the decisions for everyone else—for about 220 million people? Who is to decide? Is it more important to have sports events or improved medical care? Should we make people eat nutritious foods whether they want them or not? Who should pay for the arts? Is there one best style or color of clothing? If we had unlimited resources, there would be no problem; we would simply choose to have everything. But your resources and society's total resources are limited. How should these resources be used?

In the United States we try to let people make these decisions for themselves insofar as it is practical within the society. Then, spurred by the lure of profits, the firms within the business system compete to supply the choices you and the other people like you have made on how to satisfy your needs and wants.

For the record, there is a difference between needs and wants. A **need** is something that is necessary—something you can't get along without. Each day you need food, water, and shelter. Over the long run, you also have emotional needs such as the needs for human interac-

DID YOU EVER WONDER?
THE BEST MARKETS . . . AND THE WORST

It's no secret that air conditioners and snow shovels sell better in some cities than others. The same is also true of just about every kind of product, from popcorn to deodorants. Below are the most and least promising markets for a number of consumer products, based on a survey of 20 key cities.

	The best	*The worst*
Beer and ale (% of drinkers who consume)	Milwaukee (67.9)	Dallas/Fort Worth (44.2)
Bicycles (% adults who ever bought)	Minneapolis/ St. Paul (30)	Atlanta (18.5)
Briefcases (% adults who ever bought)	Los Angeles (12.9)	Cincinnati (6.2)
Canned chili (% of homemakers who use)	Dallas/Fort Worth (72.7)	Boston (6)
Deodorants and antiperspirants (% adults who use once a day)	Baltimore (88.1)	Minneapolis/ St. Paul (78.3)
Foreign travel (% adults who traveled in past three years)	Seattle/Tacoma (38)	Cincinnati (10.8)
Fur coats (% adults who ever bought)	Detroit (11)	Cincinnati (6.4)
Insecticides (% of homemakers who use at least once a month)	Houston (61.9)	New York (26.4)
Life insurance (% adults who currently have)	Pittsburgh (80.3)	Miami (53.4)
Lipstick (% of women using at least twice a day)	Seattle/Tacoma (58.2)	Cincinnati (35.6)
Men's neckties (% men who bought one within 12 months)	Cleveland (18)	Pittsburgh (10.2)
Motor oil (% adults who buy)	Dallas/Fort Worth (64.8)	New York (40.8)
Panty hose (% women who bought in past month)	Houston (61.1)	Miami (39.7)
Paperback books (% adults who bought in last 30 days)	Seattle/Tacoma (53.2)	Dallas/Fort Worth (31.3)
Popcorn (% adults who buy for home use)	Minneapolis/ St. Paul (54.3)	Miami (26.5)
Restaurants (% adults who visited in past month)	Seattle/Tacoma (72.6)	Washington, D.C. (54.9)
Scotch whisky (% of drinkers who consume)	New York (35.9)	Cincinnati (9.6)
Shotguns (% adults who ever bought)	Minneapolis/ St. Paul (12)	New York (3.1)
Tennis racquets (% adults who ever bought)	Los Angeles (17.5)	Cincinnati (9.8)

Source: From Niles Howard, "More Bang for the Ad Dollar." Reprinted with the special permission of *Dun's Review*, November 1978, Copyright 1978, Dun & Bradstreet Publication Corporation; data from Major Market Index 1977.

tion and achievement. A **want** is something you would like but can survive without. A want is not as critical as a need, but at times it may seem more important. Throughout this text we will tend to use the term *needs* to refer to both needs and wants.

WHAT IS BUSINESS?

You are certainly familiar with business already because it is all around you everyday. But a more formal definition is a good way to begin our investigation of the subject. **Business** is the human activity of converting resources into goods and services for the purpose of bringing about transactions that will result in a profit to the organization.

This definition involves four elements. First, it involves **human activities.** Business firms do not manage themselves, nor are they managed for themselves. Firms own land, machinery, and buildings, but all of these are managed or operated by people.

Second, it involves production. **Production** is the conversion of one set of resources into another set of resources with greater value. This may be the conversion of steel, glass, and synthetic fibers into an automobile, or the effect of some human energy and 11 herbs and spices on a bucket of chicken. The dentist who fills your tooth is involved in producing a service. Production is any activity that turns one set of resources into something more desirable.

Third, business involves exchange. **Exchange** is trading one item or service for something of value. Business firms produce items of value not for their own use, but in order to exchange them. This may be an exchange of goods or services for money, or for other goods and services.

And, finally, it involves **profits.** Business activity is undertaken to increase the financial and material welfare of the participants—to make

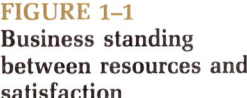

FIGURE 1–1
Business standing between resources and satisfaction

money. Profits are the rewards for doing the job right. Business includes those activities of a society that are directed toward achieving a profitable return on production and exchange.

No one designed or created the business system; it just grew up to meet the needs of people. It developed to bridge the gap between the people's needs and their self-sufficiencies—their ability to meet their own needs (see Figure 1–1). Why? Because that's where the profits are. People are willing to pay to improve their quality of life.

SELF-SUFFICIENCY VERSUS INTERDEPENDENCE

You are capable of taking care of some of your own needs. If you were stranded on an island in the Robinson Crusoe style, you would be able to take care of your basic food and shelter needs. But there are limits. There are some goods and services that are very important to your preferred lifestyle that you cannot provide for yourself, or at least you cannot provide them as easily as you can buy them. You could make your own shoes and furniture—but how well? And what other activities would you have to give up to do so?

What are your options?

What are your options in meeting your needs? The first, most basic, and most dreaded option is to do without. Let's move on from that quickly! The second choice is to be self-sufficient. You could seek to take care of yourself—to meet your own needs with your own skills, efforts, and resources. How far does that go?

In the last few years we have seen a return-to-nature trend in the United States. There is a great deal of satisfaction to be gained from meeting your own needs, but for most of us, it is not easy. Most people choose to meet those needs that they can meet most easily or from which they derive the most satisfaction. They turn to another option for the tricky and difficult needs. The return-to-nature movement has spawned entire industries to supply the materials people need to "rough it."

Your third option is to share a task with someone else. The old-fashioned barn-raising was handled this way. A person called on the neighbors to lend a hand and returned the favor at a later date. Of course, you can be sure that there were some people who were willing to be helped but never available to return the favor.

Today we have babysitting co-ops, community gardens, and other sharing ventures. When the group is small, it is easy to see that everyone is sharing the responsibility. But as the group gets larger, two things happen. First, someone must start to keep score. It becomes necessary to define each person's fair share and then to set up some way to make sure that it is delivered. Second, it leads to the division of labor and specialization.

Division of labor means breaking up the overall job into a number of defined tasks. **Specialization** involves limiting a worker to a single task or a related set of tasks so that the worker will become more skilled at that task. This leads to a state of interdependency. Each of the specialists needs all of the others to finish the job. Sharing can work well in limited areas, but as our needs become more complex, it can be very complicated. So, for most of our needs, we turn to the fourth option.

The fourth option is contracting out. You pay others to perform tasks that you do not like to do or are not able to do as well for yourself. You have, or are preparing to have, a specialty—something you can do better than you can do other things. Some people are dentists, some are carpenters, some drive trucks, some sell, some are data processors, and others are accountants.

Since it is very difficult for the accountant and the truck driver to make a direct exchange of their specialized contributions, they use money to keep score. The truck driver can even buy the services of the dentist, who in turn buys the services of the accountant. You can take the money you receive for your labors and spend it in the market-place to meet your needs as you see them. The business system is society's way of organizing interdependent human beings.

Business deserves neither the big-bad-wolf image, in which it is often portrayed, or the title of servant of the society. Business meets society's needs due to a profit motive. Profits can result only from the efficient use of resources to meet the needs of the members of the society. Business must respond to the needs of the people.

Utility

Business sells utility. **Utility** is the need-satisfying capacity of any physical thing, idea, or service. You know that some things have more utility than others. There are four different factors that combine to make up utility: form, time, place, and possession.

Form utility.   You want the right size or style of shoe, a plane ride to the correct city, or a steak as opposed to a steer. **Form utility** exists when the item has the proper characteristics to meet your needs. It is the right size, shape, color, and available in the right quantity. Services must also have form utility; that is, they must be right for the need. If you need an appendectomy, you won't be satisfied with a hearing test.

Time utility.   As you might expect, **time utility** means that the item is available when you need it. The reason why Halloween candy sells for half price on November 1 is not that it has lost its form utility—

the group agree, there can be problems. Can you imagine writing out the combined shopping list for the entire population of the United States for a year? For five years? Now think about the problems in coordinating the schedules and resources to meet those needs. What if you finally got everything settled and then discovered that you had forgotten some small but important need, such as shoelaces?

Everyone is supposed to share in the output according to need. The Communist motto is: "From each according to his ability, to each according to his need." That would work out well as long as there was enough output to satisfy everyone's needs. The tough questions arise when someone has to do without. Who should it be?

There is no perfect communism. The Russians and the Chinese practice government-controlled versions. Each year the Soviets update their five-year plan which specifies what is to be produced, with what resources, and by whom. While time will decide on the merits of each economic system, at the moment the standard of living of the average Russian or Communist Chinese citizen is far below that of the average American.

Socialism

Under **socialism,** the government owns and controls the major industries and resources, whereas smaller businesses are left to private ownership. The government decides how the critical resources are used in the primary industries. In Great Britain the government controls the coal industry, railroads, and health care and allocates resources within those industries.

The idea behind socialism is that basic human services should be available to all citizens. Beyond that, consumers are free to make their economic decisions in the marketplace. In theory, this system could be very efficient. It all depends on how well the government operates the major industries.

Table 1–1 summarizes and compares the three economic systems according to who owns the resources and makes the economic decisions.

TABLE 1–1
The alternative systems

Systems	Ownership of resourses	Economic decisions
Private enterprise	Private individuals	Individuals within laws
Communism	Group	Group or leaders
Socialism	Government/private	Government

BUSINESS AS A SYSTEM

We are all part of and dependent on the business system. It may seem that *system* is one of the most overused words, but we use the term because it is so descriptive of the way the elements of business operate. We speak of the accounting system, the banking system, the management system, the distribution system, and so on. It would be hard to imagine a functioning society if the elements of these systems—the employees, customers, material suppliers, shippers, bankers, investors, and others—were not interdependent and bound together by an objective.

Inputs, transformations, and outputs

Systems have an objective. They exist to do something. Some systems are carefully planned and designed, whereas other systems evolve, that is, come into being naturally. But, all systems have some outputs. In business systems, the outputs are products and services to be sold. Each business system produces something—transportation, peanuts, financial services, you name it. Since you can't produce something from nothing, every system requires some inputs—raw materials, energy, labor, equipment, technology, and so on. Finally, in order to produce an output from the inputs, something has to happen in between. This is true whether the output is a physical product, a service, or even an idea. You have to process the inputs in some way to produce the outputs. You have to transform the inputs to achieve the objective. So, the **systems** concept might be visualized as the input/transformation/output modules in Figure 1–3.

FIGURE 1–3

Input/transformation/ output modules for (A) an electric furnace, (B) Chevrolet Division of General Motors, and (C) a law office

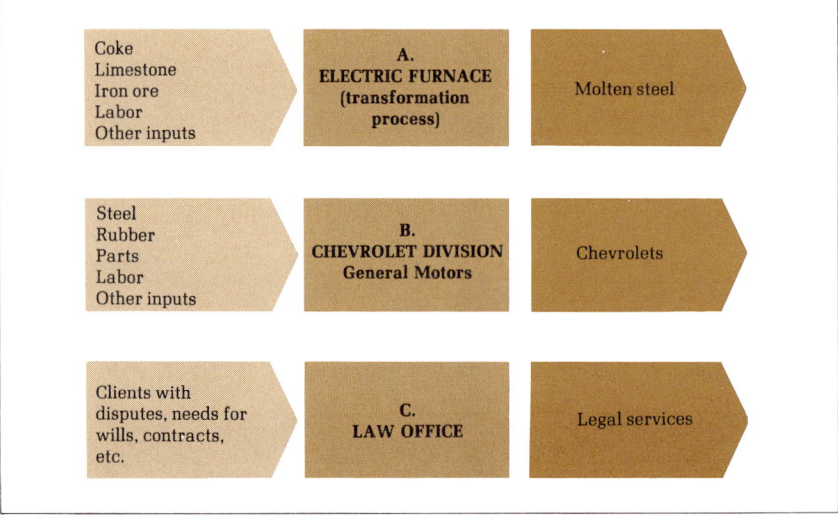

There are millions of kinds of transformation processes that follow this same form. Figure 1–3A shows the input/transformation/output modules of an electric furnace that produces molten steel. Figure 1–3B represents the Chevrolet Division of General Motors, which produces Chevys. Figure 1–3C shows the modules for a law office producing legal services. Since all business systems have these three basic modules, business analysts use this systems framework to design and analyze manufacturing plants, accounting departments, retail stores, and other organizations. The purpose is to understand the interrelationships among the elements of the system to see how they affect the output.

Interrelationships

The larger and more complex the system, the more interrelationships there will be. Nothing exists in isolation. Each system requires a variety of inputs and is affected by many external factors, institutions, and events. The price you pay for coffee in the supermarket is affected by the cost of labor, the availability of coffee substitutes, the state of the economy, the weather in Brazil, and other factors. The overall consumer price level may be affected by such things as shortages, the money supply, and government spending. It may seem that everything is affected by everything, but the value of systems analysis is that you can begin to make sense out of these interrelationships.

Suppose you wanted to make a little sense out of the energy use in your community. You would start with a list of the factors that seem to be interrelated. Let's work with energy use, the quality of the environment, and the size of the population. How do these affect each other? If energy use increases, the quality of the environment will decrease due to increased levels of smoke, auto exhaust, and resource depletion. The two factors move in opposite directions. But how would a change in the environmental quality affect the size of the population? If the environment improved, more people would choose to live in your community. If you diagram these relationships, you end up with Figure 1–4.

The arrows show how an increase in each factor affects the others. A plus sign means that an increase in one results in an increase in the other. A minus sign means that an increase in one results in a decrease in the other. You always ask what would happen if the first factor increased: Would the other increase or decrease?

But surely Figure 1–4 doesn't tell the whole story. There must be other factors involved. What about energy capacity and energy cost? You ask the same question. If energy capacity increased, what would happen to energy use? Wouldn't it tend to increase? If energy capacity increased, what do you suppose would happen to energy cost? We

FIGURE 1–4
Relationships of energy
use to quality of environment and population.
If population increases,
energy use increases; if
energy use increases,
quality of environment
decreases.

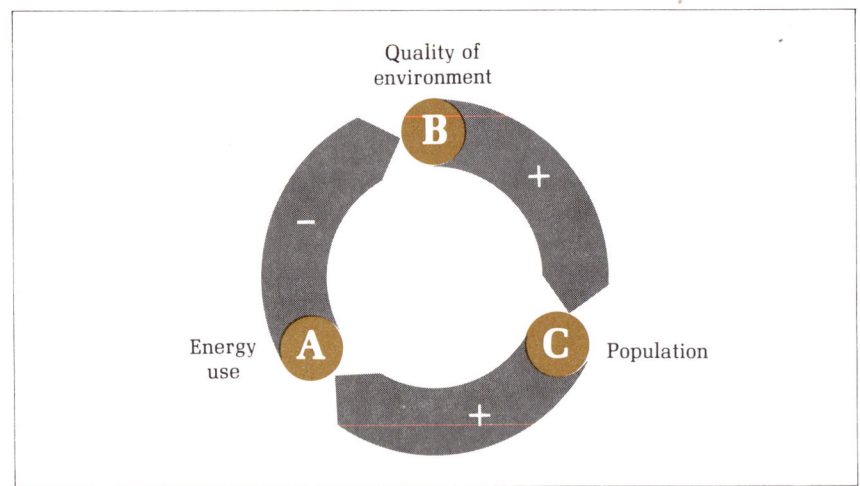

would expect that to decrease. There might be cost efficiencies or energy
price wars. Figure 1–5 shows these additional relationships.

If you put Figures 1–4 and 1–5 together into Figure 1–6, you have
the interrelationships among five factors. This could go on and on.
You could relate it to jobs, houses built, and others, but let's stop
here. You can see that the five factors are interrelated. In a way, you
can say that everything affects everything.

How do analysts use these relationships to predict things like future
energy needs? They start with diagrams like Figure 1–6 to sort out
the complex effects. While we have made casual assumptions about
the relationships, analysts attempt to test their assumptions. They then
insert whatever numbers they have to work with, such as population

FIGURE 1–5
Relationship of energy use
to energy capacity and
energy cost

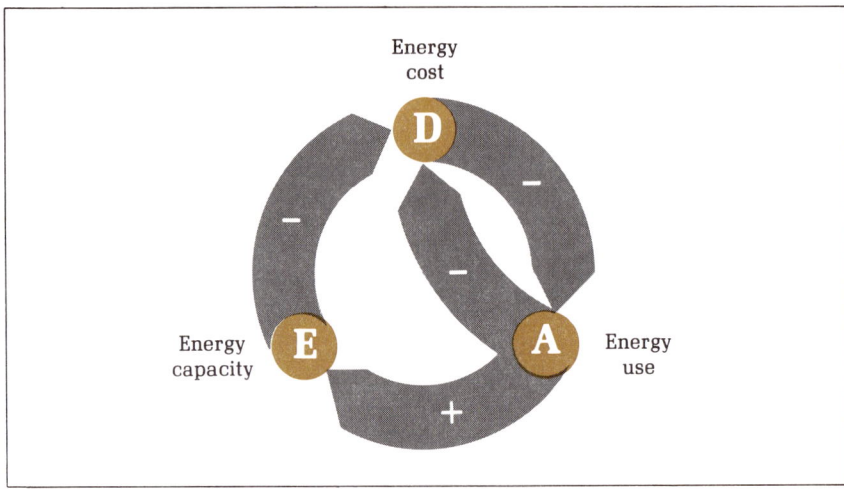

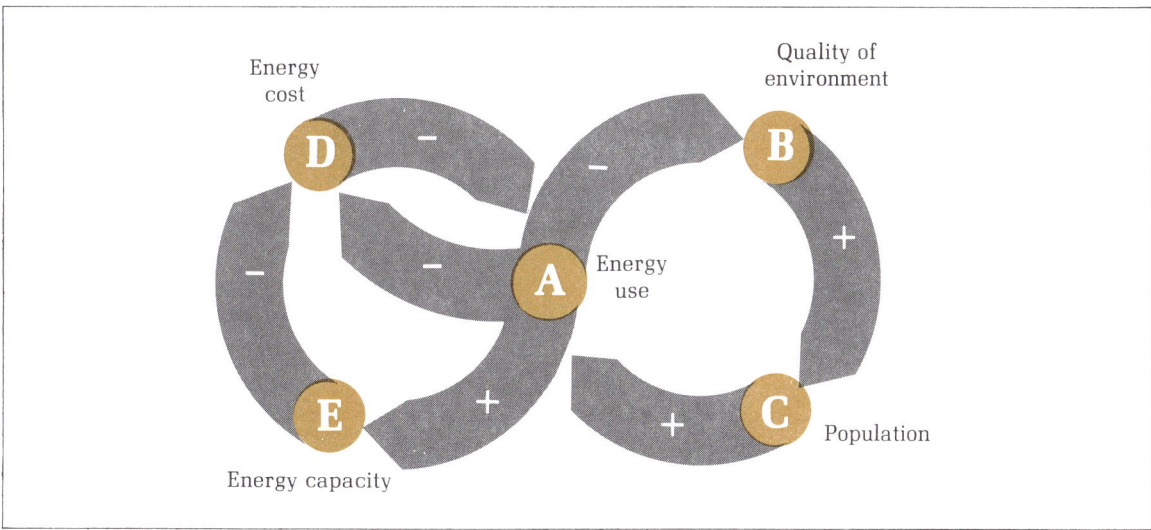

FIGURE 1–6
Combined relationship of
energy use to quality
of environment, popula-
tion, energy capacity,
and energy cost

growth rates and current energy usage. Eventually they arrive at their best predictions of future levels.

Systems within systems

Each system is complete in itself, yet most systems interact with other systems. For example, a bakery is a system. It transforms inputs such as flour and eggs into baked goods—the output. The individual bakery is a small system within the larger food industry system. Allegheny Airlines is a system that transforms planes, pilots, flight attendants, ground crews, and other inputs into air transportation. But Allegheny is only a small part of the overall transportation system, which involves not only other airlines but also taxis, highways, airports, travel agents, and other transportation-related systems.

Each of these systems makes up a unified whole, but each, in turn, is a part of a larger system. The output of a small system, like the bakery, forms an input to a larger system, such as the bakery industry. The output of the bakery industry forms an input to the still larger food products industry. The food products industry is in turn a part of the even larger system of consumer goods. The systems within systems grow as shown in Figure 1–7, until you have the entire U.S. economy made up of manufacturing, services, financial and banking institutions, and government.

The more complex a system is, the more difficult it is to predict the effect of changes within that system. That is not surprising. It fits in with what we observe about the state of the economy. We often hear on the news that one well-known economist says that we will have continued expansion, whereas another is saying that we are

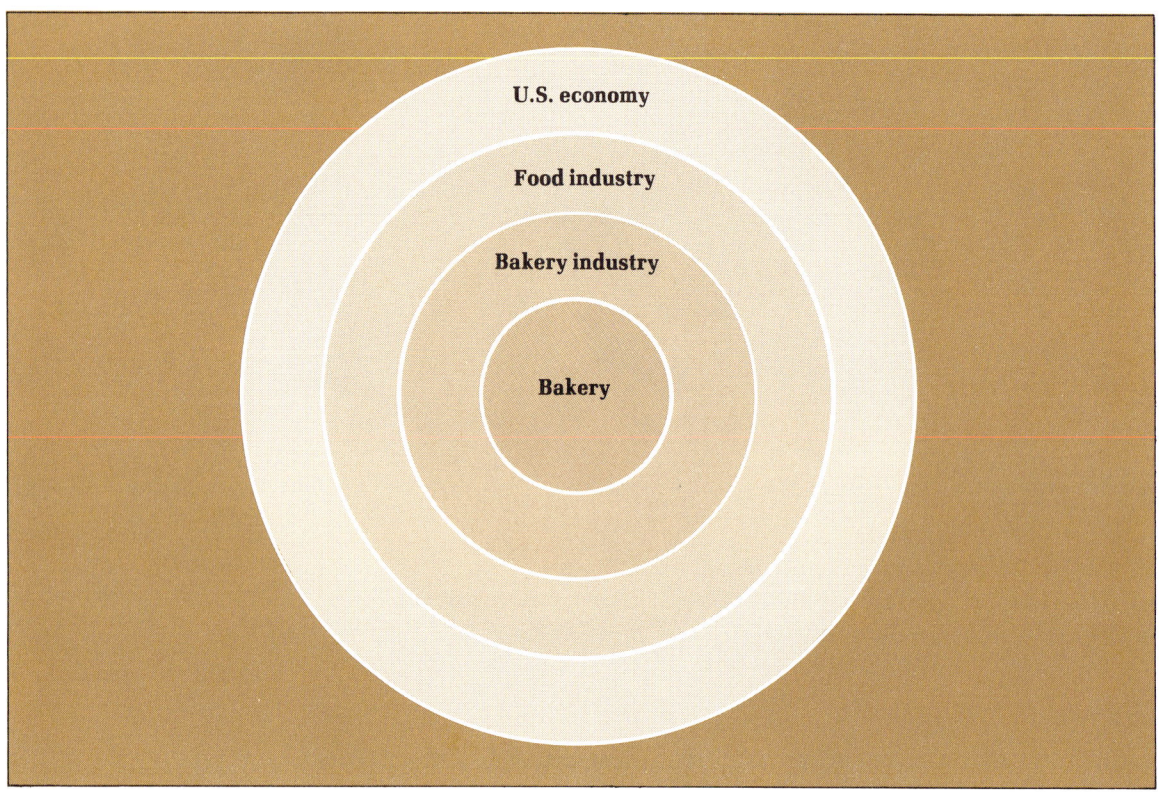

FIGURE 1–7

Nesting of systems within systems—the output of each system is an input to a larger system

headed for a recession. Competent economists can easily disagree. The economy is a very complex system that we may never fully understand.

Our purpose in this text is to help you to understand what the business system does and why it works the way it works. We will first look at the overall business community and then at the individual firms within it. We will deal with the constraints and opportunities facing large firms and small firms, firms involved in manufacturing, and firms that offer services. We will look at the inputs, the transformations, and the outputs. We will examine each of the business functions and how they fit together. We will define the roles of consumers, managers, suppliers, workers, unions, the government, and all of the other players. We will consider the events that have brought us all to this point and make a few predictions concerning the future.

SUMMARY

Every society has an economic system to meet the needs of its members. Every economic system must settle two basic questions: (1) To what use should the society's resources be devoted? (2) How will the goods and services produced by the system be divided? Every economic system also must have capital. When individuals own and control the capital, we call it *capitalism* or the *private enterprise system*. Under *communism,* the resources are held in common by all the members of the group. When the government owns and controls the basic productive resources, it is called *socialism.*

In our capitalist society, there are a lot of people who have needs and wants just like you. Most of these are satisfied through the business system. Business is the human activity of converting resources into goods and services for the purpose of bringing about transactions that will result in a profit to the organization.

Interacting with the business system is not your only option. You always have the option to do without; or you could try to be self-sufficient. A third option is to share tasks with someone else. These are possibilities, but most people choose to pay others to perform tasks that they do not like to do or are not able to do as well for themselves. The business system is actually society's way of organizing interdependent human beings. Business sells utility—the capacity of any physical thing, idea, or service to satisfy human needs. Total utility includes form, time, place, and possession utilities.

Business firms are always searching for unmet needs that they can fill and thereby earn a profit. But the business system can't do everything for everybody. This may be due to a lack of technology or because the needs cannot be met at a price that people are willing to pay.

A system is an interdependent set of components forming a unified whole, bound together by an objective. Some are carefully planned and designed, while others evolve. Systems have an objective; they exist to do something. The outputs of business systems are products and services to be sold. To produce outputs, systems require inputs and transformation processes. Each system is complete in itself, yet most systems interact with other systems. The more complex a system is, the more difficult it is to predict the effect of changes within that system. The business system is very complex. The purpose of this text is to help you to understand what the business system does and why it works the way it does.

REVIEW QUESTIONS

1. How would you define *business?*

2. How can you meet your needs? How does the business system fit in?

3. What is utility? Think of three products or services you have purchased in the last week and describe how each one provided the four elements of utility.

4. What are the differences between the private enterprise system and the alternatives?

5. What is a system? Describe two systems other than the business system.

CASES

Case 1–1. How would you like to own this bridge?

The Golden Gate Bridge, a famous San Francisco landmark, is visited by hundreds of thousands of tourists from all over the world each year. When the cable that had held up that bridge for decades was being replaced in 1976, Joe King bought 15 miles of the old corroded cable. Joe paid a flat price of $50,000 for the cable and agreed to pay the bridge authority 60 percent of any profits from the venture. He formed the San Francisco Bridge Company and began cutting that cable into 4-inch segments to be sold to nostalgic customers.

Joe offered three versions of the mounted cable segments: 24-karat gold-plated for $50, nickel-plated for $40, or the famous rust-protective orange paint of the actual bridge for $35. Then Joe invested $200,000 in advertising over a six-month period to sell the idea to the public. The profit to be split between Joe's company and the bridge authority could be as much as $4 million.

1. *What forms of utility are offered by this product?*
2. *How is Joe participating in the private enterprise system?*
3. *Do you think this product would be available in a socialist or communist system?*
4. *Should people be allowed to spend their money on a piece of slightly corroded bridge cable?*

Case 1–2. They thought he was all wet

Charlie Hall was optimistic. He was also up to his neck in Jello. The inventor of the waterbed was a design student at San Francisco State University when he made his first attempt to design a piece of furniture that conformed to the body. It was a vinyl bag filled with 300 pounds of blue Jello and styrene pellets. The Jello rotted and started to smell, but Charlie kept improving his product and ended up with the waterbed, complete with frame and heater.

He approached several major mattress manufacturers and was turned away. He started his own business but went broke. People didn't believe his claims about waterbeds, and they had all kinds of fears about flooding their houses or being electrocuted by the heater. Today waterbeds are very well accepted.

1. *Does the waterbed have greater utility today than it did when Charlie was trying to sell it?*
2. *Under the private enterprise system, Charlie was allowed to invest his money in a losing venture. Later others succeeded with his idea. Is that fair?*

chapter 2
AN ENTERPRISE AS A PART OF THE ECONOMIC SYSTEM

By studying this chapter you should be able to find answers to these questions:

1 What are the institutional characteristics of the U.S. economic system?
2 How do you measure and judge the system?
3 What are profits and the function of profits in the U.S. economic system?
4 Which industries are most profitable?
5 How are the rules for the business game set in our system?
6 What is a market clearing price?
7 How do you measure the performance of the U.S. economy? How do you know when it is doing well and when it is not?
8 What are the causes of inflation? Recession?

Terms you should know:

capital
deficit spending
entrepreneur
gross national product (GNP)
market clearing price
monopolistic competition
monopoly
oligopoly
price elasticity of demand
pure competition
velocity of money

Business could well be the single most important institution in the United States. It may characterize Americans as accurately as any other generalization. The private enterprise system and way of thinking are expressed in almost everything we do and are reflected in our form of government. Perhaps the essence of the system is that the individual firm is free to define a business opportunity and then to capitalize on it. These individual businesses add up to form our economic system.

OPPORTUNITIES GALORE

Businesspeople must be optimists by nature, for they see opportunities everywhere. Think about some of the great firms and how they started. Some began with a brilliant or even an accidental technological breakthrough, such as those that brought us telephones, light bulbs, and pocket calculators. Charles Goodyear had searched for years for a way to preserve natural rubber. Then one evening he accidentally spilled it on the stove and found that heat brought about the results he had sought. He called the process *Vulcanizing* after Vulcan, the Roman god of fire. But such dramatic breakthroughs are the exception rather than the rule. Most success stories begin when someone sees a chance to do something just a little better.

CAPITALIZING ON ADVANTAGES

A successful firm capitalizes on one or more of its advantages. It may perceive a need that is not being adequately met and move to fill the gap. McDonald's and others recognized something about human nature and eating habits. You don't always want a full-course meal at a fancy price! When you're hungry and on the run, service and a full menu are not top priorities.

Once the fast-food need had been recognized, the big chains moved rapidly to capitalize on the idea by franchising. They couldn't have locked into the potential market without franchising because they did not have enough investment capital to expand so rapidly. The idea to fill an unmet need coupled with franchising created brilliant success. We will talk more about franchising in Chapter 5. Are there still some unmet needs that could become business successes?

Sometimes a firm has control over resources that are crucial to success. Mining companies are good examples. Kennicott Copper has control over valuable deposits of copper.

Your local electric utility has a different kind of control. It has been granted a monopoly by government to generate and sell electric power in a certain area. The government grants monopoly control to avoid costly duplication of facilities. For many years, the Yellow Cab Com-

PHILIP M. HAWLEY
There are many career opportunities in retailing

Philip M. Hawley is president and chief executive officer of Carter Hawley Hale Stores, Inc., a major retailer. Unless you are from southern California, you may not recognize the company name. But you probably recognize the names of one or more of the stores that are part of the Carter Hawley Hale retailing empire that Hawley helped to build. They operate in almost all states. Here are the names of the stores: The Broadway; The Emporium; Capwell's; Weinstock's; Neiman-Marcus; Bergdorf-Goodman; Holt, Renfrew; Waldenbooks; and Sunset House.

Philip Hawley obtained his undergraduate education at Reed College, Stanford, and the University of California, Berkeley, being elected to Phi Beta Kappa at age 19 as a junior at Berkeley. Like many business leaders, Hawley is a director of several other important firms, such as Atlantic Richfield, BankAmerica Corporation, Pacific Telephone, and Walt Disney Productions.

You may think that businesspeople are so busy with their firms that they do not think about anything else, but just the reverse seems to be true. Hawley is active as a trustee, direc-tor, or member of the Music Center of Los Angeles, the County Art Museum, The Huntington Library and Art Gallery, Community Television of Southern California, California Institute of Technology, Stanford Business School, UCLA Graduate School of Management, Marlborough School, Harvard Business School, YMCA of Los Angeles, The Haynes Foundation, The California Community Foundation, The California Chamber of Commerce, and The Conference Board.

Retail stores are so much a part of our lives that you may overlook the career possibilities in this area. First, the most common small business in the country is retailing in some form. But in addition, retailing has become big business, and large retailers such as Carter Hawley Hale provide opportunities in selling, buying, and store management. Retail selling requires important personal skills and knowledge of products.

When you go into a store and see all of those products available "off the shelf," remember that buyers selected them and made important decisions about style, quality, and price. Skillful buyers can make a big difference in the success of a retail store.

A retail store has important managerial problems of billing, credit, hiring and managing personnel, security, inventory, advertising, and plant maintenance. Retailers need computers to implement their billing, credit, and accounting systems. Shoplifting and other theft are important problems. These are all problems of operations, and retail stores must train people to manage all these kinds of problems.

pany had a concession for the sole rights to operate taxis in Los Angeles. Who has the refreshments concessions at your local baseball and football stadiums? These enterprises with market control have a significant advantage in a special access to markets, and they capitalize on it.

Some firms have gained significant advantages through the develop-

ment and maintenance of superior technology. Names like IBM and Jet Propulsion Laboratories are linked with high technology. When other companies try to compete, they must overcome both the image and the reality of technological advantage.

Then there is the advantage of location. For some firms, location is a key factor in success. Have you noticed that when new shopping plazas are developed, certain chain organizations are located there? The locational advantage shows clearly when a successful business is killed because a new freeway reroutes traffic and leaves it isolated from potential customers.

Individual firms with some mission defined by an opportunity are the cornerstone of the economic system. These firms capitalize on whatever advantages they have. They may be small or large and produce any kind of products and services. They compete with each other to various degrees and in various ways. Their collective decisions have an impact on our prosperity, economic stability, and quality of life. In fact, we are affected by the economic system from the cradle to the grave.

THE ECONOMIC SYSTEM

Let's think about the U.S. economic system, its elements and flows. Who are the people involved in the system? How are the rules of the game set? How do you measure and evaluate the economic system?

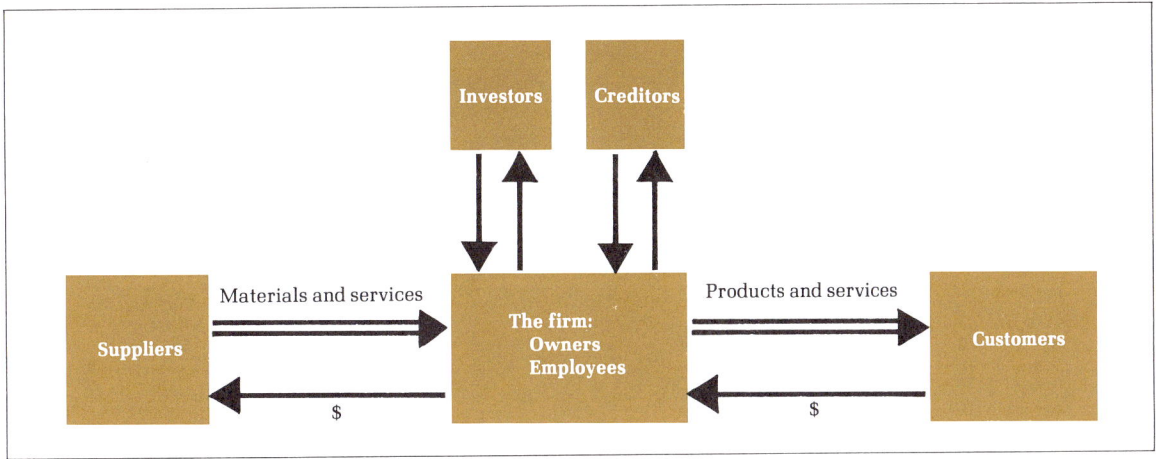

FIGURE 2-1
People relationships in an
individual firm

People

Who is involved in the system? Everyone, you say! True, everyone is involved somehow, but we can see relationships among the people by labeling them. For a given firm there are creditors, customers, employees, investors, owners, and suppliers. Their general relationships are shown in Figure 2–1. It is a simple and neat classification if you look at only one firm. But when you start to ask who's who in ten firms, the labels get mixed up. One firm's investors are another's employees, customers, suppliers, or creditors. The titles suppliers, investors, and creditors in Figure 2–1 may even represent entire firms.

When you look at a whole community or an industry, you can begin to see relationships. Who supplies whom, who owns what, who buys from whom, and who owes whom? But as soon as you start to look at broader systems, the individual faces of people blur. You begin to think of which firms supply others, to group firms by industry, and to see employees as groups called unions.

Resources

The basic inputs to an enterprise are land, labor, capital, and the entrepreneur. Economists call these four inputs the **factors of production.**

Land. The cliche "land underlies everything" is true for business. Land is the fixed resource that serves as the site for buildings, equipment, and operations. **Land** is obviously the crucial resource for agriculture and all natural resources, such as oil and mineral deposits. Urban sprawl is a current social issue—land that can produce fruits, vegetables, and meat is being plated with concrete and asphalt for highways and housing developments.

Labor.   Labor includes everyone in the company from the president to the janitor! Will further automation eliminate labor as an input? No, but it will change the nature of the labor input. Important changes in the mix of the labor input have been occurring since the Industrial Revolution by the mechanization of many jobs. There will be more on this topic in Chapter 20.

The trend has been to reduce the use of labor simply as a power source. More recently, automatic control of machines has switched the need for labor to that of overseeing the production process. Labor has not been eliminated; it has simply been converted to more interesting tasks such as design and maintenance of machines, planning, and management.

Capital.   Every enterprise requires capital. Somebody has to put up the money to buy equipment, to pay workers, to pay the rent, and to advertise. To the economist, **capital** is the productive resource, such as the machinery, not the money itself. Those who contribute the money for capital equipment and the other resources that are required expect to earn some return on those funds. Without capital, there would be no production.

Entrepreneur.   A business will not be formed unless someone brings all the elements together and organizes them into a productive system. This person is the **entrepreneur.** It might be the president of the company, but sometimes the president is a professional manager and someone else is the entrepreneur. Someone must take the risks of investing

Rewards to the factors of production

and of putting capital and personal time on the line. If the enterprise succeeds, the rewards could be great. If it fails, the capital investment goes down the sink.

Rewards. What is the incentive to each of the factors of production? Why does the entrepreneur bother? Why should labor work? Why pour in capital? Why allocate land to production? In the American private enterprise economic system, the reward system developed as follows: land receives rent, labor receives wages, capital receives interest, and the entrepreneur receives the profit or suffers the loss.

The least understood of the rewards is profit. Profit is the reward for doing a good job; it is what is left over from sales revenue after paying for the inputs of land, labor, and capital. If costs exceed revenues, then profit is negative—a loss. This is the risk taken by the entrepreneur. Think of it this way. Profit is the worth of the product or service to customers over and above costs; customers are willing to pay that much more than the bare cost of the product.

Profits control capital flows. Profits are the regulator that attracts investment capital to areas that have greater demand in the marketplace. When demand is strong, prices increase and profits usually follow. High profits attract venture capital to socially worthy needs as measured by demand and price. More product is produced, thereby increasing supply. Expanding capacity requires more capital input and risk. Low profits, or losses, would not attract investment capital.

What percentage of the sales dollar do you think ends up as profit? People often guess rather large percentages, especially for corporations. In 1976 *U.S. News & World Report* surveyed 5,448 American consumers. The median guess of profits was 14¢ per sales dollar. Women guessed higher than men, 22¢ versus 13¢. One fourth of the people estimated that profits were more than 25¢ per sales dollar. Actually, profits for all corporations average only about 3¢ to 5¢ per sales dollar.

Who makes the rules?

Business is just like any other activity. There must be a set of rules and accepted activities. In the business game, there are lots of groups that have a say in the rules.

Competitors. In most cases there are competitors who offer equivalent products and services. A competitor would not necessarily offer the same product, although it might. It might offer a product that is a substitute. For example, in transportation, the local bus company competes with private automobiles; in the energy field, natural gas competes with electricity; and so on. In the U.S. economic system, much of what a firm can do depends on what competitors can do. Competitors affect what a company does by the quality of goods and services they offer.

A firm can compete by being better—by having superior product designs, by being flexible in the kinds of products and services offered, and by making them available when customers want them. As a customer, you may select a certain car because of the features, the performance, or other aspects of quality. But an alternate model may be available on the lot now, and being able to buy close to what you want from available inventory may be the deciding factor.

In theory, a business should be able to set prices at any level. So why not set them high? If a company sets them too high, it will not be able to sell as much, and total revenue may even fall. Why do sales fall at higher prices? There are two reasons. First, customers shop around and buy from a competitor who offers a lower price. A company's volume falls while the competitor's increases. Second, there is a relationship between price and demand called the price elasticity of demand. **Price elasticity of demand** means that demand will increase for lower prices and decrease for higher prices. The effect is different for different products.

So while a business may be able to set prices, designs, and policies on inventory availability, the actions of competitors set limits on what can be done. Competition is an informal mechanism for setting the rules.

Supply and demand. Perhaps the most fundamental economic law is that "scarcity creates value." Just think—a 1957 "classic" Thunderbird brings a price of $12,000. If there is a limited number of something and it is desirable, then the value of the item is bid up. On the other hand, if the item is plentiful, such as air, then it is free or has no value in the economic sense. But, for an item to have value, people must want it. So let's start with demand.

What determines demand for gasoline at the corner station? Many different people buy gas there. The amount they use depends on many different things such as age, the nature of their work and the gas needed to get to work, income, and the type of car. Each of us has different uses for gas, and the values we place on those uses are not equal. A drive to an evening movie might not have equal value to a use related to work.

There are changes in lifestyles that could change the amount of gas we use. If you inherit a fortune, your gas consumption will increase. If you were fired, it would decrease. Let's not confuse these kinds of gas use changes with changes that result from increases or decreases in price.

If gas prices double, use will decline. This change has to do with the different values that you place on different uses for gas. You may decide to reduce your more frivolous uses, and total demand will decline. If gas prices are cut in half, the opposite happens. People will think little about using gas for the slightest whim. It's cheap and is treated that way.

Now look at the supply side in relation to price. If the price of gas doubles, you revalue your uses. But there is a second effect—the higher price provides both an incentive and the money to expand the amount produced. With more gas available at the high price, what happens? Inventories accumulate, since you (and others) have already cut out your more frivolous uses. Now, if the gas station has an inventory of gas that it cannot sell, the price will come down and provide an incentive to buy for those frivolous uses. It costs the gas station owner to hold an inventory. Conversely, if the price is high, the gas station owner will try to sell more gas to take advantage of the potential profits.

If you plot the demand versus price, and the supply versus price together, you get Figure 2–2. The **demand curve** is a schedule of the amounts demanded at various prices. The **supply curve** is a schedule of amounts offered for sale at various prices. The point where the two curves cross is called the **market clearing price,** where demand and supply are in balance. It is the price that clears the market of supply.

Now what happens if someone with the power decides to control the price and keep it below the market clearing price? You guessed

FIGURE 2–2
Supply and demand determine market clearing price

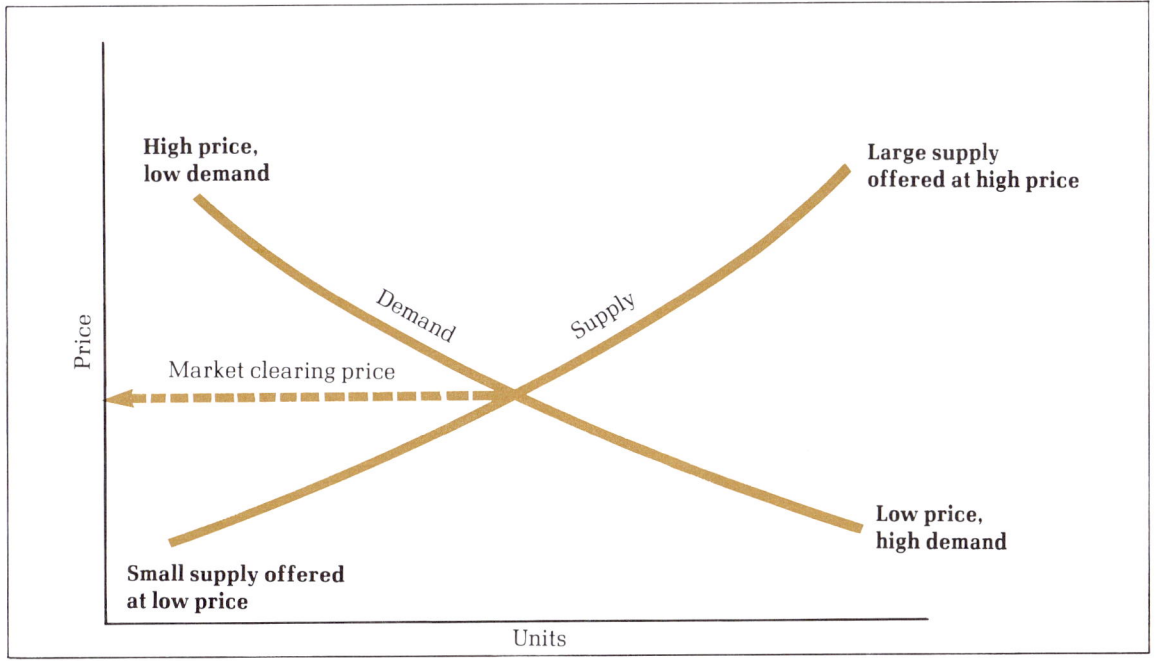

High price, low demand

Large supply offered at high price

Demand

Supply

Price

Market clearing price

Low price, high demand

Small supply offered at low price

Units

it—shortages! Why? Because at the bargain price we all enjoy our frivolous uses, and because supply will be restricted as on the supply schedule in Figure 2–2.

In the early 1970s the oil embargo provided a dramatic lesson on prices and shortages. The embargo resulted in restricted supplies. The price was not allowed to increase, however, "because it would be unfair to let oil companies gouge the public." Lines a block long at gas stations were common. But gas was still relatively cheap, so why cut out the frivolous uses? In fact, we were all paying much more for a tank of gas if we place any value on the time we wasted waiting to buy gas. If you had nothing else to do, perhaps your time was not too expensive. But if you were using your car or truck to earn a living, the waiting time was very costly. The economic moral is that we pay the market clearing price one way or another. Supply, demand, and the market clearing price are mechanisms that set some of the rules for the business game.

Government.   What businesses can and cannot do is regulated by government at all levels. There are rules for fair competition, collective bargaining, wages, pollution, taxes, profits, safety, pension plans, and sometimes prices. Managers decry the bureaucratic control placed on them but quietly take advantage of the rules when they turn out to be in their favor. For example, MEMOREX sued IBM for unfair competitive practices, taking advantage of government legal doctrine. In that situation, MEMOREX probably thought the rules were good. It is often true that government rules are there because they protect business, and business may lobby government to have rules set.

The rules of the business game are set by competitors and their actions, supply and demand, and by the government. Competitive pressures and economic laws provide informal rules that are followed because they reflect realities. Government provides formal rules.

SIZING UP AN ENTERPRISE

There are many ways to look at an enterprise. Let's take two dimensions: industry structure, and degree of competition.

Industry structure

There are almost 15 million business firms in the United States. Most of them are small businesses. Table 2–1 shows how many firms are in which kinds of business. Agriculture, forestry, and fishing involve the largest percentage, accounting for more than one out of four firms. Services such as transportation and medical care are close behind and account for another one out of four firms. Retail trade and finance,

TABLE 2–1
Number and percentage
of enterprises in
different industries

Industry	Number of enterprises (000)	Percent
Agriculture, forestry, and fishing	3,586	26.6%
Mining	86	0.6
Construction	1,099	8.2
Manufacturing	449	3.3
Transportation and public utilities	434	3.2
Wholesale trade	548	4.1
Retail trade	2,329	17.3
Finance, insurance, and real estate	1,576	11.7
Services	3,367	25.0
Total	13,474	100.0%

Source: *U.S. Statistical Abstract*, 1976.

insurance, and real estate also involve large numbers of firms. Only three firms out of 100 are in manufacturing.

Another way to look at industries is to see where the money is. Sales and profits for these same industries show a different picture. Table 2–2 shows that by far the greatest sales and profits are in manufacturing. Therefore, the relatively small number of firms in manufacturing make a great deal of money. The closest second in profits is in services, although the total sales in services is fifth. Apparently services are quite profitable.

Degrees of competition

Not all industries have the same degree of competition. Economists use a four-part classification to label industries. It ranges from pure competition to no competition at all, monopoly. Even in a monopoly

TABLE 2–2
Sales and profits for
different industries

Industry	Sales ($ billions)	Percent of total sales	Profits ($ billions)	Percent of total profits
Agriculture, forestry, and fishing ...	101.0	3.5	11.4	6.5
Mining	32.3	1.1	7.3	4.1
Construction	164.7	5.6	7.7	4.4
Manufacturing	1,017.3	34.8	65.0	36.7
Transportation and public utilities ..	192.5	6.6	10.3	5.8
Wholesale trade	431.8	14.8	15.3	8.6
Retail trade	514.8	17.6	16.2	9.2
Finance, insurance, and real estate ..	296.6	10.2	17.2	9.7
Services	170.0	5.8	26.6	15.0
Total	2,921.0	100.0	177.0	100.0

Source: *U.S. Statistical Abstract*, 1976.

though, there is competition between industries. The electric company faces competition from those who generate their own power or even use candles and kerosene lamps.

Pure competition.   When people speak of the virtues of competition, they are usually thinking about the special case of **pure competition.** Some important characteristics of an industry provide for pure competition:

1.   There are many small firms in the industry.
2.   Products in the industry are similar or identical.
3.   It is easy to enter or leave the market.
4.   Everyone knows what is available at what price.

The result of these special conditions is that no one firm can affect price by itself. The market clearing price prevails as a price-setting mechanism through the forces of supply and demand.

Pure competition is not simply an ideal. It exists in the stock market, and for many commodities, such as wheat, beef, gold, and silver. Agricultural commodities used to be traded in completely free markets, but this is no longer true because of government price supports. However, these markets operate freely as long as prices are above the support levels.

Monopolistic competition.   The conditions for **monopolistic competition** in an industry are:

1.   There are many firms, but fewer than for pure competition.
2.   Products are not identical among firms.
3.   It is relatively easy to enter markets.

Under these conditions, firms take advantage of product differences. The differences may be real, for example, the road performance of a Porsche is acknowledged to be better than that of a Volkswagen. Or, the difference may be relatively minor but is promoted by the manufacturer as being significant. Much of the advertising that you are exposed to attempts to convince you of product differences. Thus, Procter & Gamble advertises that children who use Crest Toothpaste have fewer cavities. Bufferin is alleged to be better than aspirin because it doesn't upset your stomach.

The result of monopolistic competition is that firms have some control over prices, since the products are not identical. But, they must convince you that the product differences are worthwhile, and that price differences between products are justified.

Oligopoly.   When there are only a few sellers, that is an **oligopoly.** It is usually difficult for a new firm to get started in an oligopolistic industry because of huge capital requirements. Think of trying to finance a new venture in the steel, auto, or computer industries. Even if you could finance such a venture, you would find yourself looking directly into the teeth of U.S. Steel, General Motors, or IBM. These three giants control the largest shares of the markets in their industries. In each industry, the giant along with a handful of other companies represent your competition.

As a result, in an oligopolistic industry, producers have substantial control over their prices. If you check prices in these industries, you will find them to be similar. But these prices are not market clearing prices, as with pure competition. The competitors opt for price stability. It is clear to all producers that price reductions would have to be met by all and would result in lower profits for all.

Most of the court cases dealing with antitrust—charges of monopoly and unfair competition—involve oligopolistic industries. The largest firms often feel that the reward for success is an antitrust suit filed by the government or by smaller companies in the industry.

Some of the most prominent cases in the recent past have involved IBM and Eastman Kodak. But the rewards to smaller companies for winning may be changing. After convincing a jury that Xerox was guilty of antimonopoly law violations, SMC Corp. expected to get $112 million in treble damages, which was recommended by the jury. But the judge ruled that SMC should receive no damages. The judge wiped out the damage award not on technical grounds, but because he felt that private litigants should not collect damages when it is society as a whole that suffers. Since both sides in the dispute had spent more than $20 million in legal costs and executive time, smaller companies now may think twice before suing in the hope of obtaining huge awards.[1] The idea is that the social interest is protected by government suits that have the objective of protecting society's interest. Apparently the government wants to retain a monopoly on antitrust suits.

Monopoly.   When there are no competitors, there is a **monopoly.** Legislation prohibits monopoly in the United States unless it is stamped "government approved and regulated." The managers of a firm with a monopoly can set prices at any level they feel will maximize their profits, and "the public be damned." That is why approved monopolies and government regulation go hand in hand. Services offered and prices are subject to control by state public utilities commissions, the Federal Communications Commission, and other regulatory bodies.

Most U.S. monopolies are public utilities: electric power, natural gas, and telephone services. American Telephone and Telegraph Company, "Ma Bell," is one of the largest companies in the world. Recently, Ma Bell has been put under new competitive pressure by companies like TRW, Litton Industries, and General Dynamics. The Federal Communications Commission and the new competitors seem bent on breaking up the Bell system, which provides about 85 percent of the telephone service in the United States. They want to intrude on Bell's telephone equipment supply monopoly and to duplicate long-distance phone service.

Monopoly practices. It is said that every business manager believes in competition but does everything possible to become a monopolist. Practices such as price collusion among companies and other secret agreements among firms in an industry are illegal. Actually, there may be collusion, but it is very informal and therefore legal.

Price leadership is practiced in certain industries. It works like this. A big producer like U.S. Steel is looked to as the price leader. If U.S. Steel raises its prices, the others follow in short order. There is no collusion; other companies just like to price as U.S. Steel does.

Other monopoly practices are condoned. Patents for inventions and copyrights are monopolies granted for a specific term. The rationale is that these monopolies are needed to promote technological development and creativity.

Occupational licensing is a form of monopoly control. Licensing is not limited to electricians and plumbers. Dentists, physicians, engineers, real estate agents, and many others restrict entry to their trades and professions through licensing. In exchange, they agree to certain standards of practice.

When you step back and look at the degree to which companies within an industry compete, you see a wide range extending from pure competition to monopoly. Not too much of our economy is represented by idealistic pure competition. Most of American business is involved in monopolistic competition and oligopoly. A summary is provided in Table 2–3.

TABLE 2–3
Degrees of competition in U.S. industry

	Examples	Number of firms in industry	Product characteristics	Control over pricing	Entry into industry
Pure competition	Commodities, beef cattle, gold, stocks and bonds	Many small	Similar	Supply and demand	Easy
Monopolistic competition	Toothpaste, aspirin	Many large and small	Different or can be differentiated	Some	Fairly easy
Oligopoly	General Motors, IBM, U.S. Steel	Few	Similar or different	Substantial	Difficult
Monopoly	Electric utilities, telephone companies, patents, copyrights, licensing	One	No substitute	Usually regulated	No way!

MEASURING THE ECONOMY

How is the economy doing? How do you know when it's doing well and when it isn't? There are many ways that people look at these questions. Most often people look at their own economic well-being and make judgments. If your take-home pay is increasing and if your status within the system is improving, things may look pretty good. But we have to consider broader measures to tell whether the economy as a whole is doing well. Let's examine three measures that are common gauges: gross national product (GNP), economic stability, and quality of life.

Gross national product (GNP)

Economists use GNP to determine how much the economy is actually producing, and whether or not it is expanding. The **gross national product** is the annual total market value of all the goods and services produced. Figure 2–3 shows a graph of GNP beginning in 1950. Note that GNP increases in all years. Since 1950, GNP in current money terms has increased an average of 6 to 7 percent per year, sometimes as little as 0.1 percent and sometimes as much as 15 percent.

Real GNP.   By raw GNP measures, we have had a trillion-dollar economy since 1971. But the GNP quotes current market values of goods and services, so because of inflation we haven't really done that well. Economists deflate the figures and quote GNP in terms of what you could buy in 1972. The curve of deflated or real GNP is also shown in Figure 2–3 for comparison. These figures show the real increases. The economy is expanding over the years, but not nearly so fast as indicated by the raw GNP figures. Real GNP has increased an average of about 4 percent per year, but real GNP actually declined in 1954, 1958, 1970, 1974, and 1975. So real GNP is a better measure of how the economy is doing. If it does not increase or if it actually decreases, we are not doing well at all. Recessions mean people are out of work and conditions are bad for business. On the other hand, when real GNP booms ahead as in 1976 and 1977, we get inflation. We will discuss these expansions and declines in real GNP in the section on economic stability later in this chapter.

Services versus products in GNP.   Where is the economy going in terms of the kinds of outputs it produces? Figure 2–4 shows a startling trend since 1948. Services as a percentage of GNP have increased from about 30 percent to 45 percent in 1977. Americans are buying more services, or paying more for them, or both. The latter is a good part of the change. The price indexes of services have increased 10 percent faster than general prices—over 250 percent since 1950, while consumer prices in general have increased about 225 percent. The cost of medical services has increased more than 350 percent in the same period.

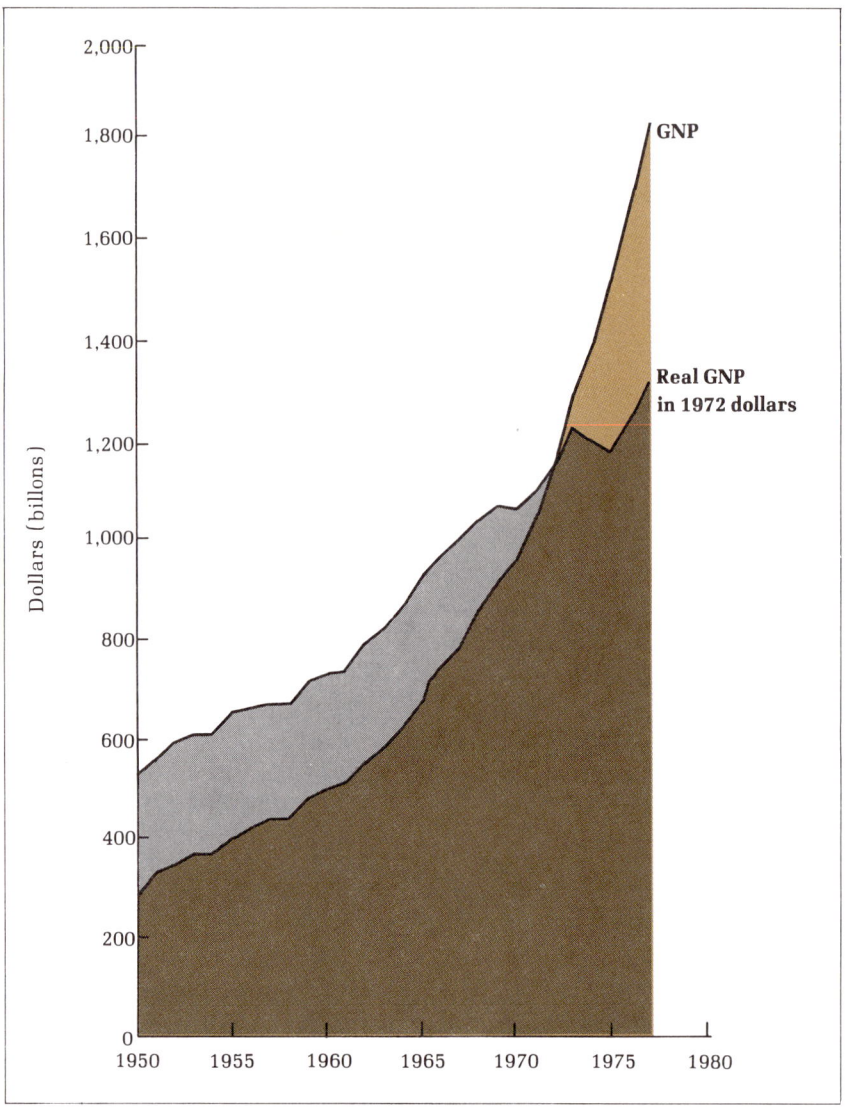

Source: *Economic Report of the President*, 1978.

In the Soviet Union, analysts do not include services in GNP, only products that you can see and feel. This concept of GNP may be realistic for the Soviets, since there are few services available there. If services were included they might not amount to much.

Productivity.   Another gauge that is related to GNP is productivity— output per hour of labor. If productivity increased, there could be an increase in real GNP with the same labor force. Figure 2–5 shows a 100-year record of productivity in the United States. There is an increase in productivity, except for declines in 1920 and 1930.

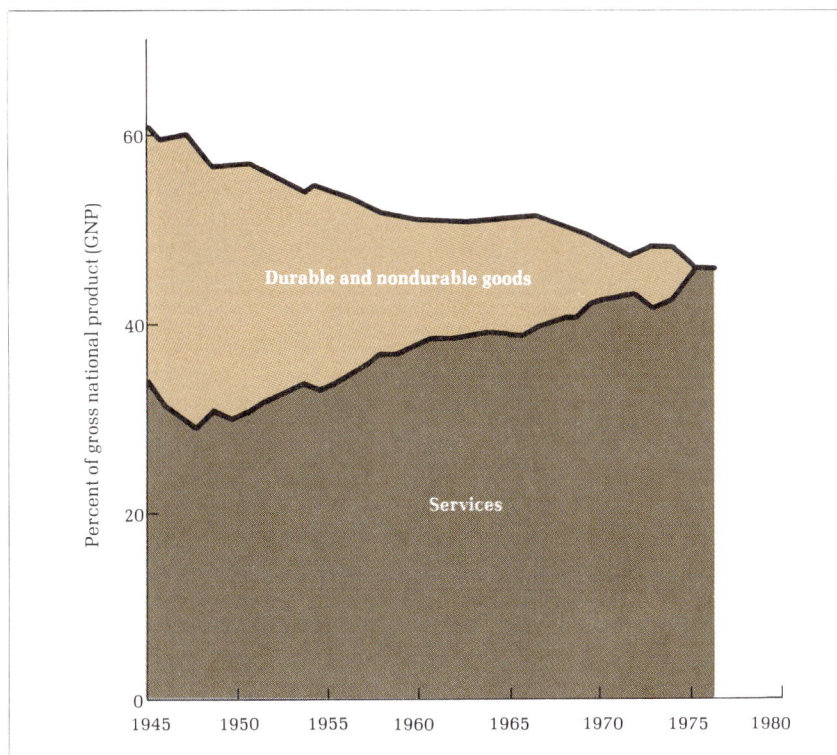

Source: *Economic Report of the President*, 1978.

FIGURE 2–4
Relative importance of goods and services output in the U.S. economy by percentage of GNP

FIGURE 2–5
One hundred years of productivity growth; output per worker-hour in U.S. manufacturing, 1870–1972

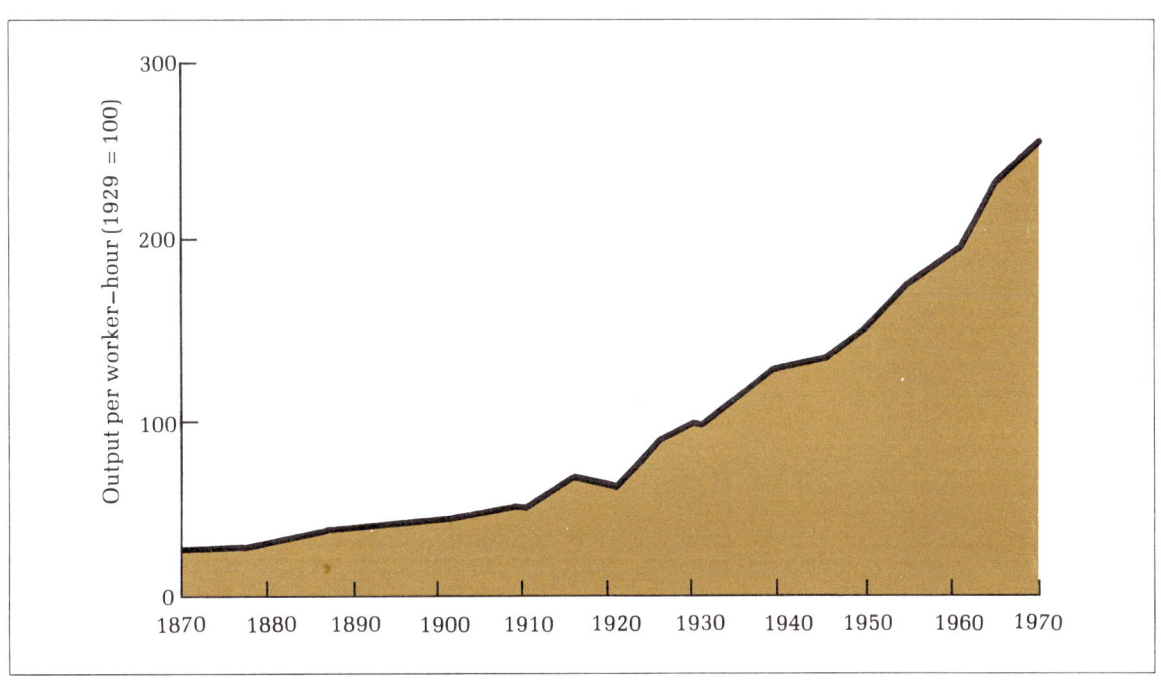

Sources: J. W. Kendick, *Productivity Trends in the United States* (Princeton, N.J.: Princeton University Press, 1961); and the Bureau of Labor Statistics.

What causes productivity to increase? Is it because employees are simply working harder? No, it represents the effects of mechanization, automation, efficient management, better education and training for workers, research and development effort, and many other factors.

Economic stability

Those ups and downs of GNP are disturbing. The ups represent inflation, and Americans are becoming more and more disturbed by its effects. The downs represent economic recessions, and we don't like them at all because economic activity slows down, people become unemployed, and economic hardship is widespread.

Economists refer to the ups and downs as the **business cycle,** although few believe that there is a regular periodic cycle. When it occurs, the economy goes through fluctuations that include periods of prosperity, recession (which can deepen into a depression), and recovery.

Recession.   If you reexamine Figure 2–3, you can see some of the effects of economic fluctuation in the real GNP curve—where the dips occur. In recent times there were recessions that involved declines in real GNP in 1970 and in 1974–75, the latter being most severe. There are other important effects of recessions that are not shown in the real GNP figures. Business sales and profits decline, and output is cut back correspondingly. The most important effect from a social point of view is unemployment, which jumped from 4.9 percent in 1973 to 5.6 percent in 1974, and 8.5 percent in 1975.

To recover from recessions, the government usually cuts taxes and may increase its spending through projects designed to put people back to work and through existing programs of unemployment compensation and welfare. The Federal Reserve Board also cuts interest rates and takes other actions to expand the money supply and make business investments more attractive.

Prosperity and recovery.   When the actions taken by government to get out of a recession begin to work, they result in expanded employment opportunities, real GNP, and business sales and profitability. Business invests in expanding capacity in response to increased sales and profitability and because interest rates are attractive to finance the expansions. Prosperity results, with lower unemployment and with people having more money to spend.

If the expansion overshoots the mark of steady growth, there is a boom. There is an initial false sense of security in a boom because people are working and have money to spend. But this is like running on a treadmill that is going faster and faster. You have to run faster just to keep up, and you finally exhaust yourself and fall. One of the associated effects of booms in recent times has been inflation.

"Why don't you look at it this way, Mrs. Peters—prices are lower today than they ever will be."

Reprinted by permission *The Wall Street Journal.*

Inflation. During the past decade the U.S. economy has suffered double-digit inflation (greater than 10 percent per year) for short periods. Inflation is usually measured by the consumer price level. If average prices are increasing 10 percent per year, but your income is increasing only 7 percent per year, it's not hard to see that you have come out badly. Inflation and its causes are a very complex subject, but let's sort out some major causes and effects.

When inflation is reduced to its simplest elements, the major causes are quite understandable. Figure 2–6 represents the "inflation machine." Assume for a moment that the value of the consumable goods and services produced is in balance with the dollars paid to all those who compete for the purchase of the goods and services. Then prices will

FIGURE 2–6
The inflation machine

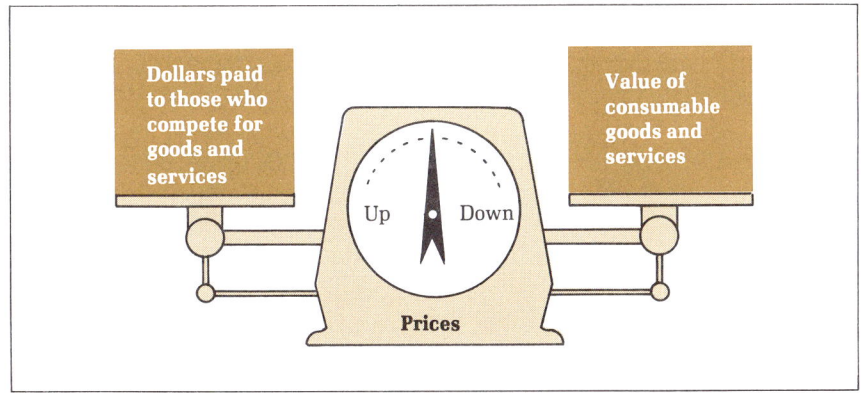

remain stable. Prices of individual items will fluctuate based on their conditions of supply and demand, but the aggregate price levels will be stable. The inflation machine is nothing more or less than a broad view of supply and demand and the market clearing price.

Now, if you load the left side of the inflation machine with more dollars than the value of the goods and services in the right side, what happens? Prices will increase! Competition for what is available will drive up the prices. Another way to load the left side of the inflation machine is for the same number of dollars to be spent with greater frequency. That is called increasing the **velocity of money.** The dollars flow through the economic system faster, and this creates a similar effect. Or, if people take money out of savings and spend it, that increases the number of dollars in competition for the available goods. The effect is the same—competition for what is available on the right side will drive prices up.

Now, let's look at a few ways in which the left side of the inflation machine can get loaded beyond the value of the consumable goods and services on the right side. The important ways are:

1. Expansion of the money supply.
2. Government deficit spending.
3. Wars.
4. Increased velocity of money and spending from savings.

The money supply. If the government expands the money supply, it dumps extra dollars into the inflation machine. The Federal Reserve System has control of interest rates and the reserves that banks can lend. If it lowers the interest rates and expands credit, then consumers can buy without having actual dollars available. So, making credit easier and cheaper to obtain has the effect of increasing the money supply and loading the left side of the inflation machine.

Deficit spending. Then there is government **deficit spending.** When government spends more than it takes in, it is just like expanding credit and therefore the money supply. It pumps extra dollars into the inflation machine and creates excess demand. This excess demand in turn puts upward pressure on prices.

Wars. Notice that the right side of the inflation machine is loaded with consumable goods and services. Now suppose that you pay people to produce something that cannot be consumed. You pay them, and their dollars flow into the left side of the inflation machine. But no equivalent products and services flow into the right side to balance. How do the war goods get consumed? Well, you blow them up, preferably in someone else's backyard!

Look at Figure 2–7 to see what happened to consumer prices during the wars in this century. Prices went up not only during wars but

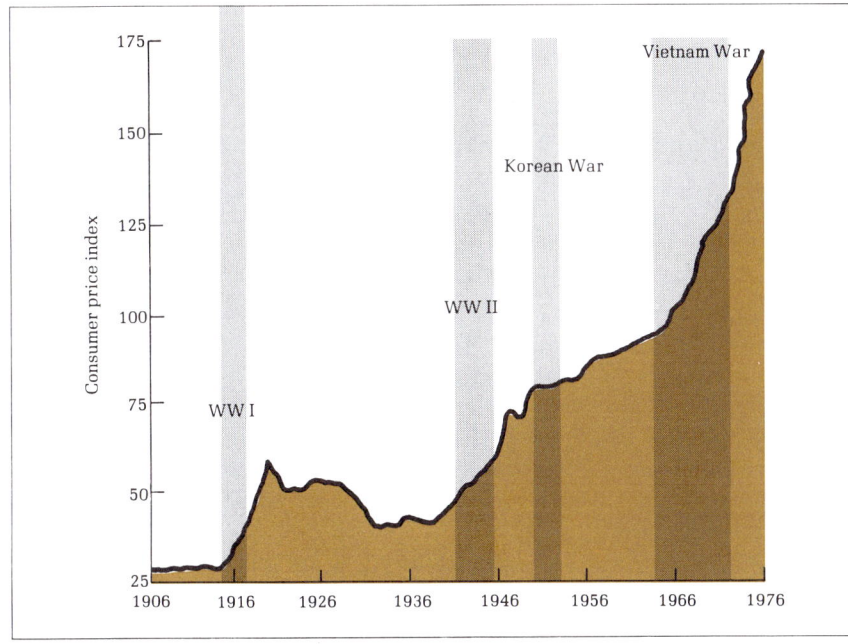

FIGURE 2–7
The consumer price index during four wars (prices in 1967 = 100)

also afterward as pent-up demand and shortages required satisfaction by the voracious inflation machine.

Velocity of money. When money in the system goes around and around faster, economists say that the **velocity of money** has increased. People can spend their money faster by dipping into savings or by saving less than usual. They might dip into savings for a variety of reasons, but an important reason related to inflation might be to beat price increases. If prices are going up, you might decide to use your savings before they are worth even less. A result, however, is that you help fuel the inflation machine.

Net private savings have been declining in the United States. The peak in recent times was about 8.3 percent of GNP in 1966, and it declined rather steadily to about 5.1 percent in 1978, which represented a 30-year low. At the same time, we know that we have had high inflation in recent times, reaching double-digit amounts at times. Saving less means more money for the inflation machine, which compounds the inflation problem. Why are people saving less? People may reason, "Why save when the value of my savings is falling because of inflation? I'll spend it now before prices go up even more. At least I'll get current value for my money!" There are also disincentives to saving, since interest on savings is taxed.

Did you know that consumers in the United States save less than people in many other industrialized countries? The 1973–77 average of savings as a percentage of disposable income was 6.7 for the United States, 10.3 for Canada, 14.1 for Great Britain, 15.2 for West Germany, 17.3 for France, and 24.9 for Japan. Some of those countries have suffered even worse inflation rates than the United States. Obviously the causes of inflation are complex and not explained only by savings rates.

Other causes of inflation. There are other important causes of inflation, such as the dramatic price increase in crude oil following the 1973 oil embargo. Crude oil prices tripled, which affected costs both directly and indirectly. More recently, the crude oil prices have rocketed above $20 per barrel, and promise to increase even more, adding to the inflationary spiral.

Productivity increases can offset modest cost increases. But during rapid inflation it becomes more and more difficult to offset cost increases by higher productivity. When productivity declines while costs are increasing, inflation is reinforced and runs wild. This actually happened in 1973, 1974, and 1975.

The wage-price spiral keeps inflation going and may accelerate it. As prices increase, workers naturally want higher wages and salaries. As business finds its costs increasing, including wages and salaries, it naturally wants to raise prices to keep from going broke. It's like a dog chasing its tail.

Getting personal with the government. Have you thought about the role of the progressive income tax in personal economic progress? A progressive income tax is one where the percent tax increases as your income increases. For example, if your taxable income was $10,000 the tax rate might be 20 percent. But if your taxable income was $20,000 the tax rate increases to 25 percent. As inflation charges on, your income goes up to keep pace. But taxes increase faster because the higher the income, the higher is the tax *rate.* Also, the higher the inflation rate, the faster you get to higher income tax brackets.

U.S. News & World Report published data showing one reason people feel pinched. They give data for an executive, a worker, and a pensioner and show what happens when prices increase 46 percent in five years (an inflation rate of 7.8 percent, compounded annually). In each case, income is assumed to increase to keep pace with inflation. Figure 2–8 shows how much all three lost in net income after taxes.

Measuring economic stability is another way of assessing how well the economy is doing. When the economy is fluctuating between wild booms and busts, it is not in control. The objective is to have a stable economy that grows steadily, perhaps at the average rate of real GNP growth of about 4 percent. It seems clear that the government still does not know how to do it. Learning how to balance the use of money supply, government spending, and other economic policies in relation to other political and economic issues is obviously not easy.

FIGURE 2–8

Why People Feel Pinched

Executive
A Corporate Manager, With Spouse and Two Children

	5 Years Ago	Now	Change
Yearly pay—	$50,000	$73,000*	Up $23,000
Federal taxes (income and Social Security)	$11,872	$21,381	Up $ 9,509
Inflation "tax"— reflecting 46% rise in prices	—	$16,295	Up $16,295
What's left	**$38,127**	**$35,324**	**Down $2,804**

Worker
A Typical Production Employe, With Spouse and Two Children

	5 Years Ago	Now	Change
Yearly pay	$7,550	$10,600	Up $3,050
Federal taxes	$924	$1,192	Up $ 268
Inflation "tax"	—	$2,970	Up $2,970
What's left	**$6,626**	**$6,438**	**Down $188**

Pensioner
A Single Person Living on Social Security

	5 Years Ago	Now	Change
Yearly pension	$2,000	$2,885†	Up $885
Federal taxes	0	0	—
Inflation "tax"	—	$911	Up $911
What's left	**$2,000**	**$1,974**	**Down $26**

* Assuming raises kept pace with inflation   † Annual rate after 6.5 percent increase in July 3 check
Source: estimates by USN&WR Economic Unit

Source: Reprinted from *U.S. News & World Report,* June 19, 1978. Copyright 1978, U.S. News & World Report, Inc.

Quality of life

Another way that we measure the economic system is in terms of quality of life. What does the economic system do to help make life enjoyable rather than a trial? This is not easy to answer, since there are so many dimensions to consider.

First, there are living standards produced directly by the economy— we can measure something here. In overall terms, our economy is successful. The U.S. economy produces living standards on a par with the highest in the world. Per capita income levels in Canada, Norway, Sweden, Switzerland, and the United States are all about the same. Still, the economic system has not eliminated poverty, ghettos, urban blight, and high unemployment rates in minority groups.

The economic system and the jobs it offers go hand in hand. People spend about 40 hours out of 168 available in the week (25 percent) on jobs. Do they gain satisfactions from their jobs, or are jobs simple and boring? Have specialization and big business dehumanized work? Are there opportunities to move up in terms of job status and pay? There is divided opinion on these questions. Many people feel strongly that this is still the land of opportunity. If you are willing to work hard, you can get ahead. These people say that if the initial job isn't the best, you can work hard and change that situation.

At the same time, surveys show worker dissatisfaction with assembly-line types of work particularly and with the feeling of being just a cog in a giant machine—a machine where you don't understand your role or your fundamental worth to the end product. The extent of these dissatisfactions was made apparent by Johnny Paycheck's roaring success with the song "You Can Take This Job and Shove It" during 1977–78.

The main institutions involved in the production of quality of life for Americans are business and government. How do people feel about these two? *U.S. News & World Report* reports the results of a survey in which 5,448 people responded to 201 questions on attitudes toward business and government. Those surveyed included all ages, incomes, and political views. The following results should give both business and government something to think about.

Attitudes toward business.   To put it in a nutshell, people do not think business contributes much to their quality of life. Quite the reverse—they were dissatisfied with the quality of products they had bought and with the inadequate resolution of their complaints. Twenty-five percent said they had complained to a manufacturer in the last year, and only 48 percent of these said they had gotten satisfaction. The feeling of having been "ripped off" seems widespread. Fifty-nine percent had returned products to retailers because they were unsatisfactory. Retailers were complimented by respondents; 78 percent of those who had returned items said they were satisfied with the way their complaints were handled. The results are summarized in Figure 2–9. The criticisms cut across a broad spectrum of values.

FIGURE 2–9
U.S. News on business images

U.S. BUSINESS—ITS STRENGTHS AND WEAKNESSES

In the opinion of 5,448 American consumers . . .

BUSINESS IS STRONGEST IN—	BUSINESS IS WEAKEST IN—
✓ Developing new products	✗ Communicating with general public
✓ Providing products and services that meet people's needs	✗ Being interested in customers
✓ Hiring members of minority groups	✗ Communicating with employes
✓ Communicating with stockholders	✗ Providing value for the money
✓ Paying good wages	✗ Dealing with shortages
✓ Improving standard of living	✗ Controlling pollution
✓ Providing fair return to investors	✗ Conserving natural resources
✓ Providing steady work	✗ Being honest in what is said about products

Source: Reprinted from *U.S. News & World Report*, September 6, 1976. Copyright 1976 U.S. News & World Report, Inc.

The responses were not all bad, however. The list of strengths in Figure 2–9 is highly complimentary on some important issues like new product development, meeting consumers' needs, hiring and pay practices, and pay and living standards. Perhaps people are saying that the basics are no longer enough—more is expected in today's world.

All in all no particular type of business was given an excellent rating. Some were thought to be good, for example, airlines and banks, but many were thought to be poor, such as auto manufacturers, oil and gas companies, auto dealers, and railroads. Figure 2–10 summarizes the overall ratings.

Attitudes toward government. People expressed considerable dissatisfaction with government. Almost a fifth of the respondents said they had complained to a government agency in the last year about delays, poor service, and errors. Only 68 percent of these said they were satisfied with the handling of their complaint. The U.S. Postal

FIGURE 2–10

HOW BUSINESSES RATE WITH CUSTOMERS

Survey participants were asked to rate the performance of 20 major industries. In the scoring system, 1 is the equivalent of a poor job, and 7 the equivalent of an excellent job. The ranking:

		Average Rating
1.	Airlines	5.17
2.	Banks	5.05
3.	Trucking companies	4.61
4.	Large department stores	4.59
5.	Tire manufacturers	4.57
6.	Retail food chains	4.53
7.	Appliance manufacturers	4.44
8.	Steel manufacturers	4.37
9.	Life-insurance companies	4.31
10.	Drug manufacturers	4.30
11.	Food manufacturers	4.23
12.	Electric utilities	4.16
13.	Construction companies	4.13
13.	Gas utilities	4.13
15.	Service stations	3.98
16.	Appliance-repair services	3.54
17.	Automobile manufacturers	3.53
17.	Oil and gas companies	3.53
17.	Automobile dealers	3.53
20.	Railroads	3.16

FIGURE 2–11

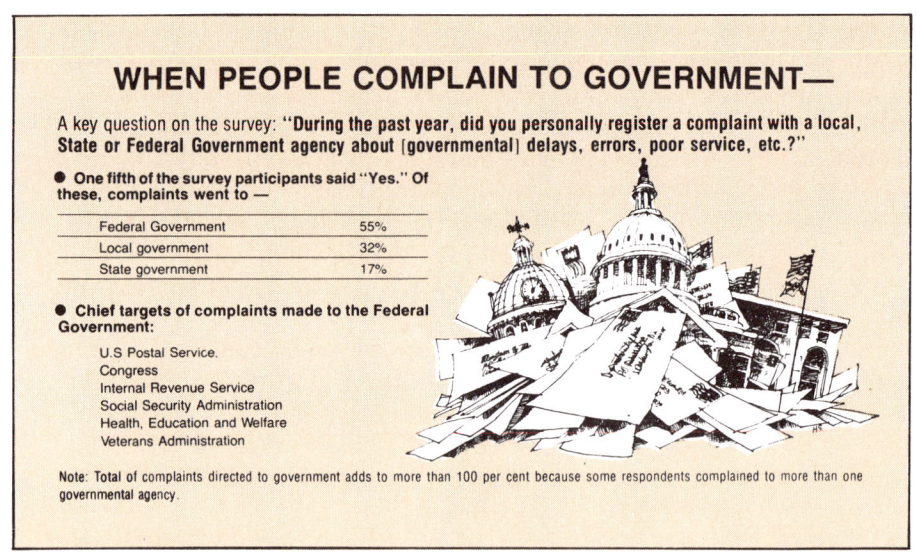

WHEN PEOPLE COMPLAIN TO GOVERNMENT—

A key question on the survey: **"During the past year, did you personally register a complaint with a local, State or Federal Government agency about [governmental] delays, errors, poor service, etc.?"**

● One fifth of the survey participants said "Yes." Of these, complaints went to —

Federal Government	55%
Local government	32%
State government	17%

● **Chief targets of complaints made to the Federal Government:**

U.S Postal Service.
Congress
Internal Revenue Service
Social Security Administration
Health, Education and Welfare
Veterans Administration

Note: Total of complaints directed to government adds to more than 100 per cent because some respondents complained to more than one governmental agency.

Source: Reprinted from *U.S. News & World Report,* September 6, 1976. Copyright 1976 U.S. News & World Report, Inc.

Service was the butt of 20 percent of the complaints (see Figure 2–11). Some people feel that private business could do better.

The passage of Proposition 13, which forced a cut in property taxes in California in 1978, is yet another strong indication of citizens' dissatisfaction with government. It has been said that the way to get a mule's attention is to hit it on the head with a board. That analogy was drawn with Proposition 13. Voters were trying desperately to get the attention of government, feeling that their concerns had been ignored.

Measures of the economy have many dimensions. We have discussed output and productivity, what violent economic fluctuations do to us, and quality of life, a rather subjective reaction to the entire result.

SUMMARY

A successful business finds an advantage and capitalizes on it. The advantage may be an unmet need, a technological breakthrough, or access to markets, such as location or a granted monopoly.

The economic system may be viewed in terms of the people involved, the factors of production, the rewards, who makes the rules, and degrees of competition. People assume multiple roles when you look beyond a single firm. The factors of production reduce to land, labor, capital, and the entrepreneur. Each has rewards, but profit to the entrepreneur is the least understood.

No single controlling body makes the rules for business. Competition and the economic law of supply and demand have an informal influence, but government also establishes rules that affect almost every aspect of business operation. One reason that government is a rule maker is that pure competition exists for only a fraction of industries. There are other business forms involving lesser amounts of competition, such as monopolistic competition, oligopoly, and monopoly.

We need to have a basis for determining how well the economic system is doing. We can look at GNP, how stable the economy is, and the quality of life. Raw GNP figures are impressive, but inflation masks their meaning. Real GNP shows whether or not more goods and services are actually produced. Productivity increases can counterbalance price increases to some extent.

When the economy is stable, real GNP increases about 4 percent per year. But typically the economy has fluctuated around a growth trend involving booms, inflation, and recessions. Controlling the economy seems to be an unsolved problem. Inflation has been a very difficult problem in the 1970s, and people are judging the economy and those who manage it by the inflation rate.

Quality of life is a diffuse concept, but if people feel that the economy doesn't produce it, something is certainly wrong. Some of the many dimensions of quality are living standards, the nature of work in the system, and how the outputs of the system are accepted. A survey indicated rather considerable consumer dissatisfaction with both business and government products and services.

REVIEW QUESTIONS

1. Think about a relatively new enterprise in your community. Does it have some kind of advantage with respect to competitors in the same field? How does it capitalize on its advantage?

2. How meaningful is it to identify people as being part of an entire industry, using a diagram like Figure 2–1?

3. What are the factors of production?

4. What are the rewards given to each of the factors of production?

5. How do you define the term *profit?*

6. Which industries yield the highest profits?

7. How does each of the following function in helping to make the rules of the business game?

   a. Competition.
   b. Supply and demand.
   c. Government.

8. Define the term *market clearing price.*

9. In terms of their numbers, what are the three most common industries?

10. What is the most profitable industry in the United States? The second most profitable industry?

11. Define the terms:

   a. Pure competition.
   b. Monopolistic competition.
   c. Oligopoly.
   d. Monopoly.

12. Define the terms *GNP* and *real GNP.*
13. What causes productivity to increase?
14. What is a business cycle?
15. What actions does government take to stimulate the economy and get out of a recession?
16. What actions does government take to cool off the economy during a boom and to control inflation?
17. What is the inflation machine? How does it work?
18. What is the role of the following in causing inflation?
    a. The money supply.
    b. Deficit spending.
    c. Wars.
    d. Increase in crude oil price.
    e. Fall in productivity.
    f. The wage-price spiral.
19. How do you measure the quality of life?
20. What do you think of Johnny Paycheck's song?

CASES

Case 2–1. Is there a need for —?

Oliver Sparks was an "electronics nut." He had all the equipment an amateur could possibly afford in his basement—test equipment, scopes, a ham radio transmitter, and two receivers. He spent all his spare time related in some way to electrical ideas. He read a variety of magazines that dealt with electronics and all kinds of practical applications of electric gadgets. Indeed, he often had ideas of his own, and constructed prototypes and tried them out.

One morning Oliver was ready to go to work, but his car would not start—the battery was dead. He got a push to the local gas station and had a recharge. It took about an hour, and he spent that time thinking about the inconvenience and time lost and what he could do about it. After all, it was an electrical problem. When he got home that night, he went directly to his basement workshop and started rigging up a way to charge his own battery at home. He figured that there would be many times when he could use the rig, especially when he had been away and his car had not been driven for awhile.

The more Oliver thought about his recharge rig,

the more he was intrigued by the fact that many people often find themselves inconvenienced by run-down batteries. He refined his rig until he felt that anyone could use it. His final design involved a plug-in unit with an electronic circuit inside that was no larger than the rechargers used for pocket calculators. On the other end of a 6-foot cord was a special plug that fit into the cigarette lighter of the car. The recharger end fit into a standard 110-volt wall plug (or an extension cord).

1. Does Oliver's recharger provide for an unmet need in our society?
2. Could a new business be founded on the basis of the home recharger?
3. How can Oliver find out whether his recharger can be exploited as a business?
4. If Oliver were to attempt to establish a new business based on the recharger, what major steps does he need to follow? How can he succeed? How can he fail?

Case 2–2. The King Tut exhibit and scalpers

The fabulous King Tut exhibit made the rounds of the larger U.S. cities in 1978–79. When it came to Los Angeles, the Los Angeles County Museum provided the space and made all the arrangements. The exhibit had been extremely popular in every other city, which provided a great deal of advance publicity for the Los Angeles event. The County Museum wanted to make the cultural event available to everyone, so it priced admission at $2. When tickets went on sale at several locations, the ticket offices were mobbed with people, some of whom had stayed up all night to maintain their places in line. Tickets were sold for every hour of the six-week engagement of the exhibit, and all available tickets were sold on the first day and a half. Everyone connected with the exhibit was delighted that so many Los Angeles citizens wanted culture in their lives.

As soon as the tickets had been sold, however, scalpers were getting as much as $30 per ticket. The news was full of statements of outrage by citizens and public officials.

1. What was the market clearing price for the tickets?
2. Should the County Museum have charged more for the tickets?
3. Is black marketeering a natural outgrowth of an attempt to control or set an artificially low price?
4. If the museum officials wanted to ensure that low-income citizens would have the opportunity to see the Tut exhibit, what other mechanisms could they have used instead of the $2 price?

chapter
3

SOCIAL
RESPONSIBILITY
OF BUSINESS

By studying this chapter you should be able to find answers to these questions:

1 Why should business be involved in socially responsible issues?

2 What are the social responsibilities of business to employees, customers, and the public at large?

3 What government agencies regulate conditions for employees, customers, and the public at large?

4 What kinds of socially responsible actions has business taken on its own?

5 What are the rights of citizens with respect to the economic system? What are their corresponding responsibilities?

6 What abuses do employees and customers indulge in which place added strains on the economic system?

Terms you should know:

Clean Air Act of 1977
Consumer Product Safety Commission (CPSC)
Environmental Protection Agency (EPA)
Food and Drug Administration (FDA)
National Minority Purchasing Council
Occupational Safety and Health
    Administration (OSHA)
Water Pollution Control Act of 1972

Why should business be interested in social issues? After all, why are people in business anyway? Isn't it to make money? Why get involved in social and environmental issues that cost money and dilute profits? Some managers feel that business should concentrate on the economic functions and not be diverted with social responsibilities. This narrow view is not representative of today's businesspeople, however.

WHY BUSINESS SHOULD BE INVOLVED

Pollution, destruction of redwood trees, and little fishes that may become extinct—what do these issues have to do with business? Since business has played a role in generating social problems, there is no justification for its inaction. In fact, there may be short- and long-range benefits to business in helping to solve social problems. Also, everyone has a stake in humanity. We are all part of the human race—breathing the same air, drinking the water, being exposed to unsafe products, and so on. We all have many roles in society as citizens, customers, investors, as well as businesspeople.

"I breathe, too, you know!"

Reprinted by permission *The Wall Street Journal*.

The multiple roles that businesspeople assume in society provide a way of seeing the reasons for their involvement. Let's look at three groups of people: employees, customers, and the general public.

ROBERT L. CHAMBERS
Making pollution pay

Mr. Robert L. Chambers is the founder and currently the chairman of Envirotech Corporation. Chambers' significant accomplishments in business began in 1947 when he founded the Magna Power Tool Corporation, the producer of the "Shopsmith." Between then and now he was president of the BSP Corporation, but for students of business, his most important accomplishment was to capitalize on pollution control.

For many businesspeople, pollution control means being controlled by government agencies, but Chambers saw opportunity. He saw an unfilled need for a "total capabilities" company that could serve the emerging pollution control market. By merging and acquiring related companies in air quality control, water quality control, instruments and controls, and mining machinery, Chambers developed a "one-stop" place for industry to shop for pollution controls.

In 1969, when Chambers founded Envirotech, it had only two other employees. In three months it was off and running with 2,000 employees; in 1979, just ten years later, there were more than 9,000 workers. It lost money at first, like almost all new businesses, but after ten years, Envirotech had total revenues of more than $50 million and a net income of more than $15 million.

EMPLOYEES

It hits close to home when you think about employees. What are the broader social issues with respect to employees? Are the jobs in the organization safe? Is one likely to be injured because of the way jobs are designed? What can be done to redesign them so they are safe? Does it make any difference if jobs are boring? Does business have a responsibility to hire minorities, women, and the handicapped?

Health and safety

Some industrial jobs have hazards associated with them. Coal miners stand a good chance of getting black lung disease and face significant risks of mine accidents. Mine accidents and black lung disease kill about 100 workers per 10,000 worker-hours of exposure, making mining one of the most hazardous industries. Recently, the cancer-causing effects of working with asbestos have become known. If you work around nuclear materials or X-ray machines, radiation exposure is a hazard. If you're a salesperson or business executive, there are health and safety hazards that come from traveling and job stress.

Business managers usually see clearly the connection between employee health and safety and the short- and long-run benefits derived from controlling health and safety hazards. Beyond humanitarian motives, poor health and safety records are costly. They result in lower productivity, higher worker's compensation insurance premiums, and possible law suits when employees are injured or disabled by work-related health problems.

Beyond the humanitarian and cost reasons, there are strong regulatory and institutional forces that demand the attention of business. The **Occupational Safety and Health Administration** (OSHA) is a government regulatory body that issues stringent regulations concerning all aspects of worker health and safety. The detailed rules and regulations were "driving managers up the wall." Finally, in 1977, OSHA recalled some 1,100 detailed safety regulations in favor of more general rules that allowed businesses some discretion in adapting to local situations.

Currently, however, OSHA is on a cancer crusade, having issued a far-reaching proposal for identifying and regulating cancer-causing substances in the workplace. OSHA plans to take the nation's dry cleaners to the cleaners. The most common dry-cleaning solvent comes in contact with 2.8 million workers in about 155,000 U.S. plants and is suspected of causing cancer. The cost of regulating the use of the solvent is estimated at $1 billion per year, with small dry-cleaning companies paying more than a quarter of the total.[1] They will probably have to install machinery that can use other solvents. Your dry-cleaning bills will be going up to help protect the industry's workers from cancer.

The other important forces demanding that business protect the health and safety of employees is labor unions. Working conditions are bargainable issues in union negotiations.

So business is concerned with the social issues of employee health and safety for several reasons: because of humanitarian reasons, because it costs money to have a poor record, and because they are forced to by OSHA and labor unions.

Meaningful jobs

The fact that employees object to boring assembly-line types of jobs is not new. In the 1950s researchers asked 180 assembly-line workers this question, "Would you say your job was interesting, fairly interesting, not too interesting, or not at all interesting?" The results became famous as a characterization of "the man on the assembly line." They showed that the larger the number of operations performed, the more often employees rated the job interesting or fairly interesting. And indeed the opposite was also true. The fewer the number of operations performed, the more often workers rated the job as not interesting.

Should business take it as a responsibility to provide interesting jobs, or should jobs be structured in a way that simply minimizes labor costs? The issue was taken up by IBM in 1950. It decided that jobs should be designed with broader scope so that employees could see more of the end product of their efforts. The term **job enlargement** was coined to describe the process and marked the beginning of a movement to increase job scope in industry. Today it is not uncommon to find employees participating in the design of their jobs and in many other decisions that used to be strictly up to management.

Hiring minorities, women, and the handicapped

"The XYZ Company is an Equal Opportunity Employer!" Companies regularly use this statement in advertising for help. It means that they are abiding by the government-enforced rules against discrimination in hiring practices. The rules say that employers should have proportions of minorities and women on their payrolls that equal the proportions in the community. The rules have been enforced particularly on the largest and most visible companies. It is not always easy for a company to follow the rules, especially if the skills required are not commonly found in members of minority groups. Many companies have had to set up training programs to develop the required skills in newly hired employees.

Employing people with physical handicaps is being recognized by many businesses as both humane and good business. Physical handicaps may limit the range of activities of an employee, but the handicapped may be fully capable of performing jobs that are designed to be within their range. Surveys have shown that handicapped employees perform extremely well.

So business accepts responsibility for employee health and safety and for increasing job satisfaction. It is in its self-interest. It may reduce operating costs or forestall liabilities, and it embraces employees as fellow human beings. Business also accepts responsibility to provide employment without discrimination.

CUSTOMERS

If employees are part of the immediate business family, then customers are no further away than cousins. Customers are dear to the hearts of business. Business must be interested in what customers need and how they are reacting to the products and services they use.

There really should be no problem. Certainly the forces of competition should make business supersensitive to what the customer needs and wants. If that's true, though, why is there a consumer movement? Why is there a **Consumer Product Safety Commission** (CPSC)? Why has there been a strong movement to establish a consumer department in the government, headed by a secretary with full cabinet status?

Toys that kill

It was a tragic Christmas for parents who gave their child a TV-promoted toy called "Battle Star Galactica." The toy fired small projectiles when a button was pressed. The parents' small child pointed the toy into his open mouth and pressed the button. The projectile became lodged in his throat, and the child died. A doctor warned that the toy was potentially dangerous because small children do put things into their mouths, and the warning was aired on the "Today Show" in September. But the warning was not heeded by the manufacturer or the CPSC, and the toy was not recalled.

Should the CPSC have recalled the toy when the warning was issued? Should the CPSC set standards for toy designs?

A U.S. Department of Commerce study released in 1976 states: "Defectively designed or produced products are estimated to kill 30,000 Americans each year."[2] Product liability costs far outweigh those related to medical malpractice which received so much publicity in the 1970s. The cost of liability insurance coverage for accidents not related to automobiles reached $1 billion in 1961, $2 billion by 1970, $3 billion by 1974, and perhaps $30 billion by 1980 according to estimates. With numbers like these, there must be a product liability problem!

The consumer movement attracted great attention with the publication of Ralph Nader's book, *Unsafe at Any Speed.* The book attacked the rear-engine Corvair, GM's first compact car, as being unstable and unsafe.

Since the 1960s the list of product safety issues has grown. First it was said that children's clothes must be treated with flame retardants—product safety, right? The flame retardant "Tris" was used widely, but then it was suspected of causing cancer. It was then banned by the CPSC, which ordered the chemical companies and retailers to help bear the cost of customer refunds. Some manufacturers were stuck with millions of dollars worth of inventory.

Then there is the question of mechanically deboned meat. Apparently the deboning equipment can get an extra 3 percent of meat from carcasses for making frankfurters, bologna, and other processed prod-

The mechanical butcher: An advance in technology, but is it good for the consumers?

ucts. But consumer groups filed suits against the use of the machines, and a Washington, D.C., judge agreed that there were hazards and banned the machines. The hazards were alleged to be tiny bone particles in deboned meat and higher fat content. Where should business stand on the issue? On one side there are potential hazards. But on the other, industry executives say that the ban cuts out edible product that costs only 18¢ to 19¢ per pound. This inexpensive meat is used in sausage to replace meat that costs 72¢ to 76¢ per pound, and this would mean lower prices for consumers.

There have also been controversies over stepladders, auto seat belts, air bags instead of seat belts, saccharin, the carpet frauds, and truth in lending. Why should business get involved? First, because there are obvious problems with some products. Second, because the cost of doing nothing is becoming prohibitive. Third, because consumer groups are becoming aggressive. And fourth, because consumers are a part of humanity, and unsafe products cannot be excused.

THE PUBLIC

Public issues of the social responsibility of business became prominent with the publication of Rachel Carson's book, *Silent Spring*. The buildup of DDT concentrations and its effect on wildlife dramatized pollution as a social issue. The reasons business should be responsive to public social issues are really similar to the reasons they should be interested in employee and customer social issues. Business helps generate the problems, businesspeople are a part of the communities affected, and all are a part of humanity.

There are often economic reasons, too. Sometimes there may be legal action by public-interest groups or government, so it may be more economical to be socially responsible than not. Competitors may force socially responsive action. For example, when Inland Steel Company cleaned up its water and air pollution in Gary, Indiana, the dirty smokestacks of their industrial neighbor, Youngstown Sheet and Tube, became even more obvious.

Sometimes, however, the economic reasons are positive. For example, Goodyear Tire and Rubber Company plans to invest $50–$100 million in energy-saving projects during the 1979–89 decade and figures to earn handsome returns on the investments. They assume that within the decade, fuel oil prices will increase by 50 percent, natural gas prices will double, and electricity rates will increase by a third. Therefore, the investments will more than pay for themselves by giving lower energy costs. Socially responsible actions and profitability can go together.

The list of public issues that involve business is very long and includes:

1. Environmental protection and pollution (endangered species, air, water, and noise pollution).
2. Urban maintenance and renewal.
3. Resource utilization, for example, energy conservation.
4. Equal employment opportunity.
5. Unemployment.
6. Fair competitive practices.

Government has taken an active role in pressing for business action, particularly regarding pollution and the environment. The **Environmental Protection Agency** (EPA) has been particularly aggressive in setting

---

THE MIGHTY SNAIL DARTER

The snail darter is a tiny fish that is on the endangered species list. Its last habitat happened to be in the way of the Tellico Dam project in Tennessee. The first obvious solution was to move the little fishes to another nice place elsewhere. But snail darters do not take well to being moved—they object by dying! So midway in the project, work on the dam was stopped by legal action. The little fishes had taken their case all the way to the Supreme Court and won. Now the Senate and the House of Representatives, which had passed the Endangered Species Act in the first place, are wondering whether the law provides for a balance between conflicting social objectives.

standards for air quality, automobile pollution, water quality, and similar concerns.

Laws have been passed to protect endangered species. Environmentalists work hard to extend the approved list of endangered species. The endangered species are sometimes on a collision course with other socially desirable projects of either private or public enterprises, however. An important public issue is not whether the endangered species should be protected, but how to balance these objectives with the costs to society.

The aerosol ban

In 1974 two University of California chemists published a theory that fluorocarbons, the propellants commonly used in aerosol spray cans, damage the protective layer of ozone in the atmosphere. Among the predicted effects was an increase in skin cancer. The ozone screen filters out some ultraviolet radiation, and the amount of radiation would increase if the ozone screen were depleted. At that time, fluorocarbons were included in about 50 percent of the aerosol market. There was an immediate reaction by environmentally minded consumers who boycotted such products.

In 1977 a ban and a timetable were announced by the **Food and Drug Administration** (FDA), the Environmental Protection Agency, and the Consumer Products Safety Commission. Manufacturing of fluorocarbons for the aerosol market would cease by October 1978, companies could not use the gas in products after December 1978, and spray cans with the gas could not be sold at all after April 1979. The aerosol ban threatened the $4.7 billion industry. The two biggest manufacturers were DuPont and Allied Chemical Corporation. The lost sales were estimated to be more than $1 billion as shown in Table 3–1.

What did the industry do? It adapted quickly by finding a technological solution. Robert Abplanalp, president of Precision Valve Corporation, announced a new valve design within one day of the ban an-

TABLE 3–1
What the fluorocarbon ban will cost industry

Industry sector	Lost sales, 1977–1980 (millions of 1976 dollars)
Marketers and captive fillers	$ 573
Chemical manufacturers	299
Container manufacturers	132
Valve manufacturers	37
Independent fillers	26
Total	$1,067

Source: Reprinted from the May 30, 1977 issue of *Business Week* by special permission, © 1977 by McGraw-Hill, Inc., New York, N.Y. 10020. All rights reserved.

nouncement. Abplanalp was the designer of the first aerosol valve. The new valve, called "Aquasol," makes it possible to use new propellants that do not damage the atmosphere.

The new propellants are less costly and promise to ease the economic impact of the ban. Industry experts expect sales to be back on track in the early 1980s. Social goals were met, perhaps saving future lives, and the economic impact was softened by a phasing out rather than an immediate ban. Business prevented a potential economic disaster by doing one of the things it does best—use technology to solve problems.

"*Eureka! I've discovered it—assuming validation by my peers, clearance from the FDA, and ambient air quality standards in production that fall within appropriate EPA guidelines.*"

The clean air act

The efforts to clean up the air were thought by many citizens to be an "act" played by both public and business officials. Indeed, smog exists in every large city. Those suffering in Los Angeles have felt for 20 years or more that nothing was really being done. But in August

TABLE 3–2
Estimated costs to fight
air pollution (in billions
of 1974 dollars)

Private spending	
Auto pollution	$ 82
Industrial pollution	$ 27
Utilities pollution	$ 32
Government spending	
Pollution from public buildings, incinerators,	
and other government facilities	$ 6
Total	$147

Source: Council on Environmental Quality. *U.S. News & World Report*, August 4, 1975, Copyright 1975, U.S. News & World Report, Inc.

1977, President Carter signed a new **Clean Air Act.** Even before that legislation, steps had finally been taken that tightened controls on permissible amounts of emission from autos, power plants, and other industrial sources.

While hardly anyone is in favor of dirty air, the clean-up costs are staggering. As early as 1974, the Council on Environmental Quality estimated that it would take $147 billion to fight air pollution. The cost breakdown in Table 3–2 also indicates the major sources of pollution.

The remedies for auto pollution are well known. Catalytic converters on new cars have met auto pollution standards. The costs to the consumer have been higher auto prices and higher costs for unleaded gas. A handful of manufacturers, such as Honda, have met the emission standards without needing converters and unleaded gas.

Industrial air pollution laws bar the construction of new plants (pollution sources) in areas where air quality standards are already being violated. This affects virtually every existing industrial community. The result of these rules is to put new pollution sources only in nice, clean places, which may have no economic advantages. EPA has finally relented by stating a new policy that allows a new pollution source to be built if the builder can show that existing pollution sources have been reduced by a greater amount than the new added source. Then, total pollution will be reduced while permitting expansion.

Under the new policy, Standard Oil of Ohio (SOHIO) wanted to build new storage tanks in Los Angeles in order to ship Alaskan oil through Los Angeles to Western Texas. In order to meet the guideline of less air pollution, SOHIO bought out owners of existing tank farms. It then shut down the old tanks in order to get EPA approval for the new ones.

The electric utility companies are a major source of pollution, and EPA has set emission standards for them. The emissions from smokestacks include both solid and chemical pollutants. Great emphasis has been placed on reducing the allowed amounts of sulfur dioxide (SO_2)

produced by burning coal. The new push to use coal as an energy source has made compliance even more difficult. Technology has produced SO_2 "scrubbers," which reduce emissions of SO_2, but cause a pollution problem of their own—scrubber sludge.

A significant problem for utilities and for many other industries is the time required for planning and constructing new power plants. As EPA establishes new standards, utilities are caught in the middle of existing expansion projects. Utilities fear that if emission standards are tightened often, they will never get their expansion projects out of the planning stages. EPA finally came down on the side of the utilities in setting its 1978 standards. It cited "potentially disruptive effects of applying the rules to projects about to begin construction." The Indiana and Michigan Power Company was granted a permit to build two huge plants within one day after the announcement of the new standards.

DID YOU EVEN WONDER?

How long does it take to choose a site and then design, plan, and build a new electric power plant?

If all you want to do is build a coal-fired power plant, it will take only seven to ten years. The first one or two years are allocated to site approvals and particularly environmental considerations.

If you want to build a nuclear plant, it takes nine to twelve years. The first two to four years are for site preparation and environmental studies.

For both coal-fired and nuclear plants, a good share of the time required after site approval is allocated to delays due to regulatory reports, inspections, and other factors related to maintaining environmental standards.

Don't drink that water!

A quaint sign in a restroom of a Janesville, Wisconsin, restaurant reads, "Please Flush the Toilet, As Beloit Needs the Water." This is a humorous reminder of the interdependence of most of our water supply systems. What we put into the system comes out in someone else's water supply, or even in our own.

The federal **Water Pollution Control Act of 1972** called for the installation of the best practical pollution control technology by 1977 and the best available technology by 1983. Industry seemed to accept the 1977 target but choked on the 1983 target. Edwin Gee, a senior vice president at DuPont speaking for industry, said that the 1983 requirement would cost $22 billion and that it represented "treatment for treatment's sake."[3]

Industry is ahead of municipalities in having 85 percent compliance with the 1977 requirement, compared with only 33 percent compliance by municipalities. In December 1977, the National Commission on Water Quality and Industry recommended a five- to ten-year postponement of the 1983 requirements. The compromise solution, however, requires that the 1983 standards be applied rigidly to a list of 129 hazardous chemicals by 1984. All other pollutants fall into a different category that must meet the "best available technology" requirement by 1987.

A great deal of progress has already been made. Water pollution clean-up programs have brought several "dead" bodies of water back to the point where they support life. These include Escambia Bay near Pensacola, Florida; Lake Erie; Salt Pond at Blue Hill, Maine; St. Paul Harbor at Kodiak, Alaska; and the Thames River in England.

A body of water as large as Lake Erie was dying in the late 1960s. Sewage and other pollutants used up the oxygen needed by fish. But now the decline in the life-support capability of the lake has been reversed. Biologists credit an extensive program to control the kind and amount of sewage, pesticides, and other toxic materials dumped into the lake. A majority of industrial violators complied by 1977. Officials are even predicting that sport fishing may be possible in the future.

The water pollution compromise between industry and the National Commission on Water Quality represents social responsibility on the part of both. By working toward a mutually satisfactory solution, their joint responsibility to the public has created a program to provide clean water at a cost that is affordable to the public.

SOCIALLY RESPONSIBLE BUSINESS ACTIONS

The news is filled with reports of conflict between business and regulatory bodies such as EPA and environmentalists. Business is often portrayed as the villain who cares nothing about protecting the environment if it costs money. But the position to "clean up at any cost" is not socially responsible either. There are extreme situations calling for extreme action, and perhaps the aerosol ban was one of these. But since the public ultimately pays the cost in higher prices and taxes, business must seek balance in solutions to public issues. Business often needs time to absorb the costs and to meet standards.

Business has made heroic efforts to clean up the environment, measured in part by the expenditures of pollution control projects. In 1974 the Council on Environmental Quality estimated that expenditures for the next ten years would be $224 billion, of which about $190 billion would be spent by industry. Some of the individual projects are of staggering proportions.

One of the largest industrial environmental clean-up projects ever attempted got under way in the late 1970s. Armco and Republic Steel

Companies jointly will spend $370 million to end the dumping of waste rock into Lake Superior and to complete related pollution control projects at the iron pellet plant of Reserve Mining Company in Minnesota. The clean-up program exceeds the cost of $350 million that was required to build the original industrial plant.

Business is investing millions in projects to save energy. Goodyear has a manager of energy conservation who states that the company is spending $64,000 to apply insulation to steam-heated tanks in Houston. But, the resulting fuel savings will total $143,000 in the first year. Similar projects in the company are equally good investments. General Electric spent $13,000 for shutdown timers on equipment in Louisville. The timers shut off machines any time they have been idle for 15 minutes, which saves about $51,000 in electricity per year. IBM is putting computers to work at energy conservation. Computers control energy use by shutting off lights or machines when they are not needed.

Industry self-regulation

Perhaps the highest order of social consciousness is to take personal initiative for social responsibility. Many industries have established their own standards for product safety and have issued "seals of approval" for products that meet these standards (see Figure 3–1). This same type of effort occurs with many services. The Fabricare Institute, an association of 1,500 California dry cleaners and launderers, has a system to help consumers who have problems with any of its members. The member has a week to reach an agreement with the consumer or the institute takes over and imposes a settlement.

Pollution control as a business

Why not start a business designed to meet an unmet need—to clean up pollution? Entrepreneurs certainly would not miss a good bet for long, and they haven't. One good example is a firm called Envirotech, which was started in 1969 by Robert Chambers. With so much money being spent in the United States on pollution control, someone must be a supplier of systems and equipment. Chambers decided to combine components like pumps, filters, evaporators, and sewage treatment equipment into a high-technology pollution control company. It worked!

Crunch on small business

Did you know that a company can finance the purchase of pollution control equipment by issuing **tax-exempt bonds?** This is an incentive to get business to cooperate with the social objectives of pollution clean-up. It works like this. The company issues bonds at interest rates

FIGURE 3–1
Industry
self-regulation

How safe?

The whirling blade of a rotary mower can cut off a toe or finger in an instant or turn a piece of wire or a pebble into a dangerous missile.

The latest industry safety standards from the Outdoor Power Equipment Institute and the American National Standards Institute considerably diminish the chances of serious accidents. They include such safeguards as a stress-tested deck that extends an eighth of an inch below the path of the blade, a trailing shield between the rear wheels to stop flying objects and help prevent your foot or hand from entering the housing, and discharge chutes angled to limit the height and distance a blade can hurl an object.

Probably 90% of mowers sold today are covered by these standards, although compliance is voluntary. Machines that do comply have this triangular seal bearing, next to the words "safety standards," the legend "ANS B71.1a-1974."

Important as safety standards may be, they are no substitute for caution and common sense. Play it safe. Read and *follow* the safety rules in the owner's manual that comes with your mower.

Source: Reprinted with permission from *Changing Times* Magazine, © 1977 Kiplinger Washington Editors, Inc., April 1977 *Changing Times.*

in the range of 5–7 percent. These are very low-cost financing rates for a company. Investors are willing to buy bonds with such low interest rates because they do not have to pay income taxes on the interest. The result is incentives for business to clean up pollution and for investors to accept low-interest, but tax-free, income.

Until recently, only large companies like Exxon, General Motors, and U.S. Steel were able to take advantage of tax-exempt bond financing. Small companies could not use the tax-exempt bonds because the costs of issuing these bonds priced them out of the market. The result was that large companies could finance expensive pollution control equipment at interest rates of only 5–7 percent, to be paid back over 20–40 years. Small companies had to use ordinary bank financing at rates of 10–12 percent over short periods like five years.

Finally, financiers realized that they were missing an opportunity. A precedent was set in the late 1970s when the California Pollution Control Financing Authority combined the financial needs of seven different companies in one $4.6 million bond offering. By combining their smaller needs into one large offering, the companies could take advantage of tax-exempt bond financing. The Small Business Administration gets into the act with a loan guarantee. The bonds cost the seven companies only about 6 percent over 20 years.

So business is really doing a great deal to be socially responsible. There are several reasons for their involvement:

1. Personal ethics and genuine feeling of responsibility.
2. Actions of competitors.
3. Industry self-regulated standards.
4. Pressures from crusaders like Ralph Nader and Rachel Carson.
5. Public-interest pressure groups.
6. Government legislation and regulation by OSHA, and EPA, and other agencies and also at the state and local levels.

The costs of socially responsible actions are enormous and are passed onto consumers in the prices of products. The balancing act that business managers must perform is to be socially responsible without pricing their products out of the market. That's why there is often foot-dragging by individual companies and industries. Business managers need to be able to absorb the costs over a period of time when faced with enormous expenses or with loss of revenue as with the aerosol ban.

Using the unique talents of businesspeople

Businesspeople often express their desire to be socially responsible through personal public service. It is very common to find businesspeople serving for no pay on commissions, charity groups, and other efforts to help solve social problems.

One such group is the **National Minority Purchasing Council,** which was established in 1972. The simple objective of the council is to increase the number of purchases large companies make from minority-owned companies. In its first year the council generated $86 million in minority purchases. This total grew to almost $1 billion in 1977.

SOCIAL RESPONSIBILITY OF CITIZENS

The great surge of social issues being thrust on business comes from reactions of individuals as employees, as consumers, and as citizens at large. These reactions have been galvanized through group action. Labor unions, consumer groups, and public-interest groups have made the collective feelings of people felt. These actions say, in effect, that people have rights that are related to the economic system. President John F. Kennedy summarized these rights in 1962 in a simple but eloquent way as:

1. The right to safety.
2. The right to be informed.
3. The right to choose.
4. The right to be heard.

Much of the pressure from people represents demand for these fundamental rights.

Citizens must accept their corresponding responsibilites if the whole system is ever going to work:

1. The responsibility to use with care as directed.
2. The responsibility to seek and process information.
3. The responsibility to compare and avoid waste.
4. The responsibility to express needs and preferences.

As individual citizens, we often only complain and expect someone else to act. But we have responsibilities, too.

Product misuse is a serious problem that can result in a product liability suit. The courts have held companies liable under product safety codes even when a consumer misused the product. The legal rationale is that misuse comes under the "foreseeable use" doctrine. It is necessary only to prove that the product was used in a foreseeable manner and that injury resulted. The fact that the product may have been misused is not given much weight, since the concept of foreseeable use has been extended to mean that the misuse was foreseeable by the manufacturer.

The potential for unethical abuse through product misuse is enormous. The total number of such suits has increased 200 percent within the past five years. Insurance premiums for product liability have soared in order to cover the cost of court awards. Manufacturers and insurance companies feel that enough is enough. They think greater responsibility should be placed on consumers to use products with reasonable care. They have even taken out newspaper ads, pleading for greater consumer responsibility. Product costs are increased by these liability costs, and we are all paying for the abuses.

Who pays the cost when a consumer makes a buying mistake? Many mistakes result from a lack of information, even when the correct information is readily available. Consumers make purchases without considering the alternatives or even without considering something as simple as the right size. Later, they return the merchandise, and the cost of processing the return must come out of the store's revenues.

There are also returns of merchandise that has in fact been used. Incredible as it may seem to many, it is not uncommon for a high-style dress to be worn to a party and returned as "unsuitable" the next day.

Have you ever been asked to answer a few questions about a product or service for a consumer survey? Many people regard these surveys as unreasonable intrusions. They refuse to answer. But think about it. How is business going to provide the goods and services you need if you keep your needs and preferences a secret?

Shoplifting and theft

If you want to hear some revealing facts, talk to a department store manager about the extent of shoplifting. Both customers and employees do it. A New Orleans supermarket chain manager estimates that 1 out of 14 people is shoplifting significantly. A Los Angeles department store manager states that his store loses more than $1 million per year in theft, or 3.4 percent of sales. Who pays for shoplifting? We all pay, through prices that are higher than they otherwise would be.

What can business do about shoplifting? Increased security of all kinds has been used: undercover agents, tagging merchandise with materials that set off alarms if taken, and others. A unique system uses muzak broadcasting "I will not steal" mixed in with the music. People do not consciously hear the message, but it is supposed to sink into their subconscious. The shoplifter is unknowingly being lulled into honesty. The system is being tested and if successful will certainly be used commonly.

Another current remedy for shoplifting is directed at screening out dishonest employees through the use of lie detectors. Montgomery Ward, a user of lie detectors, says: "From 50 to 70 percent of our loss goes to employees, and this is the same for any retailer. Shoplifters don't take you for nearly as much."[4]

A *Business Week* survey in 1978 indicated that lie detectors are being used in all types of companies: retailers, manufacturers, auto insurance companies, nursing homes, and others. A developing issue in the use of lie detectors is their legality. Is it an unconstitutional invasion of privacy or a legitimate way to screen out dishonest employees?

Muzak and Shoplifting

As reprinted from *The Sacramento Bee*, August 14, 1978.

Bad checks and other abuses

Getting a check cashed has become a hassle. In the Boston area and elsewhere, you may have to submit to fingerprinting and a "mug shot." But, if you complain, the store manager is likely to invite you to cover the burgeoning bad check account. It has been estimated that one out of every ten checks written in supermarkets bounces.

Other customers may not pass bad checks but may simply charge purchases and not pay. Credit losses are a big source of business loss. Businesses spend money on credit checks before offering people credit, but even then credit losses are substantial. A Los Angeles department store reports that it lost $480,000 in bad checks on a total volume of $30 million. It also takes credit losses on 10 to 13 percent of its credit sales, and over half of its business is done on a credit bases. The honest customers have to pay for the dishonest acts of others.

Trade secrets represent another kind of theft. A trade secret is recognized by the courts as anything that gives a company a competitive edge. In addition, it must be kept secret within the company and not generally known. It could be a formula, process, product, or technique. The "trade" in trade secrets goes on in basically two ways. A competitor or a go-between can actually steal a valuable document. This is clearly illegal. The other more common way is to hire away a competitor's executives. The executives bring the information with them, either in their heads or on paper conveniently copied on the office copier.

The courts have given injured firms strong backing in protecting their trade secrets. For example, IBM was awarded $20 million when Telex Corporation was found guilty of making off with trade secrets by hiring IBM executives away. A former manager of a Celanese Corporation plastics plant was ordered to pay that company $500,000 when found guilty of selling trade secrets to a Japanese firm.

The social responsibility of citizens is an issue that cannot be solved by legal mechanisms. It goes to the heart of "moral decay." Shoplifting, bad checks, theft of trade secrets, and product misuse are measures of people's attitudes toward the "system." Abusers often express feelings such as, "I'm being ripped off daily by the system, so why shouldn't I get my share, too?" Perhaps the depersonalized nature of large businesses has taken a cultural toll. When people steal from employers, they seem to feel that there is nothing personal about it. The employer is a big nonhuman thing, and besides the theft is nothing in relation to billion dollar sales figures.

SUMMARY

Business should be involved in social issues for a variety of reasons: (1) business has played an important role in generating problems that have broad social significance for employees, customers, and the public at large; (2) there may be short- and long-run advantages that result from involvement, and (3) we all have a stake in humanity.

For employees, the social issues are health and safety and the nature of their jobs. Working in some industries is hazardous, and special care is needed to make jobs safe. Business needs to accept responsibility for the effect of unsafe working conditions. OSHA has broad powers as a government agency to regulate conditions at the workplace. Labor unions also apply pressure to maintain safe and healthful conditions.

Customers have banned together in the consumer movement to demand social responsibility with respect to product safety and consumer fraud. The CPSC has been created to regulate and set standards.

The broadest social responsibility issues are those that affect the public at large. These issues get the most publicity, since they focus on matters of nationwide concern: environmental protection, pollution, urban renewal, energy conservation, equal employment opportunity, unemployment, and fair competitive practices. Pollution and the environment have been the most prominent issues, and EPA is the government regulator. The cost of cleaning up air, water, noise, and solid waste pollution is so enormous that it cannot be absorbed in a short time. A responsible position by business, government, and the general public recognizes a balance of social goals in which the cost to the public is one of the considerations.

Business has taken socially responsible action on its own. Business-people have participated at all levels in trying to seek solutions. Business has developed self-regulatory measures and gone into the business of pollution control. Tax-exempt bond financing of pollution control equipment has provided an incentive for business action, and this strategy is now also available to small business.

Employees, consumers, and the public also have social responsibilities. The extent of shoplifting, employee theft, bad checks, credit losses, and other abuses is shocking. While citizens have rights with respect to the economic system, they also have corresponding responsibilities.

REVIEW QUESTIONS

1. Should business be involved in broad social issues? Why shouldn't their responsibilities be restricted to the production of goods and services?

2. What is the nature of responsibilities that business has to each of the following?
   a. Employees.
   b. Customers.
   c. The public at large.

3. What is the role of each of the following in regulating business?
   a. OSHA.
   b. CPSC.
   c. EPA.
   d. FDA.

4. Can you think of any industries that have self-regulatory bodies for consumer protection?

5. Why should businesspeople serve on commissions, boards of charitable organizations, and other bodies? Should they be paid for such service?

6. President Kennedy stated the rights of citizens with respect to the economic system. Think about this statement of rights with respect to business responsibility to employees, customers, and the public at large. Do you feel that citizens' rights are being met?

7. Should business use lie detectors to screen out dishonest employees? If not, what other control measures do you suggest to reduce employee theft?

8. Since bad checks and credit losses are so extensive, should business use a cash-only system?

9. Under what conditions do you feel that business should accept the return of merchandise?

10. What position do you think business should take on the misuse of products that might result in accident or injury and resulting liability?

CASES

Case 3–1.   My business is being killed by pollution control

Rose Ferris owns and operates a small dry-cleaning business. She used to describe it as "a good clean business." But the local air pollution control officials visited her one day, and after inspecting her plant, they told her that she would have to install pollution control equipment to reduce emissions of the cleaning fluids to acceptable levels. Not only that, but she was given only six months to convert entirely to the use of different cleaning fluids that were less volatile and less lethal. Rose couldn't understand why they were "after the cleaning business." "After all," she said, "there aren't that many cleaners in town, and they couldn't be contributing very much to pollution."

The entire episode seemed like a nightmare to Rose when she received bids for the required pollution control equipment—$150,000. Also, the new cleaning fluid would cost 50 percent more than the traditional fluids she had been using.

After recovering from the initial shock, the realities hit Rose. She didn't have $150,000 to invest in the business, and she feared that she would not even be able to finance the equipment at the bank since her business was not all that profitable. The more expensive cleaning fluid would increase her operating costs and require her to raise prices. She was afraid that she would not be able to compete with the larger chain operators in the area. After 20 years in the business, she wondered whether she should quit.

1. *What is Rose's social responsibility?*
2. *Are the pollution control officials going too far? Should they be allowed to put Rose out of business?*
3. *Would it make a difference in this case if Rose operated a large, financially strong business, perhaps one of the chain operations that she referred to?*

Case 3–2.   How do you feel about the snail darter's case?

Reread the paragraph concerning the snail darter on page 66 in this chapter.

1. *What do you think are the real issues in this case between the snail darter and the builders of the Tellico Dam?*
2. *Should an economic development project be allowed to kill off an endangered species?*
3. *Should a little fish be allowed to block a multimillion-dollar economic development project that will bolster local business and provide employment for hundreds of people?*
4. *How do you balance the conflicting social objectives of protecting an endangered species and promoting economic development?*

part II

WHY:

The benefits of business

We know that business firms exist within an economic environment and that they can continue to exist only by using resources wisely to provide the utilities that people are willing to buy. But firms are owned and managed by people. Why do some people take the responsibility for setting up these organizations to meet the needs of other people? Why do other people invest their money in businesses? There are certainly risks involved.

You might say that people start businesses because they hope to make money. That probably would be right, but financial rewards are only part of the lure of starting, managing, or investing in a business firm. Those who take these responsibilities also may be rewarded with a feeling of accomplishment.

In this country we have many different types of firms. Some are small businesses owned and operated by a single person or family. Others are partnerships among a small group of people. And at the extreme there are huge corporations with hundreds of thousands of shareholders and professional managers. How do these forms of organizations differ? Why is each form appropriate in certain situations? How are the participants rewarded? These are the questions we will deal with in Chapter 4.

Can a small business survive in today's economy? There are many small business failures. One solution is franchising. Through franchising, a small business can enjoy some of the benefits of big business. Franchising is becoming so important in our country that it is the focus of Chapter 5.

Any business can continue to exist only if it is profitable. How is profitability measured? How can a firm detect problem areas and bring its financial affairs under control? How do the people who invest in businesses know whether the professional managers are doing their jobs well? Chapter 6 covers the topic of accounting—the process by which both small and large firms collect, analyze, and report the financial data on their operations.

RISKS AND BENEFITS: FORMS OF BUSINESS ORGANIZATION

By studying this chapter you should be able to find answers to these questions:

1 What is the profit motive and how is it important to a private enterprise system?

2 How do you cast dollar votes and how do your votes affect the economic system?

3 What is the relationship between risk and opportunity?

4 What are the three basic forms of business organization and how do they differ?

5 What are the advantages and disadvantages of operating under each form of organization?

6 How do corporations affect capital accumulation?

7 What are the shortcuts, combinations, and variations in organizational form and why are they used?

8 How does society benefit from business success?

9 How do successful firms return benefits to those who have shared the risk?

Terms you should know:

capital accumulation	joint venture
consolidation	limited partners
cooperative (co-op)	merger
corporation	partnership
division	private corporation
firm	public corporation
franchising	sole proprietorship
general partners	subsidiary

In 1776 the economist Adam Smith wrote a book called *The Wealth of Nations.* He described an invisible hand that guided the economic system. Now, over 200 years later, that invisible hand is still with us. It is called *self-interest.*

Every day hundreds of thousands of Americans make millions of independent economic decisions. Each person is guided by that invisible hand. It's amazing, but the system works. If we examine our system carefully, we can see two parts that fit together neatly: the profit motive and the dollar vote. The force that holds this all together is the balance between risk and opportunity.

THE PROFIT MOTIVE

A private enterprise economic system is based on the profit motive. You make a profit when you get more out of something than you put into it. Is that wrong?

Some people use terms like *profiteer* and think of anyone who would profit at someone else's expense as a villain. But there is nothing wrong with making a fair profit. Profit is only a payment for performing a service or taking a risk. When a firm or an individual performs a service that is needed by someone, there should be some return or benefit for doing so.

Just think of all the merchandise on the shelves in all the Sears, Penney's, and K marts each December. A lot of effort goes into getting those goods on the shelves. What if no one wants to buy any of it? These stores have their funds on the line and are betting that they will have what you want. In return they expect to earn a fair return on that money, to earn a profit. After they have paid the clerks, the rent, and the bills, they hope to have something left over. If they don't, do you think it would be as easy for you to do your holiday shopping next year? Profit pays the manufacturer, distributor, and retailer for performing those services and taking the risks that must be taken in order to benefit the customers.

THE DOLLAR VOTE

The other half of the picture is the dollar vote. You cast dollar votes each time you make a purchase. Americans have voted Crest Toothpaste, Sears, Levi's, and World Championship Tennis into the popular positions they enjoy today. Ipana Toothpaste, W. T. Grant, and World Football League did not get enough dollar votes and have faded into oblivion. Sellers must compete for your dollar votes. No seller can snatch your wallet and grab your dollars. You are trying to act in your own best interest guided by that invisible hand each time you decide to cast or not to cast your dollar vote.

Some of the products or services you would like to have are not available. That is because no one has been willing to take the risk that these products would earn enough dollar votes to be profitable. For example, when natural gas was cheap, it got the votes. When it became scarce and costly, more people were willing to cast their dollar votes for solar heating systems. It became less risky to design and market solar equipment.

RISK AND OPPORTUNITY

In general, there is a direct relationship between opportunity and risk. The more risky a venture is, the more profitable it can be. Of course, there is also a greater chance that it will result in a loss. Very few people would have traded places with Evel Knievel as he prepared to jump the Snake River Canyon on his jet-powered motorcycle. He was willing to take a lot of risk and he made a big profit.

Of course, there are always people who speak up after the risk to say that the rewards were too high. But in the private enterprise system,

---

MOVIE MAKING: A BIG RISK CAN LEAD TO BIG REWARDS OR . . .

There is no such thing as a low-budget movie anymore. Even so-called low-budget films cost about $3 million just for the film plus another $6 million or so for marketing. In recent years both the risks and the rewards have risen sharply. *Jaws, Star Wars, Saturday Night Fever, Star Trek,* and other hot films take in the lion's share of the box-office receipts, which can be close to $3 billion a year. But more than 200 other films fight over the leftovers.

Viewers have become much more choosy. As the price of a movie ticket has gone up, the range of television entertainment has expanded. Movie producers are trying to lessen the risk by producing more of the least expensive movies. They would rather produce three $10 million movies than one $30 million extravaganza.

Part of the problem is the time lag. *The Thornbirds* was a best-seller in 1978. Acquiring the movie rights and writing the screenplay consumed months of time. The picture was to be ready for the market by Christmas 1979, but by that time another story made it to the top of the best-seller list.

Then there are the critics. It really doesn't matter how much money or effort is poured into the picture if the early reviews blast it. A few unkind words from a reviewer in New York or Los Angeles can spell its doom. Why do moviemakers take the risk? Ask George Lucas. *Star Wars* has made him very, very wealthy.

anyone is free to offer goods or services at the prices he or she chooses. The market decides whose prices are fair. If a seller's prices are too high, the market will cast its dollar votes elsewhere.

Our economic system depends on people's desires for profits and their willingness to take risks to get them. Otherwise there would be no K mart to stock Crest Toothpaste just in case you want to buy a tube. There might not even be any Crest Toothpaste or televisions, computers, and frozen foods. At best, when you wanted something you would have to order it ahead and pay in advance.

The profit motive combats economic inefficiency. Whenever there are tasks that enough people are unwilling or unable to do for themselves, some person or firm steps in and takes a risk because of the possible profits. Sears, the largest retailing firm in the United States, was started by a person who took a risk. While working as a station agent for the railroad, Richard Sears spent his small savings to buy a dozen watches from a mail-order catalog. He then set out to find people to buy them. He took a risk and he made enough profit to try it again.

In this text we examine the factors that affect business success and the tools managers use to minimize the risks while increasing the returns. In this chapter, we will explore the forms of business organizations. We will then look at the rewards that can come to those who are willing to share the risk.

ALTERNATE FORMS OF BUSINESS ORGANIZATION

A **firm** is an organization of people and resources with the purpose of conducting a specified type of business. But not all firms are organized in the same way. The form of organization that is best for a firm of one size with one mission might not be best for another firm. A firm might even change its form if conditions change. The three basic forms of business organization are the sole proprietorship, the partnership, and the corporation.

About eight out of every ten firms in the United States are operated as sole proprietorships, but altogether they account for only 13 percent of the business transactions. Most of these are small businesses as shown in Figure 4–1. Partnerships account for about one out of ten U.S. firms and do about 7 percent of the business. Most large firms are corporations. While only one out of ten U.S. firms is a corporation, these firms do 80 percent of the business.

Sole proprietorships

A **sole proprietorship** is formed when a single person goes into business. It is the simplest form of business organization. In the eyes of

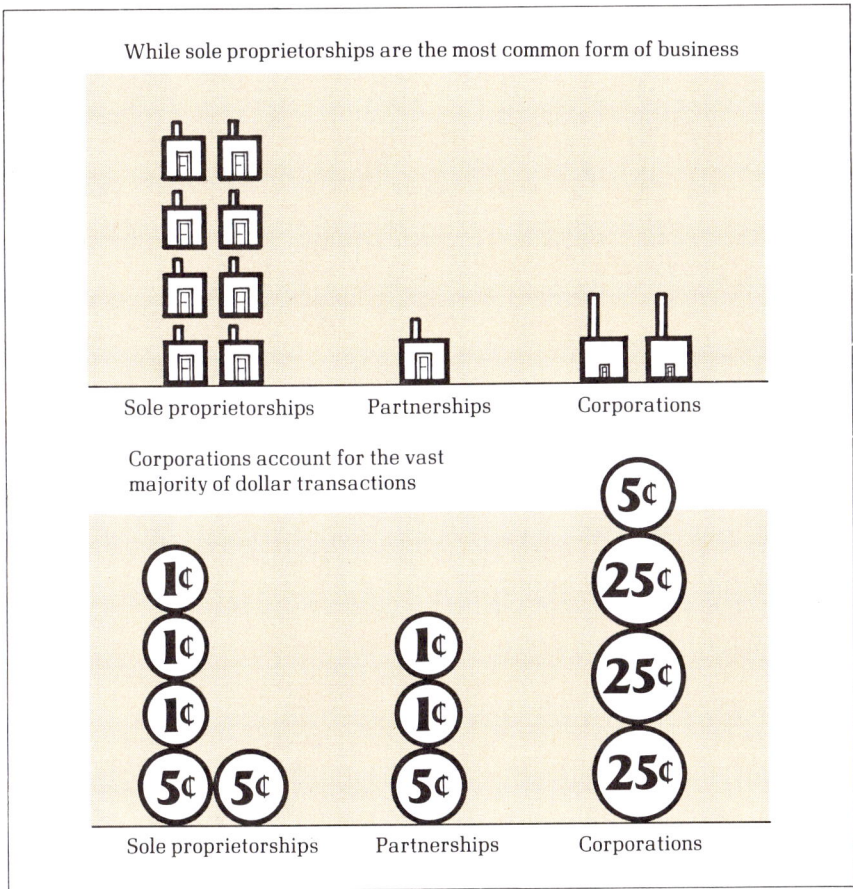

While sole proprietorships are the most common form of business

Sole proprietorships   Partnerships   Corporations

Corporations account for the vast
majority of dollar transactions

Sole proprietorships   Partnerships   Corporations

FIGURE 4–1
**There are more small
business firms, but
corporations do a major
share of the business**

the law, the tax courts, and the suppliers and customers, the owner
is the firm. The firm's income is personal income to the owner, and
the owner is personally responsible for all the debts and liabilities
of the firm. There are several advantages to this form of organization.
    Flexibility. It is easy and inexpensive to set up a sole proprietorship.
It allows for a high degree of individual control and flexibility. If you
were to go out tomorrow and open a small store with your own money,
you would be free to make all the decisions. Of course, you would
have to obey the laws and pay your taxes. Other than that, if it is
your money, you can make the decisions—you can decide on the location, the name, the hours, whom to hire, and on and on.
    If you make good decisions and the firm makes a profit, it will be
your personal income. A sole proprietor is truly self-employed. You
could decide to reinvest the earnings in the store or take them home.
This income would be taxed as personal income. On earnings up to

about $15,000, the tax rate on personal income is less than the tax rate on corporate income. This is a real advantage as long as the business is small.

THE SMALL BUSINESS ADMINISTRATION

The Small Business Administration (SBA) was established in 1953 to aid, counsel, assist, and protect the interests of small businesses. Since many small businesses face financing problems, the SBA helps small business owners gain access to capital and credit. It maintains an active loan program and has recently concentrated on loans to women, minorities, and Vietnam War veterans. Most SBA loans are made from funds supplied by local private banks under the SBA guarantee program. In effect, the SBA becomes the small businessperson's cosigner on the loan.

The SBA runs training programs and provides consulting services aimed at improving the management skills of small business owners, potential owners, and managers. Two of its programs are SCORE and ACE. SCORE is the Service Corps of Retired Executives. ACE is the Active Corps of Executives. These two groups provide volunteer counseling to small business owners. The SBA publishes a wide variety of practical guides for small businesses. Many of these guides, such as "Management Aids for Small Manufacturers," are available without charge from any of the SBA's local offices.

The SBA is also concerned about the long-range competitive welfare of small business. It conducts studies on the current and future problems and needs of the small business community and makes recommendations to other federal agencies. Part of its function is to make sure that small businesses receive a fair portion of government purchases, contracts, and subcontracts.

Source: *U.S. Government Manual, 1977/78,* pp. 625–30.

Disadvantages.   Since sole proprietorships are usually small businesses they face some special problems. One of the most critical is the shortage of capital. A sole proprietor has limited sources of funds. Many lenders avoid lending to individuals who run their own businesses. The sole proprietor is entitled to all of the profits but must also cover all the losses. A sole proprietor has unlimited liability. If the store is a failure, the creditors can collect from the sole owner. If there is not enough revenue to pay the bills, they could force the owner to dip into personal savings. A customer who slips and breaks a leg in the store can sue the sole proprietor as an individual. The owner and the firm are the same legal and financial entity.

It can also be difficult for the small business owner to get expert help in some areas of running a business. When a firm has few employees, each one must perform a number of functions and may not have the chance to become expert at any one such as personnel or advertising. In a sole proprietorship, the owner enjoys all the benefits and shoulders all responsibilities.

Partnerships

Like sole proprietorships, partnerships are usually small businesses. A **partnership** is formed when two or more individuals associate to start a firm. This can happen in many different ways. Some partnerships are formed on a handshake. Others involve written contracts that point out the rights and responsibilities of each person, such as the one in Figure 4–2.

In some partnerships the rights and responsibilities are the same for all of the partners. In others they differ. Some of today's large corporations started out as partnerships, for example, Procter & Gamble, Sears & Roebuck, Johnson & Johnson, and Bell & Howell.

Advantages. Partnerships have some of the same advantages as proprietorships. It can be fairly easy to set up a partnership. Then if it is a success, the firm's income is counted as personal income to the partners and is taxed as such.

Another advantage of partnerships is that they allow for the pooling of resources. A group of people can share their resources to set up a firm that any one of them might not be able to manage alone. These resources may include money, talents, contacts, or perhaps a well-known name.

Disadvantages. Since each of the partners contributes something of value, each one has some say about the way in which those resources are used. The partners may not be equal and some may have more to say than others, but all of the partners must be considered. This means that a partner lacks some of the flexibility enjoyed by a sole proprietor. In fact, there can be serious conflicts. Often partners find that they simply cannot get along. Sears bought out Roebuck after the two clashed over Sears's advertising policies.

Another real concern of many people in a partnership is the problem of being jointly and separately liable for the firm's debts. The partnership is responsible for the contracts made by any of the partners. There should be an agreement on each partner's fair share of the debt, but if one partner defaults, the others have to pay. The creditors can force the remaining partners to dip into their personal savings to pay off the firm's debts. It would certainly pay to pick trustworthy partners.

FIGURE 4–2
Sample partnership agreement

Articles of Partnership

THIS CONTRACT, *Made and entered into the   day of   19*
by and between

WITNESSETH: *That the said parties have this day formed a partnership for the purpose of engaging in and conducting   business under the following stipulations which are made a part of this contract:*

FIRST: *The said partnership is to continue for a term of   from date hereof.*

SECOND: *The business shall be conducted under the firm name*
of   at

THIRD: *The investments are as follows:*

FOURTH: *All profits or losses arising from said business are to be divided as follows:*

FIFTH: *A systematic record of all transactions is to be kept in a double entry set of books, which are to be open for the inspection of each partner. On   hereafter a statement of the business is to be made, the books closed, and each partner credited with the amount of the gain. A statement may be made at such other time as the partners agree upon.*

SIXTH: *Each partner is to devote a minimum of 30 hours per week to the business and to engage in no other business enterprise without the written consent of the other.*

SEVENTH: *Each partner is to have a salary of $ per month, the same to be withdrawn at such time or times as he may elect. Neither partner is to withdraw from the business an amount in excess of his salary without the written consent of the other.*

EIGHTH: *The duties of each partner are defined as follows:*

NINTH: *Neither partner is to become surety or bondsman for anyone without the written consent of the other.*

TENTH:

ELEVENTH:

IN WITNESS WHEREOF, *The parties aforesaid have hereunto set their hands and affixed their seals on this day and year above written.*

_____

_____

This concern has led to the development of variations on the standard partnership form.

Types of partners.   A partnership arrangement must be satisfactory to each partner. Some potential partners have something important to offer to the firm but are willing to assume only a limited amount of risk. Therefore, some partnerships have both general and limited partners. **General partners** have full rights and responsibilities. They have the right to participate fully in the management of the firm and have unlimited liability. **Limited partners** give up some rights in return for protection from unlimited liability. Usually they can lose only the amount they have invested in the firm.

Corporations

A **corporation** has a legal identity separate from that of its owners and managers. It is granted this identity in a charter issued by the state in which it is incorporated. A corporation is a **legal entity** capable of owning assets, transacting business, entering into contracts, and incurring liabilities. The corporation, not its owners, is liable.

Forming a corporation. A firm can start out as a corporation or switch over to that form as it grows. To form a corporation, papers must be filed with the state in which the firm is to be incorporated. This can involve complex legal actions and may require the services of an attorney. The investors are granted shares in the corporation, which are evidenced by stock certificates. They become shareholders. The **shareholders** elect a **board of directors** to represent them. The members of the board are responsible for formulating long-range policies for the firm and for hiring the managers who will make the day-to-day decisions.

Within the private enterprise segment of our economy, corporations can be private or public. A **private corporation** issues shares, but these shares are not traded on a public exchange. They are sometimes called a closely held corporation because all of the shares are owned by a small group of people. Sometimes they are all members of one family (see Table 4–1).

Advantages to the firm. A firm that has incorporated enjoys some business advantages. One of the most important is a greater capacity to raise capital. When a sole proprietorship or a partnership needs more funds, the owners must either invest more of their personal funds or try to borrow the funds. A corporation can raise funds simply by selling additional shares. This is known as *financing* and is discussed in detail in Chapter 12.

Once a firm has reached a certain size, there are tax advantages. Personal income beyond $200,000 is taxed at the rate of 70 percent. The maximum corporate income tax rate, however, is 46 percent. Another advantage is that a corporation's life can be unlimited. The lives of other forms of organization are tied directly to the lives of the owners. When one of the partners drops out of a partnership, a new partnership must be formed.

Almost all large firms are incorporated, and size itself offers some

THE BIG BOARD: THE NEW YORK STOCK EXCHANGE

On an average day $50 million worth of securities are traded by the 1,366 traders who work on the NYSE floor. If you looked down from the visitors' balcony, you might think you were late for a sports event and that the cleaning crews were fighting. You'd see groups of people in light green smocks standing around oval booths yelling at each other and waving their arms. The floor would be littered with scraps of paper. It seems confused, but it is a organized market.

The NYSE came into being in May 1792, when a group of U.S. Revolutionary War Bond traders agreed to meet at a regular time and place. From then until the 1930s, when the government acted to impose strict controls, trading continued in a boom and bust cycle. Today, most NYSE requirements and restrictions are designed to inspire the confidence of investors.

Only the securities of *listed* firms are traded. Listed firms must meet requirements that assure they are legitimate publicly traded corporations. There requirements include minimum levels of annual earnings, tangible assets, number of publicly held shares and shareholders, and market value of outstanding common stock. If a listed firm slips below these minimums, trading in its securities is suspended, or it can be delisted.

The NYSE is an association. Members must be approved by the board and purchase *seats*. The number of seats is limited to 1,366. Available seats are auctioned off to the highest bidder. Seats have sold for more than $500,000. The NYSE is the organized structure within which the traders operate. It does not buy and sell the securities. How does the trading take place?

The NYSE is an auction. It goes on each business day from 9:00 a.m. to the closing bell at 3:00 p.m. EST. The traders execute orders they get from investors. You could call a local stockbroker today and ask to buy 100 shares of Levi stock. The broker would give you the current price reported electronically from the NYSE floor. You could place an order to buy at market or to buy at a specific price. Of course, if you specify a price and no owner of Levi stock is willing to sell at that price, no trade will take place.

Your broker teletypes the order to the firm's member on the exchange floor. With orders for perhaps 100,000 daily transactions funneling through 1,366 traders, this trader is very busy. The trader proceeds to the *post,* that oval booth, where Levi is traded. At the post is a *specialist,* a member trader who is responsible for *making a market* for Levi. Each listed security has a specialist who keeps track of offers to buy and sell and can even buy and sell the security. Your trader asks for the bid and asked prices on Levi. *Bid* is what other would-be buyers are offering, and *asked* is what would-be sellers are willing to take. As your representative, a member must buy at the lowest possible price and sell at the highest possible price. If a bargain is reached, each trader notes it on a slip of paper and goes on to the next order. There is no formal contract—just some hand waving and order shouting at the post. The member then teletypes the outcome to your broker, who calls you. You have five business days to pay the broker.

TABLE 4–1
Familiar private
corporations

All the shares of a private corporation are owned by one or a few individuals who are usually members of the same family. Each of the familiar firms listed below is a private corporation with annual sales of at least $200 million.

Firm	Business
E & J Gallo Winery	Wine
Estée Lauder	Cosmetics
Hearst Corp.	Publishing
Amway	Home care products
United Parcel Service	Parcel delivery
Reader's Digest Association	Publishing
Mars, Inc.	Candy
S. C. Johnson & Sons	Wax and home care products
Hallmark Cards	Cards and novelties
Encyclopaedia Britannica	Publishing

Source: Lawrence Minard, "In Privacy They Thrive," *Forbes*, November 1, 1976, pp. 38–45.

TABLE 4–2
Twenty-five largest
industrial corporations

	Ranking in	
	Sales	*Employees*
General Motors	1	1
Exxon	2	14
Ford Motor	3	2
Mobil	4	6
Texaco	5	43
Standard Oil of California	6	114
International Business Machines	7	5
General Electric	8	3
Gulf Oil	9	57
Chrysler	10	9
International Telegraph and Telephone	11	4
Standard Oil, Indiana	12	81
Atlantic Richfield	13	71
Shell Oil	14	128
U.S. Steel	15	7
E. I duPont de Nemours	16	13
Western Electric	17	8
Continental Oil	18	97
Tenneco	19	22
Procter & Gamble	20	61
Union Carbide	21	18
Goodyear Tire and Rubber	22	10
Sun	23	133
Caterpillar Tractor	24	31
Eastman Kodak	25	15

Source: *Fortune*, May 7, 1979, p. 270.

advantages (see Table 4–2). These include economies of scale and the ability to hire management experts and specialists. But these advantages are not a direct result of the organization form. For a large firm, the advantages of incorporating completely overshadow the disadvantages. It is only for the small firm that the disadvantages are a serious concern in choosing this form of organization.

Advantages to the society.   Any society depends on capital accumulation for its growth. **Capital accumulation** means that enough funds can be collected under one group's control to begin an economic project.

DID YOU EVER WONDER

Why is the corporate tax rate different from the individual tax rate?

Individuals in the United States pay taxes according to a progressive scale. The more money you make, the higher the percentage you pay in taxes. Single people with over $2,200 in earnings beyond legal deductions are in the 14 percent bracket. They pay 14 cents on every dollar by which their taxable income exceeds $2,200. Once that gets beyond $2,700 the rate jumps to 15 percent. The maximum individual tax rate is 70 percent.

Corporations pay taxes in steps. They pay 17 percent on the first $25,000 earnings, 20 percent on the next $25,000, 30 percent on the next $25,000, 40 percent on the next $25,000 and 46 percent on all earnings beyond $125,000. With all of the news we've been getting about the earnings of corporations, why isn't the maximum rate higher?

A corporate tax structure similar to the individual tax structure would be damaging to the economy and eventually to every member of the society. The current corporate tax structure encourages corporations to reinvest their earnings in plants and equipment which will generate employment opportunities for citizens as well as produce the goods and services to satisfy the needs of the population. If the corporation keeps its earnings and reinvests these earnings, the lower tax rate applies. If it pays the earnings out in the form of dividends to the shareholders, the shareholders must pay additional taxes on those earnings at a higher rate.

Some of the underdeveloped nations of the world suffer because of a lack of capital accumulation. No one individual or group is able to come up with enough money to build a factory or set up a transportation system, so everyone is held back from private economic development. They may be forced to resort to loans from foreign governments, which often have strings attached.

There are three reasons why incorporating encourages capital accumulation. First, the corporate form of organization allows many people to share some of the benefits of ownership without the day-to-day responsibility for the management of that firm. A major corporation such as General Motors may have over a million separate owners.

Second, people with only a small amount of capital can invest. Even if you don't have enough savings to start your own business or become a partner in a firm, you may have enough to buy one millionth of General Motors.

THE COST OF PAPERWORK

The Commission on Federal Paperwork estimated that business spends $93 billion each year complying with the paperwork requirements imposed by the federal government. That's about $500 for every man, woman, and child in the United States, and it doesn't even include state and local requirements. It is difficult to add up all the costs of just the paperwork part of government regulation. Kaiser Aluminum gave a student intern the assignment of looking into the costs of reporting to the federal government. She found that Kaiser was submitting at least 10,000 reports each year to all levels of government. The reports filled about 240 file boxes each year and consumed the entire work-year of 80 employees. Kaiser estimated the cost of this paperwork to be $5 million a year.

Firms in the energy and health industries or manufacturers of products such as automobiles, which attract the attention of the Environmental Protection Agency, bear a particularly heavy burden. Eli Lilly & Company reports that more employee-hours are devoted to paperwork than to research on drugs for cancer and heart disease. It took two light trucks to deliver Lilly's 120,000-page application for the approval of a new drug for arthritis. And remember, you pay for this paperwork on both ends. The cost of the paperwork is included in the price of the products and services you buy, and your tax dollars pay the wages of the government employees who receive, read, and analyze, and file the reports.

Sources: Paul H. Weaver, "That Crusade against Federal Paperwork Is a Paper Tiger," *Fortune,* November 1976, pp. 118–21; Howard Jarvis, "The High Cost of Paper These Days," *The Sacramento Bee,* October 3, 1978; and John F. Sims, "Regulations—And What They Cost Us," *The Sacramento Bee,* September 20, 1978.

Third, shareholders are free from the high degree of risk of being a sole proprietor or a partner. Their liability is limited to the amount they have invested. Disgruntled creditors have no right to the personal assets of corporate shareholders.

Disadvantages.   There are three disadvantages of incorporating. First, it is more difficult and expensive to incorporate than to simply go into business. Even for a very simple, closely held firm, incorporating can cost $1,000.

Second, there are tax penalties. In effect, corporate earnings are taxed twice. They are taxed first as earnings to the firm. Then if these earnings are distributed to the owners, they are taxed again as personal income. A closely held corporation can avoid this by filing as a Subchapter S Corporation. Subchapter S is a special provision of the corporate tax laws that allows a closely held firm to avoid the payment of corporate income taxes on income that is distributed to owners. The owners still have to pay taxes on that income as personal income, but at least it is taxed only once.

Finally, incorporating creates a legal being that is then required to file reports with various government agencies. The most important of these are financial reports both for taxes and for the purpose of protecting investors. Before the Great Depression in the 1930s, swindlers convinced thousands of Americans to invest in firms with futures that were too good to be true. In fact, they were not true, but people invested and lost their savings. After that, the Securities and Exchange Commission was established to assure that reliable information is made available to investors.

These reports create several problems. They can be difficult and costly to prepare. There has been considerable controversy over the paperwork burden imposed on corporations by government agencies. General Motors Corporation calculates that the papers it has to prepare in order to gain certification for its cars for sale in a single year would make a stack 15 stories high.[1] Second, some of these reports are readily available to competitors. Some competitive secrets can be exposed. One of the advantages enjoyed by closely held corporations is that they are free from the reporting requirements of the Securities and Exchange Commission.

While sole proprietorships, partnerships, and corporations are the

TABLE 4–3
Advantages and disadvantages of forms of organization

Form	Advantages	Disadvantages
Sole proprietorship	Easy to set up, high degree of flexibility, single income tax	Unlimited liability, limited life, harder to raise capital
Partnership	Pool of resources, single income tax, easy to set up	Unlimited liability, limited life, harder to raise capital
Corporation	Limited liability, easier to raise capital	More complex to set up, double taxation (except Sub. S), increased reporting

major forms of organization, the economic system is adaptive. It is not limited to these forms. If none of these seems to be the right form for a particular venture, another form may be devised. Table 4–3 summarizes the advantages and disadvantages of the major forms of organization.

SHORTCUTS, COMBINATIONS, AND VARIATIONS

Sometimes a firm seeks a way to expand rapidly to meet strong market demand. In other cases, the owners of two or more firms find that they have compatible purposes and resources. How can they set up a firm that includes both? Perhaps an existing firm has grown quite complex or developed a new product or service that is incompatible with its current mission. If so, it may seek some way to keep its operations segregated while still maintaining some control. These needs have led to the development of shortcuts, combinations, and variations. The most popular are franchising, mergers, joint ventures, consolidations, cooperatives, and subsidiaries.

Rapid Expansion

When a firm wishes to take advantage of an opportunity, it has two choices. It can either build up its business in that area within the existing firm, or it can go outside. Two methods are often used.

Franchising. Franchising is a popular method of rapid expansion. In **franchising**, a person or firm with an idea but limited resources sells or rents its business system to others who will be able to come up with resources to aid in the expansion. This method has been used in industries from fast foods to auto repair. In fact, it is so important that it is the subject of the entire next chapter.

Merger. A **merger** is a combination of two corporations in which only one survives. The merged corporation no longer exists. Mergers occur when one of the two firms is considerably larger than the other. Green Giant was merged into Pillsbury. While the Green Giant brand name remains, its shareholders became shareholders in Pillsbury. There are no more Green Giant shareholders.

Mergers are sometimes called **acquisitions.** A firm might acquire total ownership of another firm or it might obtain controlling ownership, that is, buy over 50 percent of the firm's shares. Some mergers are peaceful. The managers of the merged firm are left to manage their firm with little interference, but they are able to draw upon some of the resources of the larger firm.

In other cases, the merger attempt is resisted. When there is resistance, a merger is referred to as a **takeover.** Carter Hawley Hale owns such famous local department store chains as Neiman-Marcus in Texas, Bergdorf Goodman in New York, and The Broadway in California. When Carter Hawley Hale attempted to take over Marshall Field, the dominant department store chain in Chicago, Marshall Field's managers resisted mightily. They were finally able to fend off the takeover bid.

A corporation may merge with another firm for a number of reasons. A very successful firm may buy out its suppliers or companies to whom they sell. This could be done to further cement a productive relationship. It may also be a way to capture greater control of the necessary sources of supply or to control access to the marketplace. Sears has at least partial ownership in more than 30 of its suppliers.

A merger is one way to avoid time-consuming and costly product development or to minimize the risk involved in expanding or entering a new field. At one time, Procter & Gamble sought to expand into the household bleach market. This is an area that is closely related to P & G's major markets, but in which it did not have a product. To do so it bought Clorox, the firm with the most popular household bleach in the country. But the government became concerned that P & G's action would result in a less competitive marketplace. It felt that P & G should introduce a product to compete with Clorox. So P & G had to sell Clorox.

Sunbeam wanted to diversify into new markets. A diversified firm has interests in several areas so that it is not too dependent on any one of them. Sunbeam purchased several firms including Hurst, the producers of auto transmission equipment, and Mile High Ice Machine Company, a Denver-based manufacturer of commercial ice-making machines.

Compatible purposes and resources

If individuals can benefit from becoming partners, it is logical that the same holds true for firms. Two or more firms may realize that they are trying to serve the same need and would be better off combining their efforts. Sometimes the managers of different firms learn that they each have resources that the other needs. When two or more firms become partners, it may be in the form of a consolidation, a joint venture, or a cooperative.

Consolidations. A **consolidation** is a combination of two or more fairly equal corporations. None of the original corporations survives. All the shareholders become shareholders in the new corporation. Consolidations take place for the same reason as partnerships. A consolidation allows the participating firms to share their resources.

Joint ventures. A **joint venture** is an agreement between two or more firms to commit a part of their resources to a common purpose.

This may be a temporary project or a co-owned subsidiary. A joint venture differs from a consolidation because neither firm loses its corporate identity in the process.

Joint ventures are undertaken either because neither firm is willing to take the entire risk involved in a new project or because neither of the partners has the capacity to complete the project alone. When the Ford Motor Company built an automobile plant in the USSR, the

---

THE CALIFORNIA ALMOND GROWERS EXCHANGE

The California Almond Growers Exchange is a grower-owned cooperative that produces, processes, and packages almond products under the Blue Diamond label. Since it was founded in 1910, the exchange has grown dramatically and today includes 4,700 grower members. Membership is based on a five-year Crop Agency Agreement. By becoming members, growers agree to harvest, hull, dry, and deliver their entire crops to the exchange. In turn, the cooperative agrees to process and market the crop, returning all proceeds less expenses to the producer.

The Almond Growers Exchange (AGE) serves its members' needs in a number of areas in which the individual grower's efforts would be too costly or ineffective. Since all the growers have a common interest in farm trade negotiations and farm-related legislation, the AGE represents the combined interests of the growers by supplying vital information to negotiators and legislators. Another area in which the members combine their resources to meet their individual needs is in the area of agricultural research. One recent project was aimed at finding a solution to the navel orangeworm infestation.

But AGE is perhaps best known for its efforts to stimulate demand for its members' almond products. AGE specialists create new almond products such as the flavored almond gift packs. AGE maintains an extensive advertising program and has established almond tasting rooms in major California cities and tourist areas. Together, the almond growers can accomplish many tasks that would be beyond the means of the individual grower.

Soviets insisted that the project involve local partners. Without the partners, Ford would have been unable to complete the project.

The Alaskan pipeline was a joint venture among Atlantic Richfield, British Petroleum, and several other major oil companies. This project was very risky and none of the firms was prepared to bear that risk alone. Once the project is completed, the joint venture relationship is dissolved.

Cooperatives.   A **cooperative** (co-op) is a continuing association of independent firms for a common purpose. When a firm belongs to a cooperative, it pays dues or a fee. The cooperative performs services for its members that they could not economically perform for themselves. Cooperatives are more popular in certain industries such as agriculture. The Michigan Milk Producers Association, Florida Citrus Commission, and the California Fruit Growers' Exchange are all involved in arranging for the best methods of storage, transportation, and marketing of their members' output.

Co-ops are important in industries where the producers are small and their output is similar. You can't tell one Florida juice orange from another, but the Florida Citrus Commission hopes that the "Bird," Mark Fydrich, and Evonne Goolagong-Cawley can convince you to drink more orange juice. If you do, all of their members will benefit.

Segregation with control

When a firm is compact and all of its resources are being channeled toward the same objectives, it remains as a single undivided unit. But when a firm reaches a certain size or becomes involved in a variety of products and markets, the managers may choose to reorganize the firm into divisions or to set up subsidiaries.

A **division** is a unit within the firm. Its managers are employees of the main firm and there is a direct management link. A **subsidiary** is set up as a separate firm. Its relationship with the parent firm is often more financial than managerial. As long as the subsidiary is meeting the profit expectations of the parent firm, its own management usually is free to make decisions. Either type of segregation may be necessary because of management factors or market factors.

Management factors.   The three management factors that encourage segregation are the need for evaluation, human factors, and managerial limitations. When all the operations of the firm are lumped together, it can be difficult to evaluate the return achieved from each of the different activities. One activity may be very unprofitable, but its losses might be covered up by the gains of another activity. Segregation permits more honest evaluation of each division.

Sometimes there are human factors. The divisions of some firms compete with each other. This can motivate people. Other firms see their divisions as training grounds for managers. A person can be given responsibility for a small part of the operation and grow faster. Managers of subsidiaries and divisions are responsible for their own plans and performance. Both motivation and experience are human benefits of segregation.

MARY KAY ASH

If I change my attitude I can change my life.

Photo by Bradford Bachrach.

Mary Kay Ash is chairman of the board of Mary Kay Cosmetics. She earned that position through hard work and a positive attitude. On September 13, 1963, she and her two sons started their company with $5,000, one shelf of cosmetics, and nine people. By 1976 Mary Kay Cosmetics had grown large enough to be listed on the New York Stock Exchange. Today the firm is an international organization with over 40,000 independent beauty consultants and net sales of almost $50 million.

Mary Kay Cosmetics is a direct sales organization. A direct sales organization sells to cus-tomers in many non-store settings such as door-to-door, parties, and through catalogs. Its founding idea was to provide women with the opportunity to achieve success and financial independence in the business world. Its 40,000 independent saleswomen are in business for themselves. They buy the merchandise from the Mary Kay Corporation and sell it to their customers. Women who are especially suc-cessful as Mary Kay saleswomen are awarded special prizes such as pink Cadillacs (on one-year leases which the company renews if her sales stay up), furs, and dream vacations.

Mary Kay Ash's mother had struggled to support four children and an invalid husband. Mary Kay herself became a saleswoman when she was left with three children to support and was desperate for money. She became a dealer for Stanley Home Products, a direct sales party plan company. The next year she was crowned queen at the annual sales meeting for having sold the most Stanley products for the year. After 13 years with Stanley, she joined World Gifts, a firm selling decorative accessories. There she rose to the position of national train-ing director before leaving to start her own firm.

Segregation may be necessary because the operation has grown too big and too complex to be managed from a single office. How could one person keep track of the critical day-to-day developments facing General Mills, which has operations in foods and coffee, child and adult games, clothing, and several other industries? If top management is involved in the day-to-day management in each of the different areas of the firm, it may mean that no one is watching over the firm's future course and welfare. There are limits on the extent to which a manager can be stretched and still remain effective.

Market factors.   Divisions or subsidiaries may do a better job of serving different groups of customers. Food processors find that the needs of institutional markets such as hospitals vary a great deal from the needs of household consumers. They often set up separate divisions in order to serve each market better.

Segregation helps to avoid product image conflicts. Most food processors convert the by-products of their operations into animal feeds or fertilizers. Esmark is a diversified firm that started out as the Swift Meat Packing Company. Different Esmark divisions produce the Playtex products, Peter Pan Peanut Butter, and Vigoro Fertilizers. Clearly the images, uses, and markets for these products are different enough to justify segregation within the firm.

The separate areas of the firm may offer alternatives to the consumer. General Motors has several divisions that produce cars and trucks. Cadillac focuses on luxury-car buyers, while Chevrolet aims at the mass market. Without divisions, your choices of domestic automobiles would be limited.

These are just a few of the shortcuts, combinations, and variations that are used to create the best form of organization to accomplish a specific purpose. These forms have developed because they are useful. As needs change, new forms will continue to develop. Each of these forms continues to exist because it is beneficial to the economic system, to the management, and to the owners.

REWARDS FOR THOSE WHO SHARE THE RISKS

Regardless of the form of organization, some person or persons have put up the money needed to set up each and every firm in the United States. The money used to set up or expand a business is called **capital.** Those who supply it are **capitalists.** While this term has been used in a negative way, it means only someone who has invested funds in a business.

Capitalists invest their money in hopes of realizing some return. They could have put their money in bank accounts and been assured of a fixed return. But they would be renting their money to the bank, and they would earn no more or no less than the stated interest rate. By investing their money in a business, they hope to earn more than the savings account interest rate for having taken the risk.

Who are the owners of American business?

Many people see industrial giants like General Motors, IBM, and U.S. Steel as impersonal enemies of the population. The consumer complaint segments of local news shows often portray the marketplace as a constant battleground between consumers and the business community. The announcement of a huge product recall is viewed as a victory for the citizens in their war against the greedy forces of business. A closer look at the situation uncovers not an adversary relationship, however, but an interdependency between business firms and the citizens they serve. In this battle of US against THEM, most of US are THEM and all of THEM are consumers.

Small business ownership. Almost all Americans are capitalists whether they realize it or not. Many are the direct owners of small businesses. There are about 12 million small businesses in the United States. Most of these businesses affect family members in addition to the owner. About 140,000 partnerships bring thousands of other Americans into direct ownership contact with business.

Minority and women owners. A recent development is minority business ownership. In 1972 minority ownership accounted for 4.4 percent of all firms in the United States. These firms employed just under 500,000 people and had sales of about $17 billion. It seems small, but this is a 19 percent increase over a survey made three years earlier. Most minority-owned firms were in retail trade and services. Each of these industries accounted for about 31 percent of the total minority-owned firms. Table 4–4 summarizes the data.

Women owned 4.6 percent of all U.S. firms in 1972. Again, most of these firms were in the retail trade and service industries, which accounted for 33 percent and 38 percent, respectively. Women-owned firms recorded sales of $2.4 billion.

Individual citizens are not limited to small business ownership. It has been estimated that one out of ten Americans owns at least one share of corporate stock traded over one of the organized exchanges. These are forms of direct ownership, but many people are involved indirectly as well.

Indirect involvement. Some people invest in mutual funds. These organizations collect investments from many different people and then invest those funds in corporations. If you or other members of your family have savings deposited in banks, savings and loans, or credit unions, these funds may be channeled into the ownership of corporate shares. If you have any kind of insurance or have money in a pension

TABLE 4–4
Minority-owned business firms in the United States

	Firms owned by			
	Black	Spanish origin	Other	Total
Number of firms (000)	195	120	67	382
Net sales ($ billions)............	$7.2	$5.3	$4.1	$16.6
Employment (000)	197	150	109	456

Source: *U.S. Statistical Abstract*, 1976.

fund, your money is being used to supply capital to businesses. The process by which these funds are collected and then flow into the capital stream is called *intermediation*. This topic is discussed in detail in Chapter 12.

What are the rewards?

The returns generated by a successful firm are passed out in several forms. If the firm is a partnership or a sole proprietorship, the earnings of the firm are the personal income of the owners. The owners can decide whether or not they want to take their earnings out of the firm.

When corporate earnings are passed out to the shareholders, it is called a *dividend*. Each year about one out of every ten individual tax returns lists dividend income. Dividends are not an automatic result of profitable operations. The board of directors must decide whether it is going to declare dividends and if so, how much. Dividends are paid on a per share basis; that is, a person with 1,000 shares in the firm would get a dividend check for ten times as much as a person with 100 shares. The alternative is to retain the earnings for use within the firm.

Shareholders can disagree over dividends. Some would prefer to have their earnings kept in the corporation. They believe that this will increase the value of their shares. Besides, if the earnings are paid out, the shareholders must pay income tax on them. Other shareholders are quite willing to pay the income tax in order to get some immediate return on their investment.

The declaration of dividends is a sign to the investment community that the firm is profitable. It is seen as a commitment to the shareholders. Some firms pride themselves on never having missed paying a dividend. Dividends may be paid in cash, shares of stock, or products and services. Cash dividends are the most common. Once a liquor distiller passed out fifths of liquor to its shareholders!

How profitable are the various forms of organizations?

There is a lot of variation in profitability depending on whether the firm is organized as a proprietorship, a partnership, or a corporation. Table 4–5 tells the story.

And the money goes around and around

Capitalists are not the only ones who benefit as a result of the profit motive. Each time you go to the store or pay your monthly bills, it is easy to think that money flows in only one direction—out. But where do you get your money? Before a successful business returns any profits

| | Before-tax profit (percent of sales) | |
Industry	Proprietorship and partnerships	Corporations
Agriculture, forestry, and fishing	13.4%	4.0%
Mining	14.3	23.6
Construction	13.4	1.8
Manufacturing	10.7	6.3
Transportation and public utilities	12.3	4.9
Wholesale and retail trade	7.0	2.5
Finance, insurance, and real estate	3.6	6.1
Services	33.0	2.8
All industries	12.9	4.8

Source: *U.S. Statistical Abstract*, 1976.

TABLE 4–5
Before-tax profits of proprietorships and partnerships, and corporations as a percentage of sales dollars

to its owners, it must pay its employees. When business is good, employment goes up and more people are able to share the output.

When we are in a period of prosperity, there are direct and indirect returns to citizens. Firms expand and invest in new ventures. Expansion leads to new jobs, and the new ventures can lead to greater satisfaction for consumers.

Employees often own shares in their firms, but a firm can reward its employees in other ways as well. Many firms practice profit sharing. In profit sharing some proportion of the profits is set aside to be returned to the employees. Normally the employees' eligibility for these rewards is related to their years of service and grade of pay. The rewards may be either in cash or in shares in the firm.

Profitable firms pay more taxes. The casinos in Nevada are highly profitable. They pay so much in taxes that citizens of that state pay only 3 percent state sales tax and no state income tax. Nationwide, corporations return an average of almost 50 percent of their after-expense earnings to federal, state, and local governments.

Owners and nonowners alike share in the benefits that come about when a firm is profitable. A firm makes a profit when it is able to provide products and services for which customers are willing to cast their dollar votes.

SUMMARY

People are guided by that invisible hand of self-interest as they make their independent economic decisions in our private enterprise system which is based on the profit motive and the dollar vote. Dollar votes are cast each time you make a purchase. Profit is the payment for performing a service or taking a risk. The more risky a venture is, the more profitable it can be.

A *firm* is an organization of people and resources with the purpose of conducting a specified type of business. A sole proprietorship, the simplest type of firm, is formed when a single person goes into business. This person is then entitled to all of the profits but must also cover all of the losses.

A firm formed by two or more individuals is called a *partnership*. General partners have the right to participate fully in the management of the firm and have unlimited liability. Limited partners give up some rights in return for protection from unlimited liability.

A *corporation* is a legal being with rights and responsibilities. The corporate form of organization allows many people to share in the ownership of a firm and encourages capital accumulation. There are also shortcuts, combinations, and variations in the forms of organization. These may occur because a firm is seeking a way to expand rapidly. A firm may seek some way to keep its operations segregated while still maintaining some control. Or the owners of two or more firms may find that they have compatible purposes and resources. The most popular shortcuts, combinations, and variations are franchising, mergers, joint ventures, consolidations, cooperatives, and subsidiaries.

Under franchising, which is extremely popular in the United States, a firm sells or rents its business system to others. Merger occurs when one firm buys another firm. This may be to avoid time-consuming and costly product development or to minimize the risk involved in expanding or entering a new field.

A consolidation is a permanent association in which neither firm is acquired by the other. They become partners in a single firm. In a joint venture, two or more firms agree to commit some of their resources to a common project. A cooperative is a continuing association of independent firms for a common purpose.

Some firms are organized into separate units because of market conditions or management factors. A division is a wholly owned unit of the firm. A subsidiary is set up as a separate firm.

Some person or persons have put up the money needed to set up each and every firm in the United States. This money is called capital, and those who supply it are capitalists. Most Americans are capitalists or have deposited funds in banks or insurance firms from which money flows into the capital stream.

But the capitalists aren't the only ones who benefit. The returns generated by a successful firm benefit society and the owners. If the firm is a partnership or a sole proprietorship, the earnings of the firm become the personal income of the owners. Corporate earnings are passed out to the shareholders as dividends. And even before a business returns any profits to its owners, it must pay its employees. In addition, many firms practice profit sharing, and all profitable firms pay taxes.

REVIEW QUESTIONS

1. How do the profit motive and your dollar votes interact? Why is this important to the private enterprise system?

2. Why do the potential rewards increase with increased risk? If the rewards can be great, why do so many people avoid risks?

3. What are the differences among sole proprietorships, partnerships, and corporations? What do these mean in terms of advantages and disadvantages to large firms and to small firms?

4. How does the existence of corporations affect the capital accumulation within our economy?

5. What is the difference between a merger and a consolidation? Why would a firm enter into either arrangement?

6. How do joint ventures differ from consolidations?

7. Many co-ops are in agriculture. Can you think of some other industries made up of small firms that could benefit from cooperative efforts in advertising, warehousing, or other business functions?

8. How does the average citizen benefit when business firms successfully accomplish their missions?

CASES

Case 4–1.   The case of the 100-day year

Every year one out of every five American families packs up and moves. There are several well-known and successful firms in the moving business. The problem is that for these firms, the business year is just about 100 days long. Most people want to move during the summer. Bekins is the fifth largest interstate mover in the United States. Bekins' management is concerned about three problems. First, so much of its business is concentrated in the summer months. Second, the rate of growth in the household moving business is expected to taper off. Third, interstate trucking is heavily regulated by the government. With the increased costs of labor and fuel and the possible lid on prices, Bekins could be caught in a profit squeeze.

Bekins wants to diversify, that is, to develop other lines of business. Recently Bekins acquired Data Transportation Co., a firm specializing in moving computers and others electronic systems. It also acquired a building services firm, which provides maintenance, pest control, and security services.

1. *Why would Bekins acquire these businesses rather than starting them up?*
2. *Do these businesses compliment the moving business?*

Case 4–2.   Mother Hatton and her sons

Hatton's Restaurant in Los Angeles is a family tradition. George Hatton opened the Lebanese restaurant in 1935, and it is still owned and managed by Mother Hatton and her two sons, George Jr. and Carl. The restaurant is small with only six booths and five tables besides the row of stools at the bar. The menu is limited, but most of the customers have been eating there so long that they seldom bother to look at the menu. The hours are limited. They open at 10 a.m. and close at 3 p.m. five days a week. Once a month, George Jr. comes in to open the bar to serve the lodge members who meet across the street.

The Hattons offer some special services. George Jr. often fixes a special plate of tidbits at no charge to his loyal customers. Carl regularly feeds the meters on the street in front of the restaurant so that his customers aren't ticketed. There are many busier restaurants on the street, but the Hattons aren't anxious to grow. They are happy to operate their sole proprietorship as is.

1. *Is there room in this economy for a small family-owned restaurant based on a no-growth, customer service objective?*

2. *Is a sole proprietorship the best form of organization for Hatton's?*

3. *If you were called in as a consultant, what would you discuss with George Jr?*

chapter 5

FRANCHISING: THE BIG BUSINESS OF SMALL BUSINESS

By studying this chapter you should be able to find answers to these questions:

1 What is franchising?
2 What are the four major types of franchise systems?
3 Why has franchising become so popular?
4 What are the benefits and disadvantages for the franchiser?
5 What are the benefits and disadvantages for the franchisee?
6 What is included in a franchise package?
7 How are franchises sold?
8 What are the expected trends in franchising?

Terms you should know:

business concept
"franchise ethic"
franchise system
franchising
royalty
type I franchise system
type II franchise system
type III franchise system
type IV franchise system

What do McDonald's, Holiday Inns, Inc., Avis, Century 21 Real Estate, General Motors, H&R Block, and Roto-Rooter Sewer Service have in common? They're all in franchising. To some people franchising means fast foods. But franchising is important in more than 40 industries (see Figure 5–1). Close to one third of all retail sales are made through franchised outlets. What is a franchise? Why is franchising so popular? How does it work? What is expected in the future? Those are the topics that we will discuss in this chapter.

FIGURE 5–1
Franchising is used in many different industries

WHAT IS FRANCHISING?

Franchising is big business. Franchising is also small business. A **franchise system** is a business chain made up of owner-managed outlets. Hundreds of thousands of owner-managed franchise outlets dot local communities in the United States and around the world. While each franchisee operates a small business, the franchiser may well be a major corporation such as The Coca-Cola Company or The Pillsbury Company.

Defining franchising

Franchises are so diverse that it is hard to come up with a single accepted definition. **Franchising** is a business arrangement in which the franchiser grants the franchisee the right to do business in a pre-

114

scribed manner over a certain period of time in a specified place. Franchising is one of the ways in which a firm can develop a distribution system for its products or services. Here are some of the tests by which you can tell a franchise system from other forms of distribution.

1. A **contract.** A franchise is based on a contract between the parent firm and the local franchisee. The contract states the rights and duties of each party.

2. A **purpose.** Both parties agree that their purpose is to provide for the efficient distribution of the product or service. The franchiser grants the franchisee the right to do business within a particular market area for a specified period of time.

3. **Resources.** Both parties make a contribution toward the business. The franchiser contributes such things as a business idea, a trademark, training, and advice. The franchisee usually contributes money and agrees to manage the local business.

4. A **business entity.** The franchise outlet is normally set up as a separate business with a distinct identity. It is not absorbed into the franchisee's existing business.

5. A **common public identity.** Both parties support a common public identity through the use of common trademarks, architecture, uniforms, or advertising. This reinforces recognition and acceptance.

6. A **financial arrangement.** The franchisee is an independent businessperson who expects to make a profit. The franchisee is not employed by the franchiser, but in return for the franchise rights, the franchisee agrees to compensate the franchiser.[1]

Types of franchising systems

Franchising is not new. Singer Sewing Machine Company set up one of the first U.S. franchise systems just after the Civil War. Franchising is used in many different industries. Since it is a form of distribution, franchise systems can be classified according to distribution functions. There are four types. The Singer System was an example of type I.

Type I: Manufacturer–retailer. Type I systems dominate franchising both in dollar sales volume and in number of outlets. In **type I franchise systems** the manufacturer of a product contracts with independent local businesses to distribute its products to the final customer. The most common examples are automobile dealers and gas stations (see Figure 5–2). Almost half of all franchise outlets in the United States are auto dealerships or gas stations.[2]

Type II: Manufacturer–wholesaler. Some manufacturers grant franchises to wholesalers who in turn sell to other businesses (see Figure 5–3). This is the **type II franchise system.** If you look on most cans of soft drinks you'll find a statement such as "Canned by the Dr Pepper Bottling Company of San Francisco under the authority of Dr Pepper

Company, Dallas, Texas." The bottler is an independent firm with a franchise from the soft drink manufacturer. The manufacturer sells syrup to the bottler. The bottler adds water and gas, cans or bottles the beverage, and sells it to stores and restaurants. Without a franchise system the manufacturer would either have to ship a lot of water or operate its own bottling plants in almost every city.

Type III: Wholesaler–retailer. In the **type III franchise system,** retailers retain the advantages of independence while enjoying some of the benefits of belonging to a chain. Western Auto, Ben Franklin Stores, Rexall Drugs, and Convenience Food Marts are all independently owned and operated yet project the image of a chain. The wholesaler purchases goods in quantities that allow for lower prices and coordinates national advertising efforts.

Type IV: Service/trademark holder–retailer. In **type IV franchise systems,** the real value of the franchise lies in the trademark, image, and method of operation. The franchiser is seldom a manufacturer or a wholesaler. The franchiser is in the business of selling a business system. Normally the franchiser has successfully operated several outlets and then expands by selling the system to others who wish to start their own businesses. The fast-food restaurants are the most visible type IV franchise systems. Most type IV systems deal in services rather than products (see Figure 5–4).

Type IV franchising developed rapidly during the 1950s and continues to expand rapidly today. The success of type IV systems is largely a result of the increased mobility of the U.S. population. If you are like most people, when you're on the go you like to see some familiar names. The two biggest type IV systems are McDonald's and Holiday Inn. We'll refer to them often as we explore franchising.

FIGURE 5–4
Well-known type IV
franchisers

WHY IS FRANCHISING SO POPULAR?

When you go into McDonald's you know what will be on the menu, what it will cost, and how it will taste. People older than 30 can remember when the "Billions Sold" sign in front of a McDonald's read "— Millions Sold" and was changed every few months as the total changed. Now, with almost 5,000 outlets, McDonald's sells more than 6 million hamburgers each day.[3] If it passed the 25 billion mark in December 1977, what do you suppose the total is today?[4]

Do you think that the McDonald's Systems, Inc., managers are pleased that founder Ray Kroc decided to take the franchising route back in April 1955? The franchisees must be happy. Over half of McDonald's new franchises are granted to people who already own a McDonald's franchise. Besides that, McDonald's has a waiting list of applicants at least three years long.[5] Why is everybody so eager to get into franchising?

Benefits for the franchiser

Why would someone with a successful business or a timely business idea expand by franchising rather than expanding alone? Franchising

RAY KROC

Press on! Nothing will take the place of persistence.

Ray Kroc was in his early 50s when his curiosity led him to investigate rumors of an exceptionally successful drive-in restaurant in southern California. He was so pleased with what he saw that he plunged all of his money and energies into developing a franchise system that has revolutionized the food industry. Based on the principles of quality, service, value, and cleanliness, McDonald's has become an American institution. The McDonald's network has provided opportunities for thousands of small businesspeople, and millions of young people have worked behind McDonald's counters.

Ray Kroc was a high school dropout who had supported his family through a variety of jobs as a musician and a salesman. Before jumping into the restaurant business, he had been selling paper cups and milkshake machines. It was the McDonald's brothers extraordinary purchases of paper cups that initially attracted his attention.

Serving as senior chairman of the board of McDonald's, in recent years Ray Kroc has devoted much of his energy to a wide range of civic and philanthropic projects. On his 75th birthday his friends and business associates established The Ray A. Kroc–Ronald McDonald Children's Fund to provide seed money for local Ronald McDonald houses throughout the country. With these funds, local groups of McDonald's owners can begin their campaigns to raise more funds to establish homes near children's hospitals. The purpose of a Ronald McDonald home is to provide a place where the families of children stricken with leukemia and other serious diseases can stay with or near their children at little or no cost during treatment.

provides at least four benefits: a simpler source of funds, stronger manager motivation, better local business contacts, and reduced labor problems.

Simpler source of funds. Franchising is one way to finance rapid expansion. This is very important to a small business or an individual with a great idea. It would have cost $450 million to establish the first 2,700 Kentucky Fried Chicken outlets.[6] Colonel Harlan Sanders started the business at 65 with nothing but his secret recipe and a social security check for a few hundred dollars. He slept in his car as he traveled around selling his idea. Who would have lent him even the first million dollars? He had no choice but to turn to franchisees as a source of funds.

Through franchising, a firm can get others to pay for the privilege of belonging to its marketing system. If the company owned all of its outlets, it would be burdened with all the costs. With franchising, each franchisee covers a part of the costs.

Stronger manager motivation. Imagine that you managed a business for someone else and that business failed. You might be upset, but you could find another job. Of course, if that business had been very successful, you might have been in line for a raise. But what if you owned the business? You would have a great deal more to gain and a great deal more to lose. This is the idea behind the **"franchise ethic,"** which states that franchisees are more motivated than salaried managers because they have their own money at stake. According to a top McDonald's executive, "We feel very strongly that having only owner-operators is one of the keys to success in the franchising business. They are more involved, more highly motivated."[7]

Not all franchisers agree that this is true. Some believe that franchisees are interested only in reaching a certain income level. After that, the motivation is lost. Some franchisers are simply investors who hire managers to operate their businesses. For instance, Collins Foods in Los Angeles owns and operates 216 Kentucky Fried Chicken outlets.[8] In this case the motivation would be no different than if the original franchiser had hired 216 managers.

Better local business contacts. The oil companies began franchising in the 1930s because of the need for concerned, on-the-spot managers. At that time there was strong price competition in the gasoline business. Locally owned outlets could adjust prices quicker, and their out-of-pocket costs were lower. Members of the owners' families helped out by tending the pump or maintaining the grounds.

In many towns the local people resent the intrusion of outside ownership. It may be an advantage that the franchisee is a local businessperson with local contacts. If owned by a local person, the new outlet may be accepted more rapidly.

Reduced labor problems. Whether the outlet is managed by an employee or by the owner, it has just about the same number of people doing the same kinds of jobs. Under a franchise system, however, it is much more difficult for labor unions to organize the employees. If all of the workers were employed by one system, the union could bargain with the system. Under a franchise arrangement, the union would have to organize smaller groups of employees and bargain with individual owners.

Disadvantages to franchisers

While there are notable advantages to franchisers, there are some disadvantages, too. The most important of these are limited returns and reduced control.

Limited returns. Some franchisers would have preferred to expand without franchising if they could have obtained the funds. Some firms have both company-owned and franchised units, and often the company-owned units are much more profitable. The returns from the franchised outlets are limited to the amount set by the franchise contract. As they have grown more profitable, some franchisers have started to buy back their franchises. In a company-owned store the firm gets the full benefits of increased profits. Of course, if business is bad, the firm takes the entire loss.

Loss of control. The contract specifies certain rights and duties for each party. Beyond that, the franchiser's options are limited. The franchiser can make changes only by persuading the franchisee that the change is going to result in higher sales and more profit. If it is not a part of the contract and the franchisee rejects the idea, the franchiser is powerless.

Franchising is a popular way to do business because it offers benefits that often exceed the drawbacks. These advantages are not one-sided, however.

Benefits to franchisees

Each year 500,000 new businesses are started in the United States. People are attracted by the idea of independence. They dream of making their own decisions and profiting from their own work. But half of all these new businesses fail within two years. Only 25 percent survive for five years. One thousand small businesses fail each day.[9] Franchising can improve the chances of small business success by offering a packaged business system, an accepted image, a support system, and some of the economies of scale enjoyed by larger businesses.

A packaged business system. Most small businesses are started by a person with a special interest in some product or service. This may be anything from auto repair to yogurt. While these people know a lot about their special interest, they seldom have any background in accounting, advertising, store design, personnel, operations, market research, and other critical business functions. A franchiser can offer a complete package to fill in these gaps. The franchisee can then rely on tested methods rather than learning by trial and error. Most independent small businesses are on a financial shoestring with little room for error.

An accepted image. One franchisee predicted that sales volume would drop 60 percent within a day if the Burger King sign above the door were replaced with a sign that read "Fred's Burgers." When you have a good experience with one outlet of a franchise system, you are more likely to stop at another unit. It takes months or even years for a new independent business to build up enough customers to even cover its costs, but some new fast-food franchises manage to do so on the first day.[10] Even though it's a new store, customers know of the chain.

Continuing support systems. Franchisees can call on the franchiser for many kinds of continuing support. This may be help in training employees, tax assistance, management consulting, or any other area in which a small business is less able to help itself. Each year McDonald's conducts a separate market survey for each of its franchisees.[11]

These forms of continuing support are intended to assure that the franchisee avoids problems in managing the business. The franchiser wants to be sure that the outlet continues to produce a profit. After all, the continued success of the parent company is dependent on the success of its individual units.

Economies of scale. The franchiser can offer many services for less than the same services would cost the independent business. Think about a simple plastic sign on the wall of a Baskin-Robbins outlet. If the owner of that store had to order one sign, it would be far more expensive than the per unit cost when Baskin-Robbins, Inc., orders 5,000 identical signs. Very few local businesses could afford to produce a color television commercial. A major franchiser can do so and make prints available to franchisees at a fraction of the total cost.

Holiday Inns, Inc. even designs packaged restaurants for its outlets. An innkeeper can order the package, which includes coordinated furniture, wall coverings, menus, table settings, and other accessories. In a short time and at a relatively low cost the innkeeper can switch from the Tivoli Garden to the Flying Machine theme.[12]

McDonald's ran market tests for four years before introducing the Egg McMuffin.[13] Few restaurants could afford such extensive research, but when the cost is spread over 5,000 units, it becomes reasonable. These and other economies of scale allow the franchisee to enjoy many of the benefits of a large business while maintaining some of the independence of a small business.

Disadvantages for franchisees

Franchisees also face disadvantages. The two that seem to cause the most concern are the cost of the franchise and the restrictions imposed by the franchiser.

The cost of the franchise. The greater the success of the system, the more it costs to join. Most franchisees pay an initial fee as well as some monthly charge over the lifetime of the franchise. The initial fee may be high. It once cost $950 to become a McDonald's franchisee. Today the initial fee is over $250,000.[14]

The franchisee buys into a system because it is supposed to make

DID YOU EVER WONDER?

What do popular franchises cost?

Getting into the franchise business can be expensive. Here are the most recent price tags on some of the more popular operations:

Type of franchised business	Start-up cash required ($000)			Total investment involved ($000)		
	Lowest	Median	Highest	Lowest	Median	Highest
Automotive products and services	$ 3	$ 20	$100	$ 5	$ 43	$ 500
Business aids and services						
Accounting, credit, collection agencies,						
and general business systems	1	8	50	3	15	225
Employment services.........................	2	15	40	2	20	50
Printing and copying services	5	15	25	33	39	45
Tax preparation services......................	1	2	5	1	2	8
Miscellaneous business services	1	8	85	2	5	125
Campgrounds	30	50	75	35	225	650
Construction, home improvement,						
maintenance, and cleaning services	2	10	100	4	20	450
Convenience stores	3	10	35	16	55	185
Educational products and services	1	15	75	5	30	145
Fast-food restaurants	4	20	160	14	80	515
Hotels and motels	10	100	400	60	600	1,000
Laundry and dry-cleaning services	3	15	50	10	55	85
Recreation, entertainment, and travel services	1	15	300	2	50	900
Rental services, auto/truck	8	30	50	17	80	150
Rental services, equipment	2	10	45	3	35	168
Retailing, nonfood...........................	1	20	135	2	40	280
Retailing, food						
(other than convenience stores)	1	20	100	4	50	300

Source: Reprinted with permission from *Changing Times* Magazine, © 1977 Kiplinger Washington Editors, Inc., April 1977 *Changing Times.*

it easier to be a success. If that turns out to be true, it was a good buy. But some franchises have been oversold. People have been disappointed when they were less successful than they expected.

Some franchisees have no complaint regarding the initial fee but resent the monthly charge. Once their businesses are established, they doubt that they still need to belong to the system. Remember that the Burger King franchisee believed that the franchise accounted for six out of every ten burgers sold. But there are many people who are less satisfied with their franchisers.

Restrictions and interference. Holiday Inns, Inc. advertises "No Surprises!" Their research shows that 70 percent of the people who check into hotels on any night have never been to that hotel before.[15] They are buying an unknown. Most reservations are made from out-of-town locations, so the buyer can't tell whether the hotel is a palace or a dump. Holiday Inns, Inc. has built its reputation on consistency. You are supposed to have the same quality room with the same amenities whether you are in a Holiday Inn Hotel in Detroit or San Diego.

This means that standards become very important. If you have a bad experience with the restaurant at the Holiday Inn Hotels in Elkhart, Indiana, you might give up Holiday Inns forever. There are 1,725 other innkeepers who stand to lose your business.

A standardized product is the backbone of a successful franchise system. Therefore there must be some control over the franchisees to assure that each one lives up to the standards of the system. Each Holiday Inn Innkeeper can expect three unannounced on-the-spot inspections each year.[16] McDonald's has 190 field consultants who make two three-day inspections of each unit each year. The owner gets a 17-page report that grades the quality of food, service, speed, cleanliness, and hundreds of other items.[17] This kind of supervision, although critical to the success of the system, can be annoying to the local owner.

Franchising has been successful because it has matched people who had businesses that were in need of funds with people who had funds and wanted to start businesses. It has been mutually beneficial. While there are some drawbacks and there have been some problems with specific firms, franchising continues to grow. Let's look at how a franchise system is developed.

HOW DOES FRANCHISING WORK?

The franchiser may have a successful business concept, but it must be packaged before it can be sold as a franchise. The franchiser must clearly define the salable business concept, develop a matching business system, add a support system, and set up a financial system. Only when all of these pieces are included is the package ready for sale.

A business concept

Kemmons Wilson took his family on a trip from Memphis to Washington in 1951. While other things went smoothly, he was disgusted with the quality of lodging along the way. When he returned to Memphis he defined his business concept. He was going to offer a clean, dependable, moderately priced room with extras such as a pool and free ice to attract families. He would call it Holiday Inn. The units would be located along major traffic routes. Wilson's first Holiday Inn Hotel was an immediate success.[18]

A **business concept** defines the unique benefit to be offered to consumers, the brand name or identification, and the setting. For Kentucky Fried Chicken, it is the Colonel's secret herbs and spices, the name

Kentucky Fried Chicken with the image of the Colonel, and the counter service at the building with the red and white circus tent roof.

A matching business system

Most small businesses fail because of poor management. The success of the franchiser depends on the success of the franchisees. The wise franchiser supplies franchisees with a workable business system. The objective is to help the franchisee run an orderly business. The business system includes such things as sample forms for accounting records, inventory management, personnel evaluation, correspondence with customers or suppliers, and any other paperwork that can be standardized.

The business system may also include schedules and timetables. It may suggest lead times on placing orders, hours of operation, maintenance on equipment, or advertising schedules. The purpose is to protect the new owner-manager from misjudgments.

Business systems must match the business concept. The system for a coin-operated laundry with lots of equipment and few workers would be very different from the system offered for a new Snelling & Snelling Employment Agency franchise.

A support system

The franchiser normally provides two kinds of support. *Entry support* includes all the assistance in getting the outlet set up and opened for business. This often begins with help in selecting a site. It could include guidance on selecting suppliers and employees. Most major franchise operations provide training for the franchisee and key employees. McDonald's has Hamburger University; Holiday Inn University trains 4,500 people every year; and Kentucky Fried Chicken franchisees can attend Chicken University.

When a new McDonald's opens in your neighborhood you see Ronald McDonald with free balloons for the kids, but you can't see all of the background support. Everything has been carefully planned. Advertising, training, and other guidance based on years of experience can help the new franchisee avoid opening-day disasters.

But the support should not end on opening day. The franchise agreement spells out the details of the *continuing support.* This can include additional training, promotional support, and management assistance. The franchisee can depend on the franchiser to keep track of changes in the business environment and to suggest adjustments. For example, when Wendy's Old-Fashioned Hamburgers began to take away some of McDonald's franchisees' business, McDonald's supplied its outlets with an anti-Wendy's Action Pak.[19]

Reprinted with permission from the November 22, 1976 issue of *Advertising Age.* Copyright 1976 by Crain Communications, Inc.

Some franchisees believe they would do as well without the franchise

This continued centralized support allows the local owner-manager to concentrate on the daily business of running the store. Each of the benefits that are a part of the franchise package must be clearly stated. The franchisee must know what is being offered for the money.

A financial system

If the franchise package is going to be sold, it must have a price. Most franchise arrangements provide for one or more of five different sources of revenue for the franchiser:

1. Initial franchise fees.
2. Royalties on sales.
3. Rental fees on equipment, buildings, or fixtures.
4. Markups on sales of materials, supplies, or equipment.
5. Special fees for management assistance or the use of trademarks or special processes.

Initial fee. Most franchisers collect an initial franchise fee. Holiday Inns, Inc. charges $20,000 plus $150 for each additional room over 100. These fees are in part to cover the expenses involved in setting up the new outlet. But the fee also serves another purpose—it discourages those who are not serious about running a business. From the start, the franchisee has a lot to lose.

For a new franchise system, initial fees provide the funds to promote the franchise system to other prospective buyers. Most financial systems include something beyond the initial fee, otherwise the franchiser would have to expand forever.

Royalties   A royalty is a payment of a portion of the proceeds in return for the right to do business. Royalties account for the greatest revenues to franchisers. The royalty may be a simple percentage of sales. For example, McDonald's gets 3 percent of every dollar taken in by its franchisees. It could be set up on the basis of unit sales; Colonel Sanders started out charging a nickel per chicken. Holiday Inns, Inc. charges 4 percent of the gross room revenue per month. Under a royalty system, the franchiser and the franchisee share in the ups and the downs of the business.

Rental fees.   Many franchisers rent some or all of the facilities to their franchisees. This arrangement benefits both parties. It is a continuing source of revenue to the franchiser. It also means that the franchisee can go into business with less start-up money. Instead of investing in the building, equipment, and fixtures, the franchisee can pay a much smaller monthly fee. Some rentals are set up as a fixed amount per month just as if you rented an apartment. Other rentals are based on sales volume.

McDonald's owns the facilities used by 52 percent of its franchise outlets and leases them at the rate of 8.5 percent of total sales.[20] When business is good, it is to the franchisee's advantage to pay a fixed rent. All of the extra dollars then go into profit. When business is slow, a fixed rent can be a real burden. A rent based on sales would decrease with sales, however.

Markups.   Some franchisers act as wholesalers. They purchase goods in large quantities and resell these goods to their franchisees. Other franchise systems are set up as distributorships. Amway Products, Mary Carter Paints, Dr. Scholl's Foot Comfort Products, and General Motors franchise outlets solely to distribute the products they manufacture. The revenue to the franchiser is the markup on the sale of merchandise to the franchisee.

Special fees.   In addition to other fees, some franchisers charge separate fees for the use of trademarks or patented processes. Others charge extra for management services. Many franchisers charge a fee for the use of their corporate trademark or symbols (see Figure 5–5).

Separating these fees from the general royalty payment is logical only if the benefits to franchisees are not in proportion to their sales. For example, Holiday Inns, Inc. charges a special fee for the use of the Holidex reservation system, which is the largest private communica-

FIGURE 5-5
The "great sign"

Source: Courtesy of Holiday Inns, Inc.

tions system in the world. It has 2,300 terminals and is tied into major travel agencies and airlines. Systemwide, an average of 30 percent of all reservations are made through the Holidex network, but some innkeepers get 70 percent of their reservations this way.[21] Under a separate fee setup, these people pay more.

The franchise package is a product that the franchiser is offering for sale. Franchisers care a great deal about the actions of the people who buy their franchises. Their future success rests on the success of their franchisees.

Selling the franchise package to the right people

Selling the franchise package involves marketing techniques similar to those used for any product or service. But it also involves careful screening and selection of buyers and legal precautions to protect both the franchisee and the franchiser.

The franchiser must first locate interested prospects. Then these prospects must be fully informed through a well-planned sales presentation. The next task is to select the right person to whom to sell the franchise.

Locating qualified prospects. There are several ways to attract qualified prospects. Some firms simply sit and wait. People actually seek out McDonald's. Other firms depend on referrals from current franchisees. Smaller firms set up booths at trade shows. Many firms use advertising to deliver their message.

The way a firm delivers its message depends on the type of people it wants to reach and the number of franchises it can sell. Some franchisers advertise in national newspapers such as *The Wall Street Journal*. These papers are read by people with higher than average incomes and some business experience. Holiday Inns Inc. recently ran a two-page spread stressing the bright future of the travel industry and the benefits of becoming an Innkeeper. If you were interested, you could clip the coupon and send it in with $25 for a 62-page report on the Holiday Inn System. The $25 may have appeared to offset the cost of the report, but a probable purpose was to discourage those who are not really serious. This points to the greatest disadvantage of national newspaper advertising. It can attract many people who are not qualified prospects. Yet the franchiser must still go to the expense and trouble of dealing with them.

A new franchise system needs outlets everywhere. An established system needs only a few additional outlets in selected areas. In this case, local newspaper ads may be the answer. If Roto-Rooter needs another outlet in Kalamazoo, Michigan, it can advertise in the *Kalamazoo Gazette.*

There are two kinds of specialty magazines that carry many franchise advertisements. There are newsletters that cater to people interested in business opportunities. *National Franchise Reports* and *Success Unlimited* are examples. There are also magazines in special-interest areas. Puppy Palace, Inc., might advertise in *Dog Owners Digest,* for example.

However the message is delivered, there are four common appeals that are directly related to the benefits franchisees stand to gain. With phrases such as, "Start your own profitable business," and "Earn more than ever before," franchisers appeal to the prospect's interest in enhancing income. *Income* is the most popular of all appeals.

The next most popular appeal is *investment opportunity.* A newer franchiser might stress the opportunity to get in on the ground floor—"Your chance for the investment of a lifetime."

A third appeal is *independence.* "Are you tired of taking orders? Be your own boss." Independence is one of the important benefits of small business ownership.

The fourth appeal is *reduced risk.* Some franchisers stress their national reputation and history of success. "With 20 successful years behind us, we're ready to expand."

The purpose of advertising is to stimulate interest. These ads seldom tell the other side of the story. In the end, the franchiser can win only if the franchisees know what they will get and what will be expected of them. The sales presentation is the whole story.

The sales presentation: The whole story. While advertising stresses the benefits, the sales presentation should tell the whole story. Only a dishonest operation seeks to deceive the prospect. Unfortunately, when franchising was expanding rapidly in the 1950s, some fraudulant individuals tarnished its reputation. You should be wary of any deal that is too good to be true. Figure 5–6 gives some tips for potential franchisees.

Reputable franchisers realize that it is to everyone's advantage that the prospect understands everything about the system. They are only

FIGURE 5–6
Tips for potential
franchisees

A franchise can be the key to success or it can turn out to be a nightmare. It is up to the potential franchisee to be sure to ask the right questions and check out the facts. Here are some suggestions.

CHECK IT OUT CAREFULLY

1. Have the contract evaluated by your own attorney.
2. Check to see whether you have exclusive rights to a territory. The franchiser may have reserved the right to sell other franchises in your territory.
3. Check on the circumstances under which you can terminate the agreement and see what it will cost you to do so.
4. Can you sell the franchise? Will you be compensated for any goodwill you have established?
5. Who will you be competing with? On what basis will you compete? What advantage will you gain through the franchise?
6. Have you talked with any other franchisees in this system? Select them yourself—don't settle for the ones the franchiser has suggested.
7. Check out the start-up and continuing services carefully. Don't settle for general answers—get specific.
8. Check with the Better Business Bureau, Dun & Bradstreet, and the International Franchise Association.

TAKE A GOOD LOOK AT YOURSELF

1. Do you have enough capital to survive until the revenues from the franchise exceed the expenses of doing business?
2. Are you well aware of the practices of the franchise and can you accept and cooperate with the established policies?
3. What are your advantages and disadvantages? Are you ready to run a business?

AND THE DANGER SIGNALS

1. Are you being pushed to make a quick decision? Watch out!
2. Are you going to be expected to sell franchises to other people? A pyramid scheme can't go on forever. Someone will have to pay.
3. Does it seem too good to be true? If so, it probably is just that.

interested in people who are able to make informed and rational business decisions. Falsely high expectations can lead to dissatisfaction later and create real problems in the system.

The sales presentation has to accomplish three things. First, the prospect must be informed about the general nature of franchising. Then the franchiser must inform the prospect about the industry, its practices, and its future. Finally, the prospect must understand the details of the particular system.

The sales presentation can take place in many settings. It may be in the prospect's home. Many franchise systems set up meetings with groups of prospects in a community. These may be held in hotel meeting rooms or other group settings. AAMCO Transmissions and Evelyn Wood Reading Dynamics follow this pattern.

Some firms invite qualified prospects to their headquarters for a sales presentation. Success Motivation Institute franchises people to sell its line of self-help motivational tapes and books. Prospects are invited to a three-day seminar in its offices in Waco, Texas. During this time they are exposed to all of the details of the program, meet the company officers, tour the plant, and meet established franchisees who are in town for refresher training. While this is more expensive for SMI, it provides greater control over the prospects. It also provides for a much more thorough evaluation of the prospects.

Selecting the right franchisees. Franchisers hope to sell franchises to people who will run successful businesses. The franchiser is selecting a local partner. Each firm has its own standards for the ideal franchisee. Three things that are commonly considered are financial capabilities, business experience, and positive attitude.

One purpose of franchising is to generate the funds to finance rapid expansion. Most franchisers are concerned whether the prospect will be able to come up with the needed funds. This means that the prospect should have some savings and should be able to obtain credit. The prospect should have enough money to make the initial investment and to weather a period of slow sales or an unexpected expense. It can look bad for the whole chain when one of its units goes bankrupt.

Many franchise systems require that their franchisees have had practical experience in managing a business. This need not be experience in the same industry. It is assumed that some experience helps the applicant to be more aware of the nature of the task ahead. Some franchisers prefer that the prospect has not had experience in the same industry. They are concerned that it will be difficult for the prospect to "unlearn" habits that are contrary to their system.

Franchisers search for people who will work hard and be determined to succeed. They want people who will take responsibility and show initiative. They want people who will make a positive contribution to the system. The idea for the Big Mac was actually contributed by a franchisee. But franchisers have a system and a set pattern for each task. For example, Holiday Inns Inc. has a 32-page manual on how to clean a bathroom. So they need people who will follow directions and adhere to the standards of the system.

Some franchisers are also interested in the other members of the franchisee's family. Many small businesses become family activities.

Even if none of the other family members will be directly involved in the business, their attitudes can affect the franchisee.

There are no sure ways to predict success in franchising. By evaluating application forms and personal interviewing, franchisers attempt to select people who will succeed. As franchising has expanded, many franchisers have learned from past mistakes.

WHAT CAN BE EXPECTED IN FRANCHISING?

The conditions that led to the growth of franchising in the past are expected to continue. The population is mobile, the cost of rapid expansion is high, and there are still people who see opportunities in franchising. As franchising expands, there may be any of a number of developments. Let's look at these changes on the part of franchisers, franchisees, and the government.

Actions by franchisers

Franchising has been the key to business success for many organizations that would otherwise have remained very small firms. This success can be expected to bring about several trends. First, franchising will spread to other industries. Second, organizations that have achieved financial strength through franchising may attempt to regain some of the control they lost. Finally, as more firms enter each field, the competition will increase and the weaker firms will fail.

Franchising other industries. The factors that accounted for the success of franchising in fast foods, hotels, and rental cars are present in other industries. Any industry that is made up of small outlets serving similar customer needs is subject to franchising. During the 1980s, experts predict that almost all of the nation's 250,000 independent real estate firms will join franchise systems.[22] Accounting services, health food stores, health clubs, travel agencies, and many other types of businesses are likely to turn to franchising.

Regaining control. Many of the major franchisers have found that company-owned units are more profitable. These chains have been buying back franchises or opening a higher proportion of company-owned stores. Pizza Hut plans call for at least half of its new outlets to be company-owned.[23] Wendy's bought back all of its franchises in Atlanta and Memphis.[24] As long as the franchisers can supply their own capital, they are moving in the direction of company ownership.

Increased competition. Franchising is really big business. Many of the independent chains have been acquired by major corporations. As competition has increased, it has become more difficult for a new firm to get started. Those firms that suffered from poor management or inadequate resources failed. This has left two types of franchise chains: major national franchise chains and regional chains. Some people have predicted that there will be a limit on the number of franchise outlets that can be absorbed into the economy. There is supposed to be some point at which the market is saturated. Therefore, since most of the major chains predict expansion, the level of competition should increase.

Actions by franchisees

The same factors that affect the franchisers will affect the franchisees. As the field of franchising matures, franchisees are expected to become more sophisticated. This should lead to two developments: (1) a trend toward multiple franchising, and (2) more and more franchisees joining franchisee associations. The object is to deal with common problems and to deal as a group with the franchiser.

Multiple franchising. Burger King has begun to sell franchises to local restaurant chains. A restaurant firm with eight outlets in Manhattan converted all of them to Burger Kings. Another firm converted 80 of its restaurants to Burger Kings. Both firms had been losing money. One president said, "We couldn't lick them, so we joined them."[25]

Franchisers have also been granting additional franchises to their successful franchisees. Between the move to company-owned outlets and the move to multiple franchising, there may eventually be little room for the small businessperson.

Franchisee associations. The McDonald's franchisees in northern California have formed the Northern California Association of the Golden Arches. Franchisee associations are made up of the owners of the franchises in a single system. The members share information, and in some cases the association negotiates with the franchiser on behalf of the franchisees as a group. This gives the small franchisee a stronger voice in dealing with a major corporate franchiser.

Actions by the government

As franchising becomes more important, it will bring about more action by governments at the federal and local levels. Over half the states have already passed laws that regulate franchisers. These laws apply regardless of the state in which the franchiser has its offices. For example, if Success Motivation Institute in Waco, Texas, sells a franchise to a person in Sacramento, California, the laws of the state of California apply.

Think about the problems this creates for the national franchiser. If each state had its own set of requirements, each national franchiser might have to write 50 different contracts. The only other choice would be to write out one standard contract that meets the requirements of the most regulated state and does not conflict with the laws of any other state. The relationships between franchisers and franchisees would be just about 50 times more complex. It is logical that there will be pressure for legislation at the federal level.

There will also be pressure from traditional retailers. At present franchising accounts for $1 out of every $3 spent in retail stores. If franchising continues to grow in popularity, nonfranchised retailers will try to bring pressure to curtail franchising. As franchising spreads to industries beyond fast foods and auto supplies, more and more traditional retailers will be affected.

SUMMARY

Franchising is simply a method of distribution. The franchiser grants the franchisee the right to do business in a particular way in a particular place for a given period of time. There are many different franchise arrangements. Most are based on a contract which specifies that the franchisee will distribute a particular product or service. Both the franchiser and franchisee have rights and responsibilities. Both contribute something of value. The franchiser may contribute a unique product or a business system, and the franchisee usually contributes capital and local management. Franchise agreements have been reached between manufacturers and retailers, manufacturers and wholesalers, wholesalers and retailers, and between people who had successful business concepts and others who wanted to start businesses. This last type of franchise has been growing in popularity over the last quarter century.

Franchising has become popular because it offers advantages to both the franchisers and the franchisees. It allows the franchisers to use other peoples' money to expand their businesses. Since those people have their own money in the business, they may well be more motivated than salaried managers. Franchising provides the franchisee with a tested business system and increased chances of small business success. The support system provided by the franchiser allows the franchisee to enjoy the independence of a small business along with the economies of scale of a large business.

Of course, there are some disadvantages. The franchiser is limited both in earnings and in the level of control that can be imposed on the franchise system. The franchisee must share its earnings with the franchiser and must submit to some control.

The franchiser is really in the business of selling a packaged business. The franchise package includes a business concept, a matching business system, a support system, and a financial system. The franchiser's success depends on selling this franchise package to the right people. Franchisers attempt to locate qualified prospects in a number of ways. They might depend on referrals from their existing franchisees, or they may present their message at trade shows or through advertising. In most cases franchisers try to appeal to the prospects' desires for income, an investment opportunity, independence, or association with a successful firm. The message is normally one-sided, but during the sales presentation that follows, the franchiser must present the whole story. In the past, fraudulent franchisers have misled hopeful franchisees. A deal that is too good to be true indeed may not be true.

The success of the franchiser depends on the success of the franchisees. Therefore, franchisers attempt to select franchisees who will work hard and take the responsibility for their outlets, yet be willing to listen to advice and cooperate. These franchisees must also be able to provide the necessary funds and be able to manage the day-to-day operations of the business.

Franchising is expected to become even more important in our economy. Several trends are expected. It is likely that the success of franchising in fast foods and more than 40 other industries will bring about interest in franchising in still other industries. Some firms that have achieved financial success through franchising are expected to begin to buy back their franchises. Franchisees are expected to become more sophisticated and to move toward multiple franchises and franchisee associations.

As franchising becomes more important in the economy, there will be more regulation at both the state and the federal levels. A successful form of business always draws attention, and there is no doubt that franchising has proved to be successful.

REVIEW QUESTIONS

1. Show how the tests of a franchise system apply to McDonald's.

2. What are the benefits of franchising to the franchiser? Are these still important after the chain has been established?

3. What are the benefits to the franchisee? Which benefit would be most important to you?

4. Think of three franchises you have done business with and explain their business concepts.

5. Franchising is important in more than 40 industries. How many can you name?

6. Think of your favorite hobby. If you were going to open a store to serve people with this same hobby, what kind of business system and support system would you need?

7. If your business was a great success and you decided to expand through franchising, what financial system would you set up? Explain why you would or would not include each of the five sources of revenue.

8. Look in the newspaper or some magazines and find a franchise advertisement. Can you explain why that ad was placed there? What appeal is being used?

9. Can you think of any industries that might be ready for franchising? Why do you think so?

CASES

Case 5–1.   A Big Mac without worms, please

In October 1978, the management of several hamburger chains faced a difficult problem. Rumors had been circulating that they used red worms to enhance the protein content of their hamburger meat. Supposedly this had been disclosed on "60 Minutes," the CBS network news investigation program. Of course, the rumors were untrue if for no other reason than that worms cost $5 to $10 per pound! As the largest franchise operation, McDonald's was hit the worst. It was estimated that business was off by as much as 30 percent in some locations.

The international corporate offices went so far as to get supportive letters from the U.S. Secretary of Agriculture, the producers of "60 Minutes," and even George Sroda, the self-proclaimed Worm Czar and author of a book, *Facts about Nightcrawlers.* The rumor was having the most serious effect in Kentucky, Georgia, Ohio, and Indiana.

1. *Should McDonald's attempt to deny the rumors? If so, how?*
2. *All of the franchisees contribute to the national advertising budget. Since the rumor has not affected sales in many states, should the money contributed by franchisees in those states be used to help the franchisees in the affected states?*

Case 5–2.   The 30-minute tune-up

Insta-Tune, Inc., is the largest of the fast auto tune-up chains. In three years it had set up 130 tune-up centers in gas stations that were abandoned during the oil crunch. Andy Granatelli, the former racing car driver, took part of his winnings and funded Tune Masters. Andy's company has been growing at about half the rate of Insta-Tune. The big difference is that Tune Masters has opted for company-owned units, while Insta-Tune has been franchising.

Both companies started out in California and are snapping up defunct gas stations. Insta-Tune has been spreading out to open stations in Texas, Illinois, and even Maine. Insta-Tune franchises sell for $12,500. Franchisees pay Insta-Tune 7 percent of gross revenues, a $10-a-week service fee, and $500 a month for advertising. Start-up costs are about $50,000. The sales average 12 tune-ups a day at $37.

1. *Why would Granatelli choose to set up company-owned outlets instead of franchising? What advantages are there for Insta-Tune?*
2. *The franchisee pays Insta-Tune the initial franchise price, the service fee, the percentage of gross, and the advertising fee. How do each of these affect the franchisee?*
3. *Why would anyone invest in an Insta-Tune franchise?*

chapter 6

ASSESSING EFFECTIVENESS: ACCOUNTABILITY AND CONTROL

By studying this chapter you should be able
to find answers to these questions:

1 What is accounting?
2 How do managers of the firm and outsiders
use accounting information?
3 How does a firm decide on an accounting
period?
4 What is the difference between cash and
accrual accounting?
5 How does double-entry accounting work?
6 What can be learned from a balance sheet?
7 What information is contained on an
income statement?
8 What good is a statement of changes in
financial position?
9 How do ratios help in understanding
financial statements?
10 What is the difference between private and
public accounting?
11 How does an audit protect those who use
financial statements?

Terms you should know:

accounting
assets
balance sheet
credit
debit
depreciation
expenses
financial accounting
Financial Accounting Standards Board (FASB)
income statement
liabilities
managerial accounting
net income
owners' equity
private accountant
revenues
statement of changes in financial position

business firm can continue to exist in the long run only if it makes some profit. It must eventually provide for some return to those who have invested in it. At some point, the owners and managers of a firm must stop and try to answer the big question: Are we making money?

You might think that it would be easy to answer this question. Isn't the firm making money if there is some money left in the bank account after all the bills have been paid? It would be just that simple if the firm was going out of business. If it sold everything and paid off all the creditors and investors and still had money left over, it must have made money. But the managers can't wait until they go out of business. It is important to know how well the firm is doing while it is still in business. Are earnings high enough to pay dividends to the owners? Do the managers deserve a bonus? Should the employees get raises? Is business good enough to expand? Would it be better to sell the business and put the money in a bank? Can the firm get a loan? How much are the taxes? These are just a few of the questions that must be answered.

Accounting provides answers to the financial questions asked by interested persons both within the firm and outside the firm. In this chapter we will discuss the nature of accounting, the uses of accounting information, the way the basic accounting statements are prepared, the analysis of these statements, and the role of public accounting.

WHAT IS ACCOUNTING?

Accounting provides for the continuing collection, organization, and summarization of information on the financial situation within a firm. It is a system of decisions, techniques, and practices that permits the evaluation of a firm's financial position. Accounting has been described as follows:

> Accounting focuses on the measurement and reporting, in monetary terms, of the flows of resources into and out of an organization, of the resources controlled by the organization and of the claims against those resources. In doing this, accounting collects, processes, evaluates and reports certain information. Accounting measures . . . the efficiency with which an organization uses the scarce resources available to it for carrying out its objectives.[1]

A good accounting system provides for the orderly retention of financial information on the performance of a firm. The accounting process starts with the individual financial transactions of a firm. But it isn't hard to see that simply recording each transaction could soon lead to a pile of useless numbers.

There is a big difference between accounting and bookkeeping. Book-

"These are the figures for the first three months."

Reprinted with permission from the November 1, 1976 issue of *Advertising Age*. Copyright 1976 by Crain Communications, Inc.

Without accounting, financial data could become a pile of useless numbers.

keeping is limited to the recording of transactions in the books, the firm's financial records. Once the books have been set up, few decisions or judgments are made. Today most of these operations have been turned over to machines. Accounting involves a series of steps by which similar transactions are grouped together and summarized in financial statements and reports. Accountants must make complex decisions and evaluations.

Two important areas of accounting are financial accounting and managerial accounting. The purpose of **financial accounting** is to prepare financial statements for those outside the firm, including the government, the firm's shareholders, and the general public. As long as the firm's financial statements have been prepared according to the accepted accounting practices, it is possible to make many useful comparisons.

In order to make sure that the statements of one firm can be compared with the statements of another, financial accountants must comply with strict ground rules. Can you imagine what it would be like if each firm designed its own income tax form? Standard financial statements make it possible to measure changes in the performance of the firm from one period to the next. It is also possible to compare the performance of one firm with that of other firms.

Managerial accounting provides the managers of the firm with the financial information they need to assess the potential financial impact of their decisions. For example, the managers may need special cost figures to reach a decision on a new project. While reports for internal use need not conform to outside guidelines, they often do. Such reports can be understood easily by people new to the firm. Besides, since the financial accounting information is required anyway, it is often the starting point for the preparation of managerial accounting information.

THE USES OF ACCOUNTING INFORMATION

Accounting has been called the "language of business" because it is the primary formal means by which information about a firm is communicated. Accounting information serves as a common frame of reference. It is something that all firms have in common whether they are large or small or in one industry or another. Accounting information is used by managers and their advisors. It is also used by outsiders who deal with the firm or who are affected by its actions.

Internal uses of accounting information

Managers use financial statements to assess the firm's overall performance. They can judge how well the firm is using its financial resources and answer that big question: Are we making money? But managers also use these statements and the information behind them in other ways.

Accounting information is an input to management's decision making. Cost figures provided by accounting are critical to planning and to budget preparation.

Accounting information also serves a control function. Accounting provides a financial report on the results of past decisions. At the end of each financial period, the new accounting information can be used to compare the actual results with the expected results. Sometimes these comparisons are both frightening and very informative.

Accounting allows managers to keep track of the results of business activities. It helps managers to spot problems, which can then be corrected. If one firm's financial statements are better than those of other firms in the same industry, the difference might well be better management.

Accounting information is a very important part of the communications between a firm's managers and interested outside parties. These include shareholders, lenders, financial analysts, suppliers and customers, union officials, government agencies, and even competitors.

External uses of accounting information

Every firm is evaluated by some outsiders. Even the smallest single proprietorship with no employees or creditors must at least provide

ELLEN K. LEE
Member, New York Stock Exchange

Wagner International
Photos Inc.

In 1977 Ellen K. Lee became a member of the New York Stock Exchange thereby earning the right to execute customer orders on the floor of the exchange. Ms. Lee was only the third woman to be accepted as one of the 1,366 members of the exchange. Beyond that, she was only 25 years old when she earned that honor.

Ms. Lee, Assistant Vice President, Bache Halsey Stuart Shields, Inc., joined the firm in 1974 upon graduation from Seton Hall University. At that time she took a position as trainee in the Branch Customer Services area. She had chosen the Bache position over several offers in other industries because she felt that the financial service industry offered the best opportunities for her advancement. She immersed herself in the financial world and claims, "My vocation and my avocation is finance."

Founded in 1879, Bache Halsey Stuart Shields, Inc., is a leading investment banking firm. Headquartered in New York, Bache has 176 offices in 143 cities in 11 countries. It is itself a publicly held corporation with over 10,000 shareholders and 6,500 employees including 2,500 account executives. Bache Halsey Stuart Shields, Inc., has memberships on 59 different securities, commodities, and options exchanges.

tax information to the government. The larger the firm, the more people there are who are interested in its financial performance.

Corporations with publicly traded stock are required by law to provide certain accounting information to their shareholders. To do so, they issue annual reports. While only three financial statements are required, these annual reports often include a great deal of other information on the firm. It is estimated that the average large firm prints two to three times as many annual reports as it has shareholders.[2] These reports are distributed to potential investors, libraries, and individuals who write or call seeking information on the firm.

The shareholders.   Among other things, accounting information shows the return on the investment of the shareholders. This information shows how well the firm has used the money provided by the owners. If the returns are below the owners' expectations, the owners can try to get the managers to change their strategies, replace the managers, or sell their shares in the firm.

Wouldn't you think that shareholders would pay careful attention to the information released in the annual reports? A recent study showed that four out of ten shareholders either don't read the annual report or spend only one to five minutes doing so.[3]

Even if the shareholders take no action, the release of accounting information affects them. An increase in earnings is one of the factors that can increase the market value of the shareholders' stock. On the other hand, if earnings are down, the market value of the shares may decline.

Financial analysts and potential investors. Financial analysts and potential investors use financial statements to evaluate the firm as a possible investment. If the firm looks good, more people will try to buy the stock and the price will go up. On the other hand, if the company looks unstable or financially weak, fewer people will want to be owners and the price will go down. While some potential investors try to estimate the firm's promise for the future and others may even flip a coin, analysis of the financial statements is a good way to make a decision. The statements show what the firm has actually been able to do.

Lenders. Lenders evaluate the financial statements of firms that ask to borrow money. Careful analysis of these statements shows how wisely the firm has used its funds in the past. Beyond that, lenders may continue to examine the financial statements of their borrowers over the lifetime of the loan to be sure that the borrowers are maintaining the financial strength that justified the loan in the first place.

The lender may impose restrictions on the financial behavior of a borrower. Then the lender examines the statements of the borrower to be sure that these restrictions are being met. If there are signs that the borrower is getting into trouble, the lender may be wiser to help out rather than allow the firm to go bankrupt. This might mean an adjustment of the repayment schedule or some management advice. The lenders to the Penn Central Railroad and W. T. Grant have been criticized for failing to spot the signs of trouble in time to help turn these major businesses around.

Suppliers and customers. Whether buying or selling, business firms have an interest in the financial condition of the firms with which they do business. Unless the price has been reduced, it is usually not a good idea to buy from a firm that is about to go out of business. This could cause problems with service and make the product much less valuable. When RCA got out of the computer business, it left a lot of customers with orphaned equipment. Had the customers examined the financial statements of RCA's computer division, they might have realized that the end was near.

If a supplier sells goods to a firm that is later unable to pay its bills, it could mean a big loss. Many of the firms that had sold merchandise to W. T. Grant just before it went bankrupt ended up accepting a fraction of what they were owed. They would have been much better off if they had never made the sale. Accounting information can give suppliers or customers some idea of the financial stability of the firm.

Union officials. You can be sure that before the officials of the United Auto Workers or the Teamsters go to the bargaining table on a new contract, they have been very careful to review the financial statements of the firm. Then they are able to estimate how much they think the firm can afford to pay. If the firm has had a good year and earnings have been high, the union is likely to press harder for increased wages and benefits.

Government agencies. The firm's federal, state, and local taxes are based on the figures reported on its financial statements. The tax laws passed by various government bodies affect the way in which these figures are reported. The decisions of the tax courts and the Internal Revenue Service also affect accounting practices. Observers from each of these agencies are interested in a firm's financial statements. The chance of prosecution or other penalties for noncompliance lends added importance to the accounting methods used to develop these statements.

Competitors. There are many reasons why competitors have an interest in a firm's financial statements. The financial statements of other firms in the same industry give each competitor some idea of where it stands. For example, 1978 was a bad year in the intercity passenger bus industry. Discount airfares had lured away most of its customers. The managers of Trailways Corporation might have felt that they did a terrible job of managing their firm that year since their revenues dropped off compared with those from previous years. But one look at the financial statements of the other firms in the industry, such as Greyhound, would show them that they really lost less than their competitors and were well ahead of the industry averages.

It is clear that there are many groups of people who make use of a firm's financial statements. Accurate accounting is very important to the successful management of a firm. It is with these uses in mind that each firm sets up its accounting system and prepares its financial statements. The accountants' objectives are to conform to accepted accounting principles, to meet legal requirements, and to serve the managers' purposes. The outsiders who wish to make use of these financial statements must often interpret them to find the answers to their specific questions. Before we look at the ways in which statements are analyzed, let's look more closely at the basic financial statements and how they are prepared.

THE BASIC ACCOUNTING PROCESS

Regardless of the complexity of the firm, the basic accounting process still follows the general form that was set up in the Middle Ages by a Franciscan monk named Lucas Pacioli. Among the important concepts underlying the basic accounting process are the accounting period, the accounting basis, and double-entry accounting.

The accounting period

For the purpose of reporting to outsiders, the normal accounting period is one year. While many firms choose the calendar year as their fiscal or accounting year, some account for their income over their natural business year. A natural business year is based on the normal cycle in a particular industry as shown in Figure 6–1. K mart closes its books in February after all of the Christmas returns and payments are over.

It can be very difficult to cut into the stream of events that affect a normal business. Even if the income statement is prepared in the off-season, there are ongoing expenses and revenues that do not fall neatly into one year or the next. Expenses are outflows of resources or costs for goods and services used by a firm to earn revenues. Revenues are inflows of cash and other items of value received for goods sold or services rendered. What if inventory is carried over from the

FIGURE 6–1

Different firms set up different accounting periods to meet their needs

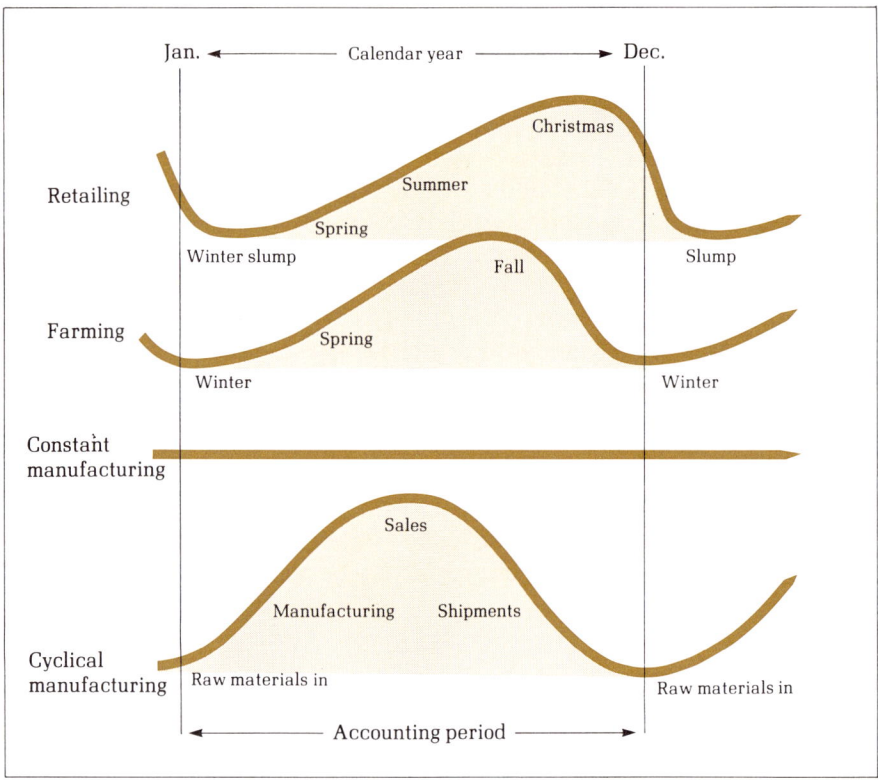

past season? Should the costs of producing that inventory be assigned to the past year?

An accounting basis

These kinds of problems cannot be solved entirely but can be minimized if the firm adopts a standard approach. There are two basic approaches to recording financial information. The first is called **cash basis accounting.** In cash basis accounting, revenue is counted as revenue when it is received, and expenses are counted as expenses when they are paid. This is the method most people use to keep track of their personal finances. If you are treated by a doctor on December 27 and pay the bill on January 2 of the next year, you would report that expense on your income tax form for the year in which the bill was paid, not the year in which you were treated.

Most firms operate on an **accrual accounting basis.** Under an accrual accounting system, revenue is counted as revenue when it is earned, and expenses are counted as expenses when the firm makes use of the goods or services bought, not when the bill is paid. If a firm sends an employee for a physical exam on December 27 and pays the bill on January 2, the expense is reported for the year in which the service was performed, not the year in which the bill was paid. Suppose you went to the department store and purchased a shirt on your charge account. That store counts that revenue in the year in which the sale was made even if your payment arrives during its next fiscal year.

While the accrual basis seems more complicated, it is used so that revenues and expenses are counted in the same period as the activities that caused those revenues and expenses. Double-entry accounting is another part of accounting that seems complex but is used for greater accuracy.

Double-entry accounting

Figure 6–2 gives an outline of the basic accounting process. It shows the path taken by a piece of financial information from the time it is created as a result of some transaction until the time it has meaning to the firm's managers or interested outsiders.

The first step in an accounting system is a journal. A **journal** is a log or diary of financial activity. From the journal, entries are separated into similar groups of transactions, which are then transferred to separate T-accounts in a ledger.

A **T-account** is a form with a title at the top of the T. Transactions that increase the value of the account are recorded on one side of the upright, and items that decrease its value are recorded on the other. There are three basic groups of T-accounts that match up with the

FIGURE 6–2
The accounting process

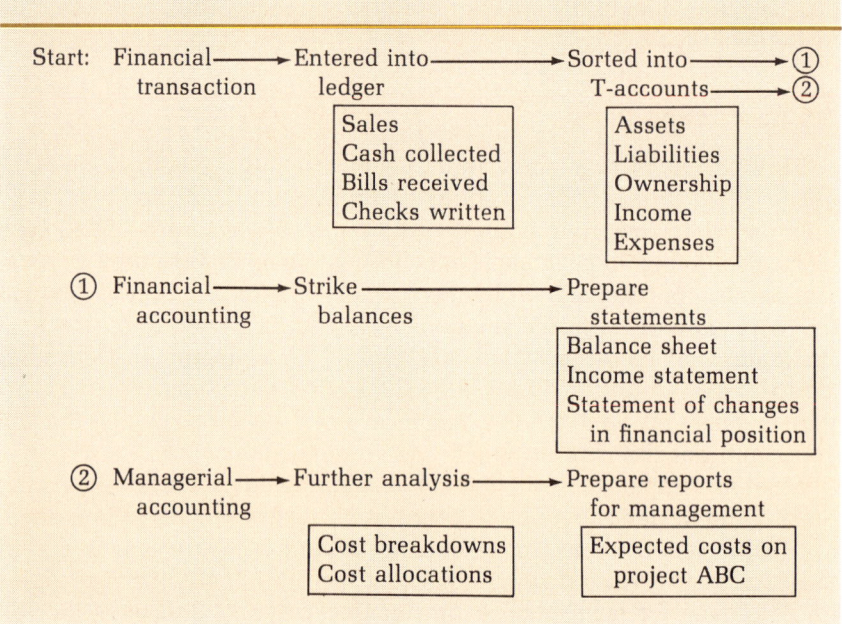

items on the basic financial statements. These are shown in Figure 6–3 and are described in detail in the next section on the financial statements. There can be as many separate T-accounts within each account group as the firm needs to meet its needs. For example, under assets—things the firm owns—there can be separate T-accounts for such things as buildings, cash, inventory, and accounts receivable.

Entries recorded on the left-hand side of the accounts are called

FIGURE 6–3
Basic T-accounts

Assets		Liabilities	
Debits	Credits	Debits	Credits
+	−	−	+

Owners' Equity	
Debits	Credits
−	+

	Increases	Decreases
Assets	Debit	Credit
Liabilities	Credit	Debit
Owner's Equity	Credit	Debit

Office Supplies (asset)		Cash (asset)	
Debit	Credit	Debit	Credit
+	−	+	−
50¢			50¢

FIGURE 6–4
Even a paperclip transaction results in entries in two accounts

debits. Entries on the right-hand side are called **credits.** The first rule of accounting is that for every debit there must be a credit. In recording each transaction, one entry is on the left side of a T-account and the other is on the right side of another T-account.

This is the reason why it is called **double-entry accounting.** If the firm pays cash for a box of paperclips, this is recorded as an increase in the asset account for office supplies and as a decrease in the asset account for cash (see Figure 6–4). The firm has shifted its wealth from one form to another.

A single transaction can result in entries in more than two accounts. If a firm buys a truck for $15,000, paying $5,000 down and signing a note for $10,000, the full $15,000 purchase price of the truck is recorded as an increase in the asset account for trucks. The $5,000 down payment is recorded as a decrease in the asset account for cash. Again, the firm's assets have been converted from one form to another. But what about the $10,000 the firm still owes? That is a liability—something that is owed—and it must be recorded as an increase in the liability account for notes payable. The sum of the entries on the left sides of all of the accounts must equal the sum of the entries on the right sides of the accounts (see Figure 6–5).

All of the firm's transactions are recorded in a journal and summarized in the appropriate accounts during the accounting period. At the end of the period the accountants use this information to prepare the financial statements.

FIGURE 6–5
A transaction may result in more than two entries

Building (asset)		Cash (asset)		Mortgage (liability)	
debit	credit	debit	credit	debit	credit
$10,000			$2,000		$8,000

THE BASIC FINANCIAL STATEMENTS

The three basic financial statements are the balance sheet, the income statement, and the statement of changes in financial position. The **balance sheet,** sometimes called the *statement of financial position,* shows the financial condition of the firm at one point in time. This may be at the end of a quarter or a year. The **income statement,** also called the *profit and loss statement,* shows whether the firm has earned net income during the accounting period. The **statement of changes in financial position** shows the firm's sources and uses of funds over the accounting period.

These financial statements are the result of the financial accounting process, which is closely guided by the generally accepted principles of accounting and constantly evaluated by the **Financial Accounting Standards Board** (FASB). Because accounting information can have very important economic impacts on broad groups of people, the FASB tends to be quite conservative and restrictive.

The balance sheet

The **balance sheet** is simply a list of the firm's assets and the claims against those assets. All the assets a firm owns have either been paid for by the firm's owners or the firm still owes money for them. Therefore, the assets of the firm balance against its liabilities and owners' equity (see Figure 6–6).

FINANCIAL ACCOUNTING STANDARDS BOARD

When the Financial Accounting Standards Board was established in 1973, it was charged with the responsibility to develop financial accounting and reporting standards that would help to maintain confidence in the reliability of financial data. The FASB is supported by the Financial Accounting Foundation, an independent body consisting of trustees representing each of the sponsoring organizations:

The American Accounting Association
The American Institute of Certified Public Accountants
The Financial Analysts Federation
The Financial Executives Institute
The National Association of Accountants

The seven board members ponder deep-seated problems facing a profession that is under constant pressure to make its numbers reflect more accurately and honestly an economic reality that grows constantly more complex. The board members are assisted by 106 full-time staff members and by an advisory council drawn from a wide cross section of businesspeople. The FASB is the accounting profession's conscientious effort at self-regulation. As long as this is effective, the Securities and Exchange Commission will keep some distance. Should it fail, the profession would be subjected to more stringent SEC regulation.

FIGURE 6–6
Assets equal liabilities plus owners' equity

Assets. For accounting purposes, **assets** are valuable resources that are owned by a firm and that were acquired at a measurable cost. These assets are recorded on the balance sheet if they can be sold or if they will be used to conduct business. They might be acquired for cash or for a promise to pay. If you put $1,000 down on a $6,000 car, you have a $6,000 asset. You acquired $1,000 worth of it for cash and $5,000 for the promise to pay. Some things that are of value, such as a good image in the community or trusted employees, do not show up on the balance sheet. They have value but were not purchased.

Problems can arise if the value of an asset changes. Should it show up on the balance sheet at the purchase price or at the current market value? The balance sheet often does not show the current fair market value of the firm's assets. This occurs because keeping these values up to date would require a great deal of estimation and guesswork. Investors and creditors could be misled if the value of assets was overestimated.

In Chapter 12 we will discuss in detail each of the types of asset and liability accounts from the viewpoint of their role in the financial management of the firm. Here we are concerned with their importance in an accounting sense, that is, how these assets and liabilities can be recorded and reported in a way that is most useful to the managers and outsiders who use accounting information.

As you can see from Figure 6–7, current and fixed assets are reported separately. Current assets are cash and other resources that are expected to be converted to cash or consumed within about one year. Fixed assets are expected to have useful lives exceeding that arbitrary one-year limit. They are to be used to produce the firm's product or service and include such things as land, buildings, and equipment. Accountants have adopted the practice of listing current and fixed assets separately because of the important issue of liquidity.

Liquidity refers to the speed with which assets can be converted to cash. When a firm is in financial trouble, it needs cash to avoid financial disaster. If all of its assets are tied up in resources that cannot be converted to cash quickly and easily at some price close to the actual market value, the firm could be forced into bankruptcy even if it has substantial assets.

Liabilities.   The claims of outsiders against the assets of the business are **liabilities.** These include everything the firm owes to everybody. If the liability can reasonably be expected to be paid off within a year, it is a **current liability**. If the firm owes a debt that is to be paid off over a period of years, the payment due in the current year is shown as a current liability and the rest of the obligation is shown as a **long-term liability.**

Owners' equity.   The **owners' equity** section reports that share of the firm's assets contributed by the owners. This share was contributed either through their initial investment or by leaving the earnings of

FIGURE 6–7
Balance sheet

DELTA COMPANY
Comparative Balance Sheet
December 31, 1979, and December 31, 1978

Assets

Current Assets:	1979	1978
Cash	$ 7,500	$ 4,800
Accounts receivable, net	8,000	9,500
Merchandise inventory	31,500	32,000
Prepaid expenses	1,000	1,200
Total Current Assets	$ 48,000	$ 47,500
Plant and Equipment:		
Office equipment	$ 3,500	$ 3,000
Accumulated depreciation, office equipment	(900)	(600)
Store equipment	26,200	21,000
Accumulated depreciation, store equipment	(5,200)	(4,200)
Buildings	95,000	80,000
Accumulated depreciation, buildings	(10,600)	(8,200)
Land	25,000	25,000
Total Plant and Equipment	$133,000	$116,000
Total Assets	$181,000	$163,500

Liabilities

Current Liabilities:		
Notes payable	$ 2,500	$ 1,500
Accounts payable	16,700	19,600
Dividends payable	1,000	700
Total Current Liabilities	$ 20,200	$ 21,800
Long-Term Liabilities:		
Mortgage payable	$ 17,500	$ 20,000
Total Liabilities	$ 37,700	$ 41,800

Stockholders' Equity

Common stock, $10 par value	$115,000	$100,000
Premium on common stock	8,500	5,000
Retained earnings	19,800	16,700
Total Stockholders' Equity	$143,300	$121,700
Total Liabilities and Stockholders' Equity	$181,000	$163,500

Source: William W. Pyle, John Arch White, and Kermit D. Larson, *Fundamental Accounting Principles*, 8th ed. (Homewood, Ill.: Richard D. Irwin, 1978), p. 606. © 1978 by Richard D. Irwin, Inc.

the firm under its control rather than distributing them to the owners. If the firm is incorporated, the owners' equity is shown as stockholders' equity. If the business is a sole proprietorship or a partnership, the owners' equity is shown as an individual person's capital.

These are the general items on a balance sheet. Clearly the balance sheet included in the annual report of a diversified firm such as the Transamerica Corporation is far more complex than the balance sheet of a simple sole proprietorship. But the basic format and the reasoning underlying its preparation are identical.

The income statement

The **income statement** matches the revenues of the accounting period against the expenses of that period. The revenue earned is matched against the costs of the goods and services used to earn that revenue. Preparing the income statement involves a series of subtraction problems. As shown in Figure 6–8, the major headings on the income statement reflect revenues, expenses, and net income.

Revenues.   The receipts from the sale of goods and services during the accounting period are the **revenues.** These may be in the form of cash or funds owed to the firm on credit sales. A firm can earn revenues without earning net income. If the firm sells its products for less than it cost to manufacture them, it has taken in revenue, but the firm's owners are no wealthier. If revenues are greater than expenses for the accounting period, the firm has net income. Of course, if expenses exceed revenues over the accounting period, the firm suffers a loss.

$$\text{Net income} = \text{Revenues} - \text{Expenses}$$

The amount of total revenue is the starting point in preparing the income statement. It is the figure from which all the expenses of doing business are subtracted to arrive at the firm's net income.

Expenses.   The cost of goods and services consumed by the firm in its efforts to earn revenues are the **expenses.** Expenses are recognized in the period in which the resources are used. This need not be the period in which the payment is made.

Land, equipment, and some other products or services have an expected life exceeding the accounting period. To fairly match expenses against revenues, there must be some way to assign a part of the cost

FIGURE 6–8
Income statement

REXEL SALES COMPANY
Income Statement for Year Ended December 31, 19—

Sales		$50,000
Cost of goods sold		30,000
Gross profit from sales		$20,000
Operating expenses:		
Sales salaries expense	$8,000	
Rent expense	1,200	
Depreciation expense, equipment	1,000	10,200
Net Income		$ 9,800

Source: William W. Pyle, John Arch White, and Kermit D. Larson, *Fundamental Accounting Principles*, 8th ed. (Homewood, Ill.: Richard D. Irwin, 1978), p. 603. © 1978 by Richard D. Irwin, Inc.

of that item to each of the accounting periods during which it will be used. Depreciation is the answer. **Depreciation** means that a portion of the cost of that item is allocated as an expense during each of the accounting periods in which it is expected to have useful life. Of course, this involves an estimate of the useful life of the item. According to Lockheed executive Roger Ulvestad, an L-1011 wide-body jet costs United Airlines $37 million and has an expected useful life of 16 years. At the end of that time, it would have a salvage value of about 10 percent or $3.7 million. Using the simplest form of depreciation, *straight line depreciation,* United could assign just over $2 million ($37 million − $3.7 million ÷ 16) as a current expense during each of the 16 accounting periods.

Net income. After subtracting all the expenses from the revenues, you are left with the amount the firm earned during the accounting period—the profits or **net income.** This is the amount available to be reinvested in the business or distributed to the owners. Net income might also be reported as earnings per share (EPS):

$$EPS = \frac{Net\ income}{Number\ of\ common\ shares\ outstanding}$$

EPS is the total net income divided by the number of common shares outstanding. This figure allows for comparisons among firms. You can divide the market price of a share of the firm's stock by its EPS to arrive at the price/earnings ratio—the firm's P/E. This figure is reported on the stock market page of many newspapers. A firm with an EPS of $3 and a current market value of $15 per share would have a P/E of 5 (15/3 = 5). The EPS is information about the firm's past performance. The price is the current market value. A high P/E ratio means that investors are expecting the firm to do even better in the future. In the late 1960s, when electronics firms were on the brink of tremendous growth, some electronic firms had P/Es of over 20.

$$P/E\ ratio = \frac{Current\ market\ price\ of\ one\ share}{EPS}$$

Statement of changes in financial position

The statement of changes in financial position is prepared to show outsiders how the firm is acquiring funds and how it is using its funds (see Figure 6–9).

Cash generated. The firm can acquire funds from four sources: they might be invested by owners, borrowed, generated internally as profit from the operations, or result from selling off assets. A firm could make its current income statement look better by selling some of its assets, but this might damage its future earnings potential. The figures under

FIGURE 6–9
Statement of changes in financial position

DELTA COMPANY
Statement of Changes in Financial Position
For Year Ended December 31, 1979

Sources of working capital:

Current operations:

Net income for 1979*	$12,200	
Add expenses not requiring outlays of working capital in the current period:		
Depreciation of buildings and equipment	4,500	
Working capital provided by operations	$16,700	
Other sources:		
Sale of common stock	12,500	
Total new working capital		$29,200

Uses of working capital:

Purchase of office equipment	$ 500	
Purchase of store equipment	6,000	
Addition to building	15,000	
Reduction of mortgage debt	2,500	
Declaration of dividends	3,100	
Total uses of working capital		27,100
Net Increase in Working Capital		$ 2,100

* Delta Company reported no extraordinary items during 1979.
Source: William W. Pyle, John Arch White, and Kermit D. Larson, *Fundamental Accounting Principles*, 8th ed. (Homewood, Ill.: Richard D. Irwin, 1978), p. 605. © 1978 by Richard D. Irwin, Inc.

Sources of working capital allow the investors and creditors to see how the funds were acquired.

Cash applied. A firm might use its cash to support its current operations, purchase fixed assets such as equipment, invest in securities, pay off debts, or pay dividends to owners. By clearly showing how the firm has used funds, this statement allows outsiders to spot any unusual uses.

Change in cash. The difference between the cash inflows and the cash outflows over the accounting period is the change in cash. An increase in cash does not mean that the firm has made a profit or that the welfare of the owners has improved. It simply means that the firm is in a more liquid position. It has more assets in an easily converted form. This could mean that it has less ability to generate income. The accountants report these changes. The reasoning behind the firm's decisions in acquiring and using funds is considered to be financial management rather than accounting.

Each of the three basic accounting statements contains information that outsiders need to judge the market value of the firm and the quality of its management. The statements must be prepared according to established guidelines, but the information may need further interpretation to provide answers to the outsiders' questions.

INTERPRETING FINANCIAL STATEMENTS

The users of financial statements are interested in the way in which the firm has used its financial resources and in the future earning potential of the firm. They are concerned about the firm's financial stability and its ability to deal with events that affect that stability. Many of these answers are found by computing ratios based on the information contained in the financial statements.

A ratio is simply a comparison of one number with another. The firm's ratios can be compared with average ratios for the industry or with the ratios of other firms. Average industry ratios are computed and published by investment information services such as Standard & Poors and Dun & Bradstreet. The four basic concerns are liquidity, leverage, activity, and profitability.

Liquidity ratios

Liquidity is a measure of the ease with which the firm can meet current financial obligations. **Liquidity ratios** measure how well the managers have balanced earning assets against liquid assets. If all of the firm's assets are tied up in buildings, land, or other fixed assets, it is in a nonliquid condition. But if all of the firm's assets are in cash, it would have no machinery or facilities to earn any income. There must be a balance.

The two commonly used liquidity ratios are the current ratio and the quick ratio. The **current ratio** compares current assets to current liabilities:

$$\text{Current ratio} = \frac{\text{Current assets}}{\text{Current liabilities}}$$

This answers the question: If this firm had to meet all of its current liabilities today, would the current creditors get their money and would the owners be protected? If the firm had to sell out in a hurry, it might have to sell some of its assets for less than a fair market value. Therefore, investors are usually happy to see that the current ratio is greater than one. On the other hand, they don't want it to be too high, since then current assets are not producing income.

The quick ratio is even a tougher test of the firm's ability to meet its current obligations. The **quick ratio,** which is also called the **acid test,** compares the firm's current assets other than inventory to its current liabilities. It is assumed that it would be harder for the firm to sell off its inventory than to sell securities or other cashlike assets.

$$\text{Quick ratio} = \frac{\text{Current assets} - \text{Inventory}}{\text{Current liabilities}}$$

Since the firm will have its inventory as a cushion to protect its investors, the acceptable quick ratio is lower than the acceptable current ratio. Investors would probably be satisfied with a quick ratio of one.

Leverage ratios

Leverage ratios compare the funds supplied by owners with the funds supplied by creditors. The most common leverage ratio is the debt ratio. It compares total debt with total assets:

$$\text{Debt ratio} = \frac{\text{Total debt}}{\text{Total assets}}$$

The **debt ratio** shows the proportion of the firm's assets that have been financed through borrowing. This ratio is very important to creditors. They want to know how well they are protected. If the firm collapses, creditors have the first claim on its assets. But if the owners' share of those assets is small, creditors will be fighting with each other. They would prefer that the owners had enough invested in the firm to cover all of the creditors' claims.

Owners like to see higher leverage when business is booming, and less leverage when business is slow. This is because the creditors' payment is fixed; it is the same whether the firm is profitable or not. If business is good, the firm is using the creditors' funds to earn profits. The extra amount beyond the creditors' fixed payment goes into earnings per share. But if business is bad, the creditors must be paid anyway. Then the owners may get nothing.

Activity ratios

Activity ratios measure how well the firm is using its resources by comparing the funds invested in various assets with the revenue generated by those assets. The two most common activity ratios are inventory turnover and average collection period.

Inventory turnover compares the funds invested in inventory with the sales revenue. A higher turnover means that the firm is making better use of its assets. It can't make any profits if its inventory just sits there. A supermarket chain should show a higher average turnover than a jewelry chain.

$$\text{Inventory turnover} = \frac{\text{Cost of goods sold}}{\text{Average inventory}}$$

Average collection period shows how fast the firm collects the money owed to it. If it is slow, the assets are tied up making interest-free loans to customers rather than producing income.

$$\text{Average collection period} = \frac{\text{Accounts receivable}}{\text{Average daily sales}}$$

If the accounts receivable—the money owed the firm by its customers—were equal to the average daily sales, the firm would have a one-day collection period.

Profitability ratios

A firm can sell a lot and still not make any money—either it isn't making enough on each sale, or it has too much invested in the assets that produce the sales. The profitability ratios that measure whether activities are profitable are the profit margin on sales and return on investment.

The **profit margin on sales** compares the actual sales revenue with the net income. This answers the question: What percentage of each sales dollar is actually profit?

$$\text{Profit margin} = \frac{\text{Net income}}{\text{Sales}}$$

The **return on investment** (ROI) is a measure of the rate at which the money invested in the firm is generating income. This ratio compares the net income with the total assets of the firm:

$$\text{Return on investment} = \frac{\text{Net income}}{\text{Total assets}}$$

You may be asking yourself whether or not you can count on the financial information supplied by firms. What good would it do to compute these ratios if the numbers aren't accurate in the first place? Accountants cannot really assure accuracy, but they can assure that the statements have been prepared according to the accepted guidelines. This is the responsibility of the public accountant.

THE ROLE OF THE PUBLIC ACCOUNTANT

Private accountants maintain the accounting systems for firms. The private accountant is employed by the firm. **Public accountants** are not employees of the firm, but they sell their services to the firm. Most states require that public accountants be certified. **Certified public accountants,** CPAs, have met requirements for education and experience, have passed a test administered by the American Institute of Certified Public Accountants, and have been licensed to practice by the state. A CPA offers management advice, tax services, and audit services. It is the audit services of the CPA that provide the assurance that the financial statements have been prepared properly.

Report of Independent Public Accountants

To the Stockholders and Board of Directors of Bache Group Inc.:

We have examined the consolidated statement of financial condition of Bache Group Inc. (a Delaware corporation) and subsidiaries as of July 31, 1978 and July 31, 1977, and the related consolidated statements of income, stockholders' equity and changes in financial position for the years then ended. Our examination was made in accordance with generally accepted auditing standards, and accordingly included such tests of the accounting records and such other auditing procedures as we considered necessary in the circumstances.

In our opinion, the financial statements referred to above present fairly the financial position of Bache Group Inc. and subsidiaries as of July 31, 1978 and July 31, 1977, and the results of their operations and changes in their financial position for the years then ended, in conformity with generally accepted accounting principles consistently applied during the periods.

New York, N.Y.,
September 21, 1978.

                                                  Arthur Andersen & Co.

FIGURE 6–10
CPA opinion

The audit

The purpose of an **audit** is to lend credibility to the firm's financial statements. The firm opens its books to the CPA, who examines them closely and then issues an opinion on the financial statements, such as the one in Figure 6–10. This opinion indicates whether the statements have been prepared in a manner consistent with accepted accounting principles. Obviously the CPA cannot examine every single transaction, but an audit often involves spot checks to be sure that recorded transactions did occur as stated on the books.

SUMMARY

Accounting provides answers to the financial questions asked by interested persons both within the firm and outside the firm. It provides for the continuing collection, organization, and summarization of information on the financial situation within the firm. Accounting is the primary formal means by which information about a firm is communicated.

The purpose of **financial accounting** is to prepare financial statements for outsiders including shareholders, lenders, financial analysts, suppliers and customers, union officials, government agencies, and even competitors. **Managerial accounting** provides the managers of the firm with the financial information they need to assess the potential financial impact of their decisions. Accounting also allows managers to keep track of the results of business activities.

Important concepts underlying the basic accounting process are the accounting period, the accounting basis, and double-entry accounting. While many firms choose the calendar year as their fiscal or accounting year, some account for their income over the natural business year. Most firms operate on an accrual accounting basis under which revenue is counted as revenue when it is earned and expenses are counted as expenses when the firm makes use of the goods or services. Each transaction results in entries in at least two accounts. The first rule of accounting is that for every debit there must be a credit.

The three basic financial statements are the balance sheet, the income statement, and the statement of changes in financial position. The *balance sheet* is simply a list of the firm's assets and the claims against those assets. The *income statement* shows the firm's net income over the accounting period. The statement of *changes in financial position* shows how the firm is acquiring funds and how it uses its funds.

The users of financial statements compute ratios based on the information in the statements. Liquidity ratios measure how well the managers have balanced earning assets against liquid assets. Leverage ratios compare the funds supplied by owners with the funds supplied by creditors. Activity ratios compare the funds invested in various assets with the revenue generated by those assets. Profitability ratios measure the rate of return achieved.

Private accountants set up and maintain the accounting systems for their firms. A CPA offers management advice, tax services, and audit services. The audit services of the CPA provide the users of financial statements with assurance that they have been properly prepared. The CPA examines the firm's books and then issues an opinion on its financial statements.

REVIEW QUESTIONS

1. What is accounting? What purposes does it serve for managers? For outsiders?

2. Why do different firms use different accounting periods?

3. What is the difference between the cash and accrual accounting bases? Why do most individuals use the cash basis of accounting while most firms use the accrual basis?

4. Set up three T-accounts labeled equipment (asset), cash (asset), and notes payable (liability). Make the entries showing that you have purchased a new machine for $5,000 by making a $1,000 down payment and signing a note payable for $4,000.

5. What is the purpose of the balance sheet? The income statement? The statement of changes in financial position?

6. Go to the library and get a copy of an annual report for a company that interests you. Can you find each of the major headings we have discussed on this firm's financial statements?

7. Look at the stock quotations in your local newspaper. Is the price/earning ratio listed? Explain the purpose of the P/E ratio.

8. Ratios are used to interpret financial statements. Explain the purpose of each of the four different types of ratios?

9. What is the difference between private and public accounting?

10. What purpose do audits serve?

CASES

Case 6–1. What do all those ratios mean?

SPURR MANUFACTURING, INC.
Balance Sheet, February 1, 1980

Assets				*Liabilities*		
Cash	$1,000		Accounts payable	$2,000	
Accounts receivable	3,000		Notes payable	1,000	
Inventory	4,000		Total Current Liabilities		4,000
Total Current Assets		8,000	Long term debt		4,000
Building		10,000	Common stock		8,000
Land		2,000	Retained earnings		4,000
Total Assets		20,000	Total Liabilities		20,000

SPURR MANUFACTURING, INC.
Income Statement for Year Ended January 31, 1980

Sales	$30,000
Cost of goods sold	10,000
Gross profit on sales	20,000
Operating expenses	
Selling expenses	10,000
Administrative expenses	5,000
Net Income	5,000

1. Calculate the following ratios for Spurr Manufacturing, Inc.:
   a. Current ratio
   b. Quick ratio
   c. Debt ratio
   d. Inventory turnover
   e. Average collection period
   f. Profit margin
   g. Return on investment
2. Briefly explain what each of those ratios told you and what you have learned about the financial condition of this firm.

Case 6–2. CSC, Inc., and its depreciation problem

CSC, Inc., is a small firm that sells communications consulting services to other businesses. Recently CSC purchased a Wang word processing system, a very sophisticated electronic minicomputer typing system. The system could have been rented for $525 per month. The purchase price was $12,000. While that is a lot of money considering the price of a typewriter, CSC management was impressed by the fact that the system is supposed to increase typing speed by as much as five times.

The system has an estimated life of ten years. At the end of that time, it will probably have a salvage value of $1,000. The president asked David Christopher to figure out the yearly depreciation expense for the accounting statements.

1. *What is the yearly depreciation using the straight line depreciation method?*
2. *Why is it important to CSC to include that depreciation as an expense during each of the ten years of the system's useful life?*

part
III

WHEN:

The timing of
business decisions

You can have a great idea, but if the time is wrong, it's not so great. The idea of solar energy is not new, but we hope your friends and relatives did not try to start a home solar heating company in the 1960s. The timing was wrong then. When is the right time? How do you know it is right?

There are literally dozens of important business decisions in which at least part of the success depends on timing. When should you introduce a new product? When should you drop a product from the line? When should you expand facilities? When should you borrow money for financing? What should be the timing of production schedules—how much to produce when? When should a machine be replaced? When should you build up inventories? When should you reduce inventories? When should you hire? When should you lay off? This is not an exhaustive list, but these are important decisions in which timing can make the difference.

All of these questions deal with what to do in the future. They ask for plans, either short or long term. But back up a bit. Plan for what? What are the goals? How are they set? Successful businesses plan for the future in order to attain goals. The mere fact of attempting to plan ahead assumes that you look ahead and try to forecast what really will happen. When will demand turn up? When will the seasonal peak occur? For longer range plans, what is happening in society, cultural values, political trends, population trends, and technological developments? Could the anticipated changes usher in new products and services and make old ones obsolete?

Good plans depend on good forecasts. Because of their importance, you need to know how business forecasts and plans to meet goals. Chapters 7 and 8 deal with these two related topics.

FORECASTING:
A LOOK AT THE
FUTURE

By studying this chapter you should be able find answers to these questions:

1 For what kinds of business plans and decisions are forecasts essential?

2 What is exponential smoothing and how does it work?

3 How would you use exponentially smoothed forecasts in business?

4 What is a causal forecasting model? Since time series and causal models are both quantitative in nature, how are they different?

5 What is the Delphi method and how is it used?

6 When are market tests and surveys useful as forecasts?

7 When is it useful to study similar products as a basis for a forecast?

Terms you should know:

causal forecasting models
Delphi method
econometric forecasting models
exponentially weighted moving average
moving average
random variation
regression analysis
technological forecasting
time series forecasting models

Forecasting is a technical subject for statisticians! Right? Yes, that's true, but it does not end there. You should know what kinds of forecasts can be made, how accurate they can be, and something about how they function. That is the minimum in order to understand how business plans and decisions are made. There are also some ways of looking into the future that are not statistical. These nonstatistical techniques provide the basis for some of the most important longer-term business decisions. You should know about them, too.

THE NEED FOR FORECASTING

You can't avoid making forecasts. You do it every time you make a decision, even though it may not be a conscious act. Decisions are meant to have an effect on something in the future. So if you decide to do A rather than B, you are forecasting that A is preferable to B. In many of our daily decisions, the forecasts involved are very straightforward, and we probably do not think of them as being forecasts. "If I fill my gas tank, I can drive to Santa Barbara." That decision involved forecasts of gas mileage and other factors such as the weather. You do not think too hard about the forecasts in such a decision, unless there are no gas stations on the way, for example.

WHAT HAPPENS IF THE PRICE OF OIL JUMPS ANOTHER 54 PERCENT?

Remember the oil embargo and what happened to crude oil prices? In 1973 crude prices were less than $3 per barrel, but in 1974 they jumped to more than $10 and have floated up year by year since 1974. What happened because of the price increase? The price of gasoline went up, of course, but so did the prices of almost everything else. We know that crude oil prices have a substantial effect on inflation in the economy, so we spend a lot of time and attention tracking the attitudes of the oil-producing countries (OPEC) so we will not be caught by surprise.

In early 1979 crude oil prices jumped almost 15 percent again to about $13 per barrel, but government economists were assuming that the price increase would be only 7 percent. Forecasters estimated that the impact of the difference between what was expected and what actually happened was to increase the U.S. inflation rate by more than 0.5 percent and decrease the economic growth rate by 0.3 percent.*

In mid 1979 OPEC increased crude oil prices *again* to about $20 per barrel, a 54 percent increase over the $13 price.

* *Business Week,* January 8, 1979.

The consequences of surprises

When the risks are great, you are likely to think carefully about forecasts. Suppose you were about to introduce a new product. You were going to produce 10,000 of them at a cost $100,000 and mount a nationwide promotional campaign at a cost of $50,000. You would not risk $150,000 without first trying to assess the market for the new product. The consequences of finding out afterward that the market was very small are too great. So you make the best forecast you can and use it as an input to the planning process. The final plan will depend on information about the expected market.

NIXON'S MEMOIRS

The hardcover edition of the Nixon memoirs hit the bookstores with a $20 price tag. The publisher had scheduled a first press run of 200,000. Nixon was paid more than $2 million for the manuscript. A paperback edition was scheduled to follow.* At the end of the first week, a media-based survey indicated that only 250 copies had been sold.

* *Time*, May 8, 1978.

How would you rate the risk in the plans to do the following?

1. Introduce a new product. Cost of initial 10,000 units is $100,000. Cost of nationwide promotional campaign is $50,000.
2. Build new plant to meet developing demand for your products in the Northwest. Investment in building and equipment is $1.5 million.
3. Float a $5 million loan to finance the development of a new product and the facilities to manufacture it. Interest rate will be 8 percent with a ten-year term. The loan agreement requires annual payments of $745,000 for ten years.
4. Accumulate 10,000 units of finished goods inventory from January through June in order to meet the expected summer seasonal sales of air conditioners. Average manufacturing cost is $100 per unit.

Each of the preceding plans assumes a level of demand. If those assumptions are not good ones, the plan is poorly based. You could be burned. Of course, careful forecasts can be in error, too, but the idea is to reduce the element of surprise.

Types and uses of forecasts

There are several ways to classify forecasts. First, how long is the forecast horizon; that is, how far in the future are you attempting to forecast? Forecast horizons are often characterized as short, medium, and long. There are no fixed limits, but a short horizon is usually considered to be from one day to a month, medium from one month to a year, and a long horizon greater than a year. Some forecasting methods are more useful for one time frame than for another.

Quantitative forecasts are based on historical data; they depend on numbers. By analyzing the historical data, you project into the future. There are two types of quantitative forecasts. **Time series forecasting models** simply project historical data foreward after processing it by some statistical analysis. For example, if you had data on the number of cars sold by Ford each month for the past five years, that would be a time series. A time series forecasting model would simply use that data to project future sales. **Causal forecasting models** correlate demand with factors in the economy that cause the demand to increase or decrease. A **model** is a device for representing a complex process or system. There are many kinds of models. Some are mathematical, such as forecasting models that represent the process of generating demand for a business.

Sometimes there are no historical data but you still need a forecast, as with a new product introduction. These kinds of forecasts are called qualitative rather than quantitative because you have no past data to go on. Qualitative forecasts are based on what experts think, on analogy with similar situations in the past, and on market assessments. The fact that they are qualitative does not mean that they are haphazard or "seat of the pants" guesses. Great care may be taken to be sure that they are consistent and carefully thought out.

Some people prefer to think about quantitative models as forecasts because they *cast forward* known historical data, and to think of qualitative models more in terms of predictions. They feel that there is more crystal-ball gazing in qualitative models. We shall use the term *forecasting* for all methods. The following sums up the classifications of forecasts:

Horizon.
  Short, medium, and long.
Quantitative.
  Time series.
  Causal.
Qualitative.
  Expert opinion.
  Analogy with similar past situions.
  Market assessments.

In general, the forecast horizon for time series analysis is relatively short, perhaps a day to a month. You can forecast that far into the future with these methods with acceptable accuracy. These short-range forecasts are useful for conducting operations, controlling inventories, scheduling, pricing, and timing special promotions. The development costs for these kinds of forecasts are low and the development time is short. A minimum of one year of historical data is required. Two years of data are needed if there are seasonal swings in demand.

The causal methods have a horizon in the short to medium range of perhaps a month to a year. They are useful for developing marketing strategies and for planning production and facilities for existing products and services. Their development costs and time are in the medium range, and several years of historical data are normally required.

Finally, the qualitative methods have the longest horizon. They are used to project one to five years in the future. These methods are useful for new products and product development, marketing strategies, pricing, and facility planning. They are relatively expensive to develop and use.

TIME SERIES FORECASTS

The difficulty in making sense of demand or sales data is that the numbers do not hold still for you. They vary—sometimes all over the graph. Perhaps they vary in some ways that allow you to make sense out of them, however. Let's look at three typical situations.

Flat average with random variations

Figure 7–1 shows the five-year record of monthly demand for product A. If you just "eyeball" the chart, you would probably say that it has no particular pattern. It isn't going anywhere—either up or down. On the other hand, monthly demand does vary. It is certainly not the same from month to month. Look at the timing of the highs and lows. It is not always high or low in some particular month or season. It just seems to jump around haphazardly. The haphazard kind of variation in Figure 7–1 is called **random variation.**

What causes random variation? Random, uncontrolled events cause random variation. For example, orders in December 1979 were relatively high because one customer sent in a large order near the end of November and the mail was late. If it had come in November instead of December, the two months would have averaged out to be almost the same. Or, perhaps the weather had an affect on people. You could have had maintenance problems in November and ended up shipping some of November's orders in December. Random variations occur for all sorts of crazy, unpredictable reasons. That's the key to how you approach forecasting in this situation. Don't try to forecast unpredictable events!

Since you cannot forecast the random ups and downs in Figure 7–1,

WARREN H. PHILLIPS
Informing people is a public trust.

Patrick D. Pagnano
for *Business Week*.

"We have long regarded Dow Jones' corporate purpose as more than that of a business enterprise alone. The important role that our publications and other products perform in informing the public, in encouraging debate on public issues, and in education is a service to our society that we regard as a public trust."

Warren Phillips heads a publishing organization that conveys the very essence of the image of business in the minds of many. When you use the name Dow Jones, you think of the Dow Jones average of blue-chip stock prices and Wall Street, the financial center of the United States. *The Wall Street Journal*, published by Dow Jones & Company, is read by businesspeople throughout the country, many of whom use it as a source of forecasting information. Indeed, *The Wall Street Journal* is read by more college business students than any other single publication related to business education. A Louis Harris survey found *The Wall Street Journal* to be the most trusted publication in the country.

But, did you know that Dow Jones also publishes *Barron's*, a string of community newspapers called the Ottaway Group, and college textbooks in business, economics, and the social sciences through the Richard D. Irwin company?

Phillips has led Dow Jones through a period of dramatic growth and change. From a technological point of view *The Wall Street Journal* is now phototypeset at a speed of 80 lines of type per minute in most plants (some newer equipment operates at 350 lines per minute), and images of the paper are transmitted by satellite to several locations. It is then actually printed at 12 sites around the country. By decentralizing the printing, Dow Jones makes it possible for you to read today's *Wall Street Journal* today. A related current problem for Phillips is delivery costs. *The Wall Street Journal* has been delivered by mail in the past, but annual postal delivery costs have risen from $6 million in 1971, to $21 million in 1977, and to over $35 million in 1979. Phillips is coping with that problem by using private delivery when it is more economical to do so. At the beginning of 1980 more than 300,000 *Wall Street Journals* were being delivered by Dow Jones itself or private contractors.

Why would a successful business and financial newspaper acquire a community newspaper publisher, a newsprint paper mill, and a textbook publisher? Just to expand profits? That would be a good reason, but in addition Phillips wanted to isolate Dow Jones from the effects of economic recession and ensure a supply of newsprint. Both the newspapers and the textbook publishing subsidiaries have demonstrated strong resistance to the effects of recessions compared with the national advertising markets that Dow Jones depends on for revenue in its other publications. Also, by acquiring a 40 percent interest in a newsprint mill, Phillips has obtained a hedge against newsprint cost increases and supply problems.

What background enabled Phillips to rise to the top of Dow Jones? First, he has been involved in publishing since he was editor of the campus newspaper at Queens College. During that same time he was a part-time college correspondent for the *New York Herald Tribune* and the *New York Times.* Following college graduation in 1947, he joined *The Wall Street Journal* as a copyreader and wrote a column. in 1949 he left to work at the copy desk of *Stars and Stripes* in Germany while continuing to contribute to the *Journal* as a freelance writer.

In late 1949 Phillips rejoined *The Wall Street Journal* as a correspondent in Germany. He then moved through positions such as chief of the London Bureau, foreign editor in New York, news editor, and managing editor, and was appointed president in 1972. Additional titles were added—chief executive officer in 1975 and chairman of the board in 1978. Early recognition of his talent came in 1958 when Phillips was chosen one of the Ten Most Outstanding Young Men in the Nation by the U.S. Junior Chamber of Commerce.

you are better off to ignore them. If you plan for them, you will simply get into trouble. So average them out and look only at average demand as a basis for forecasting and planning.

Moving averages.   You could compute the average for the entire five-year record for product A. It turns out to be 451 units, with a high of 755 in May 1977 and a low of 161 units in October 1980. But, you want to know whether or not the average is changing. **Moving averages** tell you that. It would be common to use a three-month moving average. Just average the values in the last three months as you move along. With each new month, you add in the new monthly figure and drop the oldest monthly figure, computing a new average.

Weighted monthly averages.   Now you can carry it another step. If you want to know what is happening currently, why not weight the most recent monthly figures more heavily? That is what is done in Figure 7–2. The weighting is by a formula and the result is called **exponentially weighted moving average.**

Notice in Figure 7–2 how the exponentially weighted average curve smooths out the random variations. In fact, the common name for this type of forecasting is **exponential smoothing.**

The forecast.   Figure 7–2 gives the weighted average month by month. Now if you want to forecast for the next month, what figure do you use? The last average that you computed is the best forecast for the next month. It's that simple. The whole idea is to smooth out the random variations to give you a figure to use for planning.

But, you say, "The actual figure for next month might be higher or lower than the average." True, but you have no way of knowing whether it will be higher or lower, or by how much. So you cannot plan for it. But you can plan for average conditions, with contingency plans for a demand that is higher than expected. Perhaps you carry a little extra inventory to provide for the greater demand. In fact, these inventories are called **safety stocks.**

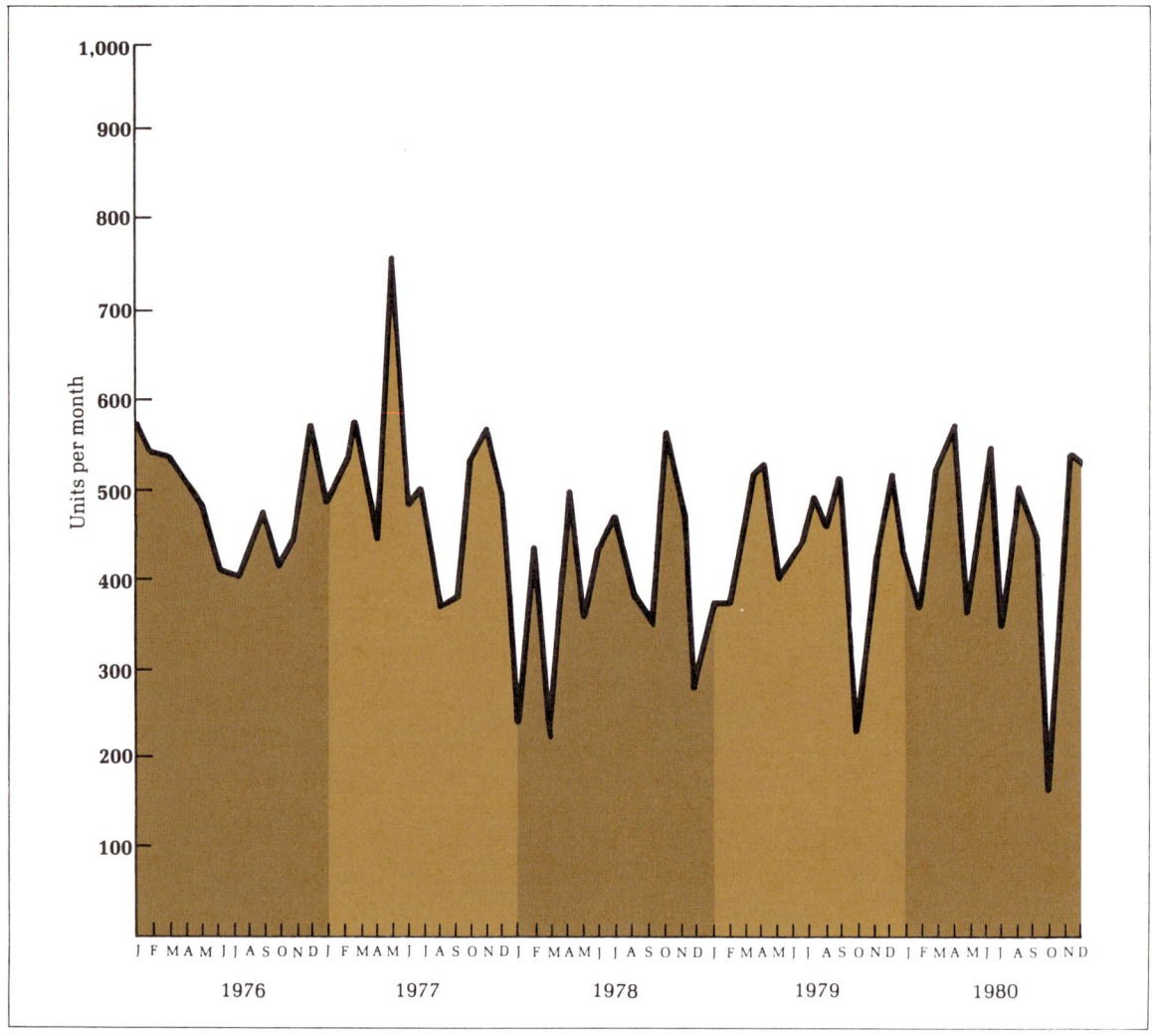

FIGURE 7–1
Monthly demand for product A, random variation

Trend with random variations

Figure 7–3 shows a five-year record of monthly demand for product B. The main difference in the pattern of demand variation between product A and B is that B has an upward trend. You can see that average demand is increasing, even though there are ups and downs. So the random variation is still there as you would expect, but the historical data show that you are making some progress toward higher sales goals with product B.

Now, you say, why not just use the exponential smoothing method to forecast for product A? If average demand is trending upward, won't

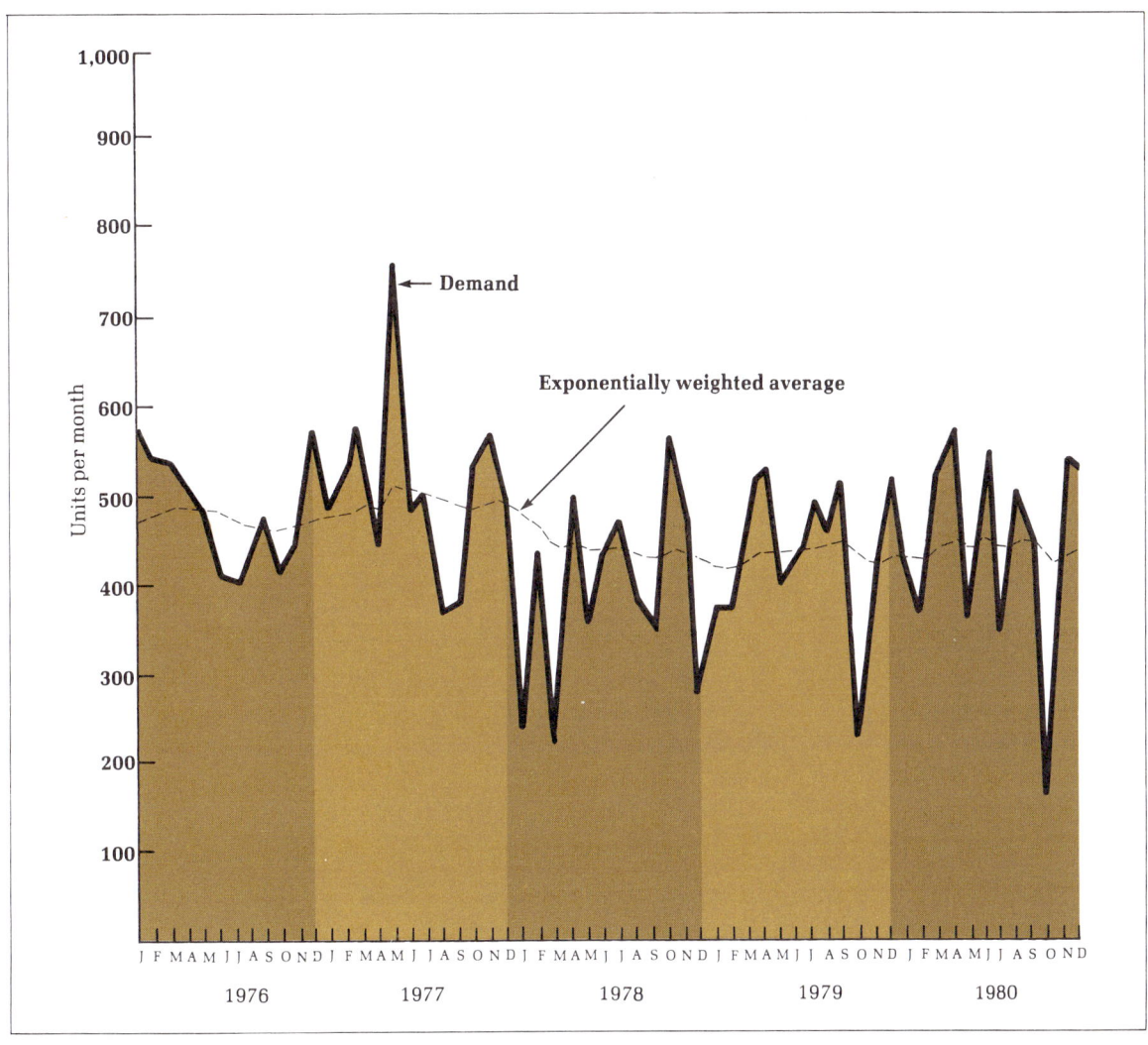

FIGURE 7–2
Monthly demand for
product A with ex-
ponentially weighted
averages shown

the predicted demand follow? Yes, it will, but it will lag behind the
actual change a bit, even though it responds to the increased (or decreased) trend in average demand. It is simple to compensate for the
lag, however. You can use similar statistical techniques, with a minor
variation to compensate.

Seasonal with random variation

The third situation is shown in Figure 7–4. Product C's demand
doesn't seem to be going either up or down. Its five-year average is

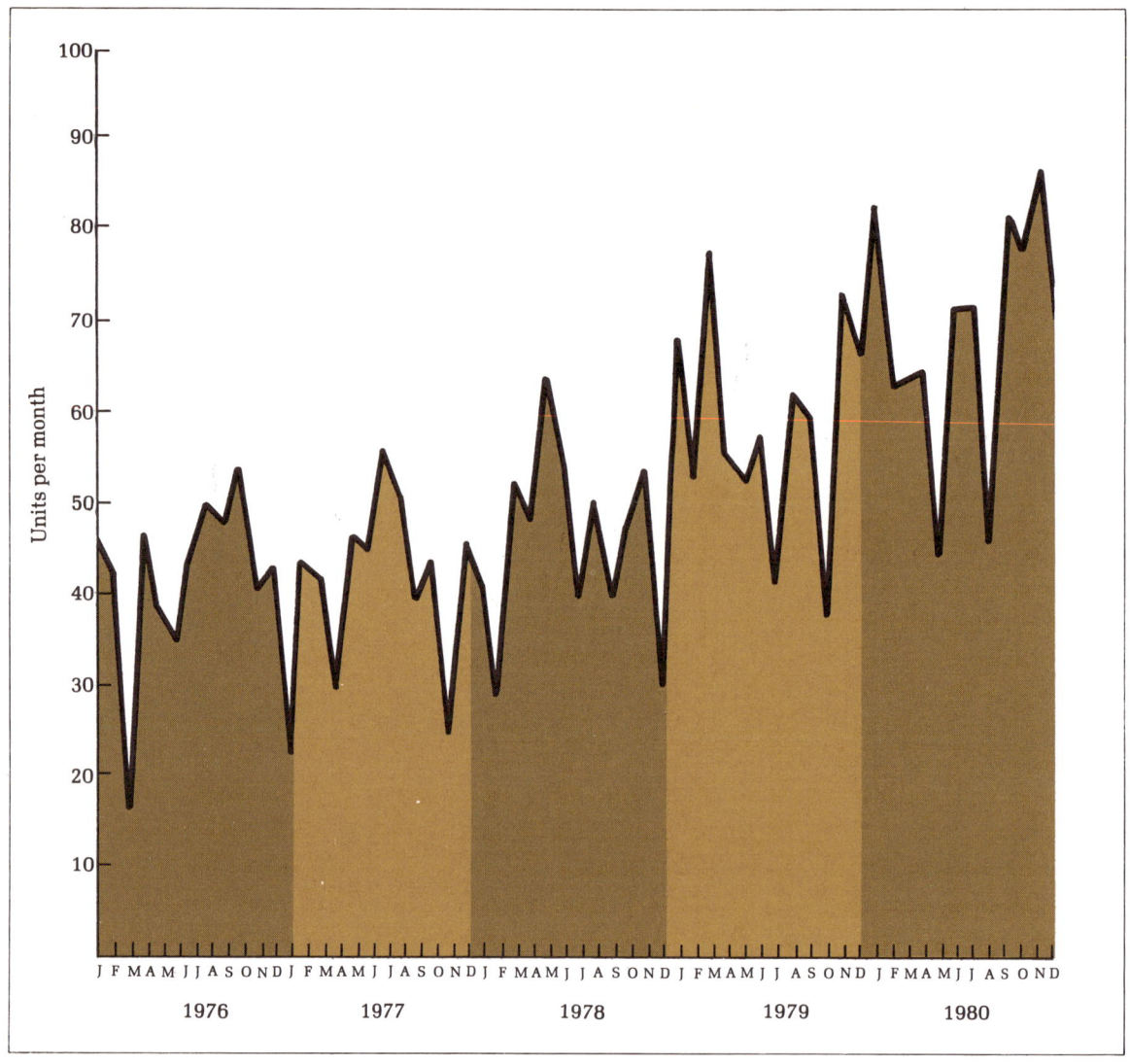

FIGURE 7–3
Monthly demand for
product B

162 units per month, and each year the average demand is close to that figure. The monthly figures jump around, but examine the timing of the peaks and valleys each year. The minimum values occur in the summer and the maximum values in the winter. There is seasonal variation. Of course, there is also some random variation. You can see that demand does not follow a rigid seasonal cycle.

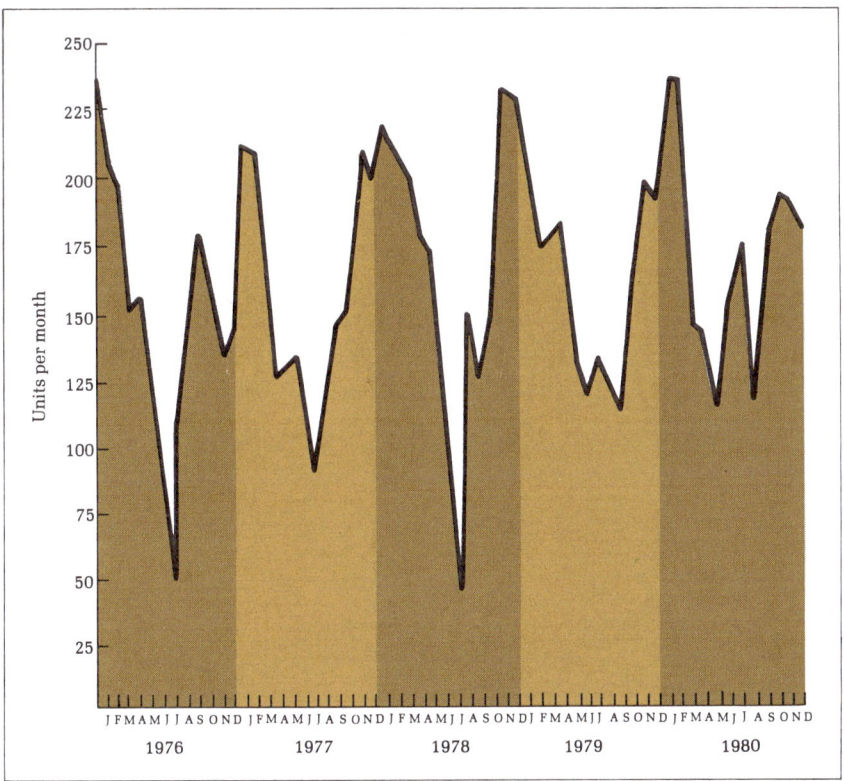

FIGURE 7–4
Monthly demand for
product C

You can forecast seasonal variation, which is what we mean when we say that demand is seasonal. Demand is expected to be high in the winter and low in the summer in this case.

Seasonal adustments. The trick in modifying exponential smoothing to take account of seasonal variations is to set up base seasonal indexes. By analyzing the historical data for your business, you can determine that on the average, January demand is 1.4 times the average, February 1.3, March 1.2, June 0.73, and so on. Then you can still use exponential smoothing, but you must modify the figures by the base series that you develop. It is more complex than the trend calculations, but it also follows a formula.

The forecast. The results of computing a seasonally adjusted exponentially smoothed average for product C are shown in Figure 7–5. The random variations are discounted as before. To forecast, you modify the smoothed average with the appropriate base series. To be sure that the base series is current, you would keep updating the indexes each year as new data come in.

FIGURE 7–5

Monthly demand for product C with seasonally adjusted expected demand computed by exponential smoothing techniques

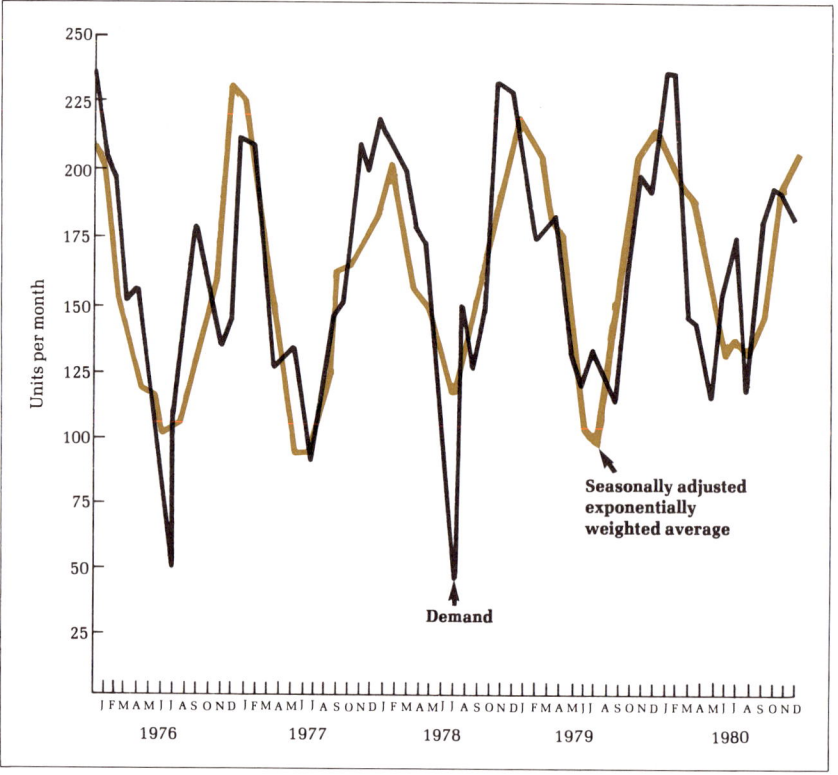

Uses of time series forecasts

You can use time series forecasts for situations where short-range planning is appropriate. A good example is for the timing of special promotions. You may want to time the promotion to boost up low sales in the summer. Also, you can use time series forecasts to plan and schedule operations for next month. How many units should you produce? Do you need to hire more workers? You can use time series forecasts as a basis for inventory control.

Time series forecasts are inexpensive to set up and maintain. You will need at least a year of historical data. If you have a seasonal pattern, you will need at least two years of data, because you need extra experience to estimate the seasonal base series.

Once they are set up, time series forecasts are easy to maintain, especially if computers are available. Some large companies maintain forecasts for 1,000 or more items. All you need to do is supply the most recent demand data to the computing system, and it will keep supplying you with forecasts.

DID YOU EVER WONDER?

How does the telephone company know how to staff the switchboards?
Staffing is quite a problem because of the great variation in the number of calls requiring operator assistance depending on the day of the week, the season of the year, and whether or not it is a holiday. For example, the highest call rate is on Christmas day, and the second highest is on Mother's Day. The lowest number of calls are made on Thanksgiving. But, in addition, the demand is seasonal. Call rates near the end of July are only about 75 percent as high as those during the Christmas peak. Also, the number of calls made on Saturday or Sunday is only about 60 percent of the calls made on weekdays.

With all that variation in demand, the only way to be sure of how many operators the telephone company needs to service callers is to have a good forecasting system. The General Telephone Company installed a statistical forecasting system that predicts the number of calls each day with an average error of only 3.5 percent. Armed with that kind of information, it provides enough operators to be sure that your call will be answered within ten seconds 89 percent of the time.

CAUSAL FORECASTING SYSTEMS

Time series methods make no attempt to explain *why* demand goes up or down. They just process the demand data and grind out a projection of what to expect next. They are simple, inexpensive, and reasonably accurate. Causal methods try to improve accuracy by constructing a theory of *why* demand changes occur. What causes demand to increase or decrease? What factors in the economy control the demand for a product? Does demand go up and down with the gross national product (GNP)? With disposable income? Housing starts? New marriages?

Regression analysis

The most common causal forecasting systems are based on regression analysis. **Regression analysis** is a method for using related information to arrive at forecasts. You find economic indicators that seem to move consistently in either the same or the opposite direction as the demand for your product. This is called **correlation.** For example, the demand for apartments is correlated to interest rates. As interest rates go up, fewer people can afford to buy houses so they rent apartments. You might find several indicators that are related. Then you develop a *regression equation* that relates the demand to these factors. A regres-

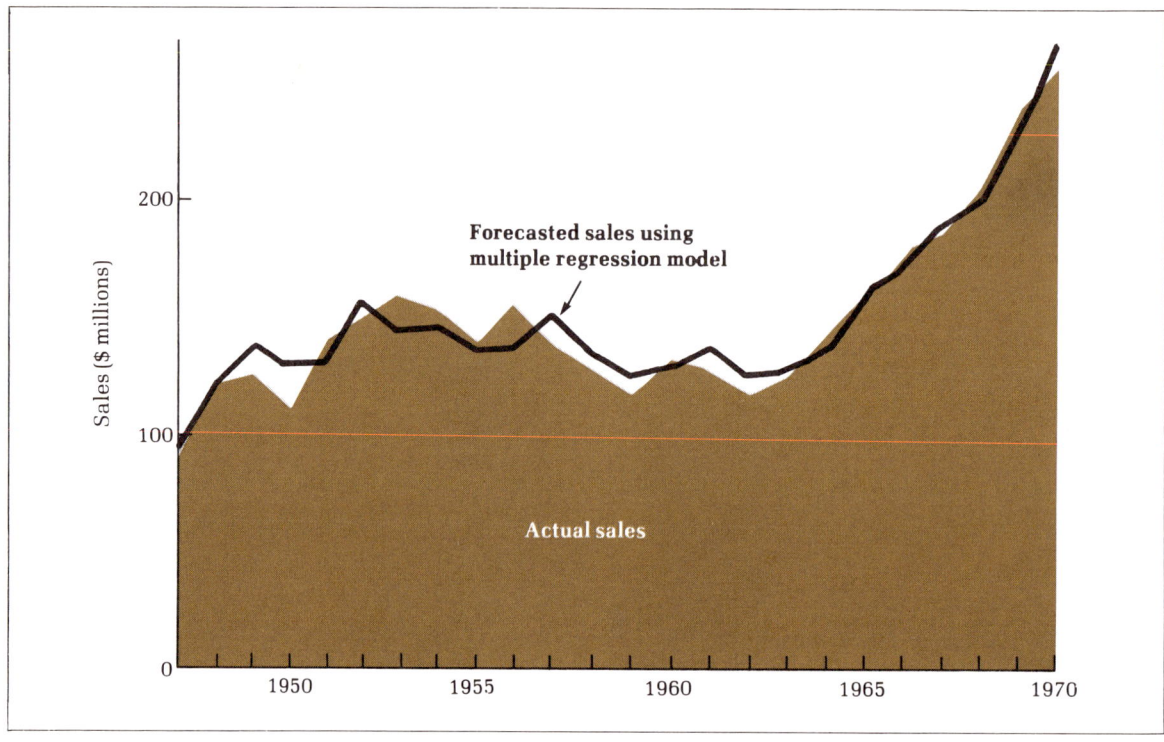

FIGURE 7–6
Forecasted versus actual sales for a furniture company

sion equation represents the line that best fits a series of data points for something like the relationship between demand for refrigerators and housing starts.

To forecast, then, you simply plug in the current values for the indicators and compute expected sales. There may be one or several economic indicators used. When more than one is used, such systems are called **multiple regression.** It sounds simple, and it is simple to use once developed, but it requires a professional statistician to develop such forecasting models.

For example, in a furniture company, sales were found to correlate with last year's sales, new housing starts last year, and amount of disposable income. These factors really makes sense. New housing starts last year are an obvious indication that furniture demand will follow. Disposable income indicates the degree to which people will be able to spend for furniture, as well as for other discretionary items. Last year's sales is an indication of the company's position and past ability to penetrate the market.

The preceding factors deal with the entire furniture market. The regression equation, however, makes the model specific to your business. The completed equation looks like this:

$$S_{\text{this year}} = -33.51 + 0.73\,S_{\text{last year}} + 0.33\,H_{\text{last year}} + 0.672\,I - 11.03\,T$$

where S is your sales, H is housing starts, I is disposable income, and T is the number of years from the beginning of the historical data. You just take the figures for the indicators from government publications, plug in last year's sales and the number of years elapsed, and compute the forecast for this year's sales. Once developed, almost anyone can use the equation to compute the forecast.

Figure 7–6 shows a 24-year record of actual versus forecasted sales for the furniture company, using the preceding multiple regression equation. The average error for the 24 years is 4.98 percent. Not bad!

Econometric forecasting models

You can carry the idea of multiple regression further and develop a whole system of equations called an **econometric forecasting model.** These equations may link the kind of sales equation shown for the furniture company to company costs, selling expenses, and prices. The idea is to reflect in the forecast the impact that increased sales would have on other factors, and vice versa.

If regression forecasting systems are complex, then econometric models are *very* complex. They are not for the average person to dabble with, but you should know about them because they are used. They have been used to forecast automobile industry sales, iron and steel scrap prices, and in other situations where the development cost was

justified. Econometric models have also been used to forecast elements of the economy as a whole. Did you ever wonder where the newcasters come up with their predictions on the economy? They probably got them from economic forecasting services available from universities and consulting organizations.

Causal forecasting models have great value to business planning. After all, if a company is trying to formulate basic strategies for marketing, pricing, and production for next year, a good forecast is really important. These models are complicated and relatively expensive to develop, but, like many things in business, you need *not* be an expert on the technical side in order to use the results.

PLANTING TREES AT WEYERHAEUSER

A large lumber company such as Weyerhaeuser has a continuing important decision—how many trees should it plant to meet demand 20 years from now? It takes that long to grow some types of trees used for lumber, and even longer for others. Guessing might not pay off too well. If the company guesses too low, it will lose market share in the future. If it guesses too high, it will invest a great deal in extra trees that it cannot sell.

In order to plan with such long lead times, the company needs to have a forecasting model that takes account of population growth, family formation, birth rates, and so on. If the lumber companies did not plan, they might lose potential business in the future, or there might be housing and furniture shortages 20 years hence.

QUALITATIVE FORECASTING METHODS

It is an interesting observation that if you want to look long range, you need to use qualitative forecasting methods. Some of the biggest and most important business decisions are based on qualitative forecasts. Examples are decisions to pour funds into a new product development or to support a new product introduction with an expensive nationwide promotion campaign. If a company decides to build a new plant to provide capacity into the 1980s, how does it forecast the need for the new capacity?

These kinds of decisions commit the company's resources and assets for some time in the future. If the strategy is ill-conceived, it may be due to the forecast that was made. If you are right in these longer-range strategies, you may be the company hero. But then, the forecasting system is a hero, too.

Why use qualitative forecasting systems as a basis for these big decisions? Sometimes you cannot use a quantitative forecasting system because either no historical data exist or projecting historical data that far ahead is invalid or very risky. But, there are some cases where a combination of qualitative and quantitative systems have been used effectively.

Executive opinion

By far the most common qualitative forecasting system is executive opinion. Sometimes this is formalized by having key executives submit their best estimates about the future. Then differences are worked out in executive committee meetings to come up with numbers that become official. Sometimes it is informal with the chief executive officer deciding what the planning-based estimates will be. The planning process then goes forward with forecast assumptions.

Technological forecasting

Technological forecasting is a term used for the longest-range predictions. The method involves the pooling of judgment of experts in looking into the future and is often called the **Delphi method.**

Sometimes, the objective of the process is to anticipate products and processes in the dynamic business environment. Sometimes the objective is to estimate market sizes and timing. The panel of experts can be constructed in various ways and often includes both insiders and outsiders.

PREDICTING AIR TRAVEL TO THE YEAR 2000

It takes ten or more years to develop an airplane that involves new technology. These planes may cost $35 million or more in current dollars. How many will be needed? The answer depends on many "iffy" factors. Will supersonic transports be used? Will the present wide-body craft be the main vehicle? Will vertical takeoff and landing planes be practical by that time? Will the costs be such that air travel will expand even more? Will airports need to be expanded and redesigned? Will we need more airports?

Who knows the answers to such questions? No one knows with certainty, but experts in the field of airplane design and production, economists, and political scientists may be able to pool their expertise and provide reasonable predictions on which flexible planning can be based. The Federal Aviation Agency, airplane manufacturers, airline companies, and the general public have a considerable stake in the plans being made.

One of the most extensive technological probes into the future was done by the TRW Company. The project involved the coordination of 15 different panels corresponding to 15 categories of technologies. The study provided the company with a basis for planning future moves into new products and technologies.

The American Hoist & Derrick Company used such methods in combination with other forecasts to look five years ahead. The first two years of actual experience compared with the forecast showed a maximum error of 3 percent.

Market surveys and research

Market surveys and the analysis of consumer behavior are valuable inputs to predicting market demand. The methods involve the use of questionnaires, consumer panels, and tests of new products and services. A company's products and services may be compared with those of competitors and the results summarized. New market segments may be tested with variations of product designs or quality levels. Then comparisons can be made with data on existing products. These kinds of data are often the best available to refine the designs of products and facilities for new ventures.

FIGURE 7–7
Typical S curve of introduction, growth, market saturation, and decline in the life cycle of products and services

Historical analogy

Sometimes you can supplement market research by looking at the performance of another related product. A good example is with color

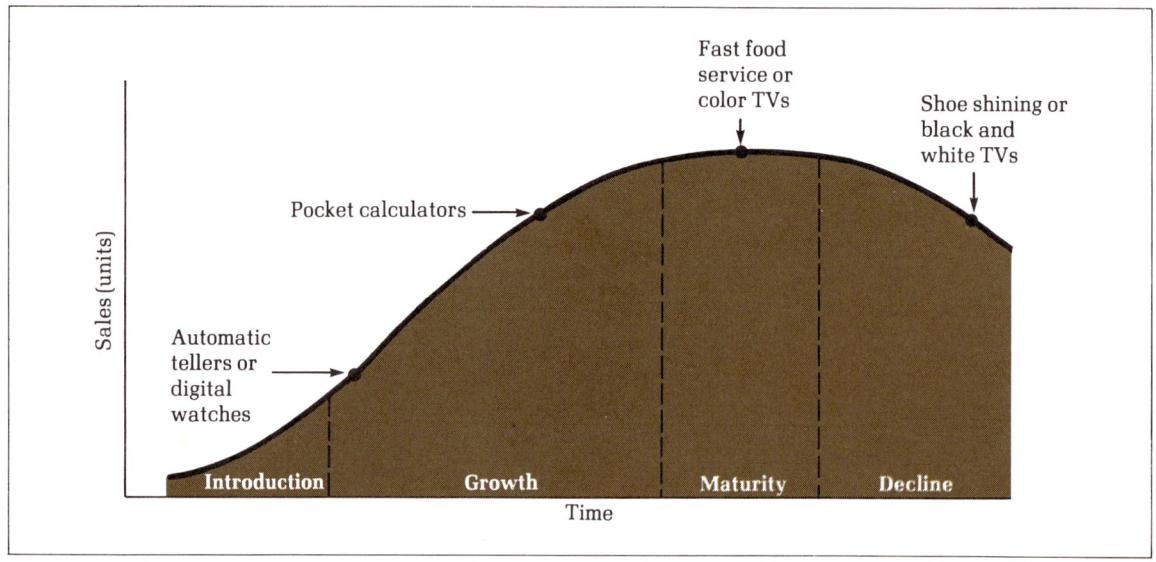

television related to its ancestor, black-and-white television. The assumption was made that the development of color television would follow the black-and-white pattern. This provided a good basis for marketing and production planning.

The related product probably had a life cycle similar to that shown in Figure 7–7, which is a typical introduction–market growth–maturity–decline pattern of sales, with typical products and services shown in each stage.

TABLE 7–1
Summary of forecasting methods

Methods	Applications	Data and information needs	Cost	Development time
Quantitative methods				
Times series				
Moving averages	Short-range forecast, 1 day to 1 month; pricing, timing of special promotions, scheduling, inventory control	Minimum of 1 year of history; 2 years if seasonal	Low	Very short
Exponentially weighted moving averages	Same as above except particularly adapted to computer application with large numbers of items	Same as above	Low	Very short
Causal models				
Regression analysis	Short and medium range of 1 month to 1 year for existing products and services; marketing strategies, production and facility planning	Several years of history, 5 or more, depending on number of variables	Medium	Medium
Econometric models	Same as for regression analysis, plus regional and national models of the economy	Same as for regression analysis	High	Medium
Qualitative methods				
Executive opinion	Medium and long range for marketing, production, and financing strategies	Variable	Low	Low
Delphi	Long-range forecasts for new products and product development, impact of new technologies, market strategies, pricing, and facility planning	Variable	Medium-high	Medium
Market tests and surveys	Long-range forecasts for new products and product development, pricing	Variable	Medium-high	Medium
Historical analogy and life cycle analysis	Same as above	Several years involving nearly complete history for an ancestor product	Medium	Low-medium

SUMMARY

Forecasting provides an essential input for many plans and decisions in business. Forecasts are needed to implement routine planning and control of inventories and raw material buying. When the risks of plans and decisions are high, much of the burden for success falls on the quality of forecasts.

Forecasting methods may be classified as quantitative or qualitative. Table 7–1 summarizes the most common types, their applications, data needs, costs, and development times. Of the time series methods, exponentially weighted moving averages (exponential smoothing) are the most popular because of low cost and short development time. This method is also well adapted to computer application, which is particularly important when large numbers of items need to be forecast.

The causal models are for medium-range forecasting and express a theory of what causes the variation in demand to occur. They require a professional statistician for development and are relatively costly but accurate. Econometric models are sophisticated and costly and at this time are not used often in business.

Qualitative methods are for medium- and long-range forecasting. Executive opinion is the most common. Delphi methods improve on executive opinion but are more costly and time-consuming. Market tests and surveys and product analogies are of great value for forecasting new products, product development, and pricing.

REVIEW QUESTIONS

1. What is the definition of the term *time series forecast?*

2. What is the definition of the term *causal model?*

3. What is random variation? How do you deal with it in times series forecasting?

4. What is a moving average? How do you compute it?

5. What is the difference between a moving average and an exponentially weighted moving average?

6. If average demand is flat and you have computed exponentially weighted moving averages, how do make a forecast?

7. How is the term *exponential smoothing* descriptive of the process that takes place?

8. If demand is essentially flat and you are using exponentially weighted moving averages, what value do you use to forecast the next period?

9. If trend is apparent in the demand data, how do you alter the basic exponential smoothing model to take account of it?

10. If demand data exhibit seasonal variations, how do you modify the basic exponential smoothing system to take seasonal variations into account?

11. What is the general field of application of time series forecasts?

12. Explain the rationale for causal forecasting systems.

13. How are econometric models different from regression models?

14. What is the general field of application of causal forecasting systems?

15. Why shouldn't one of the quantitative forecasting systems be used for long-range forecasting?

16. Explain the rationale for the Delphi method of forecasting. How is it different from forecasting by executive opinion?

17. How are market tests and surveys used for forecasting? What is their field of application?

18. What is the general field of application of qualitative forecasting methods?

CASES

Case 7–1. The Nixon memoirs

Reread the section in this chapter (page 167) about the memoirs of former President Nixon.

1. *What factors do you think might have contributed to the very small initial sales?*

2. *Was the risk taken by the publisher high or low?*

3. *Was the risk taken by former President Nixon high or low?*

4. *What sort of forecast might the publisher have used?*

Case 7–2. Auto STAMPCO—Why do I need a forecast?

Fred Benson is president of Auto STAMPCO, a small producer of stamped metal parts for the automobile industry. The company produces small holding brackets that are used in the assembly process for AMC and Chrysler automobiles.

When asked how he forecasts the volume of business to expect, Fred laughed and said, "Why do I need a forecast? I just produce what they tell me they need. Sometimes it's pretty hectic, because they seem to change their minds, but I scramble and try to make them happy."

1. *Does the fact that Auto STAMPCO produces for only two major customers eliminate the need for a forecast?*

2. *The auto industry has been able to forecast volume reasonably well using an econometric model. Should Fred Benson obtain the results of the industry forecast?*

3. *Should Fred Benson try to obtain the forecasts of AMC and Chrysler?*

4. *If Fred Benson had a forecast, would life at the plant be less hectic? What would a forecast do for him?*

**chapter
8**

PLANNING:
PLOTTING A COURSE

By studying this chapter you should be able to find answers to these questions:

1 Why do businesses spend so much time, effort, and money on planning?
2 What are planning horizons? Are they always the same?
3 How do you go about planning? What is the process?
4 How is a plan expressed to people in the organization?
5 What is a strategy in business planning?
6 What is the role of budgets in planning?
7 How do corporate, functional, and operational planning differ? How are they related?
8 What is the role of the computer in the planning process?

Terms you should know:

budget
computer-based planning
corporate planning
management by objectives (MBO)
plan outputs
planning horizon
self-audit
variable budget

Have you ever agreed to go out with friends to a restaurant and found that no one knew where it was or how to get there? Did you ever face the situation of not being able to complete your academic program because the courses you needed were not offered that term? These are both personal situations in which a little planning might have helped.

For the restaurant, perhaps each thought the other knew or would take the initiative. You need to know where the restaurant is and perhaps estimate how long it will take to get there. The travel time will also depend on the route. Simple plans could make the difference.

For the academic program, it would be helpful to know the planned schedule of course offerings in advance. If the college did not make the schedule available, then it should plan. If the schedule was available but you didn't use it, then you should have planned.

There are dozens of personal situations where you can see the value of planning. The consequences of not planning in some of these situations may be only inconvenience. You may joke about it afterwards. Sometimes, however, the personal consequences can be very bad. Not graduating on time is bad, especially if you have enough total units.

WHY BUSINESSES PLAN

Businesses spend a lot of time and effort in planning. It costs a great deal, so why do they do it? This comes back to the achievement of goals and the consequences of not planning. Think about important decisions. Should a new product be introduced? Should a product line be dropped? Should a new sales office be opened to penetrate the western states market? What are the goals of these actions? If careful plans have not been laid for these kinds of decisions, there may be severe penalties. RCA did not plan to lose $450 million on its attempt to penetrate the computer business. But did it really plan effectively when it went into the market? Did it determine how much capital was required to compete with IBM?

Not all planning that is important to business has the dramatic consequence of the RCA loss. Most planning seems fundamental to the way successful businesses are run. Haphazard operation is antibusiness in our minds. If the church dinner is well run, you may say, "It was run like a business." You probably mean that it was well planned with clear objectives in mind and well executed according to plan.

Business planning occurs in various stages, and these subplans must be coordinated. If the various parts of business seem uncoordinated, jumbled, and haphazard in the way they function, it may reflect a lack of planning. Financial plans must key in with raw material purchasing and payroll dates. Personnel plans must relate to production schedules so that there is neither too much nor too little labor available.

Production schedules must key in with sales, special promotions, and market conditions.

Businesses plan because they wish to achieve certain goals, because of the consequences of not planning, and to provide a framework for coordination among functions and subunits. Without plans there may be some bizarre results.

DID YOU EVER WONDER?

What day of the week and hour of the day are the least popular?

Here is one answer. When the King Tut exhibit tickets went on sale in Los Angeles, they were sold for each day of the week and for entry during each hour of the day in order to even out the number of viewers at any one time. People lined up for blocks, and some stayed up all night in line in order to be sure of getting their choices.

The last tickets sold were for 11:00 a.m. on a Tuesday!

PLANNING HORIZONS—HOW FAR AHEAD TO LOOK

How far into the future should a business plan? The **planning horizon** depends on the purpose. Long-range plans are fundamental to basic goals and objectives. These plans can be used in determining the nature of products, markets, locations, capacities, and so forth. Plans that extend beyond a year are generally called long-range plans. They provide the framework for shorter-range plans.

The medium range is usually considered one month to one year. There may be seasonal variations in product sales. What are the sales goals? Plans are needed to achieve them. Plans need to be made for production in relation to demand, particularly if it is seasonal. Should labor be hired for the seasonal peak, or should inventories be accumulated during the lull to be sold during the peak season? What are the risks of either type of plan? If you are canning tomatoes, you have no choice—you can them when they are ripe. But there is a choice for many businesses. The personnel, materials, and financial plans must be coordinated with the production plan. The medium-term plans need to be developed within the framework of the long-range goals and plans.

Short-range plans are made to implement goals that come from medium-range plans. These plans involve day-to-day operations in the one-day to one-month range. Examples are schedules for labor, machines, and material flow. How much planning can be done in the short range? Isn't this just the implementation of the medium-range plans? Yes, but plans can be implemented well or badly. Waiting until

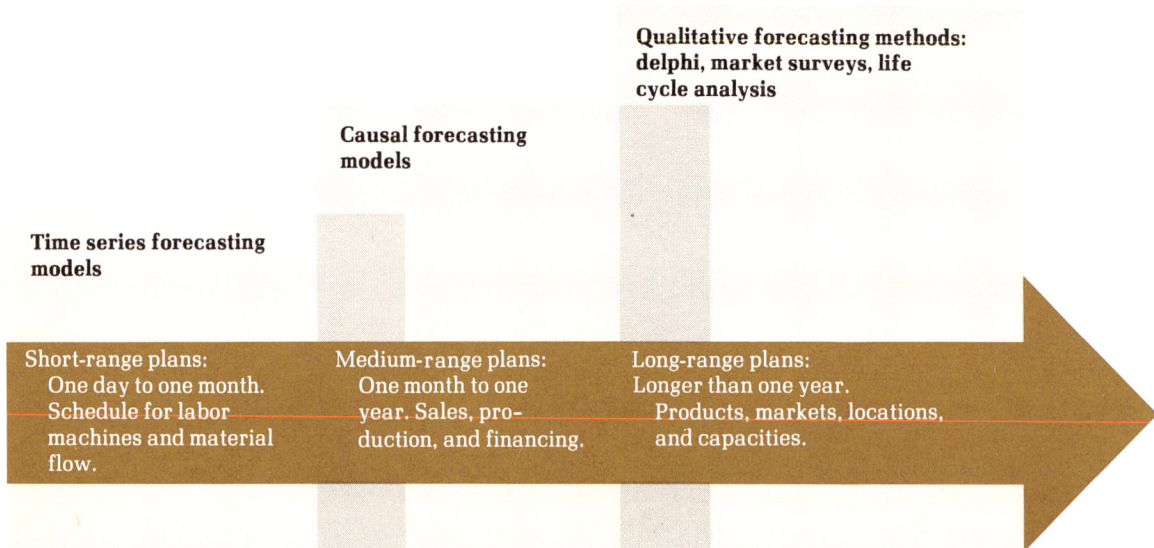

Qualitative forecasting methods: delphi, market surveys, life cycle analysis

Causal forecasting models

Time series forecasting models

Short-range plans:
   One day to one month. Schedule for labor machines and material flow.

Medium-range plans:
   One month to one year. Sales, production, and financing.

Long-range plans:
   Longer than one year. Products, markets, locations, and capacities.

FIGURE 8–1
Planning horizons in relation to available forecasting techniques

the last minute does not permit planning. If there is no lead time between planning and execution, obviously you cannot plan. That's part of the difficulty with short-range plans. Things begin to happen rapidly and if a plan was not made, you're "in the soup."

Now isn't it convenient that there are forecasting techniques that parallel planning horizon needs? Recall the time series, causal, and qualitative forecasting techniques from Chapter 7 on forecasting. Figure 8–1 relates the forecasting techniques and the planning horizons.

THE PLANNING PROCESS

While there is no formula for planning, businesspeople have done so much of it that they have thought a lot about how to do it. There are some logical steps to planning. The following process helps ensure that each step has been given enough attention.

Self-audit

Planning really starts with an examination of where a business is now. An assessment of the current status of the business is needed to know where it should be at a future time. It is necessary to be objective at this point. The slogan "Know thyself" is a good guide. A **self-audit** should determine the current status of the following factors:

1.   Financial position.
2.   Condition of facilities and equipment.
3.   Quantity and quality of personnel.

4. Appropriateness of organizational structure.
5. Major policies and strategies.
6. Competitive position.
7. Profitability of product lines.

Survey environment

What factors outside the company affect it? These factors are not under the company's control. There may be trends that it can better adapt to if it knows they are going to happen. Better yet, there may be opportunities developing. Some of the factors in the environment that might be surveyed are:

1. Population growth and movement.
2. Economic conditions.
3. Government regulations (taxes, wage and price controls, safety, pollution control, equal opportunity, and so forth).
4. Labor supply.
5. Competitors.
6. Suppliers.
7. Wall Street conditions.
8. Social values.

Objectives or goals

One value in scanning the environment is to uncover opportunities. If you consider the market, your competition, what customers want,

and your strengths and weaknesses, you are in a position to set realistic goals. Where do you want to be at a future time? What do you want to accomplish and when? These statements are the long-range goals to keep in sight when developing plans. However, there may be a difference between desire and realistic objectives. You must consider whether or not the objectives are compatible with the environmental factors and organization objectives. If they are not, the objectives need to be reworked.

The objectives selected may be of various types. They might involve increased market shares, penetration of new geographic areas or product lines, profitability goals, development of new technologies, or cost reduction programs. Forecasts are a major input to the process of setting objectives. Objectives must be realistic in terms of the future.

Resource requirements and budgets

Forecasts and objectives must be converted into actual resource requirements: labor, material, space, equipment, and other factors. Budgets are keyed in with these resource requirements. Budgets are an important expression of business plans. They state expected costs, workloads, output, and more. A budget is something that people understand. It tells them exactly what is expected of them in terms of sales, costs, and the allowed resources. The budget is the basis for controlling the plan once it is developed.

An important extension of the entire process is to develop projected financial statements that will result. What impacts would you expect the plan to have on the balance sheet, the income statement, and the statement of changes in financial position?

Plan outputs

When the plan is financially sound, it must be communicated to people in the company who are to implement it. The plan outputs may be in several possible forms: statements of objectives, policies, rules and procedures, and budgets. These outputs will be discussed in more detail in the next major section of this chapter.

Control of the plan

Plans are not made just to be filed away. They should be reviewed periodically to determine progress. If major deviations have occurred, the company must ask why. Were the forecasts correct? Have environmental factors shifted? Were the objectives realistic? Plans will need to be reviewed and updated.

Figure 8–2 is a flowchart that summarizes the planning process just discussed. Note that it provides two opportunities to rework objectives.

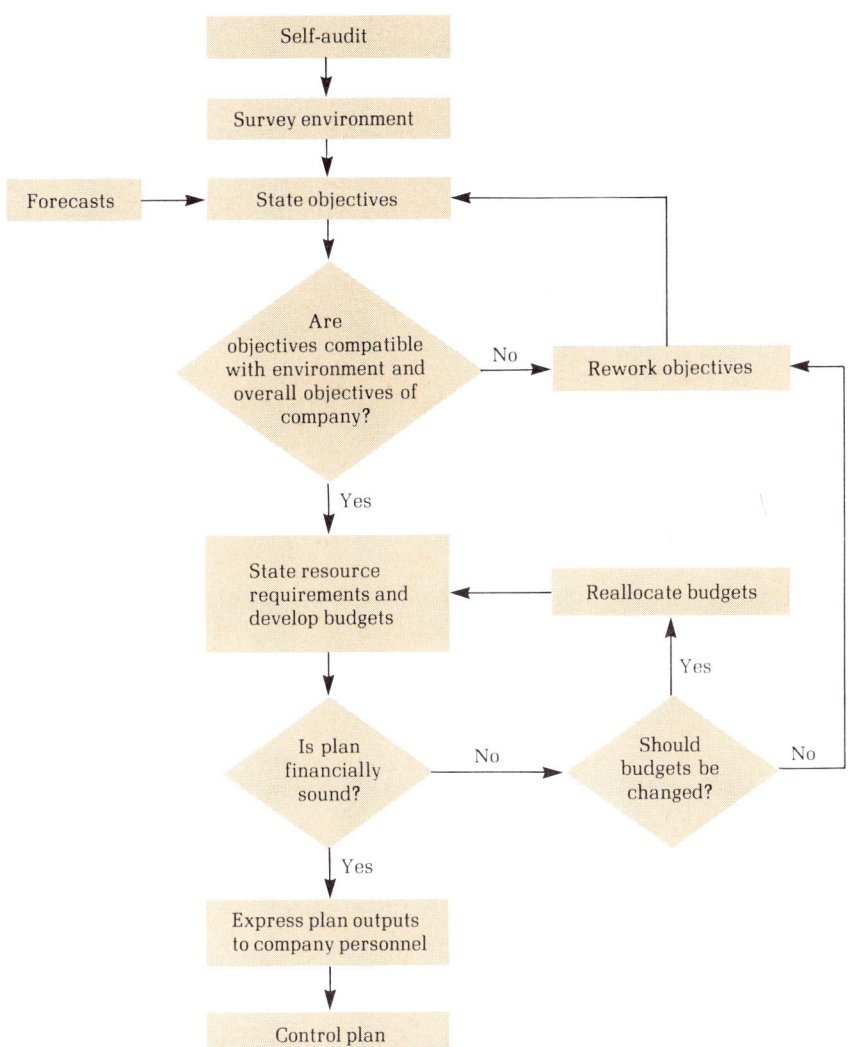

FIGURE 8–2
Flowchart of the planning
process

Adapted from: L. W. Rue and L. L. Byars, *Management: Theory and Application* (Homewood, Ill.: Richard D. Irwin, 1977). © 1977 by Richard D. Irwin, Inc.

If objectives are not compatible with the environment and with the overall goals of the organization, objectives are reworked. Also, if the plan is financially unsound and simple budget changes will not do the trick, then objectives are reworked. It is simpler, however, if the plan can be made financially sound through budget reallocations.

OUTPUTS OF THE PLANNING PROCESS

Now that you have been through the planning process, what do you have? Where is the plan and how is it expressed? There is no point in just filing it away. People must make it work. They must know what the plan is and understand it.

Statements of objectives

People need to understand where the company is expected to go; otherwise they might unknowingly be pulling in opposite directions. When President Kennedy announced the national goal of putting a person on the moon, he galvanized action to that end. People in government and business were motivated to help achieve the goal.

The plan for putting a person on the moon could have existed without the announcement, but it would have been less effective. Without the announcement, people might have wondered why large contracts were being placed by NASA. There might even have been inaccurate rumors as to what the government was up to.

Strategies and policies

Strategies are the general ways in which a company intends to achieve objectives. For example, a new strategy for Volkswagen in penetrating the U.S. auto market is to establish manufacturing plants here. In late 1979 there was even a rumor that VW wanted to buy Chrysler. The strategy carries with it the commitment of resources to achieve the objective. The action by Volkswagen of installing a U.S. plant is a concrete expression of the new strategy.

Strategies may carry with them new or changed policies. **Policies** are plans that are meant to guide people in the company. They eliminate some of the possible actions and point decisions toward the objectives of a plan. But policies should not be so restrictive that there is no room for creative action. A policy of buying only from the cheapest qualified bidder leaves a purchasing agent with an empty job and may even produce bad results.

Strategies and policies are some of the most important results of planning. They provide more specific direction than the statements of objectives, and they are the first step toward implementing the plan.

Procedures and rules

Procedures are more specific and restrictive than policies, but they reflect a planned approach. They leave little room for discretion. For example, there are procedures for hiring and layoff, purchasing, granting wage and salary increases, and so on. The term *procedures* smacks of bureaucracy, but when used appropriately, procedures reflect the best way of doing things and give consistent results. The consistency also helps to provide control. If the procedure was followed, but perhaps costs are still out of line, something must be wrong. A company without procedures probably operates in a haphazard, unplanned way.

Rules are even more restrictive than procedures. They specify exactly what to do, and often what not to do. Some of the best examples are safety rules, such as the designation of certain departments as "hard hat" areas. Plant safety may be part of an objective to enhance local image and improve labor relations. The problem with rules is that they leave no room for creative action. If there are rules for everything, then no one needs to think. And if no one thinks, then it is hard to see how goals can be achieved.

Budgets

Budgets specify sales and spending targets, or sometimes spending limits. Budgeting is often thought of as planning. It can be, if it involves the entire planning process discussed previously. Usually budgets are one of the important results of planning. Budgets make the plan specific by expressing it numerically. You know what the plan means since you have a budget for so many dollars, worker-hours, sales units, and other factors.

One important value of budgets is that they indicate expected performance. Since they are numerical, you can measure what actually occurs and compare. The difficulty with budgets is that they can put people in planned straitjackets rather than encourage creativity. Budgets are too often associated with control and budget slashes. Budget slashes may not involve carefully considered objectives that fit in with a broader plan.

Spending budgets are often constructed to key in with the volume of activity. If output geared to sales is 1,000 units per month, then perhaps the cost budget is $3,000 per month. But if activity increases to 1,200 units per month, the cost budget is automatically expanded to $3,600 per month. The sales revenue, detailed cost items, and planned profit could all vary in this way without requiring additional budget approval. These **variable budgets** provide flexibility and help plans to be achieved with a minimum effort spent in administrative wrangling.

The outputs of the planning process are statements of objectives, strategies and policies, procedures and rules, and budgets. They all express the plan but have different functions in doing so.

Communicating the plan to people in the company in these ways is important in getting their cooperation. But if people hear of the plan for the first time through the statement of a policy or the receipt of a budget, an opportunity has been missed. The entire planning process provides a framework for the people to become involved. They can be involved not only to hear an early warning of what the plan will be but also to contribute their expertise, knowledge, and creativity.

PLANNING IN ACTION

To this point we have been discussing the planning process and the outputs of planning. These topics are general and apply to all kinds of planning. Now let us turn our attention to ways of getting everyone involved in the planning process and making plans work in organizations. Then we shall see how planning occurs at various levels within an organization, and how these plans tie together. We shall also look at how computers are being used to help in the planning process.

Management by objectives (MBO)

Through **management by objectives,** all employees participate in setting objectives consistent with the overall objectives set at the top. This contributes to a feeling of shared purpose and to an understanding of a basis for evaluation. The success of MBO depends on sincere commitment and a thorough understanding of the technique.

A group of management consultants who make a business of solving the management problems of both large and small companies start off their investigation with this simple exercise. First they meet with the top managers and ask them to make a list of the objectives of the firm. Then they meet with the middle managers and make the same request. Then they exchange the lists. They claim that both the top managers and the middle managers are frequently surprised to learn what the other group has been expecting. While they may not have been working against each other, they have often been working toward different goals.

**Progress is when everyone
pushes in the same direction.**

**Lend a hand!
Do more than your share.**

Progress is when we all push in the same direction

Management by objectives (MBO) is a system that is supposed to help all of the people in an organization work toward the same goals. Each person is supposed to understand the goals, accept the goals, and direct his or her efforts toward achieving those goals.

How does MBO work?   MBO is really very simple. Have you ever watched one of the charity telethons? When Jerry Lewis or one of the local hosts gets up there and pleads, "Come on, we've just got to raise that $XXX million," it's amazing how some of the hardest hearts in the city dig into their pockets. Jerry sets the overall objective and tries to get the audience involved in it. Then, as the results roll in, they are displayed so that everyone can see how they are doing compared with the objective. Under MBO, each person in the organization is supposed to focus on definite and measurable results.

First, the overall objectives of the organization are set up by top management. Then all of the managers down the line have a voice in setting the objectives for their units. In this way, all the managers are supposed to understand the relationships between their objectives and the overall objectives of the firm. If each manager sets the objectives to be achieved within that unit, each manager must believe that those objectives are proper and attainable.

For these objectives to be meaningful, they must be operational. It's one thing to set an objective such as improving performance. That is an interesting objective, but it lacks operational meaning. An **operational objective** includes three elements: (1) it is measurable; (2) it is attainable; and (3) it includes some indication of when it is to be achieved. It might be phrased: Unit A will increase its output of product X by 200 units during the next calendar year. This objective clearly indicates what is to be measured and when. We can only assume that it is within the capacity of unit A.

MBO stresses coordination of objectives among the units of the firm. It emphasizes the measurement of performance against standards established by the individual units with the approval of top management. Is it as great as it sounds?

The benefits and drawbacks of MBO.   The basic benefit of MBO is that it focuses everyone's effort on commonly accepted goals. This improves the chances that these goals will be achieved. It contributes to the clarity of evaluation of employee performance. In general, it is expected to improve employee performance and to increase job satisfaction. But it is not without costs, and it does not always succeed.

One of the problems associated with MBO is that it takes the manager away from the task at hand in order to handle the MBO system. It involves additional meetings and paperwork. Unless top management is sincerely committed to the process, it can become an exercise in puffery. Each layer of the organization can attempt to impress the next layer with its intentions. At the end of the year, everyone may be

AN MBO SUCCESS STORY

If you take a look at the safe in a bank, you are likely to see the Diebold trademark. This firm has been making safes in Canton, Ohio, for over 100 years. Diebold's has recently initiated an MBO program in its installations and technical services division.

The process began with a series of seminars to explain MBO. These included discussions of a number of management theories, transactional analysis, and personal effectiveness, as well as goal-setting techniques. Diebold's management estimated that it would take from three to five years to fully implement the system.

According to Roger E. Calhoun, manager of the division, "Since the introduction of MBO to our division, performance on all levels has measurably improved. Management is now using the input of the productive workforce in establishing objectives, and the field managers report that the participative approach to management has assisted them in dealing with their responsibilities."

disappointed. Unless everyone understands the purpose and requirements of MBO or any other management system, there is little hope for success.

Levels of planning

Business planning takes place at several levels in the organization.

Corporate levels.   The term used for planning at the top is **corporate planning.** As you would expect, corporate planning takes place at the highest level involving basic company objectives as indicated in Figure 8–3. These objectives set the basic targets concerning markets, market shares, locations, capacities, and profitability.

Corporate planning produces plans in the form of stated company objectives, strategies for achieving objectives, policies, and broadly based budgets for the main divisions, departments, and subsidiaries. The structure depends on company size and how it is organized. Plans at this level are long range, usually looking one to five years ahead.

Such plans often involve expansion, new products and whole new product lines, and programs to penetrate new markets. Therefore, larger-scale financing is often required in the form of new stock and bond issues or longer-term bank loans. Of course, the projections in the plan are that the new ventures will produce revenues that more than cover the expansion and financing costs. Thus, an acceptable plan is one in which profitability is projected.

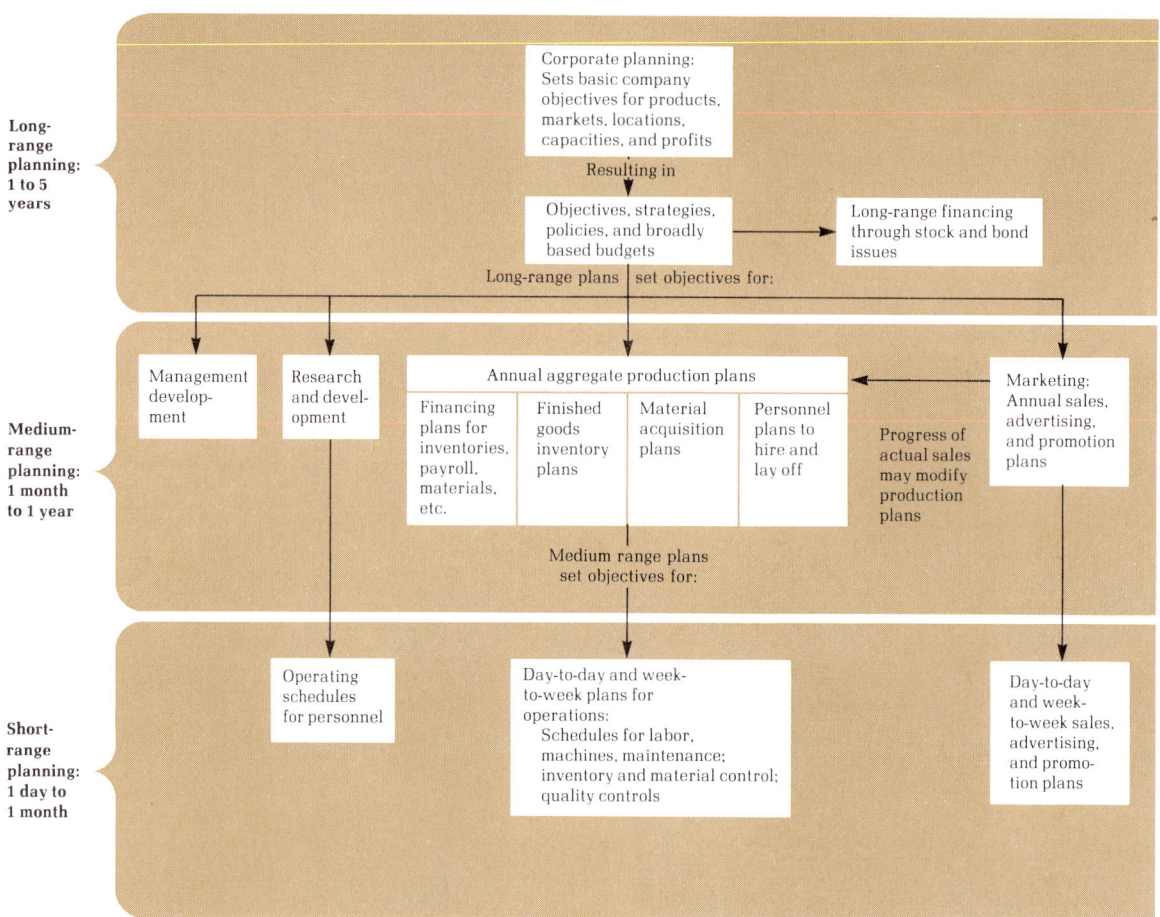

FIGURE 8–3
Long-, medium-, and short-range planning

Functional levels.   Corporate plans set the basic objectives for planning at functional levels. Functional levels deal with the basic functions of marketing, production, finance, personnel, purchasing, and research and development (R&D). The corporate plans are communicated through statements of objectives, new and revised policies, and budgets. The functional planners must develop plans that fit in with these objectives, policies, and budgets.

The sales objectives are of key importance. Their achievement will affect everything else. The aggregate production plans are based on the corporate plans in the general sense, but they are always tempered by the progress of actual sales, as shown in Figure 8–3. **Aggregate production plans** mean broadly based production plans that deal with general measures of output rather than detailed schedules. Figure 8–3 shows functional plans of aggregate production, inventories, material acquisition, personnel, and finance all tied together. This is because they are all closely related to the production activity level and must be coordinated.

Research and development (R&D) objectives are set by corporate plans. Where is the R&D effort to be placed? What new products should be developed? What product improvements are called for by market conditions? R&D must allocate its resources within the allocated budgets. This may mean new and different kinds of scientific personnel or changes in the balance of personnel.

Finally, long-range plans may call for more and better management personnel. Expansion programs mean personnel as well as facilities. **Management development** is a general term that recognizes the need to develop new personnel and to revitalize existing personnel. It may involve various educational programs, both internal and external to the company. The scarce resource in meeting corporate objectives is often personnel, especially when expansion is involved. If objectives require a change of direction, there may be enough personnel in total but with the wrong backgrounds. Management development then performs a retreading function. Functional planning is medium-range planning, in the one month to one year horizon.

Operational levels.   Finally, medium-range plans at the operational level set objectives for day-to-day and week-to-week operations. They work within the limits of objectives and budgets set by the functional level plans. Much of the operational planning is in the production function. In order to meet sales requirements and still meet cost standards, labor, machinery, and maintenance must be scheduled. Finished goods inventories and raw material levels must be carefully controlled, and plans must be made to control the intended quality levels. Other functions such as sales and R&D may also have short-range planning needs.

The general planning process discussed earlier applies to the various levels of planning shown in Figure 8–3. Note, however, that objectives are set mainly at the corporate level. Objectives at lower planning levels are fixed by the higher planning decisions. Note also that the planning horizons of long, medium, and short correspond to planning levels of corporate, functional, and operational.

Computer-based planning

Much of the planning process involves an examination of alternate proposals. But, to really evaluate the proposals means hours and hours of tedious computation. You must evaluate the effects of all the revenues and costs. It may turn out that one idea is profitable, but another is more profitable and you cannot do both. Or adjustments in a proposal may make a big difference in projected profitability.

Here is where computers come in. With a computer model of company revenues and costs, you can evaluate all kinds of proposals in a very short time. If you find one that looks really good, you can fine-tune it. So **computer-based planning** not only speeds up the process, but it also allows you to evaluate the impact of more ideas on the company's revenues, costs, and profits.

   An example.   Here's how it works. First, a computer model of the operation is built. Suppose it is the plywood manufacturing operation shown in Figure 8–4. We see that the material inputs are company-owned logs together with purchased logs as required. These materials are processed through the veneer manufacturing phase, which involves peeling—cutting a thin sheet of veneer from the surface. The veneer is then dried to a specified moisture content. By-products of the peel-dry process are lumber cores and chips, which can be sold. Plywood is then glued and pressed with veneer produced in the previous operation or with purchased veneer.

FIGURE 8–4
Flow of plywood manu-facturing operations

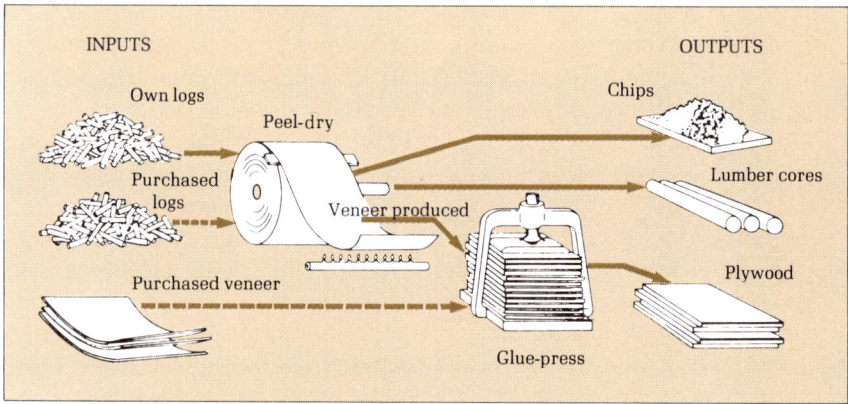

Source: Reprinted by permission of the *Harvard Business Review.* "Corporate Models: On-Line Real-Time Systems," by James B. Boulden and Elwood S. Buffa (July–August 1970). Copyright © by the President and Fellows of Harvard College; all rights reserved.

   The computer model for the plywood operation represents all of the revenues and costs in equation form. The equations are simple. Revenue comes from three sources: sales of plywood, chips, and lumber cores. Revenue for plywood is simply the quantity sold times the price per unit. Cost relationships are just as simple. Raw material costs are the products of the quantity used times the price. You represent the cost relationships that exist, whatever they are.

   The trick is to take advantage of the computer's capability to work with any set of quantities and prices you give it. So, you can work with different assumptions on quantities and prices in planning just by inserting new numbers. The model remains the same, representing the company's revenue and cost relationships. You try alternatives by representing what would happen to revenues, costs, and profits *if*

LINE ITEMS	QR1	QR2	QR3	QR4	YRT
SALES PLY	35800.0	37950.0	31200.0	33600.0	138550.0
SALES CHIPS	1350.0	1953.0	1827.0	1921.5	7051.5
SALES LUMBER	843.8	1260.0	1181.3	1260.0	4545.0
SALES ELIM					
TOTAL SALES	37993.8	41163.0	34208.3	36781.5	150146.5
D&A PLYWOOD	716.0	759.0	624.0	672.0	2771.0
COM PLY	2148.0	2277.0	1872.0	2016.0	8313.0
FREIGHT PLY	242.2	267.7	306.0	306.0	1122.0
TOT COM	3106.2	3303.7	2802.0	2994.0	12206.0
NET SALES	34887.5	37859.3	31406.3	33787.5	137940.5
RAW MATERIAL	4824.2	6831.2	6914.9	6999.7	25570.0
VENEER PURCH	8375.2	5694.1	9034.8	9252.4	32356.5
OP SUPPLIES	2860.8	3504.4	3844.5	3891.6	14101.2
LABOR	6544.8	8840.6	9181.2	9293.8	33860.4
COST ELIMIN					
COST OF SALE	22605.0	24870.2	28975.4	29437.6	105888.1
GROSS PROFIT	12282.5	12989.0	2430.9	4349.9	32052.4
FIXED COSTS	1250.0	1250.0	1250.0	1250.0	5000.0
SELLING EXP	750.0	750.0	750.0	750.0	3000.0
G&A EXPENSE	750.0	750.0	750.0	750.0	3000.0
OTHER EXPENSE	125.0	125.0	125.0	125.0	500.0
TOT IND EXP	2875.0	2875.0	2875.0	2875.0	11500.0
NET PROFIT	9407.5	10114.0	-444.1	1474.9	20552.4

FIGURE 8–5
Example of a income statement for the plywood example

the proposal were used. In planning parlance, these alternatives are called "what if" questions; that is, what would happen if . . . ?

In the plywood example, Figure 8–5 shows the income statement based on such a model by quarters, and the year-to-date totals. Quarters 1 and 2 represent actual experience in this case, and quarters 3 and

FIGURE 8–6
Sensitivity of net profit to wage rate for the plywood example

```
WAGE  R. = 5.000

        LINE ITEMS              YRT
        NET PROFIT            20552.4


WAGE  R. = 5.250

        LINE ITEMS              YRT
        NET PROFIT            18859.3


WAGE  R. = 5.500

        LINE ITEMS              YRT
        NET PROFIT            17166.3


WAGE  R. = 5.750

        LINE ITEMS              YRT
        NET PROFIT            15473.3


WAGE  R. = 6.000

        LINE ITEMS              YRT
        NET PROFIT            13781.0
```

4 represent projections based on forecasts. You can call for reports by months, quarters, or years and project as far ahead as you wish. You can call for other kinds of reports such as a balance sheet or a cash flow analysis.

Now, the great advantage of the computer model is that you don't have to refigure everything just because you get curious. For example, suppose the average wage rate is $5 per hour. You want to know the impact of various increases, so you just call for a sensitivity analysis of the wage rate. You indicate that you want year-to-date profits for the wage rates of $5, $5.25, $5.50, $5.75, and $6. Within a few minutes you get Figure 8–6 printed out. You can do sensitivity analyses on any of the variables in the model in the same way.

There are other useful commands that are just as simple. You can ask for the breakdown of sales volume. You can state a profit objective and have the computer print out the sales required and the entire profit and loss report for that objective. You can structure the model by departments or divisions, or however your company is organized. Then you can look at the impact of a proposal on a single department, on a division, or on the company as a whole.

Use of computer-based planning. Computer-based planning is in common use today. Reports have been published on the use of such models at the Xerox Corporation, in financial institutions, and for aggregate production planning. Also, there have been extensive applications in the Inland Steel Company, Potlatch Forests (an integrated forest

FIGURE 8–7
Typical corporate planning system for electric utilities

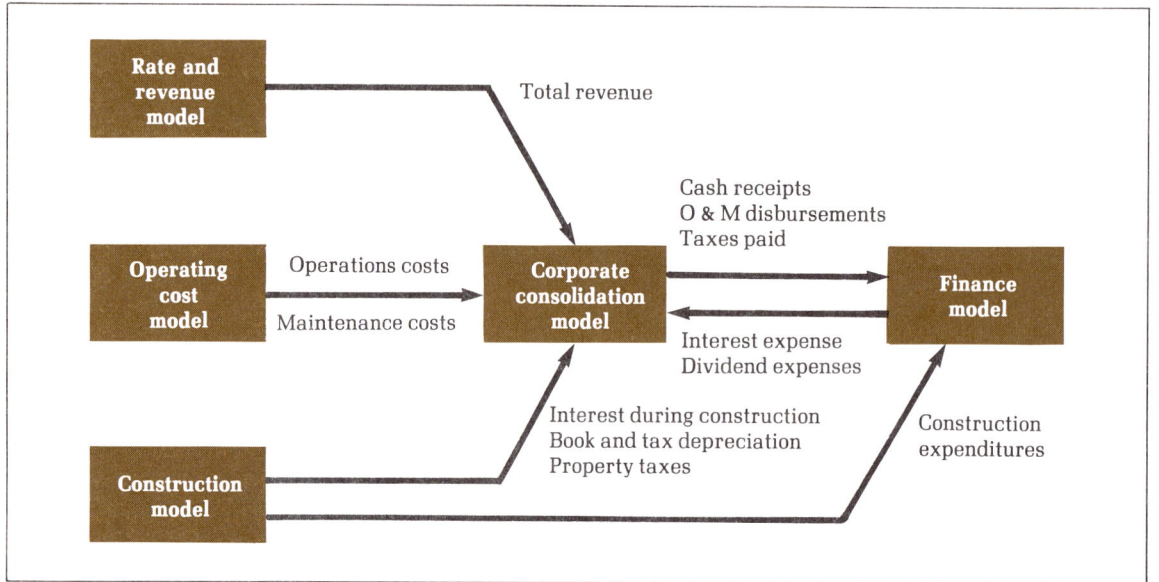

Source: J. Ogden, " 'What Happens If' A Planning System for Utilities," *Public Utilities Fortnightly,* March 1972. Courtesy of Planmetrics, Inc.

products company), the Food and Drug Administration, and electric utilities. The applications in electric utilities are particularly interesting, since this industry has been faced with rapidly changing fuel costs, continuously increasing demand, and the need to expand physical plant to meet requirements.

Figure 8–7 shows a typical corporate planning system relating five separate models. Four of the five models define separate problem areas: rate and revenue, operating costs, construction, and financing. Each model is linked to the others so that the effect of a change in plans in any one model will be reflected in the other models. The fifth model is a corporate consolidation model, which allows the examination of the effects of strategies in each area on the total organization.

SUMMARY

Planning is of great importance to business and is one of the marks of a well-run company. Businesses plan to capitalize on opportunities and achieve goals and to help achieve coordination between subunits. It turns out to be too costly not to plan!

Long-range planning sets the strategy of a company in the competitive marketplace for the next one to five years. Medium-range plans are in the one month to one year time span, and short-range plans are in the one day to one month time span. Corporate, functional, and operational plans match up with these three horizons.

The planning process is general and applies to all levels of planning. The setting of goals and objectives for the company as a whole, however, is long range and centered in corporate planning. The planning process begins with a self-audit and goes through stages of surveying the environment, stating objectives, examining the compatibility of objectives with the environment and the existing company, stating resource requirements and budgets, testing financial soundness, communicating the plan, and finally controlling the plan.

Management by objectives (MBO) is a systematic way of involving people in the planning process. The idea is honestly to get employees to help set goals that are consistent with corporate goals. If you participate in this kind of process, then you will feel a part of it and help make the plans come true.

The outputs of the planning process are the goals and objectives, strategies and policies, procedures and rules, and budgets. At each level of planning, the objectives, policies, and budgets provide bases for goals and objectives at the next lower level. Basic objectives, however, are set by top-level corporate planning. Functional plans depend on sales, but material, inventory, personnel, and financial plans must be coordinated with production plans. Planning at operational levels is centered largely in the production function.

Computer-based planning is common today. Such systems provide great speed and allow the examination of many alternatives.

REVIEW QUESTIONS

1. Do you think it is possible to plan effectively without a goal or objective in mind?

2. Businesses plan because they wish to achieve certain goals, because of the consequences of not planning, and to provide a framework for coordination among functions and subunits. Pick a personal problem in your experience in which you feel that planning can make a big difference in the outcomes. Identify the goals, consequences, and framework for coordination in the problem.

3. What are the three types of planning horizons commonly identified in business? How are they related to planning levels?

4. Identify the function of each of the following in the planning process:
   a. Self-audit.
   b. Environmental survey.
   c. Statement of objectives.
   d. Compatibility of objectives.
   e. Statement of resource requirements and budget development.
   f. Determination of financial soundness.
   g. Communication of plan outputs.
   h. Control of plan.

5. In the planning process, under what conditions would you rework objectives?

6. In the planning process, under what conditions would you reallocate budgets?

7. What is management by objectives and how does it work?

8. How are objectives set for the functional planning level? For the operational planning level?

9. Why must the plans for aggregate production, finance, personnel, finished goods inventory, and purchasing be closely coordinated?

10. Where in the planning process does computer-based planning fit in? Does it substitute for the entire process?

11. What is sensitivity analysis in computer-based planning? What is its value?

12. Suppose that an electric utility had a set of models similar to those shown in Figure 8–7. Now, suppose that it had to justify rate increases to the State Public Utilities Commission. Of what value would the system of models be in this situation?

CASES

Case 8–1. Mary Watson, the fire fighter

Mary Watson had a franchise for BURGER, a national fast-food chain. The business had gotten a good start four years ago. It was well located near Braniff Community College and Mary had worked hard to maintain quality, cleanliness, and good service.

On Monday morning after getting a quote for overhauling the refrigeration system, she exploded,

"What is going on here? The refrigerator has broken down, and where will I get the money to have it put back in shape? My bun delivery is not here and I am almost out! Three of my 'hands' didn't show, and my accountant says that costs are way up for the third quarter in a row. It seems as though that all I do is put out fires around here."

1. *What kinds of plans should Mary make?*
2. *How are these plans interlocked and related to each other?*
3. *How far ahead should Mary plan?*
4. *Is there an answer to the fire-fighting approach to managing a business, or is it a part of business life that you must put up with?*

Case 8–2.   MBO be hanged!

A consultant had just presented a report to Ronald Woods, president, chairman of the board, chief executive officer, and founder of the Ronald S. Woods Publishing Company. Woods publishes textbooks in business and economics (like this one) and is now well established as a prime publisher. It wasn't always that way, for Ronald Woods started the company from scratch and built it with energy and good business judgment. As you note by his titles, he is just about everything in the company—he makes all the important decisions. Nevertheless, he has a loyal core of admiring and competent editors, sales representatives, and production executives.

It was not unexpected to Ronald's staff that he "blew his stack" when the consultant presented a report that recommended the installation of MBO.

"What a bag of hogwash! Everyone knows what the objectives are around here—I tell them. Sure we took a sidetrack into publishing in the high school English field, and it was a disaster. I made the decision, and I take the responsibility for it. Profits are down temporarily, but they will be right back on track next year. MBO be hanged!"

1. *Does Ronald Woods understand MBO?*
2. *If it were installed, what could MBO do for Woods Company?*
3. *Can MBO work in a company like Woods?*
4. *Suppose that Ronald were about to retire from active management of the company. Would MBO be more or less important to its continued success?*

part IV

WHO:

To provide satisfaction to a market

All the efforts of the business firm are directly or indirectly related to satisfying the needs of some group of people. But there are many differences among people and their needs. People in Florida need different clothing than people in Minnesota. Older citizens' needs differ from those of infants. The consumer market is only one type of market. Few families buy computers, but business firms and governments need them. These buyers make up two other types of markets. There are also consumer, industrial, and government markets outside this country. To U.S. firms these represent multinational markets. Managers must decide which group or groups of people will be their target—the market for their goods and services. They must also try to keep up with the changes that are constantly occurring in these markets. The characteristics of these four types of markets are discussed in Chapter 9.

It is obvious that there are many different types of buyers with different needs, but some other points are not so obvious. Two people may have the same characteristics or needs but may not choose to satisfy them in the same way. Why does one family watch television, whereas another goes to a movie? These are questions of consumer behavior. All of us have been exposed to many influences that affect our spending behavior. Businesses need information on consumer behavior and buyer characteristics in order to make good decisions. To get this information, many firms conduct marketing research. Consumer behavior and marketing research are the focus of Chapter 10.

With a target market in mind and information on that market, the firm is ready to develop a marketing program. Decisions must be made on the product or service to be offered, including the branding and packaging of those goods, the price to be charged, the way in which the goods can be promoted, and the distribution channels to be used. The factors that enter into these decisions are discussed in Chapter 11.

chapter
9

MARKETS TO
BE SATISFIED

By studying this chapter you should be able to find answers to these questions:

1 What is a market?
2 What are the four major types of markets that a seller might attempt to satisfy?
3 How are markets interrelated?
4 How are U.S. consumer markets changing?
5 What types of goods and services are needed by industrial markets?
6 How important are government markets?
7 Why is there an increased emphasis on multinational markets?

Terms you should know:

accessory equipment
consumer market
common demand
demographics
derived demand
government market
industrial market
installations
manufactured parts
market
merchandise
multinational market
raw materials
services
Standard Industrial Classification (SIC)
Standard Metropolitan Statistical Area (SMSA)
supplies

Right now someone is carefully planning to get to you. It may be the manager of your college bookstore, the owner of the local McDonald's franchise, or a product manager at Procter & Gamble. Each individual firm can continue to exist only if it earns dollar votes in the marketplace. These sellers think that they have a good chance to get your vote. They will earn your votes by satisfying some of your needs better than those needs can be satisfied elsewhere.

Of course, your votes alone aren't going to keep McDonald's in business. When you buy something, you may think of yourself as a consumer, but do you think of yourself as a part of a consumer market? These sellers don't know your name, but they know a lot of other things about you. They know you as a part of a market—a cluster of people with needs for their products.

WHAT IS A MARKET?

To define a **market** as a cluster of people with similar needs is only partially correct. To be a market, the cluster must have economic strength. That means it must be made up of enough people with enough purchasing power. In addition, these people must be willing to spend that purchasing power to satisfy their individual needs.

Enough people with similar needs

For a seller to make an attempt to satisfy your needs, there must be enough other people with needs similar to yours to make it worthwhile. There is no magic number. There are very few potential buyers for Lockheed L-1011 jumbo jets, yet the market is worthwhile for Lockheed. McDonald's advises its franchisees to locate in a market of approximately 50,000 people. Procter & Gamble develops and produces products with the potential market of millions of people. Many markets that are not large enough to allow Procter & Gamble to use efficiently its mass production capacity may be quite profitable for sellers who operate on a smaller scale.

Some clusters of people have needs but are too small to attract any sellers. Painesdale, Michigan, is a small town with people who have the need for a variety of products. Yet there isn't a single store in the entire town. There aren't enough people to make enough purchases to keep a store in business. Some small towns find that they cannot attract a doctor—a seller of medical services (see Figure 9–1). There just aren't enough people to pay enough medical bills to support a doctor. To be a market, a group of people with needs must be large enough to attract a seller.

212

TOWN RECRUITING A CONVICT DOCTOR

Alexis, Ill. (AP)—Residents of this tiny western Illinois community, desperate for a physician, have voted to bring a federal prisoner here with an eye toward his settling down as their doctor.

Dr. Morris Salkind, 53, of Philadelphia, is expected to be paroled on Aug. 26 after spending two years in the U.S. Medical Center for Federal Prisoners in Springfield, Mo. He was convicted in October, 1976, on bail jumping and mail fraud charges involving making false statements about Medicaid claims.

A residents' committee from Alexis, population 946, voted Monday to have Salkind visit, possibly in September, said committee member Wes Allen. He said the group would gather donations to pay Salkind's expenses.

"The vote was to go on further with the financial aspects and bring him to Alexis for a visit because he will not make a decision until he has visited our area, and the people want to meet him before making a decision," Allen said.

Source: *The Sacramento Bee*, May 25, 1978.

FIGURE 9–1
Small town needs doctor

Enough purchasing power

The second test is purchasing power. The individuals in the cluster must have something of value to exchange for the goods and services that meet their needs. They must have something to spend. In addition, they must have the authority to spend it. While they usually spend money, there are many other possibilities. Credit is something of value, a promise to pay in the future.

In the late 1970s, Vietnam veterans were able to pay for education with their GI benefits. They weren't spending their own money. They were spending their claims against the resources of the U.S. government. If you have health insurance, you have arranged to be able to spend your claims against the resources of the insurance company in the event you have an accident or illness.

There are some clusters of people in our society who have very real needs, but because they lack purchasing power, no seller can take full responsibility for serving these people. Private firms can continue to exist only if they exchange their goods and services for something of value. In some cases, the government subsidizes the purchasing power of these people. The government Medicare program for senior citizens is an example. Private doctors, hospitals, and nursing homes are more able to serve the needs of senior citizens when Medicare increases their medical purchasing power.

Senior citizens and veterans are markets because they have both purchasing power and the authority to make purchases. They can decide whether they will make purchases and where those purchases will be made, even though they may spend resources provided by the government. To be a market, a cluster of people with needs must be large enough to have enough purchasing power to attract a seller.

Willingness to spend

Are there some things you won't buy even though you could afford them and could use them? Maybe your need isn't too pressing. You may prefer to save your purchasing power just in case you find another need is more important. Willingness to spend is one of the more difficult questions for sellers as they try to identify markets. Only rarely do people declare their willingness to spend in advance. Even then, the seller may be fooled. Some people are willing to agree that some new product or service is a great idea, but when it comes right down to getting out their wallets and spending their money on it, they back out of the market. In most cases, the seller can only estimate the willingness of people to spend their purchasing power.

A market is a cluster of people with similar needs who have both the willingness and the authority to spend their individual purchasing power to meet their needs. To be a part of a market, you need not know anyone else in that market or even realize that there are others who have needs similar to your own. Although each person acts independently, sellers view the cluster as a market because the needs and the actions taken to fill those needs are similar.

Different kinds of markets

Consumer markets are made up of people who are buying for ultimate consumption. That means that whatever utility the product or service has to offer will be used by someone for personal benefit. Most of the purchases you make probably fall into this category. You may buy a car for your own use. You might buy some food to have friends over for a party. The products may be shared with others, but they are purchased with the intent of providing personal benefits. These benefits need not be pleasant. If you were to go to a hospital and purchase an appendectomy, you would be acting as a consumer in the consumer medical market.

Not all purchasing activity is undertaken to satisfy personal needs. Some people are responsible for purchasing the goods and services that are needed by businesses and government units in the United States. The consumer, industrial, and government markets within this country are also called domestic markets. The term *domestic* simply

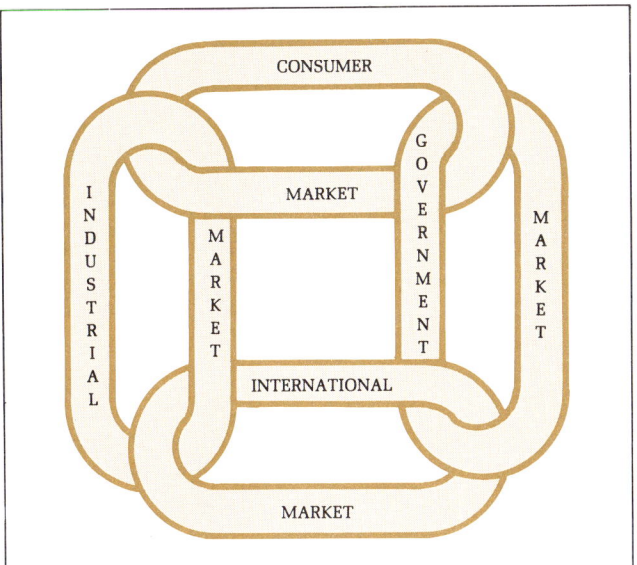

FIGURE 9–2
Four interrelated markets

means in one's own country. Multinational markets are markets outside this country. These multinational markets might be made up of consumers, industrial buyers, or government representatives. Figure 9–2 illustrates the different kinds of markets.

Industrial markets are made up of people who purchase goods and services for private businesses. These businesses may be sole proprietorships, partnerships, or corporations. The intent of the buyer is to use the goods and services to do business. Some of the purchases are for resale. Someone at your campus bookstore arranged to buy this textbook so that it could be resold to you. Other purchases are to provide the materials to produce something that will be sold later. The manager at a car wash buys water, soap, brushes, and wax to be able to sell you a car wash. Businesses also need some goods and services just to operate. Electricity, typewriters, and tax services are examples.

Government markets consist of people who buy goods and services for federal, state, and local government units. This includes everything from nuclear warheads for the Pentagon and radishes for a White House dinner to gasoline for the police cars in your community. The government buyers purchase goods and services to run the government units, which are to provide for the security, health and welfare, and governance of the citizens.

Multinational markets consist of all those people who buy goods and services to be used in a country other than the one in which the seller is headquartered. The Coca-Cola Company is headquartered in

Atlanta, Georgia. It claims that Coke is enjoyed in more than 130 countries, territories, and possessions around the world.[1] You may be a part of the multinational consumer markets for companies such as Sony, Honda, Volkswagen, or Heineken. When Lloyds of London insured dancer Fred Astaire's legs for $1 million, Astaire was a part of the famous insurance group's multinational market for out-of-the-ordinary insurance coverage. To the Japanese, Germans, Mexicans, and Canadians, we are part of the multinational markets. Multinational markets include people who buy for personal use, for industrial use, and for governments.

Interrelated markets

All of these markets are interrelated. In some cases the various buyers are competing to buy the same goods and services. They have **common demand.** During the very cold winters of 1977 and 1978, supplies of natural gas for industrial users were cut back to assure that there would be enough to heat homes. Industrial customers' needs were judged to be less critical than the needs of the consumer market. The government and industrial markets clashed over common demand for portions of the redwood forests in northern California. The logging industry wanted the land for its timber, while the government wanted to expand the national park areas. The various markets compete continuously over limited supplies of certain goods and services.

The industrial market is also related to the government and consumer markets because of derived demand. **Derived demand** means that the demand for one product or service comes about due to the demand for another product or service. Why does the Ford Motor Company buy huge rolls of sheet steel from U.S. Steel? Is it because Ford executives want to own steel? Is it because U.S. Steel needs the money? No, the demand for steel is derived or comes from the demand for automobiles. The Ford Motor Company is going to be a part of the market for U.S. Steel only as long as consumers buy Ford automobiles. The demand for other raw materials such as cotton is derived from consumer demand for the finished product. In the late 1970s cotton growers united in an effort to persuade consumers to buy shirts, pajamas, and other articles made from cotton. The demand for cotton had been declining as consumers turned to clothing made from synthetic materials. The industrial market's demand for cotton is derived from the consumer markets' demand for cotton clothing and other cotton products.

Although the domestic consumer, industrial, and government markets as well as the multinational markets are related through either common or derived demand, there are some distinct differences in these markets. Let's look more closely at some of the important characteristics of each of these four types of markets.

CONSUMER MARKETS

Whether a firm is serving a national or a local consumer market, the same factors are important. Firms that view themselves as serving a national market are constantly seeking information on the population nationwide. They are concerned especially with the changes in the rate of population growth, level and distribution of income, age distribution, and family status. These same kinds of changes take place on a smaller scale within communities and are just as important to a firm seeking to serve a local market.

Demography is the study of population factors. **Demographics** are statistics on people. These might include just about anything about people that can be counted or measured. Much of the information that is useful in measuring the potential of various consumer markets is collected according to **Standard Metropolitan Statistical Areas** (SMSA). An SMSA is a metropolitan area with a central city of at least 50,000 people. It is considered an integrated economic unit because many of the people who live in suburban areas around the central city either work or shop in the city. Some of the SMSAs include more than one city (see Figure 9–3).

As population shifts occur, the effect on some SMSAs is greater than on others. These differences may indicate to a national firm that there is reason to change the direction of its marketing effort. For example, national retailers such as Sears and Penney's are building more new stores in areas with increasing populations. A change in the demographics within a SMSA could affect the demand for the products and services offered by local firms. Let's look at the trends.

Rate of growth and distribution of the population

The population of the United States continues to grow, although at a much slower rate than it has in the past. Based on the information available in 1970, the Bureau of the Census predicted that our population would reach 225 to 238 million by 1980.[2] We fell far short of that mark with a 1980 population of just over 218 million people. Even though the numbers did not change too much, the geographic distribution of the population changed dramatically in the last decade (see Table 9–1). It is estimated that two out of every five families move at least once every five years.[3] One of the effects of this mobility is that previously pronounced regional differences in habits and behaviors have begun to disappear.

FIGURE 9–3
Standard metropolitan statistical areas

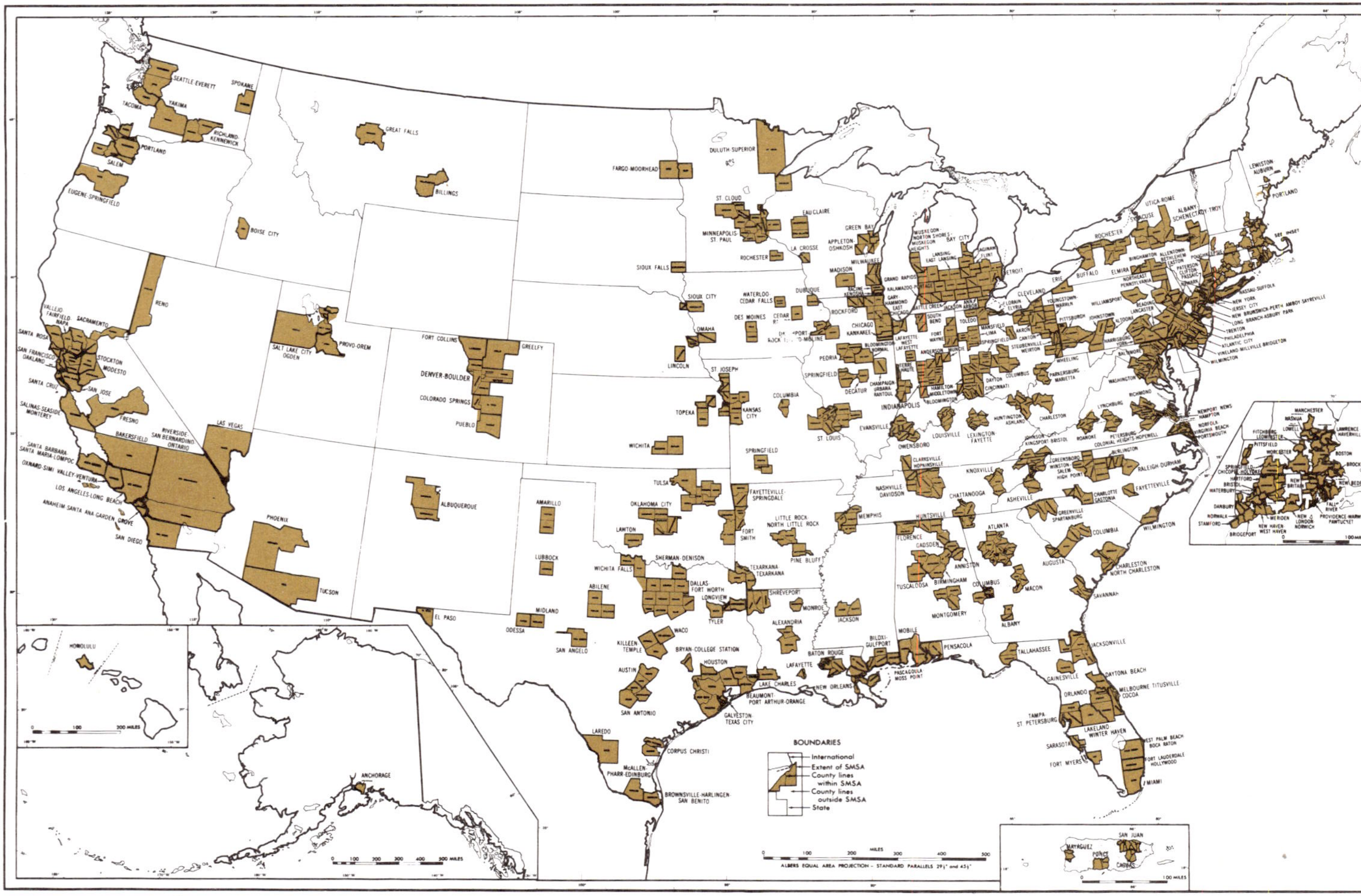

Source: *Standard Metropolitan Statistical Areas—1975*, rev. ed., U.S. Department of Commerce.

TABLE 9–1

The 25 largest metropolitan areas in 1980

Rank and area	1980 Population (000)	Percent change, 1970–1980
1 New York	9,415	−5.6
2 Chicago	6,977	0.0
3 Los Angeles–Long Beach	6,787	−2.0
4 Philadelphia	4,770	−1.1
5 Detroit	4,425	−0.2
6 Boston	3,473	1.5
7 Washington, D.C.	3,254	5.6
8 San Francisco–Oakland	3,223	3.7
9 Nassau–Suffolk, New York	2,840	5.6
10 Dallas–Fort Worth	2,680	6.2
11 Houston	2,437	21.9
12 St. Louis	2,317	−2.3
13 Pittsburgh	2,282	−5.0
14 Baltimore	2,180	5.2
15 Newark, N.J.	2,089	1.5
16 Minneapolis–St. Paul	2,053	4.4
17 Atlanta	2,008	25.9
18 Anaheim–Santa Ana–Garden Grove	1,951	37.3
19 Cleveland	1,859	−9.1
20 San Diego	1,768	30.2
21 Tampa–St. Petersburg	1,678	54.2
22 Miami	1,619	27.7
23 Denver–Boulder	1,605	29.4
24 Phoenix	1,457	50.3
25 Milwaukee	1,441	2.6

Source: "Sharp Contrasts in Metro Growth." Reprinted by permission from *Sales & Marketing Management* magazine, October 20, 1975. Copyright © 1975.

In general, people have been moving away from the mid-Atlantic and North Central states to the sunbelt areas. As states such as Arizona, Texas, and California have experienced rapid growth, the demand for housing and other consumer products to support that growth has brought about many new business opportunities.

People not only move to new SMSAs but they also move around within SMSAs. There has been a pronounced move toward the suburbs. Many large cities are plagued by deteriorating inner-city neighborhoods. As their markets move to the suburbs, retailers have been abandoning downtown locations. People in the suburbs tend to have greater purchasing power. The average suburban family income is 20 percent higher than the average urban family income, and the gap is widening.[4] Many downtown business districts are finding it difficult to compete with planned suburban shopping centers.

Population shifts affect not only the places where consumers choose to buy products and services, but also the types of products and services they buy. Both the moves to the suburbs and the relocations to more moderate climates have contributed to the increased demand for more casual clothing and furniture, and for products and services to support leisure activities. Of course, increased purchasing power is part of the reason for this increased demand.

Income level and distribution

The U.S. population enjoys one of the highest levels of personal income in the history of the world. A nation's **per capita income** is its total personal income divided by the number of people in the country. Table 9–2 shows how we compare with some of the other nations of the world.

As income increases, consumer spending patterns shift. In 1857 a German statistician named Ernst Engel observed a pattern that seems to hold true even today. Think about three broad groups of purchases; food, housing, and all others. The "all other" group includes recreation, savings, travel, cars, medical care, and all of the things a person might buy beyond food and housing. Engel observed that very poor people spent most of their incomes for food. They didn't spend a lot of money on food because they didn't have much money, but they spent a high proportion of their money on food. Rich people, on the other hand, spent more actual money on their food, but the money they spent represented a smaller proportion of their incomes. Then he noted that both poor and rich people tended to spend about the same proportion of their incomes on housing. Of course, the poor person lived in more humble housing, but it represented about the same proportion of income. What happened to the rest? For the very poor, there was nothing left. For the rich, there was a great part of their income to be spent in the all other area (see Figure 9–4).

TABLE 9–2
Selected per capita incomes (in U.S. dollars)

Country	Annual income per person
Australia	$ 6,764
Botswana	251
Brazil	1,452
Cuba	840
Denmark	8,920
France	8,610
Germany	8,797
India	161
Israel	3,529
Japan	5,990
Laos	80
Soviet Union	3,591
Sweden	10,100
Switzerland	12,646
United States	9,508

Source: *Reader's Digest Almanac and Yearbook* (Reader's Digest Association, Inc., 1979).

30.8%   19.4%   49.8% $10,000

21.6%   24.0%   54.4% $50,000

FOOD   HOUSING   OTHER

FIGURE 9–4
Poor versus rich spending today

Source: U.S. Department of Labor and The Conference Board, 200 Constitution Ave. N.W., Washington, D.C. 20210.

As the income level in the United States has increased, the demand for products and services in the "all other" category has increased. For almost two decades, the average family income has been rising. An explosive growth is expected in the number of families earning at least $25,000 a year. By 1985, almost one third of the families in the United States are expected to be in the $25,000 and over income bracket.[5] (See Figure 9–5.) People are spending a smaller proportion of their incomes on food, although they are spending more actual dollars. They have a greater proportion of their incomes to spend elsewhere.

Of course, you do not always get to choose how you spend your money. Most Americans are well aware of the difference between gross and net income, more commonly called take-home pay. **Gross income** is the amount you earn, and **net income** is the amount left after deductions. Deductions such as insurance premiums are voluntary. They are one way you have chosen to dispose of your income. Other deductions are involuntary. Federal taxes, state and local taxes, and social security taxes are taken off the top of most paychecks. The after-tax amount

1975	Income class:	1985
14%	$25,000 and over	30%
12%	$20,000-25,000	15%
18%	$15,000-20,000	17%
23%	$10,000-15,000	16%
21%	$5,000-10,000	15%
12%	Under $5,000	7%

Source: U.S. Department of Commerce, *Conference Board Record*, May 1976, p. 25.

FIGURE 9–5
The changing income pyramid: projected percent distribution of families based on 1975 dollars

is called **disposable income.** This is the amount of income that is available to be spent by consumer markets. When our nation suffers from a high rate of unemployment, the government can stimulate demand in consumer markets by cutting taxes. This increases the amount of disposable income and increases demand for consumer products. Be-

DID YOU EVER WONDER?

How do you compare with the average on consumption of common food items?

The following are average annual per capita consumptions in the United States.

Candy	16.7 lb	Coffee	560 6-oz cups
Wine	7 qt	Soft drinks	493 8-oz glasses
Orange juice	16 qt	Tea	160 6-oz cups
Red meat	165.2 lb	Chicken	43.3 lb
Fish	15 lb	Eggs	287
Butter or margarine	16.9 lb	Milk	32 gal
Cheese	20.7 lb	Yogurt	2 lb
Onions	9 lb	Mushrooms	2 lb
Rice	7 lb	Frozen vegetables	25 lb
Canned vegetables	53 lb	Bananas	19 lb
Apples	16.3 lb	Potatoes: Fresh	48.3 lb
Lettuce	22 lb	Frozen	36.8 lb
Carrots	6.5 lb	Chips	16.3 lb

Source: Center for Science in the Public Interest.

cause of derived demand, the increased demand in the consumer markets soon brings about increased demand in the industrial markets.

Most people spend the first part of their disposable income on necessities. Food, housing, and medical care are some of the common necessities. But some are more necessary than others. Food is clearly necessary, but must it be steak? We buy clothes for both protection and modesty, but is style a necessity? At some point we are spending beyond the basic necessities. Income that is available to spend out of choice rather than necessity is called **discretionary income.**

One of the reasons why so many people feel that they lack purchasing power is that they really lack discretionary income. Perhaps they have come to define some things such as televisions, washing machines, and variety in their wardrobes as necessities. Maybe they have committed themselves to fixed payments on mortgages, cars, and other installment credit. They have little left after they pay their bills.

The availability of credit has created advantages for both buyers and sellers, but these advantages have not been without costs. Credit is a way to introduce flexibility in purchasing power. It allows consumers to enjoy the benefits of various products and services while they earn the income to pay for them. Credit doesn't increase a person's purchasing power; it simply shifts it forward in time. In the end, all of the credit obligations are supposed to be paid off in money.

In fact, credit really decreases a person's purchasing power, since a part of that purchasing power is being spent to rent money. When

"Getting back to those interest rates, could you be a little more specific than 'it's going to cost a pretty penny?' "

Reprinted by permission *The Wall Street Journal.*

WHY YOU FEEL BROKE, by Sylvia Porter

Let's say that at the start of 1973, you, the breadwinner in a family of four, earned a partially after-tax income of $15,000—meaning after deduction for federal income and Social Security taxes, but not including the huge bite from state and local taxes. Let's also say that since then, your annual pay hikes have hiked your partially after-tax income to more than $22,500.

That's a hefty pay increase of over 50 percent in just five years. But it has been merely enough to keep you even in purchasing power so that your family can buy about the same marketbasket of goods and services at the beginning of 1978 as it could with that much smaller after-tax income at the beginning of 1973.

But wait. The cost of living, as measured by the official price indices, has increased "only" around 45 percent in this five-year span. How come, then, that an income rise of more than 50 percent is essential just to stay even in buying power?

The first answer is that as you move up the pay scale, you move, too, into even higher income tax brackets and your pay is subjected to even-higher income tax rates. Federal income tax rates alone squeeze more and more out of your gross, leave you with less and less for your net-after-taxes. Call it the tax-bracket "creep," as Commerce Secretary Juanita M. Kreps did the other day, or call it the progressive tax "squeeze," as I have done so often in the past; or whatever—the result is the same. As your salary or other income rises, under our progressive tax system, you pay a greater percentage of it to the federal government. The gap yawns wider and wider between your gross and your net.

This is just one reason you feel so "broke" at a time when you're earning the highest pay of your entire life.

A second answer is that on $22,500, you are paying far more in Social Security taxes in 1978 than you paid on $15,000 in 1973. Your wage base is much broader and the wage base on which your Social Security taxes are figured is slated to continue climbing relentlessly year after year. At the same time, the Social Security tax rate on incomes has been in an uptrend too. You'll be paying $1,071 in Social Security taxes this year (matched by your employer) on a wage base of $17,700. By 1982, five years from now, if your pay increases have taken you to the $31,800 income bracket, your Social Security tax will be up to $2,271, again matched by your employer.

This is a regressive tax—hitting all income brackets in a similar way—as against the progressive income tax. But the result is the same here too. As your salary or other income rises, you pay a higher Social Security tax. The gap yawns still wider between your gross and your net.

A third answer is that you are using far more services than ever before and all services cost more than ever before. Living in a "service" society commands a price and since you have chosen that life, you must pay the price demanded.

Instead of doing your laundry by hand you buy a washer-dryer and pay for that big-ticket item. You use public transportation, which has climbed in price at a pace far faster than the cost of cars. You go to the movies and pay prices that would have stunned you a mere few years ago. All these service costs have zoomed, rising at a rate far outpacing the rates of increases in other areas. And your use of more and more services seems without end.

And finally, although much more subtle, is the factor of your ever-expanding aspirations, your continual upgrading in your demands. The luxuries of yesterday are the necessities of today. You have become accustomed to yearly increases in your spending budget to new peaks, and resent any interruption in the trend. Whatever form the upgrading takes, the general rise in aspirations is undeniable. And any sudden retreats are no more than temporary.

These then are four reasons you feel so "broke" at a time when you're earning the highest pay of your entire life.

I speak for millions of you as well as for myself, I suspect, when I admit that an honest look at the way I live suggests that if I ever go broke, I'll surely be going broke in style!

Source: From *Your Money's Worth* by Sylvia Porter. Copyright 1979, Field Enterprises, Inc. Courtesy of Field Newspaper Syndicate.

you pay interest on a charge account, you are paying rent for the use of that money. A family that maintains a charge account at the department store at the normal $300 limit by paying the minimum monthly payment is really paying $54 each year to rent $300 from the store. For each $1 spent, this family receives 72¢ worth of goods and services plus the right to use those goods and services sooner. If time is important, however, the use of credit is worth the price.

The use of consumer credit has increased over the past decade. The average U.S. family now owes $1 to a creditor for each $5 of take-home pay.[6]

Average personal income does not tell the whole story. How is that personal income distributed over the population? In some countries, a few people control most of the wealth. They are able to buy luxurious homes and automobiles while others live in squalor.

The large number of people in the middle-income range in the United States has encouraged the growth of industries to mass produce consumer products. In countries where a small group controls the wealth, the rich buy from producers in other countries and the poor go without. Most of the wealthy people in the Mideast oil-producing nations drive American or European automobiles. One of the reasons why there is no domestic automobile industry is because the majority of the people

HOOKED ON CREDIT AND OUT OF CONTROL

"Charge it!" *Those two little words are so simple, until the time comes to pay. "I know," writes Mrs. Mary K. Mansour, an Akron, Ohio, reader of* Changing Times. *"I learned the hard way about five years ago. And I still have the urge to use those magic words whenever I don't have cash."*

Let her tell how it was, in her own words.

It was easy to get credit cards then. Companies were eager to process your application and encouraged you to go use them right away. I got a gold-toned card once and even was told that I was an exceptional customer. That's when the trouble began.

We had just been married and naturally wanted the best of everything all at once. We had stable income and job security. We wanted a nice home, good clothes, a few luxuries. Did our sparse wardrobes need brightening? Ah, yes, our credit cards! How easy it was to go out and buy! With every intention of paying, we soon ran up a $500 clothing bill in one store alone.

Little by little the fever crept over me. I spent much more on items I charged than if I had to pay cash. I told myself it was all right to buy the prettier $20 handbag instead of the $10 one. It wouldn't show up on my account until next month anyhow.

As the statements rolled in, I never paid much attention to balances. I merely paid the minimum required and, as far as my creditors were concerned, I could go on charging forever. They had me hooked, although I didn't realize it until years later.

When I hit my credit limit on an account, I wouldn't charge on that account for a while, until my balance got down to where I could charge again. Our balances averaged $300 to $500 for as long as we kept charging. But I was confident that all would get paid sooner or later. And my credit cards enabled me to get all I needed for myself and my family.

By then we had two children and I had no job. I got to thinking nothing of charging groceries, haircuts, plants, car repairs. Even our family doctor took credit cards.

How easy and convenient it all was. Then one day it hit us. We had $4,000 to $5,000 tied up just in charge accounts and easy payments!

We tried to figure out what we had to show for it. We couldn't account for anywhere near half of what we'd spent. The clothing was out of style, the groceries gone. In effect, we still owed our doctor. There it was, bigger than we dreamed, the bottom line telling us we were in debt and out of control.

Payments began to exceed the cash coming in. We had to juggle bills, hold off one to pay another. We got deeper in the red and could see no way out. The finance charges grew each month. There were interest charges, previous balances, service charges, late charges. We had so many bills coming in I hated to see the mailman coming. What were we to do?

A bill-consolidation loan was out of the question because, believe it or not, we had little collateral. We were too embarrassed to borrow from relatives. It was just too late.

Well, that's how it was until a year ago. We're still struggling to pay what we still owe, but we charge no more. The stress and worry about paying the bills haunted us until it actually made us sick. It was just too much to handle.

They say, "Guard your credit." You'll never know how wise that is until you've been as close to ruining it as I have. Look at those cards in your wallet. If you use them to buy things you don't really need, don't push your luck. Credit can be like a disease in a weak body. Take it from one who has been there. It's a long, rough road back from "charge it" to "cash only."

Source: Reprinted with permission from *Changing Times* Magazine, © 1977 Kiplinger Washington Editors, Inc., February 1977 *Changing Times*.

cannot afford to buy or operate an automobile. Clearly, our income distribution spreads the purchasing power more evenly over the population, thereby creating consumer markets. Of course, not all markets are growing at the same rate. The income distribution among the states shifts with changes in the population level and employment (see Figure 9–6).

Age

Peoples' needs change over their lifetimes. The cycle runs from baby food and tricycles through a heavy emphasis on education and recreation, then to houses and automobiles all the way to retirement travel and nursing homes. Age affects not only the types of products and services that are needed but also the purchasing power of the people with the needs. Income tends to increase with age until retirement.

Babies are not born at a constant rate. There tend to be fewer births when a nation is at war or suffering economic depressions, and more births immediately following wars and during periods of economic prosperity. These peaks and valleys in the birth rate persist as peaks and valleys for various age groups as the babies grow into adults.

After World War II, this country experienced a period of peace and relative prosperity, which resulted in a tremendous baby boom. That baby boom is still exerting a strong effect on consumer markets. Those babies will be in their mid-20s and early 30s during the 1980s and will be creating a baby boom of their own as they pass through the child-bearing ages. Even though each family will have fewer chil-

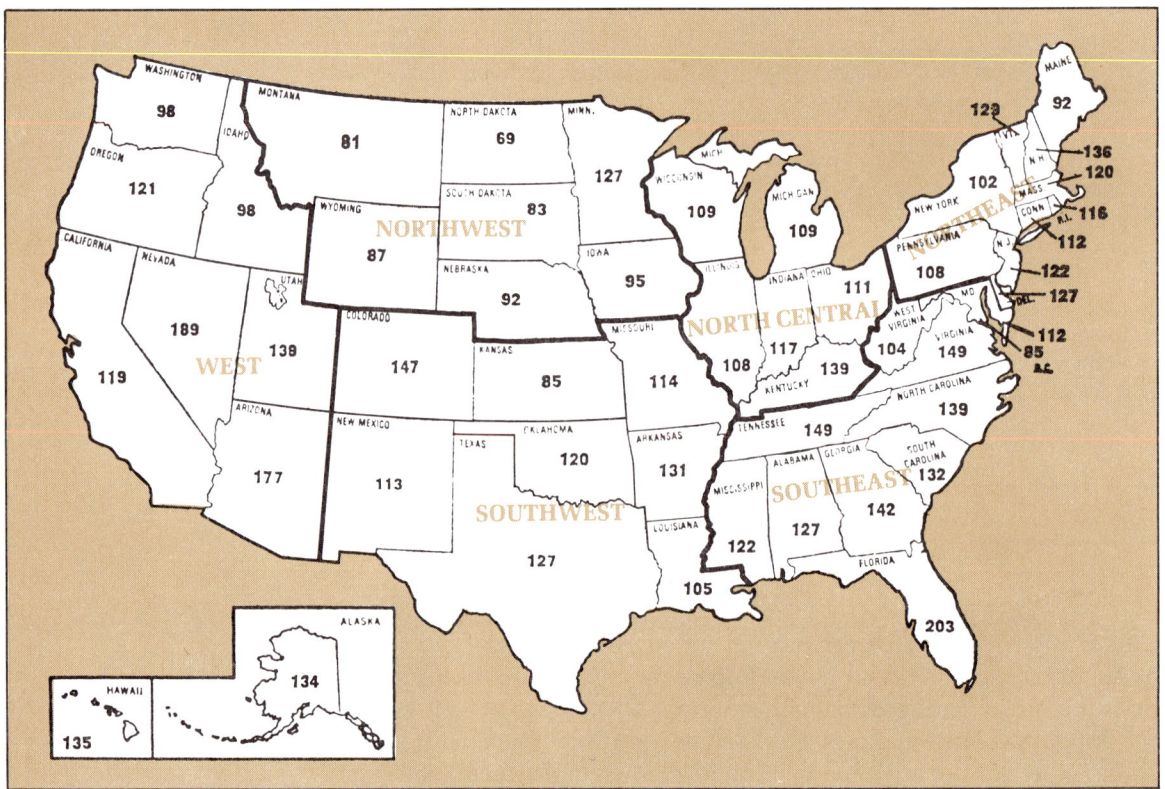

FIGURE 9–6

Where the money will be (percentage increases in personal incomes, 1969–1990)

This map shows recent projections of percentage increases in total personal income in each state from 1969 to 1990, based on 1967 dollars. The figures are the latest available from the Bureau of Economic Affairs of the Department of Commerce. However, fast-moving changes in population, energy needs, construction, and business even now are affecting the projections of what lies ahead. It is likely, for example, that projections in the Northeast and North Central regions will be revised downward and that those in the Southeast, Southwest, and Northwest will go even higher. Those for the western states probably will remain about the same.

Source: Reprinted with permission from *Changing Times* magazine, © 1976 Kiplinger Washington Editors, Inc., January 1977 *Changing Times*, p. 12.

dren, there will be so many people in the early adult group that the actual number of babies will increase. There were fewer babies born during the war years, 1941–46. This means that we will see fewer middle-aged adults and fewer teenagers, the children of these middle-aged adults. But primarily due to improved health care, there will be more people in the grandparent age range. The senior citizen group will continue to grow as a consumer market. Figure 9–7 shows a projection of the U.S. population by age groups.

While the actual birth rate is not totally predictable, sellers have a reasonable warning about the proportions of the age groups. This warning should allow them to prepare to meet the needs of these con-

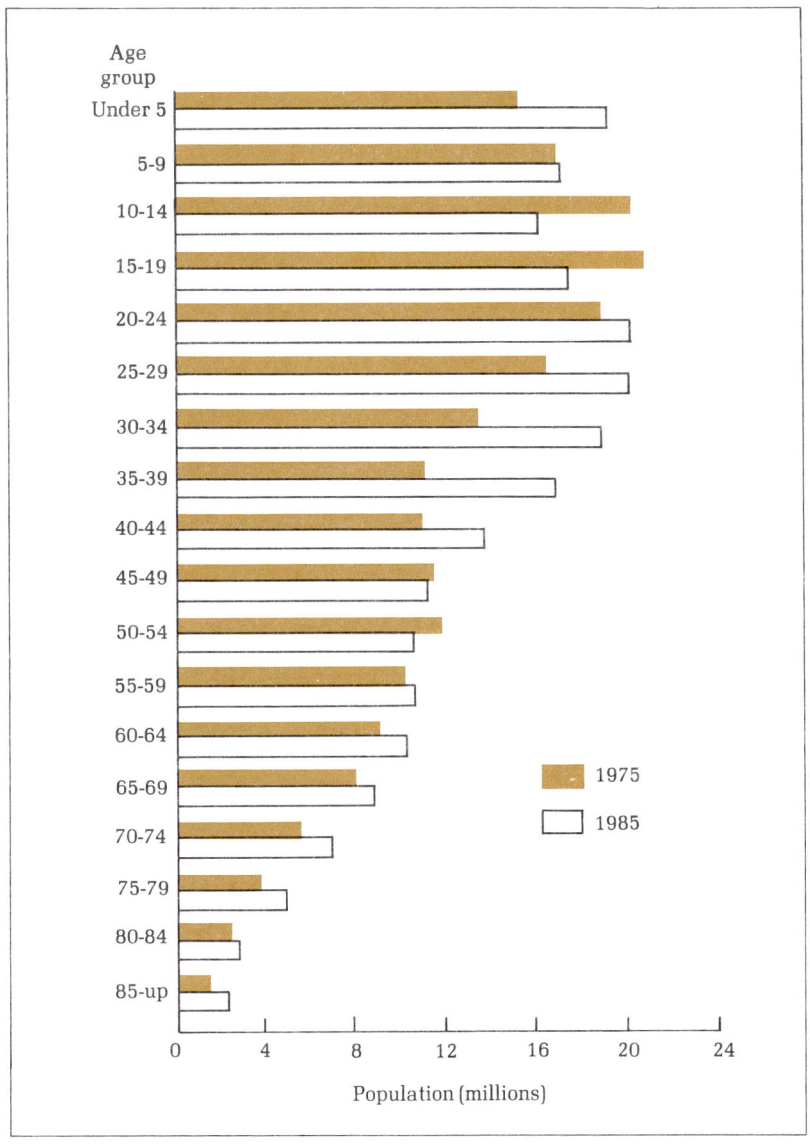

FIGURE 9–7
A look ahead at the U.S. population, 1975–1985

Shifting demographics: Population will increase from 213,446,000 to 234,067,000 during the next decade. The new mix will vitally affect markets for goods and services and alter the composition of the labor force.

Source: *Business Week*, January 12, 1976, p. 75.

sumers. Upjohn Pharmaceuticals is heavily involved in research on degenerative or old-age diseases. PepsiCo, Inc., is preparing to increase its emphasis on diet and mixer-type beverages in anticipation of the changing tastes as its primary market ages from the teenage to the adult age group.[7]

Family status

In years past, family status was fairly predictable. There were greater social penalties attached to both remaining unmarried and being divorced. With less effective birth control and lower costs of child rearing, large families and long marriages were normal.

Recent studies indicate three family-related trends that will affect

---

IS THE FAMILY LIFE CYCLE OUTDATED?

For many years marketers assumed that most people followed through a family life cycle. The traditional family life cycle had a number of stages. Your stage in the life cycle was supposed to affect the types of purchases you would make.

An overview of the life cycle

Bachelor stage; young single people not living at home	Newly married couples; young, no children	Full nest I; youngest child under six	Full nest II; youngest child six or over	Full nest III; older married couples with dependent children	Empty nest I; older married couples, no children living with them, head in labor force	Empty nest II; older married couples, no children living at home, head retired	Solitary survivor, in labor force	Solitary survivor, retired
Few financial burdens	Better off financially than they will be in near future	Home purchasing at peak Liquid assets low	Financial position better Some wives work	Financial position still better	Home ownership at peak Most satisfied with financial position and money saved	Drastic cut in income Keep home Buy: Medical appliances, medical care, products which aid health, sleep, and digestion	Income still good but likely to sell home	Same medical and product needs as other retired group; drastic cut in income
Fashion opinion leaders	Highest purchase rate and highest average purchase of durables	Dissatisfied with financial position and amount of money saved	Less influenced by advertising	More wives work				
Recreation oriented			Buy larger-sized packages, multiple-unit deals	Some children get jobs	Interested in travel, recreation, self-education			Special need for attention, affection, and security
Buy: Basic kitchen equipment, basic furniture, cars, equipment for the mating game, vacations	Buy: Cars, refrigerators, stoves, sensible and durable furniture, vacations	Interested in new products Like advertised products Buy: Washers, dryers, TV, baby food, chest rubs and cough medicine, vitamins, dolls, wagons, sleds, skates	Buy: Many foods, cleaning materials bicycles, music lessons, pianos	Hard to influence with advertising High average purchase of durables Buy: New, more tasteful furniture, auto travel, non-necessary appliances, boats, dental services, magazines	Make gifts and contributions Not interested in new products Buy: Vacations, luxuries, home improvements			

Source: "An overview of the life cycle"—William D. Wells and George Gubar, "Life Cycle Concept in Marketing Research," *Journal of Marketing Research*, vol. 3, November, 1966, p. 362. Reprinted by permission.

But how does this idea apply today? Some people still pass through all of the stages, but think about some of the common causes for variation. Some people never marry. Others marry and divorce. Others repeat the marriage–divorce cycle several times. Some couples choose not to have children. The person who marries a single parent is suddenly thrust into the full-nest stage. There have been a number of TV comedy shows based on the problems that can come up in some of these ready-made families. How do you expect to move through the family life cycle?

many consumer markets: (1) there has been an increase in the number of people who remain single and live alone or with another single person; (2) there has been an increase in the per capita incidence of divorce; and (3) there is a tendency toward fewer children per family. Each of these factors tends to distort the patterns of needs that used to be reflected in the family life cycle.

Sellers of products that tend to be "one to a household," such as dishwashers, fire insurance, or basic telephone service, tend to be more concerned about the number of households than the actual number of people. These sellers used to depend heavily on the marriage rate as an indicator of household formations. Most young people remained a part of their parents' households until marriage. During the past decade, however, the number of women under 25 living alone tripled. The number of men under 25 living alone doubled.[8]

The increasing divorce rate is another factor in family formations. In divorce, a single household suddenly becomes two households with duplicate needs.[9] As the family status changes, the market changes.

Another measure of family status is the number of children or the size of the family. The tendency in the United States has been toward smaller families. Almost half of today's families consist of only two members. In general, this means there is more discretionary spending power. Raising children is a tremendous financial commitment. It has been estimated that the parents of the average child born in 1970 will spend over $30,000 raising that child to the age of 18. With fewer children, a family spends more on each child. The average cost of getting ready for the first baby is about $700. Parents often recycle baby clothes and furniture for later children. In 1960, first babies accounted for only

The average American household consists of 2.9 persons

25 percent of the births. In 1985, 40 percent of the babies born are expected to be first babies.[10] While the number of the people in the market for baby products will increase at a slower rate, their ability and willingness to spend will increase.

Family size affects not only spending priorities but also the nature of the products purchased. Appliance manufacturers have been manufacturing smaller appliances. The smaller family needs a smaller refrigerator, generates smaller wash loads, and has less need for a nine-passenger station wagon.

Sellers of consumer goods and services watch the trends in the size, age, income, and family status of the population. These factors affect the needs of the people who make up their markets. To be able to produce or sell consumer goods and services, these sellers take on the role of buyers in the industrial market.

INDUSTRIAL MARKETS

Industrial markets are invisible to the average consumer. Most people fully expect to find the goods and services they need offered for sale when and where they want them, but they seldom stop to think of all the transactions that had to take place to make that possible. Just about the time most people start to think about buying a winter coat, people who buy merchandise for clothing stores are making decisions on the styles of clothing they will offer for sale the following spring. Orders placed by these buyers will help clothing manufacturers to estimate the amount of cotton, polyester, thread, buttons, zippers, and other materials to order from their suppliers. If demand is strong, clothing manufacturers may order additional machinery or build additional plants. Long before the ultimate consumers have any idea that they will need jeans or cars or any other consumer products, industrial transactions are taking place to assure that those products will be available. Today some farmer may have to order seed for next year's cotton crop, which will find its way to your closet as a pair of jeans two years from now.

The classification of industrial goods

Industrial markets are vast and complex. They are made up of all the people who buy the goods and services that businesses need to continue to operate and provide satisfaction to their own markets. The range of products and services would be overwhelming without some system or organization. The classification of industrial goods can help to make it more understandable. It is a way to organize goods and services needed by the industrial markets. All of the goods and services fall into one of seven categories: installations, accessory equipment, raw materials, manufactured parts, supplies, merchandise, and business services (see Table 9–3).

TABLE 9–3
Classification of industrial goods

Class	Finished goods	Repurchase rate	Cost
Installations	No	Low	High
Accessory equipment	No	Medium	Medium
Raw materials	Yes	High	Low
Manufactured parts	Yes	High	Medium
Supplies	No	High	Low
Merchandise	Yes	High	Varies
Services	No	High	Varies

Installations. Additions to the firm's facilities that are useful over an extended period of time, and set the level of operation for the firm are **installations.** To General Motors these installations might mean a new automobile assembly plant. To a pizza shop, a new oven would be an installation. If it had one oven and added a second oven, it would double its capacity.

Accessory equipment. Those goods that are used in conducting business or producing products but do not become a part of the product or change the level of operation of the firm are called **accessory equipment.** Portable business equipment such as typewriters, shelving units and racks in a retail store, electric drills, and chairs are common examples.

Raw materials. Those materials that are purchased in an unprocessed form and processed for sale by the business are called **raw materials.** The raw materials for a bakery would be flour, eggs, and other ingredients.

Raw materials are the result of farming, mining, drilling, fishing, or some other process that collects these from our environment. These materials may be processed just enough to allow for efficient storage or shipping. For example, iron ore might be formed into ingots.

Manufactured parts. Screws, sheet steel, glass, clocks, radios, tires, light bulbs, and hundreds of other manufactured parts are combined to produce an automobile. Each of these could be identified within the finished product. **Manufactured parts** become a part of another product although they retain their own identity.

Supplies. Pencils, typewriter ribbons, machine lubricants, and other operating and maintenance supplies are fairly inexpensive. However, these supplies are essential to continuing business operations. One type of supply that was taken for granted until shortages began to occur is energy. Electricity, natural gas, and water fall into the supply category. **Supplies** do not become a part of the finished product but are used in normal business operations.

Merchandise. When a department store purchases clothing, appliances, linens, jewelry, and other products in order to make those products available to you, these are industrial purchases of merchandise.

JESS BRAVO
Keep an open mind

Jess Bravo lives by one basic philosophy: "Keep an open mind. A closed mind fights changes, is inflexible, has no team spirit, won't take risks, and is without imagination. On the other hand, an open mind is exciting, assertive, very creative, and sensitive to other people. These ingredients add up to help either a business or an individual excel. People in business must remain receptive to new ideas or they are dead."

Jess speaks from experience. Mark Larwood Industries was founded in 1946 for the sole purpose of servicing title companies and county recorders by providing them with microfilm copies of official records of real estate transactions. Since then the industry has been undergoing constant change with the development of the data processing and computer industries. Mark Larwood had to be flexible enough to change its orientation from microfilm to micrographics. Had the management resisted the changes, some of which required large investments, the firm would have faded away. Instead, Mark Larwood is the most modern and most technologically advanced total microfilm service company in the nation, with six computers in three locations in northern California. The firm now serves not only the county recorders but also a multitude of government, education, and business clients.

Most people are affected by micrographics services without even realizing it. Your school records are probably on microfiche along with your class schedule, registration records, hospital records, retail records, medic-alert records, payroll reports, and hundreds of other documents that affect your life. The use of micrographics makes it possible to maintain adequate records without aggravating the paperwork problem. In one case, tax records that had filled eight file cabinets were reduced to fill a single three-ring binder.

How did Jess Bravo progress to his position as vice president of a large microfilm firm? "It's almost like the plot for a movie. A poor Mexican couple first migrated to Los Angeles and then further north with their 12 children. I was one of those children. My family settled in Milpitas near San Jose when I was five and I enjoyed a very normal healthy childhood. In high school it was a real shock when I finally learned that I was a minority." Jesse Bravo is a former professional photographer. He graduated from Brooks Institute of Photographic Arts and Sciences in Santa Barbara in 1961 and joined Mark Larwood Industries in 1969.

Merchandise consists of products that are purchased and resold in substantially unchanged form.

Services. A helpful activity performed by some person or persons who are not regular employees of the firm is a **service.** The demand for services in the industrial market has increased just as it has in the consumer market. Business services range from janitorial services for the small firm, all the way to high-priced management consulting services for major corporations. Businesses contract for services in those areas where it would not be efficient for regular employees to perform the activities. It might be that the need for the activity is too limited or irregular to justify a regular employee. Perhaps there are specialized skills involved.

Different businesses have needs for different combinations of these basic types of goods. K mart seldom buys raw materials but concentrates on merchandise. U.S. Steel is in the business of buying raw materials and converting them into manufactured products. One of the most important factors in identifying industrial markets is the type of business.

Type of business

Just think of all the different kinds of businesses you personally deal with every year. There's the bank, the supermarket, the gas station, the dentist, clothing stores, movie theaters, bookstores, insurance companies, restaurants, and on and on. You know that there are oil companies, chemical companies, farms, casinos, air freight companies, hydraulic pump manufacturers, and hundreds of other kinds of businesses. How does a seller make sense out of this variety? One system is the Standard Industrial Classification.

The **Standard Industrial Classification** (SIC) is a system developed by the federal government to organize the reporting of business information. Each major industry in the United States is assigned a two-digit number that indicates to which of the ten groups shown in Figure 9–8 it belongs. Within each major industry, the types of business are further subdivided by using additional digits.

Companies within the same SIC number tend to have similar needs. By identifying the SIC numbers that represent its potential customers, a seller can make use of a wealth of information on the industrial markets it serves. The industrial markets are complex and purchase a wide variety of products and services. A type of market with even more diverse needs is the government market.

GOVERNMENT MARKETS

Have you ever seen a highway construction sign with the phrase "Your tax dollars at work"? Highway construction is just one of the ways that the government spends your tax dollars. In 1978 the Carter administration made history by submitting the first federal budget that exceeded the half-trillion-dollar mark. That's purchasing power! Add to that the spending of 50 state governments and thousands of county and city governments, and there are a lot of tax dollars at work. Each

FIGURE 9–8
Standard Industrial
Classifications (SIC
codes) for U.S. industry

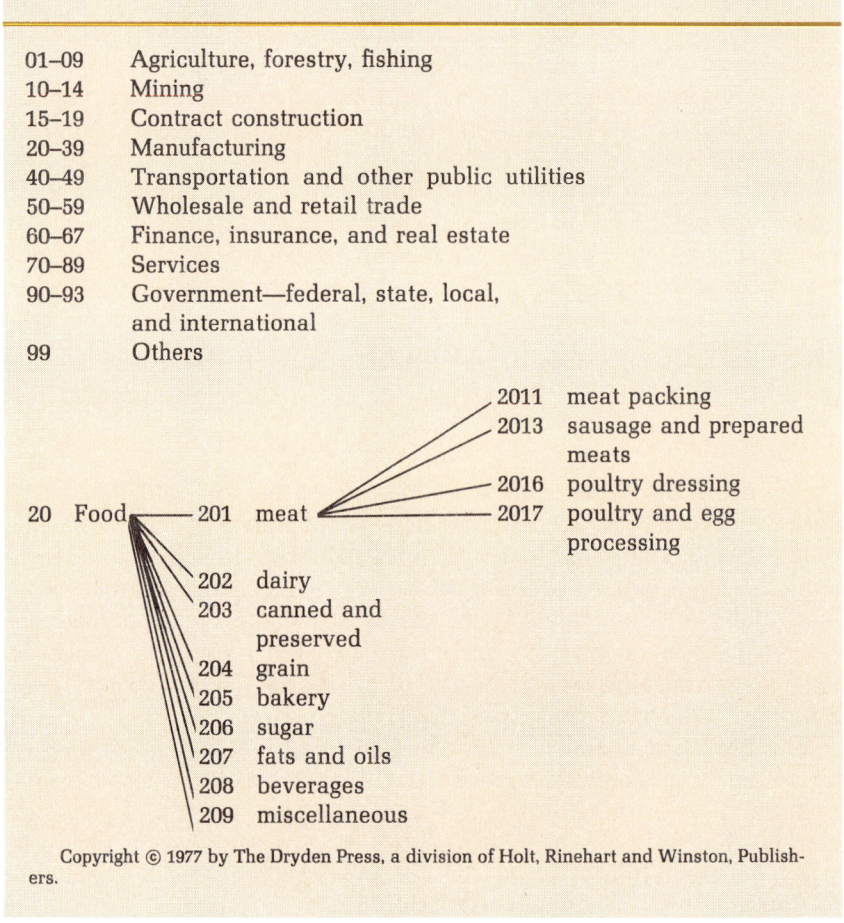

01–09	Agriculture, forestry, fishing
10–14	Mining
15–19	Contract construction
20–39	Manufacturing
40–49	Transportation and other public utilities
50–59	Wholesale and retail trade
60–67	Finance, insurance, and real estate
70–89	Services
90–93	Government—federal, state, local, and international
99	Others

20 Food
— 201 meat
— 2011 meat packing
— 2013 sausage and prepared meats
— 2016 poultry dressing
— 2017 poultry and egg processing
202 dairy
203 canned and preserved
204 grain
205 bakery
206 sugar
207 fats and oils
208 beverages
209 miscellaneous

of these governments has the authority to tax citizens in order to provide for the common welfare.

Government spending

Government markets within the United States are very important. Governments spend large sums of money on defense, education, public welfare, highways, natural resources, and health (see Figure 9–9). Really there is a government market for just about everything.

Consumers or businesspeople who do not spend their money carefully may eventually end up in bankruptcy. In contrast, while voters may recall government officials or vote them out of office, a government cannot declare bankruptcy and close down. The needs of the citizens would go on. Therefore, government buying procedures are designed with the objective of insuring efficient spending. Unfortunately, this objective is not always achieved.

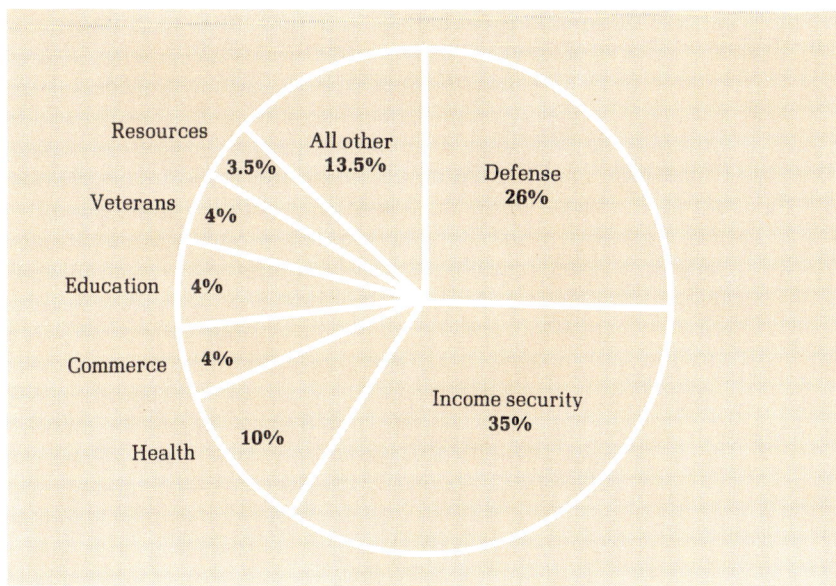

FIGURE 9–9
How the federal
government spends your
tax dollars

Source: *U.S. Statistical Abstract, 1976.*

Government buying procedures

Governments follow two basic buying procedures: bidding and negotiated contracts. In **bidding,** the government invites qualified suppliers
to submit the price at which they could deliver particular items that
have been carefully described. The competition among the bidders is
supposed to hold prices down. In some cases, there aren't enough competitive suppliers, so governments use **negotiated contracts.** The government buyers and suppliers are supposed to work out an agreement
that is fair to all parties.

Obtaining goods and services at the best price is not the only objective of government buying activities. Governments use their purchasing
powers to achieve a number of complex objectives. The first, of course,
is to acquire the goods and services necessary to support government
programs. The federal government buys food to feed military personnel,
and local governments buy fire hoses. Government spending is also
a powerful force on the general economy. Increased government spending can reduce unemployment and aid the recovery from periods of
economic recession. The government can use its spending power to
maintain the competitive balance within an industry. Some government
contracts are specifically designated for small businesses. Other contracts are limited to minority businesses or small businesses. In this
way, government spending has a social purpose.

The consumer, industrial, and government markets in the United
States represent tremendous economic activity. But ours is only one

of more than 130 nations in the world. The importance of multinational markets continues to increase.

MULTINATIONAL MARKETS

Multinational trade is a persistent economic activity. Indeed, Columbus discovered America while in search of a shorter route to India to buy spices. The British Empire was founded on multinational trade. There are substantial economic and social benefits in serving multinational markets.

There are two main reasons for the increased attention that is being paid to multinational markets. First, the standards of living in nations around the world are improving. Citizens, businesses, and governments of these nations have increased purchasing power and greater interest in the products of other nations. Second, there is increasing economic interdependence among the nations of the world. Improved communications and transportation combined with an increasing level of technology have caused many nations to grow dependent on the raw materials or manufactured products of other nations.

Improved standards of living

Economists usually divide the world's nations into three groups: developed nations, developing nations, and less developed nations. Developed nations such as the United States, the western European nations, and Japan have mature economies with a variety of manufacturing and service industries.

Developing nations have begun to develop their domestic industries, but the benefits of this development have not spread over the population. The Mideast nations are experiencing rapid growth in some areas due to the returns on their petroleum exports, but these benefits are not shared by all. Often the government of a developing nation will deliberately devote its resources to machinery and technology at the expense of consumer goods with the intention of increasing its production capabilities. This increased productivity should increase the per capita income of the population and eventually bring about greater demand for consumer goods.

Less developed nations are the have-not nations of the world. These nations are usually poor in natural resources or have been exploited by other nations. Often the population is more worried about producing enough food to feed itself today than about its future economic development.

Trade patterns

Most international trade occurs among the developed nations of the world. The United States is both the largest buyer and the largest

TABLE 9–4
Top ten U.S. trading
partners, export and
import, 1975 (in $ millions)

Exports		Imports	
Canada	$21,759	Canada	$21,747
Japan	9,565	Japan	11,268
West Germany	5,194	West Germany	5,382
Mexico	5,144	United Kingdom	3,784
United Kingdom	4,525	Venezuela	3,624
The Netherlands	4,183	Nigeria	3,282
Iran	3,242	Mexico	3,059
Brazil	3,056	Saudi Arabia	2,625
France	3,031	Italy	2,397
Italy	2,867	Indonesia	2,221

Source: U.S. Department of Commerce; and Domestic and International Business Administration, *Overseas Business Reports, 1976.*

seller of goods and services in the international marketplace. But the rate of economic development worldwide is accelerating. As a nation becomes more developed economically, it becomes a better customer for the goods sold by other nations (see Table 9–4).

SUMMARY

A market is a cluster of people with similar needs and the economic strength to meet those needs. The people must have purchasing power and the willingness and authority to spend it to meet their needs. The objective of business activity is to satisfy at least one target market.

Consumer markets are made up of people who buy goods and services to meet their own needs or the needs of individuals with whom they associate. Consumers buy goods in order to benefit from the utilities offered by those goods. Industrial buyers intend to use the goods and services they purchase to conduct their businesses. This may involve reselling the goods, processing the goods into other goods and services for sale, or using them in normal business operations. The various levels of government represent markets for goods and services that are necessary to provide for the defense and governance of the population. But not all the goods and services sold by firms within the United States are used in this country. Consumers, industrial buyers, and government officials of other countries constitute multinational markets. These markets are forever changing.

In attempting to serve the needs of their markets, sellers must be alert to changes that affect either the level or the nature of the needs of their markets. In consumer markets some of the important indicators of needs are rate of population growth, level and distribution of income, age distribution, and family status. In general, the size of our population has been growing at a slower rate than in the past, although certain groups such as senior citizens are increasing more rapidly. Income is constantly rising. As the size of the average family declines, there are more households demanding more goods and services. These increasing demands are reflected in increased purchasing on the part of both business and government.

REVIEW QUESTIONS

1. Define the term *market*. Then identify three groups of people and explain why each qualifies as a market.

2. How do consumer, industrial, government, and multinational markets differ?

3. Explain the differences in spending patterns between lower-income and upper-income consumers.

4. Discuss the expected effects on the consumer market of a shift in the U.S. population toward a larger percentage of single adults.

5. Discuss the difference between derived demand and common demand. Give three examples of each.

6. In understanding consumer markets, why might a seller use information on an SMSA rather than information on an individual city or an entire state?

7. How does consumer credit affect income? How does it affect spending behavior? What is the value of credit to the consumer?

8. You could think of your household as similar to a business. For each of the seven types of industrial goods, identify a comparable household good.

9. Think about a major consumer product. Try to develop a complete list of the transactions that probably took place to make that product possible. Be sure to consider materials, tools, services, and other necessary functions.

10. The government has a number of objectives in its buying activities. Specify those objectives and discuss ways in which they might result in conflict.

CASES

Case 9–1.   Textbooks aren't the only things to read

In 1978 Americans spent $5.5 billion on 1.4 billion books in more than 12,000 bookstores. Magazines sold 263 million issues for a total of $4 billion. Americans spent $14.6 billion on newspapers. The per capita figures were $23.80 on books, $18 on magazines, and $62.60 on newspapers.

B. Dalton Booksellers, the nation's largest bookstore chain, opened new stores at the rate of one a week. There were almost 200 separate bookclubs selling books through the mail. Some of these specialize in science fiction, religion, or mysteries. Books are available in supermarkets, drug and discount stores, airport shops, and college bookstores. And

with all these printed words, about one out of every five Americans is functionally illiterate—cannot read the directions on a can of soup.

1. *Make a list of five kinds of books, five kinds of magazines, and three kinds of newspapers. Describe the characteristics of the people in the market for each. Don't forget the industrial market.*

2. *How much did you spend on books in the past year—both texts and nontext books? What are the characteristics of the people who are part of the consumer book market?*

Case 9–2. The city might be a good customer

When Kathy Kordas graduated from school, she turned her interest in sports into a business. The physical fitness craze was in full swing. Kathy believed that the time was right to open a store that specialized in athletic shoes. It took a little while to get things organized and running smoothly, but after two years in the business Kathy had established good relations with the major athletic shoe manufacturers and had built up a respectable level of business. One of the ideas that had turned out well was to offer a 10 percent discount card to members of the local youth soccer league teams.

Then Kathy started to think about the school teams. They needed shoes, too. The problem was that this would mean dealing with the school system instead of individual consumers. Kathy knew that it could mean a lot of sales, but she was reluctant to deal with a government customer.

1. What are the risks Kathy faces if she tries to do business with a unit of government?
2. What information does Kathy need to help her decide what to do?

chapter 10
ASSESSING CONSUMER BEHAVIOR

By studying this chapter you should be able
to find answers to these questions:

1 What is the consumer buying process?
2 What is meant by hierarchy of needs?
3 How do social forces affect consumer behavior?
4 Why do business firms undertake marketing research?
5 What are the steps in the marketing research process?
6 What are secondary data, where do they come from, and why are they used?
7 What are primary data and how are they collected?

Terms you should know:

consumer buying process
culture
experimentation
family
focus group
hierarchy of needs
marketing research
observation method
panel
primary data
reference group
secondary data
social class
subculture
survey
test market

onsumers spend over a quarter of a billion dollars on mouthwash every year in the United States. Most of the products on the market consist of a pinch of flavoring and dye added to a blend of water, alcohol, and glycerin. Listerine is amber, Lavoris is red, and Listermint is green. Recently Micrin, which once accounted for one of every seven bottles sold, was taken off the market. It had been floundering among the also-rans with less than 1 percent of total mouthwash sales. In attempting to explain Micrin's lack of consumer acceptance, one advertising executive suggested that there never had been a successful blue mouthwash.[1]

Do consumers really select mouthwash on the basis of color? What causes some people to buy one brand while others swear by a different one? Is it taste? Is it price? Maybe some people buy a particular brand because they believe that it will keep them healthy. Some people may be seeking to increase their sex appeal.

Consumer behavior is not simple. A purchase is really only part of a complex process. Let's first look at that consumer buying process, then discuss the social influences that affect consumer behavior, and finally investigate the efforts of businesspeople to understand better the needs and motives that shape consumer behavior.

THE CONSUMER BUYING PROCESS

Your task as a consumer is to try to do the best job of meeting your needs within your limited budget. Like most people, you probably find that your needs are greater than the resources you have to meet those needs. So you make some effort to make the right purchases—the ones that will bring you the greatest satisfaction. Of course, the amount of effort you put into any purchase decision depends on the importance of that decision. If something costs a lot of money, will last a long time, or is likely to be noticed by others, it usually rates more purchasing effort. Most people spend a lot more time buying a car than a candy bar.

A five-step process

The normal five-step **consumer buying process** is shown in Figure 10–1. Let's imagine that you are going to buy a car and see how these steps relate to that purchase. To start the process, you must become aware of your need for a car. It may not be a pressing need. In fact, it may not even be a need in the strict sense. Without this new car, you would continue to exist. Perhaps you just want a new car. But something gets you started thinking about cars.

This moves you to the next step—you seek information. You have some internal sources of information. You already know something about cars and the local dealerships. Maybe you have bought a car

244

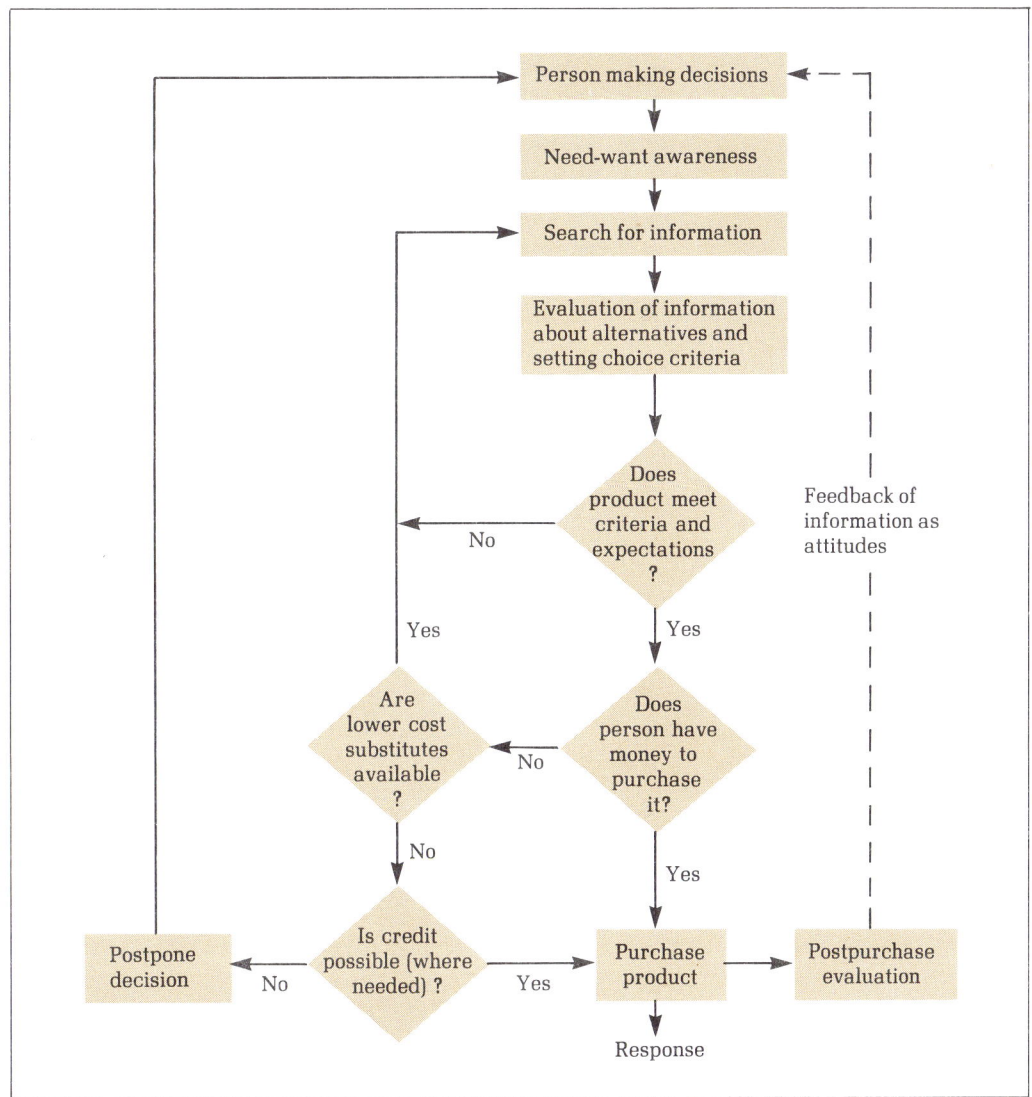

Source: E. Jerome McCarthy, *Basic Marketing,* 6th ed. (Homewood, Ill.: Richard D. Irwin, 1978), p. 164. © 1978 by Richard D. Irwin, Inc.

FIGURE 10–1
Consumer buying process

before. Maybe you have helped a friend or relative to buy a car. You may turn to external sources of information such as specification sheets supplied by the automobile companies and reports in automotive magazines. You may turn to personal sources such as friends for information and advice.

When you feel you have enough information, you move to the evaluation and choice step. You might mentally list the factors that are most important to you in your selection of a model or a dealer.

In the fourth step you make a decision and act on that decision. You may even decide not to buy any car. Regardless of your decision, the buying process is not over yet.

You begin to evaluate your decision. You may feel a little uncomfortable. Perhaps you drive to a friend's house to show off your new car, hoping that your friend will approve. You may watch car commercials even more closely than you did before the purchase and pay special attention to any positive reports on the type of car you bought. You store all of this information in your mind to be remembered the next time you need a new car.

Do you go through this process to buy that candy bar? Probably not. First of all, even if you made the wrong decision it wouldn't make a lot of difference in your life. And, since you have bought candy before, you have information stored away that allows you to make a quick decision. In fact, you have various amounts of information on thousands of buying decisions you make in your role as a consumer. In some cases this information is accurate, factual, and complete. In other cases you make decisions based on incomplete information, biased perceptions, and habit. There are even some purchase decisions in which accurate, factual, and complete information is unavailable.

Individual consumers have different tastes and preferences. While a manufacturer can list the fiber content, care instructions, and size on a pair of jeans, there are no facts about your preference for the

Different people have different needs

"Is there any brand that will give my kids LESS energy?"

Reprinted by permission *The Wall Street Journal.*

style. In most purchases there is some need to make personal judgments. Different people use different standards in making those judgments. Even if those judgments are made on the basis of incomplete information, biased perceptions, and habits, they are the best judgments if they result in your satisfaction. Some people are willing to pay a premium to be the first ones to drive the new models of automobiles each year. Other people snap up the previous year's models at reduced prices. Different people are trying to satisfy different needs.

A hierarchy of needs

All people have the same basic needs. These have been placed in rank order by Abraham Maslow into a **hierarchy of needs** (see Figure 10–2). People tend to start at the bottom of the hierarchy and focus their efforts on meeting their needs to a reasonable degree at each step before moving up to the next set of needs.

The most basic of all human needs is the need to maintain life, the **physiological need.** This need is continuous; it must be attended to daily. If it is not satisfied, other needs become unimportant. If you are hungry, thirsty, or cold, you will direct your attention toward food, water, or shelter. If your physiological needs are being met on a day-to-day basis, you can move to the next step.

Safety needs include the needs for security, stability, and protection from physical harm or danger. You are taking some precautions that your physiological needs will be met in the future. You may buy insurance or put money in a savings account. One of the values of your education is that it will increase the chances that you will be able to support yourself. The idea is to try to protect yourself against unpleasant surprises.

FIGURE 10–2
Maslow's hierarchy of needs

Self-actualization

Esteem

Belongingness and love

Safety

Physiological

JOE GIRARD

If I could do it, starting from where I did, anybody can.

Joe Girard has been listed as the "World's Greatest Salesman" in the *Guinness Book of World Records* for more than 11 years. He reached that point after having been thrown out of high school, fired from more than 40 jobs, tossed out of the army, and failing as a petty thief. In desperation, with no place to turn to earn enough to feed his family, he convinced a Detroit Chevrolet dealer to hire him as a auto- mobile salesman. He now makes over $200,000 a year in gross commissions.

Joe has a lot of techniques that account for his extraordinary success. He makes a serious effort to maintain contact with his customers. Each month he sends out a card or letter to each of the thousands of past customers on his mailing list. That customer may return later to buy another car but, more important, each customer has about 250 friends and relatives. Joe feels that a satisfied buyer is the best advertising. He pays past customers, barbers, department store clerks, and anyone else who deals with the public a bonus of $25 for each customer they direct to him.

Joe has been successful because he has seriously studied his market and has been willing to experiment with techniques to satisfy that market. He tells his story in the book *How to Sell Anything to Anybody* (Warner Books, 1977).

When you feel comfortable that your physical needs will be met on a continuing basis, you are more able to focus on your **social needs** for belonging and love. We all need to give and receive affection. This need for acceptance and association is a strong force in society. It is basic to the establishment of rules of social conduct and patterns of social organization.

Beyond the need for social acceptance are **esteem needs.** To fulfill these needs requires a sense of self-worth or achievement. This leads to a feeling of being respected by others. People who seek to be leaders or to receive recognition are trying to satisfy their esteem needs.

At the top of the hierarchy is the need for **self-actualization.** This is the need to totally utilize your abilities. It is the need that drives some people like Bruce Jenner through every grueling day of training to win the Olympic decathlon or Shirley Temple Black to serve as ambassador to Ghana when she needed neither the fame nor the money.

Most people are constantly striving to satisfy their lower-level needs and to move toward higher levels of the hierarchy. They seek out products and services that they believe will help them to meet their needs.

Individuals translate these general needs into very specific needs. The specific needs you define and the solutions you choose are in part determined by social influences.

SOCIAL INFLUENCES ON CONSUMER BEHAVIOR

The socialization process began to work on you the minute you were born and will continue throughout your life. All of us have been exposed to a variety of social influences that will affect the ways we choose to meet our needs. We are all individuals, yet we conform to behaviors found in our society. We are influenced by the norms or rules of the social groups to which we belong (see Figure 10–3). Some of these influences are broad and general. The culture, subculture, and social class provide general guidelines to acceptable behavior. Reference groups and the family tend to exercise more specific influence over our behavior.

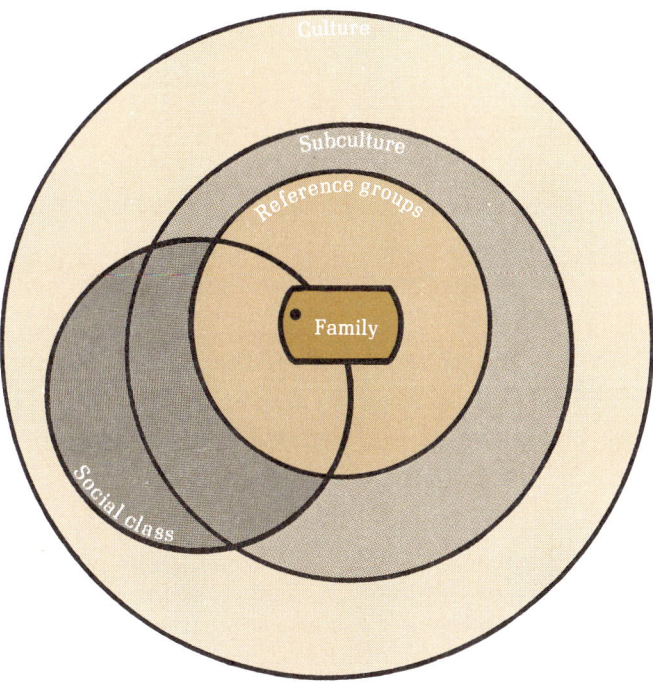

FIGURE 10–3
Concentric rings of social influence

Culture

Culture is an accumulation of solutions to basic human questions. Every culture combines five basic elements. **Technology** is the state of industrial arts. Technology answers the question of how to provide for the physical needs of the population. **Social institutions** such as the family and the educational and legal systems clarify how people are supposed to relate to one another and pass on the culture to children. A **language** serves as the vehicle for communication. **Religion** helps us to explain that which we do not fully understand. Finally, **aesthetics** provide enjoyment. Music, art, and dance are answers to the question of how to enjoy life.

The answers to these questions vary among cultures. One of the important determinants of the answers are the resources available to a group of people. We eat beef because our geography is suited to raising cattle. The Japanese and English eat seafood because they have very little land and lots of ocean. As the answers are handed from generation to generation, the origin of a practice is sometimes obscured. Many of the answers become formalized as laws or regulations.

"You fancy a bucket of penguin?"

Reprinted with permission from the May 16, 1977 issue of *Advertising Age*. Copyright 1977 by Crain Communications, Inc.

Culture sets the outside limits on acceptable behavior. These limits change very slowly in response to changes in the environment. All of the elements of a culture are related, so a change in one often produces changes in another. It's not always clear where the change began. Has the availability of convenience foods, labor-saving devices, and other technological change led to a changing role for women in this society? Maybe the changing role of women created the demand for goods and services to support a different family lifestyle. We know that the culture is slowly and constantly changing, but the rate of change is not the same among all groups.

Subcultures

Within each culture there are subcultures. **Subcultures** are groups that accept the same basic social guidelines but take a slightly different approach within those guidelines. Subcultures often develop out of religious or ethnic similarities. Attitudes of these subcultures may be reflected in choices of foods or clothing, social and recreational activities, and other practices that affect consumer behavior. For example, members of the Church of Jesus Christ of Latter-Day Saints, the Mormons, do not drink coffee, cola, or alcohol, or smoke. They also place great emphasis on the family. The values and attitudes of the subculture certainly affect the consumer behavior of the Mormons.

DID YOU EVER WONDER?

Buying behaviors differ among families. But as you can see from the table, there are some things that most of us have in common.

Product	Percent of wired homes	Product	Percent of wired homes
Refrigerator	99.9	Calculator	92.7
Black-and-white TV	99.9	Color TV	81.3
Radio	99.9	Washing machine	73.3
Toaster	99.9	Electric dryer	59.3
Vacuum cleaner	99.9	Blender	50.0
Iron	99.9	Hamburger maker	15.6
Coffee maker	99.9	Bag sealer	10.6
		Microwave oven	7.5

Social class

A **social class** is a segment of a society made up of people with similar social and economic status. Social classes are often defined in terms of family background, amount of income, and occupation. Members of a social class tend to associate with other members of that class and to develop similar patterns. The idea of social class tends to generate value judgments that are contrary to the principles of equality. But there is no evidence that a person is a better person for belonging to one social class rather than another.

Early research into social classes resulted in the definition of six groups. The characteristics associated with membership in each class are shown in Table 10–1.

In the past, social classes were studied very carefully in attempts to predict consumer behavior. But today social class may have less

TABLE 10–1
Social class characteristics

Class	Characteristics
Upper upper	Social elite of the society, inherited wealth
Lower upper	Very high income professionals, earned position and wealth
Upper middle	Professionals with good incomes, well-educated
Lower middle	Skilled working people, home and family oriented
Upper lower	Semiskilled and unskilled labor, lower income but stable lifestyle
Lower lower	Unemployed, low income, transient lifestyle

influence on consumer behavior for several reasons. First, as our population has become more mobile, a person's status in the community is less likely to be defined by the status of parents and grandparents. Second, the widespread availability of education has eased the transition from one social class to another. Third, television has increased communications and hence the similarities among classes. Finally, the vast majority of Americans are concentrated in the middle-class range. This is not to say that America is a classless society, but social class is not as useful as it once was as an indicator of consumer behavior.

Reference group

A **reference group** is a collection of people to which you look for guidance as to appropriate behavior. There are two types: aspiration groups and actual reference groups. The difference lies in whether or not you see yourself as a member of the group.

An **aspiration group** consists of people with whom you would like to be associated. You may adopt the dress or speech patterns of people in the group in hopes of being accepted. When people go to job interviews, they try to dress and act in a way that makes them seem more like people who already have that kind of job. Middle-aged weekend athletes dress in clothes that have been endorsed by their golf or tennis idols. Magazines run special features on the favorite recipes of famous people so that others can eat the same things as the people they admire. Even though you don't belong to that group, the behaviors of the people within that group affect your behavior.

An **actual reference group** is the group to which you belong. You are an accepted member of the group. It may be as simple as a group of students who regularly study together, or it may involve formal membership in an organization such as a labor union. Some of your behaviors as a consumer are influenced by your reference groups. If all your friends are going skiing, you might be influenced to go along. If a certain behavior becomes popular, many people will adopt it just to be part of the group. Every generation has had its fads. More important than keeping people warm, raccoon coats, black leather jackets, ski parkas, and Levis jackets have served as uniforms for young people.

Most people have multiple reference groups. You might adjust your behaviors slightly as you go from school to work to your home. It is not unusual that a student who has to wear business clothes to work will hurry to change into jeans before going to class. While jeans may be more comfortable, at least part of the reason is to fit in with the other students.

While you may switch reference groups over time, the effects of your contact with one particular group lingers. That group is your family.

The family

By **family** we mean the household within which you were raised. There are many ways in which your family's influence on you differs from that of larger or more distant reference groups. Your family was probably your first and most persistent reference group. According to psychologists, most of your basic values and attitudes were well established before you started school. During that time, most of a child's hours are spent with relatives. Even the children of working parents experience most of their human contacts with their parents. Your family has probably been important both to the development of your attitudes and values and to your concept of your role in the buying process.

The effect of family influence becomes very obvious when two people marry. Patterns of behavior that are familiar to one of the partners may be very strange to the other. In some families buying decisions are democratic. Everyone gets a chance to express an opinion, even the children. In other families the major decisions are made by one parent or the other. If you grew up in one environment, you may have difficulty adjusting to a different pattern. Besides that, your family helped you to develop some habits and preferences. If, as a child, you were continuously exposed to the same brand of ketchup, cleanser, or other household products, the chances are very good that you will buy those brands as an adult. Without good reason for change, most people tend to stay with the familiar.

Consumers are subject to a variety of influences as they face buying decisions. The overall culture defines the outside limits, but within those limits different people make different choices based on their own needs and the values and attitudes they have learned. The subcultures and social classes provide general guidelines, but for more specific learning experiences we depend on our reference groups and families.

THE NEED FOR MARKET INFORMATION

Businesspeople who are trying to develop products and services to meet the needs of consumers could focus on our differences. Each of us has had a unique package of learning experiences, so no two consumers are identical. To study the differences might be interesting, but it would be less useful than studying the similarities. Companies need information on the market. They use marketing research to uncover behaviors and preferences that are common to a group of consumers.

Marketing research is more than collecting statistics on consumers. **Marketing research** is the effort taken by a business firm to learn more about its present and potential customers. Businesses undertake marketing research to reduce the risk involved in making decisions. Each time a business firm makes a decision to produce a product, it is facing the possibility of wasting its resources.

The reason for marketing research

Each year American business pumps billions of dollars into researching markets. The reason is fairly clear. The failure to understand the market can be very serious. DuPont poured over $100 million into the development of Corfam, a substitute for leather. After only a few years, however, the product was taken off the market. While there are a number of reasons, one is that DuPont misjudged consumer behavior. Despite DuPont's efforts to change their habits, people bought Corfam shoes in a size that was just a little snug. After all, leather shoes stretch. Unfortunately, Corfam didn't stretch!

Campbell's Soup failed to correctly assess consumer behavior and lost millions on its Red Kettle Soups. These dry soup mixes had great ratings on flavor and some other qualities, but they took 15 minutes to prepare. A generation of Americans who were used to adding a can of water and heating soup to eating temperature in less than 3 minutes rejected the Red Kettle Soup Mixes.

A big firm may lose a lot of money on one mistake. But even smaller losses can be very serious to a small business. One out of every two new small businesses in this country fails to survive its first two years. An inadequate understanding of the market is one of the principal causes of these failures.

A superior understanding of consumer behavior has been the key to many notable business success stories. Ray Kroc noticed that although parents paid the bill, the family tended to eat at a restaurant where the kids were happy and behaved well. So he developed some techniques to attract children to McDonald's. One was simply to put the straw dispenser where children could help themselves. They used more straws, but they brought their parents back.

The Florida Citrus Commission was interested in increasing the average consumption of orange juice. Although orange juice was less expensive than some other beverages, consumers were treating it as something precious. They drank it out of small glasses and limited themselves to one glass at breakfast. Careful marketing research revealed that this behavior was related to the size of the can. When the producers introduced 12-, 18-, and finally 24-ounce cans of concentrate, per capita orange juice consumption increased dramatically.

Consumers don't buy products because they should or in order to keep DuPont, Campbells, or any other firm in business. They act in their own best interest as they see it. They buy because a product or service meets their needs and is available when, where, and how they want it at a price they are willing to pay. Through market research, a firm can increase its chances of success in meeting those needs.

How much should be spent on research?

Research can be expensive. How much should a firm invest in research? The answer depends on how much the firm stands to gain from making the right decision. Imagine that you were going to bet on a ballgame. If your team won, you could win $100, but if your team lost, you would lose $100. How much better off would you be for winning? Assuming that you are determined to place a bet, the difference would be $200. Instead of being out $100, you would be ahead $100. Therefore, you should be willing to pay up to $199.99 for perfect information on the future outcome of the game.

But there are three problems. First of all, you could probably think of a better use for $199.99. Second, you may not be able to find anyone with the information on the outcome of the game even if you were willing to pay for it. Third, if someone offered to sell you that information, what guarantee would you have that the information was accurate?

These same problems limit the amount that businesses are willing to invest in research. First, research is only one of the ways in which a firm could spend its money. Someone has to decide whether it is better to spend the firm's money on marketing research, advertising, pollution control equipment, or salaries. There are usually more uses for money than there is money. Second, some information is not available no matter what a firm might be willing to pay. There is some information that is simply inaccessible. Third, there is no guarantee that the information gathered through marketing research is perfect information. Marketing research can show only what might be expected in the future.

THE MARKETING RESEARCH PROCESS

The objective of marketing research is to come up with the most useful information on the market given the amount of time and money available. This involves more than grinding out data. The difference between information and data is that information is useful; it informs. Data are simply numbers or facts that have been assembled. Not all data become information.

The process and the techniques in marketing research are the same as research in any other field. In fact, market researchers have borrowed many of their techniques from researchers in the physical and

FIGURE 10–4
The marketing research process

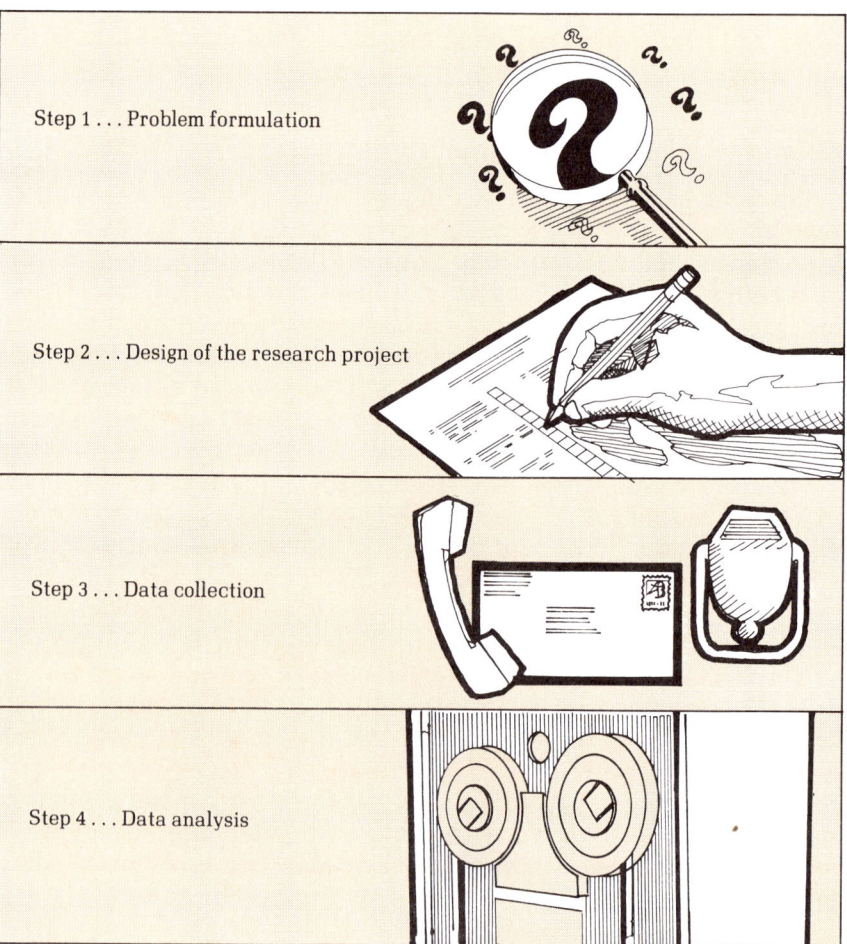

Step 1 . . . Problem formulation

Step 2 . . . Design of the research project

Step 3 . . . Data collection

Step 4 . . . Data analysis

social sciences. Research that is conducted in an organized and logical manner is far more likely to produce the desired information. Each step in the research process builds upon the step preceding it. The process begins with the formulation of the research problem. It moves to the development of a research design, then to the actual data collection according to the plan. The next step is the analysis of that data. The final step is the preparation of the research report with the desired information. See Figure 10–4 for a diagram of this process.

The formulation of a research problem

A problem is a situation involving uncertainty or doubt. A marketing research problem may involve any question about the firm's approach to the market. But not all questions merit research. To be worthy of research, there must be some choices available to the firm. If there is nothing that can be done about an unfortunate reality, it makes little sense to waste money on research. When the federal government banned the use of cyclamates, there was no reason for the cyclamate-sweetened food processors to research the reaction of consumers to the ban. They had no choice but to stop production.

Of course, the alternatives could be pleasant. A firm might have a product with many saleable features, so it could conduct research to determine which of the features should be stressed in promotions. In the problem formulation stage of research, the purpose is to clearly define the questions to be answered. One of the dangers in research is a miscommunication between the people who need the information and the researchers.

Sometimes the most obvious problem is only a symptom of another more important problem. For example, an inner-city retailer who is concerned about a decline in sales might research the prices offered by competitors in the area. The problem may really be that the customers are moving to the suburbs. Researching the wrong questions can lead only to inappropriate answers. Once the problem has been carefully defined, it is possible to develop a plan for the research.

Developing the research plan

A research plan specifies the kind of data that are needed and how and where they will be collected. Researchers use two general types of data: primary and secondary. **Primary data** are new data being collected for the specific purposes of this research project. **Secondary data** exist on file from some previous study, were collected for some other purpose, or were collected by another organization. Some research plans call for only primary or only secondary data, but most plans involve some combination.

Secondary data. It is wise to investigate available sources of secondary data before attempting to collect primary data. Why would researchers want to reuse data when they could collect new fresh data? If used properly, secondary data offer many advantages. One advantage is cost. There are many sources of very inexpensive secondary data. The U.S. government is one of the most active collectors of data in the world. The government printing offices spew forth reams of data daily. Most of these are available free at the public library.

There are also companies that specialize in collecting data for other companies. Even though they are selling these data for a profit, using these data is often less expensive than it would be for a firm to collect the data for itself. While it costs just as much for the specialized data

THE U.S. BUREAU OF THE CENSUS

The Bureau of the Census is the principal fact-gathering and statistics-publishing agency of the U.S. government. It gathers information at specific intervals on the following subjects:

Population and housing	Retail trade
Agriculture	Wholesale trade
Governments	Selected service industries
Manufacturers	Transportation
Mineral industries	Construction

A census of the population has been taken every ten years since 1790. While the initial purpose was to count noses simply to fairly allocate the seats in Congress, Thomas Jefferson pushed for the idea that the opportunity to learn more about the population should not be wasted. The data collected include age, race, education, residence, occupation, income, and many other facts that are important to government, social, and business organizations seeking to serve the public.

As the population grows, the task of collecting information becomes more complex. The need to compile census data quickly and accurately was an important stimulant to the development of the computer industry in the 1940s. In 1910 the bureau experimented with self-completed mail questionnaires to replace door-to-door interviewers. It was a dismal failure and was abandoned. But a full-scale mail test in 1970 was so successful that they began to plan to make full use of mail questionnaires in the 1980 census.

Other than the population sign on the edge of town, you may have little direct contact with the census, but it has a great effect on your life. It serves as the basis for the distribution of federal funds for important social and educational programs. It affects your voice in the federal government. And, of course, it helps the business community to be more efficient in meeting your needs.

RESEARCHERS DON'T ALWAYS AGREE

During the Vietnam War the military made extensive use of defoliants. These chemicals had been developed for the military by commercial chemical companies. One such chemical, 2,4,5-trichloroperoxyacetic acid, better known as 2,4,5-t, later became very popular as a domestic herbicide and weed killer.

In 1966 the Bionetics Research Laboratories of Bethesda, Maryland, released a report based on three years of study stating that 2,4,5-t had been shown to cause birth defects in mice. After three more years of testing, the Department of Agriculture stated that it "appeared probable that the cause was not the 2,4,5-t itself, but a contaminant in the chemical called dioxin." Dow Chemical developed a dioxin-free 2,4,5-t and tested its possible birth defect problem. Dow's tests showed no problems, but later government tests showed that the new chemical was also a probable cause of birth defects. Which results were valid?

There are several potential problems in research. These lie mostly in the scope, terminology, and methodology of research. Dow was testing for particular types of effects. The government tested for a wider range of problems. Dow used different doses than were used by the government researchers. Neither researchers were lying—they were simply conducting different research projects!

---

gatherers to collect the data, that cost is being shared by several firms.

Not only are secondary data less expensive, but they are also more readily available. On the average it takes six weeks to complete a primary research project. Compare that with how long it takes you to go to the public library.

A third reason firms use secondary data is that there may be no other choice. Some information is not available in any other form. What if you were interested in some historical fact on the population? There are also some things that people will not tell just anybody but are required to report to the government. Taxable income is an example.

There are a variety of secondary data sources. These sources are very important to the smaller firm that is less likely to have the money or personnel to conduct its own research. *Sales and Marketing Management* magazine publishes an annual "Survey of Buying Power" with data on population and spending patterns by city, county, and state. The business section of the library has a wealth of other useful information.

None of the benefits of secondary data applies, however, unless the data meet two tests: usefulness and reliability. The data may be too old to be useful. A report on eating habits in 1940 might be of little use to a person opening a restaurant today. Some data cannot be trusted. Sometimes the sources have a particular point to make or a vested interest to protect.

In some cases secondary data are all that a firm needs to reduce its risk to an acceptable level. Another important use for secondary data is as a background for further primary research.

Primary data.   Primary data can provide a firm with the answers to specific, timely questions about its market. When the research plan calls for primary data, data are usually collected from a sample. A **sample** is a small section that is supposed to represent the whole thing. It would be prohibitive for a researcher to collect data on every person in the market, so data are collected from a small group of people who are supposed to be representative. Clearly, the value of the results hinges on the degree to which the sample represents the whole market.

A classic mistake occurred just before the presidential election of 1936. A popular magazine of the times, *The Literary Digest,* took a poll and predicted that Alfred M. Landon would win over Roosevelt.[2] Are you concerned because the name doesn't sound familiar? To Roosevelt's delight, election day proved that the poll was wrong. A postmortem revealed that the sample had been drawn from the telephone book and from lists of automobile owners. Apparently no one realized that in 1936 only the more wealthy citizens had telephones and automobiles but that both wealthy and nonwealthy people voted. Indeed, Roosevelt had billed himself as the representative of the common people. Public reaction actually contributed to the failure of the magazine. Today's political pollsters are far more scientific.

Data collection

Collecting primary data involves getting information from other people. While the kinds of information needed may vary widely, there are only a few ways to go about getting it. You can ask people, or you can observe their actions. You can ask or observe either in a natural environment or in an environment that has been controlled in some way. A **survey** is simply asking questions in a natural environment and counting up the responses. When we observe the people in the natural environment, we are collecting data through the **observation method.** But when we do something to change the environment before or during the time in which the data are collected, we are using different research methods. Each of the methods has great value when used properly (see Table 10–2). Let's look at these uses.

Surveys.   The survey is the most widely used marketing research method. This is because it is the most flexible. You can always ask questions. You may or may not get the very best answers, but you can always ask. If you want to know whether a person is planning

	Question	Observe
Natural environment	Survey	Observation
Controlled environment	Focus group, panel	Experiment

TABLE 10–2
Primary data collection methods

to buy a new car, you can ask. If you need to know whether a person buys one brand of cereal or another, you can ask. If you ask the right people the right questions and they are willing and able to give you accurate answers, you will come up with some helpful data.

You can ask questions in one of three ways: (1) you can list them on a questionnaire that is mailed to people in the sample; (2) you can call and ask them over the telephone; or (3) you can appear at their door or stop them in a public place. Think about the way you might react to each of these survey methods.

Researchers send out mail questionnaires for two reasons. First, it is fairly inexpensive. With modern computerized equipment, a personalized questionnaire can be mailed to thousands of people at a very reasonable cost per questionnaire. Second, the questionnaires can be mailed to anyone anywhere in the country for the same cost. A researcher in Connecticut can survey consumers in New York and Seattle at the same cost.

Unfortunately, the response rate on mail questionnaires is very low. For every three questionnaires mailed, at least two go into the trash. How often do you take the time to carefully complete a questionnaire you receive in the mail? Of course, it varies with the length of the questionnaire, gifts offered, and your interest in the subject being studied.

Surveys provide useful data when properly designed and conducted

"...She loves me ... she loves me not ... no opinion ...
she loves me ... she loves me not ... no opinion ..."

© 1977. Reprinted by permission of *Ladies Home Journal* and Orlando Busino.

Telephone interviewing has several advantages over the mail, but it is also more expensive. Telephoning is much faster than waiting for people to return mail questionnaires. The response rate is higher also. People are more likely to cooperate with a human request for a few moments to answer a few questions.

The most expensive and flexible survey technique is the personal interview. A higher response rate is only one of the advantages of this personal contact. It also allows the interviewer to ask for explanations and to record the respondent's "body language," or nonverbal expressions. The interviewer can ask more complex questions than would be possible either on the telephone or through the mail. Of course, there is also a greater chance for the biases of the interviewer to be transferred to the respondent. People tend to answer questions in a way they feel is socially acceptable or pleasing to the interviewer. If an interviewer frowns at the answer, the respondent might change that answer.

Surveys depend on the cooperation of the respondent. People must be willing to answer the questions. This cooperation is usually minimal and temporary. There are some questioning research methods that depend on higher-level and more continuing cooperation. A **panel** is a group of people who cooperate by answering the same questions on a continuing basis. For example, an organization called National Panel Diary (NPD) maintains a panel of over 150,000 families, each of which records its purchases in particular product areas. When sellers change their selling price, product, or advertising, it is possible to measure the reaction of consumers by checking for changes in the purchasing records of panel families. Obviously NPD makes every attempt to maintain a panel that is representative of the U.S. population. Panel members receive a small payment for their cooperation.

Focus groups.   A small group of people similar to the seller's target market who are brought together in a room and asked to focus on a particular issue is a **focus group.** If, for example, the seller was interested in consumer reaction to packaging cereal in cellophane bags, the group might first be asked to discuss packaging in general. After some discussion, the trained group leader would start to move the groups attention toward food products, and then on to cereals. The comments and reactions of the participants are carefully recorded either on video or audio tape. Most focus groups are conducted in special rooms equipped with one-way mirrors so that observers can watch the whole process. Focus group research is growing increasingly popular.

Some research methods are less dependent on the cooperation of the people being studied. In fact, you may have played a part in observation and experimentation research without even knowing it.

Observation.   Gathering primary data by watching people is **observation.** Sometimes the observation is done by people and sometimes by mechanical devices. Traffic engineers put traffic counters at busy corners to measure the traffic levels and traffic patterns. Market researchers measure other human patterns. What if a paper products manufacturer really was interested in whether squeezable softness was a selling feature. If it was, it would be possible to wind the paper on the roll more loosely to achieve that soft effect. By using the survey technique, researchers could ask customers in a supermarket if they squeeze toilet tissue before deciding what brand to buy. Some people might confess, others would deny it, and others might refuse to answer. The results would be muddled. Far more accurate results could be obtained by setting up a hidden camera to record the behavior of shoppers.

Each of the research methods we have discussed to this point leads to inferences. **Inferences** are conclusions reached through reasoning. If the majority of the shoppers observed selecting boxes of cereal look at the top of the box, we might infer that price is important to the cereal buyer. We don't know that to be a fact. The shoppers may be checking to see how the box is opened. But since the price is marked on the top, it seems to be a reasonable conclusion.

Experimentation.   The only research technique that allows us to establish cause is **experimentation.** Through experimentation, a researcher can come to the conclusion that one thing causes something else. If you were thinking of investing $50,000 in designing a new package, it would be comforting to know that a new package would cause consumers to buy more of your product. The general idea behind an experiment is to measure what will happen if you make some change and compare it with what will happen if you don't make the change.

Scientists in the physical sciences can perform experiments in laboratories. They take two matched groups of rats and feed one group saccharin and rat food while they feed the other group only rat food. If the first group develops a higher rate of cancer than the second group, scientists conclude that saccharin causes cancer in rats. Marketing researchers work under more difficult conditions, but the process is the same.

The most common form of experimentation in marketing research is the test market. A **test market** is a trial run on a new product or on a change in the product, package, or advertisement. It works just the same way as the rat tests. Researchers select two or more cities for the test. Some favorite test markets are listed in Figure 10–5.

These cities have particular characteristics. They tend to be isolated. They have populations that cross many age and ethnic groups. They also have their own newspapers and television and radio stations, so that trial advertising can be limited to that area. They are usually medium-sized cities with a well-mixed population. The citizens of the test market are usually unaware of the test.

If the focus group research shows that consumers responded favor-

FIGURE 10–5
The favorite test markets

Fort Wayne, Ind.	Davenport, Iowa
Albany, N.Y.	Syracuse, N.Y.
Boston, Mass.	Denver, Colo.
Indianapolis, Ind.	Detroit, Mich.
Kansas City, Mo.	Orlando, Fla.
Nashville, Tenn.	Lima, Ohio
Dallas, Tex.	Erie, Pa.
Spokane, Wash.	South Bend, Ind.
Fresno, Calif.	Louisville, Ky.
Phoenix, Ariz.	Lexington, Ky.
Grand Rapids, Mich.	Chattanooga, Tenn.
Milwaukee, Wis.	Knoxville, Tenn.
Minneapolis, Minn.	Albuquerque, N. Mex.
Des Moines, Iowa	Lubbock, Tex.

Source: Robert Levy, "The Middletowns of Marketing." Reprinted with the special permission of *Dun's Review,* July 1977. Copyright 1977, Dun & Bradstreet Publication Corporation.

ably to the cereal in the cellophane bag, the manufacturer would submit it to a test market. The very same cereal with the very same brand name would be placed on the shelves of the very same kinds of stores at the same price for the same quantity at the very same time in two different test markets. The only difference would be that in one city the cereal would be packaged in cellophane and in the other city the standard cardboard box would be used. Researchers would measure the behavior of the consumers in the two different test markets by counting the number of cases of cereal sold. If the consumers in the cellophane market bought more cereal than consumers in the box market, the researchers would conclude that the cellophane packaging caused an increase in sales.

The biggest problem with marketing research experimentation is making sure that everything but the factor being tested is the same between the two markets. If competitive cereal manufacturers were aware that a test was being conducted, they could raise or lower their prices in one of the two markets and upset the test (see Figure 10–6).

Surveys, focus groups, panels, observations, and experimentation are some of the ways in which market researchers collect data. But, to be of value, the data must be converted into information.

Data analysis

The statistical manipulation and grouping necessary to uncover similarities and patterns among the responses of various groups of respondents is **data analysis.** It can be very sophisticated or it can be as

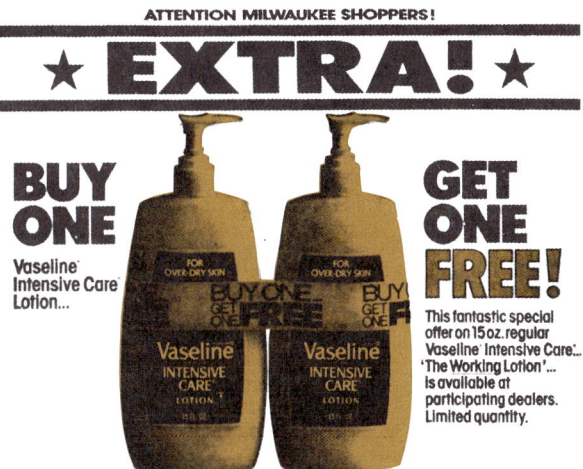

FIGURE 10–6
Competitors sometimes interfere with test markets

This half-page ad from Chesebrough-Pond's broke last week in Milwaukee newspapers, an attempt to head off Procter & Gamble's new Wondra lotion, just entering tests there. Two 15-oz. bottles are bound together for the regular price of one. William Esty Co., New York, handles Vaseline Intensive Care.

Procter & Gamble Co. is making it long-expected move into the $175,000,000 hand and body lotion business, now introducing new Wondra skin conditioning lotion into Texas and Wisconsin test markets. The product is just beginning to show up on retail shelves in Houston, Austin, and San Antonio, as well as Milwaukee, Madison, and Green Bay.

Typically, a massive advertising and promotional effort will support the effort, sources say, which appears to be specifically geared at unseating Chesebrough-Pond's Vaseline Intensive Care from its No. 1 position in the category.

In fact, Chesebrough has already started its counterattack, flooding the Milwaukee area with a buy-one, get-one-free offer for VIC, featuring two 15-oz. bottles wrapped together.

Source: Larry Edwards, ''P&G's Wondra Lotion in Test; Chesebrough Entry Fights Back.'' Reprinted with permission from the October 3, 1977 issue of *Advertising Age.* Copyright 1977 by Crain Communications, Inc.

simple as listing the number of yes and no answers to a single question. The purpose of analysis is to reach meaningful conclusions on the basis of the data. The methods used in the analysis depend on the data collection technique.

If the data were collected via survey or observation, the first step

FIGURE 10–7
Simple tabulation

A simple distribution of the responses might be enough to answer the research question. For example, a plant store owner might be interested in knowing how people learn about the store.

Question: How did you hear about this store?

Newspaper 𝚻𝚮𝚴 /
Radio 𝚻𝚮𝚴 𝚻𝚮𝚴 //
Saw it as I passed by ///
Friend or neighbor /
Referred by other store
Yellow Pages ad ////

is to **tabulate** or count up the responses. This provides a frequency distribution—a listing of the number of times each answer was given. Data are often cross-tabulated. **Cross-tabulation** is counting the answers to one question based on the answers to a second question. For example, the researchers might set up separate frequency distributions for each age group, sex, or education level.

Simple tabulation may provide the needed information. If a store owner who was concerned about the usefulness of a Yellow Pages listing surveyed customers and found that eight out of ten had located the store through the Yellow Pages, that would provide a good enough answer to the research question (see Figure 10–7).

Survey, observation, and experimental data can also be analyzed for significance. Significance tests attempt to answer the question: Have we really uncovered something or are these differences simply an accident? The data can be compared with one of many standard statistical distributions to see whether the survey has really uncovered a meaningful trend or difference. One popular method—chi-square—allows the researcher to compare the data collected with the results that were expected given the sample size and a few other factors.

Conclusions are meaningful if they help decision makers to understand the market better so that they can make better decisions. After all, the need for more information to reduce the risk involved in making decisions is the reason for the research in the first place.

SUMMARY

The consumer behavior process explains the stages through which a consumer is likely to pass when making an important buying decision.

Recognition of a need is followed by a search for information, evaluation of the alternatives, a decision and action, and finally evaluation of the outcome of the decision. Even though people have the same basic needs for physiological comfort, safety, social contact, self-esteem, and self-actualization, people choose to meet their needs in different ways.

The ways in which people define their specific needs and the actions they take to meet their needs are affected by several social forces. Among those forces are the culture, subculture, social class, reference groups, and the family. While each person is an individual, sellers attempt to define groups of people with similar needs and behavior.

Market research is the effort of sellers to better understand their markets. The purpose of research is to provide information that will reduce the risk involved in making decisions. The marketing research process is a logical and organized framework for conducting research. The first step is to clearly define the problem. Then a research plan is developed. Useful and reliable secondary data are investigated before turning to the collection of primary data. Primary data are collected through surveys, observation, panels, focus groups, and experimentation. Through data analysis, researchers hope to be able to uncover relationships that provide the information needed to aid in maing decisions.

REVIEW QUESTIONS

1. Think about your last major purchase. Prepare a list of the actions you took before and after making that purchase. How does your list compare with the five-step buying process?

2. What kind of purchases help you fulfill your needs at each level of Maslow's hierarchy of needs?

3. What are the outside limits that our culture has set on the way we meet our needs for food, clothing, and recreation?

4. Identify three subcultures and the impact each has on the food-buying behavior of its members.

5. Make a list of purchases of your actual reference groups. Do these purchases have anything in common?

6. In what ways does marketing research benefit consumers?

7. Explain the difference between primary and secondary data. When would a researcher use either secondary or primary data?

8. Have you ever been the respondent in a marketing research survey? If so, describe the subject of the study, how you were questioned, and your reactions.

9. Would your community qualify as a suitable test market? Use secondary data sources to compare your city with one of the common test market cities in terms of population size.

10. Think of some questions that a small retailer such as a clothing store owner might be able to answer through marketing research using secondary data.

CASES

Case 10–1.   The incredible edible egg

Egg consumption in the United States has been plummeting. Thirty years ago the per capita consumption was 403 eggs a year. Today the average American eats 287 eggs each year. Egg farmers are worried. The American Egg Board has mounted a $6 million advertising campaign to change the image of eggs and to educate consumers on their uses and value. The theme of the campaign has been "the incredible edible egg." The advertising stresses the egg as an inexpensive source of protein and as a versatile ingredient in many taste-tempting recipes. Changing a product's image and consumers' eating habits is not easy. It requires an understanding of how consumers view eggs and what factors are keeping them from eating more eggs.

1. *What social factors might be affecting the demand for eggs?*
2. *How does Maslow's hierarchy of needs relate to egg consumption?*
3. *How could the Egg Board learn more about the real egg-eating habits of Americans and about their real attitudes toward eggs?*

Case 10–2.   What do the consumers really want?

Even Johnny Carson wisecracks about the cost of food. But do consumers really want lower food prices or do they prefer the supermarket promotions? Acme Markets of Philadelphia plans to find out. In half of its 454 stores, all promotions will be eliminated and prices will be cut from 2¢ to 20¢ on about 600 items. The promotions and higher prices will continue in the other half of the stores. Each month the performance of the nonpromotion stores will be compared with the performance of the promotion stores. To get this program started, several decisions must be made. Should Acme alert customers to the upcoming changes? Should the nonpromotion stores be identified with a banner or sign? How should the nonpromotion stores be chosen? There may be 10,000 items in a supermarket. On what type of items should the price cuts be made? Since this test will affect the policies of the entire chain, the market research manager wants to be careful that the test is run properly.

1. *How would you answer these questions? Why?*
2. *Is this a good way to test consumers' real attitudes toward supermarket promotions? What about taking a survey?*
3. *What types of problems might interfere with the test?*

chapter
11

MARKETING
MANAGEMENT

By studying this chapter you should be able to find answers to these questions:

1 What is a marketing program?
2 Why are new products developed?
3 What does a firm consider in introducing new products?
4 What are the functions performed by packaging?
5 How does branding benefit consumers?
6 How are prices determined?
7 How do advertising media vary?
8 What is the purpose of personal selling?
9 How do middlemen earn their profits?

Terms you should know:
advertising
convenience goods
family branding
generic brand
markup
middlemen
penetration pricing
personal selling
price lining
product life cycle
resellers' brands
shopping goods
skimming pricing
specialty goods
unsought goods

T hink of all the products and services that bring you satisfaction during a normal day. You may wake up to an alarm clock manufactured in Arkansas, put on clothes from Taiwan, drink orange juice from Florida, and drive a car from Detroit. In the evening you watch a television show produced in Los Angeles, read a textbook published in Homewood, Illinois, and use toothpaste from Cincinnati. These and hundreds of other products and services are available just in case you feel the need for them.

It is no accident. This is the result of the marketing efforts of all the business firms that produce and distribute products and services to meet your needs. **Marketing** can be defined as the combination of activities directed at satisfying needs and wants through exchange processes. The purpose of marketing is to bring about transactions. Since it includes all of the deliberate efforts of firms to interact with their markets, marketing is the business activity that is most familiar to people.

Sunbeam is not trying to build up an inventory of alarm clocks at its factory in Arkansas. These clocks are being produced to be sold. You have needs that can be satisfied by some of these goods. If you need to be sure that you will wake up on time, both you and Sunbeam will benefit from a transaction. But before that transaction can take place, a number of marketing activities occur.

Marketing activities fall into four broad categories: product management, pricing, promotion, and distribution. Every firm must offer something of value to its customers. Sunbeam decided to offer clocks rather than bicycles. A magazine publisher must decide which features will attract readers. A restaurant manager might decide that a new decor will please more patrons. These are product management decisions. They affect the nature of the products and services being offered for sale.

Products are offered for sale at a price. Determining the appropriate price is a marketing activity. The price must be high enough to allow the firm to realize a return on its investment, but low enough to attract buyers. While Sunbeam can set a price on a clock, you might decide not to pay that price; then there would be no transaction.

The product must be available when and where you might buy it. Distribution activities make that possible. Distribution involves more than simply transporting a clock from Arkansas to your hometown. It involves middlemen—distributors, wholesalers, and retailers who participate in the transaction process. When you buy a Sunbeam alarm clock at your local K mart, you are dealing with a middleman.

Finally, there is the marketing activity that most people think of first—promotion. If you build a better mousetrap, the world may beat a path to your door. But then, it may not. Businesspeople promote their products and services to increase the chances of transactions.

Promotion takes many forms. The most common are advertising and personal selling.

DEVELOPING THE MARKETING PROGRAM

Marketing involves several related business activities. In the following sections each activity will be considered separately. However, it is important that you understand that these decisions are interrelated. A **marketing program** is a combination of decisions in each of these areas. It is much like a jigsaw puzzle; when the pieces fit together, the chances of success are increased (see Figure 11–1).

A marketing program is a firm's plan for approaching its target markets. It is based on an understanding of both the intended customers and the business environment. Decision makers attempt to reach the best combination of decisions on product management, price, promotion, and distribution activities.

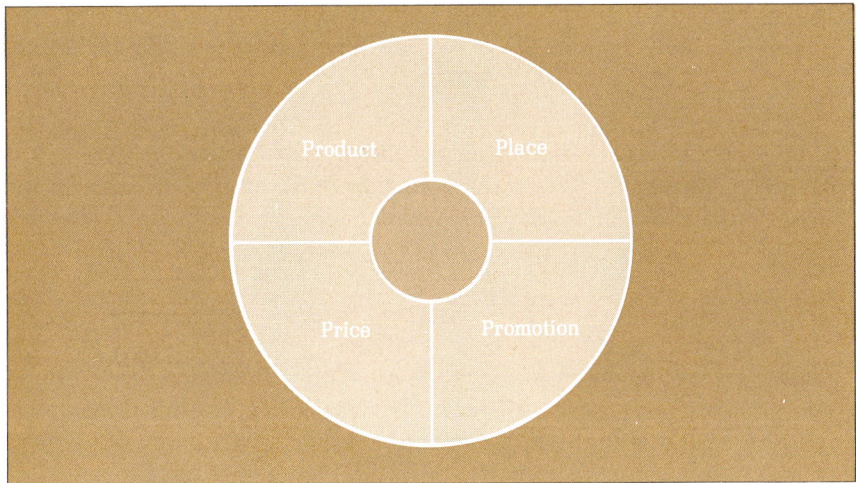

Source: E. Jerome McCarthy, *Basic Marketing*, 6th ed. (Homewood, Ill.: Richard D. Irwin), p. 40. © 1978 by Richard D. Irwin, Inc.

FIGURE 11–1
The marketing activities must fit together to meet the customer's needs.

PRODUCT MANAGEMENT ACTIVITIES

A **product** is more than a combination of metal, plastic, and glue. It is the total satisfaction you derive from your purchase. Charles Revson, the founder of the famous cosmetics firm, reportedly said, "In the factory we make cosmetics. In the store we sell hope." People don't buy just physical products; they buy the expected satisfactions of those products. Product management is determining the best way to meet the customers' needs for satisfaction.

The product is the total package of expected satisfactions.

"We feel it will convince your passengers that holding patterns actually mean more flying time for their dollars."

Source: Reprinted with permission from the August 2, 1976 issue of *Advertising Age*. Copyright 1976 by Crain Communications, Inc.

To provide these satisfactions, a firm's managers must first decide what types of products to offer and then how to package and brand those products. In the marketplace consumers react to the total product.

New product development

Every year thousands of new products and services are offered to consumers. While many of these are developed by major corporations, smaller companies and individuals also play a role. Granola was developed by an individual who later sold the rights to a major food processor. In the computer industry, there are many small businesses that press into the frontier of the technology in areas where larger firms are reluctant to assume the risks.

Introducing new products or services can be very risky. It has been estimated that eight out of every ten new products fail. But it is obvious that the parade of new products continues. Why? There are three questions involved. First, why are there new products at all? Second, why would an individual firm take the risk in introducing a new product? Finally, what is a new product?

Why are there so many new products? The basic reasons for new product development are changing consumer needs and changing technology. Consumer needs change with changes in the human environment. Some changes are social. For example, as people place a greater value on leisure and personal freedom, the demand for sports equip-

---

SUNDAY AUTO SWAP—A NEW SERVICE TO MEET AN EXISTING NEED

Have you ever wanted to sell your own car without going through a dealer? There are real problems involved. How much should you ask for it? What kinds of legal requirements must you meet? Probably the biggest problem is locating a buyer. Ginny Mills, a young woman in Sacramento, California, recognized this need and set up a service to help people sell their own cars.

First, she arranged to rent a downtown parking garage each Sunday. Then she developed a "Sell Your Own Car" kit, which includes tips on getting the car ready for sale, advice on pricing the car, and the legal papers required to complete the transaction. Finally, she advertised her service to both buyers and sellers. For $12, a seller gets the kit and the right to a space to display a car. Buyers are allowed to come in free. They show up because it gives them the opportunity to view a lot of cars in one place. It's like a giant auto flea market. Mills created a new service to meet an existing need.

---

ment, entertainment, and other health or personal development products has increased. Racquetball and hot tubs were almost unknown five years ago. Now consumer demand supports hot tub installers, equipment suppliers, and racquetball courts.

Consumer needs also change because of changes in the human physical environment. The energy shortage brought about a demand for energy-saving appliances. It also started a new industry—solar energy devices. Increased concern over water and air pollution created a market for home air and water filters. As consumer needs or preferences change, new products are developed to meet those needs.

Some new products result from changing technology. Research may lead to new products that meet long-recognized consumer needs. The need for a cure for the common cold is hardly new, yet we lack the technology to find it. Changing technology has produced products that satisfy needs that consumers always had yet were satisfied in other ways. Technology in the electronics industry has advanced to a point where functions that had required a room full of vacuum tubes can be imprinted on a tiny silicon chip. This technology led to digital watches and hand calculators. You were able to tell time and to add and subtract before, but now you can manage better.

Sometimes a change in one industry fuels changes in other industries. The widespread acceptance of easy-care synthetic fabrics in clothing led to the development of laundry detergents and equipment especially designed for these fabrics.

Why do firms respond?   Changes in consumer needs or technology underlie new product development, but why would an individual firm choose to assume the risk? Two factors are important. First, there is the recognition of opportunity. Second, there is the degree to which new products are compatible with the firm's objectives and resources.

The risk involved when Kellogg's introduces a new flavor of ready-to-eat breakfast cereal is much less than the risk faced by Sony with its Beta Max home video recorder. Shortly after Hamilton Beach introduced its Little Mac Burger Cooker, at least 15 imitations were introduced. Some firms are anxious to find new opportunities, while others play follow-the-leader. While it might be argued that any product new to a firm is a new product, most new products are imitations of established products. The question—What is a new product?—is in part explained by an idea called the product life cycle.

The product life cycle

The **product life cycle** explains the relationship between demand and profits over the market lifetime of a type of product. The demand for a product tends to increase and then decline as the product passes through the stages of its life cycle. When a product is first introduced, demand may be low because few people realize it is available. As demand grows, profits increase. But at some point demand begins to decline. Perhaps there is no longer a need for that type of product. The need for slide rules declined with the introduction of hand calculators. The stages of the life cycle are summarized in Figure 11–2.

The product life cycle does not trace the life of a single brand or model of a product. These lifetimes vary. Automobiles have been on the market for about 80 years. Sky Lab helmets had a lifetime of less than a year. There is always risk involved in introducing new products, but the risk is greater for those firms that bring out their version of a new product early in the life cycle of that type of product.

Introductory stage.   Sony introduced Beta Max during the introductory stage of the life cycle for video recorders. There was no guarantee that demand would ever reach a profitable level. Since most people were unaware of the benefits of these products, Sony had to spend over $2 million on promotion.[1] As indicated in Figure 11–2, while costs were high, sales were low. In the early years, profits were minimal.

Growth stage.   As demand grows, other producers are encouraged to offer similar products. Sony's success encouraged Zenith, RCA, and other television producers to offer video recorders. Producers entering during the growth stage avoid some of the risk encountered by the earlier entrants. They may also have the benefit of more fully understanding the need of the buyers. They may be able to improve on

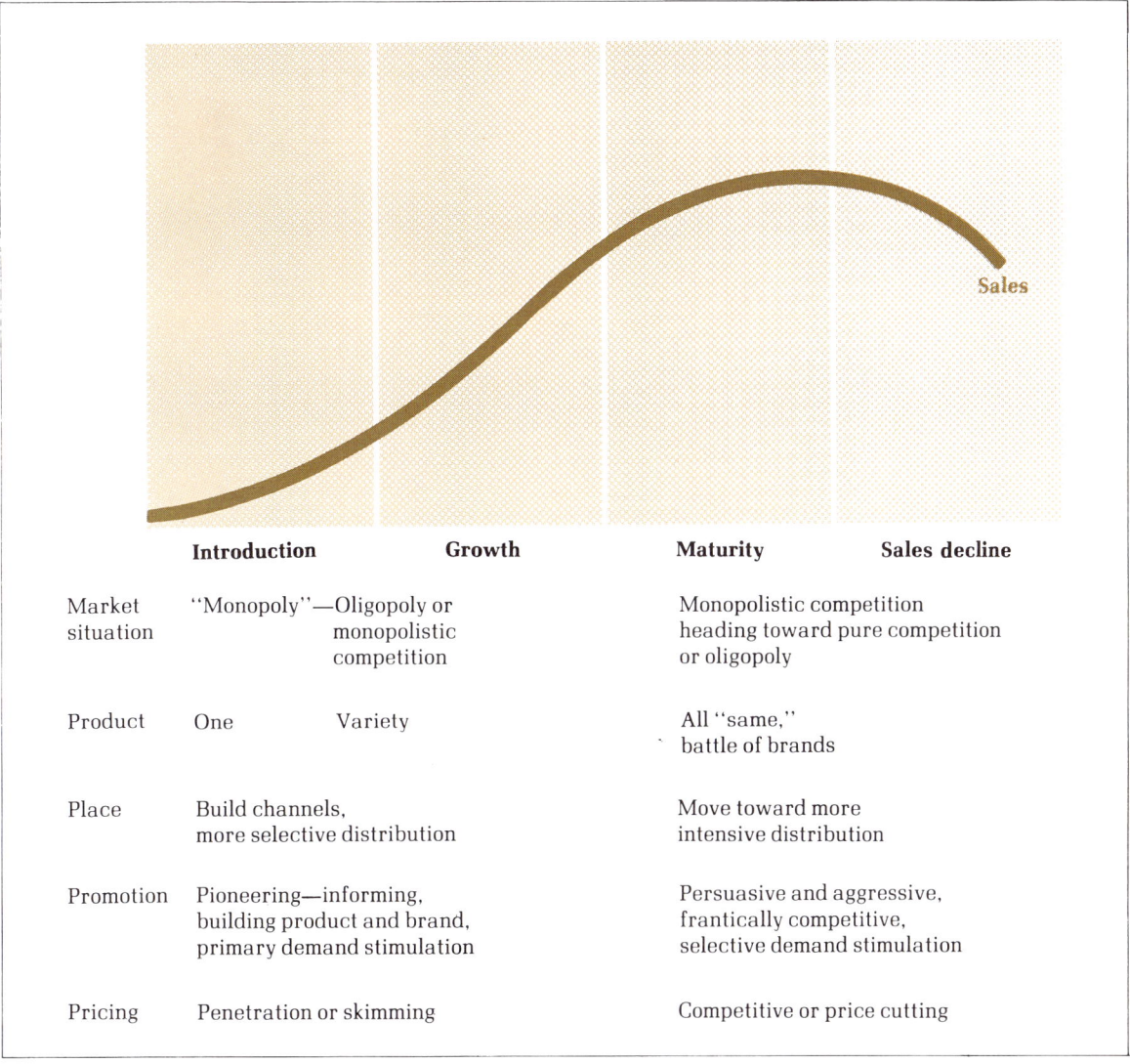

	Introduction	**Growth**	**Maturity**	**Sales decline**
Market situation	"Monopoly"—Oligopoly or monopolistic competition		Monopolistic competition heading toward pure competition or oligopoly	
Product	One	Variety	All "same," battle of brands	
Place	Build channels, more selective distribution		Move toward more intensive distribution	
Promotion	Pioneering—informing, building product and brand, primary demand stimulation		Persuasive and aggressive, frantically competitive, selective demand stimulation	
Pricing	Penetration or skimming		Competitive or price cutting	

Source: Adapted from E. Jerome McCarthy, *Basic Marketing*, 6th ed. (Homewood, Ill.: Richard D. Irwin, 1978), p. 572. © 1978 by Richard D. Irwin, Inc.

FIGURE 11–2
Typical changes in marketing variables over the course of the product life cycle

some of the features. Of course, if the first seller was very successful, competitors have to combat strong consumer loyalty.

   Maturity stage.   Products enter the maturity stage when sales stop growing. The market may be saturated. The total market for any product is like a sponge; it can absorb only so much. During the maturity stage, products may be modified to stimulate demand. Ninety-eight percent

FIGURE 11–3
**Product life cycle
extension**

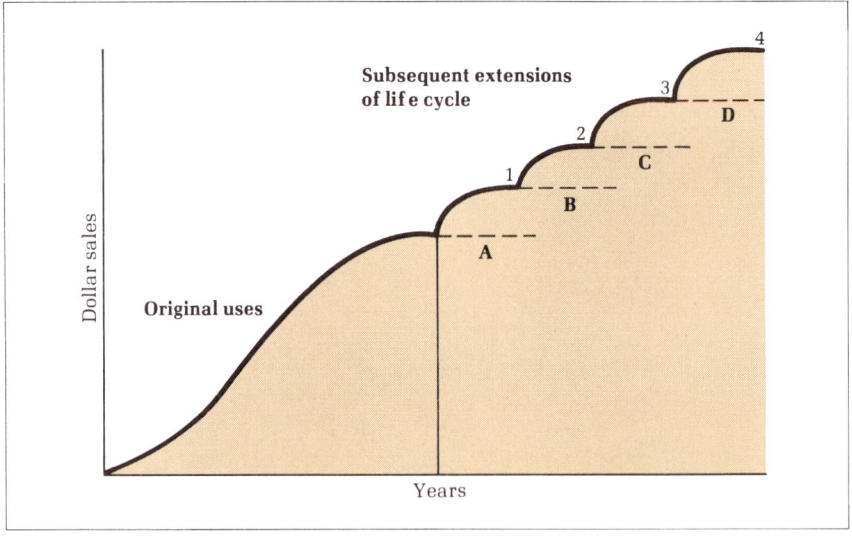

of U.S. households have a toaster. Toaster manufacturers have offered four-slice toasters, variable heat and slots for frozen pastry products, and even fashion colors to stimulate demand. These kind of changes involve little risk.

Decline stage.   In the decline stage, demand begins to slide. Some sellers drop out of the market. Others may introduce stripped-down models to sell at a lower price. Sellers may try to revitalize the market by promoting a new use of the product (see Figure 11–3). When Gerber's was worried about the declining demand for baby foods, it advertised in college newspapers that the small bottles of strained fruit and puddings made great snacks. It also promoted junior foods as convenient and nutritious light meals for senior citizens. Gerber's intention was to extend the product life cycle for these products. At the same time, Gerber's was searching for a new opportunity. Opportunity explains why a firm would develop a new product. Compatibility is important in deciding which new product to develop.

Product mix decisions

Very few firms offer a single product. Most sell some group of related products—a **product line.** Products are related because they have similar uses, are sold to the same type of customer, or are made by similar processes. A firm may offer several lines. Sunbeam sells not only alarm clocks but also kitchen clocks and decorative wall clocks. Along with clocks, Sunbeam has other lines of products. When adding new products, firms consider compatability with their existing lines.

Product line compatibility. If a firm has established a positive image in a certain market, it might introduce new products to be used by those same customers. Avon now offers jewelry along with its cosmetics to further meet the needs of its customers. Sometimes a new product or service makes use of wasted resources or by-products. A ski resort that opens its grounds to camping during the summer months is able to utilize its resources more fully.

A new product may be chosen because it needs the same type of distribution as existing products. The Hanes Hosiery Company was successful marketing L'eggs Pantyhose in supermarkets and discount stores. It has now introduced a line of cosmetics that are distributed on the same basis. Sometimes a firm will introduce new products that use the same technology as existing products. Texas Instruments introduced a line of digital watches based on its expertise in electronic circuitry.

Relationships among products can be positive. When you go to a movie theater, you expect popcorn. Levi's recently attempted to extend its very good image in casual clothing to casual shoes and socks with its Levi's for Feet. But not all relationships are so positive.

Negative relationships. Cannibalism is a negative relationship in which a firm introduces a new product with the hope of increasing its total sales, but customers see the new product as a substitute for existing products. Kodak's pocket line of cameras cannibalized its sales of standard Instamatics. Then there is the question of image. Sunbeam has an established name in electric shavers. Did you know that Sunbeam is also a leading manufacturer of animal shears? While the technology is similar, the company does not stress the relationship. In fact, it even sells the animal shears under a different brand, Shepherd. If a firm has decided to introduce a new product, one of the important decisions is how to package that product.

Packaging

Packaging adds to the satisfaction you gain from many of the products you buy. The most obvious functions of packaging are to contain and protect the product. Soda pop without a sealed container not only would run all over but would also lose its fizz. Containers for food products protect them from spoilage and contamination. Stereos are shipped with styrofoam packing to prevent damage. Small items such as Bic pens are sealed in large cardboard blister packs to protect them from shoplifters. But containment and protection are only the most obvious benefits of packaging. (See Figure 11–4.)

Packaging also adds convenience in handling and using many products. Salt comes with a shaker top, a simple dispenser. You can buy products in packages that spray, squirt, or measure their contents. Packages for products like games are designed to store the product between uses.

Some packages improve the appearance of products. Kimberly Clark packages Kleenex facial tissues in boxes that can be left in view in your home. Cosmetic manufacturers make obvious attempts to improve the appearances of their products through packaging.

Packaging can also be used for communication. Labels on packages tell you how to use the product. Labels often contain lists of ingredients or spell out the special features of the product. This information may help you to decide what to buy.

Labels provide useful information

© 1978 Universal Press Syndicate.

The type of packaging may be a factor in which product you buy or in how much you buy. Packages can be important selling tools. When soft drink bottlers switched from six-packs to eight-packs, consumption increased. Reusable packages encourage sales. L'eggs even published a booklet of craft ideas using the plastic eggs in which its pantyhose are packaged.

FIGURE 11–4
Functions of packaging

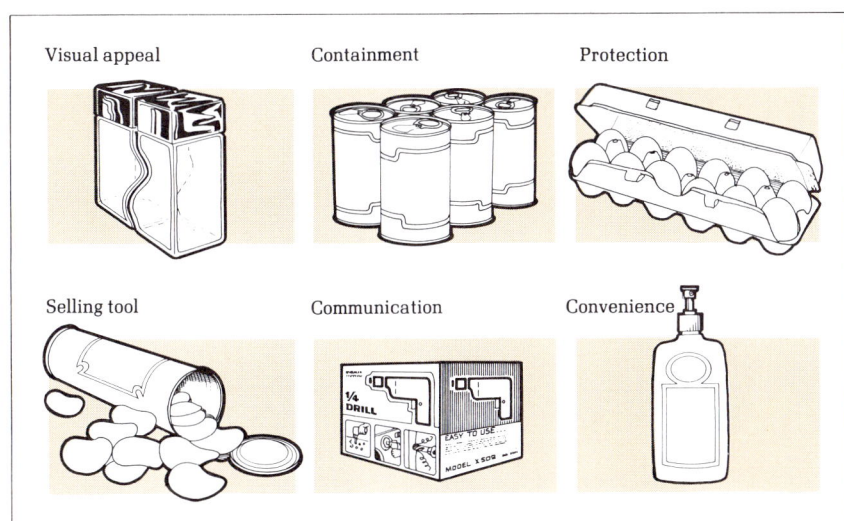

Branding

W. K. Kellogg used to inspect and sign each carton of cereal as it left his plant in Battle Creek, Michigan. Surely that sould be impossible today. However, it points out the fundamental purpose of a brand—to identify the person or organization assuming responsibility for the product or service. Branding allows you to distinguish among similar products offered by different sellers.

Since W. K. Kellogg's day, branding issues have become more complex. Both producers and consumers are concerned with brand name effectiveness, manufacturers' or resellers' brands, and brand name infringement.

Brand name effectiveness. The real test of brand name effectiveness is whether the brand name helps you to identify the products you need. If you saw a commercial for a product you wanted, you might try to find it in a store. But what would you ask for? You could identify it by its brand. If you tried the product and liked it, you could find it again in the same way. If you didn't like it, you could avoid it.

A good brand name makes identification easy. It is easy to say and easy to spell. That makes it simple to remember and use. Coke and Tide are examples. Brach's Candy is difficult to say so "BROX" is printed below the brand. A good brand name projects a positive image of the product. Kleenex on facial tissues and Frigidaire on a refrigerator offer some hint of the products' good qualities. But Frigidaire is not such a relevant brand name for the ranges and ovens offered

NO BRANDS—JEWEL STARTED IT AND OTHERS FOLLOWED

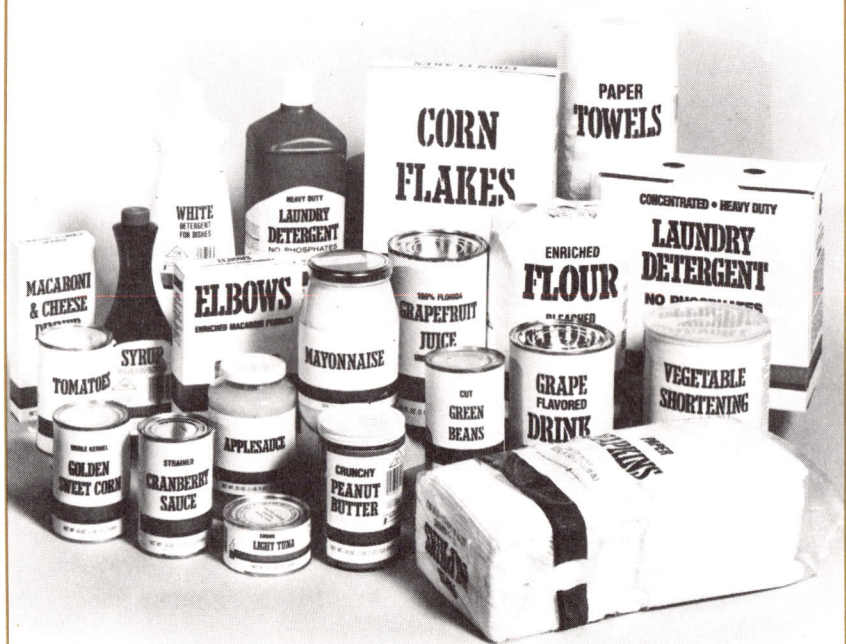

©Jewel Companies, Inc.

As inflation ate into consumers' budgets in the late 1970s, Jewel Foods, the giant Chicago-based retailer, sought a partial solution. The result was a line of "no brand name" products. Before long, other supermarket chains joined in.

The obvious feature of the no-brand line is price—a 10 to 35 percent savings over nationally advertised brands. How is this possible? There are two answers. The first is the product. While the nutritional value is the same, most generic products are the standard rather than the fancy grade. You pay less, and some of the peas, corn, and beans are less sweet and more mature. Also, there are fewer sizes and less variety. These reasons could be expected, but the next answer is less obvious.

The no-brand products are taking a free marketing ride. While brand name products must invest heavily in advertising to convince supermarket chain buyers that the consumer will buy the product from the shelf, no-brand products get free and automatic shelf space. There is little free publicity when Del Monte's has a new product, but the no-brand lines got good news coverage. The overhead costs such as product development and package testing have already been paid by the branded products. Consumers seem to be happy with the free ride while it lasts.

by that company. The Kleenex brand makes more sense on the line of disposable paper products offered by Kimberly Clark.

Just as Kleenex appears on many paper products, the Ford brand is used on cars and trucks, auto parts and accessories, and car care products. Your good experience with one of these products may lead you to buy other products with the same brand. The use of the same brand for a variety of products is called **family branding.** Some firms use **individual branding**—a different brand name for each product. Procter & Gamble offers more than a dozen different brands of laundry detergent. You would have to look closely to see that each is a P&G product. If you switch brands, P&G hopes that it will be to another P&G brand, not to the competition.

    Manufacturers' versus resellers' brands. Brands which identify the firm that sells you the product rather than the firm that made the product are **reseller's brands.** At Sears you may buy a refrigerator made by Frigidaire or Admiral but sold under the Kenmore brand. Resellers' branded products are manufactured by one firm but sold under a brand name owned by another firm. This is also called **private branding.** This practice has become more popular in recent years. What benefits does it offer to the manufacturer, to the reseller, and to you?

Manufacturers may provide products for resellers' brands because they have excess capacity. They produce more than they can sell under their own brands. They may be attracted by the security offered by contracts with a reseller. Sears can offer a small manufacturer an almost certain market for a major proportion of its output. Resellers' brands may also go on merchandise that does not meet the standards that producers have set for their own brands.

Why does a retailer like Sears bother to use its own brands? One reason is that Sears can often purchase unbranded products at a lower price than it could buy similar manufacturers' branded products. In return, Sears assumes the responsibility for the product. Sears pays for advertising and other functions such as service. Of course, if the products supplied by one manufacturer need service too often, Sears will find another supplier. Sears can switch suppliers and you will never know the difference. In fact, Sears may have several suppliers for the same product. Sears may require that suppliers produce products to its own specifications. If you want a Craftsman tool or a Kenmore appliance, you will have to buy it at Sears. While you can compare its features with those of products offered at other stores, you may find it difficult to make specific price comparisons. The use of resellers' brands ties you to a store.

How do you benefit from buying resellers' brands? The most common benefit is a lower price. This may be due to differences in quality or in advertising and service expenses. For some products, resellers' brands lack the quality image of the manufacturers' brands.

Brand name infringement.   An accepted brand name is a valuable asset, but some sellers find that their brands are too accepted. The name Kleenex, for example, seems to be more accepted than the real name for the product. Have you ever asked for a "facial tissue"? People may use the brand Kleenex to refer to Puffs, Scott Tissues, or other brands. Have you ever eaten a "gelatin" dessert? Most people eat Jello, even if it comes out of a Royal Gelatin Dessert package. A brand name that is extended to all the products of that type is called a **generic brand.** Kimberly Clark, General Foods, Coca-Cola, and Xerox hope that you will think of their brands first when you are buying the types of products they sell. However, they are very careful to protect their registered brand names from being used to identify competitive products.

COKE—PROTECTING A WORLDWIDE BRAND NAME

Have you ever asked for a Coke only to hear, "We don't have Coke. We serve Pepsi." Most customers are slightly aggravated that this minor detail is mentioned. But to the Coca-Cola people, it's a great big issue.

Each year Coca-Cola spends about $35 million advertising its name. That's a big investment. To protect that investment, Coke maintains a team of 25 people who travel all over the country ordering "Coke" in restaurants, at state fairs, at ball parks, and at other places and events. They don't drink those "Cokes"; they send them back to the labs in Atlanta for chemical analysis.

Since 1945 Coke has sued over 800 retailers for serving something other than the real thing, and it has won every suit. Does all this happen because of one misdeed on the part of the restaurant? Not quite. Before Coke sued Howard Johnson's, investigators had ordered Coke and received HOJO Cola without warning on 2,115 out of 2,480 visits.

Coke says its name is a valuable asset and that it can't afford to have people dissatisfied with another cola and blaming it on Coke. Critics claim that Coke uses this technique to scare retailers into serving Coke to avoid possible suits. What do you think?

Source: John Koten, "Mixing with Coke over Trademarks Is Always a Fizzle," *The Wall Street Journal,* March 9, 1978, p. 1+.

Some infringement on brands is deliberate. Levi Strauss has been so successful with jeans that it cannot meet worldwide demand. The company maintains eight security officers at a cost of $500,000 per year to hunt down people who are producing fake Levi's. It's not that Levi's wants people to go without jeans, but the fake Levi's fail to meet Levi's standards and cause consumer dissatisfaction.[2] This is damaging to the Levi's brand reputation. While registered brands are protected by law, the damaged firm must initiate legal action.

PRICE: HOW MUCH IS SATISFACTION WORTH?

In some European markets, an ordinary pair of Levi's sells for as much as $80. At lower prices, the demand is much greater than the supply, but at the high price, there are lots of people who decide not to buy. The Levi's are left for those who are willing to pay for them.

The interaction of supply and demand is the basis of pricing. If demand exceeds supply, prices tend to rise. If supply exceeds demand, prices tend to fall. Over a period of time, other adjustments take place. If the prices for a type of product or service are very high, the potential for profit will attract more producers. The increased supply may cause the price to decrease. If the prices are so low that the producers cannot make a reasonable profit, some will got out of business. The decreased supply will cause the prices and the profits to increase. That's the way it is supposed to work. But some factors can interfere.

Can you imagine the chaos if each time a plane left Chicago bound for Los Angeles, people had to bid on their seats? In our complex economy, total price flexibility is not always desirable. In some transactions, the final price results from bargaining between the buyer and seller. This is called **negotiated pricing.** This system is widely used in less advanced economies. It is also used in industrial and government markets where a difference of a few cents per unit can be critical. Most of the products you buy have a set price. The seller has determined the price at which the product is offered to you. You can decide whether or not you will buy it. If no one buys at that price, the seller may reset the price. This process is called **administered pricing.**

Pricing is a critical element in a transaction. How are prices determined? Let's first look at some of the general factors to be considered and then at some specific pricing practices. The seller is faced with the task of estimating the price to which you might both have agreed if you had bargained. That price would be related both to your willingness to pay and to the seller's costs.

Elasticity of demand

Your willingness to pay depends on many factors. At the top of the list is your expectation of satisfaction. Another factor is your budget. Your willingness to pay for a particular product is also affected by the availability of substitutes. All of these influence your sensitivity to price.

Willingness. Economists call this sensitivity *your* **elasticity of demand.** Consider the demand for table salt compared with the demand for T-bone steak. Table salt sells for about 20 cents a pound. Steaks cost several dollars per pound. If the price of salt doubled, would you quit using it? You may be a bit more cautious for a while, but total demand for table salt probably would not decline.

It works both ways. If the price of table salt was cut in half, you wouldn't double your use. The demand for table salt is **inelastic.** A change in price may bring about some change in demand, but that change is less than the price change. What do you think would happen if the price of T-bone steaks was cut in half? Would the demand double? It would probably more than double. The demand for T-bones is **elastic.** It will stretch in response to a price cut. Sellers consider the elasticity of demand in setting their prices.

Substitutes.   Your expectations of satisfaction, your budget, and the availability of substitutes make the difference between your elasticity of demand for T-bones and your inelasticity of demand for salt. Most people are more willing to do without T-bones than without salt. While there are certain satisfactions to be expected from T-bones, salt is more necessary. People tend to be less elastic when it comes to necessities.

While your demand for food may be fairly inelastic, your demand for T-bones is not. If the price is too high, you can switch to hamburger or other forms of protein. But there are few substitutes for salt. In a competitive marketplace, the products of one seller represent substitutes for the products of another seller.

Budget.   The impact on your budget affects your elasticity of demand. If the price of salt doubled, the total impact on your yearly

When there are few substitutes, high prices can be even more frightening.

"I'm afraid we don't yet have a scientific name for the fear of high prices."

Reprinted by permission *The Wall Street Journal.*

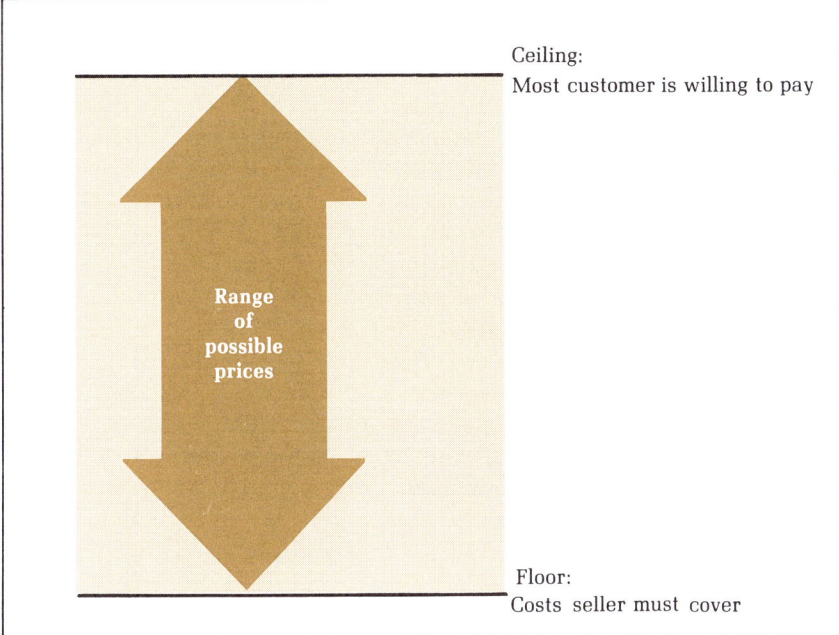

Ceiling:
Most customer is willing to pay

Range
of
possible
prices

Floor:
Costs seller must cover

FIGURE 11–5
The price must be high enough to cover the seller's costs yet low enough to attract buyers.

budget might be less than a dollar. Most people would not notice. But if the price of T-bone steaks doubled, it would rate headlines in the local paper.

While the demand for a type of product may be inelastic, the demand for a single brand is more elastic. If a single seller's price is higher than the competition's, it can mean lost sales. Some sellers accept the idea that their products are very much like the products of the competitors and compete primarily on a price basis. Other sellers attempt to emphasize the differences between their products and the products of the competition to compete on a nonprice basis.

Whether or not sellers choose to compete on a price basis, the price must cover the sellers' costs. In setting the price of a product, the highest price you are willing to pay is the ceiling, and the seller's cost is the floor. The price must fall within that range (see Figure 11–5).

Pricing new products

When a firm is introducing a truly new product, the pricing decision can be critical. Not only could the price affect the initial success of the product, but it may also affect the actions of potential competitors.

  Skimming versus penetration. If the price is set high in the range of possible prices, it is called **skimming pricing.** Only those who are willing to pay the top price for the product will buy. While there will be fewer sales, each sale will be more profitable. Of course, since the profit potential will be high, other sellers will rush to develop competitive products.

If the price is set low in the range of prices there will be less profit on each sale, but there should be more sales. This is called **penetration pricing.** The original seller penetrates further into the market before competition develops. Other companies are slower to compete because the profit potential is lower. Some sellers start off with a high price and then lower the price when competitors arrive. The consumers' willingness to pay and the sellers' costs are the bases for pricing. How are these translated into price tags on the products you buy?

Markup pricing.   The retail price you pay is equal to the basic cost of producing the product plus a series of margins called markups. A **markup** is the difference between the cost and the selling price of a product. The markup is added to cover the expenses and provide profit for the firms that make the product available to you. It may be expressed as a percentage or in dollars and cents.

The percentage method is the most popular. But percentage of what?

DID YOU EVER WONDER?
Why do prices seldom end in .00?

Most prices seem to end in .50 or .95 or something other than a whole dollar. Some of the explanations of this practice are historical and others are based on human behavior.

It could have started with Captain Macy, the founder of the R. H. Macy Company, who insisted on a rigid markup system. If the numbers came out odd, that's the way it was. Another thought is that the odd prices resulted from converting English pounds sterling to U.S. dollars during colonial trading. Since the colonial products were of lower quality, an odd ending implied a higher quality import. The third historical idea is that in the days before credit cards, odd prices forced the clerks to ring up sales in order to make change. This kept them from pocketing the receipts. With today's sales tax, this would not be a problem.

Do you really see the price $9.95 as being $9 instead of $10? That's one of the behavioral explanations. Another is that you like to get change. Maybe an odd price gives you the idea the the retailer is charging the lowest possible price. Of course, while you are waiting for your change, you might decide to buy something else.

We may not have given you the one and only reason for odd pricing, but now you can make a choice.

Source: David M. Georgoff, *Odd-Even Retail Price Endings: Their Effect on Value Determination, Product Perception, and Buying Propensities* (East Lansing: MSU Business Studies, Bureau of Business and Economic Research, 1972), pp. 14–15.

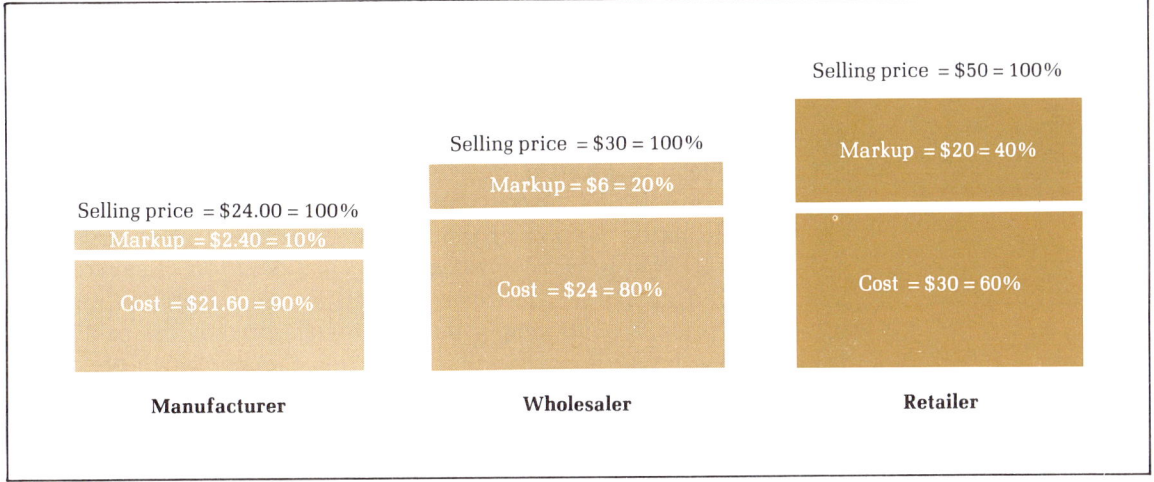

Selling price = $50 = 100%

Markup = $20 = 40%

Cost = $30 = 60%

Selling price = $30 = 100%

Markup = $6 = 20%

Cost = $24 = 80%

Selling price = $24.00 = 100%

Markup = $2.40 = 10%

Cost = $21.60 = 90%

Manufacturer   **Wholesaler**   **Retailer**

FIGURE 11–6
Example of a markup chain and channel pricing

Usually the markup is based on the selling price; that is, a 25 percent markup means 25 percent of the price on the price tag. If you intended to set a price using a 25 percent markup, how would you do it?

As we said, the selling price is equal to the cost plus the markup. If the markup is 25 percent of the selling price, the initial cost must be 75 percent of the selling price. So you need to find the price at which the cost is 75 percent. You can find this by dividing the cost by its proportion of the selling price, which is equal to 1 minus the markup percentage:

$$\frac{\text{Cost}}{1-\text{Markup}} = \text{Selling price}$$

$$\frac{\$75}{1-0.25} = \text{Selling price}$$

$$\frac{\$75}{0.75} = \$100$$

The markup method of pricing is widely used because it is simple to implement and to understand. Most sellers face the task of pricing hundreds of products. The average K mart handles 15,000 different products.[3] A standard markup makes the task much more manageable (see Figure 11–6).

Price lining. Markup pricing starts with the cost and arrives at a selling price. In **price lining,** the seller starts with the selling price and moves backward to the cost. Rather than setting a separate price for each item in the product line, the seller sets up several standard prices. Each product is squeezed into the closest price line. This system is popular with sellers of many styles or models of a product such as shoes, ties, or candy bars. It may cost Hersheys a bit more to produce a chocolate bar with almonds, but it makes sense to sell it at the same price as the plain chocolate bar.

For some products, these prices have become so accepted that they are maintained in the face of rising costs. Either the size or the quality of the product is reduced so that the seller can maintain the traditional price. Sellers held the 10 cents price on candy bars as long as they could by shrinking the size of the bars.

Setting the right price requires careful consideration of several factors involved in the sellers' costs as well as the buyers' willingness to pay the price. It's not simply that the lowest price is the best price. In fact, if the buyer is not familiar with the product, a high price may serve as a quality indicator. You might avoid a low-priced product for fear that it will not meet your needs. Some firms even stress their premium prices in their promotions.

PROMOTION

The purpose of promotion is to communicate with potential customers. There are a number of ways in which a business can do this. You are exposed to hundreds of commercial messages every day on television and radio and in magazines, billboards, newspapers, and mailers. You might encounter personal selling in a store or even at your own front door. Point-of-purchase displays and other sales promotions may catch your attention. You may see an article, a television news story, or other publicity on a firm or its products and services. Advertising and personal selling are most widely used.

Advertising

Advertising is a paid nonpersonal communication presented by an identified sponsor over an established medium. The major forms of media are radio and television, magazines and newspapers, outdoor, and direct mail. Since the purpose of each of these media is to communicate messages to you, you already know a great deal about each of them. However, you may not have organized your thoughts about the objectives of the firms that are trying to communicate with you.

Think of the messages that reach you on each of these media. How do they differ in terms of their impact, timeliness, and cost? Which ones are most effective for which types of messages? These are the kinds of questions advertisers try to answer before they spend their money on advertising. Advertising is expensive. When advertising dollars are spent wisely, both you and the advertiser benefit.

The electronic media.   When commercial television came on the advertising scene in 1946, some people predicted the end of radio. Why

BARBARA GARDNER PROCTOR
I can't be bothered with your prejudices. That's your problem.

Barbara Proctor was the first female in the country to open a full-service advertising agency specializing in marketing to blacks. But she didn't start out with the intention of creating a successful advertising agency. Raised by her grandmother in a North Carolina home with no running water or electricity, she learned the value of hard work but had no specific career objectives. After graduating from Talladega College in Alabama, she planned to return to North Carolina to teach school. But on her way home from a summer job in Michigan, she passed through Chicago. She still lives in Chicago.

She became fascinated by the music industry and soon worked herself into a position with a record company. One job led to another, and she moved through positions as a writer and jazz critic before she discovered the excitement of advertising.

When she sought to form her own agency in 1970, she applied to the Small Business Administration for a $100,000 loan. To that point the SBA had not granted any unsecured loans for a service business. "They didn't even have the right forms." She persisted and got the loan. She has used the funds wisely and was recently honored as one of a dozen women subjects in the book, *Millionairess: Self-Made Women of America.*

Beyond her success in her own business, Proctor has built a strong record of service to the community. She has served as president of the League of Black Women, on Chicago's Mayor's Advisory Committee, and on the boards of directors of Seaway National Bank, Mt. Sinai Hospital, Illinois State Chamber of Commerce, the Better Business Bureau, and the Chicago Historical Society. She has been awarded the Small Business of the Year Award and the Headliner Award by the Women in Communication, and was named by *Business Week* as one of America's top 100 corporate women.

would people listen to the radio when they could watch TV? Clearly the two electronic giants have prospered side by side. National advertisers can blanket the country by sponsoring network shows. Local advertisers can buy local spots to reach local markets. Detailed information on audiences allows advertisers to target their messages to the most likely markets.

Television and radio advertising is expensive. But advertisers rate media in terms of cost per thousand, that is, how much it costs to present the message to 1,000 people. Over 99 percent of U.S. households have both radios and televisions. More than 130 million viewers tuned in to watch "Roots," the TV drama on black ancestry. While the dollar cost of an ad in such a program is high, the cost per thousand can be low.

The popularity of these media has caused some of their more serious problems. There are only a limited number of minutes of advertising time available. As demand has grown, the price has gone up and the length of the average commercial has been shortened. You may see six messages in a minute. How many do you remember?

The print media.   The print media include newspapers, magazines, and the Yellow Pages. Print media may be more effective for communicating complex ideas. If you have an involved message, consumers are more likely to grasp it if they can read it at their own pace. While watching TV and radio is free once you have purchased a receiver, most print media are sold to consumers. For that reason, a person who reads a magazine or newspaper may be more attentive than a TV viewer. Another advantage of print media is that they tend to linger longer. An ad on the back of the *TV Guide* spends a full week in American living rooms.

Newspapers and Yellow Pages are local media. More advertising

Direct mail allows advertisers to focus on the most likely consumers.

"Listen, hon—how's this for honesty? It says, 'you are probably already a loser!!'"

Reprinted by permission *The Wall Street Journal.*

dollars are spent on local newspaper advertising than on any other medium. People turn to newspapers and the Yellow Pages for information on the local availability of goods and services. This makes them very important to small business advertisers. While a Yellow Page ad is fixed for a full year, newspapers and radio offer time flexibility. It is possible to insert or change an advertisement on very short notice.

Radio and outdoor advertising share the advantage of reaching people on the go. This can be very important to firms such as fast-food restaurants and motels. Outdoor advertising is limited to simple messages.

You may be noticing an increase in the number of catalogs, sweepstakes notices, and other special offers in your mail. Direct mail is one of the fastest growing forms of advertising. It allows an advertiser to focus on the most likely consumers. Advertisers can buy any of thousands of lists of people according to traits such as age, buying habits, and occupation. High-speed word processing equipment makes it possible to address and mail advertisements to specific individuals. While some of these messages go into the trash unopened, many receive the undivided attention of likely prospects. Table 11–1 summarizes the advantages and disadvantages of the different forms of media.

TABLE 11–1
A summary of the media

Medium	Advantages	Disadvantages
Television	Low cost per thousand, mass market, audiovisual message	High cost, temporary, limited availability
Radio	Low cost per thousand, mobile audience, short lead time	Audio message only, temporary
Newspaper	Local flavor, information source	Limited distribution, short life
Yellow Pages	Information source	Long lead time
Magazines	Color pictures, longer life	Long lead times
Outdoor	Mobile audience	Limited message
Direct mail	Specific audience	Junk mail clutter

Advertising is impersonal. It can be highly effective in communicating information on product features and availability. It helps to build brand awareness and to stimulate your interest. You can be reminded to purchase or use a product or service. Arm & Hammer reminds people to change the box of baking soda in the refrigerator. Jello runs a TV commercial at noon reminding people that they have to make the Jello if they want to enjoy it for dinner. For many products, advertising is the only persuasive force. For others, personal selling complements advertising.

Personal selling

Personal selling is face-to-face communication with a potential buyer. Personal selling is the dominant form of promotion in industrial markets. In consumer markets it is used where needs are more individual, products are more complex, or buyers tend to postpone buying. You would not need any help in buying a can of soup. But purchases of life insurance, houses, or appliances are more complex.

Metropolitan Life can advertise continuously, and most people will not seek out life insurance coverage. Many people would prefer to ignore that need. It is more difficult to postpone that purchase, however, if you are approached by a salesperson. Personal selling offers the advantage of interaction. It is the salesperson's responsibility to learn about the product and be ready to answer your questions.

You have probably encountered different levels of personal selling. The lowest level is taking orders. Most retail salespeople can help you locate merchandise and can complete the transaction. It is their duty to process your order.

At a higher level, salespeople take the responsibility for more creative solutions to their customers' needs. This is called **creative selling.** Creative salespeople are expected to be able to complete a five-step process:

1. Prospecting.
2. Approach.
3. Presentation.
4. Closing.
5. Follow-up.

Prospecting is identifying people who might have a need for the product. Insurance salespeople may use birth announcements, new car registration, or tax rolls. The objective is to identify qualified prospects—people who have the authority and the ability to buy.

The **approach** is the initial contact with the prospect. It must generate interest so that the prospect will listen to the presentation.

The **presentation** is the salesperson's attempt to deliver a message that will cause the prospect to buy. Some presentations are carefully prepared and organized routines. Others are highly individualized and responsive to the reactions of the prospect. The salesperson explains the benefits of owning the product and may even demonstrate the product. Since these benefits should be expressed in terms of the prospect's interests and needs, it is important to listen to the prospect's comments and objections. This opportunity for interaction is the principal benefit of personal selling as a promotional tool.

When the prospect seems ready, the salesperson attempts a closing. A **closing** is a request for the order. The prospect must be asked to place an order.

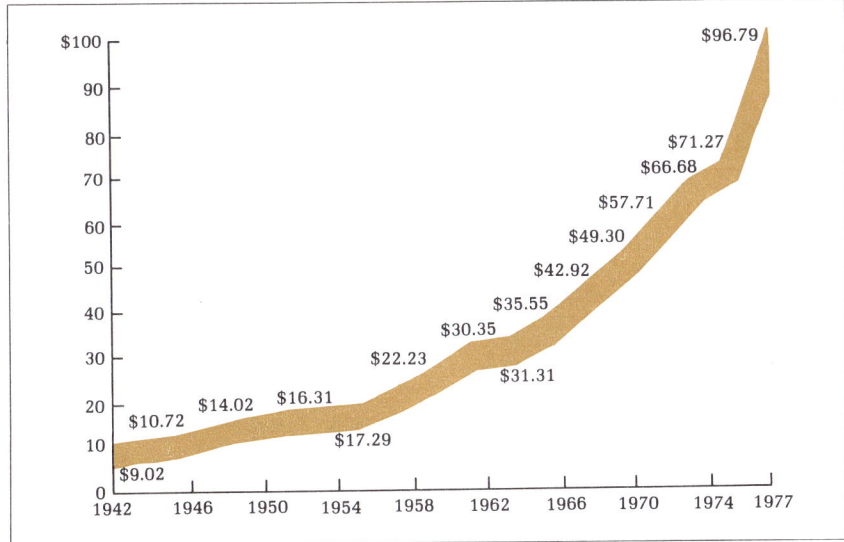

Source: *Advertising Age*, August 7, 1978, p. 14.

FIGURE 11–7
The cost of an average personal sales call increased 1,000 percent from 1942 to 1977

Follow-up involves checking to make sure that the product or service is delivered according to the contract and that the customer is satisfied with the purchase. This can lead to repeat sales. Personal selling can be very effective, but it is also very expensive, as shown in Figure 11–7.

Advertising and personal selling dominate the promotional efforts of most firms. While customers may be more aware of advertising, most firms that produce consumer products depend on personal selling to establish distribution channels for their products.

DISTRIBUTION CHANNELS

"Eliminate the middleman" is a cry of some people who are concerned about the increased costs of living. The **middleman** is not a person but one of a series of businesses that participate in the distribution process. This includes distributors, wholesalers, and retailers. If these firms were eliminated, would consumers be better off?

As an example, 80 percent of the lettuce eaten in New York City is grown in California. The selling price may triple between the field and the supermarket checkout counter. What do middlemen do to earn that much? Middlemen buy lettuce from individual farmers in order to assemble large quantities. The lettuce is then sorted by size and quality. It is shipped to New York in refrigerated cars in quantities large enough to justify economical rates. In New York, more middlemen buy crates of lettuce along with other fruits and vegetables. When New York consumers visit their supermarkets, they can select a single head of lettuce from an assortment of fresh fruits and vegetables. Where would New York consumers be without these middlemen? Would they mail in orders and receive individual heads by airmail? The price of the lettuce does triple between the field and the market, but the utility increases even more (see Figure 11–8).

FIGURE 11–8
The sorting process

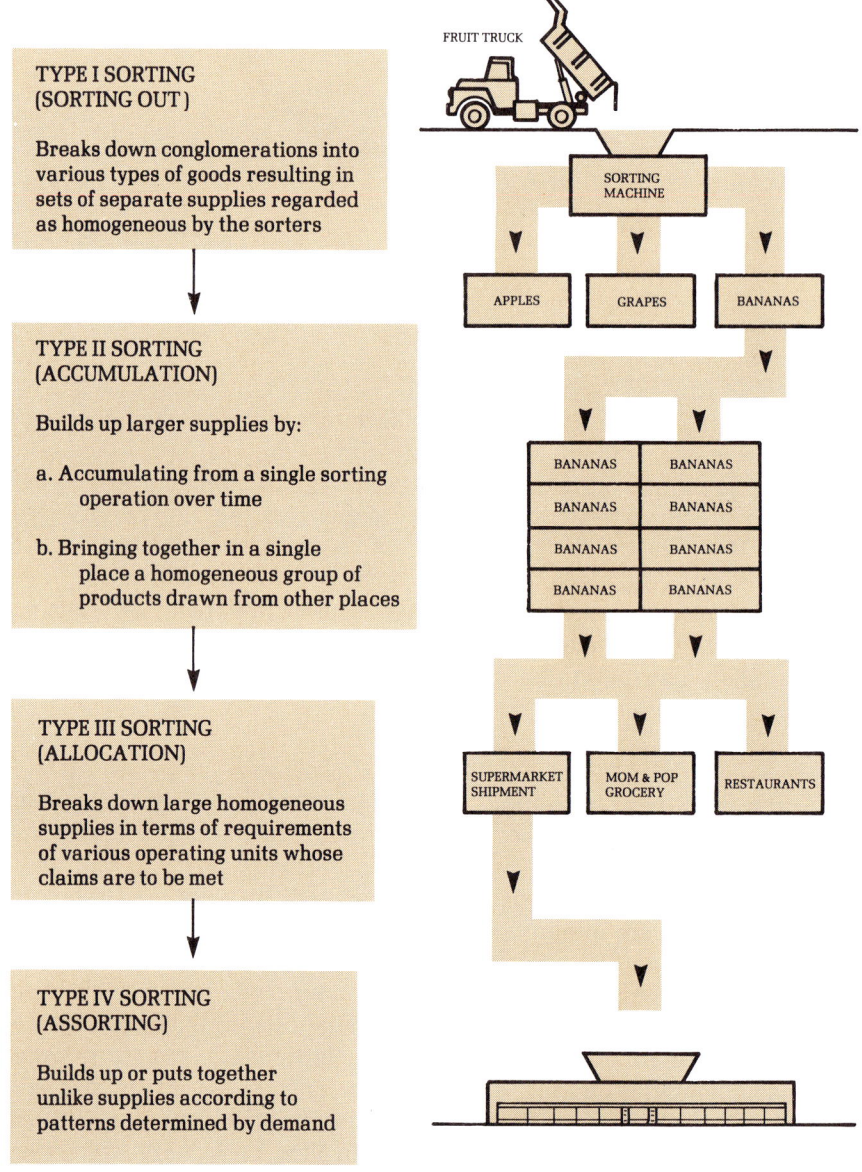

TYPE I SORTING
(SORTING OUT)

Breaks down conglomerations into various types of goods resulting in sets of separate supplies regarded as homogeneous by the sorters

TYPE II SORTING
(ACCUMULATION)

Builds up larger supplies by:

a. Accumulating from a single sorting operation over time

b. Bringing together in a single place a homogeneous group of products drawn from other places

TYPE III SORTING
(ALLOCATION)

Breaks down large homogeneous supplies in terms of requirements of various operating units whose claims are to be met

TYPE IV SORTING
(ASSORTING)

Builds up or puts together unlike supplies according to patterns determined by demand

FRUIT TRUCK

SORTING MACHINE

APPLES   GRAPES   BANANAS

BANANAS   BANANAS
BANANAS   BANANAS
BANANAS   BANANAS
BANANAS   BANANAS

SUPERMARKET SHIPMENT   MOM & POP GROCERY   RESTAURANTS

Source: Adapted from Cundiff, Still, Govoni, *Fundamentals of Modern Marketing*, 2nd ed., © 1976, p. 43. Reprinted by permission of Prentice-Hall, Inc., Englewood Cliffs, New Jersey.

Distribution can be divided into two broad areas: physical distribution and the management of distribution channels. Physical distribution is extremely important and will be discussed in depth in Chapter 18. The management of the distribution channel involves the relationships among the firms that interact to contribute to the time, place, and possession utilities of the products you buy.

Distribution and the classification of goods

The objective of the distribution channel is to provide for the greatest availability of goods and services at the most reasonable cost. The costs of distribution increase as goods are made more available. The system must balance your needs against these costs. Your needs vary with the type of product.

The classification of goods explains the relationship between consumer shopping behavior and distribution. This system defines four types of goods: convenience goods, shopping goods, speciality goods, and unsought goods.

Convenience goods.   Those products and services that most consumers prefer to purchase with minimum effort are **convenience goods.** Most groceries, toothpaste, and dry cleaning fall into this class. Sellers of these goods strive for **intensive distribution.** They try to make their goods available in all of the logical locations.

Shopping goods.   When shoppers are willing to put some effort into finding the item that best meets their needs you have **shopping goods.** They may be searching for special features, or they may be looking for the best price. Since consumers are willing to look around, sellers can use **selective distribution.** They can select a reasonable number of outlets. This is very important to sellers of more expensive products such as electronics and appliances since the costs of holding goods in inventory are high. The more sales outlets there are, the more inventory is required. These costs would be passed on to the consumer.

Specialty goods.   There are some goods for which consumers have very specific needs. They are not willing to accept substitutes. Consumers are willing to put in whatever effort is required to get the product or service they want. These products may be exotic such as rare coins, or they may simply be products that have earned a strong following. Sellers of such **specialty goods** can set up **exclusive distribution.** These products may be available in a single outlet within a market area.

Unsought goods.   There are some goods that consumers do no seek at all. These are the **unsought goods.** Regularly unsought goods are those for which consumers do not choose to recognize the need. Life insurance and encyclopedias are examples of regularly unsought goods. Emergency unsought goods are those for which the need is of an emergency nature. People do not plan ahead for fan belts for their cars or ambulance service. But when the need arises, it is critical. Regularly unsought goods require **aggressive distribution.** The seller cannot anticipate any cooperation from the buyer. This can be very costly. Emergency unsought goods must be maintained at strategic locations until they are needed.

Channel members

Products can take long or short paths to consumers. Some goods change ownership several times and other goods are sold directly to the consumer. Goods that are low in cost and are normally purchased in small quantities by a widespread group of consumers tend to move through long channels. Goods that are high in value or intended for concentrated markets usually have short channels. Services tend to move through short channels because most cannot be separated from the producers. The standard channel alternatives are shown in Figure 11–9.

Channel members are identified in terms of their role in the owner-

FIGURE 11–9
Basic channel alternatives

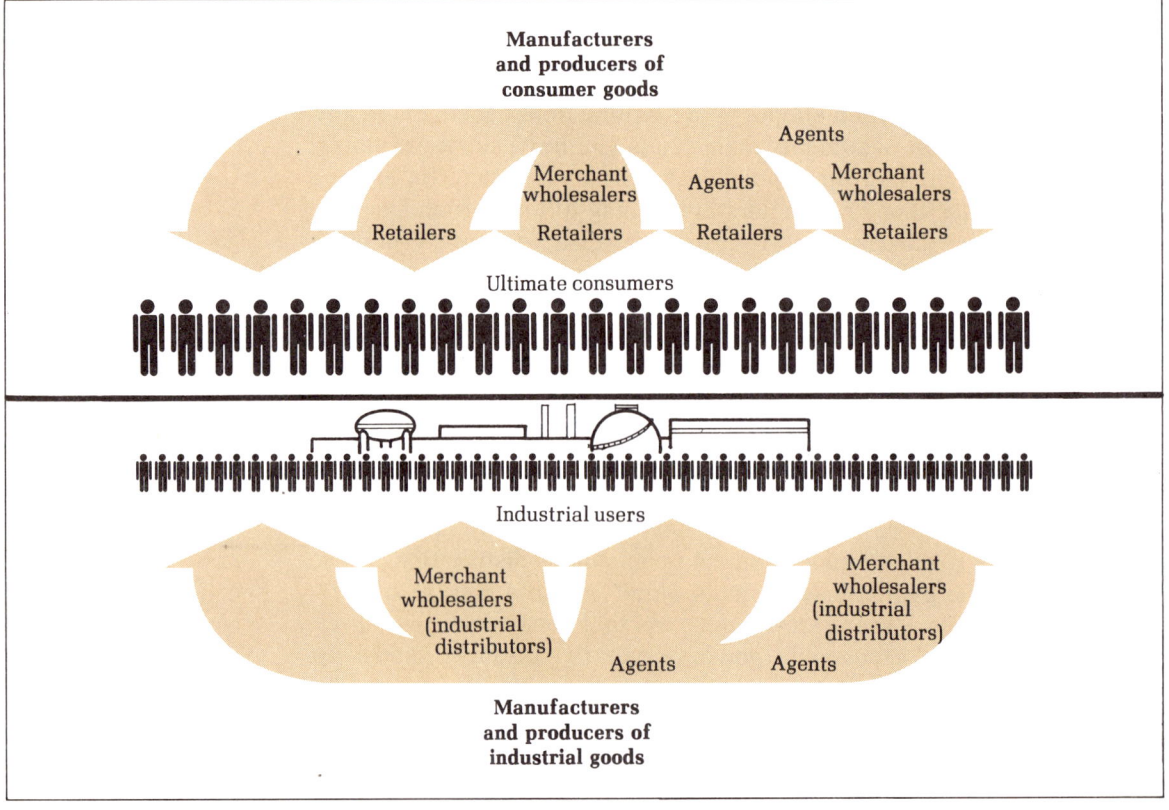

ship of the goods and their relationship to the other participants. All firms that participate in the transfer of ownership and come between producers and consumers are called middlemen. **Merchant middlemen** purchase products and sell them to the next firm or the customer. **Agent middlemen** do not own the products they offer for sale. They simply help buyers and sellers to find each other. For example, real estate agents do not own the homes they help to sell.

Retailers.   Those who sell to ultimate consumers are **retailers.** They range from giant department and discount stores such as Sears and K mart to small single-line shops such as the local shoe store. They share the purpose of providing consumers with an assortment of products and services at a convenient time and place.

Not all retailing takes place in stores. Nonstore retailing includes catalog sales, door-to-door sales, vending machines, telephone sales, and mail order.

Wholesalers.   The firms that sell to retailers are **wholesalers.** By dealing with a wholesaler, a retailer avoids the problem of dealing with many manufacturers. It simplifies the task of buying merchandise. Wholesalers buy in quantities that would be too large for the retailer to handle. They offer retailers assortments of products in the quantities they need. Few small grocery stores are interested in buying a boxcar full of cornflakes. A grocery wholesaler, on the other hand, can buy in that quantity and sell cases to the grocer along with other grocery products. **Distributors** are wholesalers' wholesalers. They provide the same type of bulk-breaking and assorting functions at a higher level.

In some channels each firm acts independently. Each chooses to deal with other firms that provide the goods and services it needs at prices it considers fair. Other channels integrate. In **integrated channels,** several levels of distribution are related through common ownership or contracts. Manufacturers such as Goodyear and Firestone maintain totally integrated channels of distribution. They produce the products and sell them to ultimate consumers through their own chains of retail stores.

SUMMARY

Business firms must interact with their markets, To do so, firms develop marketing programs. A marketing program involves coordinated decisions on product management, pricing, promotion, and distribution.

Product management includes all the decisions on the product or service that will be offered to the market. Firms develop new products to take advantage of opportunities presented because of changes in consumer needs or technology. An important consideration is the compatibility of the new product with the firm's existing business. Packaging and branding are important parts of the total product.

In a complex society prices of consumer goods are often set at a particular level rather than being established through bargaining. To set prices, sellers consider the elasticity of demand and the costs of the product. The buyer can always decide not to buy.

Promotion is undertaken to communicate with the market. The dominant forms of promotion are advertising and personal selling. Advertising allows for the widespread communication of impersonal messages. Personal selling is very important in complex buying situations.

Distribution includes both physical distribution and channel relationships. The channel for consumer goods might include distributors, wholesalers, and retailers. Channels serve the important functions of assembling, sorting, bulk breaking, and assorting.

REVIEW QUESTIONS

1. Think of a new product you've seen recently. Can you identify a change in consumer needs or technology that affected the development of that product?

2. For each stage of the product life cycle, identify a product or service currently in that stage. Why did you place each product in that stage?

3. Pick out a food product, a personal care product, and a leisure product. Describe the packages for these products in terms of the functions of packaging.

4. Name two products for which you have a favorite brand. Now name two products for which brand makes no difference to you. Why are the brands on the first two products more important to you?

5. Explain the concept of elasticity of demand using movie theaters and dentists as examples.

6. Imagine that you worked in a record shop and just received a shipment of records that cost $1.50 each. If you were asked to apply a 75 percent markup, what selling price would you set on each record?

7. What are the advantages of the print media?

8. Think of the last time you bought a product that was promoted to you through personal selling. Describe the product and the sales presentation. Explain why personal selling was used.

9. Name a convenience good, a shopping good, and a specialty good. For each one, indicate where you could buy it and explain why it is distributed that way.

CASES

Case 11–1. Pass the macadamia nuts

The macadamia nut, a high-priced alternative to chips, may turn out to be an important crop in Hawaii and may even partially replace the income lost due to the decline in the sugar and pineapple industries. Paul DeDomenico has been doing his best to make the macadamia nut into a marketing success story. Paul resigned from the presidency of the Ghirardelli Chocolate Company in San Francisco to take over Hawaiian Holiday, a major producer of macadamia nuts in Hawaii. Here is the situation he faced.

First, macadamia nuts had rarely been advertised. They had been promoted only by the airplane packets. Second, the going price was 55¢ per ounce. Third, Hawaiian Holiday had little brand recognition among potential consumers. Ninety-five percent of the company's crop was sold in bulk to food processors in Japan. Ghirardelli Chocolate Company had been a major customer. The largest producer of macadamia nuts, C. Brewer and Co., Ltd., had not been making ambitious efforts to promote the nut because its management felt that the firm would have difficulties growing and packing enough nuts to meet increased demand.

Paul is facing two serious questions. First, he needs to promote macadamia nuts but he has a limited budget. Millions of tourists visit Hawaii each year. He wants to find a way to use those tourist to spread the message about macadamia nuts. Second, he is concerned about the Hawaiian Holiday product mix. The macadamia nuts can be flavored with cheese or onion. They can also be used in candies and bakery. He is wondering if he should stick to the basic salted nuts or branch out into other products under the Hawaiian Holiday label.

1. *How can Paul get the most mileage out of his limited promotional budget? How can he take advantage of the flow of tourists?*
2. *What problems might occur if Hawaiian Holiday expands its product mix? How can these problems be minimized?*

Case 11–2. Chips in a can

Procter & Gamble is used to marketing winners. Tide, Scope, Crest, Pampers, and many other P&G products lead their industries. But potato chips have been another story.

P&G introduced Pringles in test markets in Michigan and Ohio in the early 1970s. Pringles are processed potato chips stacked in a can that looks like it should hold tennis balls. One of the reasons Pringles were packaged in a can is that it allowed for national distribution supported by national advertising. Only one other brand of potato chips, Frito-Lay, is available nationwide. Most chips are produced and sold on a regional basis because of the problems with transportation.

Sales of Pringles peaked in 1975 at $110 million and then began slipping. In 1977, P&G pumped $15 million into advertising for the product, which brought the total advertising expenditure to over $50 million. Originally, P&G had forecast Pringles sales of around $200 million a year, or about 25 percent of the potato chip market. Instead they account for about 10 percent of the market.

There seem to be several problems. One is that Pringles don't taste like ordinary potato chips. Beyond that, all the Pringles chips are identical. Apparently consumers like different sizes and shapes of potato chips. The competitions' recent emphasis on natural ingredients hasn't helped either. Retailers have been stingy with shelf space since snack foods are big items in supermarkets and Pringles don't sell as fast as some of the other chip and cracker products.

1. *What factors might be contributing to the lackluster performance of Pringles?*
2. *What opportunities are there to adjust the marketing mix for Pringles?*
3. *Should P&G just absorb its losses and get out of the potato chip market?*

part V

WITH:

Functional supports

All firms, from the smallest store to the largest conglomerate, must support their main business activities with a group of functions. First, someone must make sure that the firm has sufficient funds to operate and that the funds are used wisely. This may involve relationships with banks or other financial institutions. More businesses fail from poor financial management than from any other cause.

Second, someone must hire and train employees. Many firms find that they must deal with their employees through unions. All firms must be aware of labor legislation that affects employment activities.

Management of people on the job is another serious concern. How can jobs be structured so that people are both productive and satisfied with their work? How does the structure of the organization affect the productivity of the firm? How are employees evaluated, and how can they be encouraged to improve their performances?

Today, more than ever before, information is an important resource. It must be managed also. The widespread use of computers has made this task both easier and more complex. The objective is to have enough of the right information without suffering from information overload. While computers once were available only to large firms, today minicomputers are easing information management tasks for small businesses as well.

The support functions of finance, personnel, supervision, and information are examined in Chapters 12–15. Large firms often have departments with specialists in each of these areas, whereas a small business owner may handle each of these functions alone. All businesses must manage these support functions.

chapter 12

FINANCIAL MANAGEMENT

By studying this chapter you should be able to find answers to these questions:

1 What are the objectives of financial management?

2 What is the difference between short-term financial management and long-term financial management?

3 What factors must be considered in deciding among the short-term uses of funds?

4 What are the short-term sources of funds?

5 What are long-term sources of funds?

6 What are the long-term uses of funds and why is it wise to use long-term sources of funds to finance them?

7 What role do financial institutions play?

8 How do firms issue new securities?

Terms you should know:

accounts receivable
capital budgeting
commercial paper
common stock
current liabilities
financial institutions
financial management
intermediation
investment bankers
liquidity
retained earnings
trade credit
underwriting
working capital

How would you like to own a company that had 1,200 stores, had $450 million worth of inventory, and was ranked as the 17th largest retailer in the United States? It may sound impressive, but that is only one side of the story of W. T. Grant. In what has been called the most significant bankruptcy in U.S. corporate history, W. T. Grant closed the doors of its stores in 1975, leaving the banks with $234 million in bad loans and putting 80,000 people out of work.[1] While W. T. Grant had $512 million in assets, it owed various creditors a total of $1.2 billion.[2] There are a lot of people who were part owners of W. T. Grant. They were the shareholders of that corporation. How much do you think was left for them after the creditors got what they could?

While an autopsy showed that there were several reasons for the failure of W. T. Grant, high on the list was improper financial management. In the five years before going bankrupt, sales had actually increased 50 percent. But the amount invested in inventory increased 200 percent. In its final year, Grant's costs of extending credit to its customers increased 2,700 percent. A former finance executive of the firm said, "We gave credit to every deadbeat who breathed."[3]

K mart's management also faces an impending financial crisis. Whereas W. T. Grant could not pay its bills, K mart is generating profits faster than they can be invested. By 1985 it is predicted that K mart could be accumulating $400 million in excess cash every year.[4] Someone is going to have to find a way to use those financial resources.

THE OBJECTIVES OF FINANCIAL MANAGEMENT

Financial management is the process of effectively obtaining and using funds. To do so requires decisions in two broad areas. First, an organization could use its financial resources in several ways. Some of these uses are short-lived, whereas others involve a commitment over a long period of time. Since funds are usually limited, management often must decide among the possible uses of funds.

Second, financial managers can draw on a variety of financial resources. It is important to select the right source of funds for a particular use. The overall objective of financial management is to make the best possible use of all the financial resources available to the firm.

SHORT-TERM FINANCIAL MANAGEMENT

In order to stay in business, a firm must make a variety of financial decisions. Some of these are made daily to support the normal operation of the business. The short term is normally defined as less than one year. **Short-term financial decisions** are those that will affect the firm's sources or uses of funds for less than a year.

Financial managers must constantly ask whether an expenditure is justified. They must also be alert to the most fitting way to finance each expenditure. The real challenge is to make sure that funds are available to take advantage of opportunities while conserving the firm's financial resources. The goal of financial management is not simply to spend less but to spend the money where it will be the most useful. The financial manager must maintain a balance between liquid and nonliquid assets.

A **liquid asset** is cash or something of value that can be converted easily to cash. It is also important to balance secure investments with lower returns against more risky investments that may earn a higher return. Let's look at how these considerations affect the manager's decisions on the short-term sources and uses of funds.

Short-term uses of funds: Working capital management

Working capital is the pool of assets available to meet the firm's day-to-day financial needs. Working capital management is the administration of these short-term assets. There are four major types of short-term assets: cash, accounts receivable, inventory, and short-term investments. They are called short-term because they are normally exchanged or converted into cash within the period of one year. Each of these assets has some use, but each also has some drawbacks. The financial manager's objective is to have an adequate but not an excessive level of each of these short-term assets.

Cash.   In deciding how much of the firm's financial resources to hold in cash, the financial manager must balance the benefits of liquidity against lost opportunities. **Liquidity** means that an asset can be traded rapidly at a reasonably certain value. Most people will readily accept cash at the current value. Nonliquid assets are more difficult to exchange. Either it takes time to find a buyer or the value is not fixed. A firm's liquidity increases as it holds more of its assets in cash.

There are three reasons to hold cash. The first is that a firm needs cash to pay normal day-to-day bills. The second motive is as a precaution. The more predictable its expenses are, the less cash a firm needs to hold. Speculation is the third reason to hold cash. Cash is the most easily traded asset. The firm is in a better position to take advantage of any opportunity that arises if it has a cash reserve.

But cash does not earn returns; cash itself is nonproductive. It contributes nothing to the profitability of the firm. Besides, a firm can actually lose money by holding cash if the value of the dollar declines due to inflation. By maintaining an excessive cash balance, a firm loses out on opportunities to use those funds productively.

Accounts receivable.   Most firms sell on credit. **Accounts receivable** are the funds owed to a firm by those who purchase its products or services. When a company grants credit, it ties up its own resources. It is, in a sense, lending money to its customers.

When you buy a product on credit, the retailer lends you something of value. In some cases you pay interest on that loan, but in many cases you are allowed to take a month to pay without incurring any finance charges. Why do businesses grant their customers credit? Wouldn't it be better for the retailer if you paid cash? After all, some people never do pay their bills.

Sellers generally grant credit because it is to their competitive advantage. Reinker's Market is a small grocery store near Cleveland. It doesn't have the greatest variety, parking is awkward, and the help is overworked. It is just a few blocks from a big, modern K mart Foods. Yet, Reinker's is almost always crowded. It's not the price, the quality, or the variety that draws the crowd. Reinker's offers credit. Since none of the other grocers in the area does, Reinker's has a competitive advantage.

If all the other sellers are granting credit, customers will expect it. With more liberal credit policies, a seller may even be able to attract some buyers who were unable to obtain credit elsewhere. Easier credit terms could result in increased sales volume. But, the increased sales must be balanced against the costs of granting that credit and the chances of bad debts.

A firm can increase its accounts receivable by liberalizing its credit terms. It can give credit to buyers who were not able to meet the previous higher standards. As the standards for granting credit are lowered, most firms find that they have more bad debts—accounts that are not paid off.

A second way to increase accounts receivable is to increase the amount of time that customers have to repay the credit. A third approach is to lower the interest rate. An increase in the time limits or a decrease in the interest rates will mean that it costs the firm more to extend credit. More funds are tied up in accounts receivable and are not available for other uses such as buying the goods and services it needs to do business.

Inventory.   An **inventory** is the stock of goods or materials. There are three different kinds of inventories: raw materials, work in process, and finished goods. To a large extent, the amount and type of inventory depend on the nature of the business. A department store has more of its funds invested in inventory than a movie theater does. Beyond that, a store concentrates on finished goods, whereas a manufacturer has greater inventories of raw materials and work in process.

Since holding inventories involves a variety of costs, managers try to own just the right amount to be able to conduct business. Inventory control will be discussed in detail in Chapter 17. Here we are concerned with the funds tied up in inventory.

If a firm has too much of its short-term assets in inventory, it is in a nonliquid position. A slowdown in sales could force the firm into a position where it couldn't pay its bills. Have you ever seen a liquidation sale? The firm needs cash fast because its creditors are demanding immediate payment. So it sells merchandise at reduced prices to become more liquid. Surely this is not the most profitable way to do business.

There are also some very good reasons to hold larger inventories. First, there may be some savings in buying goods in large quantities. It may be more economical to ship in bulk, or the seller may offer a discount. Second, there is a safety factor. During the months before the contract talks come up in the steel industry, most of the users of steel begin to stockpile supplies. They buy more steel than they need in order to protect themselves in the event of a strike. If there is a strike, they can continue to produce their products and pay their workers. If there is no strike, they will have more money invested in steel inventory than they should. But no one can be certain of the future. A firm might also increase its inventories in anticipation of a surge of demand. Retail stores try to fill their shelves in anticipation of the Christmas buying splurges.

Short-term investments. After decisions have been made on the appropriate levels of cash, accounts receivable, and inventory, the firm might have some funds left. These funds should be put to use. Rather than letting excess funds be idle, firms make short-term investments in such things as U.S. government treasury bills. These securities earn some interest and can be sold on short notice. They serve as a reserve behind the cash balance.

Large corporations are usually more active in short-term investments than are small businesses. First of all, a shortage of working capital is one of the most common problems faced by small businesses. It's less likely that there are funds left over. Second, there are more short-term investment options open to large businesses. Some of the more common short-term investments are sold in units of $1 million. That's fine for General Motors, which may have millions on hand to meet its weekly payroll. If GM can invest that money for only a few days, the returns are substantial.

Financial managers spend most of their time making decisions on working capital management. But balancing the levels of cash, accounts receivable, inventories, and short-term investments is only half of the task. The other half of short-term financial management involves decisions on the sources of short-term funds.

Management of current liabilities: Short-term sources of funds

Current liabilities are financial obligations that the firm expects to pay off within a year. The firm can obtain funds from four major sources:

trade credit, short-term loans, accrued wages and taxes, and commercial paper. Let's look at the characteristics of each of these sources and the factors to be considered in obtaining short-term funds.

Liabilities are financial obligations.

"Hold it, gentlemen, hold it! I had it the wrong way around. It isn't **assets** that are in excess of ninety-seven million. It's **liabilities!**"

Drawing by Chon Day; © 1969 The New Yorker Magazine, Inc.

Trade credit: Managing accounts payable. **Trade credit** is a loan from the seller to the buyer. It is the buyer's side of accounts receivable. The seller doesn't really give money to the buyer, but allows the buyer to delay the payment of the bill for goods. In effect, the seller finances the buyer's inventory.

Trade credit is the most common source of short-term financing. It accounts for about 40 percent of the short-term liabilities of nonfinancial firms.[5] It is even more important to smaller firms because some of the other sources of short-term funds are less available to small businesses.

Trade credit is granted for a specific period of time, which normally has two parts. Most sellers allow the buyer a short period of time during which a discount applies. It is to the buyer's advantage to delay payment until the end of this discount period. But the advantages of the use of trade credit disappear as the buyer moves into the second part of the period when the discount no longer applies.

Let's assume that you had purchased some printed programs for a show being sponsored by your school. You were granted the credit terms, 2/10; net 30. This means that you can deduct a 2 percent discount from the total bill if you pay it within 10 days. If you do not, the entire amount is due by the 30th day. If the bill is $1,000, you could save $20 by paying it on or before the 10th day. That may not seem like a lot, but let's calculate the interest rate. If you wait until the 30th day, you will have had the use of $1,000 for an additional 20 days. Since there are 18 of these 20-day periods in a year, the annual interest rate is 18 times the 20-day rate. In this case, the effective annual interest rate would be 36 percent. That's quite a penalty for

---

FLOOR PLANNING: ONE WAY TO FINANCE INVENTORY

Have you ever driven past an automobile showroom or an appliance store and mentally added up the value of the inventory just sitting there. How does the retailer afford it? In many cases the answer is floor planning, in which the bank puts up the money for the inventory. It amounts to a continuing loan secured by merchandise. Of course, when the merchandise is sold, the dealer is supposed to pay off the bank. One of the characters in Arthur Haley's novel *Wheels* got in a jam that way.

> "Yolanda worked for the downtown bank which Smokey dealt with, and which financed his dealer's inventory of cars. . . . 'Our adjusters are planning some surprise dealer stock audits,' she advised him on the phone last night. 'I thought you'd want to know—your name is on the list. . . .' "

When Smokey called for the bookkeeper's report, he found he was "out of trust."

> " 'Out of Trust' meant that Smokey had sold cars, but had not turned the proceeds over to the bank which had loaned him the money to buy them to begin with. The cars were the bank's security against its loan; therefore, since it had not been informed otherwise, the bank believed the cars were still safely in Smokey's inventory. In fact, $43,000 worth of cars were gone."

Smokey's "solution" was to call several recent buyers and offer a special free checkup. The cars were then cleaned up and on the lot when the auditors arrived. It makes good reading in a novel, but wouldn't work too well in real life. Look at what it requires—an insider in the bank, cooperative customers, close-mouthed employees, and stupid auditors.

failing to take the discount. But, if you don't pay by the 10th day, you might as well wait until the 30th day. You might as well use your high-cost $1,000 loan for the full 20 days.

Not all trade credit has a time limit. Some goods are sold on a consignment basis. If the seller is not in a strong position to persuade the retailer to handle merchandise, the seller might agree that the retailer will make the merchandise available in the store but will not pay for it unless it is sold.

Some major manufacturers consign merchandise to small retailers whose working capital limitations would not permit them to carry the merchandise otherwise. Sunbeam manufactures a line of small appliances that are provided to small hardware and gift shops on consignment. One of Sunbeam's biggest problems with this is determining when payment is due. Some merchants sell the products and then hang on to the funds. To solve this, Sunbeam maintains a crew of telephone operators who regularly call the consignment merchants to check on sales and encourage prompt payment. Sunbeam can afford only a certain amount of interest-free loans.

Short-term loans.   Loans from commercial banks are the second most common source of short-term funds. Whereas trade credit is an accepted part of most buyer–seller transactions, a financial manager must make a special effort to arrange for a loan. It is the borrower's responsibility to convince the lender not only that the money will be returned but also that it will be returned on time with interest. Firms that are financially secure are able to arrange larger loans at lower interest rates.

The two most common forms of bank loans are term loans and lines of credit. A **term loan** is for a specific amount of money with a specific due date. Some term loans are unsecured. The loan is granted based on the creditworthiness of the firm. A secured loan requires that the borrower pledge collateral to obtain the loan. **Collateral** is something of value. It may be physical assets such as equipment and inventory or financial assets such as securities or a bank passbook. If the borrower defaults—fails to pay off the loan—the lender can claim the collateral. Borrowers prefer unsecured loans.

A **line of credit** is a commitment to the borrower by the bank that a certain amount of money will be available at a given rate of interest for a specific period of time. The borrower can then choose to borrow any or all of those funds at any time during that period. Lines of credit are normally set on a yearly basis. If the borrower needs more money than the limit allows, additional approval is required. You may have a similar limit on your bank charge card.

A firm uses a line of credit if it knows that it will need funds to finance expenses, but it isn't quite certain when those expenses will be incurred. For example, a furniture store might receive shipments of furniture at various times throughout the year. It may not be convenient to arrange financing each time, yet to borrow all of the money and hold it in the form of cash would not be good working capital management.

Accrued wages and taxes. Wages that employees have earned but that have not yet been paid are **accrued wages.** If you work, you are probably paid once a week. Unless you are paid in advance, you are actually loaning money to your employer. If you work on Monday but aren't paid until Friday, your employer has borrowed your Monday wages for four days. When there are hundreds of employees involved, the amounts can be substantial. If your employer paid you on a daily basis, the money would have to come from some other source. Of course, the bookkeeping could be prohibitive.

Taxes represent a similar source of funds. Firms must pay social security taxes, income taxes, and other taxes to federal, state, and local governments. Tax liabilities accumulate on a continuing basis but are usually paid once every three months. These accrued taxes are a source of funds.

Commercial paper. Unsecured promissory notes in amounts of $100,000 or more are **commercial paper.** (see Figure 12–1). It allows a

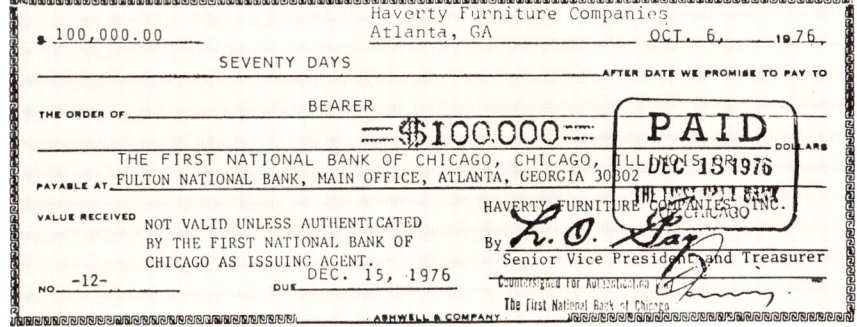

FIGURE 12–1
Commercial paper

major corporation to borrow directly from other major corporations. Large nationally known corporations issue this commercial paper, which has a life of three to six months. It is a negotiable or easily exchanged asset. It may change hands several times before it is redeemed by the corporation that issued it. Corporations issue commercial paper instead of borrowing in other ways because the interest rate on commercial paper is generally slightly lower than rates on other loans. In addition, it is generally quicker and less expensive than other sources.

In the short run a firm might draw upon trade credit, short-term loans, or accrued wages and taxes. If the firm is large and well known, it might issue commercial paper. Short-term liabilities are normally paid off within a year. But not all of a firm's projects can be completed within a year. Short-term financial management is the process of effectively obtaining and using funds in the short run. What about long-term financial management?

LONG-TERM FINANCIAL MANAGEMENT

Financial managers also make decisions that affect the firm beyond that imaginary one-year cutoff. The decisions that affect the firm over one to five years are sometimes called intermediate-term financing but are essentially the same as long-term decisions. These decisions result from a need to maintain a competitive position in a changing market. Perhaps the firm needs to expand the scope of its operations.

When a firm encounters long-term uses of funds, it is wise to seek out long-term sources of funds. In that way a firm can have some assurance that the cost of funding will stay the same over the life of the project. If short-term financing was used for a long-term project, the money would run out before the project was finished. What would happen if no new source was available? It could be serious, since long-term uses of funds affect the firm's future.

Long-term uses of funds

While financial managers spend most of their time on short-term working capital management, long-term uses of funds are important because they usually involve large amounts of money. **Long-term uses of funds** are investments that are expected to sustain or improve the productivity of the firm in the future. The process of deciding among long-term uses of funds is called **capital budgeting.** Capital investments usually fall into one of the following four categories: replacements, expansion into new products, expansion in existing products, and safety and environment.

Replacements.   Assets wear out or are damaged and must be replaced to maintain the productivity of the firm. A dry-cleaning firm might replace its old delivery truck. When a freight train derails, the railroad may find itself in need of new cars.

Some replacements increase productivity. A firm might replace serviceable but outmoded equipment with more efficient, modern versions. As computer technology continues to advance, many firms are replacing older systems with newer systems that are both faster and have greater capacity.

Expansion of existing products or markets.   In 1977 K mart opened a new store on the average of once ever 1.6 days.[6] New K marts offer the same types of products and services to the same types of customers. B&J Toys is a plastic injection molding company that produces plastic trucks and other toys. Its biggest customer is K mart. As K mart expands, it buys more of B&J Toys' trucks. B&J Toys has invested in additional plastic injection molding equipment to increase its production capacity. Both K mart and B&J Toys are making long-term uses of funds to expand within existing products and markets.

Expansion into new products or markets. To develop new products or approach a new market, a firm might invest in new equipment or facilities. It might also buy another company that is already in that business. The Coca-Cola Company diversified into the wine industry by buying Taylor Wines and Sterling Winery.

Safety and environment. Some expenditures are not intended to bring about increased productivity or sales, but they are necessary to comply with the firm's sense of social responsibility or to meet external requirements. These might be imposed by the government, by labor agreements, or by the firms' insurance companies. To obtain kidnapping insurance for key executives, some firms have been required to invest in "hardened" limousines costing over $50,000. These have special bulletproof glass and bodies and other equipment out of a James Bond movie.

Between 1970 and 1975, U.S. Steel invested $127 million for water pollution control equipment and $288 million for air pollution control equipment.[7] That's a notable use of funds. Increasingly, firms are using funds to invest in long-term projects designed to protect their facilities, their workers, or the environment.

Long-term uses of funds affect the productivity and the profitibility of a firm well into the future. Since these decisions involve a long-term commitment, they must be made with care. As the time involved increases, the risk is generally greater and the manager must deal with more unknowns. Managers attempt to reduce some of the costs and risks of capital expenditures by obtaining appropriate long-term financing.

Long-term sources of funds

Capital—long-term funds—can be obtained in three ways. It can be generated internally. Reinvested profits are called retained earnings. It can be borrowed through debt financing. The third source is equity financing obtained in exchange for part ownership of the business. Most firms use some combination of these three.

Three factors are very important in making long-term financing decisions. The most obvious is the cost involved. A second factor is the effect on the current owners and managers of the firm. Finally, different sources of capital involve different degrees of risk.

Internal financing. If a firm is profitable, the managers can choose to do one of two things with those profits. They can distribute the profits among the owners of the firm or reinvest the profits in the business. **Retained earnings** are profits that are reinvested in the business. Financing through retained earnings is not costless. While there is no direct price to be paid, there are opportunity costs for the owners. This means that if the earnings had been distributed, the owners could

FIGURE 12–2
Bonds

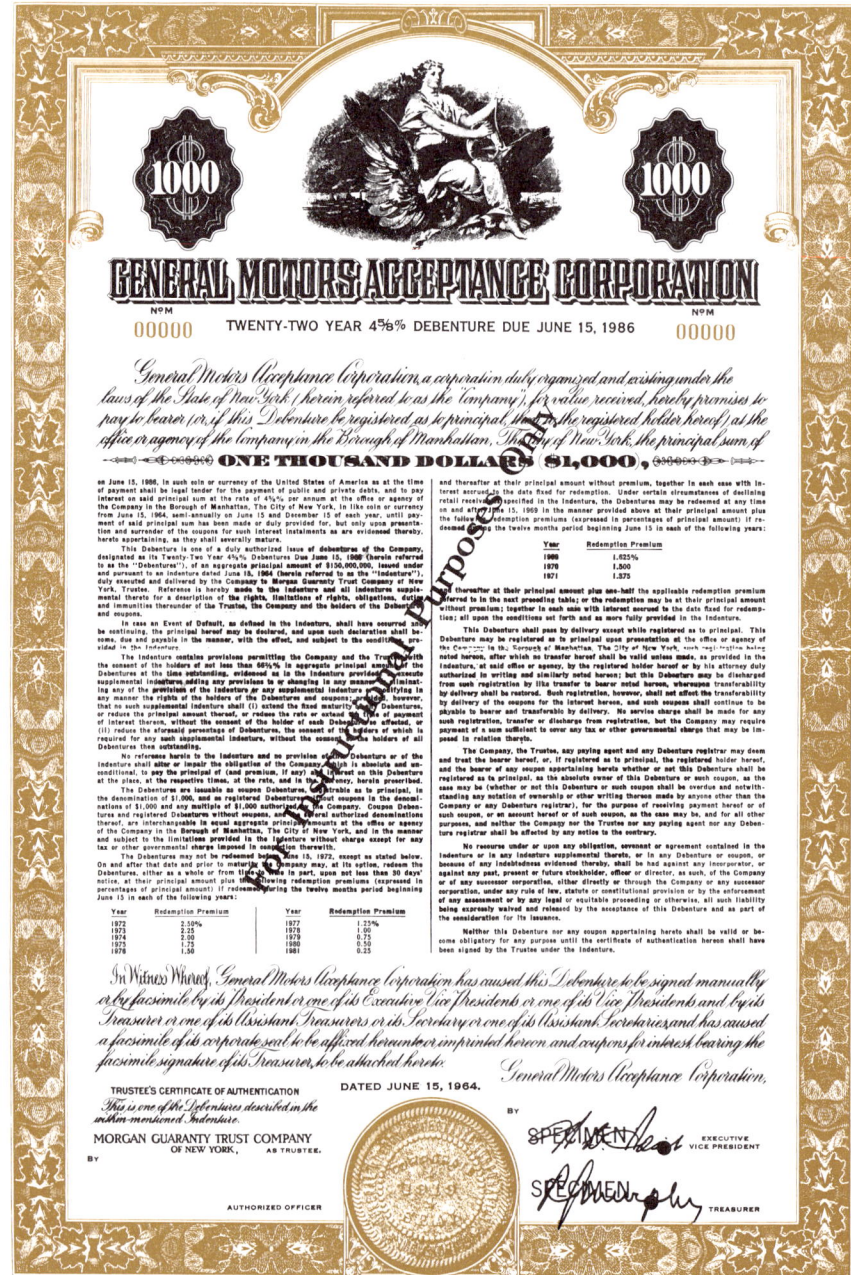

have used them in other ways. Internal financing allows the owners to maintain the same level of control over the firm. There is little risk involved.

Debt financing. A firm can raise capital by borrowing. This often is done by issuing bonds. **Bonds** are long-term notes payable (see Figure 12–2). They carry a specific interest rate and a specific maturity date. Where does debt stand in terms of cost, effects on owners, and risk?

There are two interesting points about the cost of debt. First, interest paid on debt is tax deductible. Second, once the bonds have been issued, the cost of debt is fixed. It can be accurately predicted. Even if the firm is extremely profitable, bondholders are not entitled to additional benefits.

The actual interest rate a firm must pay to borrow money depends on the general state of the economy and the credit standing of the firm. Firms try to avoid issuing bonds when interest rates are high. If a firm plans to issue bonds it will make an effort to upgrade its credit rating.

If the firm is borrowing a large amount, the lenders may impose special restrictions. For example, the firm might be prohibited from selling specific assets. Other than these restrictions to protect their investment, bondholders do not participate in the management of the firm. The owners and managers maintain control.

Payments of interest and the repayment of the amount of the loan are fixed legal obligations. When these are due, the firm must pay. This involves risk. If these obligations cannot be met, the lenders can legally file claim to the assets of the firm. Since lenders would prefer to be paid back with interest, there is a limit to how much debt a firm can obtain. As the amount of debt increases, lenders will demand higher interest rates to offset the increased risk. At some point, the cost becomes prohibitive.

Equity financing. A firm can raise equity capital by selling additional shares of ownership in the firm. In sole proprietorships or partnerships, this may mean that the current owners invest additional personal savings in the firm. Or, it may mean that new partners are brought into the firm. In the case of a corporation, it means issuing additional shares of stock.

While there may be some legal fees or other charges, equity has no fixed cost to the firm. The real cost is not in money but in control. As new owners are brought in, the existing owners must share both control of the firm and earnings of the firm.

Equity financing offers several advantages. First, it does not commit the firm to fixed payments. Earnings are paid to shareholders in the form of dividends. If there are no earnings to be shared by the owners, the firm can skip dividend payments. Second, there is no fixed maturity date. While individuals may sell their shares to other individuals, the firm does not have to buy back any shares. Third, additional equity

FIGURE 12–3
Stock certificate

financing generally improves the credit standing of the firm. If a firm goes bankrupt, the claims of lenders are satisfied before the owners get anything. The more owner money there is in the firm, the better the chance each creditor has of being paid off.

All corporations issue common stock and some also issue preferred stock (see Figure 12–3). Common and preferred refer to the owners' rights in the distribution of earnings and assets. Preferred shareholders have preferential rights. **Preferred stock** is sold with a specific dividend rate. Before any earnings can be distributed to common shareholders, the preferred dividends must be paid. In most cases these preferred rights are cumulative; they add up. If the company skips paying a preferred dividend, it must make that up and pay the current preferred dividend before common shareholders are paid. Holders of **common stock** share "in common" in any additional earnings that are distributed.

You may be wondering why anyone would buy anything other than preferred stock. Wouldn't it be much safer to have these preferred rights to the earnings? It would be safer, but remember, there is a premium on risk. These preferred rights are limited. If the preferred dividend rate is 8 percent, that's all you will get. If the corporation is tremendously profitable, you will still get only 8 percent. Common shareholders take the risk of earning nothing, but they hope to share the greater profits.

Firms issue preferred stock as a compromise between debt and equity financing. While it is equity, preferred shareholders normally have no voting rights. Common shareholders assume the greatest risk and therefore have more voice in the affairs of the firm. Like debt, preferred stock has a fixed maximum cost, which is the specified dividend rate.

Each night your newscaster reports the volume on the "Big Board." "Trading was moderate on the New York Stock Exchange with 15 million shares changing hands." Does that mean that American corporations sold 15 million shares of ownership to raise equity capital that day? Not at all. It simply means that 15 million shares changed hands. When you buy stock through one of the several national or regional stock exchanges, you are buying "used" stock. You are not buying that stock directly from the corporation but from one of the shareholders

DID YOU EVER WONDER?

Why do they talk about the bulls and the bears?

Stock market analysts often refer to investors as bulls or bears and talk about bull markets and bear markets. Merrill Lynch, Pierce, Fenner and Smith, the nation's largest stock brokerage, ran a television commercial with a thundering herd of bulls and the line "Merrill Lynch is bullish on America." Why?

In recent years the bull, with its horns pointing skyward, has come to be a symbol of optimism and the attitude that prices of securities will rise. Bears, on the other hand, with claws pointing downward, symbolize a pessimistic attitude that the securities prices will decline. Investors who are buying in anticipation of rising prices are bulls, while those who are selling their securities are bears. But there are many other possible symbols such as rams and turtles or mountaineers and divers. Why are bulls and bears used?

In the early 17th century the London Stock Market was granted a crest and a coat of arms by the English monarchy. As is customary with English crests, it depicted several animals. The three chosen were the bull, the bear, and the stag. It is from that crest that the symbolism was adopted. In the English market the stag symbolized anxiety and unsteady behavior.

Source: F. E. Armstrong, *The Book of the Stock Exchange* (London: Sir Isaac Pitman's Sons, Ltd., 1934), pp. 102–103.

of that corporation. Your money goes to that shareholder, not into the corporation treasury.

Even though the action on the stock exchange does not directly result in new debt or equity financing, the firm's managers are very interested in what happens to their stock on the market. They watch both the number of shares traded and the price at which those shares change hands. By doing so, they are more able to judge the price at which new shares might be sold. The market price of the firm's shares is an indication of investors' attitudes toward the firm.

Managers are also concerned if there is a sudden increase in the trading of the firm's shares. It could mean that some other organization is attempting to gain control or take over the management of the firm. Existing managers will generally resist takeover attempts.

The daily action of the stock exchanges is in the news each night because it is of interest to many Americans. Not only is it an indicator of the health of the economy, but about one out of every ten Americans owns stock. An exhibit in Chapter 4 explained the activities of the largest stock exchange—the New York Stock Exchange—and the roles of the various institutions and individuals who participate on the exchange. Let's consider the way firms can raise new equity or debt capital.

Issuing new securities

If a firm decides to issue new securities, it might turn to an investment banker. Investment bankers do not actually make long-term investments or act as banks. **Investment bankers** are specialists in issuing new securities. Let's follow the steps necessary to offer a new issue of securities to the capital market. This process begins with the pre-underwriting conference and ends when the securities have been sold to investors. Three separate functions are involved: counseling, underwriting, and distribution.

Counseling.   At the pre-underwriting conference, representatives of the issuing firm meet with the investment banker. They discuss the details and conditions. What is the best type of security to offer given the needs and financial standing of the firm? How much capital is needed? How does the state of the economy affect the timing of the action?

Investment bankers are affiliated with the brokerage houses that serve the general public. Merrill Lynch, Bache, E. F. Hutton, and other major brokerages have investment banking divisions. Therefore, they often have access to research that could be useful to the managers of the firm. If the firm decides to issue securities, the parties negotiate an underwriting agreement. The investment banker continues to assist the issuing firm with the legal paperwork and the preparation of the registration statement that must be filed with the Securities and Exchange Commission. This statement is examined by the SEC for omissions and misrepresentation. Until this registration process is complete, no stock may be sold.

Underwriting.   There are risks involved whenever a new issue of securities is offered in the investment marketplace. It may not sell as soon as expected, or the market value may decline. This would result in a loss for the issuing firm. **Underwriting** is the process of guaranteeing the initial sale of the securities at a fixed price.

On the day of issue, the underwriter purchases the entire issue of securities from the issuing firm at a price that is lower than the market value of the securities on that day. The difference between the purchase price and the market value is specified in the underwriting agreement. The difference is less for firms that are well managed and financially sound than for firms that are unknown or in financial trouble.

Distributing.   At this point, the issuing firm has its money and the underwriter owns the securities. The underwriter contacts individuals or organizations that might be interested in the issue. Whatever happens now benefits or damages the underwriter. If there are delays or declines, the underwriter loses. If investors snap up the securities at or above the market value on the day of issue, the underwriter enjoys the profits.

FINANCIAL INSTITUTIONS

Imagine that you had $100 for which you had no immediate need. If you tried to invest it all by yourself, you might run into some problems. First, $100 may not be enough to justify shopping around for someone in need of funds. Second, you may not even know where to look. Third, how would you handle the legal matters? Fourth, you might want some assurance that you wouldn't lose your money. There are many other obstacles that could interfere with your efforts to invest your $100. There are also lots of other people who have the same needs.

When there is a need, there are firms that make a business of serving that need. The economic system has a need for the efficient movement of funds among the various participants in the system. These include individuals, businesses, and governments. Financial institutions serve that need.

There are a large number of financial institutions in our economy. While they compete in some areas, each type of institution offers a different combination of financial services. The basic financial function of all the institutions is to collect funds from those with money and to invest funds in those in need of financing. **Financial institutions**

A. W. CLAUSEN
The world's biggest bank

A. W. Clausen is president and chief executive officer of the largest privately owned bank in the world. He was educated at Carthage College and received a law degree from the University of Minnesota. Reflecting the international scope of his organization, Clausen is a director of the US–USSR Trade and Economic Council and the National Council For US–China Trade and is co-chairman of the Japan–California Association.

The banking industry and the Bank of America have gone through great development and change as the scope of banking operations has expanded to include branch banking and credit card systems. At the same time, technological change has made computers, computerized check clearing, and electronic funds transfer realities. The Bank of America has been a leader in these industry developments.

Career opportunities in banking follow three main streams: operations, credit, and systems. The *operations* of a bank or branch involve what you see when you go to the bank. Tellers are there to provide banking service to you, but in addition there are people behind the scenes who help make the whole system work. These operations officers manage branch operations by hiring and training people, organizing the work to be done, coordinating the work of others, and generally carrying out the bank's policies and procedures. Positions in operations lead to higher-level positions as branch and regional managers.

Career opportunities in *credit* involve the loan functions of a bank. Lending officers spend considerable time working directly with customers, discussing their requirements, and developing financial plans to meet their needs. They analyze loan applications and financial statements to determine whether or not a loan should be granted, and they track the progress of customers who have been granted loans. The progression of jobs after initial training may be from loan officer for smaller accounts to larger ones and then to business accounts. These positions may be springboards to higher-level positions as branch or regional managers.

Career opportunities in *systems* reflect the computer age in banking. These systems must be designed and maintained. Designing systems for a bank requires a great deal of knowledge about the way a bank must operate, including its policies and procedures as well as rules and regulations established by state and federal laws. Jobs include analyst, systems analyst, and higher-level systems management positions.

blend together all of the funds deposited by their customers and invest those funds in the name of the institution. This process is called **intermediation.** The major financial institutions include commercial banks, life insurance companies, savings and loan associations, private pension funds, and credit unions.

Commercial banks

In that they provide such a variety of financial services, **commercial banks** have been called the department stores of finance. Commercial banks serve both consumers and businesses. They accept deposits from some customers, and lend funds to other customers. Most of those funds are deposited into two types of accounts: savings and demand accounts, which are commonly called checking accounts.

Commercial banks are in business to make a profit. They borrow funds from depositors in exchange for interest. They rent funds to their borrowers by charging interest. (see Figure 12–4). They offer their depositors interest, security, and convenience. Banks are private firms, but they are heavily regulated by government agencies. These regulations restrict bank investments to debt securities. Banks are the largest single suppliers of long- and short-term loans to businesses, governments, and consumers.

FIGURE 12–4
Commercial bank intermediation

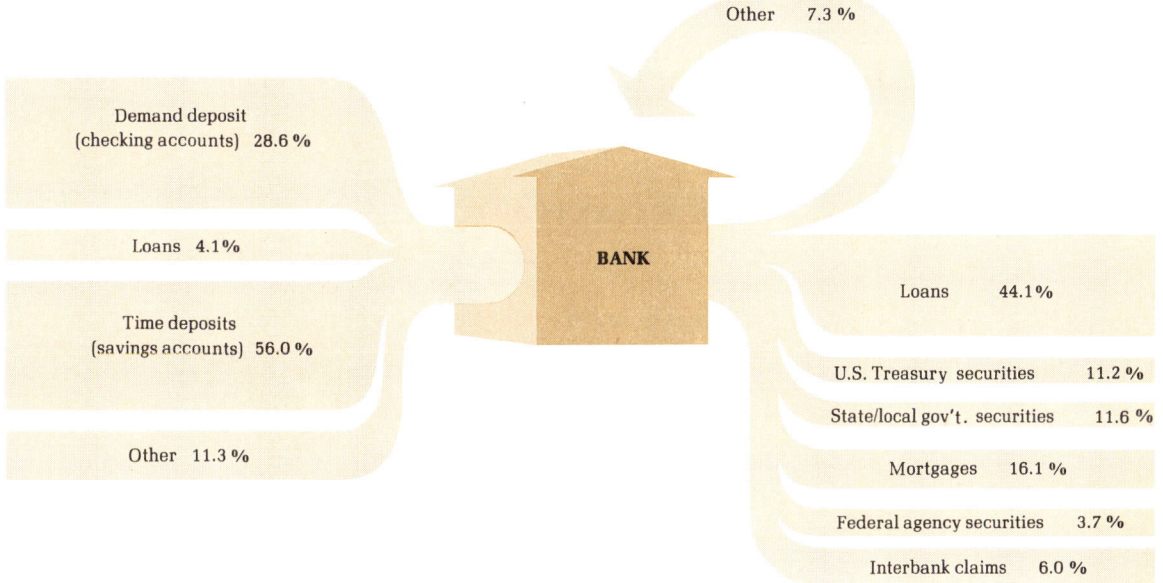

Other   7.3 %

Demand deposit
(checking accounts) 28.6 %

Loans   4.1%

Time deposits
(savings accounts) 56.0 %

Other   11.3 %

BANK

Loans   44.1%

U.S. Treasury securities   11.2 %

State/local gov't. securities   11.6 %

Mortgages   16.1 %

Federal agency securities   3.7 %

Interbank claims   6.0 %

Life insurance companies

It is easy to imagine that life insurance companies collect premiums just to pay them out to the beneficiaries of their policyholders in the form of death benefits. But the collection of premiums and the payment of benefits do not match perfectly. Life insurance companies invest the funds that would otherwise be idle (see Figure 12–5). If they invest wisely, their policyholders benefit. If they can earn money on your premiums, those premiums need not be as high.

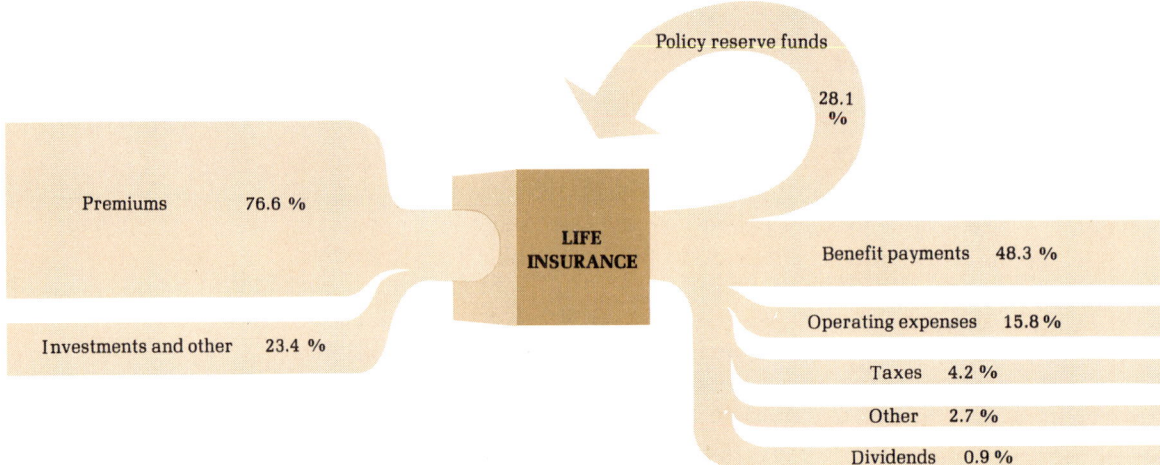

FIGURE 12–5
Life insurance
intermediation

Life insurance companies are able to predict their inflows and outflows of funds quite accurately. This allows them to commit funds to longer-term investments. By law they can invest only a small portion of their assets in common stock because of the risk involved.

Savings and loan associations

Many people do not distinguish between banks and savings and loans, but the differences are important. **Savings and loans** are much more specialized. Just as their name suggests, they collect savings and they make loans (see Figure 12–6). They do not offer checking accounts,

FIGURE 12–6
Savings and loan
intermediation

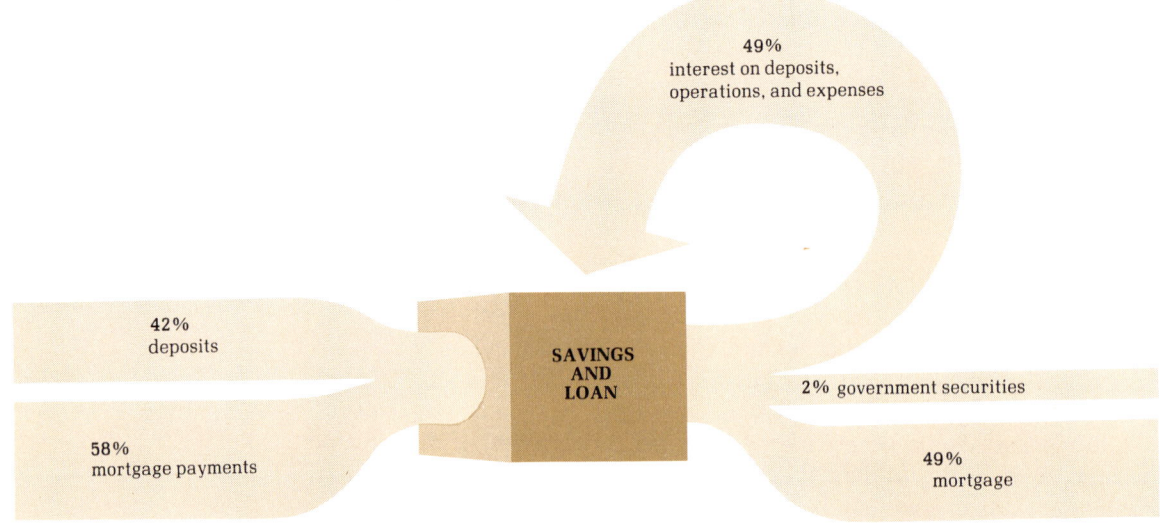

Source: *Savings and Loan Fact Book.*

although they have tried to develop systems to allow for fast and easy withdrawals from savings accounts.

Savings and loans specialize in home mortgage loans. When the demand for housing is strong, savings and loans prosper. But since mortgages are for as long as 30 years, savings and loans are not able to adjust quickly to meet changes in demand.

Private pension funds

Most people are covered by some pension fund. A **pension fund** is a group savings plan for the purpose of providing retirement or survivors income. Private pension funds are set up to collect regular contributions from employees and their employers.

You might expect that pension fund investments would be similar to those of the insurance companies. But pension fund managers are not restricted by law to limit their investments in equities. In fact, private pension funds invest heavily in equities that can offer much greater returns on investments.

Credit unions

A **credit union** is a cooperative thrift and loan society. It is composed of people who have a specified shared interest. Usually this is a common employer or membership in a church or union. Names such as the Detroit Teacher's Credit Union, Procter & Gamble Employees Credit Union, and Electrical Workers Credit Union show these relationships.

Members of credit unions deposit their money by purchasing ownership shares. In turn, each member may borrow from the association (see Figure 12–7). Credit unions do not make loans to nonmembers. Income from loans and other investments is used to pay dividends to the members.

FIGURE 12–7
Credit union intermediation

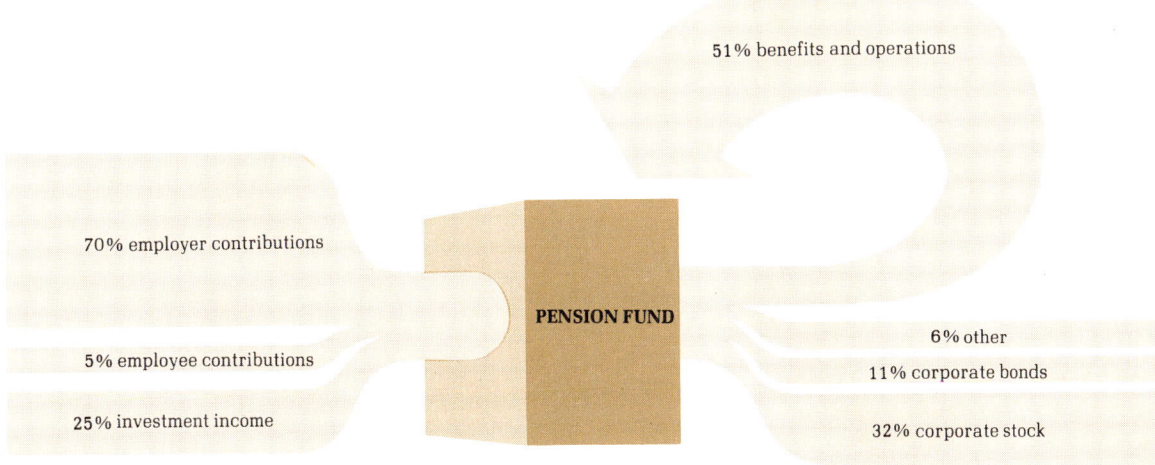

51% benefits and operations

70% employer contributions

PENSION FUND

5% employee contributions

25% investment income

6% other

11% corporate bonds

32% corporate stock

Source: Figures 12–4, 12–5, 12–7, Federal Reserve System flow of funds data.

Credit unions are owned, operated, and controlled by their members subject to government regulation. While most of their loans are to consumers, credit unions can invest in government securities, high-grade bonds, and even time deposits in commercial banks.

Some of your money may help finance long- or short-term business assets through any of these financial institutions. But once you turn your money over to an institution in return for interest, insurance coverage, or other promised future benefits, you have very little control over how that money is invested. You assume little risk and you are allowed little control. In the intermediation process, the institution stands between the suppliers and the users of funds. If you go to a bank for an auto loan, your contract is with the bank. You don't know and don't even care how the bank obtains the funds.

SUMMARY

The overall objective of financial management is to make the best possible use of the financial resources available to the firm. Short-term financial decisions relate to the firm's sources or uses of funds for less than a year. In deciding among the short-term uses of funds, financial managers attempt to balance the needs for liquidity and security against the needs to earn returns on short-term assets. They try to maintain adequate but not excessive levels of cash, accounts receivable, inventories, and short-term investments.

Short-term sources of funds include trade credit, short-term loans, accrued wages and taxes, and commercial paper. Cost and availability are important factors. Trade credit is the most important short-term source for small businesses. It can be very costly. Commercial paper funds are practical only for major corporations.

Firms use long-term funds to replace assets, to expand in new or existing products or markets, and to invest in long-term projects to protect their facilities, their workers, or the environment. Long-term financial needs are best met with long-term funding. Capital can be obtained through internal financing, debt financing, or equity financing. Financial managers must consider the costs of financing, the effect on the owners of the firm, and the risks involved.

Firms can meet their needs for long-term funds by issuing securities. Investment bankers specialize in assisting firms in this process. They provide counseling, underwriting, and distributing services. This reduces both the risk and the inconvenience for the firm.

Financial institutions serve the need for an efficient way to move funds among the various participants in the economic system. Some of the major financial institutions are commercial banks, life insurance companies, savings and loan associations, private pension funds, and credit unions. These institutions provide an intermediation process. They collect excess funds from some members of the system and make it available to meet the financing needs of other members.

REVIEW QUESTIONS

1. Evaluate each of the four types of short-term assets according to liquidity. Why is liquidity both good and bad for the firm?

2. How can a firm increase its accounts receivable? What are the advantages and drawbacks of a higher level of accounts receivable?

3. A small business was granted the credit terms 3/15: net 30 on a $1,000 purchase.
   a. Explain what the terms mean.
   b. What is the dollar amount of the discount?
   c. If the discount is not taken, what is the effective annual interest rate?

4. What is the difference between an unsecured term loan and a line of credit?

5. Consider each of the four types of short-term assets and four types of short-term liabilities. Can you name personal assets and liabilities that are similar? (Hint: Your groceries are inventory.)

6. Look through *The Wall Street Journal, Forbes, Business Week,* or other business periodicals for an example of each type of long-term financial use.

7. Compare internal financing, debt financing, and equity financing in terms of the effect on the current owners of the firm.

8. If you were buying stock, would you buy common or preferred stock? Why?

9. Pick one of the five financial institutions discussed in the chapter and explain how it participates in the intermediation process.

10. Explain the functions of an underwriter in the process of issuing new securities.

CASES

Case 12–1. Burger Country

Don Price and his two sons are opening an independent fast-food restaurant called Burger Country. The building is in a good location and one of Don's sons has had ten years of experience at McDonald's.

The start-up costs are substantial. The building and land are being leased from Burger Chef on a nine-year basis. Don estimates that the equipment will cost about $60,000 new and $25,000 used. Don needs new signs that will cost over $10,000. During the first month, advertising will be about $3,000 and supplies will cost about $5,000. Don has some savings to invest, but he will need some financing. He figures he'll be lucky if he breaks even the first year.

1. *What financing options should Don consider?*
2. *The paper goods supplier offers terms of 2/10; net 30 on Don's $800 order of napkins and other paper goods. Should Don take the discount? How much will he save?*

Case 12–2. Channell Consulting

Joan Channell is a financial consultant who specializes in the problems of small- and medium-sized corporations. Recently she was called in to advise the management of a small corporation that produces natural foods products to be distributed through supermarkets.

Demand for the firm's products has been increasing rapidly. To keep up with this demand the firm must either rent or buy a larger plant and more equipment. This will also mean increased inventories of raw materials, goods in process, and finished inventory. The managers are concerned about how to finance the costs of the expansion.

1. *What are the options? Should the managers seek out long- or short-term financing? Does it differ if they buy or rent?*

2. *Would this be different if this were a closely held corporation operating under Subchapter S.? (You might check back to Chapter 4.)*

chapter
13

PERSONNEL MANAGEMENT

By studying this chapter you should be able to find answers to these questions:

1 Why are job descriptions important?
2 From what sources do firms recruit new employees?
3 What are the steps in the normal employment process?
4 What types of training are used in industry?
5 Why are some people paid a salary while others get wages, fees, or commissions?
6 What determines the level of compensation?
7 Why are fringe benefits included in most compensation plans?
8 Why do unions exist?
9 What laws affect labor–management relations?
10 How do unions organize workers?
11 How does the collective bargaining process work?

Terms you should know:

apprentice
binding arbitration
craft unions
industrial unions
interviews
job description
jurisdictional dispute
labor union
local union
National Labor Relations Act, 1935
Norris-Laguardia Act, 1932
recruiting
resumé
Taft-Hartley Act

In the spring of 1864, a Wells Fargo stagecoach was stranded by an unexpected mountain snowstorm. The driver, John Valentine, picked up the mail sacks and made his way on foot down from the Sierra Nevada high country to the foothill town of Placerville, California. His devotion to his job caused him to become one of only a handful of people ever to cross the Sierra Nevada Mountains on foot during the snow season. He went on to serve as president of Wells Fargo from 1892 to 1901.

John Valentine

Courtesy of Wells Fargo Bank

Cassie Hill's husband was the Wells Fargo agent in Roseville, California. When he died suddenly in 1885, she took over the office. Some people assumed that her service would be temporary. After all, she had five children at home. Instead, Cassie Hill served as the Wells Fargo agent for 23 years.

The efforts of John Valentine and Cassie Hill illustrate a very important point. An organization depends on people. Every firm has to decide what jobs need to be done and then find the right people to do them.

Many people think of personnel management as hiring and firing people. Those are important, but there's more to it. **Personnel management** is the process of building and maintaining a productive group of employees. The objective is to employ an adequate number of competent and motivated people. Personnel managers must recruit and hire the right people and help workers to develop their potential. Finally, they must design and coordinate a fair and meaningful system of rewards and benefits.

Cassie Hill

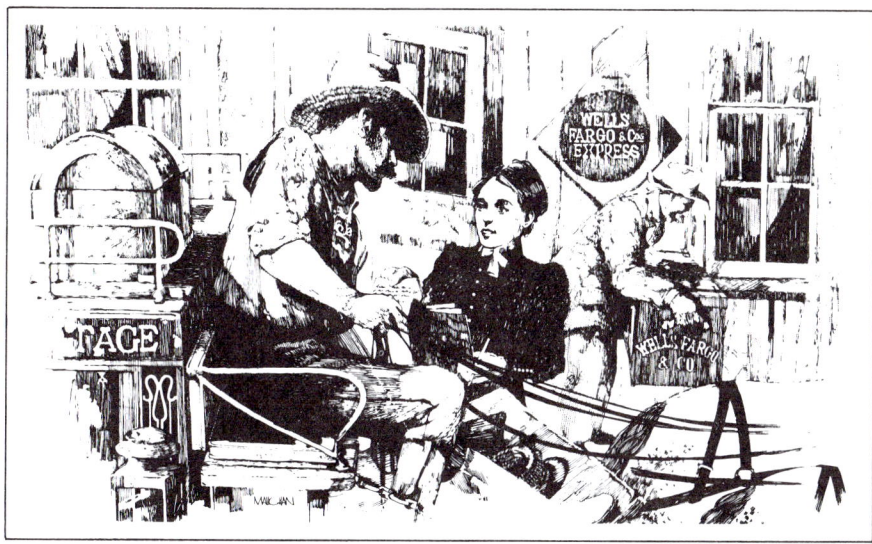

Courtesy of Wells Fargo Bank

At the end of this text you will find an appendix on careers in business. It has been included to provide you with information to help you find a position that will be satisfying and utilize your skills and education. Both employers and employees benefit when people are well suited for their positions. In the broadest sense, personnel management is the effective utilization of human resources.

Personnel policies and actions have direct effects on people's lives. Personnel actions are subject to external restrictions intended to assure safety and fairness. Government agencies and labor unions are major sources of external influence. Reaching agreements with these outside agencies and making sure that the terms of those agreements are carried out are important personnel functions.

Personnel management is an ongoing process. In a very small firm the owner makes personnel decisions. As a company grows, personnel duties are assigned to other people. Larger firms have personnel departments with specialists in personnel management. In this chapter we will look first at the way people are hired and trained. Then we'll consider the ways in which people are paid for their work. Finally, we will examine the role of labor unions and labor–management relations.

QUALIFIED PEOPLE TO FILL THE FIRM'S NEEDS

All firms need new employees. For some firms this is a continuing need. Industries such as encyclopedia sales are known for high turnover and are constantly hiring to replace employees who quit. Other industries such as electronics expand rapidly and need more employees. Even in a stable industry such as banking, people retire.

Forecasting personnel requirements

Personnel managers try to forecast staffing needs. Some firms use formal personnel planning to predict the firm's employee needs. Some of the data used in personnel planning are the firm's sales forecast, the corporate growth rate, the industrywide employee turnover rates, past retirement patterns, and general economic forecasts.

Some industries have highly predictable fluctuations in employment needs. Seasonal industries such as resorts, canneries, retailers, tax services, and construction firms increase their hiring activity just before their busy seasons. In most industries, personnel needs are less predictable. The accuracy of the personnel forecast depends on the accuracy of forecasts developed in other areas of the firm. General forecasts can be converted into hiring plans when the positions to be filled are described in detail.

Job descriptions

A **job description** is a written statement covering the duties of the position (see Figure 13–1). It describes the duties to be performed and the skills required of the person holding the position. It may also describe the working conditions and the physical and mental demands on the employee. Maintaining job descriptions is a continuing task. The nature of jobs change because of new equipment or methods, company expansion, or hundreds of other events.

A job description serves two purposes. First, it helps to clarify the work to be performed. This can make it easier to describe the type of person needed to fill the job which is important if a supervisor is depending on the personnel department to find a person for the position. Without a clearly written job description, hiring is a guessing game.

The second purpose of a job description is to help the employee to better understand what is expected on the new job. Clear job descriptions can help to minimize misunderstanding which can result in turnover. Would you accept a job with an employer who could not tell you what you would be expected to do? A well-written job description paves the way for recruiting.

Recruiting

Recruiting is the process of attracting qualified applicants. The sources tapped and the methods used depend on the needs of the firm. Major firms such as IBM, AT&T, and Procter & Gamble recruit

FIGURE 13–1

Sample job description

Norton Company
Position Description

Title: Sales Supervisor   Date: June 27, 1975
       Abrasives Marketing Group

Incumbent: Interviewer: B.C. Hammond

Reports to: District Sales Manager   Approved: (1)
            Abrasives Marketing   (2)
            Group

ACCOUNTABILITY OBJECTIVE

Ensure optimum sales and market participation at minimum sales
costs within the territory for the sale of assigned abrasive
products.

DIMENSIONS - Annual Sales Volume - $300,000 - $600,000

                Products ⊸ Coated Abrasive Division and Grinding
                           Wheel Division products and in some
                           cases, AMD products.

SPECIFIC ACCOUNTABILITIES

1. Meet or exceed sales targets for the sale of assigned
   abrasive products.

2. Develop and maintain close personal relationships with
   distributor management and sales personnel and all key
   customer personnel.

3. Recommend distributor appointments or cancellations in
   the territory.

4. Ensure that Norton obtains the maximum results from
   distributor efforts.

5. Ensure the training of distributor personnel.

6. Ensure that the District Sales Manager is currently and
   fully informed on key market conditions and all activity
   of the Sales Supervisor.

7. Meet or exceed established goals for sales credits and
   allowances in the territory.

8. Provide market information on customer needs.

Courtesy Norton Company

continuously. They have people who specialize in recruiting. Firms that need to hire many people may run advertisements stressing the benefits of working for them. These are not limited to a specific position. The purpose is to generate a continuing flow of qualified applicants.

A small business may limit its recruiting efforts to the classified ads or a sign in the window. Attracting a large number of applicants could create problems. For example, when the long-range weather forecasters predicted a third year of drought for the Sierra Nevada mountains, the owners of a small ski resort decided not to hire in advance. When a major storm hit suddenly, however, they needed about 30 employees in a hurry. A TV news reporter in a nearby city broadcast the story. The poor owners were swamped with hundreds of applicants who jammed the parking lot and tied up the phone lines. There was hardly room for paying customers!

The objective of recruiting is to stimulate a sufficient number of qualified people to apply for the position. If too few apply, the firm must either leave the position vacant or fill it with a person who may not be the best qualified. To attract unqualified people is a waste of time for everyone.

To avoid this, many smaller companies use employment agencies. An employment agency can serve the same purpose for a smaller firm that the company recruiter serves for a larger firm. But the larger firm pays the full salary and all the fringe benefits for the recruiter's undivided attention. The smaller firm pays a much smaller fee for the services of an agency. In return, the small firm's manager is spared the time and effort needed to attract applicants or to interview unqualified people.

There are four major sources of qualified applicants: (1) people who are already employed by the firm may be ready for a transfer or promotion; (2) some firms recruit their competitors' employees; (3) people may be recruited from firms in other industries; and (4) there are nonbusiness sources such as schools and the military. To reach these prospects, an employer might post notices, run advertisements in newspapers or trade journals, or make personal contacts. Some firms in high turnover industries such as real estate and insurance even use TV advertising to recruit.

From within.   There are some real benefits in promoting current employees. A policy of promoting from within can be good for morale. It tells employees that good work will be rewarded. It is a way for the firm to realize some added benefits on its investments in training. This person has a personnel record and can be more fully evaluated. A current employee also knows the firm and its policies.

But promotion from within can cause problems. The people who were not promoted could be resentful. The firm could miss a chance to bring in new people with fresh new ideas. A strict policy of promotion from within could retard the development of current employees if they feel protected from external competition for higher-level jobs. Another problem is that some people find it hard to adjust to a new status in the same firm. When a person is promoted to a supervisory position, it can be hard to give up the behaviors that went along with the former position. Sometimes other people have a hard time accepting the newly promoted person in the new position. Each of the sources of applicants has both advantages and disadvantages.

From competitive firms. The major advantage of hiring someone from another firm in the same industry is experience. It is quite common for employees of firms in the data processing industry to have some IBM background. IBM runs a fine training program. Many smaller firms that cannot afford the training expense make a special effort to recruit people with this type of training and experience.

For lower-level positions, experience reduces the need for training. At higher levels, however, other questions arise. What would happen, for example, if a firm hired a design engineer from the research department of its major competitor? Could that person provide information on the competitor's plans for future products?

In 1977 The Pillsbury Company hired the senior executive vice president of McDonald's as president of its Burger King subsidiary. Shortly thereafter Burger King introduced the Burger King Magic Magician to compete with Ronald McDonald for the loyalty of millions of hamburger-eating children. This was not the work of the new Burger King president alone. After he made the switch to Burger King, several other McDonald's executives followed.[1] To protect against this, some firms require that employees with access to company secrets sign an agreement not to accept a position with a competitor for a certain period of time after leaving the firm.

From other industries. Experience is important, but the industry in which that experience was gained may not matter. If so, a firm might recruit people from firms in other industries. A keypunch operator with experience at a bank might easily switch to a steel company. If the recruiting is not limited to one industry, the pool of applicants is much larger. There are many specialized fields such as chemical engineering, marketing research, or accounting in which the person's knowledge of the field is far more important than experience in a specific industry.

From nonbusiness sources. Fortunately, there are some positions for which potential is more important than experience. You can look around and see that students who are about to graduate are eager to find jobs that will allow them to use their increased abilities. People returning to civilian life after military service have similar needs. People in both of these groups may be more open to recruiting efforts than people who are already working.

Often they have knowledge or skills that eliminate the need for expensive training programs. For example, the airlines depend on the military to supply pilots. The military trains people for numerous other jobs as well. For the employer this is much the same as hiring trained people from other firms, but instead of having to lure them away, they are ready to leave anyway.

The objective of recruiting is to locate qualified people and interest them in the available positions. In most cases, a person's qualifications for a position do not depend on age, sex, race, religion, or unrelated physical handicaps.

Selecting the right person for the job

If the recruiting efforts have been successful, the employer has several applicants. Figure 13–2 shows the steps between the completion of the application blank and final placement in the position. An applicant might be rejected at any step in the process. As the process continues, the group of applicants is slowly reduced to a single employee.

FIGURE 13–2
Steps in the selection process

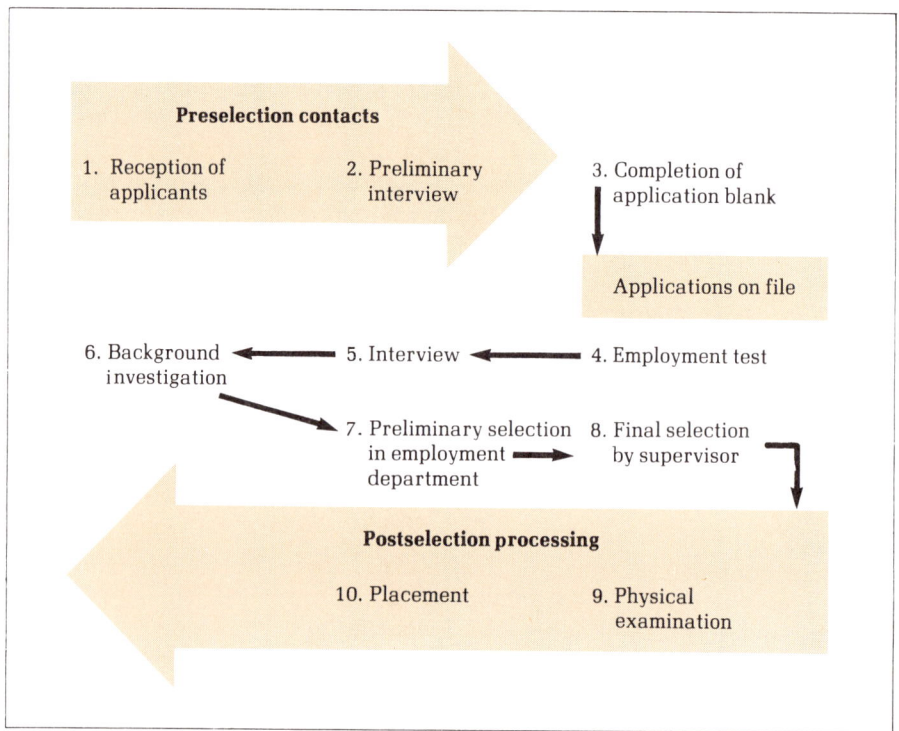

Source: Adapted from Herbert J. Chruden and Arthur W. Sherman, Jr., *Personnel Management,* 5th ed. (Cincinnati: Southwestern Publishing Company), 1976.

Application blanks. Application blanks are an easy way to collect standard information. Most firms use application blanks even if the applicant has submitted a personal resumé. A **resumé** is a summary of education, experience, and other qualifications that has been prepared by the job seeker. Tips on preparing resumés are presented in

EQUAL EMPLOYMENT OPPORTUNITIES

Equal employment opportunity is the law. During the 1960s and 1970s various state and federal laws were passed for the purpose of guaranteeing equal employment opportunities to all people regardless of race, sex, religion, age, or nonjob-related handicaps. There are a variety of agencies that attempt to enforce these laws, but progress has been slow.

The enforcement of equal opportunities takes two forms. Agencies such as the Equal Employment Opportunity Commission (EEOC) investigate complaints filed by individuals who believe that their rights have been denied. From the beginning the EEOC has been bogged down by a backlog of cases. It has made some progress in major cases such as the AT&T case, which resulted in the payment of over $15 million in back wages to individuals who had suffered wage discrimination. This enforcement depends on the individuals' ability to recognize that their rights have been denied and their willingness to make the effort to file the necessary papers.

Under the Federal Contract Compliance Act of 1971, any firm doing business with the federal government is supposed to work toward a balance among its employees that matches the minority group proportions in the surrounding community. The firm is supposed to take affirmative (positive) action to hire minority workers. This requirement has caused paperwork headaches and majority group backlash. There are no easy solutions, but increasing awareness is slowly bringing changes in traditional patterns. The goal is the fuller utilization of our most important resource—people.

"Hi there! I understand you're an equal opportunity employer!"

Reprinted by permission *The Wall Street Journal.*

the appendix on careers. Application blanks assure employers that no important facts have been omitted and allow for comparisons among applicants.

Employment tests.   Testing may be the next step. Job-related tests range from skill tests such as typing to tests of intelligence or psychological traits. Some tests are very useful. A position may require typing at 80 words per minute. If a typing test shows that the applicant can type only 30 words per minute, would you hire that person?

A **valid test** measures factors that are related to success on the job. In recent years the validity of some tests has been challenged. Tests that measure social conditioning or other factors not related to job success may result in discrimination against minority groups. Employers must now prove the validity of employment tests. This requirement has substantially reduced the use of these tests.

A good test is also reliable. **Reliability** means that the employer can count on the test to measure the same factors in the same way each time it is given. If two people with equal skills take the test, they should receive equal scores. Some tests are very reliable but lack validity. For example, two candidates for a sales position could be given a typing test. It might fairly measure their typing skills, but those skills have nothing to do with the job. Other tests are valid but lack reliability. The employer must be careful that tests are both valid and reliable. Otherwise testing not only is a waste of time and money but also interferes with the selection process.

"Do you have any other qualifications other than good vibes?"

Interviews.   Face-to-face meetings between the applicant and someone from the firm are **interviews.** The purpose is to find out more about the applicant and to allow the applicant to learn more about the firm and the job. It's a two-way process.

Interviews vary in rigidity. Some are highly structured, as when the interviewer follows a list of specific questions in a specific order. Interviewers using a moderately structured approach have a plan and seek certain answers but may vary the questions. An unstructured interview is more like a friendly conversation. The objective is to arrive at an overall picture of the applicant.

Background investigation.   Most people try to state their qualifications in a positive but honest way. But people have been known to stretch the truth. Employers make some checks on the applicant's background by asking for college transcripts, letters of recommendation, or other documents. Experience can be verified by a phone call to a past employer. Failure to check on such matters can expose the firm to serious risks.

ALL THAT GLITTERS IS NOT GOLD

When Bob Harris took the job as weather forecaster for a New York radio station and the *New York Times,* he claimed that he had a doctorate in meteorology. It turned out that that was just a bit beyond the normal resumé puffery. His knowledge came from a lot of experience and self-study. When the facts were discovered, "Dr. Bob, the weatherman" lost his job, and the station was faced with explaining his disappearance.

Preliminary selection.   Someone has to decide who is going to get the job. If it is a high-level unique position, the entire selection process might take place in the division in need of the new employee. The personnel department's role might be limited to processing the paperwork. The new Burger King president was probably selected by an executive committee. In most cases the personnel department makes a preliminary selection and sends two or more finalists for interviews with the supervisor of the specific area.

Final selection.   Most supervisors have the right to make the final choice. If the supervisor was careful to spell out the duties, requirements, and working conditions, there is a good chance that one of the finalists will get the position. If the supervisor listed one set of decision factors but judges on some other basis, the selection process could break down. The system depends on the communication between the supervisors and the personnel department.

Training: Toward a fuller utilization of human resources

Training programs are expensive. The direct costs include the salary or fees paid to the trainers and the price of the materials or training equipment used. Some firms invest in films, video tapes, recording equipment, and even special facilities and mock-up equipment. American industry spends billions of dollars each year on employee training programs.

Then there are the indirect costs. Many of the hours employees spend in training programs are hours off their jobs. Facilities and personnel that could be devoted to direct profit-making activities are assigned to training. Why?

Training programs may be costly in the short run, but in the long run well-designed training programs pay off for both the employers and the employees. The most obvious payoff is in increased productivity. Well-trained employees can accomplish more. For a manufacturer this means fewer rejects. If employees deal directly with customers, there should be increased customer satisfaction. Training can contribute to improved employee morale and reduced employee turnover.

The costs of training can be more than offset by the direct and indirect savings and the increased productivity. Of course, this happens only if the training is well designed to meet the needs of the employees. Employees need training for various reasons. Some employees are new to the firm. Others change jobs within the firm. If new machinery or techniques are adopted, the employees need to be trained. At certain intervals, employees may need to brush up on their skills. Too many accidents or rejects may be a sign that more training is needed.

There are many training methods. The type of training used depends on factors such as the number of people to be trained, the specific objectives of the training, the skill levels of the trainer and the trainees, and the time and expense involved.[2] Some common types of training are on-the-job training, conference training, classroom training, apprenticeships, and company-sponsored outside training.

On-the-job training.   On-the-job training allows people to learn by performing a task under normal conditions along with experienced employees. It is the most widely used training method. The trainee has the chance to feel productive, and the direct costs are low.

But the benefits of on-the-job training depend on the skills of the experienced employee who is in charge. It can result in passing on bad habits. It is not recommended in cases where an error could result in serious loss, damage, or injury.

Conference training.   When trainees can learn from the experiences and ideas of other employees, conference training is useful. The members of the group discuss a specific topic or problem under the guidance of a discussion leader. Not only can the trainees learn from each other, but they also have the chance to feel that their ideas are appreciated. Conference training can be very useful for newly promoted supervisors.

Classroom training. You have firsthand experience with classroom training. The business version is very much like the college classroom. There are lectures, films, reading and writing assignments, and all of the other educational techniques with which you are so familiar. The trainer can cover a great deal of material in a controlled setting. It can be interesting and informative, or it can be irrelevant and boring. It is used when a large group of people have the same training need at the same time.

Apprenticeships. An **apprentice** is a person who serves as a helper to a person skilled in a trade in order to learn that trade. Apprenticeships are used when skills are best learned by imitation and guidance. The learning period can last several years. Most apprentice programs are set up by unions. A person may have to serve as an apprentice to earn the right to join the union. Apprenticeships are common in trades such as plumbing, bricklaying, and printing. While the apprenticeship training is not formally conducted by the firm, the firm provides the working situation and benefits from the increased availability of skilled workers.

Company-sponsored outside training. There are many ways a firm can support its employees' interests in training outside the firm. Professional organizations often schedule meetings and training programs. A firm can pay all or part of the expenses of employees who choose to participate. Many companies help their employees to finish high school or college. Most of these firms pay a part of the expenses, and some firms allow time off for classes.

The objective of all training methods is improved performance. Improved performance can result from improved skills, understanding, or attitudes. Training is one way for a firm to encourage employees to develop.

WAGE AND SALARY ADMINISTRATION: THE REWARD SYSTEM

Financial rewards are important because of what they can buy, but that is just the tip of the iceberg. Think of all the other messages that are wrapped up in a paycheck. A paycheck puts a number on an employee's worth to the firm and in the social structure. It is a measure of status. Most people are very serious and very sensitive about their paychecks. The way in which wages and salaries are administered can have a great effect on employee morale and productivity.

A compensation system should be equitable, motivate employees, conform to the law, and keep labor costs under control. Those objectives do not always seem compatible. In setting up a compensation plan, employers consider the basis for compensation, the level of compensation, and fringe benefits.

The basis for compensation

Three compensation plans are in common use: time units, time periods, and direct measures of productivity. Let's look at the types of compensation plans and the reasoning behind each.

Time units. Financial rewards that are based on time units are called **wages.** A major advantage of this plan is that it is simple to understand and simple to administer. The wage rate is multiplied by the number of time units worked, usually measured by the hour.

Time unit plans are logical when the rate of work is set by something or someone other than the worker. An auto assembly worker assembles automobiles at the rate of the assembly line. If the person who installed antennas worked faster than other workers, there would be little benefit. There is no reason to install more than one per car. The group rate determines the individual's rate.

Time unit plans are also used when the work schedule is irregular. Supermarket checkers, babysitters, and clerks all work on irregular schedules. They are called in to work when the need for their services arises. The easiest way to determine the amount to pay these people is to base it on units of time. The advantage of this system to the employee lies in being paid for the number of hours actually worked. A person who works more hours is paid more. From the employer's viewpoint, the benefit is that employees are not paid if they don't work.

Time periods. Under a time period plan, employees are paid from one date to another date regardless of the amount of time they work between those dates. Some people are paid by the week and others by the month. These financial rewards are called **salaries.**

Salaries are used when the hours of work are so regular that there is little reason to count. Clerical workers normally work a 40-hour week. It's easier to pay them on a weekly basis. If they are absent too often, they may be fired.

Salaries are the dominant form of compensation for management personnel. It is assumed that they will be on duty during normal working hours. But more important, it is very difficult to measure the actual productivity of managers. It isn't how many hours they work but how well they perform that makes the difference. Salaries are logical when it is difficult to measure the individual's contribution.

Direct measures of productivity. Financial rewards based on direct measures of productivitiy are called *wages* or **commissions** depending on whether the workers produce or sell the firm's products. Those who produce on a piecework basis are paid wages. People who sell products and services are often paid a commission.

The productivity plan is logical if an individual's productivity can be fairly measured. It provides an incentive to increase productivity. The employer benefits by paying only for the output produced. This plan can cause serious problems if the employee must perform a variety of duties. The employee has one objective—to produce whatever is being measured. Employees cannot be expected to perform any functions not directly related to that output.

A combination. Since each plan has some benefits, some employers combine a base salary with some payment based on output. This offers the security employees need along with the incentive for superior performance. Whatever plan is used, someone still has to determine the actual rate per hour or the salary level.

The level of compensation

A firm must set a wage or salary level that will attract and retain competent employees, yet keep labor costs at a reasonable level. To do so, employers consider the cost of living, conditions in the labor market, the prevailing wage rate, and the firm's ability to pay.

The cost of living. As the cost of living increases, you need more money to maintain the same standard of living. If employees are forced to reduce their standards of living, it could result in high levels of employee turnover or low morale. Most union contracts include escalator clauses which require automatic wage increases tied to some index such as the consumer price index. Table 13–1 shows the relative costs of living in 12 U.S. cities for a family of four with a house and two cars.

TABLE 13–1
Costs of living in a dozen U.S. cities

City	Estimated cost	Percent of average
Los Angeles	$28,425	131%
Washington, D.C.	27,220	124
San Francisco	27,014	123
Chicago	26,587	121
Cleveland	25,243	115
Dallas	**22,017**	**100**
Cincinnati	21,797	99
St. Louis	21,420	97
Atlanta	21,231	97
Denver	21,116	96
New Orleans	20,228	92
Louisville	19,889	90

Source: Compiled by Runsheimer & Co. and reported in *Dun's Review*, April 1978, p. 63.

Conditions in the labor market. The price of diamonds, the rate of interest on loans, and the price of labor all depend on supply. If there are hoards of people eager to work, employers will have to pay less for labor than if there are few people available. If there aren't enough jobs to absorb the people who are trained for those positions, the compensation rate will decline. Since there are more people who are willing to live in Colorado or California than in Alaska, workers in Alaska are paid more. Higher pay was one of the ways the companies building the Alaskan pipeline attracted workers to Alaska. More people can perform as secretaries than as surgeons, so surgeons are paid more.

Prevailing wage rate. Once the firm has gone through the process of recruiting, selecting, and training employees, it is usually wise to retain those employees. Employees will stay with a firm only if it is in their best interest. If other firms in the area or in the industry are paying more for people with the same skills and experience, employees will be tempted to switch. Therefore, a firm should pay wages that are competitive in the industry and geographic area.

Ability to pay. Regardless of other factors, a firm cannot pay more than it can afford. The problem is that it may not be clear to employees whether the firm is unable or just unwilling to meet demands for increased wages.

The cost of living, the conditions in the labor market, the prevailing wage rate, and the firm's ability to pay affect the level of compensation. But wages and salaries are only part of the package.

Fringe benefits

Employers provide many benefits beyond wages and salaries. While fringe benefits packages vary widely, there are five major categories:

1. Legally required benefits—unemployment insurance, social security, and worker's compensation.
2. Private welfare and security programs—pension plans, life and health insurance payments.
3. Pay for time not worked—holidays, vacations, sick leave, and rest periods.
4. Extra compensation plans—profit sharing, savings plans, suggestion awards.
5. Employee services—subsidized cafeterias, discounts on purchases of company products, educational assistance.[3]

Providing these benefits can represent a substantial cost to the firm. The average weekly bill per employee for fringe benefits in the United States ranges from less than $50 in department stores to more than $100 in the petroleum industry.

Why are these resources devoted to fringe benefit programs? One important answer is our tax system. Fringe benefits and wages are both tax-deductible expenses for the employer, but the employee must pay taxes on wages. Most fringe benefits are tax-free, however. Another factor in favor of fringe benefits is that it is hard for employees to provide the same benefits on their own. Individual health and life insur-

Did You Ever Wonder?

How much do employers pay for fringe benefits and how is the money spent?

Employee benefits average about one third of payroll costs nationwide. The level of benefits varies by industry. The following list shows the average weekly dollar amount of benefits by industry:

Petroleum	$101.54	Printing and publishing	$69.87
Chemicals	96.31	Paper and lumber	66.29
Machinery	80.04	Wholesale/retail trade sales	53.75
Food/tobacco	73.50	Hospitals	42.38
Banking	72.02	Department stores	41.17

Here is the way those dollars are spent.

Private pensions
15.5%

Paid vacations
14.5%

Workers'
compensation
3.5%

Profit sharing
3%

Unemployment benefits
2.9%

Social security
16%

Insurance
14.5%

Paid rest periods
10%

Paid sick
leave
3.4%

Bonuses/
awards
1%

All other
16%

ance policies offer less coverage at higher costs. Labor unions are perhaps the most important force behind the increased cost of fringe benefits in this country.

UNIONS

Organized labor is a powerful force in our economy. About one out of every four American workers is a union member. Almost all the nation's basic industries are unionized. A strike in the coal, steel, transportation, or automobile industries can cripple the nation. Union leaders therefore can exert strong pressures on both business and government. To understand the role of unions, let's first look at why they exist and how they are organized, and then examine the relationships between employers and unions and the legislation that affects those relationships.

Why do unions exist?

Unions developed during a time when many employers gave little thought to the welfare of their workers. Neither business nor government acted to improve working conditions. Individual workers were powerless against their employers. A **labor union** is a group of workers who have united to exert collective pressure to achieve and maintain benefits for themselves. Unions negotiate with employers to reach labor agreements that provide improved working conditions and benefits.

Unions engage in political activities such as endorsing political candidates and encouraging prolabor legislation. They exert political pressure in areas such as trade, education, and the environment if they believe the results will affect their members.

Another major purpose of labor unions is to continue to exist. Unions try to organize nonunionized workers. In recent years unions have focused on white-collar workers, including government employees. Unions are often in conflict with employers who frequently oppose unionization. Unions also conflict with each other in jurisdictional disputes. A **jurisdictional dispute** occurs when two or more unions are in competition to represent a group of workers. Many of these disputes are the result of the organizational structure of labor unions.

The structure of labor unions

There are two forms of labor unions: industrial and craft unions. **Industrial unions** are formed on the basis of the industry in which the members are employed. They are open to both skilled and unskilled workers in those industries. Industrial unions predominate in mass production industries such as automobile and steel manufacturing. The

United Auto Workers and United Steelworkers are two major industrial unions.

Craft unions are organized on the basis of the type of work performed by their members. All members in a craft union perform the same type of work. The Brotherhood of Electrical Workers and the Machinists are craft unions. Who should organize the machinists at an auto assembly plant? Should they be under the jurisdiction of the United Auto Workers or the Machinists Union?

The basic unit of both industrial and craft unions is the local union. A **local union** is the organization to which the individual union member belongs. These locals are then affiliated with a national union, most of which are affiliated with the AFL-CIO—an association of unions. The local members elect officers and conduct activities on the local level. They select delegates to represent them at national AFL-CIO conventions. Most members never participate in the affairs of the national union.

A part of the dues paid to the local unions goes to the national union and the AFL-CIO. When one local union goes on strike, it can

TABLE 13–2

Nation's largest labor unions

	Membership		
	1964	*1974*	*Change*
Teamsters	1,507,000	1,973,000	Up 31%
Auto Workers	1,168,000	1,545,000	Up 32%
National Education Association	903,000	1,470,000	Up 63%
Steelworkers	965,000	1,300,000	Up 35%
Brotherhood of Electrical Workers	806,000	991,000	Up 23%
Machinists	808,000	943,000	Up 17%
Carpenters	760,000	820,000	Up 8%
Retail Clerks	428,000	651,000	Up 52%
Laborers	432,000	650,000	Up 51%
State, County, Municipal Employes	235,000	648,000	Up 176%
Service Employes	320,000	550,000	Up 72%
Meatcutters	341,000	525,000	Up 54%
Clothing and Textile Workers*	560,000	517,000	Down 8%
Communications Workers	294,000	499,000	Up 70%
Hotel and Restaurant Workers	445,000	452,000	Up 2%
American Federation of Teachers	100,000	444,000	Up 344%

* Created in June 1976 by the merger of the Amalgamated Clothing Workers and the Textile Workers.

Source: Reprinted from *U.S. News & World Report*, October 4, 1976, p. 31. Copyright 1976 U.S. News & World Report, Inc.

draw upon some of these collective resources to support that strike. Of course, that is only if it is an approved or legal strike. There are other benefits of affiliation. A local union lacks the strength to affect national political policies, but the combined groups can exercise political pressure. The larger and more diverse the group, however, the greater are the opportunities for disagreement. In a disagreement in 1968, the United Auto Workers left the AFL-CIO. Table 13–2 lists the largest U.S. labor unions.

Labor union history has been stormy. Before turning to the current concerns of unions and the present pattern of union–management relations, let's look at the forces that have shaped the labor movement.

LABOR RELATIONS THEN AND NOW

Throughout its history, the labor movement has attracted the serious attention of supporters and enemies. Unions have been molded by people and by social and economic events.

Labor legislation

In 1842 a Massachusetts court ruled that unions were legal, but in other states union activities still could result in heavy fines or prison terms. Ninety years passed before unions won legal protection from the federal government. Legislation passed in the 1930s allowed for the growth of unionism and still serves as the guidelines for union activity.

Why is it that after 90 years there was a sudden surge in public support for unionism? First, the nation was suffering through the Great Depression. With one out of every four people out of work, millions of people had firsthand knowledge of the need for job security. Second, strikes in the auto, coal, steel, and railroad industries had ended in violence and widespread publicity on employer unfairness to workers. Finally, new leaders had taken over the unions. They had studied labor's past failures and were better prepared to manage unions. These factors set the stage for the passage of three important acts.

The Norris-Laguardia Act of 1932. Union supporters fought for 14 years to pass this bill.[4] Three points were critical to union organization. First, it outlawed *yellow dog contracts* which require workers to sign a pledge not to join unions in order to be hired. Second, it limited the use of court orders against unions. Before the act, an employer could easily get a judge to issue an injunction. Third, anyone arrested for union activities could request a jury trial. The **Norris-Laguardia Act** gave unions the legal protection to organize, but did not require employers to recognize unions.

CESAR CHAVEZ

If you're outraged at conditions, then you can't possibly be free or happy until you devote all your time to changing them and do nothing but that.

Cesar Chavez, president of the United Farm Workers of America, AFL-CIO, founded and leads the first successful farm workers union in U.S. history. Born in Yuma, Arizona, Chavez began as a migrant farm worker at the age of ten. His organizing abilities were developed with the Community Service Organization (CSO), a barrio-based self-help group that was forming among California Mexican-Americans in the 1950s. Chavez served as the national director of CSO in the late 1950s and early 1960s, but his dream was to create an organization to help the farm workers with whom he identified. Since CSO would not commit itself to organizing farm workers, Chavez quit his job, moved his wife and family of eight children to Delano, California, and founded the National Farm Workers Association, a forerunner of the United Farm Workers of America.

Nonviolence was the keystone of Chavez's philosophy, and in 1965 strikers took such a pledge. Chavez conducted a 25-day fast in 1968 to reaffirm the UFW's nonviolent philosophy. Robert Kennedy called Chavez "one of the heroic figures of our time" and flew to Delano to be with him when he ended the fast. Chavez stated, "For us, nonviolence is more than academic theory, it is the very life blood of our movement."

The organizing years for the union attracted nationwide attention. In a bitter conflict with grape growers, Chavez led a five-year strike-boycott. In October 1975, a Louis Harris poll showed that 17 million Americans were honoring the grape boycott. The boycott was finally resolved when both the UFW and growers supported a new California collective bargaining law. Chavez is now moving to organize farm workers in other states.

The National Labor Relations Act of 1935. The **National Labor Relations Act,** also called the Wagner Act, outlawed many common anti-union activities. Employers were no longer allowed to discriminate against union members, spy on unions, or unfairly interfere with union organizing. Second, it required the employer to bargain with a union that could prove it represented a majority of the employees. This time employers could not ignore unions since the act set up an independent agency to monitor union representation elections. Today the National Labor Relations Board **(NLRB)** continues to regulate labor–management relations to guard against unfair practices.

Under these laws, unions grew stronger. In fact, when a long coal strike in 1946 brought the nation to the brink of disaster, many people felt that unions had grown too strong.[5] Antiunion legislation followed.

The Taft-Hartley Act.   The **Taft-Hartley Act** prohibits unions from refusing to bargain with employers, from using force or threats in organizing, and from a number of other unfair practices. Because of the public concern over paralyzing strikes, this act gives the federal government the power to call for an 80-day cooling-off period if a strike threatens the national welfare. The strikers are supposed to go back to work while both sides continue to bargain. While this has worked in some strikes, in 1978 striking coal miners simply refused to obey the law.

Current management–labor relations

The basic task of the local union is to negotiate and enforce the labor agreement between its members and their employer. Since this constrains the personnel practices of the firm, union organizing efforts or contract demands are often resisted.

Union organizing.   Organizing is serious business. The American Federation of Teachers spends about $30 million a year organizing teachers. Major unions use complex information-gathering techniques to locate groups of workers who are ripe for unionizing. Most organizing efforts are led by well-trained, full-time organizers who guide local volunteers in publicity, motivation, and union management. Several unions may be trying to organize the same group of workers. Each organizing team is trying to get 30 percent of the workers to sign its union recognition cards (see Figure 13–3). Then it can ask the NLRB to call for a representation election.

After a period of campaigning by the union and management, a secret-ballot election is held under NLRB supervision. If more than 50 percent of those voting favor the union, the firm must recognize it

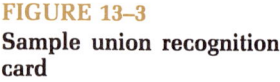

FIGURE 13–3

Sample union recognition card

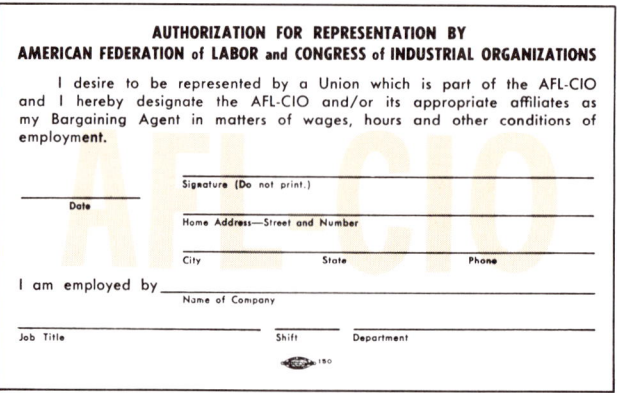

as the bargaining agent. Under the Wagner Act, firms are restricted in what they can say and do about union organizing. But recently unions have won only about half the NLRB elections.[6] Eastman Kodak, IBM, and Texas Instruments are three major employers who have been avoiding unions successfully.

Collective bargaining. Collective bargaining is the basic strength of labor unions. By negotiating for its members as a group, a union is able to gain benefits that individual workers may be unable to achieve. Through the collective bargaining process, the union and the firm reach a labor agreement that is acceptable to both sides. Over the past 40 years, laws and customs have molded a standard pattern for collective bargaining.

First each side studies the other side's position. The union studies the company's finances and plans, while the firm studies union contracts reached with other firms in the industry. When union and management negotiators meet at the bargaining table, each side makes an opening statement, then the union presents a detailed list of demands. The firm counters with its list of proposals. Each list includes some unrealistic points that later will be traded away to reach a settlement. Both sides retire to study their positions and prepare counterproposals. The process continues until they reach an agreement or a deadlock. If no agreement is reached, the issues may be submitted to **binding arbitration.** In binding arbitration an impartial outsider is called in to settle the issues, and each side agrees to abide by the arbitrator's decision. Most contracts are settled without serious conflict, but there are exceptions.

Throughout the process, each side issues public statements and tries to gain support from the workers, the press, or the public. The union tries to show that it is protecting its members' rights. The firm may try to weaken the union's support. Lockheed once mailed each of 8,500 members of one local a 108-page copy of its proposals. Lockheed claimed that the union had not fairly informed its members of the company's position.

Each side has weapons that it can use to bring pressure on the other side. The union can call for a **strike vote.** If the majority of the members agree, they refuse to work until a contract is signed. During a strike, the union sets up a **picket line.** Striking members patrol the firm's entrances and discourage customers or other workers from dealing with the firm. Members of nonstriking unions often will honor the picket line. Finally, the union can stage a boycott. A **boycott** is an effort to discourage customers from buying the firm's products. During a strike at the *Sacramento Bee* newspaper, strikers went door to door asking people to cancel their subscriptions.

The firm can continue to operate during a strike. In some industries, such as hospitals, it is critical to maintain partial operations to protect customers or facilities. If the firm can maintain operations, a strike is less likely to cause management to give in at the bargaining table. Some firms shut down completely during a strike. This may be to avoid violence or because it is impossible to operate. It can also be a useful technique. Nonstriking workers who are put out of work or customers who are forced to do without the firm's products bring pressure on the union to settle. If there is a serious threat to the nation's economy, the government can take action under the Taft-Hartley Act.

Current labor issues

Unions have made major gains in working conditions and wage levels. While other issues will continue to be important, the major thrust of bargaining has now shifted to job security. As automation has increased productivity, more goods can be produced with fewer workers. If people lose their jobs, unions lose their members and their strength. To protect jobs, unions must further restrict the firm's flexibility in personnel management. Unions are striving to gain more control over the number of workers required to do a job and the number of hours worked. For example, the number of workers needed to run the presses was the major issue in the strike that shut down the major New York newspapers in 1978.

A shorter workweek is another union goal. If the unions can force a 30-hour week, it will take four workers to do the job that had been handled by three workers. If a plant employs 1,000 workers, this means over 300 new jobs. Of course, labor costs would increase.

A guaranteed lifetime income is being discussed. In 1976 the United Steelworkers negotiated a contract with major gains in unemployment benefits, special pensions for plant shutdowns, and other income-security provisions.[8] Unions are expected to continue to seek benefits and security for their members.

SUMMARY

Every firm must employ an adequate number of competent, motivated people. Personnel managers forecast the personnel needs of the firm and then try to fill those needs. Once a job description has been prepared, qualified applicants must be recruited. Applicants may come from within the firm, from other firms in the industry or other industries, or from nonbusiness sources. They are tested and interviewed in an attempt to select the right person for the job.

Firms support training programs in order to make better use of their human resources. The training may be in a realistic setting as is the case with on-the-job training and apprenticeships. Or training may involve conferences, classroom lectures, or outside schools.

Employees may be paid on the basis of units of time, a time period, or productivity. The level of compensation depends on conditions in the labor market, the prevailing wage rate, and the firm's ability to pay. Most employees also receive a variety of fringe benefits.

About one out of four American workers belongs to a union. Unions engage in collective bargaining with employers to provide for improved working conditions and benefits for their members. Workers belong to local unions, which in turn belong to national unions. Most national unions are affiliated with the AFL-CIO. Union activities are protected under the Norris-LaGuardia Act, the National Industrial Recovery Act, and the National Labor Relations Act. This provides the strongest protection for unions. When unions seemed to be growing too strong, Congress passed the Taft-Hartley Act to give the government more control over unions.

Unions have continued their organizing efforts. Recently they have concentrated on white-collar workers. Collective bargaining continues to be a major benefit that a union can offer its members. In future bargaining, unions can be expected to concentrate on job security and lifetime income protection.

REVIEW QUESTIONS

1. Why is a job description important in hiring? Could you write a job description for the position of student?

2. Think about the kind of job you would like to take when you graduate. Why would a firm wishing to fill that kind of position recruit you instead of a person from the three other sources of applicants?

3. Think about the experience you have had in looking for a job, even a part-time job. Did the potential employers follow through the steps in the employment process? If some steps were skipped, explain why.

4. What are the advantages of each of the five types of training? Describe a situation in which each would be used.

5. Make a list of five different jobs and the type of compensation plan for each one. You can find some examples in the classified ads. Why is that plan appropriate to the position?

6. If your employer was going to increase your total compensation by $10 per week, would you rather have it in money or in fringe benefits? Why?

7. What is the difference between an industrial union and a craft union?

8. Why have unions been granted legal protection under the Norris-Laguardia Act and the National Labor Relations Act? How do those acts, which are almost a half century old, affect you today?

9. Why is job security such an important issue in collective bargaining?

CASES

Case 13–1.   To join or not to join?

Mike just started a new job in the sporting goods department of a major department store. After he had been on the floor for a few days, he was approached by one of the other clerks about joining the retail clerks' union.

Mike's mother is a grade school teacher who is represented by the American Federation of Teachers. During the past year the teachers in her district went out on strike and were eventually successful in getting wage increases and more sick leave and retirement benefits. Mike's father manages a small service company and often complains about the problems

he has with deliveries because of what the members of the Teamsters Union are allowed and not allowed to do under union contracts.

Mike likes his job and feels that he is being paid fairly. He thinks he might want a career in retailing. He really doesn't know what to do about joining the union.

1.   What would you tell Mike to do?
2.   What are the advantages of belonging to a union?
3.   What are the disadvantages of belonging?

Case 13–2.   Eenie meenie miny moe

To finance her way through school, Marilynn used to photograph weddings. When she graduated, she opened a small studio and found that she had enough business to pay the rent and make a small profit. She could increase her sales if she didn't have to take care of all the appointments, billing, and other telephone and paperwork for the business. After careful evaluation of the situation, Marilynn has decided that she should hire a receptionist.

Marilynn has never had an employee. She has never hired anyone. She wants to make a good decision for several reasons. She doesn't want to have to fire anyone, she can't afford to pay someone who

can't do the job well, and she doesn't want to waste time training the wrong person.

1.   Use your imagination and develop a job description for Marilynn's new employee.
2.   What sources should Marilynn use to find applicants? Why?
3.   If you were Marilynn, what would you be looking for as you evaluate prospective employees? What questions would you ask?
4.   What should Marilynn do to be sure that she is an equal opportunity employer?

chapter
14

MANAGING PEOPLE

By studying this chapter you should be able to find answers to these questions:

1 What is management?
2 Why is management needed?
3 How do early studies of management affect management thinking today?
4 What is it about the task that affects the style of management used?
5 What is it about the structure of the organization that affects the style of management used?
6 How do leaders get the power to lead?
7 What are the different leadership styles?
8 What are the advantages of centralized or decentralized authority?
9 What are the characteristics of a good employee appraisal system?

Terms you should know:

centralization
Hawthorne effect
Hawthorne studies
hierarchy
leadership
line personnel
management
scientific management
span of control
staff personnel
theory X leaders
theory Y leaders

The Queen of Hearts in *Alice in Wonderland* used an interesting management technique. When a worker displeased her, she simply shouted, "OFF WITH HIS HEAD!" While this may solve some of the nation's unemployment problems, it is probably not the best approach to managing people!

Queens of Hearts

Any group needs management. Someone must take the responsibility for coordinating the activities of other people to achieve the goals of the group. This is true for a baseball team, the March of Dimes Telethon, the crew on a submarine, and a work group within a business firm. The people who work in your bookstore need management just as much as the hundreds of workers on a single production line at General Motors.

You have probably had some experience working in groups. You may have noticed that some groups work better together. They get more done and seem to have a better time doing it. This is true even if the people in the other groups are just as capable. A firm may own equipment, stock inventory, and make great plans, but these can't insure success without a productive work force.

Have you ever been treated rudely in a store or bank? Have you been to a restaurant where the service was poor? One study of a serious oil spill at a drilling platform in the North Sea showed that lack of proper management was at fault. The crew was inadequately trained, and routine maintenance had been neglected. But most crucial, the person in charge had been on duty for 30 hours straight without sleep. Human error was at least in part to blame for the disaster.[1] Incidents such as this point to the importance of responsible management.

WHAT IS MANAGEMENT?

Management is the process of facilitating goal setting and integrating human and material resources to achieve goals. The objective is not only to get things done but also get things done better. But *better* could mean a lot of things. It could mean faster or with less error, or perhaps it means with less danger or fatigue for the worker. To have either more satisfied customers or less employee turnover is another form of better.

While it may be easy to see the need for management, it can be more difficult to see the best way to manage human resources. Do you really understand why you put your best effort into one project yet neglect another? Different people have different needs. You may even have different needs at different times. One person wants to be praised, another wants to be paid, and a third wants to have close friends.

The management of human resources may be the most controversial of all areas of business, because there are so many differences of opinion. People can agree that $100 invested at 7 percent will earn less than if it had been invested at 12 percent for the same period. They can agree that a product should be made out of plastic instead of cloth. But people seem to have problems agreeing on what makes people tick.

You can imagine that it would be better if all people enjoyed their work. After all, most people spend half their waking hours at work. If workers were more satisfied, there might be fewer recalls and product defects. Since people are hired to do a job, you would probably agree that management should provide for a fair and predictable level of output. Wouldn't customers be happier if workers were pleased with the work they did? Wouldn't you prefer that the clerk at Sears smiled while taking your money? Let's take a look at a bit of management history before we turn to some of the management ideas that are widely accepted today.

THOUGHTS BEHIND MODERN MANAGEMENT

People have been studying management for almost a century. Step by step we are learning more about how to deal with the human elements of business. The technology in an area such as aerospace builds on both past practical experience and laboratory study. The same thing is true in the growth of understanding of human behavior at work. What we know today is a mixture of practical experience and research. There have been both planned studies of management and reports written by managers on the basis of their own practices.

Some people have focused on individual workers or on the interactions between workers and their supervisors. Others have looked at organizational structures and patterns of communication and authority. Some of these efforts have been worthwhile, while others have been deadends. Of the very early studies, two efforts stand out. Scientific management and the Hawthorne studies have had a lasting influence and may well affect the kind of management you will encounter in your work.

Scientific management: One best way

Some early managers behaved a little like the Queen of Hearts. While they did not behead workers, they did fire them. With no unemployment benefits, the results could be just about the same. Sweatshop conditions and worker unrest were far too common. The first efforts to study management took place in this setting. The focus was on increasing the productivity of the unskilled worker.

Had forklife trucks been invented in the late 1800s, Frederick W. Taylor might have missed his chance to become the father of scientific

FIGURE 14–1
The one best way

1. Select best workers
2. Observe and time
3. Combine best moves into pattern
   PLANNING DEPT.
4. Teach other workers
5. Everybody's happy!

management. Much of the work that is now mechanized was then done by hand. Taylor's efforts to get this work done better developed into the idea of **scientific management.** His idea of *better* was to systematically get the most output from every person and machine on the factory floor. His goal was to achieve the maximum prosperity for both the owners and the workers.

Though trained as an engineer, Taylor started out as a laborer in a steel mill. The work was unpleasant and the rewards were small. When he was promoted to supervisor, he was determined to increase productivity. He thought he could eliminate all the wasted time and effort he had witnessed as a worker. First he tried being stern and demanding with his workers. That only caused conflict. Then he came up with the idea that the firm could afford to pay the workers more if they would work more efficiently. Pay was to be based on piece rates.

Armed with a stopwatch, Taylor set out to find the "one best way" to do each job. First he would observe his best workers and carefully record and time each of their movements. It is because of this careful observation and measurement that his system was called scientific

TABLE 14–1
The basic hand movements of manual work

Therblig	Objective
1. Grasp	To gain control of an object
2. Position	To line up, orient, or change position of a part
3. Pre-position	To line up part or tool for use in another place
4. Use	To apply tool
5. Assembly	To assemble parts or objects
6. Disassemble	To separate objects
7. Release load	To release a part or object
8. Transport empty	To reach for something
9. Transport loaded	To change location of an object
10. Search	To seek to find an object
11. Select	To locate an object from a group of objects
12. Hold	To hold object in fixed position and location
13. Unavoidable delay	To wait for other body member or machine as a part of the work movement
14. Avoidable delay	To wait for other body member or machine not a part of the work movement
15. Rest for fatigue	To remain idle as a part of the cycle to overcome fatigue
16. Plan	To determine course of action
17. Inspect	To determine quality of item

Source: Marvin E. Mundel, Motion and Time Study, 5th ed. © 1978, pp. 294–97. Adapted by permission of Prentice-Hall, Inc., Englewood Cliffs, New Jersey.

management. Next he would combine their best movements into a single pattern; this was the "one best way" (see Figure 14–1). Finally he would teach this new pattern to the other workers. He came up with some amazing results. He once taught a person the "one best way" to load 92-pound chunks of metal called pig irons into a boxcar. The person's daily total skyrocketed from 12.5 tons to 50 tons. If that person worked a 12-hour day, that would be one pig iron every 40 seconds! Amazingly, the worker performed better because of better management methods.

Taylor had many followers who also believed that it was the manager's responsibility to train workers to be more efficient. Frank and

---

The Gilbreth's really believed in their motion studies and applied them at home with their 12 children. Their children reported:

Our house at Montclair, New Jersey, was a sort of school for scientific management and the elimination of wasted motions—or "motion study," as Dad and Mother named it.

Dad took moving pictures of us children washing dishes, so that he could figure out how we could reduce our motions and thus hurry through the task. Irregular jobs, such as painting the back porch or removing a stump from the front lawn, were awarded on a low-bid basis. Each child who wanted extra pocket money submitted a sealed bid saying what he would do the job for. The lowest bidder got the contract.

Dad installed process and work charts in the bathrooms. Every child old enough to write—and Dad expected his offspring to start writing at a tender age—was required to initial the charts in the morning after he had brushed his teeth, taken a bath, combed his hair, and made his bed. At night, each child had to weigh himself, plot the figure on a graph, and initial the process charts again after he had done his homework, washed his hands and face, and brushed his teeth. . . .

Yes, at home or on the job, Dad was always the efficiency expert. He buttoned his vest from the bottom up, instead of from the top down, because the bottom-to-top process took him only three seconds, while the top-to-bottom took seven. He even used two shaving brushes to lather his face, because he found that by so doing he could cut seventeen seconds off his shaving time. For a while he tried shaving with two razors, but he finally gave that up.

"I can save forty-four seconds," he grumbled, "but I wasted two minutes this morning putting this bandage on my throat."

It wasn't the slashed throat that really bothered him. It was the two minutes.

Source: Specified excerpt from pp. 2–3 in *Cheaper by the Dozen* by Frank B. Gilbreth, Jr. and Ernestine Gilbreth Carey (Thomas Y. Crowell) Copyright 1948, © 1963 by Frank B. Gilbreth, Jr. and Ernestine Gilbreth Carey. Reprinted by permission of Harper & Row, Publishers, Inc.

Lillian Gilbreth tried to define and measure every motion made by workers. They called these elements of motion *therbligs* or "Gilbreth" backwards (see Table 14–1). They carefully studied the actions of bricklayers and were able to reduce the number of motions needed to lay a brick from 19 to 5. Not only did the workers get more done, but they got it done with less effort. These studies were the beginning of time and motion studies, which are still conducted today.

Boxcars are now loaded by machine, so what does the work of Taylor and his followers mean to you? First, scientific management raised questions. The business world began to wonder about improving management instead of carrying on past patterns. Second, Taylor's lack of lasting success helped people to realize that money is not the only motivator. There are mental factors that affect human behavior on the job. Whereas Taylor's system left a gap in this respect, one study became famous and changed the course of management thinking.

The Hawthorne studies: A turning point

The objective of the **Hawthorne studies** was to test the effect of changes in the physical working environment on worker productivity. The studies were part of a 15-year research project conducted by Western Electric at its Hawthorne plant in suburban Chicago, where more than 30,000 workers assembled telephone equipment. It wasn't the actual studies that brought about the change; it was the erroneous reports written by a person who had access to some of the information.

Elton Mayo reported that one of the findings was that during the survey the workers increased their output because they knew they were being studied. It made them feel important. The idea that people respond favorably to attention and humanized supervision came to be known as the **Hawthorne effect.** This broadened management thinking about what motivates workers. Publicity over the Hawthorne effect ushered in a new era in management. A new emphasis was placed on the worker as a person. This led to many studies of the social forces in the work situation and opened the door to modern management.

THE MODERN MANAGEMENT ENVIRONMENT

Modern managers recognize that workers are human and have a variety of needs. This is not to say that money is not important. It is! But it is just one of many needs that workers expect to satisfy on the job. There have been a number of attempts to develop management systems that satisfy all of these human needs while accomplishing the objectives of the organization.

Management is sometimes a balancing act (see Figure 14–2). The

FIGURE 14–2
Management involves tradeoffs

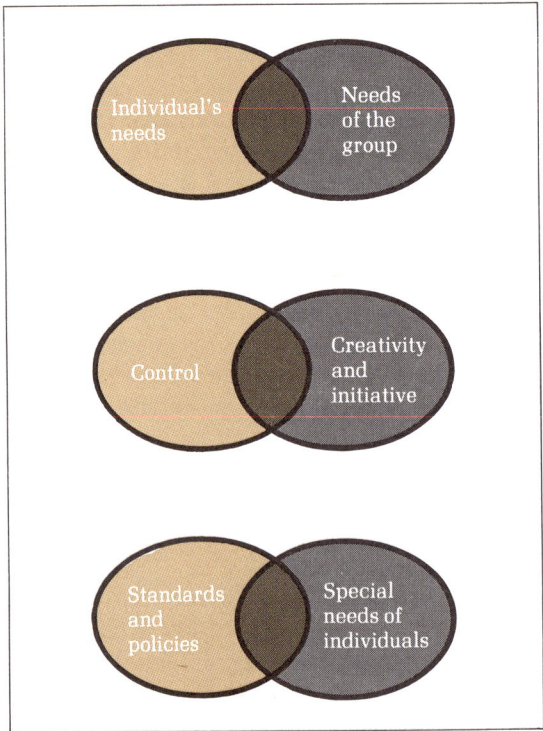

needs of the individual must be balanced against the needs of the group. There must be some control, but control can stifle the workers' creativity and initiative. Rules, policies, and standards may be needed to assure fair treatment for all, but these may not allow the manager to respond to the special needs of individual workers. What works well in one situation may not work well in another.

Not only must the manager balance these factors, but the best management system also depends on the nature of the task and the structure of the organization.

The nature of the task

We all know that there are thousands of different jobs. We also know that there are different styles of management. What is it about these jobs that affects the style of management? Three important factors are the degree to which the job is defined, the level of contact between the worker and the manager, and the need for coordination among workers.

Degree of job definition. In the Kellogg's cereal plant in Battle Creek, a worker sits staring at the 3-feet-wide conveyor belt carrying freshly

FIGURE 14–3
Job definition continuum

Low	*Medium*	*High*
"Get the results": writer, detective, engineer, physician	"Here are some suggestions": retail clerk, grade school teacher	"Do it this way": production line worker, tollgate tender

roasted cornflakes from the ovens to the packages. The clearly defined task is to watch for any change in color or quality. A clerk on the floor at Neiman-Marcus in Dallas is to be on the job during certain hours to serve customers but is also expected to decide whether it is time to straighten up the stock or call a good customer about some new merchandise. Think about the writers for a TV comedy series. The director and producer could care less about the time or place or the way the writers work as long as they deliver the script on time. Each of these jobs is managed, but the styles differ (see Figure 14–3).

Level of contact.   Some workers are subject to continuous contact with their managers. Secretaries are within close range of their bosses, and supervisors maintain a vigil over a production line. Other workers are on their own much of the time. A police officer or a salesperson performs with little direct contact with management. There are many degrees of contact between workers and management (see Figure 14–4).

Need for coordination.   To get a newspaper out on time each day requires a high level of coordination among the various workers, from the editor on down to the press operator. Each person's work depends on someone else meeting a deadline. But agents in a real estate office are far less dependent on each other. While they may at times cooperate, if one person in the office was missing, the work would go on in a fairly normal way. (See Figure 14–5.)

Each of these factors affects the manager's task. The supervisor of a production line must make sure that everyone does exactly what is supposed to be done and does it on time. The sales manager must make sure that the sales people are inspired to keep on the job even though no one is watching. The manager at the newspaper must strive for the necessary level of cooperation. Each of the managers is getting

FIGURE 14–4
Level of contact continuum

Low	*Medium*	*High*
Seldom: outside salesperson, police officer, truck driver	On and off: professor, construction worker	Constant: office worker, production line worker

FIGURE 14–5
Need for coordination
continuum

Low	*Medium*	*High*

Independent action:
    professor,
    accountant
	Some dependence:
	    secretary,
	    construction worker
		Strong dependence:
		    newspaper staff,
		    data processor

things done through people, but since the things to be done differ, the managers' roles also differ.

The structure of the organization

The manager's role is also affected by the structure of the organization. If each member of the organization could have equal authority and responsibility, there would be no need for a formal structure. Have you ever seen such a situation? A convent has a mother superior and the sisters. The military has generals and privates. The college has a dean and instructors. Social and professional organizations elect officers from among the members. Organizations develop structures.

Relationships within an organization are formalized in order to clarify authority and responsibility. Can you imagine what it would be like if anyone in the Army was allowed to holler CHARGE? The structure shows who is supposed to do what and who reports to whom. The way a firm is organized affects the options of its managers.

Most firms depict their structure on an organization chart. While this chart may just look like a bunch of little boxes connected by solid and dotted lines, it can reveal quite a lot about the firm. Some of the important concerns are the span of control, the hierarchy, line and staff relationships, and the basis for organization.

Span of control.   How many people could you supervise? You might answer, "It depends." That's true—it depends on many factors (see Figure 14–6). **Span of control** refers to the number of subordinates under the direct control of a supervisor. Many studies have been made to try to come up with the optimum number. The experts suggest that may be any number less than 15, depending on several factors. A supervisor might be expected to handle more subordinates if they are doing similar tasks, they are well trained, and there is a good system for communication. If the workers are involved in many different tasks, are new on the job, or are physically separated, the manager's task is more difficult. Normally, the span of control decreases as managers move from lower-level to higher-level jobs. Of course, a lot depends on the abilities of the individual manager.

Span of control affects both the manager's activities and the costs. Clearly a manager with 5 subordinates is able to spend more time

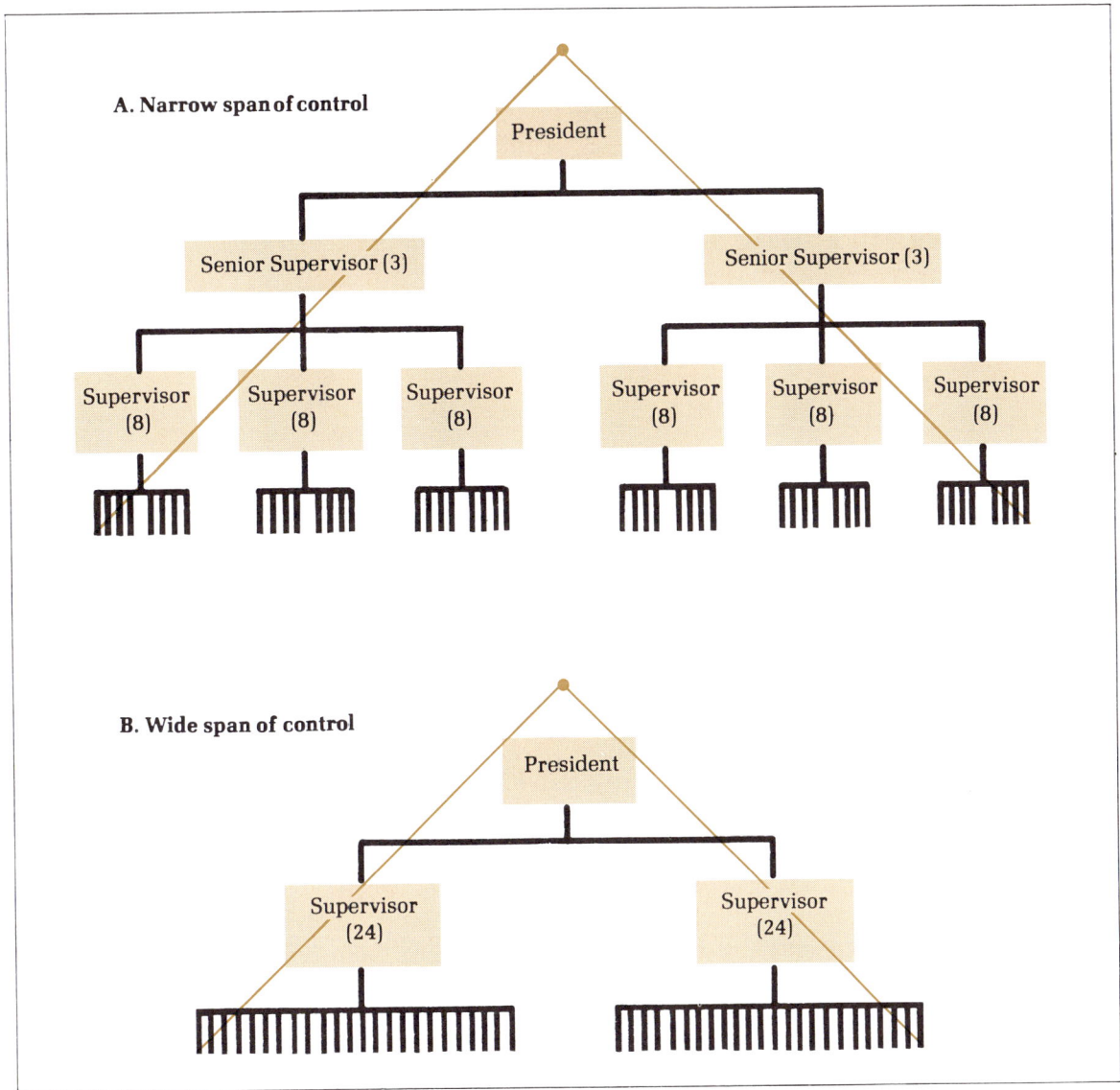

A. Narrow span of control

President

Senior Supervisor (3) Senior Supervisor (3)

Supervisor (8) Supervisor (8) Supervisor (8) Supervisor (8) Supervisor (8) Supervisor (8)

B. Wide span of control

President

Supervisor (24) Supervisor (24)

Source: J. Gibson, J. Ivancevich, and J. Donnelly, Jr., *Organizations: Behavior, Structure, Processes,* rev. ed. (Dallas, Tex.: Business Publications, 1976), p. 228. © 1976 by Business Publications, Inc.

FIGURE 14–6
Span of control diagrams

with each one than is a manager with 20 subordinates. But look what that does to costs. If the firm employs 40 production workers with a span of control of 20, it needs to pay only 2 supervisors. If the span of control is 5, the firm needs 8 supervisors.

Supervisors' salaries are not the only costs to be considered. If less attention results in low morale or lower productivity, overall costs

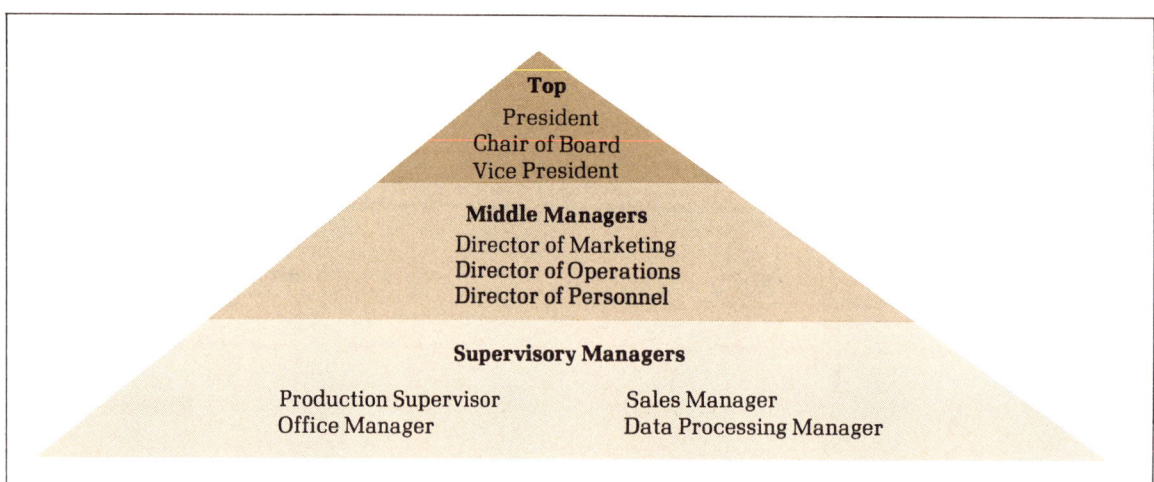

FIGURE 14–7
Top/middle/supervisory management

could increase. The span of control also affects the number of levels in the hierarchy.

Hierarchy.   A **hierarchy** exists when there are levels of power. This means that some people are subordinate to other people within the organization. The concept of hierarchy is basic to a formal structure. While there may be many levels in an organization, management is normally divided into top management, middle management, and supervisory management (see Figure 14–7). Top management includes presidents and vice presidents. Supervisory managers direct the actions of people who are at the first level or have no one working under them. Middle management includes everybody else.

Your position on the hierarchy can be quite important. Usually the higher you are, the more status you have and the greater are your rewards. Of course, the responsibilities are also greater.

The number of levels in an organization depends on both its size and the complexity of its mission. Some very large organizations even find it necessary to use numbers to express the hierarchichal positions. A clerk typist might be a grade 3, whereas a financial analyst might be grade 11. While it seems impersonal, this system allows a position in one area such as finance to be compared with a position in another such as marketing. At Sperry Vickers Corporation, a financial analyst is "equal" to a sales engineer B since both are grade 11 positions.

Most smaller firms are much less formal. There is no need for numbers to know that the president has more authority than the sales manager. But there are still questions among the other levels. How does the authority of the sales manager compare with that of the personnel manager?

Line and staff relationships. The plant manager is in a line position, whereas the personnel manager is in a staff position. What does that mean? **Line personnel** are directly in the mainstream operations of the firm. If the firm's reason to exist is to produce and sell a product, line positions include the production supervisors, the vice president of production, the sales manager, and the salespeople. **Staff personnel** advise and assist line personnel. Staff positions might include the personnel manager, the data processing manager, the accountant, and the market research manager. Line managers generally are responsible for making decisions and directing the overall operation. Staff managers direct their units but also make recommendations outside their departments.

In smaller firms most of the positions are line positions. For example, almost all the employees of a small grocery store are directly involved in stocking and selling groceries. If the store needs help in market research or advertising, it might buy these services from an outside agency. When it comes time to hire a new employee, the manager takes some time off from the checkout lane or stockroom to interview. As a firm grows, its needs for these services grow with it. At some point there is enough need to hire someone full-time just to handle research, personnel, advertising, or accounting.

The basis for the organization. Most organizations are divided into departments. Each unit has some responsibility of its own yet is interdependent with the other units. As you might have expected, there is no best way to divide the organization into working units. Two firms of the same size in the same industry might be organized on different bases. There are four methods that seem to be quite common.

The first is by function. Under this system there may be separate departments for production, sales, transportation, personnel, finance, and research. The finance manager is in charge of a group of people who are all involved in financial tasks, while the sales manager is in charge of salespeople. This system offers the benefits of specialization. People within a unit are able to share equipment or help each other with projects. Of course, the finance people spend most of their time with the other finance people, and the research people are with the researchers. This system might interfere with communications among people with different areas of expertise. The functional system is one of the most common, however. Figure 14–8 shows a function-based organization chart.

A second form of departmentalization is by product type. This almost divides the firm into separate smaller companies. The employees are organized into teams with overall responsibility for a particular group of products (see Figure 14–9). Each team includes people with different areas of expertise, and each is responsible for the profitability of its product group. This system is usually workable only in a large firm.

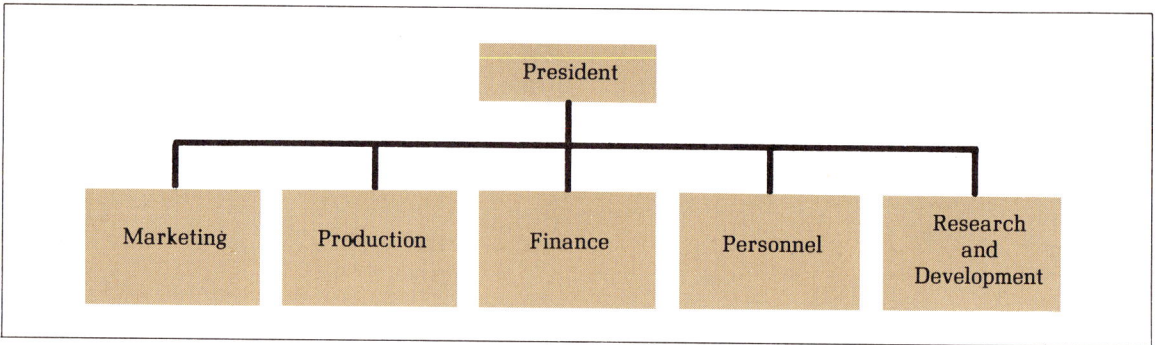

FIGURE 14–8
Departmentalization along functional lines

A firm might also be organized on the basis of territories (see Figure 14–10). This is appropriate when the conditions in the regions vary a great deal. Each division can concentrate on the problems and opportunities unique to its territory. This arrangement is used by several major retail chains. It places the emphasis on the local market. Of course, it means that the local manager must be able to handle the wide range of problems that arise. This arrangement can cause problems in communications between the regional managers and the main office. In order to do the job well, the regional manager must have the authority to make decisions. This can make it more difficult for the main office to exercise control over the regions.

Finally, the departments might be set up by type of client (see Figure 14–11). A real estate firm might have residential and commercial divisions. A food processor might have one division for consumer foods and a second that serves institutions. Banks are divided into commercial divisions to serve business customers and retail divisions to serve consumers. Some publishers have different divisions to serve the high

FIGURE 14–9
Departmentalization along product lines

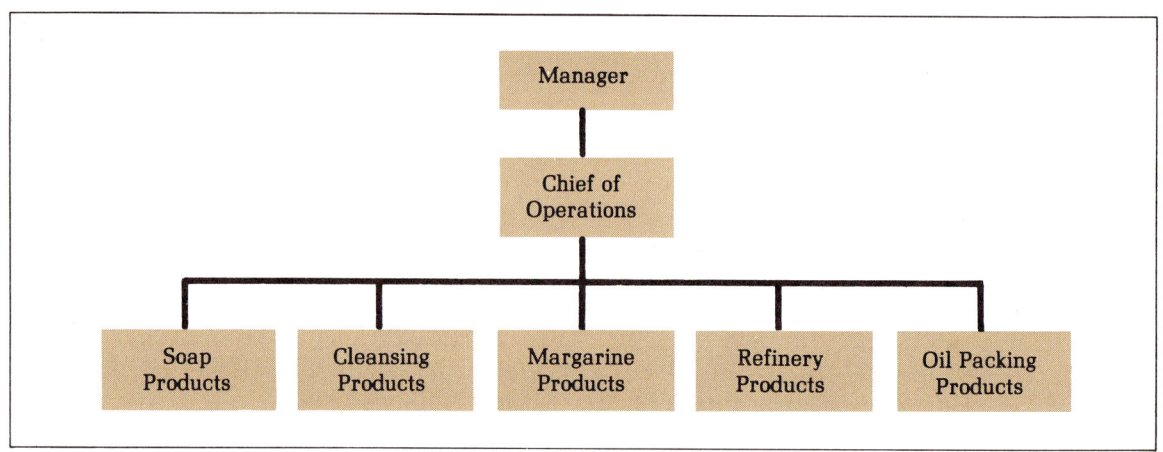

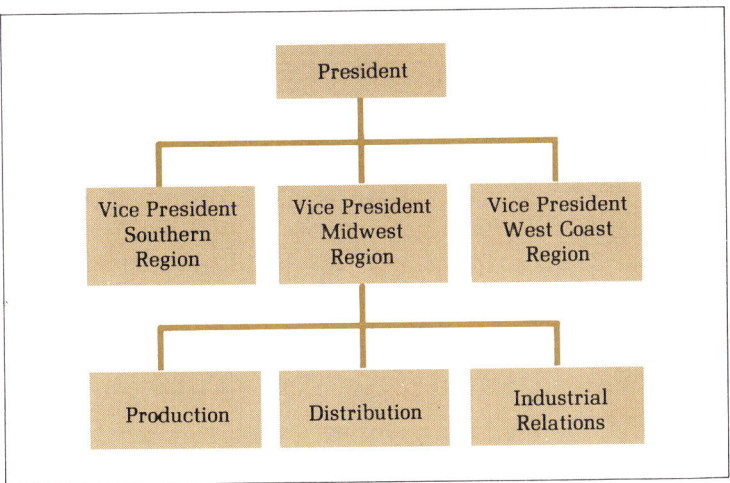

FIGURE 14–10
Departmentalization
along geographic lines

school, grade school, and college markets. This method may be logical
if the buying patterns or needs of the various customers are different
enough to deserve different treatment. It allows each division to focus
on the needs of its own group of customers. The problem with this
system is duplication of effort. For example, a publisher's representative
who works out of the elementary/high school text division might drive
right past your college in order to call on a customer, yet a college
division representative might have to come from another city to visit
your professor.

Clearly, there are many different types of jobs and kinds of organizations. While these result in the use of a variety of management patterns,
all managers face the same basic issues.

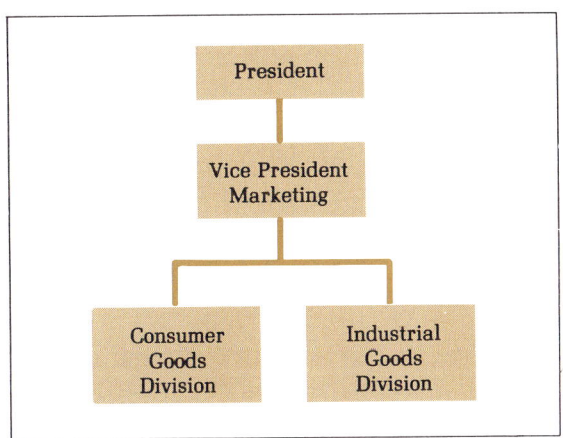

FIGURE 14–11
Departmentalization
along customer lines

MODERN MANAGEMENT ISSUES

Management involves getting things done through people, but people are not machines. A machine is designed or programmed to perform a specific function and is then turned on. As long as it is supplied with the needed energy and raw materials, it is expected to perform at the predicted rate. It might break down or get out of adjustment, but it can't complain. Getting things done through machines is a one-way relationship, but people interact. The communications are two-way. A machine does not care who flipped its switch, but people care about their managers. A machine doesn't care about its performance, but people do. Because people aren't machines, managers must be concerned about the important issues of leadership, authority, and performance appraisals.

Leadership

Leadership is the ability of one person to guide a group of people toward some goal. A leader is one who inspires people to work together to accomplish some task. Leadership is one of the duties of the manager. Managers act in a leadership role when they communicate plans and help employees to develop and maintain interest and enthusiasm for reaching the group's goals. But managers are not the only leaders in the work group. There are both formal and informal leadership roles. The manager may be the formal leader, but another member of the group might emerge as the informal leader. This is because leadership is a form of power and there are several sources of power.

Sources of leadership power.   There are at least five sources of power in a group. **Rewards** are a form of power. One person can influence another by promising something desirable. The manager has some control over rewards such as pay increases, promotions, or good assignments. Of course, the opposite is **punishment.** A manager can exercise

---

SOURCES OF POWER THROUGHOUT HISTORY

Various historical figures have been noted for the use of one of the sources of power. Here are some examples:

Power source	Famous leaders
Reward	The Pied Piper
Punishment	Adolph Hitler, King Henry VIII
Expertness	Moses, Ben Franklin
Legitimacy	Queen Elizabeth III, the popes
Charisma	Martin Luther King, John F. Kennedy

control by threatening to withhold rewards or even to fire an employee. Some managers control with **expert** power. They know more about the task than the other members of the group do. Other managers use **legitimate** power. They have a rank or status that causes workers to feel that they ought to do as they are directed. Finally, there is **charisma**—the ability to lead because others want to follow. Some managers are in control because they have earned the admiration of their employees. Each of these sources of power leads to a difference in leadership styles.

Theory X and Theory Y

Leadership styles. Leadership styles might be described in terms of the leader's attitude toward the subordinates. One system divides leaders into the theory X and theory Y types. **Theory X leaders** believe that workers dislike work, are lazy, want to avoid responsibility, and are interested only in job security. **Theory Y leaders** believe that workers are interested in meaningful work, are willing to accept responsibility, and look for chances to show their abilities and ingenuity. You can probably imagine the leadership styles that result.

Theory X managers tend to rely on punishment and legitimate power. Theory Y managers are more likely to include subordinates in the decision-making process. They believe that this is rewarding to the employees and results in better performance.[2]

But there are more than two styles of leadership. Another group of researchers uncovered a series of leadership styles used by managers (see Figure 14–12). At one end they found the boss-centered leader, who watches employees closely and makes all the decisions. At the other end is the subordinate-centered leader, who focuses on the human aspects of the job. The subordinate-centered leader may set out the objectives but will then allow the employees as much freedom as possible in completing the task.[3]

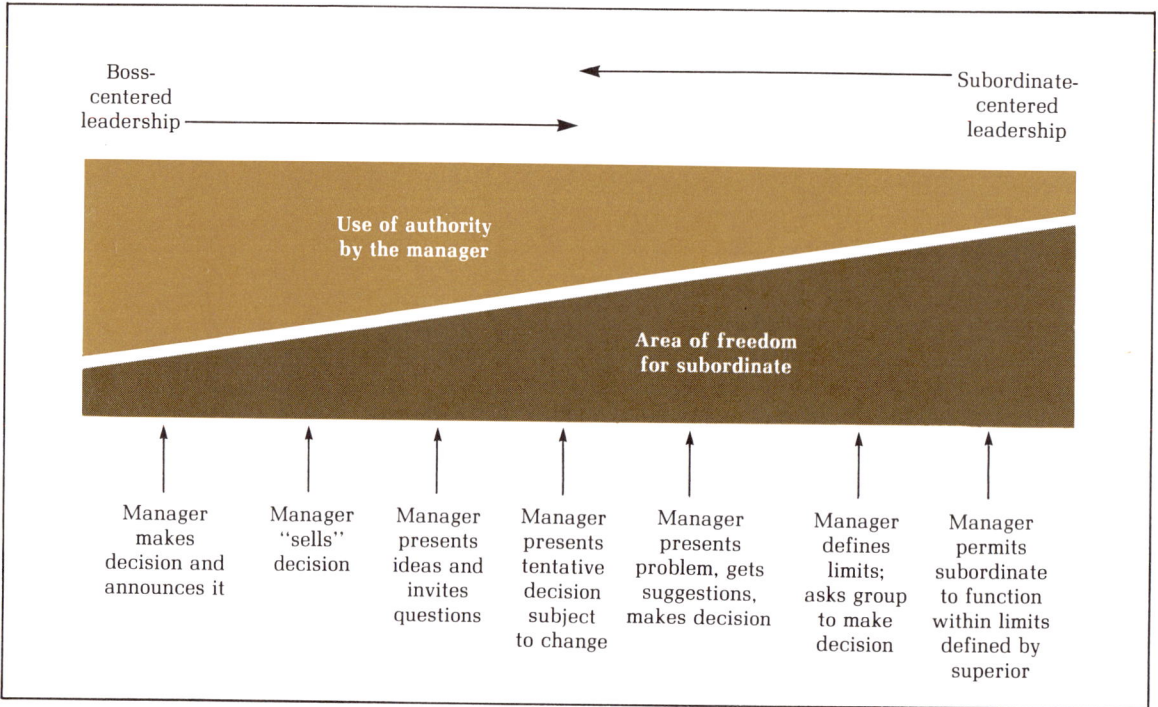

Boss-
centered
leadership

Subordinate-
centered
leadership

Use of authority
by the manager

Area of freedom
for subordinate

| Manager makes decision and announces it | Manager "sells" decision | Manager presents ideas and invites questions | Manager presents tentative decision subject to change | Manager presents problem, gets suggestions, makes decision | Manager defines limits; asks group to make decision | Manager permits subordinate to function within limits defined by superior |

FIGURE 14–12
Continuum of leadership behavior

Many of the studies on management have found that the theory Y approach or the subordinate-centered management style results in higher levels of employee satisfaction and output. But this type of leadership requires that the manager be willing to share some of the decision making with the employees. This is a question that all firms must face.

Centralized versus decentralized authority

Centralization refers to the extent to which authority is concentrated in one or few a positions. In a decentralized organization, decision-making is pushed downward in the hierarchy. On the other hand, some firms are highly authoritative. Someone at the top makes all the decisions and everyone else is supposed to follow orders. In other firms, middle- and lower-level managers are encouraged to make as many decisions as they can.

There are both benefits and drawbacks to each approach. In a decentralized firm, decisions are made by people who are close to the situation. That may be the production supervisor in the plant or the branch manager in another city. Since they are at the scene, they may be aware of some facts that are not quite so clear to someone higher up in the organization. They may be able to adjust more rapidly to changes in local conditions. For example, Penney's decentralizes advertising decision making. If it snows in Peoria, the local manager can run an ad on snow blowers. By the time headquarters forwarded approval, the snow could have already melted.

The benefits of centralization are based on three points. First, there may be factors important in reaching the decision that may not be clear to the local or lower-level manager. For example, there may be some plans that have yet to be announced. Second, there are some good reasons why the various units should operate in the same way. If the firm is planning a national advertising campaign, each office should have the same items on sale at the same time. Third, top management may prefer that middle and supervisory managers devote all their efforts to day-to-day operating questions and leave the decisions on personnel management, product design, marketing strategies, and other important questions up to the top managers and the specialists who have been hired to do those jobs.

There is no perfect level of centralization of authority. Centralization improves control, while decentralization provides added input and causes employees to become more involved in their work. The best level for any organization depends on many factors, including the need for quick on-the-spot decisions and the need for consistency among operating units. Having some control over the job can add to employee satisfaction. Another factor that contributes to employee satisfaction is a fair and meaningful employee appraisal system.

Employee appraisal

Employee appraisal is a continuous process whether or not it is formalized in a periodic evaluation. Most organizations do provide for a formal review at certain intervals. The main purpose of employee appraisals is to provide for improvement in performance. It is not unlike the grading system at the college level. You may work harder because you know a grade is coming and also work harder afterwards because you felt good about your grade.

What do you expect from the grading process? First, you expect that the grades will be assigned fairly. Two people who perform at the same level should receive the same grade. Second, you expect to know the basis on which the grades are given. If you have studied hard and done well on tests but at the last minute you learn that the tests don't count and the grade will be based on class participation, you are sure to be upset. Finally, if you are having difficulty in a course, you expect some suggestions that will help you to improve.

Your expectations about grades are just the same as an employee's expectations about an appraisal. The evaluation should be fair, based on established standards, and result in suggestions for improvement.

FIGURE 14–13
Sample employee evaluation form

Form 3891 Rev. 11/77

PERFORMANCE REVIEW AND APPRAISAL
EXEMPT PERSONNEL

TO: DATE:

ROUTING: REVIEW DATE:

RETURN BY:

NAME: _____ DIVISION: _____

JOB TITLE: _____ TIME IN POSITION: _____

GEOGRAPHICAL LOCATION _____

A.   RESULTS VS. JOB REQUIREMENTS (from job description) AND PERIOD OBJECTIVES

Attained: _____
_____
_____
_____
_____
_____

Additional Accomplishments _____
_____
_____
_____
_____
_____
_____
_____

Not Attained _____
_____
_____
_____
_____
_____
_____

FIGURE 14–13
(continued)

B. INDICATED ABILITIES AND QUALIFICATIONS

Strengths: _____
_____
_____
_____
_____
_____
_____

Improvement Needs: _____
_____
_____
_____
_____

C. SPECIFIC RECOMMENDATIONS and plans for performance improvement and/or the development of career growth potential. (Plans might include such things as outside education, in-house training, on-the-job coaching, reading, or job rotation.)

Actions To Be Initiated By Supervisor, Employee, or Other Parties	Person(s) Initiating Action(s)	Date For Initiating Plan(s)

D. GROWTH POTENTIAL for larger responsibilities in the same area or other types of work.

Is the person ready for new responsibilities immediately? Please describe. _____
_____
_____
_____

At what point might the person be ready for new responsibilities? Please describe. _____
_____
_____

Are the person's expressed career goals consistent with your observation? _____
_____
_____
_____

A fair system.   Most systems are formalized to provide some degree of fairness. In the absence of a formal system, evaluation can be casual and subjective. Some people are noticed and others are ignored. Employee evaluation forms are one attempt to increase fairness. Most forms require that the manager score each employee on several factors, which may include job performance, attitude, and improvement (see Figure 14–13).

Clearly the evaluation depends on careful attention on the part of the manager. In some cases it is quite easy for managers to evaluate employees. The task has been clearly defined and there are measures of the employee's performance. For example, a salesperson is expected to sell. At the end of the period, there are records of exactly how much that person sold. On the other hand, it is much more difficult to evaluate the performance of a bank teller. How much work did the teller do compared with what could have been done? Unless the manager received complaints or praise, there is no way of telling how satisfied the customers were with the services provided by that teller. Of course, the teller and the salesperson should both know what is expected of them.

DID YOU EVER WONDER?

Where did the term *boycott* originate?

Sometimes, regardless of the efforts of both managers and workers, there are irreconcilable differences. There are some problems that have no easy solutions. One of the tools that has been used in some of these situations is the boycott. In the late 1960s there was the grape boycott while the United Farm Workers sought union recognition by the vintners in California. The textile workers have staged boycotts against some of the major manufacturers of sheets and other cotton products. Consumers launched a nationwide meat boycott in the mid-1970s to protest the high price of beef. The supporters of the Equal Rights Amendment boycotted meetings and conventions that would have brought dollars to the economies of states that had failed to pass the ERA. The farm workers boycotted again in the late 1970s in an effort to bring pressure against the lettuce farmers. A boycott is an organized campaign to discourage consumers from purchasing the products of the manufacturers involved in the dispute. Boycotts have proved to be an effective form of economic pressure.

The term *boycott* originated almost 100 years ago in Ireland when tenants of Ireland's County Mayo ostracized a land agent by the name of Charles Boycott because he refused to lower rents. The tenants simply refused to pay.

Established standards. An evaluation should hold no surprises. When you get your grades, you should have a pretty good idea of what to expect. There certainly are borderline cases, but to do your best you must know what is expected. The same thing is true on the job. If a manager expects an employee to do a good job, that employee must know what is expected and what will be judged. A smart employee might even ask to see a blank copy of the evaluation form long before the evaluation.

Suggestions for improvement. Evaluation is a continuous process. As soon as one evaluation period is over, the next begins. Some evaluations are held solely for the purpose of determining raises or promotions. Others are intended to help the employee to do a better job or to better understand what is expected on the job. If an employee is performing well, there may be no suggestions for improvement on the present job, but there may be some areas in which this person could improve and qualify for a better job. A good manager is interested in developing people up to their potential. Both the manager and employees benefit if employees are encouraged to use all of their abilities.

"I know I'm overqualified, but I promise to use only half my ability."

Reprinted by permission *The Wall Street Journal.*

Both managers and employees benefit when employees use all their abilities.

People are not machines and they care about the way in which their managers behave. Good leadership, some sharing of authority, and helpful performance appraisals contribute to the employee's feeling of worth and positive attitude toward the job.

SUMMARY

Management is the process of facilitating goal setting and integrating human and material resources to achieve goals. The objective is not only to get things done but to get things done better. The need for management in any group is clear, but the best way to manage is not so clear. People have been studying management for almost a century. Taylor searched for the "one best way" through scientific management. Like Taylor, the Gilbreths focused on stretching human output to the maximum. But reports from the Hawthorne studies opened a new era. With the increased emphasis on workers as human beings, the task of managing becomes more complex.

There is no one best style of management because there are many different types of working situations. Some tasks are clearly defined with a high level of contact between the worker and the supervisor and a need for coordination among workers. Other jobs are loosely structured. The way in which the firm is organized also affects the manager's options. The span of control, the number of layers in the hierarchy, and the manager's line or staff responsibilities result in variations in management patterns.

Gettings things done through people involves interaction. This brings up the issues of leadership, centralized authority, and performance appraisals. Leadership is the ability to guide a group toward a goal. Leaders exercise control over a group because they have some power. That power might come from rewards, punishment, expertness, legitimate status, or charisma. There are different styles of leadership. On one hand, theory X leaders rely on punishment and legitimate power because they believe that workers try to avoid work. On the other, theory Y managers believe that interesting and meaningful work is rewarding in itself and that employees seek chances to show their abilities. Actually there is a continuum of leadership styles.

Centralization refers to the extent to which authority is concentrated in one or a few positions. Centralization provides for control and consistency. Decentralization can provide flexibility and cause workers to feel more involved with their work, thereby improving performance. The purpose of employee appraisal is to evaluate the performance fairly according to established standards in order to provide for improvement.

REVIEW QUESTIONS

1. Is management important to all groups? Why?
2. How does management work in a church, a scout troop, a store?
3. Why did scientific management fail? Would you like to work under such a system? Why or why not?
4. Have you experienced the Hawthorne effect? Describe the situation.

5. Pick three familiar jobs and rate each one on its degree of job definition, level of contact, and need for coordination.

6. Draw an organization chart for your college. Write down your thoughts on the span of control, hierarchy, line and staff relationships, and basis for organization. Compare your chart and opinions with others in your class.

7. Think of a situation in which you acted as a theory X or a theory Y leader? Why? Was it you, the group, or the situation?

8. Do you think centralized or decentralized authority is better? Under what conditions?

9. Why are employee appraisals important to the employee? To the employer?

CASES

Case 14–1. Office Products, Inc.

Stanley Bartkowski is the marketing manager for Office Products, Inc. When Stanley was promoted to that position two years ago, the sales force was organized on the basis of products. Paper, file folders, order blanks, and other paper products were in one group. Small desk items such as staplers, letter openers, paperclips, and pens were in another. The third group was larger office equipment such as paper cutters, binding machines, and collaters. File cabinets and chairs were included in the office furniture group. The last group was the electronics group, which covered calculators, time clocks, and small security systems. The salespeople in each group have the opportunity to learn everything there is to know about that type of product and the competitors.

Stanley recently attended a business products trade show. During the show he visited the booths of most of his competitors. He began to notice that most of the competitors seemed to be organized on a customer basis. One salesperson takes the firm's entire line to a particular customer. Most of the firms had specialists in government offices, school offices, doctor and lawyer offices, small business offices, and corporate offices. Stanley is worried that his system is less efficient.

1. *What are the advantages of each system?*
2. *What problems would Stanley face if he switched to a customer-based structure?*
3. *What would you tell Stanley to do?*

Case 14–2. From sales to sales management

Judy Olson was one of the first women to be hired for a sales position with a major electronics firm. She had been trained as a teacher but then found that there were no teaching jobs available. It turned out to be a blessing in disguise, as Judy was very successful in sales. She made good use of all the communication and organization skills she had learned. By the end of her first year, she was consistently in the top five producers out of the 100 salespeople in the western region.

Then Judy was offered a promotion to sales manager for a smaller office. She was thrilled. But now she had to ask herself about becoming a manager. Judy would be responsible for hiring, training, and motivating the salespeople and the clerical/administrative people in the office.

1. *Evaluate the characteristics of the sales (line) job and the clerical/administrative (staff) job. What does this tell Judy about her responsibilities as a manager?*
2. *How well do you think a theory X approach would work with both jobs? A theory Y approach?*

MANAGING
INFORMATION

By studying this chapter you should be able to find answers to these questions:

1 What is the difference between data and information?
2 What are the qualities of good information?
3 What are the activities in the information management task?
4 How did modern computers develop?
5 How do computers work?
6 What is the binary number system and why is it important?
7 How are computers controlled by human operators?
8 How are computers useful to business today?

Terms you should know:

binary number system
central processing unit (CPU)
data
flowchart
hardware
information
input unit
output unit
program
software

Have you ever been aggravated with a computer? Computers seem to be the focus of the frustrations some people feel with the faster pace and less personal nature of modern society. They are often shown as having almost mystical powers. Computers have generated both animosity and respect.

Some people think computers have all the answers.

"The true meaning of life? Sure, just a second. . . ."

Reprinted by permission *The Wall Street Journal*.

Computers are sophisticated machines that have carried us into a new era of information management. Through the use of computers, we can perform amazing information-processing feats. But computers are just the tools to be used in information management. They are useless and sometimes even dangerous without an understanding of the purpose of information management.

THE PURPOSE OF INFORMATION MANAGEMENT

Information is a resource of great value. To make the most of any resource requires management. You are constantly managing information. You take in signals and cues from your environment and try to organize them into meaningful patterns. This helps you to decide what to do and what not to do. An organization is faced with the same task. The purpose of information management is to provide the organization with the highest-quality information upon which to base its actions.

To achieve this it is necessary to find answers to several questions. First, just what is information? How is it different from data? Second, what tasks are involved in information management?

What is information?

The term *information* comes from the word *to inform*. **Information** is that which informs or helps you to understand some event or situation. The terms *information* and *data* are often used interchangeably, but their meanings are quite different. **Data** are raw, unprocessed facts. They have been organized only insofar as it makes them easier to

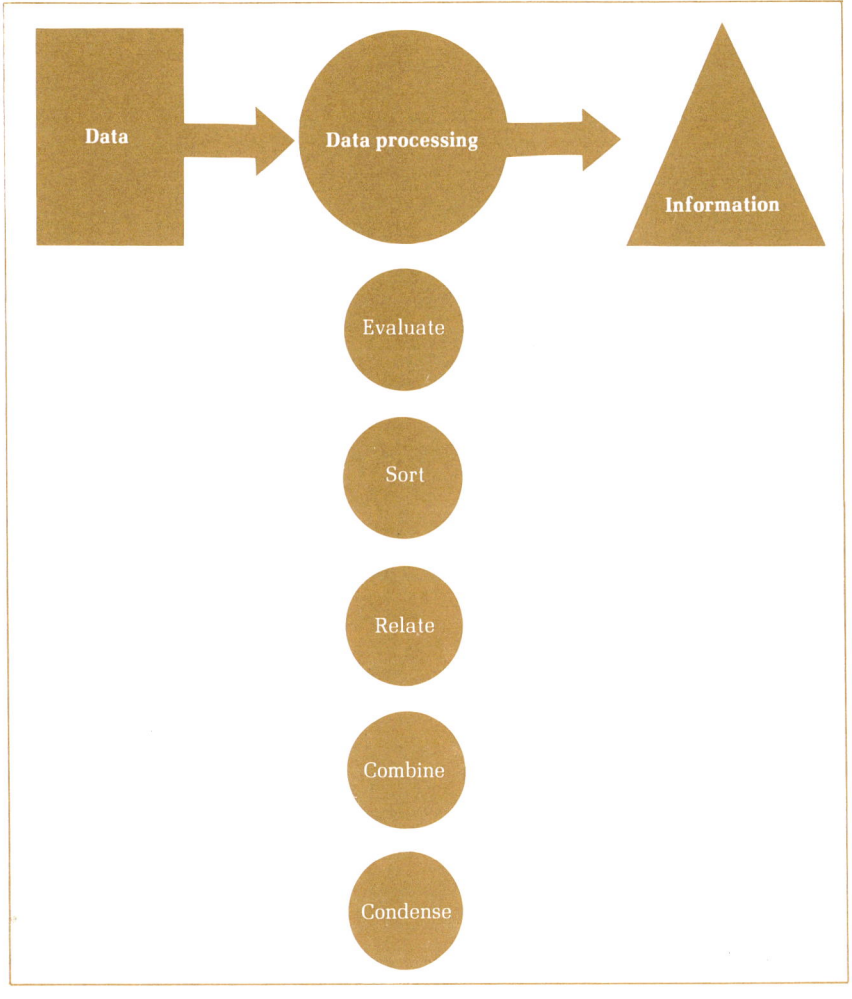

FIGURE 15–1
Converting data into information

collect or store. For example, the registrar's office probably has your records filed alphabetically. The fact that your last name begins with a certain letter has little meaning in terms of any decisions to be made. The school isn't going to decide to graduate only those students whose last names begin with a letter between A and L.

Data that have been processed or related, sorted, screened, evaluated, combined, or otherwise manipulated may become information (see Figure 15–1). To be able to inform, processed data must have certain qualities. They must be timely. Have you every heard of Monday morning quarterbacking? It's always easier to see what should have been done when the event is over. To qualify as good information, data must be both up to date and available when they are needed.

Timely data are useful only if they can answer a question. The data must be relevant. If you are trying to decide what kind of car to buy, it wouldn't do much good to read the most current road test results on motorcycles.

To be processed into good information, the data also must be accurate. Inaccurate data can be more harmful than useful. There are many people who have lost their money by betting on a sure thing. There are many ways that inaccuracies can creep into data. The collection

There are many sources of errors.

"It may be a simple, mechanical error, but according to our computer there is no Edgar P. Dawson, Apartment 5B, 112 East 17 Street, New York, New York 10003."

Reprinted by permission *The Wall Street Journal.*

methods may be biased or the wrong sources used. Maybe there were simple clerical errors.

Finally, the information should be as complete as necessary. This creates a problem because the more complete it is, the more the information costs. In some cases, however, the information is worth the price. If a company is facing a major investment or a life-or-death matter either for the firm or for its workers or customers, the cost of extra information is justified. For many less important decisions, the idea is to collect just enough information to give a pretty good idea of the probable outcome. How does a firm manage to come up with timely, relevant, accurate, and complete information?

The information management task

You are performing all of the basic information management tasks daily, but you have had so much practice that you seldom think about it. Much of your information processing is informal. In business the tasks are more formalized for several reasons. There are more people involved with more information to manage. In many cases there are legal requirements to be met. When several people have to use the information, it can be important that they all use a common system. Regardless of the degree of formality, however, there are four related information management activities that must be covered (see Figure 15–2).

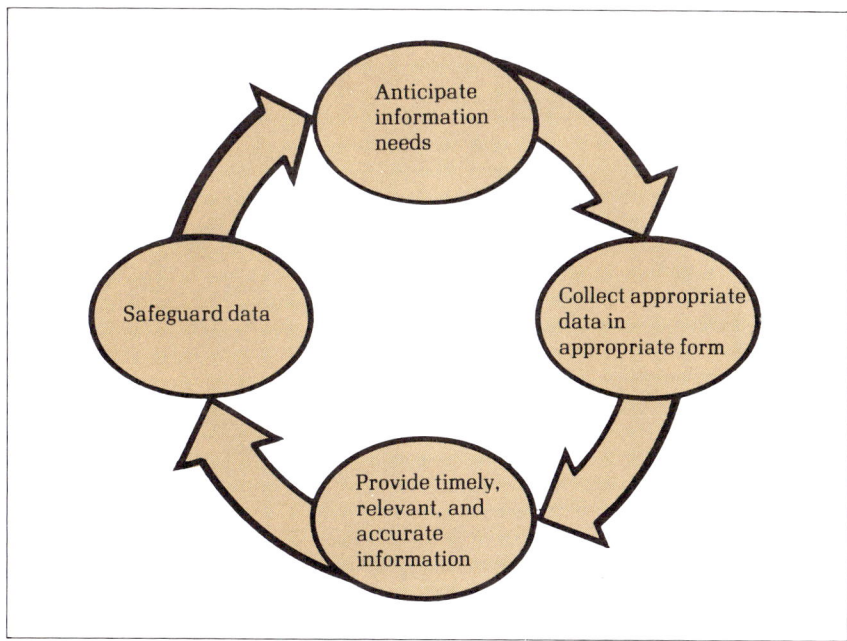

FIGURE 15–2
The information management task

First, there must be some decision about what information is and will be needed. Second, appropriate data must be assembled. Third, the data must be processed into meaningful information which is then transmitted to those who need it. The fourth and final information management activity is the safeguarding of the data.

Anticipating information needs. There are two issues involved in anticipating information needs. One is to assure the availability of relevant data and the other is to guard against being buried in data that have no use. This requires both planning and screening.

Information is not always readily available. There is some time lag. To make the best use of the information resources, the firm must anticipate upcoming information needs and begin to compile and process the data so that the information will be available when needed.

While it is easy to see the problems of not having enough information when you need it, it is more difficult to see the problem of information overload. Most businesses are constantly receiving data. Screening data is like walking a tightrope. On the one side is the problem of compiling and storing data that will only take up space and be of no future use. Even with improved systems for storing data, this is a waste. On the other side is failing to capture data that will be needed later.

Some data cannot be reconstructed if they are allowed to escape from the system. For example, if a bakery kept records of its sales only on a total daily sales basis, the management could not go back and reconstruct the separate sales of jelly donuts and brownies. If these sales were not recorded separately, the information is lost forever. The firm must constantly seek a balance between information overload and information shortage.

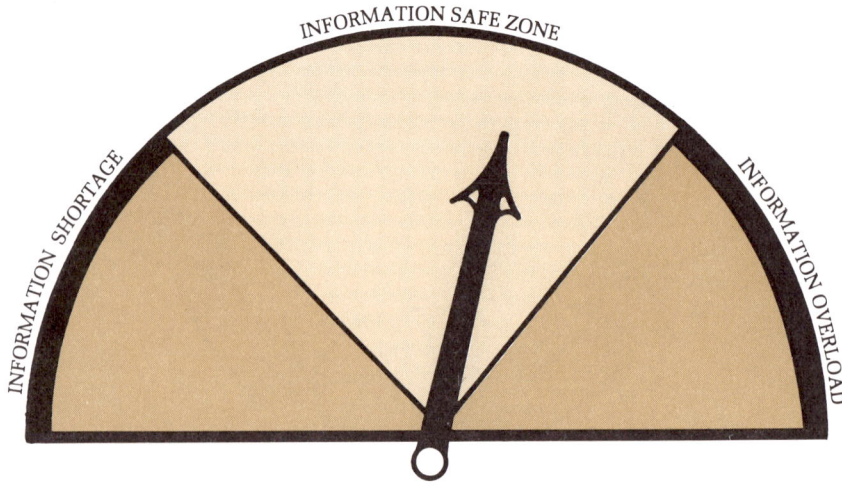

Too much is just as dangerous as too little

TABLE 15–1
Sources and forms
of data

	Internal	External
Operational	Units sold, units shipped, inventory, payroll	Price index, industry sales
Maintenance	Accident reports, return on investment, revenues and expenses	Wage rates, interest rates

Collecting the data. There are several forms of data to be collected. These come from sources both internal and external to the firm (see Table 15–1). First, there are *operational data*—all the data that arise as part of the firm's normal business activities. There are internal data such as the number of units sold, the number of parts shipped, the payroll, or other matters related to the operation of the business. The firm might also monitor outside data sources, such as the government wholesale price index, or other economic data on business in general or on its specific industry.

Beyond operational data there are *maintenance data.* These are not on washing windows or oiling machines but on the maintenance of the organization. There are a number of outside groups that require information from the firm, including shareholders, creditors, and the government. The amounts of data can be significant. It has been estimated that it costs business $40 billion each year to make reports to various levels of government.[1] Internally the firm must collect data for taxes, affirmative action reports, annual reports to stockholders and other interested observers, negotiations with labor representatives, and relations with other outsiders. To maintain itself, the firm must also collect external data regarding interest rates, wage rates, and other factors that could affect its future. These data are not useful in terms of the major business of the firm, but failure to process information in these areas could lead to serious problems.

Providing the information. The entire purpose of information management is to provide the right information to the right people at the right time. But that can be a complex job. Sometimes there are conflicts between the people who process data and the people who need information. If the users aren't careful to ask for exactly the kind of information they need, they can end up with lots of data that are either irrelevant or in the improper form. For example, a firm in the appliance industry purchased a special report on blenders from a firm that specialized in gathering and processing data. While the appliance firm was interested in kitchen-style blenders, the report was on conical blenders—

a special roller-like blender used in the cosmetics industry. Clearly the data were irrelevant.

Safeguarding the data.   Safeguarding data is important from the viewpoint of both maintenance and security. *Maintenance* is preserving the data in a condition in which they can be used at a later date. *Security* involves protecting the data from unauthorized access, modification, or destruction.

The first question to be asked is whether the data should be maintained. The next question is in what form. Storage problems increase with the level of detail. For example, all the data on last year's payroll could be stored in one number—the total of all wages and salaries paid out. At the opposite extreme, every payment to every employee could be recorded separately. The first approach would be economical in terms of the costs of data storage. All the records for the firm for five years could be kept in a shoe box. The problem is that they would be worthless.

If the data are to be maintained in order to be used again, there must be some system for retrieval. There must be some way to get to the data when they are needed. Part of the maintenance activity is to set up a coding system so that data can be located. This is very much like the Dewey Decimal System which helps you to locate books in the library. If you can't get data when you need them, they are useless.

Finally, maintenance involves physical protection. Some major firms keep their important data stored in special air-conditioned vaults with elaborate fire protection systems. Sometimes the value of data becomes painfully evident only after they have been lost or destroyed.

Each episode of "Mission Impossible," a once-popular TV show now seen late at night, started off with the important information being transmitted to the hero via a tape recording. Each tape was rigged to "self-destruct" a few seconds after it was played to keep it from falling into enemy hands. As our ability to process data increases, the importance of providing for the security of data increases.

Many of the important facts about your life are stored in the data files of the school system, hospitals, courts, the military, or other private and government agencies. To protect your privacy, these organizations have a responsibility to develop adequate security systems to assure that only those with a legitimate right to use the data can gain access to them.

Not only is your privacy a problem, but data also must be protected from those who would use them to cheat others. As more and more transactions are handled electronically, there have been incidents of crimes that occur simply by manipulating the data. Embezzlement and corporate sabotage can be simple matters of rearranging the data.

Many firms do not yet have a formalized information management

---

THE DIAMOND-STUDDED COMPUTER CAPER

Stanley Mark Rifkin was a computer consultant. He worked for a firm that provided services to banks and other financial firms. While at Security Pacific National bank in Los Angeles on October 25, 1978, he was able to observe the bank's secret security code. The code is so important that it is changed daily to avoid misuse. Later that day, Rifkin placed a telephone call impersonating a bank officer. Using the secret code, he arranged to have $10.2 million transferred to an account at a New York City bank. He then withdrew the money from that account and flew to Zurich, Switzerland, where he bought $8.1 million worth of small polished diamonds.

But greed got the best of Stanley. Believing that his computerized crime would go undetected, he smuggled the stones back into the United States. A man in Pennsylvania owed Stanley $6,000 and Stanley wanted to collect. It took the bank ten days to realize that the money was missing, but it didn't take the FBI long to locate the computer bandit. The Pennsylvania man was happy to turn him in! Rifkin faces a maximum sentence of ten years in prison and/or a $10,000 fine. And who says crimes doesn't pay? There is a good chance that the bank will come out ahead. By the time the trial is over and the diamonds are handed over to the bank, their value is expected to be almost $13 million.

Source: "FBI Arrests Suspect in Bank Funds Theft and Finds Diamonds," *The Wall Street Journal*, November 7, 1978, p. 17.

---

system. Information management is one of the newest areas of business. Areas such as accounting and production management have been well recognized throughout the history of business. It is only in the last few decades, however, that information management has been recognized as an important business function. Clearly the increased attention can be traced to the increased capabilities of electronic computers.

THE TOOLS OF INFORMATION MANAGEMENT

Computers make it possible to process vast amounts of data very rapidly and accurately. Although a "computer foul-up" is a common excuse for a problem or error, it is often an excuse. Computers simply perform according to human instructions. The information that results is only as good as the data and instructions that the human operators supplied. GIGO stands for *Garbage In, Garbage Out*.

Computers are fascinating machines. While at one time they were the expensive property of big firms, today they are widely used by firms of all sizes (see Figure 15–3). In fact, home computers have recently

FIGURE 15–3
Computers in use: Units go up . . .

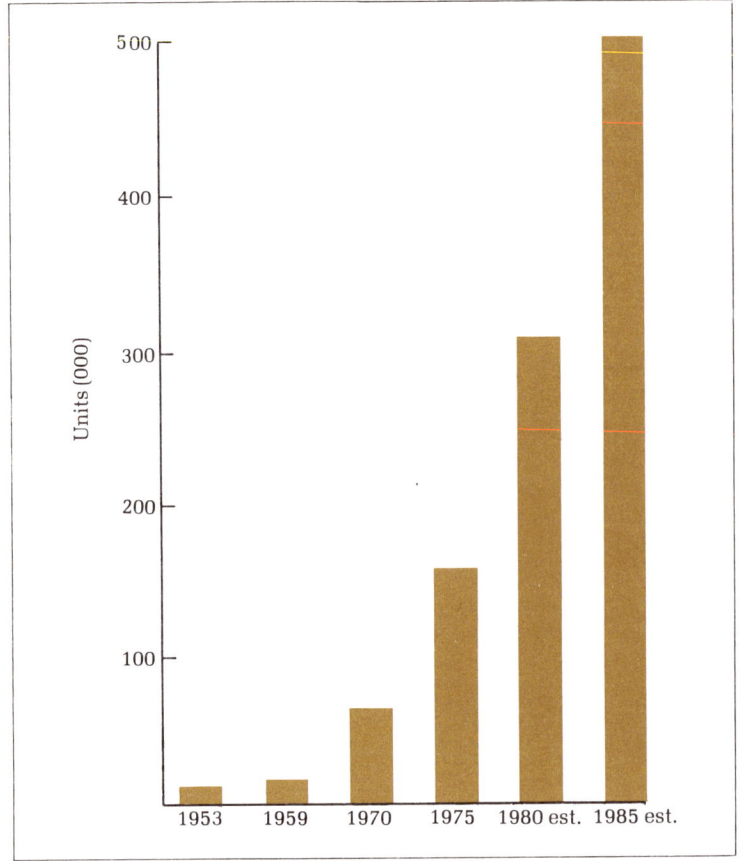

There were only about 50 computer systems in use a quarter of a century ago. Now there are some 155,000 and the total may soar to 500,000 by 1985. By one estimate, there will be one computer installation for every business with more than 50 employees.

Sources: From "Getting Control of the System." Reprinted with the special permission of *Dun's Review*, July 1977, Copyright 1977, Dun & Bradstreet Publication Corporation; data, Advanced Computer Techniques.

become available at a price not much beyond that of a color television. This will open up all sorts of personal telecommunications possibilities.

To better understand the use of computers in business today, let's look at the development of modern computers, the way computers work, and the uses to which they are put.

The development of modern computers

At one time in history information was chiseled onto a stone tablet. Not only was it slow, but just imagine how much room it took! IBM recently announced a technological development that allows all the names and numbers in the 1,076-page Brooklyn telephone directory to be squeezed into a space about the size of the bell-and-circle symbol on the front cover.[2]

Between the stone tablets and today's electronic digital computers businesses passed through several stages of data processing. Each of these has a use today. First was the manual method—the use of paper and pencils to record and manipulate data. This can be both slow and inaccurate. On the average, humans make 8 errors in every 100 items recorded.

Early improvements on the manual system came about because of the census. As the population grew, the task of making census reports became totally unmanageable. Hundreds of clerks painstakingly

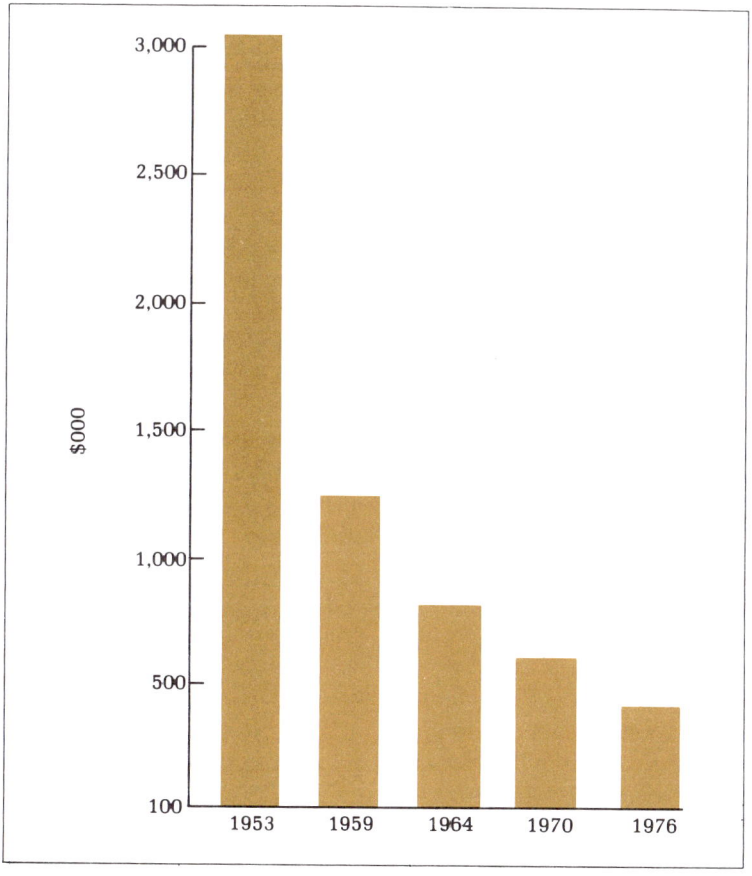

FIGURE 15–4

. . . While prices go down

Computer prices have come down dramatically. The average system cost about $3 million back in 1953. Today, the price of a typical unit is about $350,000, less than a tenth of the original cost.

Sources: From "Getting Control of the System." Reprinted with the special permission of *Dun's Review*, July 1977, Copyright 1977, Dun & Bradstreet Publication Corporation; data, IBM price lists and A.C.T. estimates.

marked tallies on carefully ruled sheets—卌.卌.||. A single tally sheet had 600 spaces where a clerk checked off the proper combination of age, race, and sex. The 1880 tally was so slow that it was feared that the 1890 census might not be completed before 1900. Clearly something had to be done.

A young statistician named Herman Hollerith came up with an idea. He developed the first punch card system. While primitive by today's standards, it saved the government about $5 million on the 1890 census. To tabulate the 1890 census of 62 million people took only one third as long as it had taken to do the 1880 census of 50 million people.[3]

It wasn't until 1952 that the first computer, Univac I, was installed for commercial use at General Electric. It used vacuum tubes like the old radios and by today's standards was huge and slow. When transistors were introduced in the early 1960s, computer speeds increased up to 1,000 times. Since then computers have become smaller, faster, more powerful, and more affordable (see Figure 15–4).

Since 1952 there have been at least four generations of equipment. Each generation was marked by a major technological breakthrough. In 1952 it cost $1.26 to perform 100,000 computations. Today that cost is down to about half a cent.

The improvement in speed has been even more drastic. First-generation computers were able to perform calculations in thousandths of a second—milliseconds. That means those computers could do in 1 second what it would take a hard-working human about 20 minutes to complete. Today's computers work in billionths of a second—nanoseconds. If you could do one calculation per second and worked ceaselessly without eating or sleeping, it would take you 30 years to do what that computer can do in 1 second. That's speed! With prices and performance improving constantly, it is estimated that by 1985 there will be 1 computer installation for every business with more than 50 employees.[4]

How computers work

Computers are not nearly so complicated or mysterious as the cartoonists imply. They are simply devices that accept data, process data, and produce results according to the instructions they are given. Let's look first at the basic structure of digital computers. Then we'll examine the input, control, and output functions of the computer.

The basic structure of computers.   There are many types of computers, but they all have the same basic requirements. A computer solves problems electronically by adding, subtracting, multiplying, and dividing. It can also do other manipulations such as counting, comparing, and moving data.

There are two interacting elements that comprise the total computer system. The actual equipment with its mental frame, wiring, circuitry, and lights is called **hardware.** The complementary supplies and instructions are called **software.**

To function, a computer must be able to read in data and instructions. This is the purpose of the **input unit.** The computer must have the capacity to store data and instructions and to perform the needed calculations. The computer works so fast that it is impractical for humans to direct these calculations at the time they are being performed. Therefore, the computer must have an internal control system. The storage, arithmetic-logic, and control functions are handled by the **central processing unit** (CPU). Finally, the computer must write out meaningful results. The **output unit** translates data from the computer's machine language into a form that can be understood by humans or other computers. See Figure 15–5.

The CPU has been called the heart of the computer. The input unit enters data into the internal storage of the CPU. The internal storage also holds the instructions. The capacity of the storage, which is sometimes called the computer's **memory,** is an important measure of the size of the computer. As the computer performs, data are passed back and forth between the arithmetic-logic unit and the internal storage. The actual processing takes place in the arithmetic-logic area of the CPU.

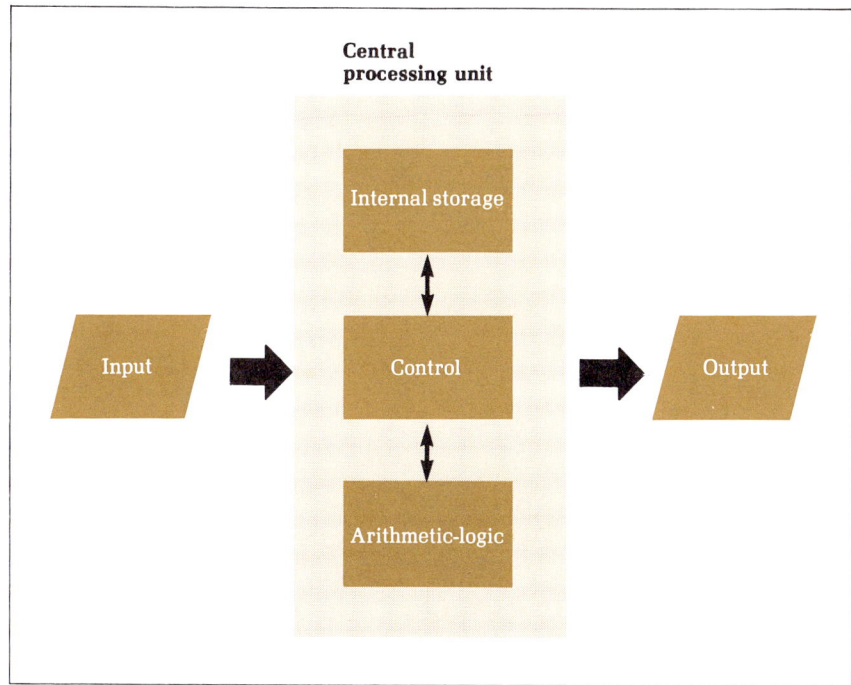

Central
processing unit

Internal storage

Input

Control

Output

Arithmetic-logic

FIGURE 15–5
Basic components of a computer system

The computer only does as it's told.

"I'm sorry to say, Mr. Wilcox—our computer seems to have taken a personal dislike to you."

Reprinted by permission *The Wall Street Journal.*

The arithmetic-logic unit performs all the arithmetic required by the instructions. It can also perform logic operations such as comparing two items of data for alphabetical or numerical sequence. During this entire process, the control unit performs the vital function of directing the overall performance of the other units. The computer executes instructions one at a time in order exactly as they have been written

FIGURE 15–6
Input devices—machine to machine

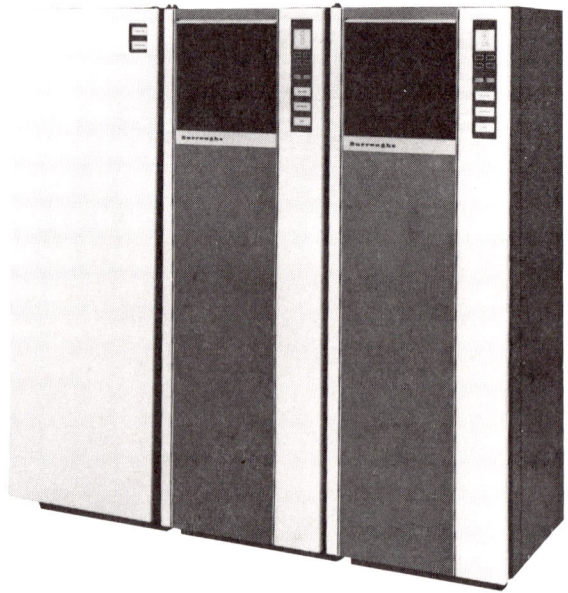

by the human operator. It only uses the data that humans have supplied. The computer is impartial and does only what it is told to do.

The input functions. As yet no computer fully understands human speech or handwriting, so the input device is used to convert data and instructions into a form that the computer can understand. The input unit is used to provide the CPU with the data to be processed and the instructions for processing them. Input devices include keyboards, punched card readers, magnetic disk units, magnetic tap units, punched paper tape readers, optical scanners, magnetic ink character readers, light pens, or mark sense readers (see Figure 15–6). Since the input device is often the slowest part of the computer process, there has been a great deal of effort devoted to creating faster and more convenient input devices.

The type of device used depends on at least three factors. The first is the source of the data. When data are being transferred from one computer to another, one of the machine-to-machine systems such as magetic tapes or magnetic disks can be used. If the data are created by people, as is the case when you take a test or write a check, one of the human-to-machine systems such as mark sense answer sheets or magnetic ink could be used. These must be fed into an input device to be read into the computer. None of these would work at the checkout counter of a retail store. There a scanner reads the price and inventory information from the uniform product code on the label.

A light pen is used because humans and computers speak different languages.

Reprinted by permission *The Wall Street Journal.*

DID YOU EVER WONDER?

How is magnetic tape magnetized?

How are data recorded on magnetic tape? Magnetic tapes, cards, and disks all depend on magnetic core. Magnetic core is the most frequently used internal storage medium. A magnetic core memory is made up of a large number of very small rings of ferromagnetic material. These rings are strung on wires as shown in the accompanying illustration. Each ring is called a *core*. Each one represents one bit of data—either a 0 or a 1.

A single core is magnetized when electric current is sent through one horizontal and one vertical wire. It can be magnetized in either direction. If it is magnetized clockwise, it is "on" and represents a 1. If it is magnetized counterclockwise, it is "off" or a 0. The whole process takes less than a millionth of a second.

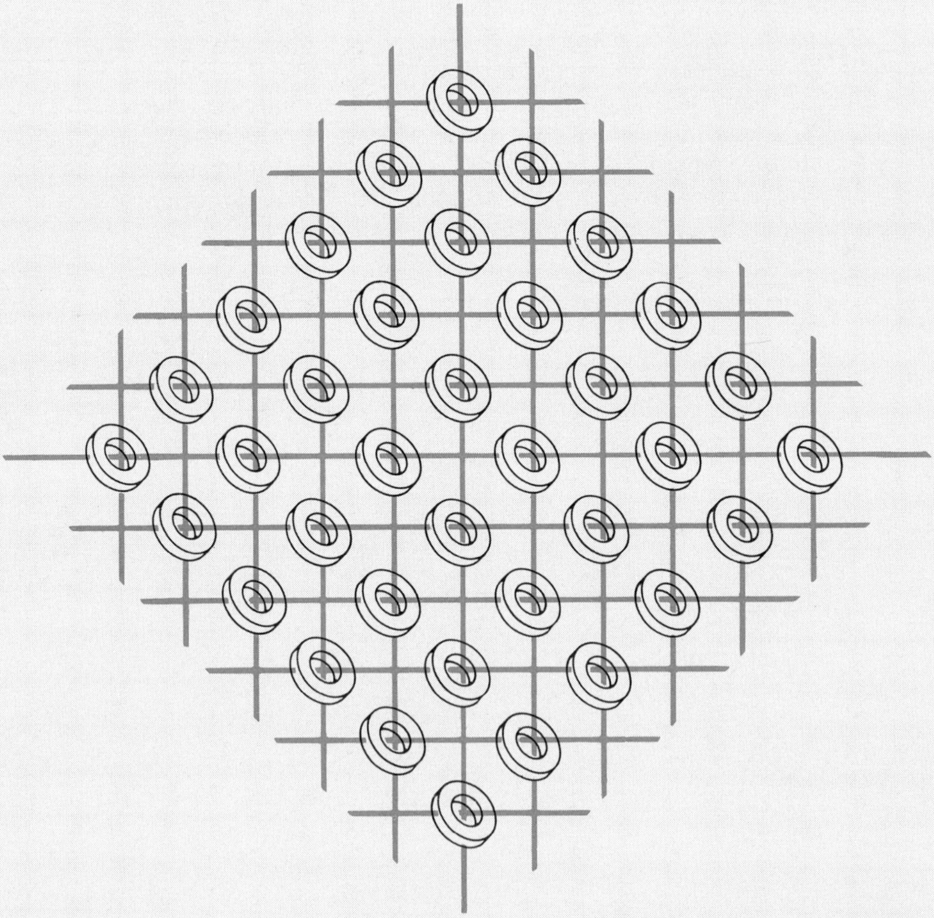

The other factors that affect the choice of an input unit are speed and cost. To enter data via a keyboard unit or a punched card unit is much slower than entering through a magnetic device.

As computers have become more powerful and more available, they have also become easier to use. At one time only very skilled technicians could communicate with computers. Today you can hold an almost-human conversation with a computer. The problems arise because of the computer's binary nature. Computers operate on a very simple principle. Everything inside the computer is a yes/no situation. All data are recorded and manipulated using the **binary number system,** which uses only 0 and 1.

To communicate with the computer, every piece of the data must be reduced to *bits.* A bit, which is short for *bi*nary digi *t,* is a fragment of data that can be represented by a yes or a no. A computer can have the capacity to store millions of bits of data in its memory bank. Each bit has an address, so the computer can search out that address as instructed and then determine whether that bit is yes—1—or no—0. All the data and manipulations of the computer are represented by strings of 0s and 1s.

THE BINARY NUMBER SYSTEM

In most of our daily activities we use the decimal number system, which is based on 10. It uses 10 digits—the numbers 1 through 9 and the 0. The binary number system uses only the number 1 and the 0. Here is how you count your fingers in binary. Can you count your toes also?

1 . . . 1	6 . . . 110
2 . . . 10	7 . . . 111
3 . . . 11	8 . . . 1000
4 . . . 100	9 . . . 1001
5 . . . 101	10 . . . 1010

To convert human thinking into a form that can be understood by the computer requires special computer languages. Among the more popular are FORTRAN—*FOR*mula *TRAN*slation, COBOL—*CO*mputer *B*usiness *O*riented *L*anguage, and BASIC—*B*eginner's *A*ll-purpose *S*ymbolic *I*nstructional *C*ode. These languages have very rigid rules, but they are becoming more simplified and easier to use.

The language is the bridge between human symbolic language and machine language. In the early days of computers, the human had to walk almost all the way across the bridge. But as the performance

FIGURE 15–7
The responsibility for
translating symbolic
language to machine
language has been trans-
ferred to the computer.

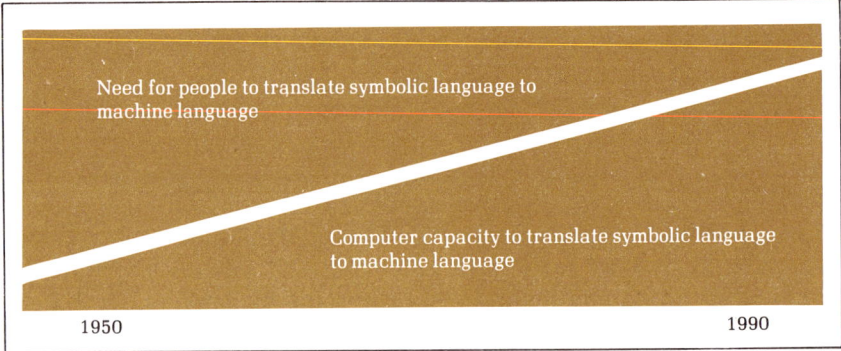

Need for people to translate symbolic language to machine language

Computer capacity to translate symbolic language to machine language

1950   1990

and capacity of computers have improved, computers have become more able to assume the translation burden (see Figure 15–7).

Directing the computer.   There are four steps in solving a problem by computer:

1.   Clearly define the scope of the problem.
2.   Develop a flowchart.
3.   Write a program.
4.   Develop a data base.

It seems obvious that you must know what you are trying to do before you can decide how to do it. The problem must be clearly defined to avoid arriving at the wrong results. In a recent government-sponsored study, the problem was to identify underdeveloped areas that might need federal grants. The researchers measured several factors and input the data. Everything worked well until the results came back. Among the areas named was an exclusive ocean-front area north of Los Angeles. The researchers had defined the problem as finding areas with little or no industry to provide employment. The residents of this area had zoned it against any industrial use but were certainly far from needy.

Many computer-related problems can be avoided through flowcharting. A **flowchart** is a diagram of the steps to be followed in arriving at a solution (see Figure 15–8). It is like a road map. It is used to keep track of the intended process. An error in the order of the steps or a missed step might be spotted in the flowchart, thus saving hours of wasted effort. The flowchart shows the general plan to solve a problem, but a computer must follow very specific instructions.

A series of detailed instructions is called a **program** (see Figure 15–9). A computer does not think and must be instructed to make every single step in solving a problem. Nothing can be assumed. Developing a workable program can be a time-consuming and tedious task. Each step can involve a series of substeps.

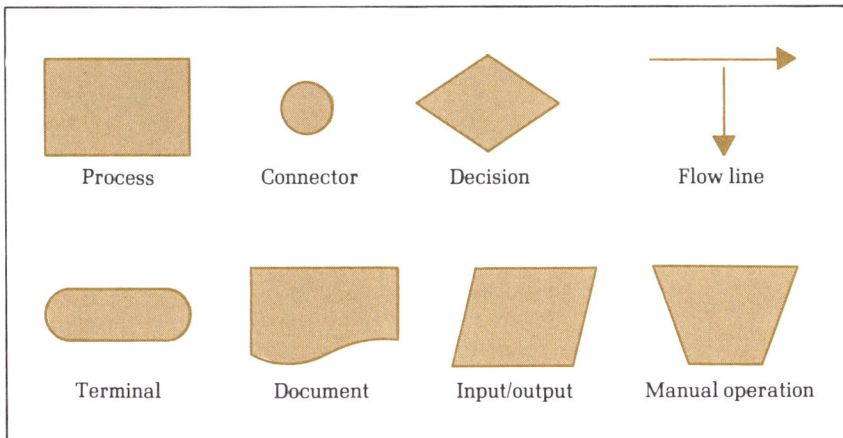

FIGURE 15–8
Common flowchart symbols

Process Connector Decision Flow line

Terminal Document Input/output Manual operation

Dealing with a computer is like dealing with a beginner. You have to tell it everything; you have to teach it every step. The computer can learn, but it can't call upon its own learning. It can store programs in its memory, but you must then instruct it to retrieve a program from memory.

Very few people can write a complex program with hundreds of steps without making at least a few errors. These errors are called *bugs*. Every program must be tested and "debugged" before it can be used to process data.

FIGURE 15–9
The procedure segment of a program used to evaluate potential vendors.

```
117700/                                                                          00021005011
117800••••••••••••••••••••••••••••••••••••••••••••••••••••••••••••••             00021005011
117900                                                                           00021005011
118000PROCEDURE DIVISION.                                                        00021005011
                                                                     SEGMENT 0002 IS 0051 LONG
118100                                                                           00021005014
118200 100-MAINLINE-SECTION SECTION.                                             00021005014
118300                                                                           00021005014
                                                                     START OF SEGMENT AT (01,005)
118400 110-MAINLINE-PROCESSING.                                                  00051000011
118500                                                                           00051000011
118600     OPEN INQUIRY VENDORDB.                                                00051000011
118700     OPEN OUTPUT INTERIMFILE.                                              00051002A11
118800                                                                           00051002B11
118900     PERFORM 1100-CREATE-SORT-FILE UNTIL END-OF-FILE.                      00051002F10
119000                                                                           00051003211
119100     CLOSE VENDORDB. CLOSE INTERIMFILE.                                    00051003513
119200                                                                           00051004710
119300     PERFORM 2100-SORT-AREA.                                               00051004812
119400     OPEN INPUT INTERIMFILE, OUTPUT PRINTFILE.                             00051004B10
119500                                                                           00051005014
119600     MOVE "NO " TO END-OF-FILE-SW.                                         00051005413
119700     PERFORM 3100-PRINT-REPORT UNTIL END-OF-FILE.                          00051005813
119800                                                                           00051005811
119900     CLOSE PRINTFILE, INTERIMFILE.                                         00051005E13
120000                                                                           00051005F15
120100     STOP RUN.                                                             00051006111
120200                                                                           00051006212
120300••••••••••••••••••••••••••••••••••••••••••••••••••••                       00051006212
```

GRACE MURRAY HOPPER

I'm not contented being a spectator.

In 1969 the Data Processing Management Association awarded its first Computer Sciences Man of the Year Award, and the honor went to Captain Grace Murray Hopper. This is only one of the many awards she has received over her career in recognition for her outstanding contributions to the field of computer sciences. In 1971 the UNIVAC Division of Sperry Rand Corporation even initiated the Grace Murray Hopper Award for young computer personnel.

Captain Hopper has truly been a pioneer in computer sciences. After graduating from Yale with a Ph.D. in mathematics, she taught at Vassar until she joined the Naval Reserve in 1943. There she was involved in the military's early efforts at developing electronic data processing capacity. In 1949 she joined Eckert-Mauchly Computer Corporation as senior mathematician and participated in the development of UNIVAC I, the first large-scale commercial computer. That company was later acquired by Sperry Rand Corporation. When Captain Hopper retired in 1971 she was head of the programming division of Sperry Rand.

Her major contributions have been in the area of developing the language capacity of computers. She invented the first practical computer compiler, a high-level computer program that enables programmers to write in an easier language rather than starting from scratch each time. She was one of the prime movers in the development of COBOL (computer business oriented language). It is largely because of her efforts that today we can communicate with computers in a simplified manner.

It may sound like you would have to spend all your time writing programs, but it's not that bad. A vast array of programs are available for sale. These "canned" programs are widely used. You simply write enough instructions for your computer to use the canned program. Most minicomputers installed in medium and small firms depend heavily on canned programs for performing payroll, inventory control, and other normal business functions. Then all that is needed is the data.

Finally: The output. Many devices that are used to input data also serve as output devices. The output might be either in machine-to-human form or in machine-to-machine form (see Figure 15–10). Machine-to-machine forms are punched cards, punched paper tape, magnetic tape, or magnetic disks. Output in any of these forms could serve as input data for another computer or at another time.

If the output is to be used by humans, it might be via a line printer, which produces the familiar green-lined computer printouts, or one

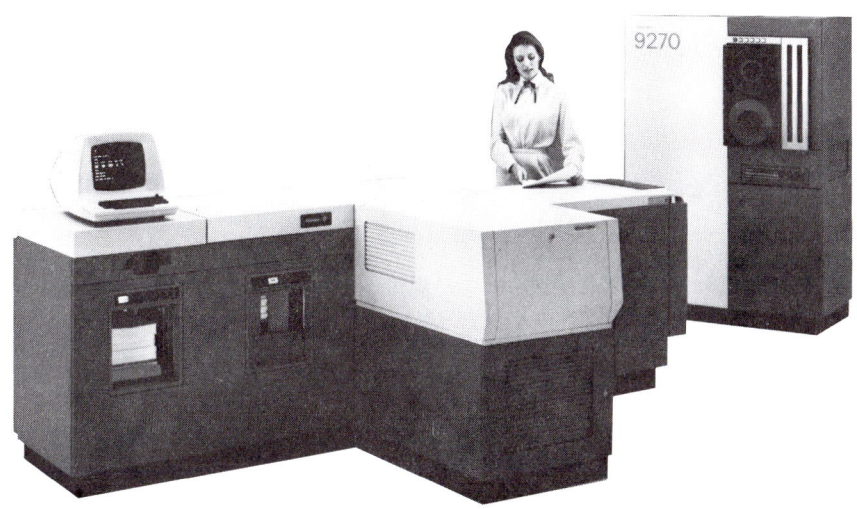

FIGURE 15–10
**Output devices—
machine to human**

of the cathode-ray tube video display screens that resemble small televisions. A long report that must be used by many people or several times would be printed out. Video displays are more common where someone needs a quick answer to a short question, such as at the airline ticket counter.

Applications in business today

With the use of computers increasing so rapidly, it is clear that business is finding many new ways to benefit from their fast and accurate data processing capacities. While these benefits were once available only to large firms with lots of money to spend on computer systems, the recent growth of the minicomputer has made computers available to many small businesses. Some minicomputer systems cost as little as $15,000. Small businesses that do not wish to own and operate their own systems can rent computer services from computer service bureaus. A monthly printout detailing the important financial aspects of their businesses can be available for a cost of less than a clerk's wages for a week.

It might be easier to list the instances in which a computer has no use than to list all the possible applications. Computers are used in all kinds of businesses for almost any problem that can be reduced to data form. DuPont has even used the computer to come up with names for its new fabrics. The name *Qiana* was developed that way. Note that the computer was not told that *u* always follows *q*.

Most computer applications fall into one of seven categories. The computer can play the role of production supervisor, record keeper, researcher, problem solver, communicator, librarian, and simulator.

As production supervisor.   Computers are used to monitor many different aspects of the production process. Giant oil refineries are run by just a few people with the aid of computers. Computers are used to keep track of inventories, production schedules, machine scheduling, and many other complex tasks. Some of the computers used in production are analog rather than digital computers. *Analog computers* measure and control some physical condition. The thermostat on a furnace is a device of that type.

As record keeper.   Computers are the least costly and most efficient way to handle large amounts of routine paperwork. Tasks such as billing customers, preparing payrolls, and maintaining employee records have been turned over to computers. Since this is the area in which you are most likely to run into a computer, it is the area where the frustrations develop. Remember, that computer only does what its human operators tell it to do.

As researcher.   Computers are used in scientific and technical laboratories to solve problems in physics, chemistry, and any other area of engineering or mathematics. The pace of research has increased dramatically as a result. In the past some problems were unsolvable because it was impossible to perform the billions of calculations needed to check out various combinations and alternatives. Computer-assisted research has led to new products and services to satisfy human needs.

As problem solver.   Businesses are also using computers to solve problems outside of laboratories. Information helps executives to make

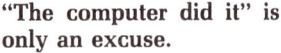

"The computer did it" is only an excuse.

"Who says I can't argue with a computer?"

decisions in all areas of the business—from the location of new facilities to the choice of the best supplier of raw materials. The ability to monitor market conditions and the performance of each area of the firm allows decision makers to act before serious problems develop.

As communicator. Business can transfer information to where it is needed almost instantly through the use of computers. All the reservation systems for airlines, hotels, and sports events are examples. Systems of this type allow a stock broker to have instant access to stock market information and a sales representative to check on inventories before promising delivery to a customer.

As librarian. The amount of data available is growing at an almost unbelievable rate. Just think of all the books, magazines, and government publications that are published daily. Old-fashioned filing systems cannot keep up with the mountain of data. The computer has the ability to store vast quantities of data and serve as a librarian by offering rapid retrieval of the desired material.

As simulator. Many events that are too dangerous, too costly, or too difficult to test as an actual physical model can be reduced to mathematical representations. Then researchers can try various solutions without the problems, costs, and dangers involved in a real trial-and-error approach. This is called **simulation.** The conditions of the environment are input into the computer. Have you seen the commercials that show snow tires being tested on a computerized treadmill that has been programmed to duplicate road conditions?

This same idea can be extended to purely mathematical models. The computer can be programmed to duplicate the economic environment, and various tax or employment proposals can be tested. As our economic forecasting abilities improve, it is easier for firms to make plans for the future.

SUMMARY

Information is an important resource and, like any other resource, must be managed wisely. Information management consists of a series of interrelated tasks. It is necessary to anticipate information needs and collect the appropriate data to provide for timely, accurate, relevant, and sufficient information. This information must be transmitted to those who need it to make business decisions. Too little information can lead to problems, but so can too much. Once the information has been transmitted, the data must be safeguarded from both physical damage and unauthorized use.

Computers are our most powerful data processing tools. But computers only follow directions and process data supplied by people. (Remember GIGO!) Computer technology has advanced rapidly since the first commercial installation about 30 years ago. They are now smaller, faster, more powerful, and more affordable. It is estimated that there will soon be one computer installation for every business with more than 50 employees.

Computers read in data and instructions through input devices, store and process them in the central processing unit, and write out results through output devices. All of this depends on the binary number system. Since people don't think in that system, there are a series of languages to help people communicate with computers. A list of instructions to a computer is called a program. There are many canned programs available to meet the standard needs of many businesses.

Businesses use computers in many ways. Some computers are used to monitor production processes. Record keeping and the accounting system are other important computer applications. Computers are used to solve problems in laboratories and in executive offices. Many of our complex communications systems depend on computers. Computers make it possible to store vast quantities of data in a very small area and retrieve data rapidly when needed. Finally, computers can be used to simulate real-life situations. This is as close as we have ever come to being able to predict the future.

REVIEW QUESTIONS

1. What is the difference between data and information?

2. How do data become information? What are the qualities of good information? Think of a decision you made in the last week and identify some data that did not qualify as information.

3. Have you ever been subject to an information overload? Describe the situation.

4. Think of three situations in which data about you or your activities are entered into a computer. What input devices do you think are used? Why did you select those?

5. Repeat Question 4 for situations in which you receive computer output.

6. Make up a flowchart for the activity of studying for a test. Start with TEST ANNOUNCED and end with TEST TAKEN.

7. What do you think are the advantages and disadvantages of canned programs?

8. Make a list of the computer applications with which you come in contact at school, on your job, or in the community.

CASES

Case 15–1. Burger country revisited

Don Price and his sons were busy setting up their fast-food restaurant as indicated in the case at the end of Chapter 12. But when Don wasn't at the restaurant, he was on his job as dean of computing sciences for the community college. Don's primary profession was in data processing. He couldn't wait to apply his knowledge of data processing to the restaurant business.

But data processing can be expensive. Don could collect and analyze mountains of data, but he realized that he was in the business of selling hamburgers and chicken, not processing data.

1. *From what you know about the fast-food business, make a list of all the kinds of data Don might collect.*
2. *To what uses might each kind of data be put?*
3. *What problems could Don encounter with information overload?*

Case 15–2. Cleary College

Luis Hernandez, the assistant registrar of Cleary College, had read several articles on the privacy issue. Most of the articles stressed the responsibility of both public and private organizations to protect the privacy of people about whom they collect data. Luis had brought up this issue at the monthly meeting in his department. He had pointed out that there were laws protecting the rights of college students. He felt that the college was lax in the security of its records on the 11,000 students who attended on either a full- or part-time basis.

The registrar, Helen Stone, had dismissed these concerns. She took the position that no one was particularly interested in the data on the students and that there was little in the records that could be harmful even if it were published in the local paper. Luis was concerned both for the students and for the college, which he felt could be held liable.

1. *Think about all the kinds of data that might be on file about you in the registrar's office or offices of your college. What outside groups might find those data useful and in what ways?*
2. *Are there any ways in which you could be harmed if the college was lax in the security of those data? Do you think Luis' concerns are valid?*

part
VI

HOW:

**Managing the
productive system**

In Chapter 1 we talked about society's needs and business as a provider. It is this providing function that we want to look at now. Business *provides* through productive systems. You need a productive system to make things like cars, washing machines, and even toothpaste. We call these kinds of productive systems *factories*.

But what about all the businesses that provide a service, like banks, clinics, and schools? Do they have productive systems? Yes, they certainly do. They all need some kind of system to provide the services they offer. That is the reason we use the general term *productive* instead of *production*—because it applies to all kinds of businesses.

So what are productive systems? They are the systems businesses use to create the goods and services we all consume. These productive systems convert raw materials or whatever is being processed to products and services. They do this by using labor, machines, supplies, and energy.

The productive system is the converter that transforms the thing being processed in some way. It may transform the shape, chemical composition, information, or location. Things may be assembled, as with automobiles, or disassembled, as with meat packing. If you are making bread, there is a chemical and physical change. If you are cashing a check at the bank, there is a change in the information in your account and a change in the location of the cash. If you are having your gas tank filled, there is a change in the location of the gas and a change in cash.

The difference between success and failure depends on how well you use the resource inputs—labor, materials, machines, and energy. First you have to have a physical system that makes sense. The work must be organized in an effective way. You have to worry about flow patterns. Should the activities follow in a straight-line fashion like a cafeteria? Or should you put all of the similar activities together, as in a hospital where there is a separate department for x-ray, pharmacy, laboratory, surgery, intensive care, and so on? The way you arrange the flow will have a big impact on the way jobs are designed. And, by the way, where should you locate this productive system and why? These are the kinds of issues we will cover in Chapter 16.

In Chapter 17, we will begin our discussion of the way you operate the productive system. You need raw materials and supplies, but how much? How do you get the best prices? How much do you order at one time? The purchasing function will be the focus of this chapter.

Now, given the system design and the raw materials, how should you plan operations? What capacity do you need for next month or even six months in the future? How many workers do you need, and by what schedule? If you operate a fast-food service 24 hours per day, 7 days per week, you have one problem. If you operate a machine shop 5 days per week, you have quite a different problem.

There is also the question of the seasonality of demand for what you are producing. If the product is a standard item, you may want to let finished goods inventories accumulate during the slack sales season. Then you can sell them off when demand is high. It could be less expensive on balance to have the products available from inventory. If you do not produce a standard item, you may not want to risk producing to inventory. If you offer a service, you can't produce to inventory. You produce the service when it is demanded, or you may lose sales.

Then there is the question of the quality of the goods and services produced. What quality levels are appropriate? How do you control these quality levels? All these topics will be discussed in Chapter 18.

Finally, you may think that once the product is produced the productive system is done with it. Not so, since it is not yet in the right place. Recall that in our definition of productive systems we included a change of location as one of the possible transformations. You have to distribute the product in an effective way. The term *effective* means to distribute it at a low cost and to have it available in the right place at the right time. So you need to design a physical distribution system. These topics will be treated in Chapter 18 also.

chapter 16

FACILITIES PLANNING: LOCATION AND DESIGN

By studying this chapter you should be able to find answers to these questions:

1 What is the basis for selecting a given plant location?
2 How is the location for a service operation different from that for a manufacturing operation?
3 How do you determine the relative importance of costs versus subjective factors in selecting a location?
4 How do you determine the capacity required?
5 How are processes and physical layout related to job designs?
6 Under what conditions would you use functional layout? Product layout?
7 In a functional layout, how can you determine which departments should be adjacent to each other?
8 What are the concepts on which assembly-line balance is based?

Terms you should know:

functional layout
job enlargement
job specialization
load summary
locational choice
plant efficiency factor
product layout
production line
scrap factor

If you are going to process something to create a product or service, you must be concerned about physical facilities. You must think about where to locate the system and how big it should be. Then you must determine the processing sequence, design the jobs, and relate these details to the layout. Facility designs can have an extremely important impact on production costs. Once the system is installed, it is difficult and costly to change locations and the basic facility design. Therefore, careful initial plans are worthwhile.

Some of the old formulas for choosing plant locations are changing. For example, it used to be common for manufacturing plants to be relocated in the South, or for foreign locations to be considered to take advantage of lower labor costs. Now the situation has reversed. Foreign companies are locating their plants in the United States, and the South is saying "Yankee, go home."

Foreign companies such as Volkswagen and Honda are finding it economical to build locally for manufacturing products for the U.S. market. The favorable West German and Japanese monetary exchange rates in relation to the U.S. dollar are part of the reason. Foreign companies can buy parts in the United States and build here at a lower cost than they can build cars in Germany or Japan and ship them here. The first Volkswagen assembly plant in New Stanton, Pennsylvania, ran into some unexpected local reactions, however. On the one hand, the plant would provide 5,000 new jobs in an area that was relatively depressed. On the other hand, some people were unhappy about having industry in a quiet rural area, and controversy developed over who Volkswagen should hire for the jobs—local people or people brought from Detroit and elsewhere. The director of the Pennsylvania Human Relations Commission said that Volkswagen was not in compliance with affirmative action requirements, and people were picketing the plant. Volkswagen found that operating in a foreign environment has its problems.

The cool reception given companies who want to locate in the South seems to come from local politicians and businesspeople. Wage rates are still lower in the rural South than in the United States in general. These influential locals want to keep it that way. For example, the Brockway Glass Company of Brockway, Pennsylvania, wanted to relocate in Roxboro, North Carolina. Ezrà Bowman, a local street cleaner, got excited when he saw the possibility of increasing his earnings from $2.70 to a probable $4 per hour at the new bottling plant. But the County Economic Development Commission turned down Brockway's bid to move in. The reasons given were that while Brockway would have brought 300 new jobs to the town of 8,000, it also would have brought its wage scales and its union. The feeling is that the higher wages and union activity soon put pressure on local business to match the wages and have to deal with union activity, too. *The Wall Street Journal*

416

DR. AN WANG
The technology is developing rapidly

Dr. An Wang founded Wang Laboratories in 1951, incorporated it in 1955, and recorded sales of $1,628,387 in 1964. By 1977, Wang was firmly established as a leading manufacturer of business computers, with 50,000 computer systems installed and sales of over $135 million. Wang was educated at Shanghai's Chiao Tung University and received a Ph.D. degree in physics from Harvard University.

Wang was a pioneer in the development of the magnetic core memory which helped make large-scale computers an economic reality. But while a handful of manufacturers such as IBM, Sperry Rand, and Honeywell were going after the large-scale computer installations, Wang was busy developing small all-purpose computer systems. As early as 1972, Wang was the first to offer a high-level computer language such as BASIC on small business computers. Now the minicomputer market is one of the fastest growing sectors of the industry. Technology has developed so rapidly that you can have a computer sitting on your desk that is as powerful as one that filled a whole room in the early 1970s.

Word processing is another new application of computer technology. We think of computers as processing numbers and numeric information, but the same technology has been adapted to typesetting and now to the office typing pool. Newspapers today set type with electronic typesetting machines, and book printers use similar sophisticated typesetting machines. Businesses today may have word processing centers, which replace the old typing pool. In a word processing center, you type at an electronic keyboard. Then what you typed is displayed on a video screen and stored on a magnetic disk. These systems have powerful editing capabilities for the correction, insertion, and deletion of material. These and other powers allow you to perfect a document, changing it to reflect all kinds of variations and updates. When you want printed copy, you simply press the right buttons and it is printed at a speed of 480 words per minute.

Wang Laboratories is a leading manufacturer of word processing systems. The manuscript for this book was prepared on a Wang word processing system and was typeset on an electronic typesetting machine.

The computer industry has many paths open for careers. Perhaps the most visible one is in computer programming, but you do not need to be in the computer manufacturing industry to work as a programmer. Programmers are needed wherever computers are used. Computer manufacturers have careers available in marketing and sales, production and operations, accounting, and personnel, just as any manufacturer would. But since the computer manufacturing industry is still expanding and finding new applications, there are extraordinary career opportunities in innovative fields.

says that the episode illustrates a little-known but widespread attitude in the South.[2]

WHERE TO LOCATE FACILITIES

Look around and ask yourself why certain businesses selected their locations. Banks and supermarkets, for example, seem to serve local areas and are usually located in shopping areas along with other similar retail stores and service organizations.

Manufacturing plants are much less likely to serve local areas. They seem to serve regional, national, and even international markets. So if a plant serves a national market, the location problem seems rather tricky. Raw materials must be transported to the plant, and the finished product must be transported to distribution points around the country. Also, other costs, such as labor, power, and taxes, might be quite different in different locations. Finding a location that minimizes the sum of all these costs may not be easy.

Locational choice

You may wonder whether location is all that important in the success or failure of a business. After all, television and radio plants are found in a variety of locations in the United States, plastics raw material plants are in several areas of the country, and plastics molding plants are everywhere. On the other hand, aluminum reduction plants are not found just anywhere, and neither are steel plants or beer plants. Why have these industries developed their peculiar location patterns?

Factors of great importance to a particular industry may eliminate most of the possible locations. For example, mining depends on the availability of raw materials, beer depends on water, and aluminum reduction requires an energy source. Therefore, mining occurs where the deposits are located, beer near good water supplies, and aluminum reduction plants near hydroelectric energy sources. How about service and retail establishments? They are oriented to consumers or clients, so they are located wherever the users are located.

One unique example of a location based on the availability of raw materials hit the news as "Daniel Ludwig's Floating Factory." Ludwig, a very rich industrialist, had decided to exploit 500,000 acres of timberland he owned in the Brazilian wilderness. A pulp plant was needed near the site of the timber. But how do you build a pulp plant at a site 250 miles inland on a tributary of the Amazon River? Ludwig's answer: Have it built as a floating plant in Japan and tow it 15,000 miles to its destination. At the site a docking area had been built for the plant and its separate floating 55,000-kilowatt power plant. The plant was floated into position over 4,000 pilings. The water around

TABLE 16-1
Measures of profitability in choosing locations

Situation	Quantitative measure of profitability
Both prices and costs vary in different markets and locations	Compare profitability in alternate locations
Prices are the same in all markets	Compare costs for alternate locations
Both prices and costs are the same in all markets and different locations	Use personal preference for a given location
Different locations do not affect costs, but revenue varies for different locations, as with retail store location	Compare gross revenue for alternate locations

the pilings was then drained, and the plant and power unit were in position. The plant went into operation in 1979 and by 1981 it will turn out 750 tons of paper pulp per day—enough to make a single strand of toilet paper stretching 61 times around the world!

If some technical factor such as raw material location, water, or energy does not determine location, then manufacturing industries may choose a site because of transportation concerns. That is, they would choose locations that minimize overall transportation costs.

Now think about what is the basis for choosing a good location. In general, a company wants to choose a location that will give maximum profits. But, if the prices in all markets are the same, then the problem is simplified a little and the firm can just compare costs in different locations.

If both prices and costs are the same in different markets and locations, then personal preference is a reasonable basis for the decision. As a matter of fact, many great businesses have developed in locations where the boss wanted to live. Obviously location was not very important to the success of those businesses.

Firms also may be faced with a situation where costs are the same in all locations, but gross revenue is different in alternate locations. The revenue could be different either because prices vary or because different locations draw more business. In this situation, the firm may just select the location that produces the largest gross revenue. This is the case for services and retail businesses. Locations near the users produce the largest revenue, so decentralized facilities make sense. For example, Sears stores are located where the people are. In large urban centers, Sears has more than one store. The decentralization puts Sears stores in close contact with more people.

Table 16-1 summarizes these measures of profitability used in choosing business locations. Businesses cannot measure everything about alternate locations by revenues and costs, however. There are subjec-

tive factors of importance—such as adequate transportation facilities. Here we are talking not only about the personal preferences of the owners for a place to live, but also about factors that make one location more desirable than another by affecting some aspect of operations. Attracting and keeping good employees could be important to operations, for example.

An industrial plant location example

The Woods Furniture Company is located in an industrial district of Los Angeles. Several problems have led to a decision to relocate. First, the present building is old, inefficient, and too small. Business is good and there is no room left for expansion. Also, labor costs in Los Angeles are high and the products require a good deal of labor input. How should Woods go about finding a new location?

First, after a general screening, the company may find several sities or towns that seem attractive. The Woods Furniture Company found three such cities in addition to its present location. The company must then measure and compare objective costs for the three sites.

Objective costs.   General appeal may mask some important differences between cities, so it is a good idea to survey the costs that would occur in each location. For Woods the important cost factors are labor, transportation, real estate taxes, state taxes, and electric power prices. Other costs such as raw material prices are the same for all locations. Now Woods needs to translate the cost rate in each

TABLE 16–2A
Objective costs
(in $ millions)

	Labor	Trans-porta-tion	Real estate taxes	State taxes	Electric power	Total objective costs
City A, current location	3.45	0.50	0.10	0.08	0.06	4.19
City B	1.50	0.60	0.03	0.02	0.04	2.19
City C	1.60	0.70	0.05	0.04	0.07	2.46
City D	1.85	0.60	0.06	0.05	0.05	2.61

city into the actual cost of producing the product. For example, the labor rate must be multiplied by the number of hours of labor that Woods needs to produce one unit. This is important in order to reflect the proper weighting of each cost factor in each city.

The results are shown in Table 16–2A. First, it appears obvious that Woods is paying a dear price for the current location. This high cost for Los Angeles reflects both the high cost of the area plus the inefficiencies of the present plant. On the basis of the surveyed costs, would you select city B? The costs for city B are $2.19 million per year, which is $270,000 less than those for city C, the next best. Costs in city C would be 12.3 percent higher than those in city B. Costs in city D would be 19.2 percent higher than those for city B. Is city B the best choice?

Subjective factors. Before deciding, Woods should look at some other aspects of each city. After all, everything cannot be measured in dollars. Not only that, but Woods should attempt to measure long-run costs as well as immediate costs. Therefore, Woods must try to predict the impact of some of the subjective factors that may affect future costs. Factors such as the attitude of city officials toward a new factory site may be an indication of future tax rates. Poor local transportation facilities may mean future company costs to bridge the gap. A short labor supply may cause labor costs to be bid up beyond the rates surveyed. A local supply of unskilled labor may indicate future training costs. Thus, whereas objective costs may point to one city, subjective factors may be the basis for a decision to select another.

For Woods, Table 16–2B summarizes the ratings given to all four cities. The first five factors are rated on a scale of excellent, plentiful, very good, good, adequate, and fair. The sixth factor—union activity—is rated as active, significant, moderate, or negligible. City B, which was on top in terms of objective costs, does not rate as well as cities C or D on factors that may affect future costs. Somehow Woods must

TABLE 16–2B
Subjective factor ratings

	Labor supply	Type of labor	Attitude of city officials	Transportation facilities	Recreation facilities	Union activity
City A, current location	Plentiful	Excellent	Good	Very good	Very good	Active
City B	Adequate	Good	Good	Good	Good	Significant
City C	Plentiful	Excellent	Very good	Very good	Very good	Negligible
City D	Plentiful	Excellent	Very good	Good	Very good	Negligible

trade off the objective cost advantage against the subjective factor disadvantages in order to decide.

These differences in objective costs and subjective factors are the bases for choices of business locations. Sometimes very careful studies are made, as with the Woods Furniture Company example. Many times, however, managers simply make overall judgments about alternate locations with all of the factors in mind.

How much capacity?

Demand for products and services may vary, which makes the capacity decision difficult. If demand is seasonal, a firm has a choice. It can set up for the seasonal peak or produce for some average level. The strategy depends on how much capacity costs compared with the costs of other ways of meeting output requirements.

For example, in Figure 16–1, the level of seasonal sales builds up rapidly to a peak during July and August. The business could build a plant with a regular capacity of 150 units per month and a peak capacity of 180 units per month if overtime is used. But it would cost a lot to build such a large plant, and it would be fully utilized only three months of the year. What would happen during the other nine months? Would workers be laid off?

There are other possibilities. For example, the average sales are 115 units per month. If capacity was set at the average rate, the business would produce too much during January, February, and March, and also during September through December. The excess inventory produced during the slack months would then be available for sale during the months of April through August. Workers would have stable employment, but the firm would be taking a risk on the large inventory.

Carrying inventory costs money too, so the problem is in balancing costs. If capacity is set for the peak, it requires expensive plant investment and high costs of layoff, hiring, and training. On the other hand, there are no inventory costs and no risk of carrying inventories. If

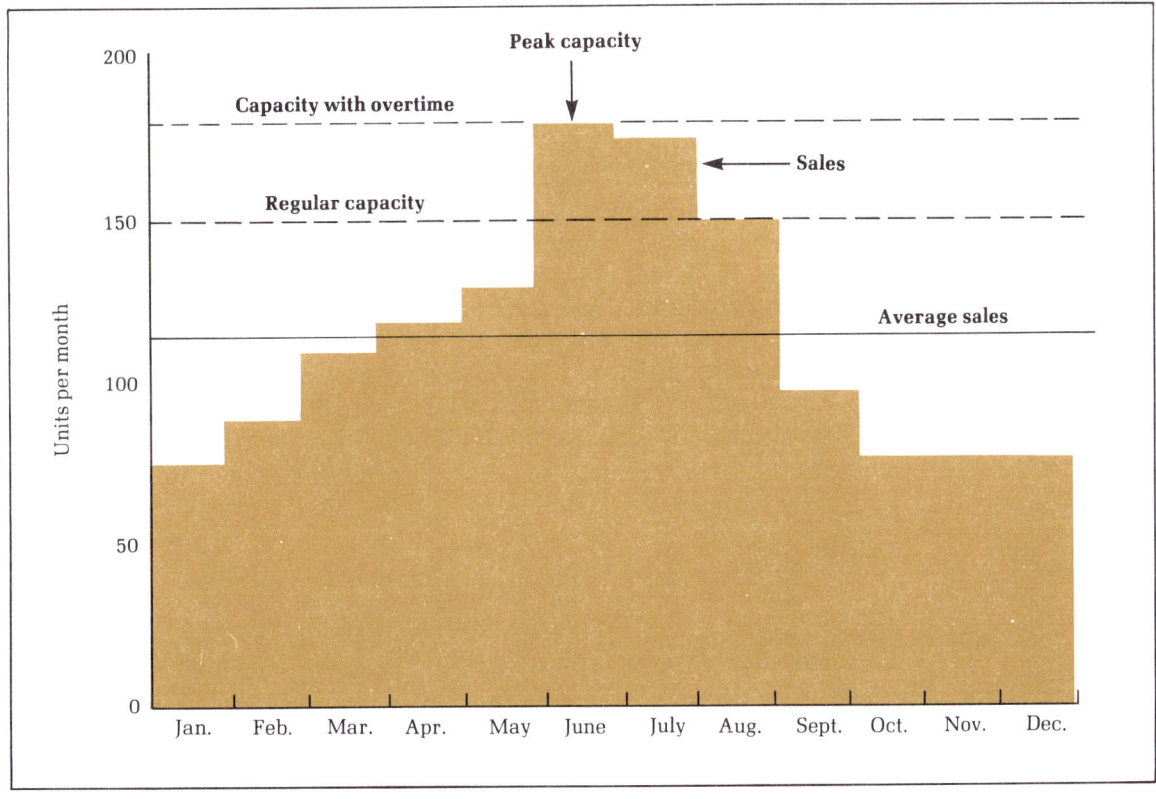

FIGURE 16–1
Capacity in relation to seasonal sales

capacity is set for the average sales level, plant investment and costs of layoff and hiring are low, but inventory costs are high. What should the company do? It depends on the kind of business and the relative costs involved.

Service businesses have unique capacity problems. In the fast-food business, the important sales variations may depend on the day of the week and the hour of the day. Friday, Saturday, and Sunday may be the big sales days, with sharp peaks near the lunch and dinner hours. McDonald's sells 40 percent of its hamburgers on weekends. Of course, hamburgers cannot be produced in advance during the slack periods; people want freshly prepared, hot food. Furthermore, there can be no real backlog in demand. People may be willing to wait a few minutes, but if the wait is long, they will go to a competitor and perhaps never come again. To customers, the fast-food business means that it will be fast and they will not have to wait.

Now how does this business set capacity? It almost has to be near peak demand. It may be possible to schedule more labor to take care of the peak—perhaps using overtime and part-time labor. But the physical facility must be set for the peak unless the business is willing to risk losing some sales. Regardless of the choice, however, the capacity will be idle a good share of the time.

Future capacity

Should a business build capacity to match present demand experience or take account of some future needs? Successive units of capacity will not be equally expensive. At any one level, there may be idle capacity in certain equipment classifications. Therefore to move to the next level may not entail the purchase of these equipment items. Where capacity is built to match some forecast of future needs, it is common to buy equipment for current needs only. However, there is enough building space so that additional equipment can be added as needed.

Capacity units

A company needs a unit of capacity that is meaningful for the particular system—one that can be translated into requirements for workers, machines, and space. In manufacturing systems some aggregate unit of capacity per time period is usually chosen, such as tons of steel, tons of dog food, number of automobiles, or machine-hours available. In service systems, the units might be numbers of beds in a hospital, numbers of students in a school, or numbers of tables, seats, or meal servings in a restaurant. In merchandising operations, the units might be square feet of selling space or display area.

Output potential is a good general measurement of capacity, since it can be converted easily to a physical capacity equivalent, such as the number of machines required. Knowing the number of machines required in various classifications will be important in actually developing a physical layout. Everything must be translated into physical units of capacity. In making this translation, a consideration of two factors reduces the utilization of equipment: the plant efficiency factor and the scrap factor.

Through the **plant efficiency factor,** a business expresses how many available hours are unusable because of scheduling delays, machine breakdowns, maintenance, and other problems. Plant efficiency factors may vary with the type of equipment and the company, but they range from 50 to 80 percent. Suppose that 100 outboard motors per week translates into the need for 550 milling machine hours per week. A firm with 70 percent plant efficiency then must increase milling machine capacity because 30 percent of the hours are lost. So actually 688 hours are needed.

Through the **scrap factor** a company recognizes that some bad parts will be produced. If a decision has been made to design a plant to build 100 outboard motors per week, that obviously refers to good motors—free of defective parts. Therefore, some of the milling capacity will be used to produce scrap. If the firm expected 3 percent scrap in the milling operations, then the 688 hours of available machine hours must be increased to 709 hours.

Now, getting down to machinery needs, suppose the company expects the machines to work 75 hours per week on two shifts. Taking both the plant efficiency and scrap factors into account, it will need $709/75 = 9.45$ milling machines. But it will have to have either 9 or 10 milling machines; there cannot be 9.45. If the company decides on 10 machines, there will be some idle capacity. If it decides to squeeze by with only 9 machines, there will probably be some bottlenecks now and then, which might be filled in with overtime work.

PROCESSES, JOBS, AND FACILITY LAYOUT

If a company knows the capacity it needs, how can it be put together into a system? The goal is to determine how the work will be done. Which machines should be used? How should the work be shared between workers and machines? Should jobs be specialized with each worker doing a small part of the process? What should be the work flow and layout?

Processes and jobs

The technology of the industry is the starting point. If the products require wood as a material, then basic woodworking machines determine a great deal of how the work must be done. For a bank, computers, data processing equipment, and general office equipment are determinants. If the product is an assembly of purchased parts, then the technology is centered in how the item is designed and must be assembled. Usually, however, there are alternate ways that the processes and jobs can be designed.

Thinking about the workers and the job structure, you can specialize or have one worker do many things. There are some advantages to **job specialization.** First, if a worker does just a small defined task repetitively, the job is easy to learn. Also, there are usually many people who can do such jobs because they do not require much job knowledge or skill. Third, if a worker does just one or a few tasks repetitively, that person does not have to spend much time getting organized to change from one task to another. Finally, the pay requirements for a job are dictated by the highest skills required in the job, even though some of the tasks may require only basic skills. With specialization, many of the resulting jobs can be constructed to have only basic skills, thus requiring lower wage rates. Only a few jobs will have higher skills with higher wage rates, so on the average rates will be lower.

On the other hand, highly specialized jobs are boring. Workers cannot see what is really being accomplished, and they may not feel that they have contributed much to the final product and to the organization. Good examples of specialized jobs are found in auto assembly lines. An auto assembly line job may be to assemble the wheels on the right side of each car that comes by. A general trend in the past 150 years, beginning with the Industrial Revolution, has been toward job specialization.

The opposite concept involves doing the whole job, rather than just a small part of it. A worker, or a team of workers, may assemble the entire car rather than just put on the wheels! Obviously, a job can be structured somewhere in between the two extremes of specialization and doing the entire assembly. The advantages of jobs with broad content are essentially the disadvantages of specialization. Broad jobs are more interesting because they involve more variety and responsibility. If there is a quality problem, you know who is responsible. On the other hand, broad jobs require higher skills and job know-how. It is harder to find qualified people and it will take longer to train them. Also, as we mentioned in regard to job specialization, broad jobs contain tasks with higher skills and thus normally require higher pay rates.

In recent years, there has been a reversal of the job specialization trend of the past 150 years. It is called **job enlargement.** Many businesses have purposely reorganized the work so that jobs have broader scope. The Swedish firm that makes Volvos is experimenting with team assembly. They wanted to recapture interest in jobs, feeling that job specialization had gone too far. This trend emphasizes that there are at least two forces that help determine the way jobs are designed: technology and human values. That is why the systems that produce goods and services are often called sociotechnical systems. The name recognizes that the needs of both must be served.

OPERATIONS PLANNING

A road maintenance supervisor hired a new worker to paint the center stripe on the road. At the end of the first day the supervisor was delighted—the new worker had painted a full mile and a half of center stripe. But the supervisor became puzzled because the second day the worker painted only three quarters of a mile, the third day one quarter of a mile, and the fourth day just 50 feet. Burning with a mixture of curiosity and anger, the supervisor finally asked why the worker's productivity was falling off so drastically after such a great start. The answer was: "Well gee, don't forget that I am getting farther and farther from the can."

Pollution and recycling processes

Recently environmentalists have had an impact on the design of processes. There have always been waste products from productive systems, but usually there was no attempt to control waste products unless a by-product had an obvious market. Wastes were disposed of in the cheapest possible way—dumped into rivers and the atmosphere.

Now waste disposal is regarded as part of the system design. Waste is processed so that it produces no harmful effects. In many instances the need to take waste disposal into account has led to the conversion of wastes to useful products. Landfill dumps have been found to produce a useful burnable gas, although it has not yet been economically profitable. A UCLA engineering professor found a way to make building blocks from manure. What next?

Facility layout

The basic physical flow patterns are related to the process and job design types we discussed earlier. Layout patterns are classified as functional or product.

"It may satisfy the clean air people, but the
clean water people will never dig it!"

Reprinted by permission *The Wall Street Journal*.

FIGURE 16–2
**Functional layout—
machines and processes
are arranged in functional
groups.**

Functional layout. Figure 16–2 shows the physical arrangement for
functional layout, also called *process layout*. Equipment of the same
functional type is grouped together, milling machines all in one place,
inspection in one central department, and so on. The processing of
an individual job then moves from one operation to the next as needed

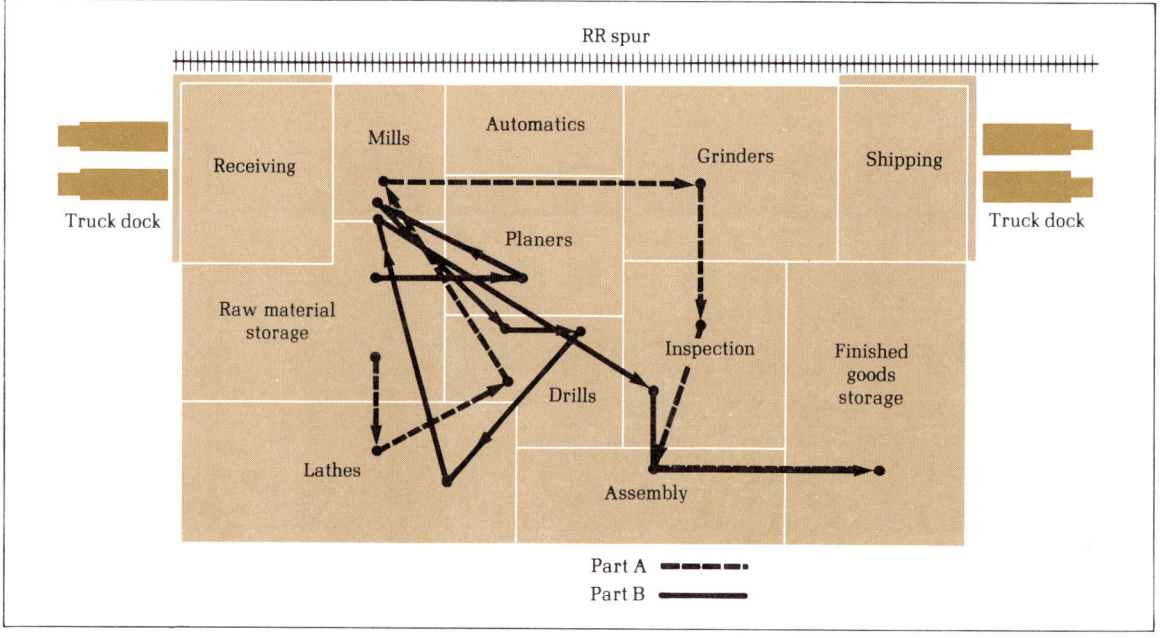

by the way the item is designed. In Figure 16–2 two illustrative parts and their routes through the system are shown.

Thinking in terms of our previous comments on processes and job design, functional layout assumes that all the functional skills and expertise are available in each of the departments. Therefore, an X-ray department of a hospital normally offers a broad range of radiology skills. A physician can call for virtually any kind of X-ray and expect it to be performed.

Functional layout is common in practice. Examples are in manufacturing, hospitals and medical clinics, large offices, municipal services, and libraries. In each of these situations, the work is organized according to the function performed. Table 16–3 gives a summary of typical departments in several common systems. In all these types of systems, the thing being processed (part, product, information, person) goes through a processing sequence. The work to be done and the processing sequence vary depending on the objective. At each service center, you must state what is to be accomplished, and this determines the processing details and the time required.

How does a business know when to use functional layout? First, it usually involves a situation where routes through the system depend on requirements. The situation calls for flexibility. To obtain reasonable utilization of workers and equipment, the idea is to assemble the skills and machines to perform a given function in one place and to route

TABLE 16–3
Typical departments in functional layout systems

System	Typical departments
Machine shop	Receiving, stores, drill, lathe, mill, grind, heat-treat, inspection, assembly, ship
Hospital	Receiving, emergency, wards, intensive care, maternity, surgery, laboratory, X-ray, administration, cashier
Medical clinic	Initial processing, external examination, eye, ear, nose and throat, X-ray and fluoroscope, blood tests, electrocardiograph and electroencephalograph, laboratory, dental, final processing
Engineering office	Filing, blueprint, product support, structural design, electrical design, hydraulic design, production liaison, detailing and checking, secretarial pool
Municipal offices	Police department, jail, court, judge's chambers, license bureau, treasurer's office, welfare office, health department, public works and sanitation, engineer's office, recreation department, mayor's office, town council chambers

TABLE 16–4
Why choose functional
layout?

1. Product and service designs may change.
2. Routes through the system vary depending on the individual processing requirements of orders.
3. It gains reasonable utilization of employees and equipment by grouping types of processes in one place.
4. It minimizes investment in equipment that would be underutilized
   if it were specialized.
5. There is increased flexibility.

the items through the departments as needed. If departments were
arranged in the processing sequence, many kinds of skills and machines
would be duplicated. Thus, when flexibility is the basic requirement,
functional layout is likely to be the most economical (see Table 16–
4).

The problem in arranging a functional layout is to determine which
departments should be adjacent to each other. Since the routes through
the system vary, a careful study of the relative location of departments
is needed.

An example. Suppose you were the business manager of a private
industrial medical clinic. You perform service under contract to a number of other businesses. These services include medical examinations
for new employees and annual physicals for key employees of the

FIGURE 16–3
Layout of an industrial
medical clinic

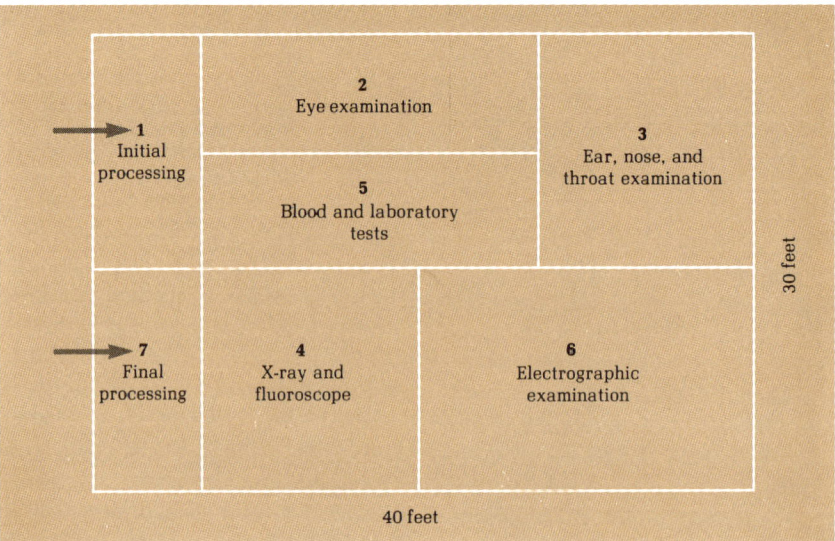

same firms. You perform five types of examination sequences depending on the contracts. The clients walk from one examination department to the next.

When you started the business, you had 1,200 square feet of available space and located each examination department in an area that fit the required space, as shown in Figure 16–3. However, clients are complaining about excessive walking to get through the procedures. You decide to see whether you can improve the situation.

You collect data on the frequency of travel per month between all possible combinations of departments as shown in Table 16–5. This is called a **load summary.** The load summary data could be computed by knowing the number of individuals processed per month under each of the different types of contracts, or by keeping track of what happens to people during a sample period of time.

With the data from Table 16–5, you can rearrange the layout so that the departments that do business with each other are closer together, as in Figure 16–4. In the figure, almost all departments are adjacent to the departments that involve trips back and forth. Only departments 2 and 4 have a longer trip, as indicated by the dashed line.

Sometimes the layout doesn't make sense to people who are not involved in the business especially when they have a long trip such as between departments 2 and 4. But the manager had to carefully choose which departments would have the longer travels. If the manager had put departments 2 and 4 side by side, then some other departments would have longer travel between them. Actually the choices made are good ones because there are only 100 trips per month between

TABLE 16–5
Load summary of number of trips per month between all combinations of departments

From departments	To department							Area requirements (square feet)
	1 Initial processing	2 Eye exam	3 Ear, nose, and throat	4 X-ray and fluoroscope	5 Blood and lab tests	6 Electrographic tests	7 Final processing	
1. Initial processing		400	100	100				100
2. Eye exam			200	100	100			150
3. Ear, nose, and throat				200	100			200
4. X-ray and fluoroscope					300	100		200
5. Blood and lab tests						300	200	150
6. Electrographic tests							400	300
7. Final processing								
								1,200

FIGURE 16–4
New layout of industrial medical clinic

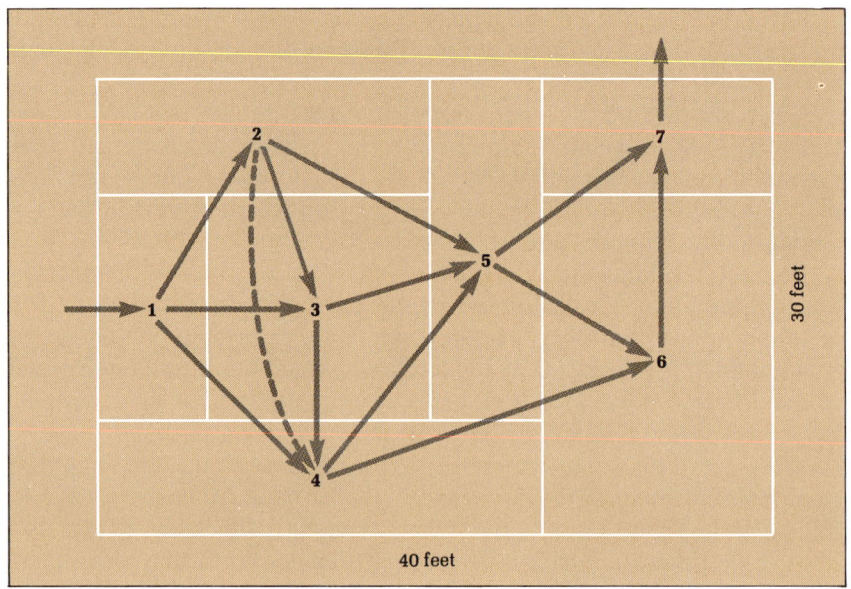

FIGURE 16–5
Product layout—machines and processes are arranged according to the sequence of operations.

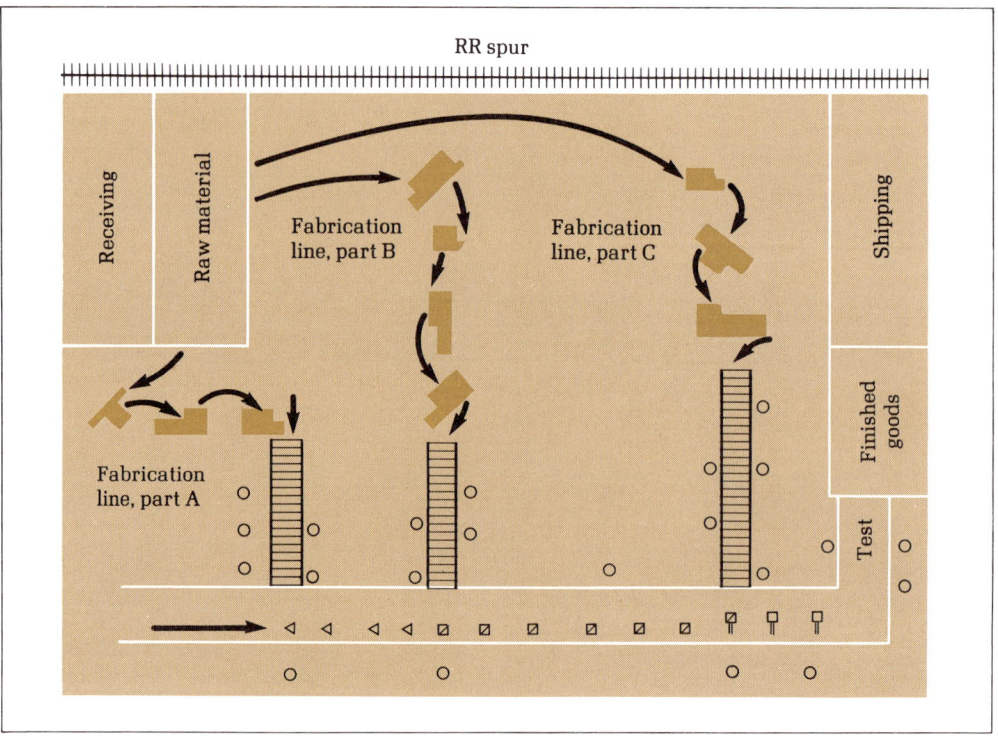

departments 2 and 4. Other arrangements would have had more nonadjacent trips.

Product layout.   Figure 16–5 shows a **product layout** arrangement. Machines and other equipment are arranged according to the sequence of operations required to fabricate and assemble the product. Machines and workers are specialized in specific operations. The part or product moves from operation to operation on conveyors or other devices, resulting in a production or assembly line. While most line operations are found in manufacturing, the idea of direct flow has been applied to some nonmanufacturing activities. For example, a cafeteria line and a dry-cleaning operation are both applications of the **production line** concept.

Why would a business decide to use product layout (see Table 16–6)? If there is a large volume involved, a product layout can get very good utilization from both employees and equipment. On the other hand, since the investment in plant and equipment is large, there must be good balance between operations in order to obtain good utilization. Balance in a line refers to the need for each operation in the sequence to have equal capacity so that a smooth flow results. There also must be relatively stable demand for the product or service in order to get good equipment utilization. A business probably couldn't justify a permanent line set up for manufacturing a fad or novelty product like hula hoops. Manufacturers would probably also think twice about line operations if they could not be assured of a continuous supply of material, since shortages can interrupt the entire system. Finally, companies need to take account of the possible negative worker reaction to line operations.

Given the decision to develop a product layout, the major problems are deciding on a production rate for the cycle time and subdividing the work so that a smooth flow can result. The subdivided activities need to be balanced so that each operation has an equivalent capacity. Getting the line balanced is important, and businesses spend a lot of time and effort to do it. The reasons become clear if you have ever observed a poorly balanced line. Have you ever eaten in a cafeteria

TABLE 16–6
Why choose product or line layout?

1. If volume is large, specialization of employees and equipment may be justified.
2. Demand for products and services is stable.
3. It results in better utilization of employees and equipment with high volume.
4. It minimizes investment in equipment with high volume.
5. Design of products and services is stable.
6. Continuous supply of materials is not a problem.

where serving the main dish took a little longer than the other operations? Customers have to wait at this bottleneck and grumble about the service. Meanwhile, the other servers are standing around waiting, too.

SUMMARY

If you are going to produce a product or a service, it will require facilities. Your first question is where to locate the facility. Sometimes location is really important and is dominated by a technical or market factor. Sometimes the best location is determined by trying to minimize the transportation costs of raw materials coming in and finished goods being shipped out.

In trying to decide between alternate possible locations, it is common to compare costs in each location. Labor, transportation, real estate, and state taxes, and utilities are the common costs. The issue is how the costs in each location translate into costs of your product. In addition, though, there are many subjective factors that need to be assessed. For example, locations for fast-food operations require an easy way to get in and out and plenty of parking.

The second major facility planning issue is to determine how much capacity is needed both now and in the future. Here you need to be concerned about how you will operate. If sales are seasonal, it may be expensive to provide the peak capacity required. In addition, the plant will be partially idle much of the time. Therefore, it may be more economical to use overtime, multiple shifts, and outside subcontracting to smooth the capacity requirement. Also, workers will have more stable employment. If you operate a service system where there are no finished goods inventories, you may have no choice but to set capacity for the peak need periods.

Often the processes required can be organized in different ways. The relationship between workers and machines and the impact on job design will be affected by the processes. Also, the nature of the layout has an important relationship to job designs. In functional layout, work is done in functional departments and jobs tend to be broad in scope. In product or line layout, jobs tend to be specialized.

An important problem in functional layout design is the relative location of departments. Since the general need is for flexibility and routes through the system will vary, you need to study flow patterns to determine the best location for each department.

In product or line layout, the location of each operation is determined by the sequence of operations on the line. Then the main issue is line balance. A balanced line is one in which the capacity of each station is equal.

REVIEW QUESTIONS

1. What does it mean if location is said to be "oriented" toward some factor such as water, energy, or transportation? Does it mean that the factor is the only one used to determine location?

2. If your location problem is such that all you need to do is compare costs in different locations, what does that indicate about prices in the alternate locations? If your location problem is such that all you need to do is compare gross revenues in alternate locations, what can you say about costs in the different locations?

3. How can subjective factors affect longer-run costs in different locations?

4. Under what conditions would you set capacity to match the peak demand that you expect when sales are seasonal? Under what conditions would you set capacity at some average level?

5. Define the *plant efficiency factor*. The *scrap factor*. How do these factors affect the capacity you need?

6. What are the advantages of job specialization? Job enlargement? How do you define the term *socio-technical system?*

7. How do you define the term *functional layout?* Under what conditions should functional layout be used?

8. In a functional layout, the routes that different orders follow through the system vary. How then can you determine the relative location of departments?

9. Define the term *product layout.* Under what conditions would you use product layout?

10. What is meant by the term *line balance?* Describe the process of balancing an assembly line.

CASES

Case 16–1. Townsend goes south?

Townsend Textiles is an old-line textile firm that has been located in New England for the last 75 years; the plant and equipment all seemed to be at least 75 years old, too. Three generations of Townsends had managed the company, but it had recently been sold to outsiders who had new capital and planned to rebuild the company, starting with its outmoded physical plant.

The new president felt that the old plant was hopeless. It was bursting at the seams and could not be expanded. He had located a piece of property about five miles out of town that would be adequate for the company's needs, including room for expansion.

At that point, the sales manager came to the president with a deal that she had uncovered. The town of Pocatello, North Carolina, was eager to attract new industry as a part of an economic development plan. The inducements were quite substantial, including a free site large enough for a new plant, options to buy adjacent land (owned by the mayor) for future expansion within five years at an attractive price, and no city taxes for five years.

1. *Is the proposal by the town of Pocatello attractive enough to counterbalance the costs of moving from New England? How can you tell?*
2. *What additional information should the president obtain in order to evaluate the proposal?*
3. *How should Townsend make this important decision?*
4. *What subjective factors should influence the decision?*

Case 16–2.   The Twentieth-Century Medical Clinic

A group of doctors organized The Twentieth-Century Medical Clinic according to a concept that held promise for reducing operating costs, thereby increasing profits. The clinic offered physical examinations to business firms that needed such services for new employees and for annual physicals for continuing employees.

The new idea was to arrange the examination steps and tests in production-line style. All individuals would be given the same set of tests. The new system was organized around a central equipment core that rotated so that the equipment for each test came in sequence in each examination room for use. Eight examination rooms were located in a circle around the equipment core, and the examination equipment was divided into eight groups. Each of the eight equipment groups was then available in sequence to each examination room for a fixed amount of time until the core turned again, making the next group available. A medical attendant competent to administer the tests was available in each room, and a doctor screened the results and made the reports to participating companies. Eight-room modules could be added to provide as much capacity as needed.

1. *What kinds of problems do you anticipate in the operation of the new system?*
2. *Do you think that the system should be less costly to operate than the traditional clinic mode of giving physical examinations?*
3. *How do you feel about the application of production-line methods to medical practice?*

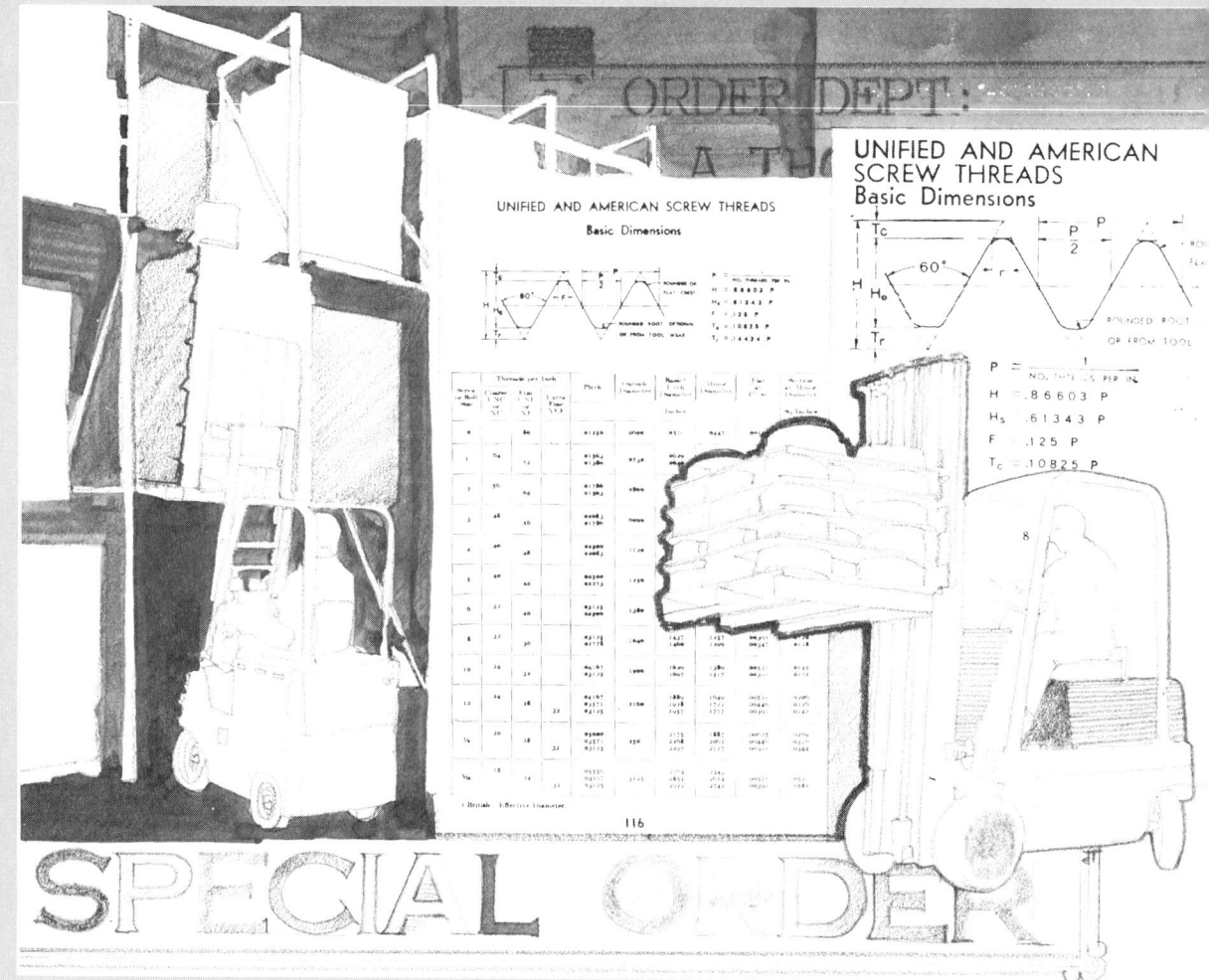

chapter
17

RAW MATERIALS:
THE PURCHASING
FUNCTION

By studying this chapter you should be able to find answers to these questions:

1. When should a manufacturer buy an item rather than make it?
2. What are the sources of information for determining specifications for what a company buys?
3. Should all orders be handled the same way? What about large orders? Small? Repeat? Special orders?
4. What is an economic order quantity?
5. What is hedging and how can it be used effectively?
6. How do you know which vendor's bid is best when there may be fixed charges and discounts in the bids?
7. What is reciprocity and when should it be used?

Terms you should know:

bill of materials (BM)
blanket contract
economic order quantity (EOQ)
forward buying
hand-to-mouth buying
hedging
incremental cost
inspection report
open-end contract

purchase order (PO)
purchase requisition (PR)
receiving report
reciprocity
release orders
specifications
standardization
vendor

The formula for making money in business is simple. Offer a good product at the right price, sell hard, and spend wisely! The purchasing function centers on spending wisely.

Of course, it varies with the type of business, but buying materials and supplies can account for a large share of costs. Buying wisely is especially important for manufacturing firms. Up to 60 percent of their costs are spent on materials, parts, and supplies. In service organizations, direct materials are not a factor, but there are supplies that must be used to provide the service. These supplies can be very expensive for health services, for example.

The importance of the purchasing function to the success of the productive system and the business goes beyond just costs. Material must be of the right quality. Material that does not meet quality standards is just like not having it at all. You cannot use it! Or, if you use poor-quality materials, customers will react by choosing better products.

Finally, materials must be bought in the quantities and at the time needed. The flow of raw materials must key in with the production schedule. If a company is short of material, it cannot produce or it may not be able to complete products. Completing them later requires special handling and setups and will probably cost more. If shortages hold up production, workers are either idle or disgruntled when they are sent home.

So the purchasing function is important from three main points of view: cost, quality, and timely performance. That's why having just an order clerk to do the buying may not be good enough. A business needs someone who knows the materials to be bought, knows quality and how to ensure that the company gets it, knows how to negotiate a fair contract, knows how to anticipate time and cost problems, and knows how much to order at one time to keep material flowing.

MAKE OR BUY?

A nagging question is always before the purchasing agent. If you have production capability, why not use it to make the item you propose to buy? The first question to ask yourself is: What business am I in? If you are going to consider making the item yourself, it ought to be closely related to your products. Or there must be another really important reason for making it yourself, like ensuring quality control or supply.

Economic analysis

Most people in business agree that cost should be the basis for make or buy decisions. If a part can be bought cheaper than it can be made, buy it! The kind of cost comparison needed, however, can be confusing. Every situation must be analyzed in terms of the incremental costs involved. A company must ask: If I buy this part instead of making it, how much do I really save? Are these cost reductions greater than the costs of buying the item? Conversely, if a firm presently buys an item, what actual added costs will be incurred? Are these costs less than the cost reductions it will experience by stopping purchase of the item?

These issues sound simple enough, but the difficulties come in interpreting them. For example, if there is already idle capacity, the cost of making will look more attractive. On the other hand, if equipment, floor space, and supervision must be acquired, the analysis would have to reflect this fact.

If a company considers buying an item for $2 that it now makes for an average manufacturing cost of $2.25, it had better look closely at the overhead cost items. It is likely that very few of the overhead cost items will truly be reduced by buying the part. The supervision, floor space, and general factory overhead will probably remain as continuing cost items. If the equipment is still useful, the company will probably keep it too. The incremental cost figure to be compared with the $2 per piece purchase cost may begin to look more like $1.50. The continuing costs of equipment and buildings and the realistic facts of idle capacity are strong pressures for continuing to make instead of buying.

Noneconomic and intangible factors

A business may be influenced by a number of noneconomic factors in formulating a make or buy policy. It may manufacture in-plant in order to control quality closely. Reliability of supply can be another controlling factor. It may manufacture in-plant in order to control trade secrets. The business may buy outside because a supplier holds an important patent, or because it may be able to maintain flexibility with alternate sources of supply. Companies dealing with large defense contracts must often subcontract as a contract condition.

Make or buy policies

Most companies follow a basic policy that places the economic criterion in the driver's seat. They wish to vary from this policy only when a limiting noneconomic factor has been consciously or unconsciously equated to a cost disadvantage. Although make or buy policies commonly assume the outside purchase of the great bulk of standard items such as nuts, bolts, switches, and valves, the policies are likely to vary somewhat as plant load changes. It is common to make parts

TABLE 17–1
Factors that may influence make or buy decisions

Economic advantage
Quality considerations
Reliability of supply
Need for alternate supply sources
Control of trade secrets
Research and development capabilities of a supplier
Retention of goodwill
Reciprocity—buying from a customer
Desire to specialize activities
Imposed subcontracting, as with some government contracts

for which basic processes are already available. But, when the plant load requires overtime, outside buying expands.

Businesses often buy when they could make simply to retain the goodwill of an important supplier. Also, arrangements are made with customers, each giving the other some of their business. This is called **reciprocity,** and we will discuss it later in the chapter. Finally, make or buy decisions are often based on policies of specialization and concentration of effort in some one basic line of products. Table 17–1 is a list of factors that influence make or buy decisions.

DID YOU EVER WONDER?

How many different parts and materials go into cars and airplanes?
A typical General Motors car has 15,000 parts and materials.

A DC-10 jetliner has more than 210,000 parts and materials, not including the engines. Each different type of rivet, bolt, and screw is counted only once. But if you add up just the fasteners (rivets, bolts, screws, etc.), there are more than 1,750,000 of them.

THE PURCHASING PROCESS

One way to get a handle on the purchasing function is to look at what needs to be done. Take a rather ordinary request for an item and see who must get involved and what they do. Figure 17–1 is a flowchart that traces the major events. First, the need arises someplace in the business for some item. It is not stated explicitly in Figure 17–1, but someone specified what was needed, and a **purchase requisition** (PR) was issued to the purchasing department. If the specifications

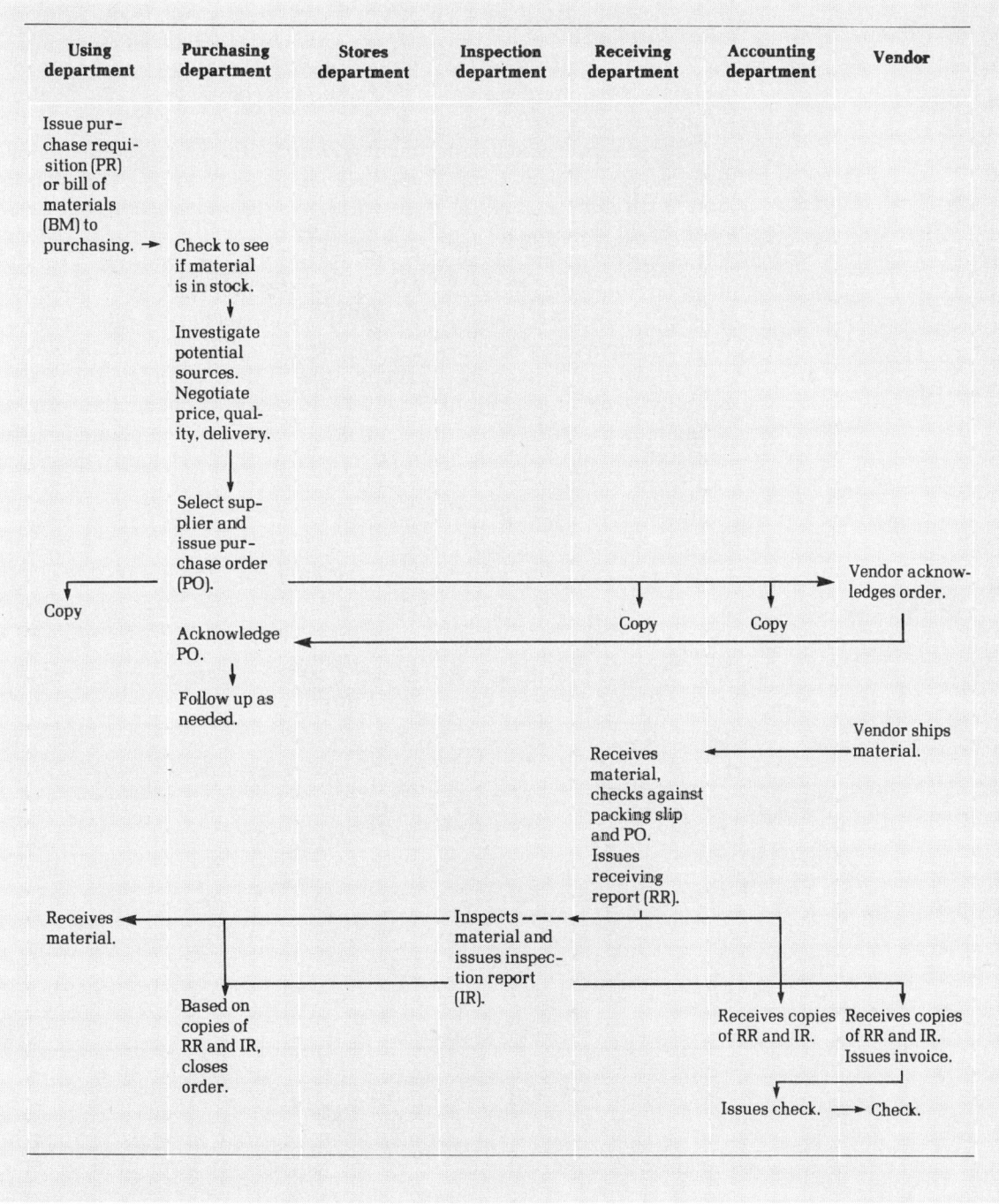

FIGURE 17–1
**Flowchart of basic
purchasing system**

are not contained or are not explicit, the purchasing department will need to clarify them. In some cases the need could be for a whole list of items related to the product, and the issuing department may simply send a **bill of materials** (BM). The BM contains the specifications of the items.

Then the purchasing department goes to work. It may sound obvious, but the first logical thing that must be done is to see whether the item is already in stock. It might be available under a different name, or the user department may just be unaware that it is in stock. Some of the really important activities of the purchasing department include investigating potential sources and negotiating on price, quality, and delivery. Based on these negotiations, a **purchase order** (PO) is issued to a vendor with copies sent to the using, receiving, and accounting departments. A **vendor** is a company that sells something. The vendor acknowledges the order to receiving. Purchasing then follows up on the order as needed. The follow-up may involve all the characteristics of the order but is particularly concerned with the delivery date.

The vendor ships the material, checking the contents against the enclosed packing slip and the PO. The receiving department then issues a **receiving report** (RR). The inspection department checks the quality against specifications and issues an **inspection report** (IR). Copies of the RR and IR are transmitted to the purchasing and accounting departments and to the vendor. The using department receives the material. The vendor issues an invoice to accounting, which then issues a check to the vendor. The purchasing department closes out the order and the process is complete.

This process sounds very mechanical, and it is for run-of-the-mill orders. Some of the problems already have been indicated. The following is a list of the important problems that occur in purchasing:

1. Determining the needs and specifications of items.
2. Soliciting proposals and bids.
3. Dealing with different kinds of orders.
    a. Large orders for continuing requirements.
    b. Special orders for equipment and other high-value items.
    c. Run-of-the-mill orders—how many to order at one time?
    d. Items of small value, exceeded by the cost of ordering.
4. Generating and evaluating reliable sources of supply.
5. Negotiating contracts.

Determining needs and specifications

Supervisors of departments are normally authorized to originate requisitions for materials needed. They may simply send a material requisition to the stores department. Standard items may be carried in stock. If the item is not standard, or if it is out of stock, the request converts to a purchase requisition. Sometimes purchase requisitions originate in using departments. For example, requests for new typewriters might come from the office manager, steel supplies from the production department, and so on.

It is the responsibility of the purchasing department to anticipate the needs of using departments. Many items are used by several departments, and the purchasing department must order for all of them. If the purchasing department waited for each to place a requisition, there would probably be too many rush orders. This means extra costs. Also, since the purchasing department is in close touch with price trends and market conditions, anticipating needs can have important advantages. Purchasing may order in advance to anticipate market shortages and increased prices.

Specifications.   Written descriptions of materials are called **specifications.** The purchase requisition requires a description of what is wanted. Often the purchasing department will have to give a more detailed specification of the item in order to get exactly what is wanted. Specifications describe in detail requirements such as chemical content, surface hardness, tensile strength, moisture content, and heat content. These requirements are often stated in such a way that the inspection department can test to see whether the requirements are met when the material is received. Sometimes specifications must state character-istics that are not easy to describe. A surface may be required to be "reasonably free from surface defects"; a finish may be a "smooth satin finish"; a specially made product may have to be of "good and workmanlike quality."

Sometimes a purchasing department has a choice of using a brand name item or ordering the equivalent through specifications. Such choices are available for a range of products such as wire, chemicals, cement, flour, tool steel, cutting oils, grinding wheels, and paint. When a company buys a large quantity of items by specification, it may save money. It can get exactly what it wants. Trademark items may not be just right for the job. Sometimes they are better than needed or sometimes not good enough. On small orders, specification buying will probably cost more than buying trademark items. If the vendor has to make a special run of materials in order to meet specifications, the cost will be high. Therefore, the general guidelines used are to buy by specification for large quantities and by trademark for small quantities.

There are three major sources from which specifications may be derived: (1) individual standards set up by the buyer; (2) standards established by certain private agencies—users, suppliers, or technical societies; and (3) government standards. Individual standards set by the buyer require extensive consultation among users, engineering, pur-chasing, quality control, suppliers, marketing, and possibly the ultimate consumers. This is an arduous and expensive task. It is often more economical to use the standard specifications set and used by others.

Standardization.   The term **standardization** means agreement on sizes, designs, and quality aspects. The idea is to reduce the number of sizes, designs, and quality levels. If products can be designed to take advantage of standardization, the costs of materials used will be somewhat lower than those required for special specifications.

Dealing with different kinds of orders

There are many kinds of orders—those for materials that are used continuously, one-shot orders for equipment, the run-of-the-mill repeat orders. All of these cannot be handled in the same way.

Large orders for continuous use.   Raw materials used in products always must be available. Production schedules must be met and these materials are the basis for action. The purchasing department has its own files and lists of things to buy, and it knows how much to buy based on the production schedule.

Most of these items are bought on **blanket** or **open-end** contracts that may cover an entire year. These kinds of contracts leave quantities and delivery times to be set as the materials are needed. Even the purchase price may be left open. Purchasing sends out estimates of expected requirements several months in advance. Then it can send out weekly or monthly **release orders** that give the vendor detailed instructions on delivery quantities and schedules.

Contracts for these kinds of high-volume items are open for bid, periodically. The company establishes a relationship with a good supplier, and it expects dependability in quality, quantity, and delivery. It may want an alternate supply source, however, for protection in case one supplier has a strike, a disaster, or other problems. It is with these large-volume items that a purchaser may indulge in forward buying and speculation.

Forward buying means that a company buys more than it needs just to make production requirements. The basic reasons for forward buying are to assure supply and, secondarily, to anticipate price movements. There is an element of speculation in the latter. If you are speculating that there will be price changes, this can affect the timing of purchases. You can either buy forward, if you expect the price to increase, or indulge in **hand-to-mouth buying** if you are expecting price decreases. In either case, purchasing should take as its first responsibility the maintenance of supply for the production process.

If a company uses raw materials that are subject to wide price variations, it may try to minimize the risk of loss by **hedging.** This can be done when there is a "futures" market for the item. The most common type of hedging is to purchase and sell the same amount of the item in the present and futures markets. By executing the two transactions at the same time, a company can protect itself against future price movements. It minimizes the possible losses or gains that might result from speculation. If a business wants to make money from the product rather than from market speculation, hedging might be an important means of protection.

As a simple example, suppose that you use silver as a raw material in a product. The price of silver goes up and down like a roller coaster, and you want to protect yourself from these price changes. You buy and sell the same amounts in the cash and futures markets in a pattern like this:

	Cash market	Futures market
June 1	Buy at $4.50 per ounce	Sell September silver futures at $4.60 per ounce
July 10	Sell at $4.40 per ounce	Buy September silver futures at $4.50 per ounce
Result	Loss of 10¢ per ounce on cash transactions	Gain of 10¢ per ounce on futures transactions

The net gain or loss from the four transactions is zero. The price changes have had no effect on raw material costs. It is not always possible to balance the transactions perfectly as in the example because the cash and futures prices do not always move by exactly the same amount. But you often can come close.

Special orders for equipment.   These kinds of orders can also be large, in that they can involve a lot of money. Sometimes a great deal of engineering work may be needed to specify exactly what is wanted. This is one kind of situation for which a company may want to have vendors bid based on a careful proposal.

Run-of-the-mill repeat orders.   These are usually middle-sized orders that are often placed with the same vendors. Each new order describes again the product and specifications, indicating the quantity and delivery date. It is common to ask more than one vendor to bid, and the contract usually goes to the lowest dependable bidder.

Since these items are used in reasonable quantity to justify repeat ordering, how many should a company order at one time? Suppose it uses an average of 6,000 of an item per year. Should it order one month's supply, six months' supply, a years' supply, or two years' supply? If the company orders too many, it must keep them in inventory for a long time and that costs money. On the other hand, it costs a substantial amount just to place an order. There are clerical costs of everyone involved and the costs of following up on the order to make sure it is received when needed. The economic order quantity concept is useful in determining the amount to order in such situations.

Economic order quantities.   Did you ever wonder why companies order the particular quantities that they do? They don't just pick a number out of the air. They are likely to order the quantity that balances the annual ordering costs against the annual inventory costs. That quantity is called the **economic order quantity** (EOQ) and represents the order quantity that strikes a balance between these two costs.

Suppose that it costs $20 just to place an order. If a company orders only one month's supply at a time, the annual ordering cost is $240. If it orders three months' supply at a time, the annual ordering cost is only $80. Obviously if it orders 12 months' supply at a time, the annual cost is only $20. The annual ordering cost decreases as the amount ordered at one time increases, as shown in Figure 17–2. So from the point of view of ordering costs, a company benefits by placing larger orders.

The factor that prevents a company from ordering extremely large amounts at a time is that it costs money to hold inventory. The inventory costs are made up of storage, interest, spoilage, inventory taxes, and other expenses. These costs are proportional to the size of the inventory, and that depends on how much the company orders at one time. If it orders two months' supply instead of one, average inventory costs

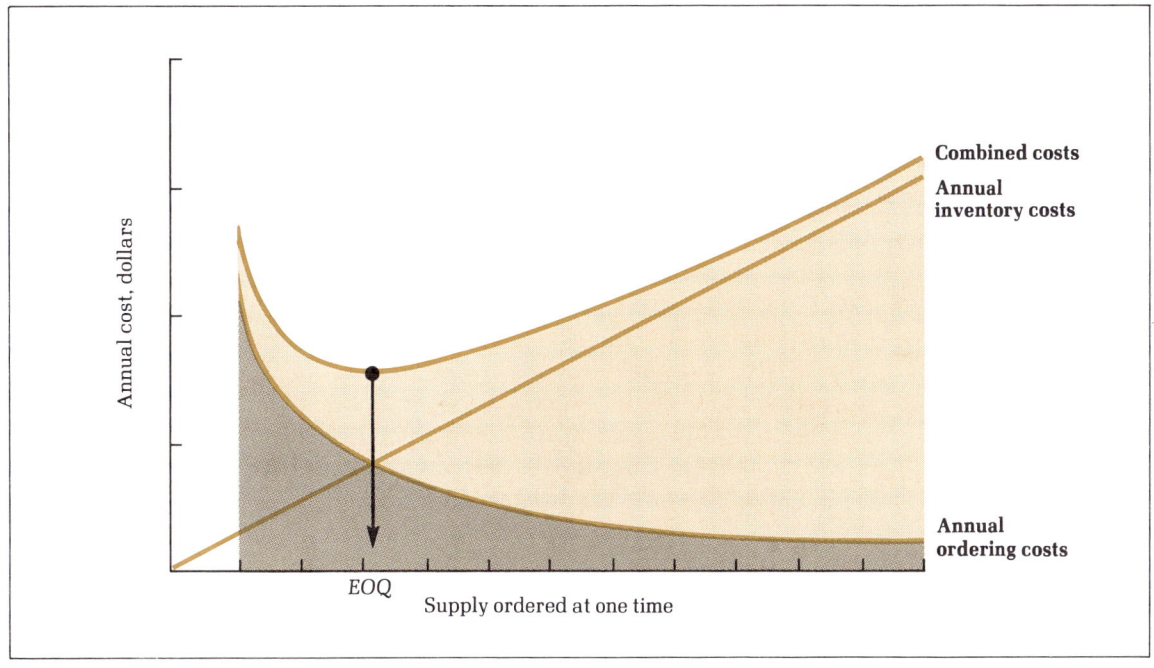

FIGURE 17–2
Annual ordering costs,
annual inventory costs,
combined costs, and the
economic order quantity
(EOQ)

double. The annual inventory cost curve is also shown in Figure 17–2. Costs increase in proportion to the size of the supply ordered at one time. So from the point of view of inventory costs, a company should order only small amounts at one time.

Neither of these costs can be ignored, so the EOQ concept results from adding the two costs together for each quantity ordered at one time. The result is the combined cost curve in Figure 17–2. The sum of the two costs falls to a minimum when the two costs are about equal, and that's a good way to think about it. These minimum-cost order quantities are called EOQs.

There are other guides to the quantities to order at one time. For example, some products are packaged in standard quantities. There are bundles, barrels, tons, and other measures. If an order is for only part of a standard package, the price per unit will probably be higher. Therefore, the actual order quantities should be adjusted when necessary to coincide with standard quantities. Another basis for selecting order quantities is transportation. Perhaps a full-carload freight rate applies to orders of a certain size or greater. Then, if the order is already close to that quantity, purchasing will probably want to consider ordering the larger quantity in order to obtain the better freight rate. Raw materials ordering may be based on a production schedule. A company may want to take the production order quantities into account when ordering raw materials. Finally, even when EOQs are used, a company may wish to round off the number of units to some logical round number.

Small orders. If it costs $15 to write purchase requisitions and orders, how does a company handle orders for items that cost only 50¢ or $1? It cannot establish a lower limit and say that it will not order anything unless it has at least a certain value. Some low-priced items may be important and they may even be rush orders. Usually companies let these orders follow through the regular procedures. There may be ways of reducing their average costs, however. For example, a company might reorder little things relatively infrequently but in larger quantities. Even if it ends up throwing away part of them, it has saved extra ordering costs. Or, a company can let individual departments buy small orders out of petty cash. Another possibility is to issue blanket orders with suppliers. Then the buyer can just order by telephone without making out a purchase order each time.

Soliciting proposals and bids

In theory, a company should get bids on everything. We have already commented on the small order, however. Bidding would make no sense there and would just increase costs. Bids are probably not asked for on some middle-sized orders either. Flipping through two or three catalogs can provide price comparisons, and the purchasing agent should have a good idea of what are good prices, since these kinds of items are ordered regularly. Occasionally, bids help to peg current prices. Reliable suppliers whose general price structure is known are often used.

For most middle-sized orders and for almost all large and special equipment orders, the practice is to get bids. Company forms calling for bids, quotations, or proposals are commonly used. These forms call for standardized information so that comparisons of bids can be made. The forms also let the supplier know that the bid is going to be compared with others—calling for a "sharpening of the pencil." In general, the buyer should select the low bid, provided the supplier is reliable. There may be good reasons why the low bidder should not be chosen, however.

Generating and evaluating reliable suppliers

How does a purchasing department generate a list of suppliers? Personal experience and the experience of others are a good place to start. The department should keep a record of that experience. Files can tell who has given satisfactory and unsatisfactory performances on price, quality, and on-time delivery. Good performance should be rewarded, but beware of past bad performance. Also, when business-people get together to talk about common problems, suppliers can be one subject of conversation.

Comparing bids. If you have three bids on an order, to whom should you award the contract? Reliability is most important if the price differences are small. Will each bidder deliver on time? How do you tell for sure? Will the materials pass inspection? If not, will the vendor take care of the problem without a hassle? Will the vendor cooperate with schedule changes and rush orders? The answers to these questions are hard to predict, but past experience and the experience of others may help.

Assuming suppliers are equal on the above factors, then it comes back to price. In simple situations, a single number on the bid may tell the price story. Sometimes, however, there are complications such as fixed charges and discounts. Then you have to do some figuring to find out which bid is the best deal.

For example, suppose you get bids on a part to be made outside. For that kind of job, it is common to find a "tool charge." The vendor must make up special tools to do the job, and there is a separate charge for it. In addition, the price per unit may depend on the size of the order. The supplier can give a discount for larger volumes because more efficient equipment can be used, or other costs get averaged over a larger quantity. You get a break—or at least you may get part of it. Below are bids from three suppliers on such an item.

			Discounts	
Supplier	Tool charge	Unit price	Unit price	Volume over
A	$220	$0.80	$0.70	1,000
B	320	0.72	0.60	3,000
C	180	0.96	0.85	500

If you want only 600 units, the total costs from each of the three suppliers are: A—$700, B—$752, and C—$690. Supplier C has the lowest bid made up of a fixed tool charge of $180 plus $0.85 per unit, or $180 + 0.85 × 600 = $690. But, if you want 2,000 units, the costs are: A—$3,720, B—$3,320, and C—$4,430. Supplier B is now the lowest bidder. So, it is tricky. You have to compute the total costs for each supplier at the quantity you want in order to be sure.

Actually, you can draw graphs like Figure 17–3 to show just where each supplier provides an advantageous quote. Supplier C has a low tool charge and has the best overall price up to 250 units. Between 251 and 500 units, supplier A is best. Then supplier C's discount takes

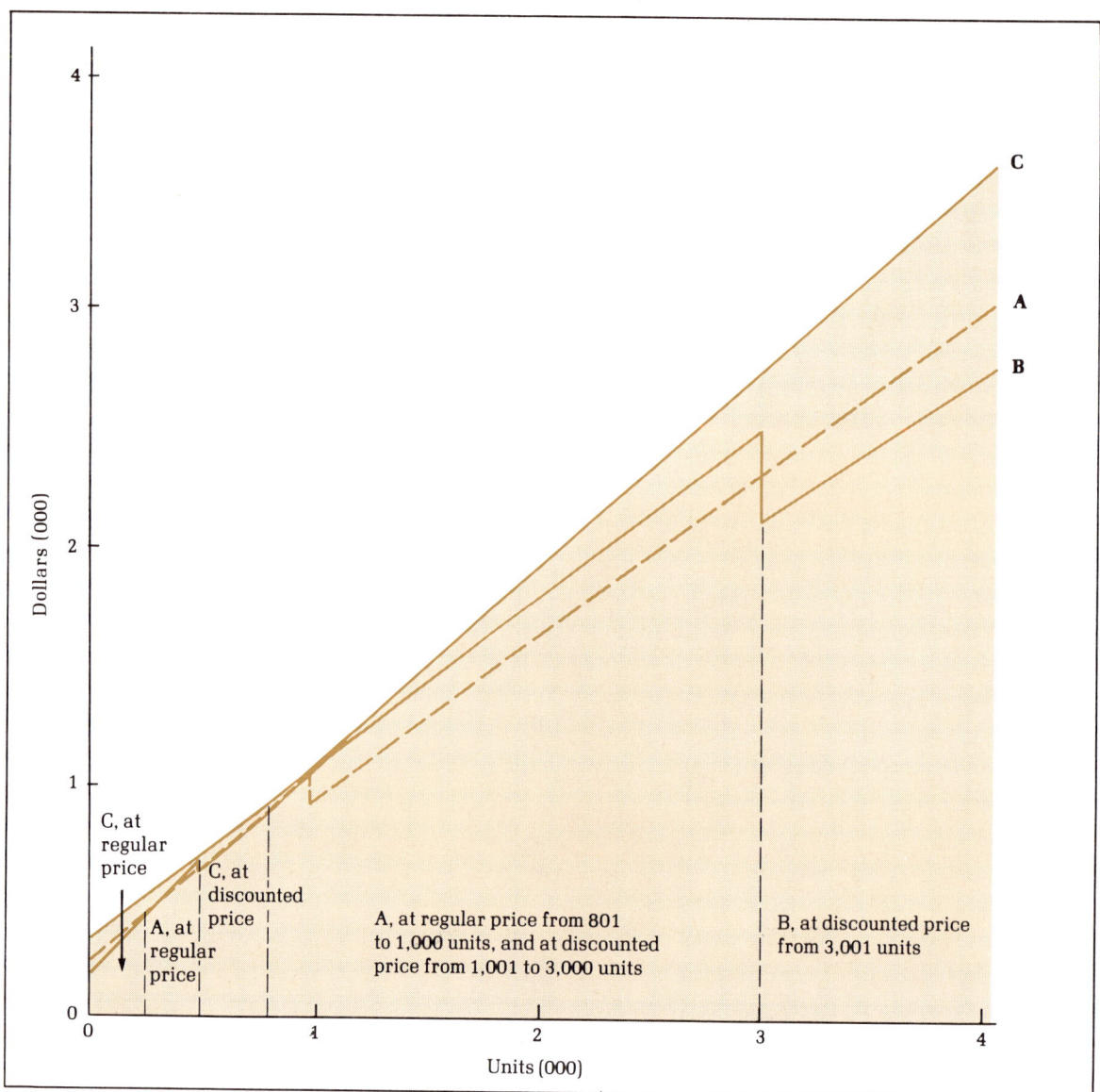

FIGURE 17–3
Total costs for three suppliers for different quantities

over and is best from 501 to 800 units. Supplier A has the lowest price from 801 to 3,000 units, and supplier B is best for only large orders above 3,000 units.

Why would the bids be so different? It does not mean that supplier B is trying to "gouge" with its large tool cost. Supplier B is probably tooled up for large orders and gives good prices for them, supplier C is good for some but not all order sizes in the low range, and supplier A serves the middle range.

Reciprocity and other objectives.   What should a company do if one bidder is a particularly good customer? Should it make a decision based on this relationship? Or, should it just look at the cold facts and be hard headed? After all, the company is in business to make a profit. Awarding the customer the contract is called **reciprocity.** It is a common business practice.

Most purchasing agents do not like reciprocity because it reduces their flexibility. Also, there can be abuses. But by and large the practice makes sense if the special customer's bid is in the ball park and is reliable for quality and delivery. After all, to save a few pennies on buying something but losing a good customer doesn't add up to good business sense. In the long run, the company may be better off recognizing that it may have to buy from someone, so why not scratch the customer's back a little?

There are other long-range objectives that may be partially satisfied through the selection of suppliers. If the quality of materials is of great importance, a firm may be better off to pay slightly more. It may thus be able to help retain and build a quality image.

Sometimes a supplier has important research and development laboratories that the buyer cannot afford to maintain. The buyer may be able to get some testing done through the supplier that will contribute to its own quality or product development. In the long run, dealing with that supplier may help achieve a better marketplace image.

A reliable supplier from the point of view of delivery can be important to a buyer. One of the largest printers in the country has a reputation for the very highest quality and claims that it has never been late with a promised order. What a reputation! It has a continuous backlog behind each machine, and it gives priority to its good customers. If you gave your work to that printer, you could count on receiving your order when it was promised. That reliability could contribute in turn to your reliability with your customers.

SUMMARY

The purchasing function provides the raw materials that feed the productive system. Even service organizations buy supplies, and sometimes these supplies are costly and crucial to the operation.

In a manufacturing business, there is always the temptation to make an item rather than buy it if the business has the know-how. But, it is important to make careful cost comparisons between make and buy alternatives. It is incremental costs that count, but firms also may be swayed by important noneconomic and intangible factors.

The overall purchasing system must be kept in mind. Several departments are involved: the user department, purchasing, stores, inspection, receiving, accounting, as well as the vendor.

There are several different kinds of orders, and they should not all be handled in the same way. Buyers handle large orders for continuously used materials quite differently than special orders for equipment or periodic orders. Small orders are a "pain," but they may be for important materials. Repeat orders raise the question of the number to order at one time and bring up the issue of the most economical quantity to order.

With large orders of continuously used materials, a company may find that price movements force it to consider either forward buying or hand-to-mouth buying. Should it really be speculating? If there is a futures market, it may decide to hedge as a protection from losses due to price changes.

Careful analysis of bids can produce economies. The best bid is sometimes masked by the fixed charges and price-volume discounts. A buyer needs to compute the total cost of each bid to be sure. But the lowest bid is not necessarily always the one accepted. A good customer may be one of the bidders and so reciprocal arrangements may be fruitful. There are also a number of longer-term objectives that may be partially achieved by selecting bidders who may not be lowest in direct costs.

REVIEW QUESTIONS

1. What is meant by the term *incremental cost?* How is it applied in make or buy analysis?

2. What are the noneconomic and intangible factors involved in formulating make or buy policy.

3. Under what conditions should you buy trade-marked items? Items by specification?

4. What are the major sources of specifications? Should you develop your own specifications or use standard ones?

5. What are blanket or open-end contracts? Under what conditions are they used in purchasing?

6. Define the term *forward buying.* Is it different from speculation?

7. What is meant by *hedging?* How can hedging be used to minimize risks if raw materials are subject to large price variations?

8. Define the term *economic order quantity* (EOQ). Under what conditions might you use EOQs?

9. What bases might you use for determining the quantities of run-of-the-mill items to order at one time?

10. How should small orders for inexpensive items be handled? What are the bases for comparing different suppliers' bids? How do fixed charges and discounts enter into the comparison of alternate bids?

11. What is reciprocity purchasing? Under what conditions should it be used?

CASES

Case 17–1.   Don't miss the opportunity for discounts!

Bill Scoof is the purchasing agent for Drugs International. His philosophy is to take advantage of price discounts whenever possible. "Why pay more for the stuff we buy. Sometimes I stretch a bit and buy a year or two supply of an item in order to get a really good price, but I seldom do that for anything where we might change the specifications, resulting in obsolescence. Being willing to buy in quantity gives me real bargaining power with vendors—they love me."

Bill was considering a deal offered by a vendor of an important raw material used in several products by Drugs International. Bill figured that the vendor had been stuck with an oversupply. It was the only way he could explain the fantastic price for

10,000 pounds. It represented a 30 percent discount compared with the price for his usual order of 1,000 pounds (about three months' supply). If he buys the 10,000 pounds, there is a problem in finding a place to store it, however, since the receiving room and storage space are just about full.

1. *Should Bill reject the offer to buy 10,000 pounds?*
2. *Does your answer to question 1 change if you are sure that the material will not spoil and is not subject to obsolescence?*
3. *How will Bill's decision look if business volume increases? Decreases?*
4. *What policies should a business have concerning price discounts?*

Case 17–2.   Be independent—Make it yourself!

Jack Young is the production manager of The Pumpo Pump Company. The company makes a variety of pumps, manufacturing some of the main parts and buying standard items that are assembled into the pumps. Jack had a good system for planning and

scheduling the parts that were manufactured in the plant, but he had trouble with several suppliers of parts. He felt that reliable suppliers are worth their weight in gold.

One particularly bad day Jack found that three

different parts that he needed to complete orders for pumps were behind their promised delivery schedules. This meant that Jack would not be able to meet the promised delivery dates for the pumps. He was really steaming when he went into the staff meeting held each week by the plant manager. He laid out the problem of being late with the pump orders. This set Bill Connors, the sales manager, into a tirade since he had promised the customers just last week that the pumps would be delivered on time. He said that it was happening too often, and his customers might well give their business to competitors. Jack's answer was, "I can make those parts in plant, but you know very well that we buy them from the Oxnard Company because they buy pumps from us. That's a deal that you made, Bill, not me." He then turned to the plant manager and said, "I want authorization to make those parts in-plant. I want to be independent of Bill's friends."

1. *Should the plant manager authorize Jack to make the parts rather than buy them?*
2. *What should Bill Connors's position be? If the parts are made in-plant, he should get more reliable promised delivery dates for his customers, but then he may lose the business of the Oxnard Company.*
3. *What factors should influence the plant manager's decision?*

OPERATIONS
PLANNING AND
CONTROL

By studying this chapter you should be able to find answers to these questions:

1 What is the meaning of aggregate planning in business? How can it be used to consider alternate planning in business?

2 What is a master schedule?

3 How can you schedule a machine that is used for several different products?

4 What are the functions of inventories in a manufacturing business? In a service business?

5 What is a fixed-quantity inventory control system? A periodic inventory control system?

6 How does the reliability system help maintain quality standards?

7 What are the functions of field warehouses? Where are they located in relation to producing plants?

8 What are distribution territories?

9 When should regional warehouses be used?

Terms you should know:

acceptance sampling
aggregate planning
control chart
cycle inventories
field warehouse
finished goods inventories
fixed-quantity reordering system
in-process inventories
level production
machine schedule
master schedule
normal capacity

overhaul
periodic reordering system
physical distribution system
pipeline inventories
preventive maintenance
production requirements
regional warehouse
replacement
safety stocks
service level
seasonal inventories

A company can design and locate facilities and negotiate contracts with suppliers for raw materials and supplies, but that is only preparation for production. There is no production until the company begins to operate its system. In this chapter we shall discuss the operation of the system, including the physical distribution of the output.

Figure 18–1 shows the whole productive process in terms of physical flow. Raw materials flow in from vendors. The vendors are outside the business, but they have a direct affect on it. Then the materials flow through the system and end up as finished goods in the factory warehouse. These goods have no value, however, until they are available to users. Therefore, there must be a physical distribution system. The productive system might include distribution warehouses that serve specific geographic areas.

A company must first decide at what level it should operate. So it needs to be able to forecast requirements. Given the forecast, it must

FIGURE 18–1
Physical flow from vendors through manufacture to finished goods storage.

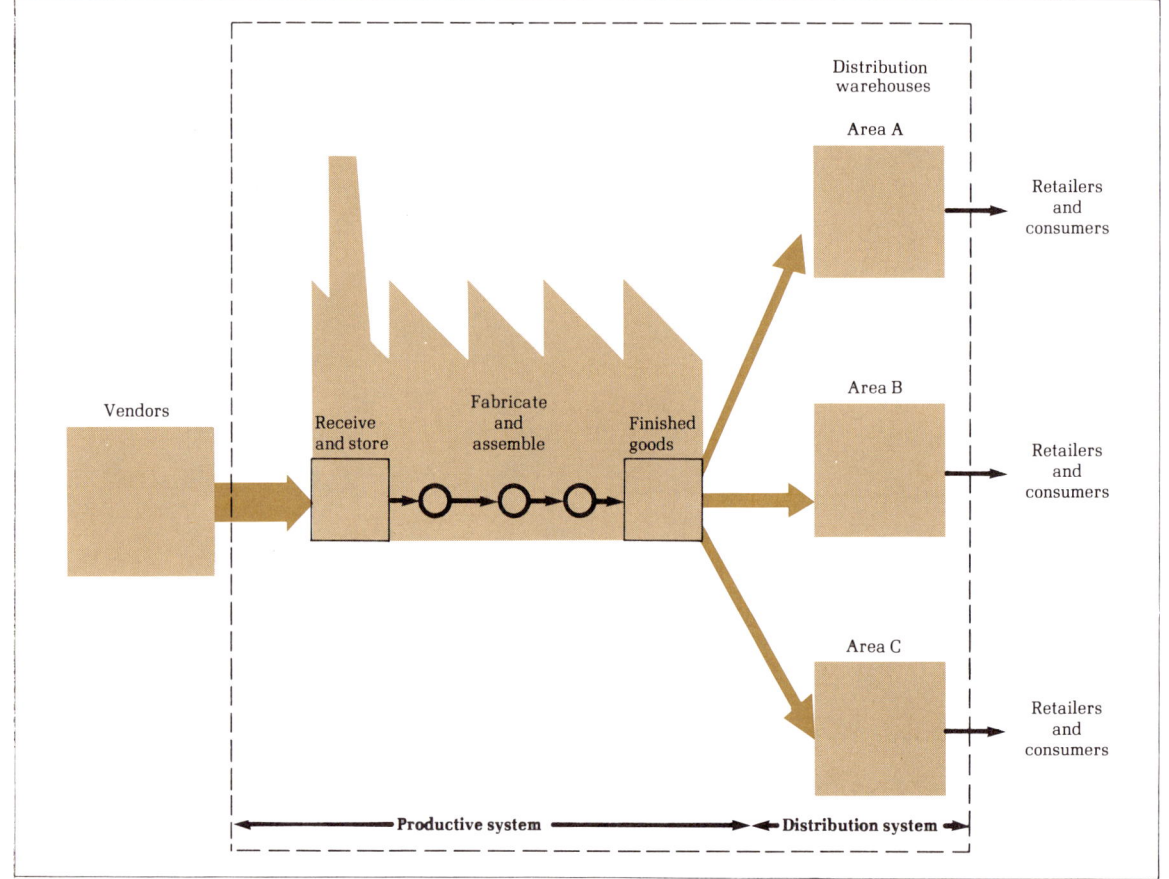

WILLIAM K. and JOSEPH COORS
Cash for cans

While William Coors has the title of chairman and chief executive officer and Joseph Coors is president and director, the two brothers state that they operate the office of the presidency jointly. The Coors brothers have been controversial figures in business because of their adherence to a policy of distributing the famous Coors beer only in the western states, because of their strong views concerning the private enterprise system, and because of the recent labor strife in their brewery at Golden, Colorado.

Coors's product distribution problem stems from the fact that it operates a single large brewery (the largest single-site brewery in the country). Therefore, it has maintained a policy of adding to its marketing area only by expanding into states adjacent to current marketing areas. But Coors beer became so popular that some distributors and retailers were "bootlegging" Coors beer for resale in the East. The Coors brothers went to court in Texas and Wyoming, and the courts upheld their right to restrict sale to their marketing areas.

Coors has been environmentally oriented for a long time. In January 1959, Coors established its Cash-for-Cans recycling effort, being the nation's first brewery to market aluminum cans. Since only a small fraction of all beverage cans in use at that time were aluminum, the recycling effort was discontinued. But the Cash-for-Cans program was set in motion again in 1970, and all Coors distributors began paying 10 cents per pound for the return of all aluminum beverage cans (both beer and soft drink cans). Over 6 million pounds of cans were returned that year. Subsequently the price offered increased to 15 and then to 17 cents per pound, and by 1977 the annual returns had increased to over 84 million pounds. The brewing industry uses more than 25 percent of the entire output of the aluminum and steel can industry.

The environmental awareness of the Coors company has also caused problems. To eliminate the consumer practice of littering by throwing away the metal opener tabs, Coors used a new opening called the Press Tab II. It attributed part of a sales decline in 1977 to the new tab, which consumers disliked, and Coors quickly redesigned the opener.

The Coors brothers pride themselves on producing beer that contains only natural ingredients with no preservatives or additives. Another source of pride is the fact that over 100 years ago the original Adolph Coors, a German immigrant, was able to achieve the American dream in establishing the Coors Company. His self-sufficiency is maintained in the operating philosophy of the company. For example, the Coors brothers continue to follow the practice of financing all expansion primarily through the reinvestment of profits rather than going to banks or capital markets for investment funds.

decide how to meet those requirements. Should it hire more workers, lay off, use one or more shifts, use overtime, or produce in advance of requirements and accumulate finished goods inventories?

Then the business gets down to actually scheduling how much of each product to produce in each time period. This is called master scheduling. The **master schedule** provides the background for more detailed decisions on controlling inventories, scheduling critical machines and personnel, maintaining the equipment, and controlling quality. That whole process produces output that can then be distributed.

AGGREGATE PLANNING

The term **aggregate planning** means broad-level planning for production. The first thing the company needs is a unit of output to use as a planning base. In the steel industry, plans are made in terms of tons of steel; in the fast-food business, it might be persons served; in a hospital, it might be bed occupancy-days; gallons of paint in the paint industry; machine-hours in mechanical industries. Many manufacturing firms probably simply use hundreds or thousands of units, even though there may be different sizes and types. For example, General Motors may use a certain number of passenger vehicles for planning, although some are four-door sedans and others are vans.

Forecast of requirements

The forecast is then developed in terms of the unit selected. Forecasting for only a month in advance may not be adequate. A company

TABLE 18–1
Production days, expected production requirements, and production requirements per production day

(1) Month	(2) Production days	(3) Expected production requirements	(4) Production requirements per production days, (3) ÷ (2) (rounded)
January	22	5,000	227
February	20	4,000	200
March	23	4,000	174
April	19	5,000	263
May	22	7,000	318
June	22	9,000	409
July	20	11,000	550
August	11	9,000	818
September	20	6,500	325
October	22	6,000	273
November	22	5,000	227
December	18	5,000	278
Total	241	76,500	

probably should think in terms of at least 6 to 12 months as a forecast horizon. The forecast helps to define the decisions that will have to be made. Suppose there is a forecast of how many units you need to have available each month, as in Table 18–1. Now you can talk in terms of **production requirements**—what is required of the productive system each month.

Column (2) of Table 18–1 shows immediately that there are a variable number of production days in each month. There are 23 production days in March but only 11 in August since the plant is shut down for two weeks that month for vacations. Expressing the production requirements per production day as in column (3) will aid in effective planning.

Did you ever wonder what businesses do about producing to meet seasonal requirements? They have to either produce some units before they are needed and store them, or gear up to produce at very high levels during the peak season.

Alternate plans

Figure 18–2 shows a graph of the requirements curve. The **normal capacity** is 500 units per production day, and the capacity with overtime is 600 units per production day. With normal capacity, requirements can be met for all months except July and August. In July, the company can meet the requirement of 550 units per day by using overtime. But

FIGURE 18–2
Requirements per production day, level production plan, and intermediate production plan

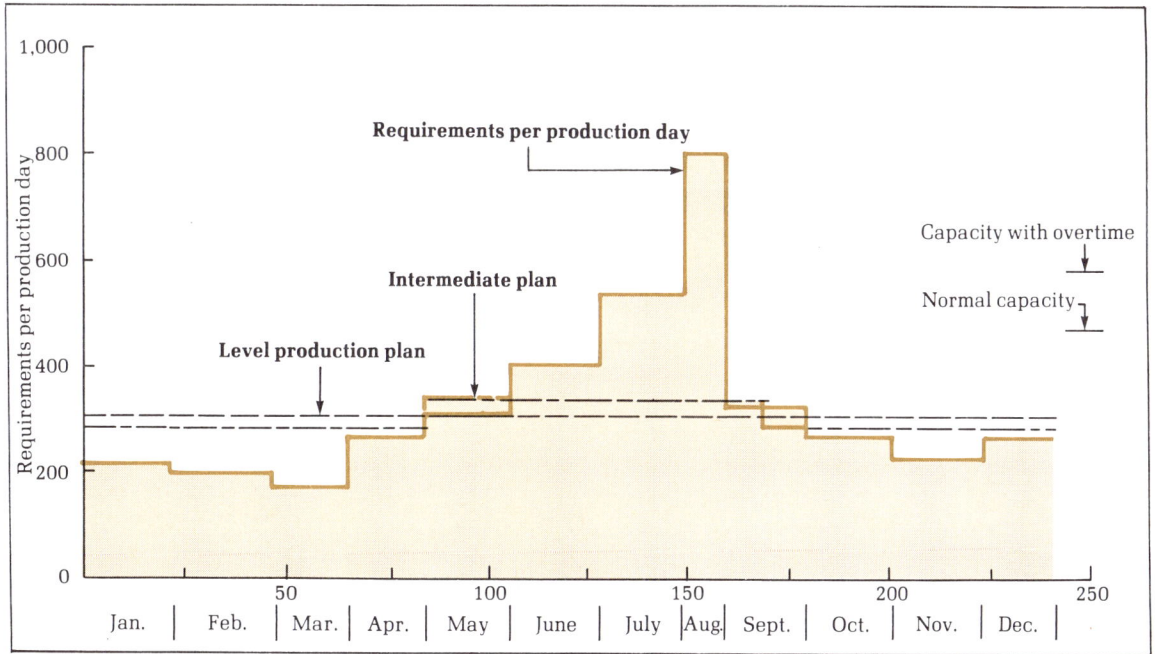

the August requirement of 818 units per day cannot be met, even with overtime. Therefore, alternate plans must be considered.

The easiest way to meet the annual requirement of 76,500 units is to establish an average level of production at 76,500/241 days = 317.43 units per production day. This schedule is called **level production** and is indicated by the dashed line in Figure 18–2. With level production, the company would produce more than needed in January through April and in October through December. The plan would be to sell off this seasonal inventory of 12,343 units during the peak period of June through August. This is a simple production schedule, but there is a risk in carrying inventory. The inventories cost money. On the other hand, it also costs money to hire and layoff people and to have them work at overtime rates during the peak season.

A compromise would be to go between the level plan and the plan that simply follows requirements. An intermediate plan is also shown in Figure 18–2. It produces as follows: 300 units per production day in January through April (84 days), 350 units per production day in May through September (84 days), and 300 units per production day in September through December (73 days). The intermediate plan offers stable employment. Extra production can be achieved solely through overtime work. There are still seasonal inventories, but they are not as large as with the level production plan.

A company would have to compare the two plans in terms of inventory and overtime costs to see which one would cost less. It also could generate other plans in the same way that might be acceptable. The best plan for a given business depends on the relative costs of carrying inventories, paying overtime premium, and hiring and laying off people if necessary. Computer programs are used in some businesses to help generate these minimum-cost aggregate plans. Similar considerations are required in deciding what physical capacity to build. In operations, however, a new aggregate plan must be generated or updated periodically, perhaps monthly.

MASTER SCHEDULES

The aggregate plan is useful in setting the production strategy, but a company then must break it down into the schedules for each product.

TABLE 18–2
Aggregate plan

	Initial	Period 1	Period 2	Period 3
Aggregate forecast	—	1,200	1,100	800
Production	—	1,000	1,000	1,000
Aggregate inventories	800	600	500	700

TABLE 18–3
Forecasts for hoes, rakes, and shovels

Period		1				2				3			
Week	1	2	3	4	5	6	7	8	9	10	11	12	Total
Hoes	100	100	100	100	100	80	75	75	75	75	65	50	995
Rakes..........	150	125	125	100	75	75	75	65	65	65	60	50	1,030
Shovels	75	75	75	75	100	120	125	135	135	60	50	50	1,075
Total	325	300	300	275	275	275	275	275	275	200	175	150	3,100
Period total		1,200				1,100				800			

For example, the aggregate schedule might call for 1,000 units in planning period 1, where the planning period might be a month or perhaps a four-week period. If there were three products (hoes, rakes, and shovels), the more detailed master schedule would indicate the quantities of each of the products to be produced in each week of the planning period. The master schedule must be consistent with the aggregate plan.

Assume that the aggregate schedule calls for level production during a three-period planning horizon. The periods of planning horizons are often months or four-week periods. The four-week period is quite convenient since it breaks the year into $52/4 = 13$ equal periods. Assume that there are three four-week periods in the planning horizon. Then the aggregate plan may be as in Table 18–2.

Now the forecast must be broken down on a weekly basis for the three products. Suppose that the composition of forecasts is as shown in Table 18–3.

The aggregate schedule by planning periods was to be level at 1,000 units per period. The aggregate forecasts are declining, but the forecasts by weeks for the three products follow different patterns, with the forecasts for hoes and rakes declining. The forecast for shovels shows an increase during the second period but declines rapidly in the third period.

The master scheduling task requires the construction of schedules for each of the three products consistent with the aggregate plan and forecast. Table 18–4 shows a master schedule that fits these requirements. The production plan indicates an initial cycling between the three products, with productive capacity allocated to one of the products each week. In the fifth week, the strategy changes to cycle shovels every other week. The schedule then takes account of the high forecast requirements for shovels during the fifth through ninth weeks. In the

TABLE 18–4
**Master schedule for
three products,
consistent with
forecasts and aggregate
production plan**

Period		1				2				3		
Week	*1*	*2*	*3*	*4*	*5*	*6*	*7*	*8*	*9*	*10*	*11*	*12*
Hoes, production	—	—	250	—	—	125	—	125	—	250	—	—
Rakes, production	—	250	—	250	—	125	—	125	—	—	250	—
Shovels, production	250	—	—	—	250	—	250	—	250	—	—	250
Total production	250	250	250	250	250	250	250	250	250	250	250	250
Aggregate plan	250	250	250	250	250	250	250	250	250	250	250	250
Deviation from plan	0	0	0	0	0	0	0	0	0	0	0	0

tenth week, the schedule returns to a three-week cycling of the three products.

Production lot sizes

Notice in Table 18–4 that several weeks' supply of each product was run. For example, hoes had a lot size of 250, although the forecast was for only 100 per week during the first five weeks. There are several reasons for operating this way. First, note that capacity per week in the aggregate plan is only 250 units, or 1,000 units per period. If the company is using its capacity for one product, obviously it cannot also be using it for another. It must stay within its capacity limitations.

Table 18–4 indicates that the company turned over all of its capacity to one product in each week in period 1. It could have divided capacity among two or more products as in period 2. But each time the company sets up equipment to run a product, it costs money for setup. So it should not set up for really small lots unless it is necessary in order to meet requirements.

On the other hand, if a company produces only in very large lots, it increases inventories. Inventories cost money, too. Therefore, in selecting production lot sizes, a company must try to balance the costs of setup and inventory, just as in purchasing raw materials. Look back in the last chapter at Figure 17–2. The EOQ concept applies to production lot size also.

The considerations for a company in setting the size of production lots are setup and inventory costs, capacity limits, and the need to meet requirements. There are some other factors, too, such as rounding to numbers such as 50 or 100, adjusting to quantities that can be transported between operations easily, and sometimes taking account of machine scheduling.

Machine scheduling

Scheduling individual machines can be important if the machine is critical. Being *critical* means there is limited capacity; that is, the machine must be scheduled carefully to get enough of all the products through. If the machine is used only for one product, the schedule may still be critical, but it is simpler. When the machine is used for several different products, scheduling is more complicated.

Suppose a machine must be set up to run four different products. The lot sizes for each product are set using the criteria just discussed. There is enough capacity to meet the annual requirements of all four products. But look at Figure 18–3. Product 1 is run, which takes perhaps 21 days to complete. The inventory of product 1 is built up as shown.

FIGURE 18–3
The machine cycling problem. Products 1 and 2 run out of stock before they can be run again.

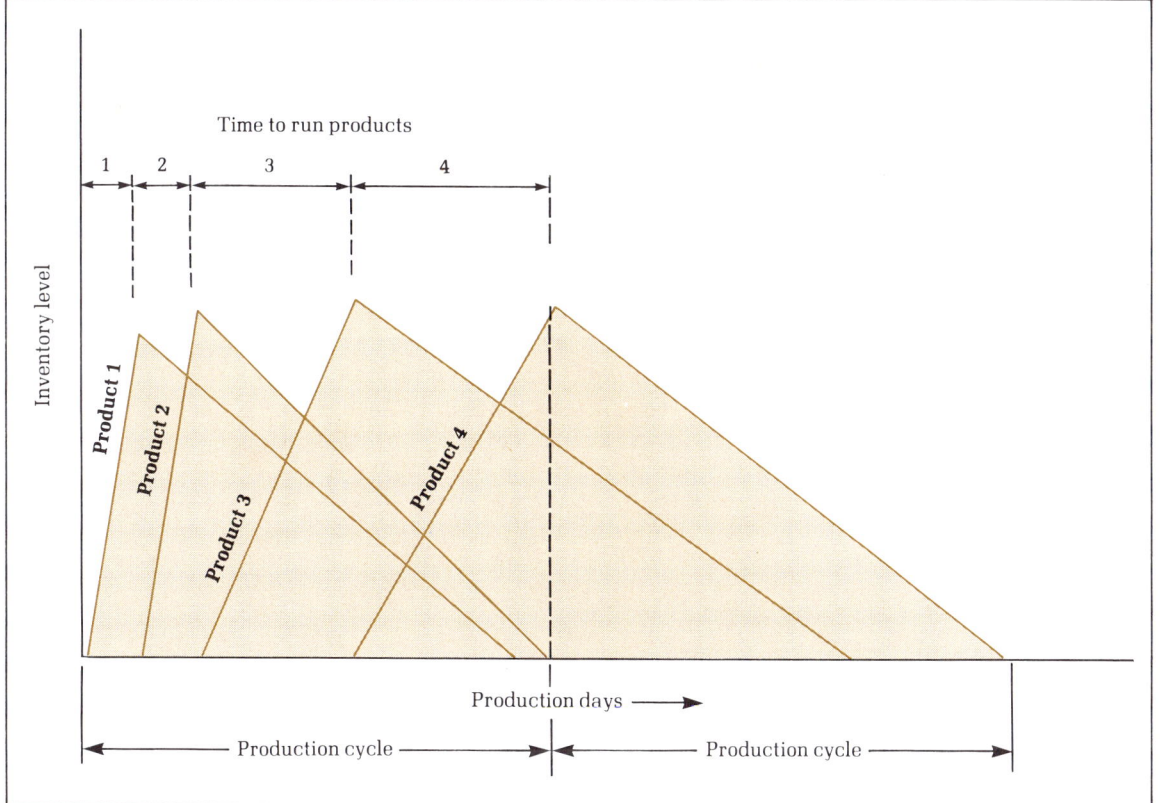

When the lot for product 1 is done, the machine is set up for product 2, and so on for the four products.

When the production run for each product is completed, the inventory is drawn down by usage according to the demand rates for each product. But what happens? Products 1 and 2 run out of stock before the completion of the production cycle.

Something is wrong with the way the production lot sizes were set. The limited capacity of the machine was ignored, and the planner didn't take account of all the products to be run. A simple way out, provided there is enough total capacity, is to set lot sizes jointly. We stated initially that there was enough capacity to meet the annual needs of the four products. So all lot sizes can be set equal to the same number of days or weeks of supply, provided the number of days or weeks of supply is greater than the production cycle time. Now the system will operate smoothly, and the inventory for each product will last at least as long as the production cycle.

SCHEDULING PERSONNEL AND WORK SHIFTS

Scheduling personnel

Scheduling operations and machines set basic work requirements. But people must run the machines and perform other work. For those businesses that operate eight hours per day, five days per week, this poses no problem. But problems can arise in businesses that operate seven days per week with two or three shifts. Many service businesses, such as food and health services, have the seven-day problem. Some manufacturing businesses operate seven days per week in order to get good utilization of their huge investment in plant and equipment.

People in our society normally work about 40 hours a week, with two days off. There is a preference for having the weekend off. But if the business operates seven days per week, not everyone can have the weekend. Also the day shift is preferred to the second and third shifts. The preferences are often satisfied for those who have seniority and by other agreements. It is essential that there are enough but not too many workers for all days of the week. It can get complicated if there are too many rules about who gets preferences.

Scheduling shifts

The previous problem is compounded if a business requires a 24-hour operation. Did you ever wonder why the telephone company offers low long-distance rates after 5:00 p.m., before 8:00 a.m., and on weekends? Figure 18–4 suggests some of the rationale. The switchboard load varies tremendously for directory assistance, coin telephone dial-

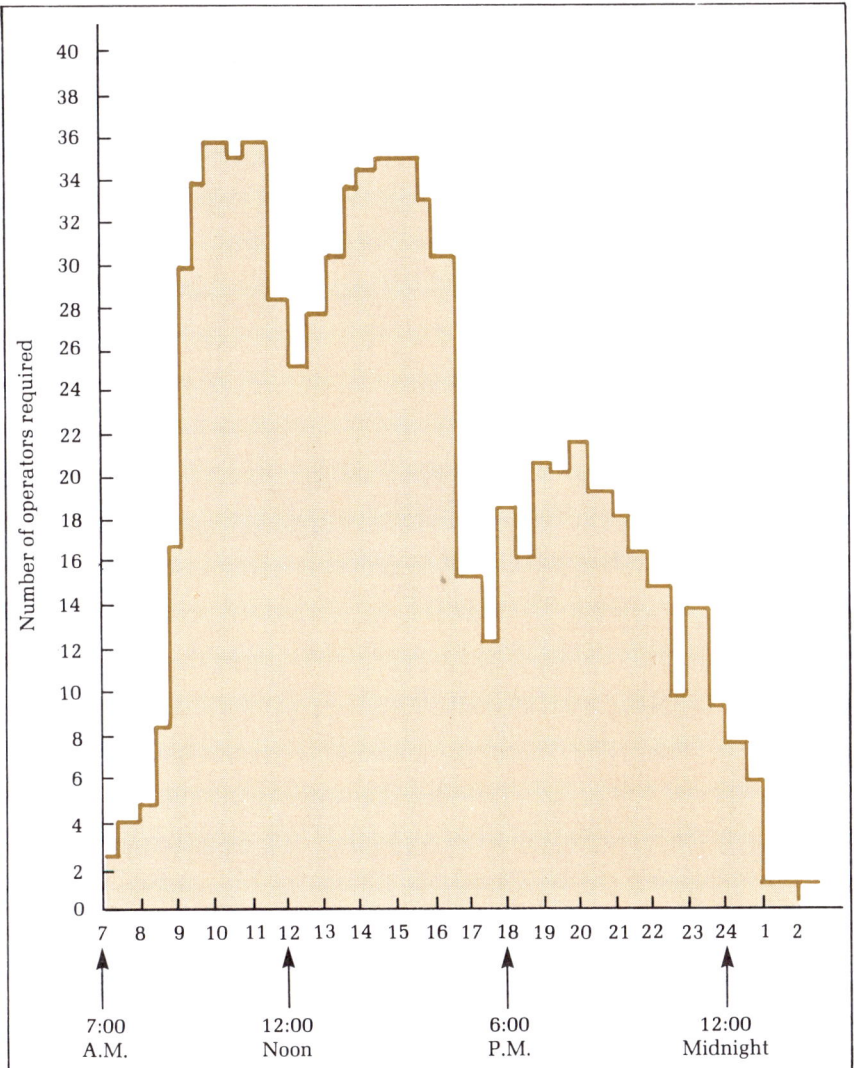

FIGURE 18–4

A typical operator requirements curve for a large telephone exchange

ing, and long-distance toll call assistance. After 5:00 p.m., the number of operators required drops off dramatically and is even lower from midnight to 8:00 a.m. Also, the Saturday and Sunday load is only about 60 percent of that experienced during the week. The attractive phone rates are an incentive for the public to smooth the workload.

Given a workload pattern like the one in Figure 18–4, a company must somehow schedule operators in shifts. The more different kinds of shifts there are, the easier the scheduling will be. For example, if shifts have different lengths—six, seven, or eight hours—it will be easier. Also, split shifts ease the scheduling task. A split shift is one in which the lunch break is longer than the usual hour or half-hour. Finally, if part-time operators can be used, some of the most pronounced peaks can be staffed more easily.

DID YOU EVER WONDER?

Which are the busiest days for different businesses?
Think about how you would schedule people to meet the needs for the regular days as well as the busy days.
The telephone company. The largest number of operator-assisted calls are on Mondays and Tuesdays at about 10:00 a.m. But the busiest day of the year is Christmas.
A department store. Saturdays, but the busiest day of the year is the day after Christmas for the sales.
A car wash. Fridays and Saturdays.
A gourmet restaurant. Friday and Saturday evenings.
A bank. Fridays, especially in the afternoon.

CONTROLLING INVENTORIES

A manufacturing business has inventories at several points in the production schedule. First, there are the purchased materials and components. Then throughout the productive system there are partially completed products. These are called **in-process inventories.** Finally, there are **finished goods inventories.** These finished goods may be at the end of the productive process at the factory, or some may be located out in distribution warehouses.

In a service business, inventories are probably less of a problem. Supplies are still needed, however, and they can be critical to the company's business. The lack of supplies could mean lost sales. On the other hand, a company does not want to be overloaded with supplies because there is a cost of carrying them.

All these inventories need to be controlled or they will get out of hand. Remember, it costs money to maintain inventories. On the other hand, if inventories are not there when they are needed, that can cost, too. There must be a balance between these extremes, and that is what inventory control is all about.

What inventories do for you

Inventories seem to have gotten a bad name. It does cost money to carry them, but they perform very important functions, so just trying to keep them as small as possible may not make sense.

First, think about inventories as they flow through the system. Raw materials are stored on the way to operations. Later they flow through the productive process as in-process inventories to be converted to finished goods. Then the finished goods flow on out to the distribution points and to the ultimate consumer. All these inventories are called **pipeline inventories.** They are required for production. Their aggregate size is proportional to production rates. The more a company produces, the larger is the pipeline inventory required. A business cannot increase production without increasing pipeline inventories.

Pipeline inventories represent the minimum possible inventory level, even for a company that operates on a hand-to-mouth supply basis. But in addition, there are other kinds of inventories that are used to make operations more efficient. Recall the ideas we talked about concerning how many items to order at one time, both in purchasing and in deciding on production lot sizes. A company should order in batches because it is cheaper. As long as it is going to order (or set up a machine), it should obtain a reasonable quantity. These kinds of extra inventories are called **cycle inventories** because they are ordered periodically.

Then, a company should keep extra inventories to prepare for the *variations* in usage. A business cannot always predict just when it will have a surge in demand. These inventories are called **safety stocks.** They allow a firm to give off-the-shelf service to customers and to make sure that there are no stock shortages in the production process.

Finally, there are **seasonal inventories.** Recall that when we discussed aggregate plans, one strategy was to accumulate inventory during the slack sales periods. These inventories are then sold off during the peak season. Seasonal inventories allow a company to stabilize employment and reduce other costs such as overtime, second shift premiums, and hiring and layoff.

You can see that inventories are useful. In controlling them, a company should make sure that inventories are maintained at the best levels. Best here means neither too much nor too little.

Control systems

There are two common ways to set up inventory controls. Both set control levels, but they replenish stocks in different ways.

The **fixed-quantity reordering system** establishes a safety stock level and an order point level. Whenever inventories fall to the order point level, an order for a predetermined amount is issued. This strategy is illustrated in Figure 18–5. The order is received after the **supply lead time** and inventory levels bounce back up. Then the cycle repeats. The order point is set equal to the amount that the company expects to use during the lead time, plus the safety stock. The safety stock is set based on experience or a study of stockouts. The order quantity

FIGURE 18–5
Fixed-quantity order
control system. The same
amount *Q* is ordered each
time inventory levels fall
to the order point. The
amount *Q* is received
within the lead time, and
inventory level is
increased to maximum for
that cycle.

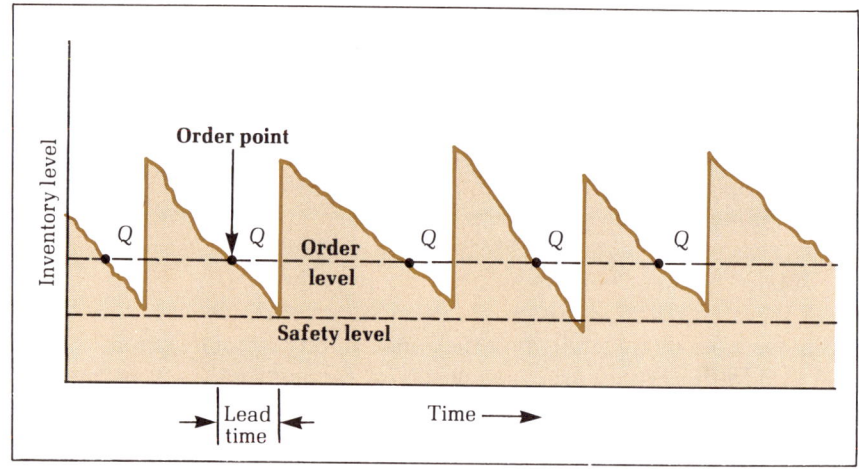

FIGURE 18–5
Fixed-quantity order
control system. The same
amount Q is ordered each
time inventory levels fall
to the order point. The
amount Q is received
within the lead time, and
inventory level is
increased to maximum for
that cycle.

is set by experience, standard quantities, or the EOQ concept. In the fixed-quantity system, if usage happens to be high, the system merely orders more often to compensate. If the usage drops off, orders are placed less often.

The **periodic reordering system** places orders according to a fixed-cycle schedule—perhaps each two weeks. A company simply orders what it has used during the period, allowing for expected use during the supply lead time. The amount ordered brings inventory levels back to the intended maximum. If usage increases, the system compensates by ordering that much more. Figure 18–6 shows how inventory levels fluctuate with a periodic system.

The periodic system is good particularly for higher-valued items. A company reviews what has happened during each period, so there

FIGURE 18–6
Periodic order control
system. Orders are placed
each two weeks, but order
sizes vary to compensate
for variations in usage in
previous period.

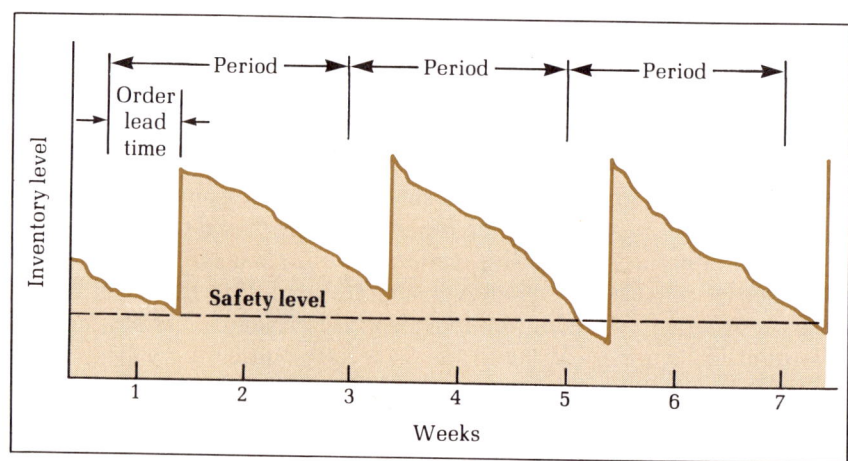

is a record if usage begins to change rapidly. The periodic system is also good when many items are ordered from the same supplier. If the orders can be grouped together, and there may be freight cost advantages. A supplier is also made more aware of the company's value as a customer when an order is for several items.

QUALITY CONTROL AND MAINTENANCE

We have dealt with controlling how much to produce and when to produce it. Another dimension for control is quality. Quality does not just happen; it must be designed into the product in the first place. Then, a company must make sure that the quality is actually what was intended. The highest quality is not always the best. Quality should match the product's expected use.

A product design may have the right quality level, but if the workers are not motivated and trained, and if the plant and equipment are not maintained, the result will not have the intended quality. So quality rests on a three-legged stool: product design, people, and maintenance. Quality control techniques are ways of finding out how a company is doing, and taking corrective action when needed.

Keeping the productive system reliable

If the system is reliable, it will produce the specified quality. The general quality control scheme is shown in Figure 18–7. A company

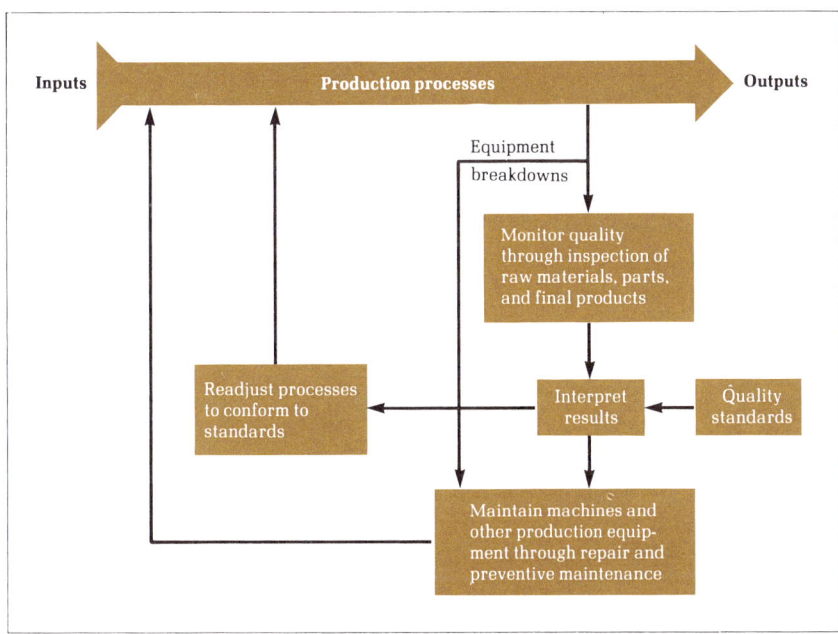

FIGURE 18–7
Relationship of quality measures, product quality standards, and maintenance in keeping a productive system reliable

monitors quality by inspection methods, measuring whatever aspects of quality are required. Then it interprets the results obtained in comparison with the product standards and specifications. If the product does not meet the standards, the company can either readjust processes or decide to improve equipment performance through maintenance. The maintenance also results in adjustments to the process. Alternately, if a machine breaks down it is repaired, which results in processes being put back on track.

Quality control techniques

Quality control techniques are concerned with the monitoring and action shown in Figure 18–7. All of the measurement techniques used by inspectors are involved. When these measures are made, they result in a conclusion about whether or not standards are met. Or they may indicate how far from standard the item is.

Statistical quality control has to do with the interpretation of the measurements. Two basic statistical quality control techniques are in common use: acceptance sampling and statistical control charts.

Acceptance sampling is used when the parts are already produced, and the inspector wants to decide whether or not the entire lot is good. A random sample is taken from the lot and inspected to determine the number of parts that are defective. Then, by referring to tables, the inspector can determine the probability that the entire lot meets standards of acceptability. If the result is acceptable, the entire lot is accepted without further inspection. If not, either the parts are sent back to the supplier or the entire lot is inspected to screen out bad parts.

Control charts are used to monitor the output of a process as it progresses. If the manufacturer can be alerted that the process has gone out of control, then the process can be stopped and corrections made before too many bad parts have been produced.

Statistical control charts are set up with upper and lower control limits for dimensions or whatever is being measured. These control limits are set so that there is a small probability of getting a measurement beyond the control limits if the process is in control. When a measurement occurs that is outside the control limits, the inspector knows that something is wrong. The manufacturer can investigate and make adjustments, sharpen tools, or do whatever is necessary to put the process back on track.

A company can put more and more effort into quality control. But there is some balance between the cost of letting some defective parts pass and the cost of inspecting to find them. The trouble with letting defectives pass is that someone finds them, and it is probably the customer. In today's world of consumer consciousness, the company could get involved in product liability suits and product recalls.

"This just in: The inhabitants of the planet Earth have been recalled
for the correction of a major defect."

Reprinted by permission *The Wall Street Journal.*

On the surface, it may appear that quality control concepts are applicable only to hard products. Actually, the same concepts can be applied to service-oriented systems for which measures of quality are often not so objective. Personal contact may emphasize the way service is given, for example, even though the service was technically adequate. Waiting time is often a criterion for service quality. In medical service, measures of incorrect diagnosis may be used. In banks, waiting time at windows and clerical errors might be quality measures.

The maintenance function

Quality control procedures are designed to track characteristics of quality and to take action to maintain quality within limits. In some instances the action called for may be equipment maintenance. The maintenance function then acts in a supporting role to keep equipment operating effectively to maintain quality standards.

Alternate policies for maintenance may be appropriate, depending on the situation and the relative costs. First, is routine **preventive maintenance** economical, or will it be less costly to wait for breakdowns to occur and then repair the equipment? Preventive maintenance involves maintenance procedures and designs to prevent breakdowns, such as the replacement of parts before they actually wear out. When should a company use preventive maintenance? How large should maintenance crews be in order to balance downtime versus maintenance crew costs? When should a company overhaul or even replace a machine?

If a machine breaks down in a fairly predictable pattern, preventive maintenance may be a good solution. By having a preventive maintenance cycle that anticipates breakdowns, a company can prevent disruptions and downtime costs. Crews may be able to perform preventive maintenance on weekends or during night shifts and thus not interfere with production.

The size of maintenance crews is often an issue. Larger crews are costly, but they repair equipment more quickly and minimize downtime costs. On the other hand, large maintenance crews are likely to be idle for a substantial part of the time. Small maintenance crews cost less and are kept busier. Of course, the small crew gives poorer maintenance service, resulting in larger downtime costs. So, a company must try to achieve a balance between maintenance crew costs and downtime costs.

Sometimes more drastic maintenance actions are economical. A company may find it more economical to renew machines through **overhauls** or **replacement.** As equipment ages, its operating costs increase due to higher maintenance. Figure 18–8 shows that operating costs are temporarily improved by preventive maintenance, repair, and overhaul. There is a gradual cost increase until replacement with a new machine is finally justified. The decisions concerning the choice between repair and overhaul normally occur at the time of a breakdown. Many organizations have regular schedules for overhaul. For example, trucking companies may schedule major engine overhauls after a given number of miles of operation. These major preventive maintenance actions are meant to avoid breakdowns and downtime at inconvenient times.

FIGURE 18–8
Operating costs increase with time. Temporary improvements result from preventive maintenance, repair, overhaul, and replacement.

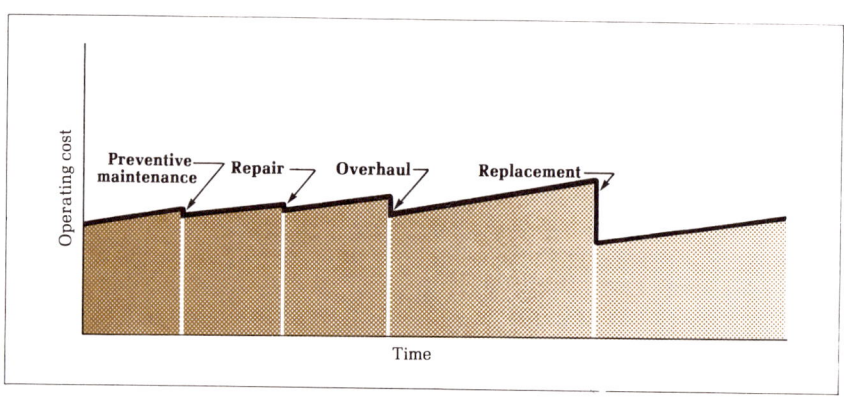

PHYSICAL DISTRIBUTION SYSTEMS

Physical distribution of finished goods has been estimated to cost about $200 billion per year in the United States alone. The cost to get the product to the place where it is finally sold can exceed the cost of production. Does this mean that something is drastically wrong, or is the system simply inefficient? Neither is necessarily true. The characteristics of products (size, weight, density, obsolescence, perishability, and other factors) have a great bearing on the required mode of transportation, speed, and storage.

In establishing a physical distribution network, a company must think about time, cost, and service level. The term **service level** means the percentage of demand that can be covered directly from inventory. How these three factors are balanced depends on the kind of business involved. In a business like clothing, the consumer usually can substitute easily. So the product must be available or sales will be lost. Freight costs for clothing are small, and a store is likely to make the tradeoffs necessary to offer off-the-shelf service. On the other hand, people who want Cadillacs want nothing but Cadillacs. They will probably wait for delivery to get exactly the options wanted. Transportation costs will probably dominate the thinking about the distribution system design. Delivery and speed might dominate in the decision if the product involved is perishable. Live lobsters from Maine are sent to California by air.

DESIGN OF PHYSICAL DISTRIBUTION SYSTEMS

The central factors in designing a distribution network are the number and location of the field distribution points. A related issue is the size of geographic areas and which warehouse is to service which communities near the margins between areas. If a business has more than one plant, there must be a more complex network. In addition to the previous issues, there is the question of which plant supplies which field warehouse? Finally, a consideration of the modes of transportation used is important regardless of the distribution network.

Distribution from a single plant

If a business has just one plant from which to distribute, its decisions are not simple, but perhaps they are as simple as they can be. Keeping in mind transportation cost, speed, and dependability, the company must decide which modes of transportation to use. It must decide on the number of field distribution points and carve out territories. It must also decide which products to ship to which warehouse. It may even have some warehouses supply others for certain products.

Number and location of warehouses.   The objective is to balance costs and service. A large number of warehouses should improve service, but they will cost more to establish and operate. A small number reduces costs but results in poorer service to customers. Each company must compare alternatives and make judgments.

If its market is concentrated, a business will want to locate warehouses near the concentration points. If the market is more dispersed, it will want to think more in terms of theoretical centers of markets.

FIGURE 18–9

Territories separated by lines of equal transportation cost

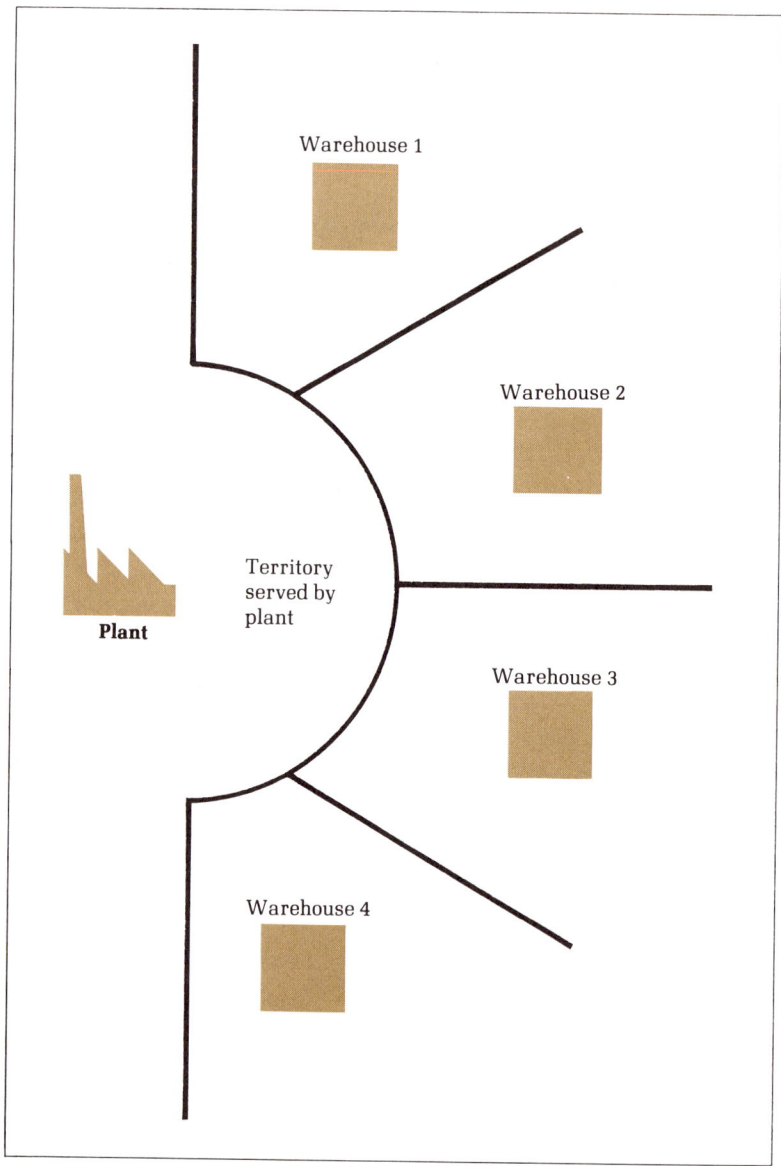

Location of warehouses, however, will still be based at hubs and will be between the plant and the market center.

Territories. In structuring territories to be served by warehouses, a company must first consider the cost to service the entire system. A town near the border between two territories may be assigned to one territory for a variety of reasons, including simple convenience. Figure 18–9 shows five territories, including the one served directly by the plant. The lines that separate territories were plotted to show approximately equal transportation costs from the distribution point. But in finally deciding on territories, a company would not necessarily follow the smooth territorial lines. Perhaps state lines nearly coincide with some equal transportation lines. The way that rail lines and truck routes actually run might be another deciding factor.

Regional distribution points. Suppose that some products do not have a large market in all territories, or that a territory is a long distance from the plant. For such situations, a business may use some distribution points as regional warehouses that serve their own territories plus serving other field warehouses for some items. This allows the company to consolidate low-volume stock items at fewer stock points, rather than trying to carry everything everywhere.

Distribution from multiple plants

Businesses often find it worthwhile to decentralize production operations. With regional plants a business may not want to produce all products in each plant. It can specialize a little. Because of regional locations, multiple plants can reduce distribution costs and may also give better service. But now there is a more complex distribution problem. Planners need to consider plant locations and warehouse locations together. Which plants should ship to which warehouses? Since each plant may not make the complete line, where should stocks be held for the special products? The best combinations are seldom obvious.

Suppose you have two plants that are specialized. Plant A makes product A and plant B makes product B. Each plant could ship directly to the field warehouses, as in Figure 18–10 *(top)*. Another pattern is to have plants A and B ship a portion of their output to each other, as in Figure 18–10 *(bottom)*. Then each plant could ship both products to warehouses near it. For example, plant A could ship both products to warehouses 1 and 2, and plant B to warehouses 5, 6, and 7. Warehouses 3 and 4 are close to having equal transportation costs from both plants. So those two warehouses could be supplied directly by each plant.

There is still a third common pattern involving regional warehouses. Figure 18–11 shows that plants A and B cross-ship to each other. Plant A then ships both products to regional warehouse I, which ships in

FIGURE 18–10
(Top) Each plant ships its individual product to each warehouse directly, and *(bottom)* plants A and B cross-ship to each other and serve only certain warehouses.

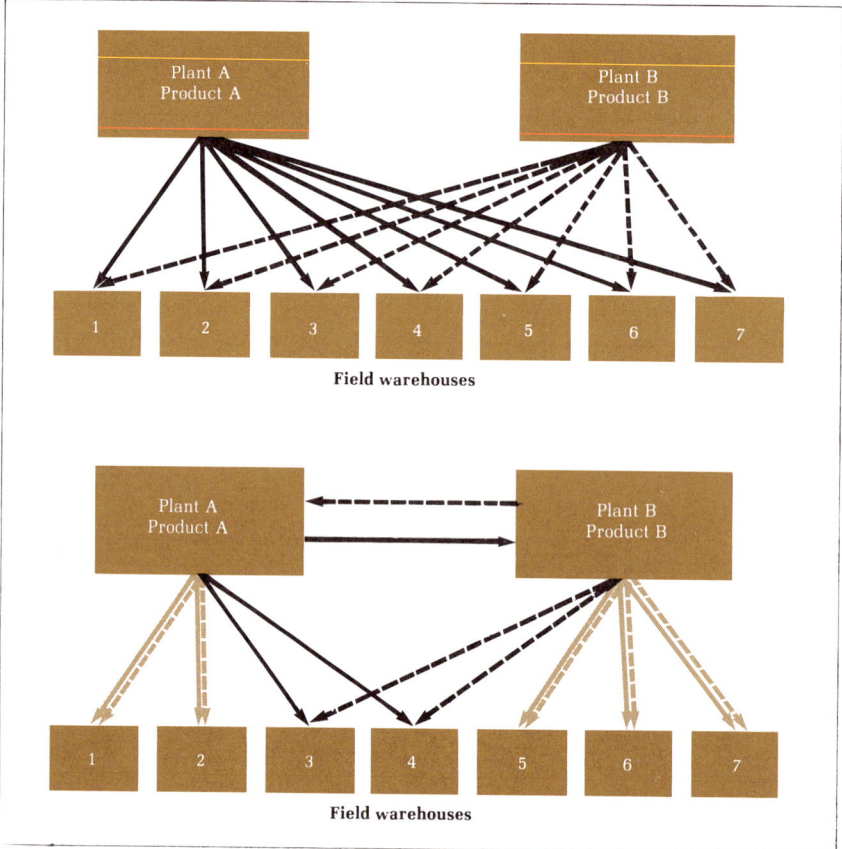

FIGURE 18–11
Plants A and B cross-ship to each other. Each then ships both products to regional warehouses I or III. Each plant ships its product directly to regional warehouse II. Regional warehouses serve field warehouses with both products.

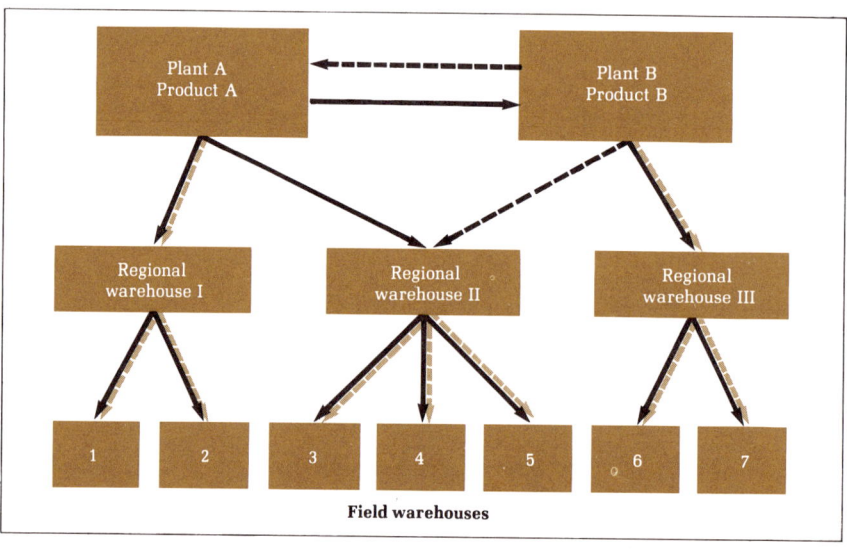

turn to field warehouses 1 and 2. Plant B has a similar pattern with respect to regional warehouse II, which then supplies field warehouses 3, 4, and 5.

Evaluating distribution alternatives

Which distribution alternative is best for a particular business? There are several factors that must be taken into account. Some require a lot of computation to see how costs change with different structures and transportation modes. Other factors, such as service level, damage, and degree of control, require judgment and consideration of tradeoffs with cost.

There have been startling results from studying distribution systems. For example, Hunt-Wesson Foods produced several hundred items at 14 locations and distributed them through 12 regional distribution centers. It grouped the products into 17 classes and the markets into 121 customer zones. It then computed the costs, which considered 45 possible field warehouse locations. It finally found a plan that reduced distribution costs by several million dollars per year and gave improved service to customers.

The Ralston Purina Company reexamined its field warehouse locations and reported results for one region that was supplied by several plants for different products. As a part of the study, various inventory service levels were also examined. The company found it could save $132,000 per year by consolidating five field warehouses into three. It also found that it should carry field warehouse inventories to serve customers off the shelf 85 percent of the time.

You can see that distribution systems are costly, but a well-designed system can cost much less than one that is merely good. The original distribution systems of both Hunt-Wesson and Ralston Purina were undoubtedly good, but the complex nature of the distribution system makes it worthwhile to study and reevaluate them carefully.

Ordering structure and system inventory

How does the field warehouse or a regional warehouse know when to replenish its stocks? Should a company hold most of its inventory at the regional or plant warehouse level, or should it keep it out in the field warehouses close to the ultimate user? These are additional issues in the design and operation of a distribution system.

The field and regional warehouses use inventory control systems similar to those discussed earlier in this chapter. Since there is a steady flow of products, each level in the system can combine orders for different products to reduce freight costs. Therefore, a periodic reordering system that places orders for all products weekly or biweekly fits in very well. But notice the time lags in the illustration of this process in Figure 18–12.

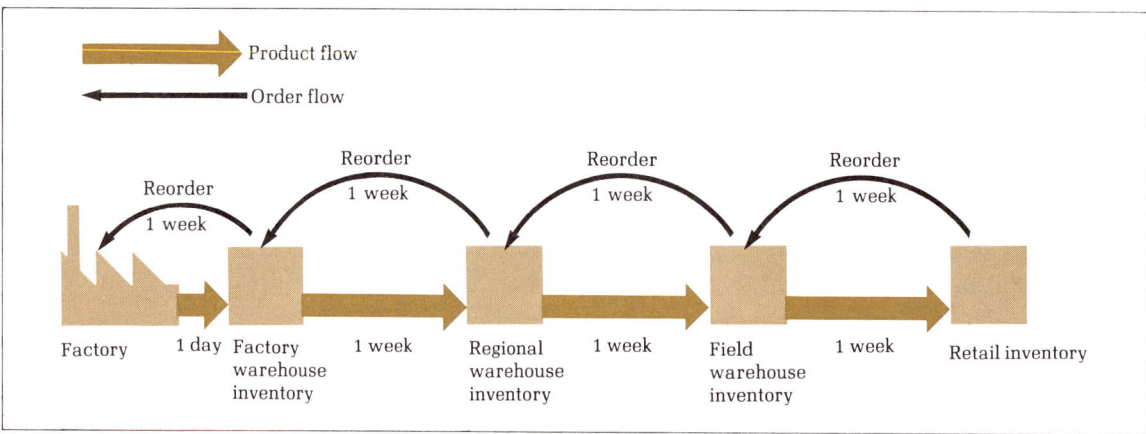

FIGURE 18–12
Structure of products and inventory reorder flow in a multilevel distribution system

In the flow of products and inventory reorders in a multilevel distribution system, there are inventories at each level, including the retailer. It takes time to determine reorder needs and to convey that information with an order to the next level. Then it takes more time to actually transport the materials. You can see that the assumed time lags cause a problem, especially if demand is changing.

If demand is increasing or decreasing at the retail level, the factory will not hear about it until four weeks have passed. This is a good reason for having a separate information system that directly feeds back the information about retail sales. When a consumer buys a large or small appliance, there is usually a card to return to the manufacturer as a warranty registration. An important use of that information is to short-circuit the type of information chain shown in Figure 18–12.

There are four stock points in the distribution system of Figure 18–12. Planners must decide how much safety stock to keep at each level. If it is all pushed out to the retail level, the stock would be close to the point of sale. But the independent retailer probably does not want to carry all that inventory. Besides, some flexibility is lost if the inventory is all at the retail level. Suppose that there is a big sales surge in Chicago, but inventory is spread all over the map. By keeping some of the safety stock upstream, there is enough flexibility to meet changing demand patterns downstream.

SUMMARY

Forecasts are crucially important in order to operate a productive system effectively. They become the basis for plans and schedules. Given plans and schedules, there is a basis for controlling output levels, schedule performance, inventories, and quality.

Every business needs some overall unit of output to make aggregate plans for employment, production levels, inventories, and the use of overtime or second shifts. Then it can break down these *aggregate plans* into *master schedules* that show how much of each product to produce and when. The master schedule is consistent with aggregate plans but takes account of *production cycling* and the lot sizes of individual products.

Critical machines need to be carefully scheduled. This is especially important when production is approaching the capacity of a machine or when the same machine must be set up to run a given number of weeks of supply of each product in order to ensure a cycle without stockouts.

Scheduling personnel and work shifts can be difficult with 7-day-per-week operations. Each worker normally wants two consecutive days off, even though weekend time off may not be available. Businesses operating 24 hours a day and 7 days per week pose even more difficult problems, especially if daily and weekly loads vary. Then work shifts must be scheduled to meet the load as well as satisfy all work rules. Seniority is a common basis for passing out the best schedule to certain workers.

The specified quality of output is important and may be *the* factor to control in some businesses. In order to control quality, a company must have information concerning the actual quality of incoming materials, the quality produced by processes, and the quality of the final product. *Statistical quality control* techniques, such as *acceptance sampling* and *control charts,* are effective aids. Equipment maintenance is an important support to the quality control system. Preventive maintenance may be economical in some situations and may not disrupt operations.

Physical distribution completes the productive system process by making products available where and when they are needed. In the design of a physical distribution system, important issues are the number and location of warehouses and geographic territories. When there are several specialized plants, the distribution network is more complex. Common solutions involve cross-shipping between plants and using regional warehouses.

Ordering in multilevel distribution systems tends to follow a chain of ordering decisions. Information feedback on actual retail sales can improve the data needed to program factory output.

REVIEW QUESTIONS

1. Define the term *aggregate planning*. What aggregate unit of output would you suggest for the following kinds of businesses: banking, a hospital, dog food manufacturer, a machine shop?

2. Why is planning on a monthly basis likely to lead to problems? Does planning on the basis of the production day available meet the problem? How?

3. What is the advantage in using a 13-period annual calendar that results in each period being four weeks?

4. What is a master schedule and how does it compare with the aggregate plan?

5. What are the considerations in setting production lot sizes?

6. If you set production lot sizes independent of each other, you may find that you run out of stock on one or more items before the production cycle is complete. How can you set production lot sizes to avoid stockouts of items before the end of the production cycle?

7. What personnel scheduling problems result when a business operates seven days per week? Twenty-four hours per day?

8. Define the term *pipeline inventory*. If production doubles, what happens to the level of pipeline inventories?

9. Define the term *cycle inventory*. How is the level of cycle inventories related to the average size of orders?

10. Define the term *safety stock*. What is the function of safety stock?

11. What is a fixed-quantity reordering system? How do you compensate for an increase in usage with this system?

12. What is a periodic system of inventory control?

When would you use it, and what are its advantages?

13. What is the general structure of the reliability system? How do the quality control and maintenance systems work together toward a common objective?

14. What is acceptance sampling? If the result of acceptance sampling is to reject the lot, then what happens?

15. What is a statistical control chart? If a measurement goes outside the control limits, what kinds of action might you take?

16. Define the term *preventive maintenance*. Under what conditions might you use preventive maintenance?

17. If markets are concentrated, what are logical warehouse locations?

18. Where should warehouses be located in relation to the plant and the market center?

19. What should be the basis for determining distribution territories?

20. Under what conditions are regional warehouses appropriate?

21. When would cross-shipping between plants be appropriate in a distribution system?

22. What are the bases for evaluating alternate distribution systems?

23. What are the effects of a chain system of inventory replenishment in a multilevel distribution system?

24. Where should safety stocks be located in a multilevel distribution system? Why?

CASES

Case 18–1.   Mix and bag

The Mixing and Bagging Company had a simple production process; it mixed various kinds of animal feed and bagged them in 100-pound sacks for sale. There was a large hopper into which workers loaded the ingredients according to predetermined formulas. Then the materials were dumped into a mixer below and mixed for ten minutes. When a batch was mixed, the material was fed by conveyor to a bagging machine where 100-pound bags were filled, sewn closed, and moved to the warehouse for shipment to customers. When a run for one formula was completed, the hopper and mixer were cleaned and set up to run another formula. The same equipment was used for all formulas.

The supervisor had divided the products into three classes: three high-demand, four medium-demand, and three low-demand products. In order to keep inventories at reasonable levels, he scheduled production runs of 4,000, 2,000, and 1,000 bags for the high-, medium-, and low-demand products, respectively. For example, he would set up and run a high-demand product for 4,000 bags before resetting up to run another product.

The foreman said that he had the place "humming" but complained that the plant manager was always telling him to produce a given order first because the item had run out of stock. "Every order

can't be first," he said. The foreman felt that the runs were too short. He felt that he was always changing over to produce a different product. He wanted to make the run sizes 10,000, 5,000, and 1,000. He felt that he could sandwich in the low-demand items easily if they were about to have a stockout.

1. *Why are stock shortages occurring?*
2. *Would it help to make the run sizes larger?*
3. *What kind of schedule should be designed in order to cycle the several products through the same equipment?*

Case 18–2. Should I produce for stock or only for special orders?

The Dynaflap Company has traditionally made its large float valves to customer order only. The average price of the valves is $50, and the president, Burly McFadden, feels that the inventory costs would be too high if he tried to make them available from stock. "When I produce to firm customer orders, I don't take risks."

But the demand for such valves has been growing. Dynaflap has a good reputation in the field and has been enjoying some sales increase, but a larger share of the increase has been going to "a young gunslinger" in the field who makes valves available from inventory. The newcomer can give fast service. Many customers seem to like the idea and actually pay

about a 10 percent premium for the good service. These developments have set Burly to rethinking his long-standing policy of producing only to special order.

1. *What are the risks for Dynaflap in maintaining its present policy?*
2. *What are the risks for Dynaflap if it decides to make its valves available as off-the-shelf products?*
3. *Will there be a loss of flexibility if Dynaflap changes to a "to stock" producing policy?*
4. *What information does Burly need to make the best decision?*

part VII

WITHIN:

The environment of business

Each firm exists within the environment. Some of the many forces and influences in the environment offer opportunities, while others impose constraints. One force that cannot be ignored is the force of government. Why is government so involved in the affairs of the business community? Governments at the local, state, and national levels have the power to tax and restrict business activities in almost every area. They also have the resources to assist the business community by supporting research, providing information, and maintaining order through the court system. Chapter 19 explains the evolution of government involvement in the private enterprise system and gives you some idea of the way government affects the business environment.

Firms also exist within the social system. Our social system is made up of ongoing developments in technology, communications, social structures such as education, and many other complex fields. A change in one area, such as the mechanization of agriculture, brings about other changes, such as the urbanization of the population. The story goes on and on. Throughout this text we have focused on understanding business today. Chapter 20 deals with the forces that have shaped the business community as it is today and the forces that will possibly affect business in the future.

GOVERNMENT: RESTRICTIONS, TAXES, AND SUPPORT

By studying this chapter you should be able to find answers to these questions:

1 Why has the role of government been steadily increasing?
2 What are the different roles that government plays?
3 What major legislative acts have paved the way for government's current role in regulating the economy?
4 What is the intended purpose of business-related government activity? Why is the government involved at all?
5 What agencies are responsible for protecting you today?

Terms you should know:

Clayton Act, 1914
exclusive dealing
Federal Trade Commission Act, 1914
Food and Drug Administration
Pure Food and Drug Act, 1906
Robinson-Patman Act, 1936
Securities and Exchange Commission
Sherman Act, 1890
trusts
tying contracts
Uniform Commercial Code

About 4,000 years ago, Hammurabi, King of Babylonia, set up his famous code. Along with the law of an eye for an eye and a tooth for a tooth, he set forth what was probably the first government ruling on product liability. He declared that if a house fell down and killed the occupant, the builder should be put to death. Government has been involved in the affairs of the business community ever since.

We have taken only a few brief glimpses at the third partner in our economic system—the government in all its many forms and levels. We all know that this partnership is not without its conflicts and disruptions, but it has a positive side, too. The government offers advice and guidance to both buyers and sellers. It also makes an effort to support business activities that it believes will contribute to a strong productive economic system. The government steps in to regulate business and it shares in the rewards through the power to tax.

If you listen to the news and read the paper, you have lots of chances to see how stormy this partnership can be. It may seem that the government and the business community are constantly at each others' throats. But then at other times it seems that government and big business are conspiring against you. When one regulation contradicts another, you get the idea that government's right hand doesn't know what its left hand is doing.

FIGURE 19–1
Layers of Government

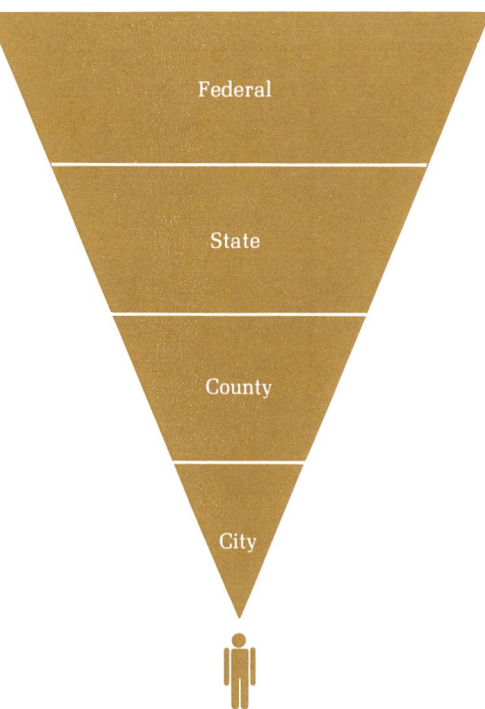

Every four years when we elect a new president, we hear that things are going to be different—not just different, but better. High on the list of promises are more jobs, less taxes, less red tape, a cleaner environment, and safer products and services. It sounds good, doesn't it?

This scene is repeated in state capitals and in cities and towns across the nation. But no new elected official starts out with a clean slate. There is a long history of government involvement in the affairs of the private business community. Some of this has been worthwhile, and some has led to complex, wasteful overregulation. To begin with, there are many layers of government. At this moment you may be within the control of a city government, a county government, a state government, and the federal government (see Figure 19–1). These can have conflicting powers and concerns.

In this chapter we will look at three questions about the government's role. First, if ours is a private enterprise economy, why is the government involved at all? Second, what are the major landmarks in the early phase of government's intervention in the economy? Finally, how well is government achieving its purposes today?

WHY IS THE GOVERNMENT INVOLVED?

The Constitution gives the government the responsibility to provide for the common defense and to promote the public welfare. A healthy economy is the best guarantee of being able to provide for the long-run well-being of the population. In order to provide for other defense and social welfare programs, the government is an important customer for the products and services provided by private firms. You may ask why the role of government always seems to be increasing. Why does government seem to be involved in so many different aspects of the business system?

Government's increasing role

Since 1776, private economic activities have been subject to U.S. government regulation. Through the 1880s, most controls were exercised by the individual states. But in the 1890s, the federal government began enacting business legislation. At first this was limited to the control of monopolies. Over the years, however, the objectives have become more complex and the role of the government in the economic system has steadily expanded. We have turned to government to do some of the things that are beyond our capacity as individuals. We hope that government authority can make the economy deliver results that a market economy left to itself would not produce.

The distance has increased.   Had you lived 200 years ago, you would have known producers personally. They would have lived in your village. It didn't take long for the news to spread if the blacksmith was making inferior horseshoes. Informal local pressure was enough to keep most producers and shopkeepers in line.

As the economy has matured into a factory system, the distance between the producers and the consumers has increased. Factories are located where they can serve larger markets. This permits the mass production that allows you to enjoy a higher standard of living, but it also creates a separation between you and the producer. This leads to a breakdown in the producer/consumer relationship. It interferes with the personal evaluation and local pressure system of control. This distance makes it more difficult for you to get all of the information you need to make wise buying decisions.

Simpler products for a simpler lifestyle.   Another reason why we need more government intervention now is that our products and services are more complex. There was only so much to learn about wheat flour and a plowshare. Besides, the average family made or grew many of the things it needed. Today you buy hundreds of complex products and services. You may be an expert on groceries but know nothing about textiles. Your friend may know a little about automobiles and a lot about dentists.

Even if you studied the products and services you need, there are some facts that you cannot uncover for yourself. Could you do the tests to get the vital information you need on foods, drugs, and product safety? Nobody knows everything about all the products and services he or she needs.

Changing values.   Another reason for increased government activity is to protect those who know little about *any* of the products and services they need. As a society, we have increasingly come to believe that our weaker members should be protected. This is not so in many other nations today, nor was it true in most nations in the past. The poor, the unintelligent, the old, and the very young either were left to the care of their relatives or were left with no care at all.

Today we depend on the government to step in and protect those who cannot protect themselves. Standards are set for childrens' toys and sleepwear to protect children even from their parents' ignorance. The government inspects nursing homes and restaurants, factories and amusement parks, in an attempt to protect the population.

And there are more of us.   The population keeps growing and using up scarce resources at an increasingly fast rate. There are few frontiers left to conquer. We now realize that we are going to have to take care to preserve what we have.

This requires a massive overhaul of the economic system. Goods that were free or cheap, such as energy, water, and clean air, are suddenly costly. Is it realistic to expect individual firms to suddenly and voluntarily take on the responsibility for cleaning up all the damage that has ever been done to the environment? Who is responsible and how should that responsibility be carried out? There are no simple answers.

The distance between producers and consumers, the complexity of our lifestyles, a greater awareness of the needs of all the people in the society, and greater demands on our economy have caused us to turn to the government. We expect government to do some of the things we are not able to do alone.

Some conflict must be expected. In effect, we have two entirely different mechanisms struggling for control of the economic system: government and business. Which one will provide the best economic decisions for fairly allocating society's resources? The government responds to the ballot and the lobby. The business community responds to market forces. The increased government intervention shows that the United States is handling more and more economic decisions through the political process.

Government's varied roles

Government plays a number of roles that affect the overall economic climate, the future of entire industries, and even the decisions facing a single firm. The actions of government fall into four broad groups: watchdog, referee, tax collector, and business booster.

A watchdog. Government monitors business actions that are beyond your view or control. This extends to almost all the business functions we have covered in this text. A firm may have to be licensed by either the city or state before it can open for business. Then the government tries to make sure that investors can get accurate financial reports. In marketing, the government monitors product quality and safety, prices, and product information. In finance, there are limits on financial institutions and controls on interest rates. When businesses acquire resources, build facilities, and engage in transportation, the government is concerned with environmental protection. A firm's personnel actions are checked for fair employment practices. There are very few, if any, business activities that escape the watchful eye of at least one government agency.

Usually the government sets up standards and then tries to make sure that these standards are met. For example, to be called a cherry pie, a 7-inch crust must contain at least 23 cherries. To be awarded a government contract, a firm must employ women and minorities. City health inspectors check to see that restaurants meet sanitary food-handling standards. New drugs undergo rigid testing before they can be used on humans. These are all areas where it would be hard for you to watch out for yourself.

A referee. Firms are in competition with each other. Someone has to set up the rules and then watch the action to be sure that those rules are being followed. Sometimes there are good reasons to change the rules.

The government assumes the task of maintaining a fair and competitive economic environment. The laws describe what is and is not fair. The idea is to see that no firm gets to the point of being uncontrollable. If there is no competition, the government will turn to other methods of control. It might set up agencies such as the Public Utilities Comissions which must approve any rate changes proposed by public utilities. Or it might force the firm to break up into smaller competitive units—a threat that is constantly held over the head of IBM and General Motors.

While the federal laws apply in all the states, state laws have differed widely. The resulting problems led to the development of the **Uniform Commercial Code.** The Uniform Commercial Code was first drafted in 1952 and has since been adopted in all states except Louisiana. It applies to business transactions and contracts.

The tax agent. All government activities have costs attached. Someone has to pay the bill. The government has the power to tax, but taxation is more than collecting enough money to run the government. The types and amounts of taxes that are imposed have a great impact on the marketplace.

Taxes may be imposed either on the basis of benefits or on the basis of ability to pay. Gasoline is taxed to provide funds for highway

DID YOU EVER WONDER?

What standards must a food meet in order to earn its name?

Here are some of the standards. Regulations also specify the exact test to be made to assure that the foods meet these standards.

To be called	*It must*
Maple syrup	Contain not less than 66 percent soluble solids derived from maple sap
Soda	Be carbonated with not less carbon dioxide than the amount that will be absorbed by the beverage at a pressure of one atmosphere and a temperature of 60°F
Mixed nuts	Be a mixture of four or more shelled tree nuts with or without shelled peanuts; none of the four may constitute less than 2 percent or more than 80 percent of the weight
Oysters extra large	Be such a size that one gallon contains not more than 160 oysters, and a quart of the smallest oysters selected should contain not more than 44 oysters
Asparagus canned	Be labeled stalks/spears if cut from 3¾" or more upper end, be labeled tips if cut from 2¾" to 3¾" upper end, and points if less than 2¾" upper end
Fruit cocktail canned	Contain between 30 and 50 percent peaches, 25 and 45 percent pears, 6 and 16 percent pineapple, 6 and 20 percent grapes, and 2 and 6 percent cherries
Cracked wheat	Be cracked so that not less than 90 percent passes through a #8 sieve and not more than 20 percent passes through a #20 sieve
Raisin bread	Have at least half as much raisins as flour by weight
Blue cheese	Contain not more than 46 percent moisture and have spores of the mold *Penicillium roquefortii* added
Fruit sherbet	Contain between 1 and 2 percent milk fat; the quantity of fruit ingredients must not be less than 2 percent for citrus sherbets, 6 percent for berry sherbets, and 10 percent for all other fruits
Whole milk	Contain not less than 3.25 percent milk fat
Condensed milk	Contain not less than 8.5 percent milk fat
Nonfat dry milk	Contain not more than 1.5 percent milk fat

building and maintenance. The taxes fall most heavily on those who use the most gasoline and supposedly gain the most benefits from the highways. When taxes are based on property values or income, it is assumed that the burden falls on those who are the most able to pay. But taxes have other effects on the economy. The taxes on cigarettes and alcohol are a major part of the price of those products. The government affects the demand for these products through tax policies.

The tax policies of states and local communities affect decisions on where to build stores and factories. California has an inventory tax whereas Nevada does not. Many firms that serve the California market locate their warehouses just across the state line in Nevada to avoid this tax. There are many types of taxes as shown in Table 19–1.

A business booster.   One valuable by-product of the actions of the government is the accumulation of a wealth of data on the economy. The Department of Commerce, the Department of the Interior, and other agencies compile data. These are then available through the Superintendent of Documents and many libraries nationwide. None of the firms that use these reports could collect that quality and quantity of data for itself. It either could not afford it or could not gain access to the data.

Data collecting is just one of the government services to business. The list of other services is almost endless. Since many have nonbusiness benefits as well, you may overlook their economic impact. The National Air and Space Administration weather reports aren't just to tell you whether it will be a good weekend for a picnic. They are critical to industries from airlines to commercial fishing to drive-in movies.

Other services are invisible to those outside the industry. The Depart-

TABLE 19–1
Government receipts by type of tax

Type	Percent federal	Percent state
Individual income tax	43%	25%
Corporate income tax	15	9
Employment tax (social security)	30	6
Excise tax	4	
Estate and gift tax	2	2
Customs duties	1	
Sales tax		31
Licenses		7
Property tax		2
Gasoline		9
Alcohol and tobacco tax		5
Other	5	4
	100	100

JUANITA KREPS

We must encourage business to perform well all those activities which serve to improve human welfare.

In January 1977, Juanita Kreps became both the first woman and the first economist to hold the post of Secretary of Commerce. This was but one in a series of "firsts." She was the first woman to serve as vice president of Duke University, to hold Duke University's highest professorship, and to be appointed to the board of directors of the New York Stock Exchange and several other corporations. She has been awarded the North Carolina Public Service Award, the Brotherhood Award from the National Conference on Christians and Jews, the Woman of the Year Award from *Ladies Home Journal,* and several honorary degrees.

Many of her efforts have been directed toward the problems of the aged and economically disadvantaged people. She was born in a mining town and educated at Berea College in Appalachia during the Depression. She went on to earn her Master's Degree and Ph.D from Duke. She has written two books, *Sex in the Marketplace: American Women at Work,* and *Lifetime Allocations of Work and Income.* She also has coauthored three books and edited several others.

Secretary Kreps functions as the President's principal contact with the business community and as a strong advocate of U.S. trade at home and abroad. She sees the main goal of the Department of Commerce as facilitating economic and technological development. It should channel information about the needs and concerns of the business community to the federal government and explain the administration's views to business.

The Commerce Department plays a vital role in promoting foreign trade. Economic cooperation among nations facilitates optimal use of the world's limited resources as well as fostering interdependence which is a major force in promoting peaceful international relations. The Commerce Department seeks to bring multinational marketing opportunities to U.S. business, particularly to small companies. Secretary Kreps has sought to help build a private enterprise system that develops greater human potential and strikes a balance between technical and economic concerns on the one hand and social and human concerns on the other.

ment of Agriculture tests soil samples for farmers. The Department of International Business Assistance sponsors trade fairs to help small businesses expand into international markets. The government channels funds into research. Most of the research into new technologies is funded at least in part by federal money. These government research contracts support research facilities that can then be used for private research and development.

Several major industries depend on government business. Without government contracts, the aerospace and maritime industries would be in serious trouble. McDonald Douglas Aircraft is the largest U.S. defense contractor. Three fourths of its $3.5 billion in annual revenues come from government contracts. Farm price supports are an example of government intervention when a vital industry is in trouble. Such action can foster healthy cooperation or create unhealthy dependency. When Lockheed flirted with bankruptcy and was bailed out by the federal government, the critics called it unhealthy.

The government may also be involved when a major firm negotiates a contract with a foreign government. When U.S. grain cooperatives reached agreements to sell U.S. wheat to the USSR, the government was involved.

"Why doesn't Russia buy a million tons of U.S. spinach?"

Reprinted by permission *The Wall Street Journal.*

The government plays many roles and, in theory, each of these roles has merit. There is a need for a force to protect the rights of the citizens, maintain a competitive environment, and provide advice and support to the business community. But there is some question as to how well the government has been able to fulfill these roles.

Before we look at how well the government is doing today, let's look briefly at five major laws that were passed more than 40 years ago but continue to affect our lives today.

LANDMARK LEGISLATION

We can look at some of the actions of the past to prepare ourselves to deal with the future. While the situation will never be exactly the same, the pattern is repeated. It starts when some event causes a flare-up in some lingering problem. This serves as a rallying point for a group of interested people who bring pressure on the government which finally acts. Let's look at the legislation, the problems behind it, the pressure groups, and the impacts.

The Sherman Antitrust Act of 1890

The competitive system depends on the independent action of firms. In the late 1800s, some firms discovered that it was to their advantage to combine their efforts. They could then squeeze special deals out of their suppliers and customers and split up the rewards. These combinations were called **trusts.** To form a trust, firms pool resources which are then managed in the common interest of owners. The agreement among the firms is often kept a secret.

The **Sherman Act** was aimed at controlling trusts. It labeled any "contract, combination in the form of trust or otherwise, or conspiracy in restraint of trade or commerce" as illegal. It also outlawed unregulated monopolies. The Sherman Act was the federal government's first large-scale intervention in private business. It came about because some firms had grown financially powerful and were using that power to monopolize the markets.

How the problem flared up. The Sherman Act was passed as a result of the great activity in mergers and trust formations. Trusts had formed in the railroad, tobacco, and petroleum industries, among others. When trusts gained control of an industry, they tended to raise the prices and reduce the quality of the products and services offered to consumers. When these trusts became too ambitious, the public pressured for trustbusting. Public unrest was so great that the Sherman Act passed in Congress with only one dissenting vote.

The trustbusters. The public was scared. People could see what was happening, but it wasn't clear where it would end. John D. Rockefeller's Standard Oil was a great example. In 1870 it accounted for less than 5 percent of the petroleum industry, but by 1880 it controlled 85 percent of the industry and was growing even more powerful.

Pressure to bust the trusts came from all the groups that were being hurt: the consumers, the small businesses that were being squeezed out of the market, and the firms that supplied the trusts and were being forced to give them preferential treatment and prices.

The impact. The Sherman Act was not very effective since it did not clearly state what was a violation. But it did get things started by declaring the government's intention to maintain competition. After several years with few results, the people were ready for stronger measures. The result was the passage of two very important bills in the same year.

The Clayton Act and the Federal Trade Commission Act of 1914

The Clayton Act and the Federal Trade Commission Act were a package. The **Clayton Act** spelled out the market behaviors that restrained trade and provided more muscle to deal with violators. The **Federal Trade Commission Act** set up the Federal Trade Commission (FTC) to enforce the Clayton Act and to protect honest businesses from unfair competitors.

The Clayton Act outlawed tying contracts, exclusive dealing, and price discrimination. It gave the government muscle to step in when a trust was dealing unfairly with its customers or squeezing price concessions out of its suppliers.

Tying contracts and exclusive dealing are tricks to restrict the options of buyers. With **tying contracts,** the seller supplies the retailer with one product only if the retailer agrees to buy another product as well. The products are tied together. Usually a retailer is forced to stock a less competitive product to get a supply of a hot item. This restricts the retailer's freedom of choice.

In **exclusive dealing,** a seller refuses to deal unless the buyer promises not to deal with any of the competitors. Have you heard the slogan "Quaker State—the asked-for motor oil"? That came about because the major oil companies had forced their dealers into exclusive deals on motor oil. A dealer who carried another brand such as Quaker State had to hide it and sell it only when a customer asked for it.

On price discrimination, the Clayton Act says: "It shall be unlawful for any person engaged in commerce to discriminate in price between different purchases of like grade and quality where the effect of such discrimination may be to substantially lessen competition or tend to create a monopoly."

The problem intensifies.   In 1890, when the Sherman Act was passed, there were about 5,000 independent firms in the United States. In 1904, 300 corporations controlled about two thirds of the nation's economic output. U.S. Steel had swallowed up about 600 independent steel producers. It was this concentration of economic power that led to pressures for government control.

The pressure groups.   In 1892 the issue was big enough to spawn a third political party—the Populists. They campaigned for more government action but lost the election. However, by the election of 1912, all three parties favored increased government action.

The impact.   Evidence of the past and current actions of the Federal Trade Commission (FTC) is all around us. Since 1960, the government has brought major restraint of trade cases against IBM, Xerox, and AT&T. It was the FTC that forced P&G to give up Clorox. The FTC will be discussed more later in this chapter.

The Robinson-Patman Act of 1936

In 1934 an FTC report concluded that the growth of chain stores threatened the existence of small businesses. This was partly because suppliers were forced to grant unjustified price concessions to large buyers. The problem was most acute in the food industry. The **Robinson-Patman Act,** which has been called the "Anti-A&P Act" in honor of the largest chain at that time, was passed to protect small business.

The problem. Wright Patman said that the act was designed to protect the independent merchants, the public they serve, and the manufacturers from whom they buy from exploitation by the chain competitor.[2] The real problem was that the large chains, with the support of the consumers who bought their goods, were driving the small food stores out of business with practices that were considered to be unfair. For example, Morton Salt offered a 15 percent discount to quantity buyers, but only five stores in the United States bought enough to earn that discount and all of them were chains.

In 1934 the United States was in the depths of the Great Depression. Whether or not the growth of chain stores was really "exploiting" the public and creating unemployment, the time was ripe for regulation. Citizens were looking to the government for some kind of relief.

The pressure groups. Retail and wholesale grocers were the first to move. They formed organizations such as the Independent Grocers Association (IGA) to bargain with manufacturers and to lobby in Congress. Then they worked to turn public sentiment against the absentee owners of chain stores. Even today the IGA slogan is "Buy from the Local Guys." In 1935 the U.S. Wholesale Grocers' Association wrote the first draft of the Robinson-Patman Act and gave it to Congressman Wright Patman.

The impact. To see the impact of the Robinson-Patman Act we have to ask what might have happened had it not been passed. We know only that today we have a mixture of major retailers and small retailers. We might have had no small business left at all. The Robinson-Patman Act is the government's basis for monitoring business pricing behavior today.

These four acts were all passed to maintain a fair and competitive business environment. Let's look at a fifth act now—the first action on consumer protection.

The Pure Food and Drug Act of 1906

The **Pure Food and Drug Act** was the government's first effort to provide for the inspection of food and drug products to protect the public. The **Food and Drug Administration** (FDA), which we will look at more closely later in this chapter, was set up to enforce this act.

The problem.   As the nation changed from a small town and farm base to an urban, factory-oriented economy, the need for preserved food products increased. People were just as concerned about food prices as they are now, so the food industry was very cost-conscious. There was less understanding of the long-run health effects of food additives, but this does not excuse conditions that by today's standards can only be described as disgusting. The public finally demanded protection following the publication of Upton Sinclair's novel, *The Jungle,* which described conditions in a meat-packing plant.

The power of the pen.   Sixty years before Ralph Nadar stirred public action with his book *Unsafe at Any Speed,* Upton Sinclair roused such a furor that Congress acted within a year to pass the Pure Food and Drug Act. From the accompanying boxed excerpt, you can see why the public demanded action.

UPTON SINCLAIR'S DESCRIPTION OF SAUSAGE MAKING

There was never the least attention paid to what was cut up for sausage; there would come all the way back from Europe old sausage that had been rejected, and that was moldy and white—it would be dosed with borax and glycerine, and dumped into the hoppers, and made over again for home consumption. There would be meat that had tumbled out on the floor, in the dirt and sawdust, where the workers had tramped and spit uncounted billions of consumption germs. There would be meat stored in great piles in rooms; and the water from leaky roofs would drip over it, and thousand of rats would race about on it. . . . The packers would put poisoned bread out for them; they would die, and then the rats, bread, and meat would go into the hoppers together.

Upton Sinclair, *The Jungle* (New York: Harper and Brothers, 1951), p. 135 (original 1906).

The impact.   The Pure Food and Drug Act was a landmark in consumer protection. But, while the Sherman Act was not clear enough, the Pure Food and Drug Act was too specific. It listed several substances that were covered by the act, but newly developed chemicals were not covered. Also, it did not prohibit the use of these chemicals. It required only that they be listed on the label so you could see what you were getting. Finally, admendments in the Food, Drug, and Cosmetics Act of 1938 corrected these shortcomings.

HOW WELL IS GOVERNMENT DOING?

It is easy to scream that the government programs have been a failure, but that may be too harsh a judgment. While it is tempting, it is far from responsible or constructive. We must judge the government's performance in relationship to the problem. Just look at the task.

First, we expect the government to define a complete set of continuing solutions that will be fair to each of the 220 million citizens and especially to each one of us. There are no easy answers to that problem. Second, these solutions must be within the scope of economic reality. This means that we do not want any tax increases. Beyond that, they must not lead us into either inflation or recession. Finally, the solutions should not expose us to threats from other nations. The government can't simply divert all defense funds into social welfare programs. This task begins to look like the impossible dream.

There is no great truth or solution that is being hidden from us. Sometimes no one knows the truth. How would you act if you had the final say on drug tests? Suppose one of the drug firms came up with a cure for cancer. Would you order the full testing program? It would take several years. Would you deny this cure to thousands of cancer victims who couldn't wait for years? In the past, rushing wonder drugs to the market has resulted in epidemics of birth defects and other widespread problems. What would you do?

These are difficult questions. When government serves any of its roles—watchdog, referee, tax collector, or business booster—some people are happier than others. Abraham Lincoln's statement still holds true: "You can please some of the people all of the time, and you can please all of the people some of the time, but you can never please all of the people all of the time."

The intentions of the government are set forth in one of three ways: (1) stated in an executive order from the president, (2) spelled out in legislation from the Congress, or (3) implied in a court decision from the judiciary branch. Regardless of their origin, these intentions must be carried out by some agency, commission, or administration. We have had a glimpse of two of these—the FTC and the FDA. To get a better idea of how government is doing today, it is useful to investigate the major agencies that enforce government policies. The seven major agencies that have the greatest impact on the business community are the FTC, FDA, EPA, OSHA, EEOC, SBA, and the SEC. Is it any wonder that businesspeople sometimes feel overregulated? It's hard enough to keep the regulators straight!

In Chapter 3 you read about some of the activities of the Environmental Protection Agency (EPA) and the Occupational Safety and Health Administration (OSHA). In Chapter 13 you had a glimpse of the Equal

Richard D. Wright, *The Providence Journal Bulletin*

Employment Opportunity Commission (EEOC). In Chapter 4 there was a feature on the Small Business Administration (SBA). Now let's look at the remaining agencies.

The Federal Trade Commission

The basic objective of the Federal Trade Commission is to maintain a competitive American economy. It has a variety of duties, but all focus on protecting the private enterprise system from being damaged by monopoly or restraints on trade, or corrupted by unfair or deceptive trade practices.

When the FTC was set up in 1914, it was given two unusual and

TABLE 19–2
Recent consumer
protection legislation

Year	Act
1966	Fair Packaging and Labeling Act
1966	Child Protection Act
1966	Cigarette Labeling Act
1967	Wholesome Meat Act
1968	Wholesome Poultry Products Act
1968	Truth in Lending Act
1969	Child Protection and Toy Safety Act
1970	Fair Credit Reporting Act
1970	Poison Prevention Packaging Act
1972	Consumer Product Safety Act

important powers. The first was the power to set up its own guidelines as to which actions were unfair methods of competition. The second was the power to act *before* actions occur rather than prosecuting later. In 1930, the FTC powers were expanded to allow it to act wherever deception of the public was involved. Some of the functions of the FTC that affect you are to:

1. Promote free and fair competition.
2. Safeguard the public from false advertising.
3. Prevent price discrimination.
4. Guard against unregulated monopolies.
5. Regulate packaging and labeling of certain consumer products.
6. Achieve truth in lending.

Uncovering fraudulant mail-order schemes, deceptions such as payola in the record industry, false advertising, and medical quackery is included in the FTC's responsibility for consumer protection. Investigations conducted by the FTC have led to a number of significant pieces of legislation (see Table 19–2).

The FTC has the power to order a firm to cease and desist an unfair practice, to divest itself of a subsidiary or cancel merger plans, or even to undertake corrective advertising.

The Food and Drug Administration

The FDA is a part of the Department of Health, Education, and Welfare. The FDA has two objectives. The first is to prevent the distribution of foods, drugs, and cosmetics that are unsafe for humans. The second is to assure that sellers tell the truth about these products.

Some of the ways in which the FDA protects you are to:

1. Inspect manufacturing facilities for sanitation standards.
2. Monitor testing of new drugs.

3. Develop product standards.
4. Develop radiation exposure standards.
5. Test products for toxic substances.

It is in performing this last function—testing for toxins—that the FDA has ordered the elimination of such products as cyclamates as artificial sweeteners, sodium nitrites in hot dogs, and other substances suspected of causing cancer.

DID YOU EVER WONDER?

What do the MDR and RDA charts mean?
On many of the food products you buy, you can find a chart showing the proportion of your minimum daily requirements (MDR) of vitamins supplied by a single serving. Where did those figures come from? The Food and Drug Administration has the responsibility for approving the labels for foods and food supplements. It is the FDA that requires that nutrient contents be expressed in terms of MDR per serving, per 100 grams, or per recommended dosage. One MDR is the amount of a vitamin or mineral that FDA studies have shown is needed to prevent symptoms of deficiency and to provide a small margin of safety.

MDRs differ from recommended dietary allowances (RDA). The RDAs were established by the Food and Nutrition Board of the National Research Council, which is not a government agency. The RDAs are based on daily nutrient allowances adequate for the maintenance of good nutrition. MDRs are the least with which normal people can manage, whereas RDAs are established as nutritional goals.

The Securities and Exchange Commission

The **Securities and Exchange Commission** (SEC) protects you in a far different way. It protects you from security fraud and swindling. It is the duty of the SEC to assure that investors get full and honest information on security offerings. The SEC also regulates the practices in the securities market.

The SEC was established in 1934 at the depth of the Great Depression. The beginning of that depression had been marked by a stock market crash. Much of the blame for that crash fell on a lack of regulation of the market which allowed swindlers to operate freely. After the crash, individual savers were afraid to invest in securities, so industry lacked the capital to recover and reemploy the population. Establishing the SEC was an effort to restore investor confidence in the securities market.

Today all new issues of securities that will be offered to the public must be registered with the SEC. False registration statements can result in a prison term. The "insiders" in a corporation, such as the officers and top managers, are required to report to the SEC whenever they personally buy or sell shares in the firm. These reports are made public to protect you from a situation where the insiders know that there will be a big profit in a few months and buy out your shares while the price is still low. Another situation is one where the insiders are selling because they have information that will cause the price to fall.

But are we cooperating?

The SEC also registers stockbrokers, mutual funds, and other people and institutions that participate in the securities markets. It has broad rule-making authority in almost all areas of the U.S. securities markets.

There are many government agencies that are in some way involved in consumer protection or in protecting the competitive economic system. There has been a great deal of progress since 1890, but the progress has been only in response to pressure. Some consumers have always been concerned about safety, but that is not enough. For example, although there is proof that using seat belts saves lives, when they were offered as an option in the early 1960s, few people ordered them. Even today many people avoid wearing them. In 1964 the Surgeon General released the report that cigarette smoking causes cancer. After only a brief dip, cigarette consumption increased. In 1972 the standards for flammability in children's sleepwear took effect. Many parents rushed out to buy the last supply of flammable sleepwear for their children. After all, it cost less. Before 1970 industry was prepared to offer home smoke alarms which could save countless lives. There was very little market interest. It wasn't until California passed a law requiring smoke alarms in all houses built after 1975 that there was sufficient demand to justify production. The government acts only in response to pressure and can protect us only if we are both willing to be protected and willing to protect ourselves.

SUMMARY

We have turned to the government to do some of the things that are beyond our capacity to do as individuals. It is the government's responsibility to provide for the security, health, and welfare of the citizens. The government offers advice and guidance to both buyers and sellers and supports business activities that contribute to a strong productive economic system.

There is a long history of involvement by each of the many layers of government. In 1890 the federal government enacted the Sherman Act. Since then, government objectives have become more complex and the role of the government in the economic system has steadily expanded. The increased distance between producers and consumers, the growing complexity of our lifestyles, a greater awareness of the needs of all people in the society, and greater strains on our economic system have caused us to depend on the government. The activities of government fall into four broad categories: watchdog, referee, tax collector, and business booster.

The Sherman Act was aimed at controlling trusts, although it was not very effective. The Clayton Act and the Federal Trade Commission Act were a package. The Clayton Act spelled out the market behaviors that were in restraint of trade and gave the FTC more muscle to protect honest businesses from unfair acts of competition. The Robinson-Patman Act, the "Anti-A&P Act," was passed to protect small businesses from price discrimination that left them at a disadvantage in relation to the chain stores. The Pure Food and Drug Act was the government's first effort to provide for the inspection and labeling of food and drug products.

The task of protecting a competitive economy and its consumers is complex. There are many different agencies involved. Seven agencies that have had great impact on the business community are the FTC, FDA, EPA, OSHA, EEOC, SBA, and the SEC. Four of these were discussed in earlier chapters.

The Federal Trade Commission's objective is to maintain a competitive American economy and to act wherever deception of the public is involved. It has the power to set up its own guidelines on unfair methods of competition and to act to head off violations *before* they occur. The FDA has two objectives: to prevent the distribution of foods, drugs, and cosmetics that are unsafe for humans, and to make sure that sellers tell the truth about these products. The SEC protects you from security fraud and swindling by assuring that investors get full and honest information on security offerings and by regulating practices in the securities market.

REVIEW QUESTIONS

1. What factors have caused the increase in government intervention in our private enterprise economy?

2. What are the four major roles played by government? Give two examples of each.

3. What pressures led to the passage of the Sherman Act? How effective was it?

4. Why was the Clayton Act passed? How is it related to the Federal Trade Commission Act?

5. What is a tying contract? What is exclusive dealing? How do they restrain trade?

6. What was the purpose of the Robinson-Patman Act? Why was it supported by the Wholesale and Retail Grocers Association?

7. What conditions led to passage of the Pure Food and Drug Act?

8. What are the responsibilities of the Federal Trade Commission?

9. What are the responsibilities of the Food and Drug Administration?

10. How are you protected by the Securities and Exchange Commission?

CASES

Case 19–1.   Beyond kicking the tires

There are more than 60,000 used-car dealers in the United States. Harry Finkelstein has been in the business for 11 years. He buys most of his cars at the auto auctions and keeps about 50 in inventory. His cars are from four to ten years old and sell for $500 to $2,500. In a normal month he sells about 15 cars. He works alone and takes home about $20,000 a year.

Harry tries to be honest with his customers. One of Harry's biggest problems is the paperwork that goes along with selling a car, but he agrees that most of it is needed to guard against selling stolen cars and other problems. Now the FTC is taking an action that really upsets Harry. It is proposing that all used-car dealers must disclose in writing on a window sticker whether 60 different automobile functions are *OK* or *Not OK,* what is wrong, and how much it will cost to fix it. The FTC estimates that the cost of inspection is $15 per car. The National Independent Automobile Dealers Association says it will average $200 per car and will only raise the cost to consumers. Harry figures that this could put him out of business.

1. *Do you think that this kind of regulation will eventually help or hurt consumers?*

2. *If Harry writes to his congressional representative, what should he say?*

3. *Is there a better way to protect the used-car buyer from the dishonest dealer?*

Case 19–2.   Is deregulation the answer?

Herb Rowen manages a travel agency. In the late 1970s the Federal Aviation Administration deregulated airline fares. Up to that time, airline prices had been strictly controlled and airline routes had been closely regulated. Airlines had to accept low-traffic routes such as the Akron–Roanoke route to earn the privilege of serving high-traffic routes such as the New York–Miami run. Now, with deregulation, airlines started to carry more passengers than ever before. They promoted special fares and special routes. Thousands of people were flying less expensively and visiting places they had never thought possible. But Herb wasn't convinced that the deregulation was good all the way round.

First, the changes meant that people like Herb made more money but had lots more problems. More people were traveling, but there was such a confusion of fares that he had to spend all his time trying to keep up. Many travelers seemed suspicious and hostile. They doubted that he had given them the best price. Passengers who did not qualify for discounts felt cheated. Herb started to think about the other problems caused by this deregulation.

The intercity bus business was suffering and started offering special flat fares like "Anywhere we drive for $69." Former bus customers were now flying. The airports were suffering. As airlines added new routes, there was great pressure on airports that lacked the gates, baggage facilities, parking, and other services needed to accommodate the sudden surge of travelers. In short, the deregulation created a mess.

1. *Should a critical industry such as airlines be heavily regulated?*

2. *Can you think of other effects of the deregulation?*

3. *How might deregulation be more smoothly handled?*

AN ONGOING
SOCIAL SYSTEM:
THE PAST AND
THE FUTURE

By studying this chapter you should be able to find answers to these questions:

1 How do the threads of technology, politics, and social development weave together in business history?
2 What is a colonial economy?
3 What developments marked the first stage of the Industrial Revolution?
4 What developments signaled the second stage of the Industrial Revolution? Which ones were extensions of progress made in the first stage? Which were discoveries and technological breakthroughs? Social and political changes?
5 When and why did corporations become the dominant form of business organization?
6 How do we know that we are now in the third stage of the Industrial Revolution?
7 What changes can you expect in the future?

The business system is only one part of the social structure, but it is a very important part. It is with us every day of our lives in many different ways. It is a part of life today and it has been a strong force in the development of our society. When Alex Haley wrote *Roots,* he traced his heritage from tribal life in Africa, through the slave days in the Old South, on to the Civil War, and up to recent days. While he was reporting on a social history, most of the factors that affected his heritage were tied to the business system.

In this text we have focused on the current contributions and operations of the business system. In the first chapter we noted that business exists to meet the needs of the population. That is true today and has been true in the past. We have every reason to believe that it will continue to be true in the future.

Of course, we haven't totally ignored history. At several points we have had glimpses of the effect of history on the current business scene. We reviewed the earlier ancestors of our modern computers. We looked at the beginnings of labor unions, and we touched on early management studies and modern production techniques. You know that Lucas Pacioli set up double-entry bookkeeping in the 1500s and that Upton Sinclair provided the fuel for the Pure Food and Drug Act in 1906. In this chapter, let's tie some of those historical threads together and then take a peek at what might be the business picture in the future.

Business history has been affected by individuals, events, and changes in other fields. It is almost impossible to sort out the interactions or to report them separately. It is even more difficult to pin down causes and effects. Many advancements required parallel developments in many different areas. As you read this chapter, try to appreciate that business has affected the society and that the society has affected business.

There are several threads running through business history. The first is the *growth of technology.* Technology can be divided into engineering, energy, production, transportation, and communications developments. Technological progress means that business is more able to meet human needs today than ever before.

The second thread is the *advancement of the political/economic framework* of the nation. Our productive capacity has influenced and been influenced by political and economic developments, including laws and wars.

The third thread is *social development.* This includes the growth of social awareness and responsibility. It also involves the social adaptation that has occurred as our economic system has matured. The level of education, the life expectancy, the health, and the attitudes of the population have interacted with these other changes.

Today's affluent citizens have more expectations than any people

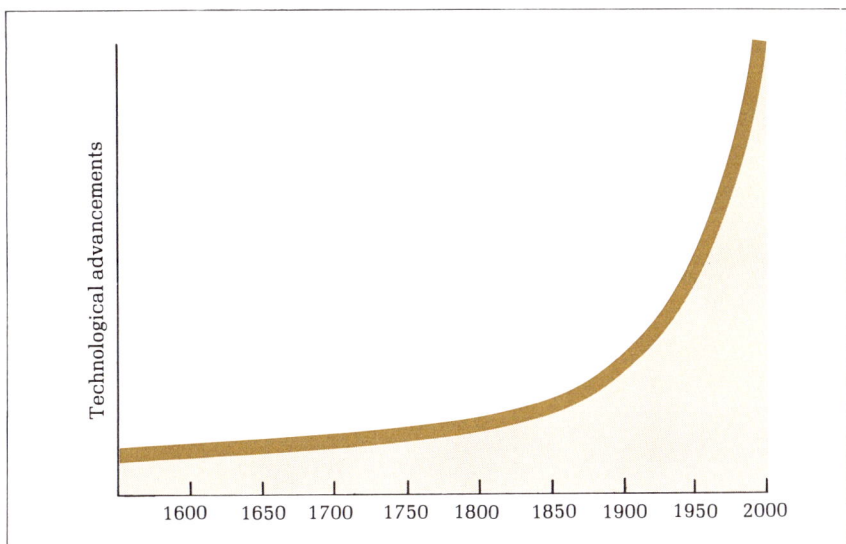

in history. You expect to have your needs satisfied, and you are not at all willing to do without. Fortunately, as human needs have become more complex, our abilities to meet those needs have increased. The prospects are both exhilarating and frightening. Ninety percent of the products available to you in stores today were unheard of only ten years ago. The pace of life is accelerating (see Figure 20–1).

There is more to do, more to learn, more to enjoy, and more to fear today than at any time in history. Problems that in the past were distant and unimportant are brought to us each evening on the television news. The challenge you face is to balance the increased opportunities against the increased risks.

As we look back at history, it helps to divide it into periods. While some dates stand out, most events are the culmination of a series of smaller events and pressures. Our domestic economy has passed through three stages to reach the stage it is in today. These stages are shown on the time line in Figure 20–2. The stage of the economy affects the welfare of the society. It determines the focus of business interests, the type of employment, and the level of productivity.

A COLONIAL ECONOMY

You know that we declared political independence in 1776, but our economic independence did not result from that declaration. A *colonial economy* is one that serves another more economically advanced nation as a source of raw materials and a market for finished products.

FIGURE 20–2
The four stages of the U.S. economy

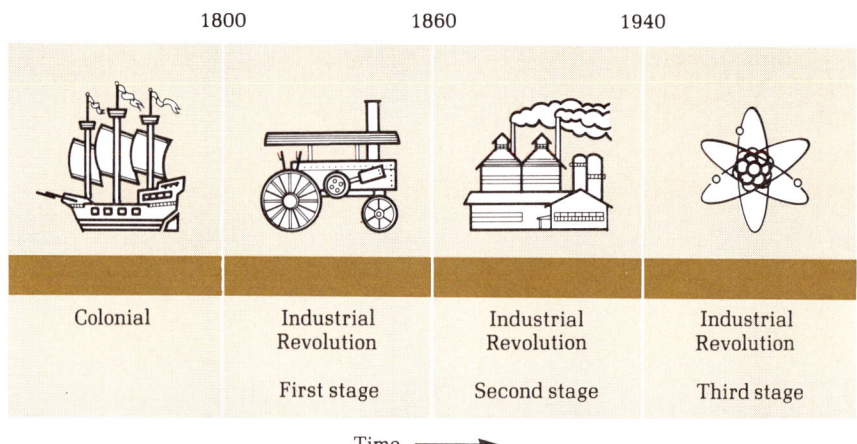

| 1800 | 1860 | 1940 |

Colonial   Industrial Revolution — First stage   Industrial Revolution — Second stage   Industrial Revolution — Third stage

Time ⟶

Even after the United States became politically independent, our economy was based on the sale of crops and raw materials to England and other European nations. We also depended on imports of finished products to meet our needs (see Figure 20–3).

Therefore, the important U.S. business interests were in large farms and plantations and in shipping. Manufacturing was of the small-shop variety, often involving only the proprietor and an apprentice. Most small shops were in the worker's homes, most people lived in rural areas and worked on farms, and most jobs were at low skill and low pay levels.

The per capita productivity was low. Production depended on human or animal power, and a good share of the output was shipped to England. In fact, our transportation system was so poor that it was easier to ship crops across the ocean than to ship them overland. Tobacco, cotton, and other agricultural crops were the raw materials for British mills and factories. The British had already entered the first stage of the Industrial Revolution.

THE INDUSTRIAL REVOLUTION: FIRST STAGE— 1800–1860

America was a good source of raw materials and a ready market for the finished products of the more industrialized nations. To protect this, these nations conspired to delay our industrialization. It was against the law to take the plans for machinery out of England, because machinery is one of the keys to industrialization. The plans for the weaving machine were actually smuggled out by Eli Whitney. But in about 1800, we moved into the first stage of the Industrial Revolution.

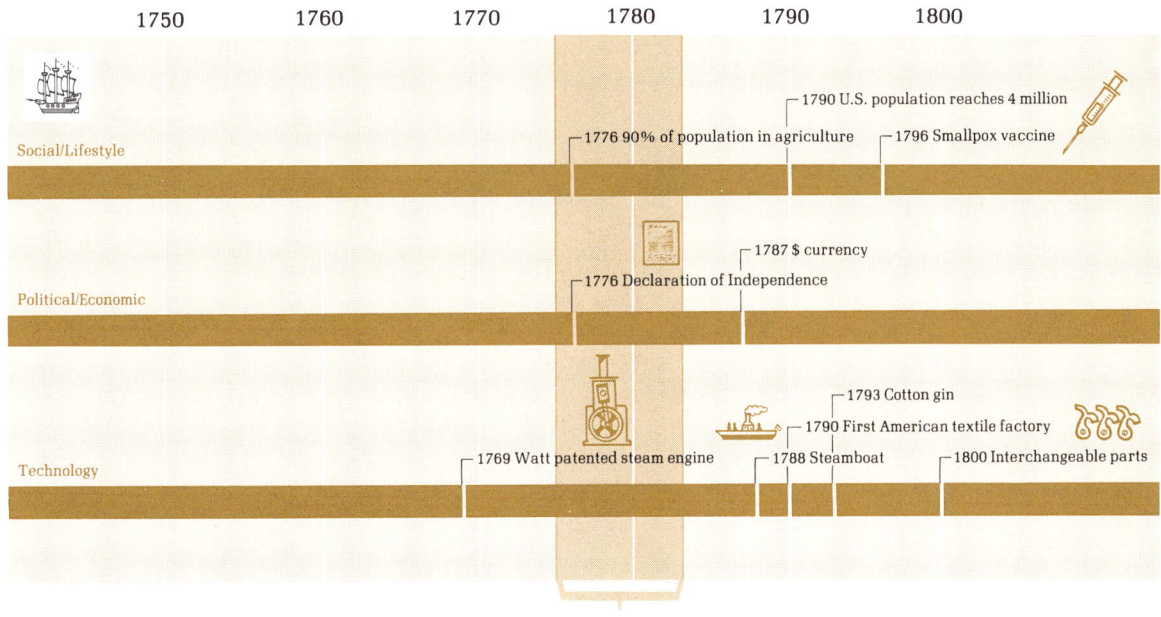

1775-1783 Revolutionary War

FIGURE 20–3
Colonial stage time line

The first steps toward industrialization

Several developments contributed to our industrialization during the period between 1800 and 1860. Productivity increased dramatically. There were also important changes in the social and business structure of the United States. You can imagine how each of the following advancements affected the economy:

1. The mechanization of industry and agriculture.
2. The application of power to industry.
3. The speed-up in communications and transportation.

Business opportunities and the society's economic advancement had been limited earlier by low productivity. There had been no way to multiply human effort.

The development of the factory system

Before mechanization and the use of power other than humans and animals, there had been little advantage to building factories. Increasing the number of people working in one place did not improve productivity; it only increased the transportation problems. In addition, before the mechanization of agriculture, there were few people to work in factories. Most people had to work in the fields just to produce enough to keep the population fed. In 1800, each farm worker could produce

FIGURE 20–4

Persons fed per farm-worker (including the farmworker), 1800–1970

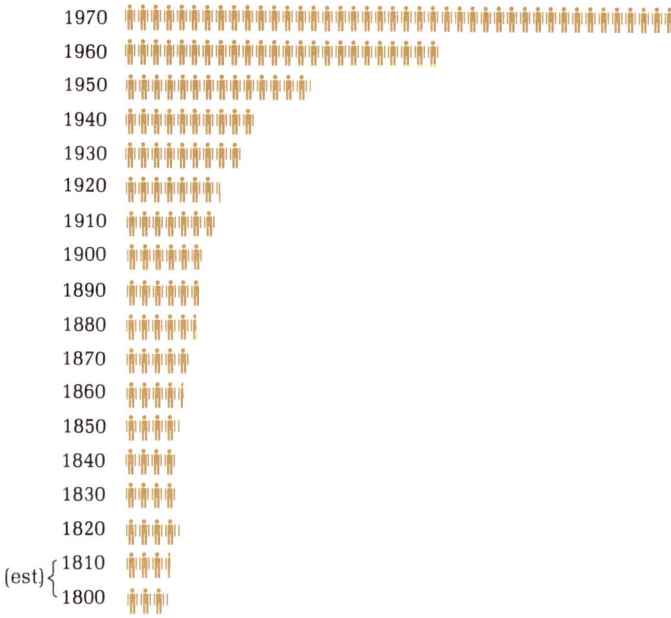

enough to feed 3 people. With the use of machines, the situation changed. In 1975, each farm worker produced enough to feed about 50 people (see Figure 20–4).

A machine could dramatically increase the productivity of not just one worker but of many workers. Machinery brought about the factory system. This was coupled with increased capitalistic control over nearly all economic activity.

It required capital to buy machinery. This need for capital affected the business structure and led to the growth of corporations. Until the early 1800s, proprietorships and partnerships were the dominant forms of business, but by 1850, corporations began to dominate business. As is still the case today, there were more proprietorships and partnerships, but corporations were larger and accounted for most of the business activity. Capitalists took the risk of setting up the plant, and the workers left home to work in factories.

As workers clustered around factories, the nation began the shift from rural to urban life (see Figure 20–5). This increased the needs for transportation and communication. The growing economy required a way to move needed supplies into the cities and to move the output of the factories to markets in other cities and other countries. Look carefully at the time line in Figure 20–6 to see some of the events and inventions that marked Stage I of the Industrial Revolution.

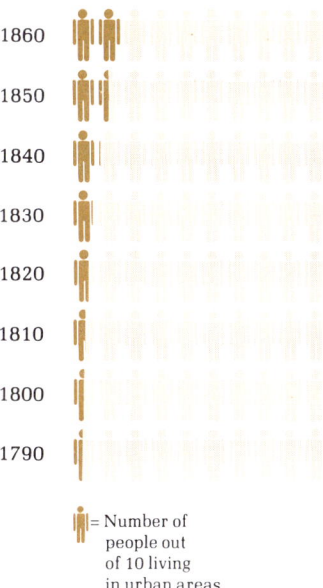

FIGURE 20–5
Urbanization of the population, 1790–1860

1860

1850

1840

1830

1820

1810

1800

1790

👤 = Number of
people out
of 10 living
in urban areas

FIGURE 20–6
**Industrial Revolution:
Stage I**

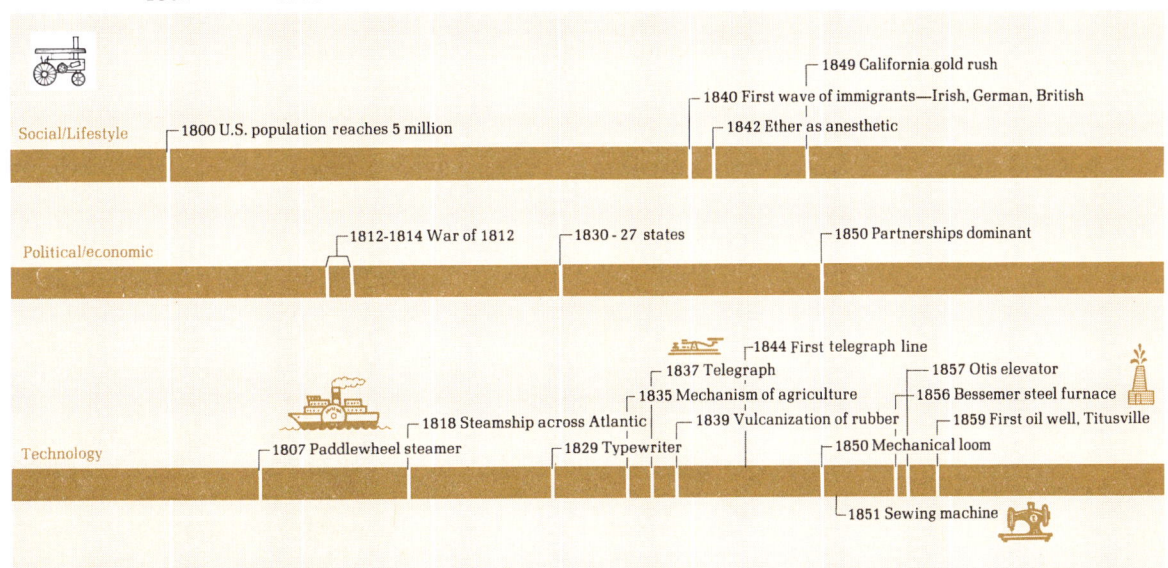

1800   1810   1820   1830   1840   1850   1860

Social/Lifestyle
1800 U.S. population reaches 5 million
1849 California gold rush
1840 First wave of immigrants—Irish, German, British
1842 Ether as anesthetic

Political/economic
1812-1814 War of 1812
1830 - 27 states
1850 Partnerships dominant

Technology
1807 Paddlewheel steamer
1818 Steamship across Atlantic
1829 Typewriter
1844 First telegraph line
1837 Telegraph
1835 Mechanism of agriculture
1839 Vulcanization of rubber
1850 Mechanical loom
1857 Otis elevator
1856 Bessemer steel furnace
1859 First oil well, Titusville
1851 Sewing machine

THE INDUSTRIAL REVOLUTION: SECOND STAGE— 1860–1940

During the second stage we completed the move from an agricultural economy to the most advanced industrialized nation in the world. This required not only machinery but also the development of social and economic support systems. Not everyone was happy with the changes. A major force leading to the Civil War was the crumbling of the old economic system.

Once the first steps had been taken, the rate of change accelerated. Inventions were refined, the shift from rural to urban living continued, the population grew, and the economy expanded. There are several developments that marked the second stage of the Industrial Revolution. Some of these were extensions of progress made in the first stage, some resulted from discovery and technological breakthroughs, and others were related to the changing social and political structure of the country.

Extensions and effects

Several of the trends that began in the first stage accelerated. Among these were:

1.   The improvement of machinery.
2.   Improvements in transportation and communications.
3.   The continued growth of the corporate form of organization.

During the second stage there were extensions on the basic mechanical principles. Once you discover how to use steam power to propel a ship, it isn't long before someone applies the same idea to a manufacturing plant. Then someone else looks for a better way to make steam, and on and on. Henry Ford observed the way a carcass passed through a meat-packing plant and applied the principle to automobile assembly. Before long he had set up a line that could produce a model-T Ford in 1 hour and 35 minutes.

The development of automatic machinery paved the way for mass production (see Figure 20–7). It made sense to build larger and more centralized factories. This meant that more and more materials had to be transported to the factories and that finished products had to be transported greater distances. This put strains on the transportation and communications industries which responded with improvements.

Greater productivity also required larger pools of capital. Corporations grew larger by selling stock to individuals with savings. The stock market and the banking facilities grew to meet the needs for financial services. The government's role in regulating these financial institutions increased, and the government also stepped up its participation in the

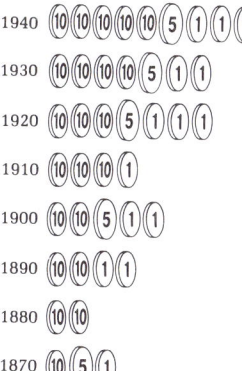

FIGURE 20–7
Productivity Index, 1870–1940 (in 1958 dollars)

business community. Individual citizens could have little impact on big business.

Technological breakthroughs

While some developments just move ahead in small steps, others make leaps or start off in new and different directions. Some of the leaps that took place during the second stage were:

1. The widespread substitution of steel for iron.
2. The substitution of gas and oil for coal.
3. The development of industrial and agricultural chemistry.

In 1856 Sir Henry Bessemer developed a process whereby a jet of air was blasted into molten iron to eliminate carbon. This blast furnace process cut the cost of producing steel by 85 percent. Between 1880 and 1914, U.S. output of steel increased more than 1,750 percent. The use of steel made it possible to build higher-quality machinery and improve production even more.

Until 1859 petroleum had been considered an oddity. It had been available only in small amounts, and its outstanding use had been as tonic in medicine shows. But then major oil fields were discovered in Titusville, Pennsylvania. This stimulated efforts to find uses for oil. The search resulted in the invention of the internal combustion engine in 1876. By the turn of the century, Rudolf Diesel had made his contribution, and diesel engines extended the capabilities of our railroads.

Parallel advancements were occurring in the field of chemistry. Agricultural chemists developed substances that could control insect pests, which had sharply reduced crop yields. They also developed stronger and more productive strains of seeds and livestock. Industrial chemists were working on substances that would be considered primitive today

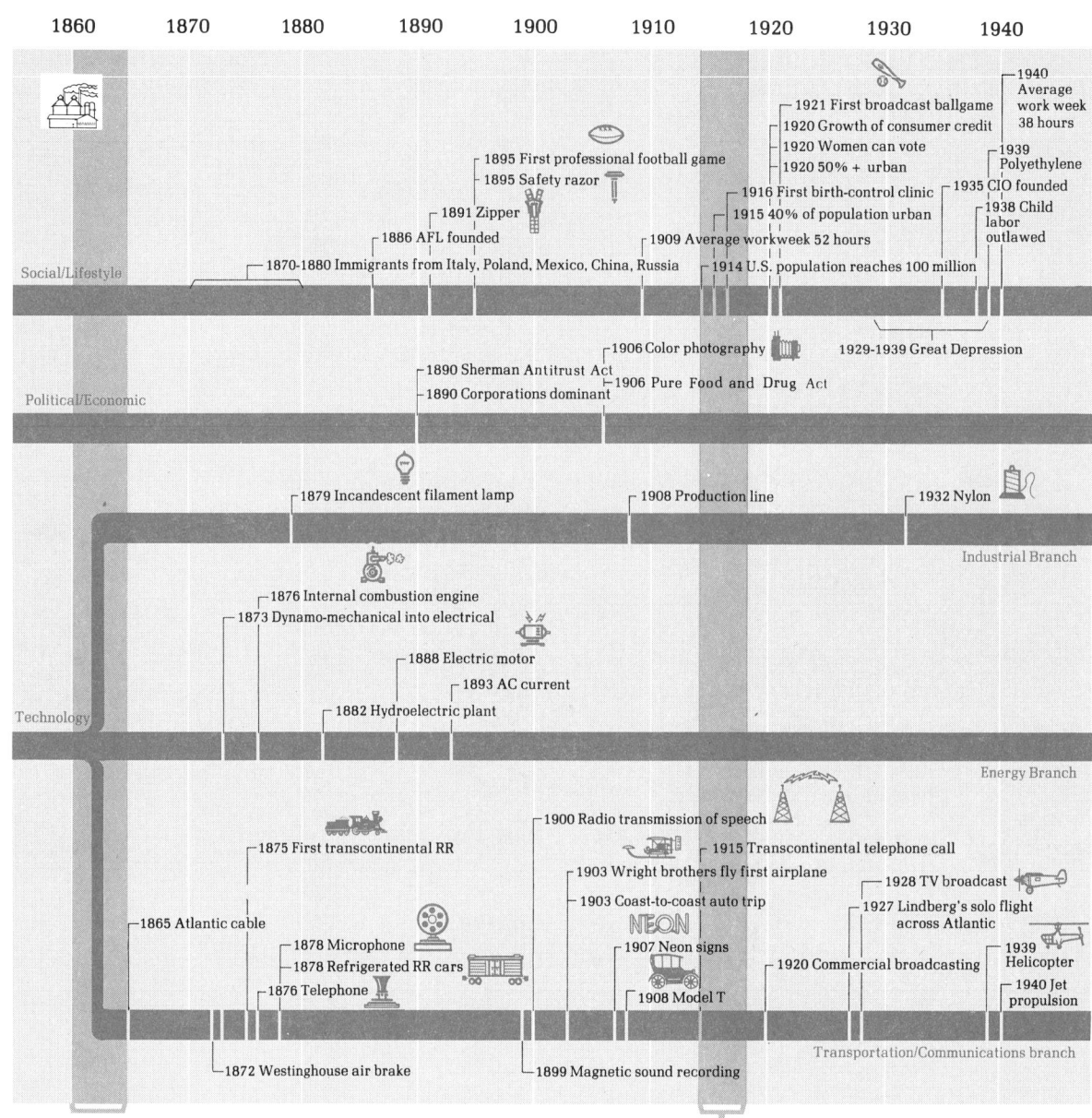

1860   1870   1880   1890   1900   1910   1920   1930   1940

Social/Lifestyle

1921 First broadcast ballgame
1920 Growth of consumer credit
1920 Women can vote
1920 50% + urban
1916 First birth-control clinic
1915 40% of population urban
1909 Average workweek 52 hours
1895 First professional football game
1895 Safety razor
1891 Zipper
1886 AFL founded
1870-1880 Immigrants from Italy, Poland, Mexico, China, Russia
1914 U.S. population reaches 100 million

1940 Average work week 38 hours
1939 Polyethylene
1935 CIO founded
1938 Child labor outlawed

Political/Economic

1906 Color photography
1906 Pure Food and Drug Act
1890 Sherman Antitrust Act
1890 Corporations dominant
1929-1939 Great Depression

Industrial Branch

1879 Incandescent filament lamp
1908 Production line
1932 Nylon

Technology

1876 Internal combustion engine
1873 Dynamo-mechanical into electrical
1888 Electric motor
1893 AC current
1882 Hydroelectric plant

Energy Branch

1900 Radio transmission of speech
1915 Transcontinental telephone call
1875 First transcontinental RR
1903 Wright brothers fly first airplane
1903 Coast-to-coast auto trip
1928 TV broadcast
1927 Lindberg's solo flight across Atlantic
1865 Atlantic cable
1878 Microphone
1878 Refrigerated RR cars
1907 Neon signs
1920 Commercial broadcasting
1876 Telephone
1908 Model T
1939 Helicopter
1940 Jet propulsion

Transportation/Communications branch

1872 Westinghouse air brake
1899 Magnetic sound recording

1861-1864 Civil War   1914-1918 World War I

FIGURE 20–8
**Industrial Revolution:
Stage II**

but that dramatically improved the economy's capacity to feed and clothe a growing population.

Social changes

At the same time, the social structure of the country was changing. During the second stage there were many important developments, such as:

1. The development of a public education system.
2. The growth of the labor movement.
3. The urbanization of the population.

As the use of automated machinery increased, the nature of employment changed. People were no longer used mainly as a source of physical power. The need for skilled workers, clerical workers, and managers increased. Public education increased the abilities of the work force. It also led to a more thoughtful market for the outputs of the business system. Figure 20–8 shows other changes that occurred during this stage.

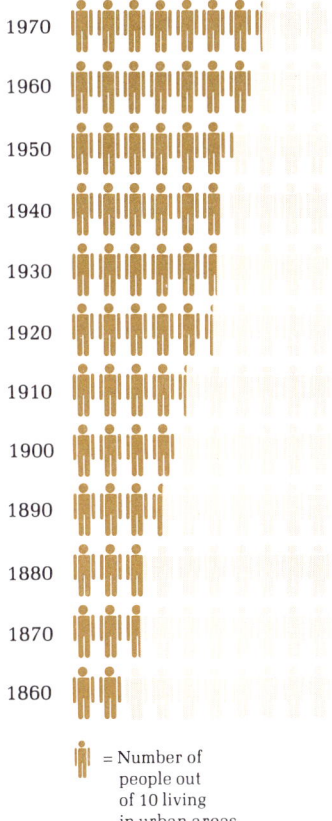

FIGURE 20–9
Urbanization of the population, 1860–1970

As the trend toward the specialization of labor and increased productivity continued, labor rightfully came to expect a fair share of the rewards of the system. Primarily through unionization, workers gained increased benefits, protection, and earnings.

By the end of the second stage of the Industrial Revolution, the U.S. population had increased to 132 million, and about six out of ten people lived in urban areas (see Figure 20–9). The cities provided concentrated work forces and marketplaces and also had to face the attendant social problems such as the need for housing, police and fire protection, and better distribution systems. The trends might have continued at a steady rate, but several forces were at work to move the economy into the third stage of the Industrial Revolution.

THE INDUSTRIAL REVOLUTION: THIRD STAGE— 1940–TODAY

In 1940 the world was on the brink of great change. Just months before, scientists had first split the atom and opened up the Nuclear Age. In laboratories there was continuing research into the new realm of electronics. The capacity was developing and might have been realized anyway, but World War II unlocked a flood of attention to increased productivity and scientific advancement.

Scientific advancement

The list of scientific advancements since 1940 is staggering, as you can see from the time line in Figure 20–10. Advances in one area spill over and bring even greater benefits in another. Aviation scientists gave us jet propulsion. Not only did that affect transportation, but through aerospace research it also resulted in satellite communications. When the Wright brothers flew that plane at Kittyhawk in 1903, they couldn't have even imagined that 77 years later Americans would sit in their living rooms and enjoy live coverage of the Olympics in Russia.

You can look around and see the benefits you enjoy due to the scientific advancements that have occurred in just the past quarter century. Business interests played a part in most of these developments.

Human advancements

The social and human advancements have been as important as the technological advancements in the third stage of the Industrial Revolution. Today we hear a great deal about the rights and the dignity of employees. We hear about equal opportunity and product safety. We are concerned about truth-in-lending and decaying inner cities. The list goes on and on. You may find yourself wondering how we ever let ourselves get into the present mess.

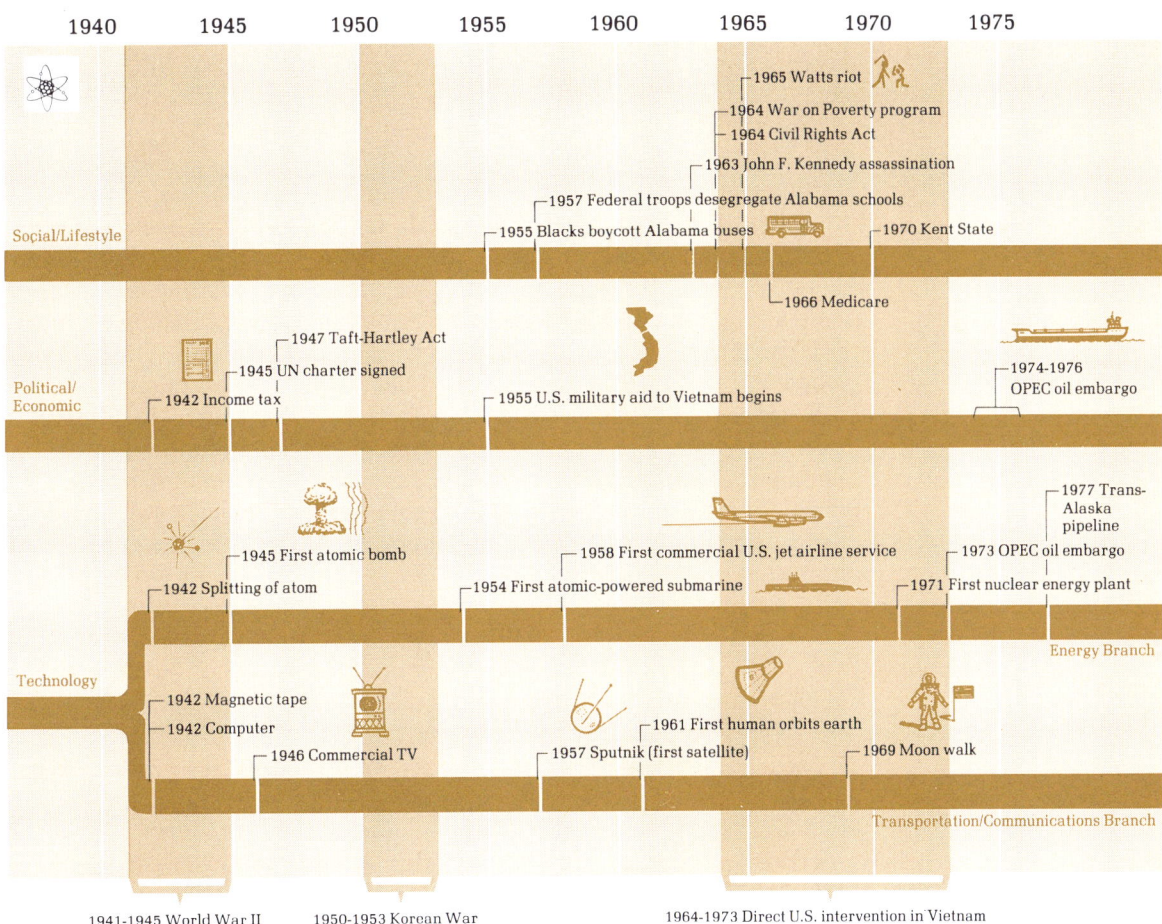

| 1940 | 1945 | 1950 | 1955 | 1960 | 1965 | 1970 | 1975 |

Social/Lifestyle

┌ 1965 Watts riot
├ 1964 War on Poverty program
├ 1964 Civil Rights Act
├ 1963 John F. Kennedy assassination
├ 1957 Federal troops desegregate Alabama schools
├ 1955 Blacks boycott Alabama buses   ├ 1970 Kent State
└ 1966 Medicare

Political/ Economic

├ 1947 Taft-Hartley Act
├ 1945 UN charter signed
├ 1942 Income tax
├ 1955 U.S. military aid to Vietnam begins
├ 1974-1976 OPEC oil embargo

Technology

├ 1945 First atomic bomb
├ 1942 Splitting of atom
├ 1958 First commercial U.S. jet airline service
├ 1954 First atomic-powered submarine
├ 1977 Trans-Alaska pipeline
├ 1973 OPEC oil embargo
├ 1971 First nuclear energy plant

Energy Branch

├ 1942 Magnetic tape
├ 1942 Computer
├ 1946 Commercial TV
├ 1961 First human orbits earth
├ 1957 Sputnik (first satellite)
├ 1969 Moon walk

Transportation/Communications Branch

1941-1945 World War II   1950-1953 Korean War   1964-1973 Direct U.S. intervention in Vietnam

FIGURE 20–10
Industrial Revolution: Stage III

Our system is far from perfect, but its problems are not new. The difference is that today we talk about them. And we have made a great deal of progress. A hundred years ago a much higher proportion of people suffered from substandard housing, nutrition, education, and employment. The infant mortality rate in the United States today is about 18 per 1,000 live births. In 1940, the number was 47 per 1,000. In 1925 an average worker had to work 53 minutes to earn enough to buy a dozen eggs, but today that has been reduced to 13 minutes.

EXPECTATIONS OF THE BUSINESS SYSTEM

You have needs and you expect to have those needs met through the business system. You also have a right to expect that you will be able to breathe clean air, drink clean water, be safe from dangerous working conditions, be treated fairly in the marketplace, and have fair employment opportunities. What can you expect of the business system in the future?

Increased automation

You can expect increased automation in every stage of business from the processing of raw materials to the billing of customers. As a part of automation, you will be dealing with more computerized facilities in your role as a consumer. Some banks and supermarket chains have already introduced automated tellers and check-cashing systems. You can expect that this will become more widespread within a few years. We will move even closer to becoming a cashless society.

We have the capacity to develop equipment that will relieve humans from monotonous and unpleasant work. As the cost of labor increases, more and more firms will view this expensive equipment as a suitable alternative. This will free human labor for more advanced employment. But, of course, it will mean that there are fewer and fewer jobs for untrained or unskilled people.

A shorter workweek

There has been a steady decline in the length of the average workweek for a century, and you can expect that trend to continue. Even in those cases where the same number of hours are worked, there will be greater flexibility in scheduling. Pressure toward the shorter workweek will come from several sources.

First, labor unions will turn to this as an added benefit for their members. Beyond a certain point, money is less effective as a motivator. Most people would prefer more free time to enjoy what they have. Staggered working hours would also relieve some of the traffic burden on freeways. It would bring some relief from the peak energy usage patterns that result when most people prepare dinner between 5:30 and 7:00 p.m.

A growth in franchising

Franchising will grow even more important in retailing and in service businesses. It will offer the opportunity for small business to compete with big business.

Increased attention to world markets

With improved communications and the increasing standard of living worldwide, there will be more attention paid to world markets. Even smaller businesses will serve markets in foreign countries.

Greater government intervention

There is no indication that there will be any change in the pattern of government intervention in the business system. The three-way standoff among the forces of big business, big government, and big labor will continue. Government will continue to make inroads into the private enterprise economy.

Exploding world population

While the U.S. population has shown definite signs of leveling off in size, the same is not true worldwide. There will be increasing population problems, especially in the developing nations. This population growth combined with increased expectations will result in even greater pressures on the world's limited natural resources. This will mean even greater demands for improved technology in the areas of energy utilization, food production, health care, and communications.

Human rights

As the standard of living in our nation and in nations around the world increases, there will be greater attention paid to human rights. This will be reflected both in employment opportunities and in the variety of services available. We will see even greater concern for senior citizens, minorities, and children.

Better management of business

People entering the business system are better trained, and the concepts and techniques of management are improving rapidly. We know more about production systems, consumer behavior and marketing, physical distribution, finance, personnel and managing people, and so on. What is more, we know how to integrate all of these elements into a smoothly functioning system. Business management has become a profession, and students like yourself enter the business system with better training than ever before, and higher aspirations that are sure to improve the management of business in the future.

SUMMARY

You are a part of the business system. You are certainly a consumer and observer and will probably participate as an employee and an investor. At the beginning of this text, we suggested three reasons why you should study business. Throughout this text we have discussed the WHAT, WHY, WHEN, WHO, WITH, HOW, and WITHIN of business. You have been exposed to the concepts, terms, and underlying logic of business. In the appendix following this chapter are many suggestions on finding careers in business.

The business system is a very important part of the social structure, and it will continue to be important in the future. Business history has been affected by individuals, events, and developments in other fields. There are three important threads in business history: (1) the growth of technology, (2) the advancement of the political/economic framework of the nation, and (3) social development. While some historical dates stand out, most events are the culmination of a series of smaller events and pressures.

Our economic independence did not result from the Declaration of Independence in 1776. We still had a colonial economy serving other more economically advanced nations as a source of raw materials and a market for finished products. Our economy was dominated by large farms, plantations, and shipping. The per capita productivity was low.

Around 1800 the first stage of the Industrial Revolution began causing important changes in the social and business structure of the United States. Among the most notable were the mechanization of industry and agriculture, the application of power to industry, and the speed-up in communications and transportation. Machinery brought about the factory system, and levels of productivity increased dramatically. This also led to increased capitalistic control over nearly all economic activity. As the workers clustered in factories, the nation began the shift from rural to urban life.

The second stage of industrialization completed our move from an agricultural economy to the most advanced industrialized nation in the world. Around 1860 the rate of change accelerated. Inventions were refined, the shift from rural to urban living continued, the population grew, and the economy expanded. Improvements in machinery, transportation, and communications brought about increased productivity and a higher standard of living.

Automatic machinery paved the way for mass production, which required larger pools of capital. Corporations became the dominant form of organization. The stock market and banking facilities grew to meet the needs for financial services. The government stepped up its participation in the business community. Technological advances included the widespread substitution of steel for iron and also of gas and oil for coal. There was great progress in the areas of industrial and agricultural chemistry.

Socially, the second stage was marked by the development of a public education system, the growth of the labor movement, and the urbanization of the population with attendant social problems such

FRANK BORMAN
Constantly looking to the future

You probably remember Colonel Frank Borman as the commander of the Apollo 8 space flight—the first manned lunar orbital mission. That event attracted worldwide attention. Today he is a businessman and head of one of the largest airline companies in the country. He is still attracting attention but in a much different way. You hear of Colonel Borman in the news taking a position on deregulation of the airline industry, or you hear of Eastern Airlines' attempts to merge with other airlines in order to improve its position when and if deregulation does occur.

The airline industry is regulated by the Civil Aeronautics Board (CAB). In order for an airline to provide passenger service between two cities, it must apply to the CAB for approval.

There is a long, complicated process to obtain approval. Colonel Borman says that the CAB exerts strong pressure on those applying for routes to favor fare discounting, even favoring fare-reducing proponents in awarding new routes. The CAB did deregulate the air cargo industry. All U.S. ports are now open to any all-cargo operation that wishes to serve them, and the companies have freedom in setting rates. Making air cargo service more available to more places aids business in product distribution. Colonel Borman feels that the same philosophy will be applied more and more to passenger service.

Colonel Borman graduated from West Point in 1950 and later obtained a Master of Science degree in Aeronautical Engineering from California Institute of Technology. He was an Air Force officer from 1950 to 1970, serving as a fighter pilot, a flight instructor, a professor at West Point, a test pilot, and finally in his well-known work in the space program. Since 1970, however, Borman turned his attention to the airline business and moved rapidly to his present position as president and chief executive officer of Eastern Airlines.

as the need for better housing, police and fire protection, and better distribution systems.

The third stage of the Industrial Revolution began with the splitting of the atom and the opening of the age of nuclear power and electronics. Business interests have played an important role in the scientific advancement of this and past stages. But, the social and human advancements during stage III have been important, too.

What can you expect of the business system in the years to come? You can expect increased automation, a shorter workweek, a growth in franchising, and increased attention to world markets. There will be many changes in the environment within which business operates.

You will see greater government intervention, an exploding world population, and greater attention to all areas of human rights. Today there is more to do, more to learn, more to enjoy, and more to fear than ever before.

REVIEW QUESTIONS

1. What were the technological, political, and social conditions during the colonial economy period?

2. How did conditions change during the first stage of the Industrial Revolution?

3. How did the second stage of the Industrial Revolution differ from the first? What important developments occurred?

4. What stimulated the growth of corporations?

5. What events marked the beginning of the third stage of the Industrial Revolution?

6. What do you think have been the three most important scientific advancements during the third stage?

7. Do you agree with our predictions of what you might expect from business in the future? Why or why not? Can you add any to the list?

CASES

Case 20–1.   Spare parts for humans

When our body parts begin to fail, why shouldn't we have spares just as one might replace the carburetor in a car? The human body parts industry was almost nonexistent 15 years ago, but now it is a $700 million industry growing at the rate of 15 percent per year. Most of the 200 companies in the business are small and privately owned, but their success is attracting the attention of large acquisition-minded firms.

Parts made from plastics, nylon, stainless steel, and tanned animal tissues are implanted to replace hip and knee joints, heart valves, and many other human parts. But there are several problems facing these small firms. Imagine the potential for product liability. Some of the smaller firms can't even get product liability insurance, and when they can, the cost is high. Spare parts are heavily regulated by the FDA as ethical drugs. It takes about five years and $5 million to bring a new product to market. In some cases there are also attitude problems. Some people cringe at the thought of having a pig valve implanted in their heart.

1. *How has this industry been the result of technological, communications, and social developments?*

2. *What effect will this industry have on future developments in society?*

Case 20–2.   Twenty years from now

History is supposed to teach us a lesson about the future. In the mid-1950s, David Sarnoff, the chairman of RCA, made a speech in which he predicted what will be going on "Twenty Years from Now." Following are some of his predictions for the 1970s along with the actual outcome.

1. *What problems face anyone who attempts to predict the future? Why did some of Sarnoff's predictions fall short?*

2. *Make your own list of ten predictions for the end of the 1980s.*

Prediction	Outcome
Nuclear power for industries, homes, planes, trains, and cars	Sixty-five plants produce less than 13 percent of U.S. electric power
Global television	On target, with sattelite transmission
Household chores done electronically	Programmable microwave ovens, and home computers that can control a few household chores, but that's about it
Weather forecasts a year in advance	Remember the winters of 1977 and 1978?
Greater importance of public opinion in politics because of improvements in data processing	True in the United States but not worldwide

GLOSSARY

A

Acceptance sampling A statistical quality control technique in which a sample is inspected and, based on the results, a decision is made whether or not the entire lot is good or bad.

Accessory equipment Goods that are used in conducting business or producing a product, but that do not become a part of the product or change the capacity of the firm.

Accounting The system of decisions, techniques, and practices that allows for the continuing collection, organization, and summarization of information on the financial situation within the firm.

Accounts receivable Funds owed to a firm by those who purchase its products or services.

Accrual accounting System in which revenue is counted as revenue when it is earned rather than when payment is received, and expenses are counted as expenses when the firm makes use of the goods or services, not when the bill is paid.

Accrued wages Wages that employees have earned but that have not yet been paid.

Activity ratios A measure of how well the firm is using its resources by comparing the funds invested in various assets with the revenues generated by those assets.

Administered pricing The seller has determined a set price at which the product is offered to you, and you can decide whether or not you will buy it.

Advertising Paid nonpersonal communication presented by an identified sponsor over an established medium.

Agent middlemen Firms that do not own the products they offer for sale but that help buyers and sellers to find each other.

Aggregate planning Broad-level planning for production.

Aggressive distribution The seller actively seeks out potential buyers.

Analog computers Computes by making measurements on some parallel physical system. A slide rule is an analog computer.

Apprentice A person who serves as a helper to a person skilled in a trade in order to learn that trade.

Approach The salesperson's initial contact with the prospect to generate interest so that the prospect will be willing to listen to the sales presentation.

Assets Valuable resources owned by a firm that were acquired at a measurable cost.

Audit To lend credibility to the firm's financial statements, the firm opens its books to the CPA who examines them closely and then issues an opinion on the financial statements.

Average collection period Length of time it takes the firm to collect money owed to it.

B

Balance sheet (statement of financial position) Statement that shows the financial condition of the firm at one moment in time.

BASIC *B*eginner's *A*ll-purpose *S*ymbolic *I*nstructional *C*ode, one of the simpler computer languages.

Bidding   Qualified suppliers submit the price at which they could deliver particular items.

Bill of materials (BM)   Statement containing the specifications related to items requisitioned.

Binary number system   The number system used by computers that uses only 0 and 1.

Binding arbitration   An impartial outsider is called in to settle the issues and each side agrees to abide by the arbitrator's decision.

Bit   Short for *bi*nary digi*t*, a fragment of data that can be represented by a yes or a no.

Blanket (open-ended contracts)   Contract for commonly used materials in large quantity, which may cover an entire year. These kinds of contracts leave quantities and delivery times to be set as the materials are needed.

Board of directors   People elected by shareholders to represent them and to be responsible for formulating long-range policies for the firm and for hiring the managers who will make the day-to-day decisions.

Bonds   Long-term notes payable.

Boycott   An effort to discourage customers from buying a firm's products.

Budget   A list of intended expenditure limit which serves as the basis for controlling a plan once it is developed.

Bugs   Errors in a computer program.

Business   The human activity of converting resources into goods and services for the purpose of bringing about transactions that will result in a profit to the organization.

Business concept   The unique benefit to be offered to consumers, the brand name or identification, and the setting.

Business cycle   The ups and downs in measures of business activity.

C

Capital   Wealth or resources that will be used to produce goods or services.

Capital accumulation   Enough funds collected under one group's control to begin an economic project.

Capital budgeting   The process of deciding among long-term uses of funds.

Capitalists   Those who invest their resources in business.

Cash-basis accounting   System in which revenue is counted as revenue when it is received and expenses are counted as expenses when they are paid.

Causal forecasting models   Models that correlate demand with factors in the economy that cause the demand to increase or decrease.

Centralization   The extent to which authority is concentrated in one or few individuals.

Clayton Act (1914)   Legislation that spelled out the market behaviors that were in restraint of trade and provided more muscle to deal with violators.

Clean Air Act (1977)   Federal legislation giving authority to EPA to clean up air quality.

Closing   A salesperson's request for the order.

COBOL   *CO*mputer *B*usiness *O*riented *L*anguage, a computer language designed for business uses.

Collateral   Something of value pledged as security against a loan.

Commercial banks   Firms chartered by the federal or state government to provide a variety of financial services for both consumers and businesses, including accepting deposits from some customers and lending funds to other customers.

Commercial paper   Unsecured promissory notes in amounts of $100,000 or more by which major corporations borrow directly from other major corporations.

Common demand   Various buyers are competing to buy the same goods and services.

Common stock   The basic class of stock in a corporation through which shareholders share "in common" in earnings that are distributed.

Communal system   Economic arrangement in which everybody owns everything.

Competitors   Those who offer equivalent products and services.

Computer-based planning   Planning process in which the results are expressed as a computer model.

Consolidation   A combination of two or more fairly equal corporations in which none of the original corporations survives and all of the shareholders become shareholders in the new corporation.

Consumer markets   People who are buying whatever utility the product or service has to offer for their own personal benefit.

Consumer Product Safety Commission (CPSC)   A federal government commission established to protect consumers from unsafe products.

Control charts   A statistical quality control technique to monitor the output of a process.

Convenience goods   Those products and services that most consumers prefer to purchase with the minimum effort.

Cooperative (co-op)   A continuing association of independent firms for a common purpose.

Corporate planning   Planning at the top levels of a business.

Corporation   A legal business identity granted in a charter issued by the state in which it is incorporated. It is separate from its owners and managers and capable of owning assets, transacting business, entering into contracts, and incurring liabilities.

Craft unions   Unions organized on the basis of the type of work performed by their members.

Credit union   A cooperative thrift and loan society composed of people who have a specified shared interest.

Credits   Entries recorded on the right-hand side of the accounts.

Culture   An accumulation of solutions to basic human questions.

Current liability   Financial obligation that the firm expects to pay off within a year.

Current ratio   Compares current assets with current liabilities.

Cycle inventories   Inventories that result from periodic ordering.

D

Data   Raw unprocessed facts that have been organized only enough to make them easier to collect or store.

Data analysis   The statistical manipulation and grouping necessary to uncover similarities and patterns among the responses of various groups of respondents.

Debits   Entries recorded on the left-hand side of the accounts.

Debt ratio   Measure of the proportion of the firm's assets that have been financed through borrowing.

Deficit spending   The government spends more than it takes in; it is just like expanding credit and therefore like expanding the money supply.

Delphi method   Technological forecasting methods.

Demand curve   A schedule of the amounts demanded at various prices.

Demographics   Statistics on people.

Demography   The study of population factors.

Depreciation   Allocating a portion of the cost of an asset to each of the accounting periods in which it is expected to have useful life.

Derived demand   The demand for one product or service comes about due to the demand for another product or service.

Discretionary income   Income available to spend out of choice rather than necessity.

Disposable income   The after-tax amount available to be spent by consumer markets.

Distributors   Wholesalers' wholesalers.

Division   A unit within the firm in which managers are employees of the main firm and there is a direct management link.

Division of labor   The overall job is broken up into several defined tasks.

E

Econometric forecasting models   A causal forecasting system that is based on a system of regression equations.

Economic order quantity (EOQ)   The order quantity that balances the annual ordering costs against the annual inventory costs.

Elastic demand   A change in price brings about a more than proportionate change in demand.

Elasticity of demand   The measure of the buyers' sensitivity to price.

Entrepreneur   A business will not come into being unless someone brings all of the elements together and organizes them into a productive system. That person is the entrepreneur.

Environmental Protection Agency (EPA)   A federal government agency with powers to control pollution and other threats to the environment.

Exchange   Trading one item or service for something of value.

Exclusive dealing   A seller refuses to deal unless the buyer promises not to deal with any of the competitors.

Expenses   Outflows of resources for goods and services used by an entity to earn revenues.

Experimentation   The research technique that allows a researcher to establish causation because of controls on the research environment.

Exponential smoothing   Forecasting based on exponentially weighted moving averages.

Exponentially weighted moving average   A method for weighting the most recent demand data more heavily in time series forecasts.

F

Family branding   The use of the same brand for a variety of products.

Federal Trade Commission Act (1914)   Legislation to set up the Federal Trade Commission (FTC) to enforce the Clayton Act and protect honest businesses from unfair competitors.

Financial accounting   Preparing financial statements for those outside the firm including the government, the firm's shareholders, and the general public.

Financial Accounting Standards Board   Seven-member committee that constantly evaluates and establishes the generally accepted principles of accounting.

Financial institutions   Commercial banks, life insurance companies, savings and loan associations, private pension funds, and credit unions, which blend together all the funds deposited by their customers and invest those funds in the name of the institution.

Financial management   The process of obtaining and using funds effectively.

Finished goods inventories   Inventories of the finished product at the end of the productive process at the factory or in distribution warehouses.

Firm   An organization of people and resources with the purpose of conducting a specified type of business.

Fixed-quantity reordering system   Inventory control system in which a fixed quantity is ordered each time an order is placed.

Flowchart   A diagram of the steps to be followed in arriving at a solution.

Focus group   A small group of people who are similar to the seller's target market and are brought together in a room and asked to focus on a particular issue.

Follow-up   Checking to make sure that the product or service is delivered according to the contract and that the customer is satisfied with the purchase.

Food and Drug Administration (FDA)   Part of the Department of Health, Education, and Welfare that tries to prevent the distribution of foods, drugs, and cosmetics that are unsafe for humans and to assure that sellers tell the truth about these products.

Form utility   The item has the proper characteristics to meet your needs.

FORTRAN   *FOR*mula *TRAN*slation, a complex computer language.

Forward buying   Buying somewhat more than you would need just to meet production requirements.

Franchise ethic   The idea that franchisees are more motivated than salaried managers because they have their own money at stake.

Franchise system   A business chain made up of owner-managed outlets.

Franchiser   A person or firm with an idea but limited resources. It sells or rents its business system to others who will be able to come up with resources to aid in the expansion.

Franchising   A business arrangement in which the franchiser grants the franchisee the right to do business in a prescribed manner over a certain period of time in a specified place.

Functional layout (process layout)   The physical arrangement in which equipment of the same functional type is grouped together.

G

General partners   Those who have full rights and responsibilities to participate fully in the management of the firm and have unlimited liability.

Generic brand   A brand name that is extended to all the products of that type.

Government markets   People who buy goods and services for federal, state, and local government units.

Gross income   The amount you earn.

Gross national product (GNP)   The annual total market value of all the goods and services produced in a country.

H

Hand-to-mouth buying   Buying barely the amount needed, usually in anticipation of a price decrease.

Hardware   The actual computer equipment with its metal frame, wiring, circuitry, and lights.

Hawthorne effect   The idea that workers respond favorably to attention and humanized supervision.

Hawthorne studies   A 15-year research project conducted by Western Electric at its Hawthorne plant to test the effect of changes in the physical working environment on worker productivity.

Hedging   A technique for minimizing losses if you use raw materials subject to large price variations.

Hierarchy   Levels of power.

I

In-process inventories   Inventories of partially completed products

Income statement   (profit and loss statement) Statement that shows whether or not the firm has earned net income during the accounting period.

Individual branding   A different brand name for each product.

Industrial markets   People who purchase goods and services for private businesses.

Industrial unions   Unions formed on the basis of the industry in which the members are employed.

Inelastic demand   A change in price brings about some change in demand, but that change is proportionally less than the price change.

Inferences   Conclusions reached through reasoning.

Information   That which informs or helps you to understand some event or situation.

Input unit   The device by which a computer system reads in data and instructions.

Inspection report (IR)   A report issued by the inspection department checking the quality against specifications.

Input unit   The device by which a computer system reads in data and instructions.

Installations   Additions to the firm's facilities that are useful over an extended period of time and set the capacity for the firm.

Integrated channels   Several levels of distribution related through common ownership or contracts.

Intensive distribution   Distribution to make goods available in all of the logical locations.

Intermediation   The process of blending together all of the funds deposited by customers and investing those funds in the name of the institution.

Interview   Face-to-face meeting between the applicant and someone from the firm.

Inventory   Stock of goods or materials in the form of raw materials, work in process, and finished goods.

Inventory turnover   Comparison of the funds invested in inventory with the sales revenue.

Investment bankers   Specialists in issuing new securities.

J

Job description   A written statement covering the duties and responsibilities of the position.

Job enlargement   Name given to recent trends in job design toward less specialization.

Job specialization   A common mode of job design in assembly lines.

Joint venture   An agreement between two or more firms to commit a part of their resources to a common purpose.

Jurisdictional dispute   Two or more unions in competition to represent a group of workers.

L

Labor   The human factor of production.

Labor union   A group of workers who have united to exert collective pressure to achieve and maintain benefits for themselves.

Land   The fixed resource that serves as the site for buildings, equipment, and operations.

Leadership   The ability of one person to guide a group of people toward some goal.

Level production   An aggregate production plan that meets annual requirements by producing at the average monthly or weekly level throughout the year.

Leverage ratios   Comparison of the funds supplied by owners with the funds supplied by creditors.

Liabilities   The claims of outsiders against the assets of the business.

Limited partners   Those partners who give up some rights in return for protection from unlimited liability.

Line of credit   A commitment to the borrower by the bank that a certain amount of money will be available at a given rate of interest for a specific period of time.

Line personnel   Those who are directly in the mainstream operations of the firm.

Liquid asset   Cash or something of value that can be converted easily to cash.

Liquidity   The convenience and speed with which an asset can be traded.

Load summary   Data on the frequency of travel per month between all possible combinations of departments.

Local union   The organization to which the individual union member belongs.

Long-term uses of funds   Investments that are expected to sustain or improve the productivity of the firm in the future.

M

Maintenance data   Data collected to meet requirements of the organization to report to the shareholders, creditors, labor representatives, and government and to deal with changes in the business environment.

Management by objectives (MBO)   All employees participate in setting objectives consistent with the overall objectives set at the top.

Managerial accounting   Providing the managers of the firm with the financial information they need to assess the potential financial impact of their decisions.

Manufactured parts   Parts that become part of another product while retaining their own identity.

Market   A cluster of people with similar needs who have both the willingness and the authority to spend their individual purchasing power to meet their individual needs.

Market clearing price   Price at which demand and supply are in balance. It is the price that clears the market of supply.

Market mechanism   The economy is directed by the individual decisions of people freely trading their resources in the marketplace.

Marketing program   A combination of decisions on product, price, distribution, and promotion through which a firm plans to approach its target markets.

Marketing research   The effort taken by a business firm to learn more about its present and potential customers.

Markup   The difference between the cost and the selling price of a product added to cover the expenses and provide a profit for the firms that make the product available.

Master schedules   A breakdown of the aggregate schedule into the schedules for each particular product.

Merchandise   Products that are purchased and resold in substantially unchanged form.

Merchant middlemen   Firms that purchase products and sell them to the next firm or to the customer.

Merger   A combination of two corporations in which only one survives.

Middleman   Not a person, but one of a series of businesses that participate in the distribution process, including distributors, wholesalers, and retailers.

Model   A device for representing a complex process or system.

Monopolistic competition   The conditions for monopolistic competition in an industry are: (1) many firms, but fewer than for pure competition; (2) products not identical among firms; and (3) relative ease of entry to markets.

Monopoly   Industry in which there are no competitors.

Moving average   A method of smoothing the effects of random variation in demand.

Multinational markets   All those people who buy goods and services that will be used in a country other than the one on which the seller is headquartered.

N

National Labor Relations Act (1935, Wagner Act)   Legislation that outlawed many common antiunion activities such as discrimination against union members, spying on unions, and unfairly interfering with organizing. It required the employer to bargain with a union that could prove it represented a majority of the employees.

National Minority Purchasing Council   An organization with the objective of increasing the number of purchases large companies make from minority-owned companies.

Need   Something that is necessary, something you can't get along without. (See also "want")

Negotiated contracts   Buying agreements reached

when there aren't enough competitive suppliers to allow for bidding.

Negotiated pricing The final price results from bargaining between the buyer and seller.

Net income (profits) The amount left after subtracting all the expenses from the revenues.

Normal capacity Capacity without overtime.

Norris-Laguardia Act (1932) Legislation that outlawed *yellow dog contracts* (which required workers to sign a pledge not to join unions in order to be hired), limited the use of court orders against unions, and provided that anyone arrested for union activities could request a jury trial.

O

Observation Collecting primary data by observing people in the natural environment.

Occupational Safety and Health Administration (OSHA) A government regulatory body that issues stringent regulations concerning all aspects of worker health and safety.

Oligopoly An industry in which there are only a few sellers.

Operational data The data that arise as part of the firm's normal business activities.

Operational objective Goal with three elements: (1) it is measurable, (2) it is attainable, and (3) it includes some indication of when it is to be achieved.

Output unit The device through which a computer translates data from machine language into a form that can be understood by humans or other computers.

Owners' equity That share of the firm's assets contributed by the owners either through their initial investment or through retained earnings.

P

Panel A group of people who cooperate by answering the same questions on a continuing basis.

Partnership A business formed when two or more individuals associate.

Penetration pricing The price is set low in the range of prices so there will be less profit on each sale, but there should be more sales.

Periodic reordering system Inventory control system in which orders are placed in a regular time cycle.

Personal selling Face-to-face communication with a potential buyer.

Personnel management The process of building and maintaining a productive group of employees.

Picket line Striking members patrol the firm's entrances to discourage customers or other workers from dealing with the firm.

Pipeline inventories Inventories necessary to fill the production and distribution pipelines.

Place utility The item is available where it is useful.

Plan outputs Statements of objectives, policies, rules and procedures, and budgets.

Planning horizon The length of time into the future for which a plan is made.

Plant efficiency factor Capacity allowance given to recognize the effect of scheduling delays, machine breakdowns, maintenance, and other plant problems.

Possession utility The right to use the item to satisfy your needs.

Preferred stock Shares sold with a specific dividend rate.

Presentation The salesperson's attempt to deliver a message that will cause the prospect to buy.

Preventive maintenance A maintenance cycle that anticipates breakdowns, in order to prevent disruptions and downtime costs.

Price elasticity of demand Demand will increase for lower prices and decrease for higher prices. The effect is different for different products.

Price lining The seller sets up several standard prices, and each product is squeezed into the closest price line.

Primary data New data collected for the specific purpose of a certain research project.

Private accountants The persons who are employed by the firm to maintain the accounting systems.

Private corporation (closely held corporation) A corporation that issues shares that are not traded on a public exchange.

Product The total satisfaction derived from the purchase of goods and services.

Product layout (line layout) Machines and other equipment are arranged according to the sequence of operations required to fabricate and assemble the product.

Product life cycle   Explains the relationship between demand and profits over the market life of a type of product.

Production   The conversion of one set of resources into another set of resources that has greater value.

Production line   A production process that uses a product layout.

Production lot size   The quantity of a product that is produced at one time.

Production requirements   What is required of the productive system during each period, translated from the forecast that allows for production lead times.

Productivity   Output per hour of labor.

Profit   The reward for doing a good job in running a business; what is left over from sales revenue after paying for the inputs.

Profit margin on sales   Comparison of the actual sales revenue with the net income.

Profitability ratios   Measures of whether activities are profitable.

Program   A series of detailed instructions for a computer.

Prospecting   Identifying people who might have a need for a product or service.

Public accountants   Persons who are not employees of the firm but sell their accounting services to the firm.

Public corporation   A corporation that has no restrictions on the trading of its shares that are usually traded on one of the organized stock exchanges.

Purchase order (PO)   An order issued to a vendor.

Purchase requisition (PR)   A request to purchase an item issued to the purchasing department by another internal department.

Pure competition   A situation among competitors in which the following conditions prevail: (1) there are many small firms in the industry, (2) products in the industry are similar or identical, (3) it is easy to enter or leave the market, and (4) everyone knows what is available at which price.

Pure Food and Drug Act (1906)   The government's first effort to provide for the inspection of food and drug products in order to protect the public.

Q

Quick ratio (acid test)   Comparison of the firm's current assets other than inventory with its current liabilities.

R

Random variation   Haphazard variation for which there is no good explanation. It may be due only to chance.

Raw materials   Materials that are purchased in an unprocessed form and are processed for sale by the business.

Receiving report (RR)   A report issued by the receiving department verifying the items and the quantity received.

Recession   Periods involving declines in real GNP.

Reciprocity   Awarding orders to a supplier who is also your customer in order to retain that customer's business.

Recruiting   The process of attracting qualified applicants.

Reference group   A collection of people to whom you look to for guidance as to appropriate behavior.

Regression analysis   A causal forecasting method.

Resumé   A summary of education, experience, and other qualifications that has been prepared by the job seeker.

Resellers' brands   Identification of the firm that sells you the product rather than the firm that made the product.

Retailers   Firms that sell to ultimate consumers.

Retained earnings   Profits that are reinvested in the business.

Return on investment (ROI)   A measure of the rate at which the money invested in the firm is generating income.

Revenues   Inflows of cash and other items of value received for goods sold or services rendered; the receipts from the sale of goods and services.

Robinson-Patman Act (1936)   Act designed to protect the independent merchants, the public they serve, and the manufacturers from whom they buy, from exploitation by the chain competitor. It was passed after a FTC report on chain stores concluded that the growth of chain stores threatened the existence of small business.

Royalty   A payment of a portion of the proceeds in return for the right to do business.

S

Safety stocks   Inventories held to give off-the-shelf service to customers and to make sure that there are no stock shortages in the production process.

Savings and Loans   Specialized financial institutions that collect savings and make loans primarily for home mortgages.

Service   A helpful activity performed by some person or persons who are not regular employees of the firm.

Scientific management   The idea of systematically getting the most output from every person and machine on the factory floor to achieve the maximum prosperity for both the owners and the workers.

Scrap factor   Capacity allowance given to recognize that some bad parts will be produced.

Seasonal inventories   Inventories accumulated to meet seasonal sales requirements and to allow stable employment and reduce costs such as overtime, second shift premium, and costs of hiring and layoff.

Secondary data   Data that are on file from some previous study, were collected for some other purpose, or were collected by another organization.

Securities and Exchange Commission (SEC)   Federal agency that protects citizens from security fraud and swindling by assuring that investors get full and honest information on security offerings and by regulating the practices in the securities market.

Selective distribution   Distribution that makes goods available at a reasonable number of outlets.

Self-audit   The determination of the current status of all important aspects of the firm.

Service level   The percentage of demand that can be covered directly from inventory.

Sherman Act (1890)   Legislation aimed at controlling trusts. It labeled any "contract, combination in the form of trust or otherwise, or conspiracy in restraint of trade or commerce" to be illegal and outlawed unregulated monopolies. It was the federal government's first large-scale intervention in private business.

Shopping goods   Goods characterized by consumer willingness to make comparisons and to put some effort into finding the item that best meets needs.

Short-term financial decisions   Decisions that will affect the firm's sources or uses of funds for less than a year.

Skimming pricing   Strategy in which the price is set high in the range of possible prices.

Social class   A segment of a society made up of people with similar social and economic status.

Socialism   Government ownership and control of the major industries and resources.

Sociotechnical system   A term used to reflect the fact that the forces that determine a given job design are both human or social and technological.

Software   Supplies, programs, and instructions for computers.

Sole proprietorship   The simplest form of business organization formed when a single person goes into business.

Span of control   The number of subordinates under the direct control of a supervisor.

Specialization   A worker is limited to a single task or related set of tasks and is expected to become more skilled at that task than at other tasks.

Specialty goods   Goods for which consumers have very specific needs and are not willing to accept substitutes.

Specifications   Written descriptions of materials.

Staff personnel   Those who advise and assist line personnel.

Standard Industrial Classification (SIC)   A system developed by the federal government to organize the reporting of business information.

Standard Metropolitan Statistical Areas (SMSA)   An economically unified metropolitan area with a central city of at least 50,000 people.

Standardization   Agreement on sizes, designs, and quality aspects.

Statement of changes in financial position   A statement that shows the firm's sources and uses of funds over the accounting period.

Subcultures   Groups that accept the same basic social guidelines but take a slightly different approach within those guidelines.

Subsidiary   A unit of a corporation that is set up as a separate firm.

Supplies   Materials that do not become a part of

the finished product but are used up in normal business operations.

Supply curve   A schedule of amounts offered for sale at various prices.

Survey   Asking questions in a natural environment and counting the responses.

System   An interdependent set of components forming a unified whole and bound together by an objective.

T

Taft-Hartley Act (1947)   Legislation that prohibits unions from refusing to bargain with employers, using force or threats in organizing, and engaging in a number of other unfair practices.

Technological forecasting   The longest-term predictions that may depend on technological innovations.

Term loan   A loan for a specific amount of money with a specific due date.

Test market   A trial run on a new product or a change in the product, package, or advertisement.

Theory X leaders   Those who believe that workers dislike work, are lazy, want to avoid responsibility, and are interested only in job security.

Theory Y leaders   Those who believe that workers are interested in meaningful work, are willing to accept responsibility, and look for opportunities to show their abilities and ingenuity.

Time series forecasting models   Models that project historical data forward after processing it by some statistical analysis.

Time utility   The item is available when you need it.

Trade credit   A loan from the seller to the buyer.

Trusts   Firms that pool resources, which are then managed in the common interest of owners.

Tying contracts   The seller supplies the retailer with one product only if the retailer agrees to buy another product as well. The products are tied together.

Type I franchise system   The manufacturer of a product contracts with independent local businesses to distribute its products to the final customer.

Type II franchise system   The manufacturer grants franchises to wholesalers who in turn sell to other businesses.

Type III franchise system   The wholesaler contracts to sells goods to retailers who are independently owned and operated yet project the image of a chain.

Type IV franchise system   The real value of the franchise lies in the trademark, image, and method of operation.

U

Underwriting   The process of guaranteeing the initial sale of a company's securities at a fixed price.

Uniform Commercial Code   First drafted in 1952 and since adopted in all states except Louisiana, these regulations apply to business transactions and contracts.

Unsought goods   Goods that consumers do not seek because they do not choose to recognize a need for them or because the need is of an emergency nature.

Utility   The need-satisfying capacity of any physical thing, idea, or service.

V

Variable budget   A budget constructed to vary with the volume of activity.

Velocity of money   The rate at which money goes around and around through the economic system.

Vendor   A company that sells you something.

W

Want   Something you would like but can survive without.

Water Pollution Control Act (1972)   Federal legislation giving the government authority to control pollution in inland waterways.

Wholesalers   Firms that sell products to retailers.

Working capital   The pool of assets available to meet the firm's day-to-day financial needs.

Notes

Chapter 2

1. *Business Week,* January 15, 1979.

Chapter 3

1. *Fortune,* July 3, 1978, pp. 86–90.
2. Reported in *Advertising Age,* February 28, 1977, p. 24.
3. *Business Week,* December 12, 1977.
4. *Business Week,* February 6, 1978.

Chapter 4

1. Government Intervention," Business Week, April 4, 1977, p. 47.

Chapter 5

1. Adapted from E. Patrick McGuire, "Franchised Distribution," A Research Report from The Conference Board, 1971, p. 3.
2. "Franchising in the Economy: 1974–1976," USDC, 1976, p. 31.
3. "There's More to Fast Food than Big Mac and Chicken," *Fortune,* March 1977, p. 213.
4. "McDonald's Grinds out Growth," *Dun's Review,* December 1977, pp. 50–52.
5. Ibid., p. 51.
6. McGuire, "Franchised Distribution," p. 7.
7. Linda Snyder, "The Right Way to Invest in Franchise Companies," *Fortune,* April 24, 1978, pp. 89–90.
8. Thomas J. Murray, "Franchising Comes of Age," *Dun's Review,* August 1977, pp. 58–60.
9. "A Pledge from Washington to Help Small Business," *Nation's Business,* July 1977, p. 31.
10. "Fast Food Franchisers Squeeze out the Little Guy," *Business Week,* May 31, 1976, pp. 42–48.

11. "McDonald's Blends New Products with Savvy Merchandising," *Business Week,* July 11, 1977, pp. 56–60.
12. Judson Gooding, "HI: The Relentlessly Ordinary Secrets of a Great Innkeeping Success," *Across the Board,* January 1978, pp. 7–14.
13. "McDonald's Blends New Products," p. 58.
14. "McDonald's Grinds out Growth," p. 51.
15. Holiday Inn advertisement, *The Wall Street Journal,* February 13, 1978, pp. 16–17.
16. Gooding, "HI," p. 12.
17. "McDonald's Blends New Products," p. 59.
18. Gooding, "HI," p. 9.
19. Paul Ingrassia, "Whopper War: Burger King Begins Big Hamburger Fight against McDonald's," *The Wall Street Journal,* April 5, 1978, p. 1.
20. "McDonald's Blends New Products," p. 59.
21. Gooding, "HI," p. 11.
22. Murray, "Franchising Comes of Age," p. 58.
23. "Pizza Hut Builds on the Appetite for Ethnic Foods," *Business Week,* July 11, 1976, p. 48.
24. "Fast Food Franchisers Squeeze out the Little Guy," p. 48.
25. Ibid., p. 42.

Chapter 6

1. Glenn A. Welsch and Robert N. Anthony, *Fundamentals of Financial Accounting,* rev. ed. (Homewood, Ill.: Richard D. Irwin, Inc., 1977), p. 3.
2. Ronald Alsop, "Annual Reports Now Doing Double Duty for Many Concerns," *The Wall Street Journal,* March 16, 1978, p. 1+.
3. Ibid., p. 1.

Chapter 9

1. *The Coca-Cola Company: Portrait of a Worldwide Company* (Atlanta: The Coca-Cola Company, October 1971), p. 22.

2. U.S. Department of Commerce, Bureau of Census, *1970 Statistical Abstract of the United States,* 91st ed. Washington, D.C., 1970, p. 6.

3. Fabian Linden, "The Geography of Demand, 1975," *Conference Board Record,* August 1976, pp. 40–44.

4. Fabian Linden, "Economics of Cities and Suburbs," *Conference Board Record,* March 1976, pp. 42–45.

5. Fabian Linden, "Family Income—1985," *Conference Board Record,* May 1976, pp. 24–27.

6. U.S. Department of Commerce, Bureau of the Census, *1976 Statistical Abstract of the United States,* Washington, D.C., 1976, p. 492.

7. "How the Change Age Mix Changes Markets," Business Week, January 12, 1976, pp. 74–77.

8. U.S. Bureau of the Census, "Current Population Reports: Household and Family Characteristics," No. 311, August 1977, p. 20.

9. "Changes Age Mix Changes Markets," p. 74.

10. Ibid., p. 75.

Chapter 10

1. Jane Rockman, "Who Remembers Micrin? One Opinion: There Has Never Been a Successful Blue Mouthwash," *The Sacramento Bee,* January 15, 1978, p. B9.

2. "Landon Keeps Digest Poll Majority," *The Literary Digest,* October 24, 1936, pp. 9–10.

Chapter 11

1. "Hotter Competition in Video Recorders," *Business Week,* April 25, 1977, p. 36.

2. "How Levi's Created a Ring of Counterfeiters," *Business Week,* September 5, 1977, p. 27.

3. Eleanore Carruth, "K mart Has to Open Some New Doors on the Future," *Fortune,* July 1977, p. 154.

Chapter 12

1. "Investigating the Collapse of W. T. Grant," *Business Week,* July 19, 1976, pp. 60–62.

2. "Dividing Up What's Left of Grant's," *Business Week,* March 1, 1976, p. 21.

3. "Investigating the Collapse," p. 61.

4. Eleanore Carruth, "K mart Has to Open Some New Doors on the Future," *Fortune,* July 1977, pp. 144–54.

5. Eugene F. Brigham, *Financial Management: Theory and Practice:* (Hinsdale, Ill.: The Dryden Press, 1977), p. 386.

6. Carruth, "K mart Has to Open Some New Doors," p. 146.

7. "U.S. Steel's New Approach to Pollution," *Business Week,* November 29, 1976, p. 87.

Chapter 13

1. Adapted from Herbert Chruden, Personnel Management, 5th ed. (Cincinnati: Southwestern Publishing Co.), p. 136.

2. Ibid., p. 182.

3. Ibid.

4. "Labor Wins 14-Year Fight for Norris Injunction Bill," *Business Week,* March 16, 1932, p. 20.

5. "Rise of Union Power: Ability to Paralyze the Nation," *U.S. News & World Report,* May 24, 1946, pp. 13–14.

6. James C. Hyatt, "Firms Learn Art of Keeping Unions Out; Figures Indicate They're Passing the Course," The Wall Street Journal, April 19, 1977, p. 40.

7. "Why Lockheed's Strike is a 'Holy War'," *Business Week,* December 19, 1977, p. 31.

8. "Hard Line on 'Lifetime Security'," *Business Week,* October, 1977, pp. 33–34.

Chapter 14

1. "Keeping Informed: Updates on Management," *Management Review,* January 1978, p. 4.

2. Douglas McGregor, *The Human Side of Enterprise* (New York: McGraw-Hill, 1960), pp. 33–34 and 47–48.

3. Rensis Likert, New Patterns of Management (New York: McGraw-Hill, 1961).

Chapter 15

1. Forest Woody Horton, "Reducing the Federal Paperwork Burden," *Datamation,* April 1978, pp. 139–44.

2. "Computer Circuitry Advance Announced by Scientists at IBM," *The Wall Street Journal,* May 10, 1978, p. 40.

3. Herbert Scott, *Census, USA: Fact Finding for the American People, 1790–1970* (New York: Seaburt Press, 1968), p. 57.

4. Donald D. Spencer, Computers in Action: How Computers Work (Rochelle Park, N.J.: Hayden Book Company, Inc., 1974), p. 22.

Chapter 16

1. *Business Week,* February 6, 1978; and *The Wall Street Journal,* April 5, 1978.

2. *The Wall Street Journal,* February 10, 1978.

Chapter 19

1. "McDonald Douglas' Cool Cautious Strategy," *Forbes,* May 29, 1978, pp. 27–28.

2. Earl W. Kintner, *A Robinson Patman Primer: A Businessman's Guide to the Law against Price Discrimination* (New York: McMillan, 1970), p. 128.

Case 19–1—Lawrence Minard, "This Cream Puff Is Certified Fresh by Uncle Sam," *Forbes,* December 11, 1978, pp. 38–39.

Chapter 20

Case 20–1—Steven Solomon, "Spare Parts for Humans," *Forbes,* May 29, 1978, pp. 52–54.

Case 20–2—"The Future That Never Came," *Forbes,* July 10, 1978, pp. 51–52.

Cover art

Robert Heindel, courtesy of Dow Jones, Inc.

Chapter opening illustrations

John Thoeming

Text design

Petey Erickson

APPENDIX
Planning your business career

The average American adult spends 10,000 days on the job. We work for a variety of reasons, not the least of which is to bring home a paycheck to pay the bills. But some people find their work very satisfying, while others merely endure it. In fact, too many people find that their work does not add to their happiness. Most people would not choose the same work if they could do it over again, yet they feel trapped in their jobs and unable to switch to something better. A better job does not mean simply work that is better paid. There are many dimensions of work. This appendix is provided in hopes that you will make a serious effort to evaluate career opportunities in relation to your own skills, preferences, and talents in order to find the position that is best suited to you and that will bring you the greatest level of satisfaction, in addition to paying the bills.

A career versus a job

The terms *career* and *job* are often used interchangeably, but there is a distinct difference. A job is a piece of work that is completed for a fixed price. It implies that the relationship is temporary and at a fixed level. A career, on the other hand, is a course of action throughout life. It implies a longer-term relationship that builds over time. One person may have worked at a summer job such as serving tables, pumping gas, or washing cars only to make money and with little intention of carrying on in that line of work. Another person may have worked behind the counter at a fast-food restaurant in order to gain the experience to go on and manage such a restaurant and then perhaps become the owner of a franchise. The first person had a *job*, whereas the second person was starting out on a *career*.

545

Job characteristics

There are thousands of different career possibilities in business. The challenge is to find the career best suited to your interests, talents, skills, and values. The good news is that 98 percent of all graduates who want jobs will be able to find them. The bad news is that one out of every four graduates will not get the kind of job he or she wants. Let's look at some of the characteristics by which a job might be measured. Some of the more important ones are earning potential, level of security, rate of advancement, level of supervision, degree of interaction, and prestige.

Earnings. Earnings are the most quantifiable measure of a job, and therefore they tend to get a lot of attention. But earnings can be quite complex. Refer to the special box on fringe benefits in Chapter 13. Are you better off to earn fewer dollars yet have better insurance protection? In Chapter 13 there is also a table of the costs of living in 12 U.S. cities (Table 13–1). Are you better off to earn $10,000 a year in Atlanta or $15,000 a year in New York? Are you better off to start in a higher-paid position with smaller yearly raises or a lower-paid position with the promise of a higher income many years later? Our point is that in evaluating earnings, you cannot consider simply the expected first year's take-home pay. Other factors to consider are base salary or hourly rate, local cost of living, fringe benefits package, and future income and potential.

Level of security. A few years ago there was a song "Do You Know the Way to San Jose," which told the sad story of a young person who had traveled to Los Angeles to become a "star" only to wind up "parking cars and pumping gas." While some stars make it big, a lot of hopefuls would have been much better off pursuing less glamorous but more predictable careers. Job security refers to the extent to which you can count on your income to continue at some stable level. Long-term contracts negotiated for unionized workers offer some security. Positions in larger firms or in government service are often thought to offer security. Self-employment or small businesses generally offer less security.

Rate of advancement. The level of security is often inversely related to the rate of advancement. Rock singers have little security, but if they are lucky they may skyrocket to stardom. It can take years and years to climb step by step through the bureaucracy of the government or the hierarchy of a major firm. On the other hand, if you start your own business, you can appoint yourself president. Of course, you can also lose your shirt. Another factor that determines the rate of advancement is the rate of growth of the industry. When an industry is expanding, it is much easier for an employee to move into a supervisory or managerial slot.

Level of supervision. Some workers are subject to constant supervision and guidance. There is always someone to tell them what to do and whether they have done it well. Some examples of such workers are production line workers, retail clerks, and office personnel. Other people are left to work on their own with a minimum of direct supervision. They may have certain jobs to complete and may file reports on those jobs, but they complete the work unsupervised. The person who services appliances for your local department store's customers, the outside salesperson, and truck drivers perform without direct supervision.

Degree of interaction. Employees who are directly supervised also tend to work in stable work groups and to develop a sense of belonging. They see the same people everyday and may develop a feeling of being a part of that group. Outside workers such as salespeople may see many people regularly but lack the continuing group interaction. Some other workers such as park rangers in fire towers may spend days without seeing other people.

Prestige. Different positions carry different levels of prestige in the community. The prestige need not be directly related to the earnings potential of the position. In San Francisco, bus drivers earn more than teachers, but teaching is generally considered to have more prestige. Many entertainers earn more than judges, but judges may have more prestige. Prestige is a measure of the regard that the community in general holds for a position.

You may be thinking of getting a job, but you may ask yourself whether that job represents a step in your career or just a job. Each job can be measured according to these characteristics. There are no good or bad scores, just scores that do or do not match your interests, talents, skills, and values. Let's look more closely at how people are rewarded for their work.

WHY

People expect to be rewarded for their work. These rewards come in many forms. The most obvious is the paycheck. The average college graduate can expect lifetime earnings of about $750,000, or about $4 for every $3 earned by the average high school graduate. There are also personal benefits to be derived.

Compensation systems

There are several methods of compensation which were discussed in detail in Chapter 13. In general, though, you might be paid a salary—a fixed amount over a certain time period, a wage—a fixed amount per hour, or either a piecerate or a commission—an amount per unit of output. Each has advantages. A salary is a guaranteed amount provided you perform normally. If you perform above average, you will have to wait for a salary increase. A wage means that you will be paid more if you work more. But if your hours are cut for any reason, you will earn less. Construction workers are not paid if rain makes it impossible to work. Piecerates or commissions mean that you can give yourself a raise by working harder. They also mean that any slow-down in your output will be penalized by a cut in pay.

Personal benefits

There are some rewards that cannot be measured in dollars. Your work will be a big part of your life. Most adults spend almost half of their waking hours on the job. Wouldn't it be nice if you enjoyed it? One professor claims that he enjoys his work so much that he feels that he should wear a mask everytime he stops in the office to pick up his paycheck.

Some of the personal benefits that fortunate people derive from their work are a feeling of contributing to the welfare of others, feelings of personal growth and accomplishment, friendships with co-workers, opportunities for self-expression, and pride.

WHO

There is an old saying that one man's meat is another man's poison. It can mean that a position that one person finds stimulating and fulfilling may seem offensive to another person. Think of the characteristics we discussed in the first section of this appendix. Some people enjoy the sense of adventure that comes from a lack of security, whereas others would have ulcers within weeks. Some people are comforted by supervision, while others feel constrained. What do you like?

Matching the person to the job

A few people are lucky enough to fall into a position that is everything they ever wanted. For most of us, however, finding the right position takes a little work. You must take the responsibility to match yourself to the right job. Who else has as much to gain from your personal success as you do? Who else cares as much as you do? Later we will mention some of the people to whom you can turn for help, but remember, in the end it is your responsibility. You must evaluate your personal preferences, interests, talents, skills, and values. You must decide whether you want to relocate or live where you do now for the foreseeable future. You must decide whether you want to climb the corporate ladder or become part of a small business enterprise.

Special talents and skills

One important step is a self-audit. As you begin to plan for your career, you should make a conscientious effort to explore your interests, talents, skills, and values. It may help to sit down with a pencil and paper and make a list of the talents and skills you have to offer. Why should an employer hire you? You also need to consider your own interests and values. There is no "best job" but there is a job that is best for a particular person. Here are some things to consider.

1. What projects, awards, hobbies, and other activities have you pursued during the past three to five years?
2. What work experience have you had?
3. What extracurricular activities have interested you?
4. Can you rearrange the above activities in order of preference? What skills were required for each? Do you seem to prefer one type of environment to another?

The idea is to look for patterns. Are you always happy when you are working with numbers? Do you like to work alone or with other people, inside or outside, on a regular schedule or in spurts, with machinery or paper? This is no time to be shy.

WHEN

You may be a bit skeptical at this point. After all, you may already have a job or it may be a little while until you graduate. You may be asking whether it is worthwhile for you to begin to prepare to find the right job. There are two answers to that question. Sometimes people get locked in too early. As a child you might have confessed to an interest in some position such as a nurse, fire fighter, engineer, or police officer, and your family may expect to hold you to that ideal. Perhaps you have been encouraged to follow in the footsteps of one of your parents or another relative. Maybe you are being guided toward a career that someone in your family always wanted but could not have.

On the other hand, many students reach graduation day with no idea of where to go. Have they failed to take advantage of the many opportunities to make important steps toward their preferred careers? According to one placement director, "The difference between being able to get a job and not being able to get a job after graduation in 99 percent of the cases boils down to one thing—planning."

Steps in career preparation

Between 1980 and 1985 almost 6 million college graduates will enter the labor force. Even if you are not yet ready to step into your first serious position, you can be taking some steps to make yourself more employable. There are some things that all employers value. Among those are a spirit of cooperation, a sense of duty and responsibility, and a willingness to put in a little extra when needed. You can be building a record to show future employers that you are a good bet. You might even get involved in a student organization, assist a volunteer project in the community such as the Muscular Dystrophy Telethon, or show these qualities through your performance on your current job.

If you already have some idea of the type of work you would enjoy, you can be gaining some valuable experience while you finish your education. For example, if you have decided that you would be well suited for sales, a part-time job in some type of sales would be a valuable asset. Another possibility is an internship or co-op program through your college.

Every year more than 200,000 students gain direct work experience through co-op programs. Business and government agencies cooperate with more than 1,000 colleges in providing paid work experiences compatible with the students' program of study. Students alternate between full-time work and full-time studies. In an internship program, students work part-time while attending classes. Some of these positions turn into full-time jobs upon graduation. If this interests you, check to see whether these programs are available through your school.

Timing your career search

The biggest barrier to finding a satisfying position is a lack of information. You should begin to watch for information on job opportunities and job characteristics now so that you will be ready to seek out the position that is right for you. You might be surprised to find out how long it can take to find the right job. You might be able to find just any job in a week or two, but to find the job that is right for you can take months. Often people start too late and then in desperation they finally take a job that is just satisfactory. They end up spending their lives in that mediocre position.

You should begin your search for information about different jobs at least a year before you will be ready to begin work. You should begin to prepare your resumé several months before so that you will have time to think it over and seek the advice of the counselors in the campus career center. They will have the time to work with you if you go to them early enough.

You should begin to interview one to three months before you are ready to take a job. It can take a long time to process paperwork and to get listed on the payroll. There are a lot of things you can do to improve your chances of getting the job you want.

WITH

One thing you can do is to take advantage of the people and tools that are available to help you find the best job for you. These resources are often overlooked, but remember, they exist to be of assistance to people like you. You have nothing to lose but a few hours of time.

People who can help

As a college student, one of your first stops should be the campus career center. There you will find specialists in career planning. Stop in to see them early enough so that they can help you. One career center director reports that each year about a third of the graduating class wakes up less than a month before graduation and begins to look for jobs.

These specialists might ask you to do a few things on your own behalf, but don't give up. Fill in the forms or sign up for the precounseling sessions. Remember, you are the one who has the most to gain! The counselors will listen to you, may offer you some direct advice, and will probably be able to point you toward some sources of information. Some other sources you might find useful are listed at the end of this appendix.

Tools that can help

Your counseling center may have a group of interest and aptitude tests that can help you to discover more about yourself and clarify your aptitudes and interests. Many counseling centers conduct special classes on interviewing or on special career opportunities. These courses take some time and offer no credit but may well turn out to be an important investment in your future.

HOW

Once you have gathered some information on yourself and the job market, how do you put it into action? How do you get started? What does the actual interviewing process involve? There is still some preparation for you to do to get ready. Remember, you only have one chance to make a good first impression.

Precontact preparation

Before you step into an interview, you have two important responsibilities. The first is to prepare the resumé that will introduce you to the employer. The second is to find out something about the employer. According to one employment expert, your resumé probably has ten seconds to make an initial impression on an employer. It must communicate positive skills and results (see Figure A–1). Here are some tips:

1. Don't start writing until you have compiled a list of your skills, accomplishments, and experiences. Then pick and choose the most relevant aspects for the job target.
2. Present your accomplishments in terms of the employers' needs, not just by title.
3. Eliminate unnecessary information such as height, weight, race, desired salary, marital status, number of children, and place of birth.
4. Limit your resumé to one page in length.
5. Use action words such as *created, organized,* and *managed,* but don't be either cute or stuffy.
6. Strive for a professional appearance. Have your resume typed with no errors on an electric typewriter with carbon ribbon and have it printed on good-quality white or cream paper. Mimeographs are not acceptable!

Most resumés include references. You should try to name people whose opinions will be respected by the employer and who will present you in a positive way. It is also a good idea to supply a mixture of references. You might use an instructor, a former employer, and a family friend. To improve your chances, be sure that you ask each of your references for permission and that you supply each one with your resumé and some information on the type of position you are seeking. Many students use at least one of their instructors as a reference. Just think of how many references an instructor is expected to write each year! During a year you may have to remember the names of only three to five instructors, while the instructor is trying to keep track of several hundred students.

If you are interviewing on campus, the career center probably has some information on the company on file, but you have to ask for it. You can also check on the company through some guides such as *Standard & Poor's* or *Moody's,* which can be found in most libraries. Ask the librarian to help you. If it is a local firm, you might check with the chamber of commerce or look for articles in back issues of the local paper. In addition to finding out about the company, try to find out something about the industry. Look in the *Reader's Guide to Business Periodicals* or *The Wall Street Journal Index* for articles on the industry. You will have a head start on the other job applicants if you know enough about the company and the industry to ask a few thoughtful questions. It shows that you care whether or not you get the job.

FIGURE A–1
Representative resumé

Home address	Your name	Office address
Home phone		Office phone

Job objective

A position of *(name of position)* within the *(name of department)* that will lead to *(brief description of your future goals)*.

Educational background

(Name of degree)—(date of degree)—(name of issuing institution). Majored in *(name of major field)* with a minor field of study in *(minor field)*.

Studies at the university included courses in *(relevant course), (relevant course)*, and *(relevant course)*. Plan to attend *(name of school)* graduate school during the evening session of September 19XX.

Business experience

19XX to present—*(name of current position)—(name of company)*. Job duties include sole responsibility for the *(type of work you do)* function. Spent six months developing a *(any special projects or accomplishments)* program for the company.

19XX to 19XX—*(name of position)—(name of company)*. Job duties included the *(type of work)* as well as direct supervision of *(number)* people. Resigned to complete college full time during the day session.

Military service

19XX to 19XX—*(final rank attained)—(branch of service)*. Attended *(type of training)* school for one year in the service. Learned techniques relating to *(mention civilian job counterpart of what you learned)*. Service encompassed a one-year tour of duty in Europe. Honorable discharge.

Honors and activities

(Mention major awards, prizes, interests, and activities.)
(Mention organizations that you are affiliated with if relevant to business activity.)
(Mention any specific abilities you have that may relate to job duties.)

Personal data

(health status)—(date of birth)—(willingness to relocate and travel)—(any other personal data that may be applicable to this job., i.e., driver's license, foreign languages spoken, etc.).

References

Suitable business and personal references will be submitted upon request.

Source: Adapted from Michael J. Freeman, *Writing Résumés, Locating Jobs, and Handling Job Interviews* (Homewood, Ill.: Learning Systems Company, 1976), p. 9.

Interviewing

Before you go in for an interview, ask yourself why people are hired. Are they hired because they need a job? No, they are hired because someone feels that the firm will be better off with them than without them. Your job is to convince the recruiter that you will be good for the firm. This means that you are both willing and able to do the job well. The recruiter will probably interview five people on the day of your interview. You have to make sure that you stand out as the best person for the job. This means that you must ask yourself: Why would I hire me? Then you have to make sure that you give your answer to the interviewer. Interviewers ask standard questions. You can answer with a few words or a simple yes or no, but then you won't stand out. If you take each question as an opportunity to divulge some important information about your abilities, you will be better off.

One way to get a feel for interviewing is to watch television talk shows. Some guests answer vaguely, mumble, or give the shortest possible response. Others get involved in the interaction with the host and seem natural and relaxed as they deliver their messages. Each guest is there for a purpose such as plugging a book or movie or alerting the public to some cause. The good guests manage to get their messages across without making the host work too hard. You have the same task—to deliver the message that you are the best possible person for the job without making the interviewer work too hard.

The more prepared you are, the easier it will be. Do you think that the president stands up before the White House Press Corps for a news conference without thinking about the questions that might be asked? No, he has his best answers prepared and is just waiting for the opportunity to use them. You can do the same thing. Here are a few of the interviewers' favorite questions. Prepare your own answers for them, but remember to do it from the point of view of the interviewer.

1. Why do you want this job?
2. Why do you think you are qualified for this job?
3. What are your major weaknesses?
4. Where do you plan to be five years from now?
5. Are you willing to relocate?
6. What was the most important thing you learned in college?
7. What is the best book you ever read? Why?
8. What person has been the most influential in your life? How?

Not easy, are they? Remember, interviewers are looking for evidence that you are mature, industrious, honest, conscientious, able to work well with others, and all of those other good things. They want to be sure that they won't be sorry if they hire you. That means that your answers, your appearance, and your behavior should all work together to make the recruiter comfortable with the idea that you are the best person for the job. Your objective is to get either a job offer or an invitation to a follow-up interview, but don't expect either on the spot. The interviewer probably will promise to be in touch.

There are many other practical hints on interviewing that you can get from your professors, counselors at the career center, or some of the career books listed at the end of this appendix.

Postinterview follow-up

Once the interview is over, some people go home and sit on their hands. That's not the way to get the job. First of all, a thank-you letter is in order (see Figure A–2). After all, the interviewer took the time to meet you. Second, the interviewer may have asked you for some additional information, so be sure to supply it promptly.

FIGURE A–2
Postinterview letter

Elaine Bari
24 Westgate Rd.
Teaneck, N.J. 07663

Mr. Adam Judes
Leachim Electronics Corporation
16–32 Park Avenue
New York, N.Y. 10007

Dear Mr. Judes:

I am writing to thank you for the time and courtesy you afforded me during my recent job interview with Leachim Electronics Corporation.

Since the interview I have read the literature you gave me and have thought about the prospects of working with your company. I am still very interested in a position and hope to hear from you soon.

Thank you again for your time and effort.

Sincerely,
Elaine Bari

Source: Michael J. Freeman, *Writing Résumés, Locating Jobs, and Handling Job Interviews* (Homewood, Ill.: Learning Systems Company, 1976), p. 68.

WITHIN

Seriously consider the environment within which you will be seeking a position. First of all, there are more people than jobs. Second, there are thousands of different kinds of positions from which to choose.

Third, economic, social, and technological changes cause shifts in the numbers of jobs in various fields. In the early 1960s we couldn't train engineers fast enough, but in the late 1960s some of these engineers ended up driving cabs. The same kinds of problems have occurred with teachers and in other fields. You need to keep an eye on the future as well.

Sources of information

Table A–1 lists some sources of information. Remember, you have the most to gain if you are able to find the right job. It's not easy, but it is worth it. You might try to get together with some of your classmates and share the job of writing for the information.

TABLE A–1
Information sources

Organizations that provide helpful career literature

American Institute of Certified Public Accountants
1211 Avenue of the Americas, New York, N.Y. 10036

National Association of Accountants
919 Third Avenue, New York, N.Y. 10022

American Advertising Federation
Bureau of Research
1225 Connecticut Avenue, N.W., Washington, D.C. 20036

American Association of Advertising Agencies
200 Park Avenue, New York, N.Y. 10017

American Bankers Association
1120 Connecticut Avenue, N.W., Washington, D.C. 20036

National Consumer Finance Association, Education Services Division
1000 16th Street, N.W., Washington, D.C. 20036

American Federation of Information Processing Societies
210 Summit Avenue, Montvale, N.J. 07645

Association for Systems Management
24587 Bagley Road, Cleveland, Ohio 44138

Data Processing Management Association
505 Busse Highway, Park Ridge, Ill. 60068

American Society for Public Administration
1225 Connecticut Avenue, N.W., Washington, D.C. 20036

Institute of Life Insurance
277 Park Avenue, New York, N.Y. 10017

Financial Executives Institute
633 Third Avenue, New York, N.Y. 10017

Administrative Management Society, Publications Department
World Headquarters
Willow Grove, Pa. 19090

American Society for Personnel Administration
19 Church Street, Berea, Ohio 44017

Public Relations Society of America
845 Third Avenue, New York, N.Y. 10022

National Association of Purchasing Managements
11 Park Place, New York, N.Y. 10007

National Secretaries Association
2440 Pershing Road, Suite G-10, Kansas City, Mo. 64108

Sources of information on careers in manufacturing

American Institute of Industrial Engineers
25 Technology Park/Atlanta
Norcross, Ga 30092

American Management Association
Career Information Services
135 West 50th Street, New York, N.Y. 10020

National Career Information Center
American Personnel and Guidance Association
1607 New Hampshire Avenue, N.W., Washington, D.C. 20007

American Petroleum Institute
2101 L Street, N.W., Washington, D.C. 20037

American Iron and Steel Institute
1000 16th Street, N.W., Washington, D.C. 20036

American Society of Mechanical Engineers
345 East 47th Street, New York, N.Y. 10017

American Society for Engineering Education
Suite 400, 1 Dupont Circle, Washington, D.C. 20036

National Association of Wholesaler-Distributors
1725 K Street, N.W., Washington, D.C. 20006

American Institute of Baking
400 East Ontario Street, Chicago, Ill. 60611

American Paper Institute
260 Madison Avenue, New York, N.Y. 10016

National Society of Professional Engineers
2029 K Street, N.W., Washington, D.C. 20006

Manufacturing Chemists Association
1825 Connecticut Avenue, N.W., Washington, D.C. 20009

American Chemical Society
1155 16th Street, N.W., Washington, D.C. 20036

American Society for Testing and Materials
1916 Race Street, Philadelphia, Pa. 19103

Society of Manufacturing Engineers
20501 Ford Road, Dearborn, Mich. 48128

TABLE A–1 *(continued)*

Aerospace Industries Association of America
1725 De Sales Street, N.W., Washington, D.C. 20036

National Aerospace Education Association
Middle Tennessee State University, Box 59, Murfreesboro, Tenn. 37132

Forging Industry Association
1121 Illuminating Building, Cleveland, Ohio 44113

Graphic Arts Technical Foundation
4615 Forbes Avenue, Pittsburgh, Pa. 15213

Society of the Plastics Industry
355 Lexington Avenue, New York, N.Y. 10017

Manufacturers' Agents National Association
Suite 509, 3130 Wilshire Blvd., Los Angeles, Calif. 90010

National Association of Manufacturers
1776 F Street, N.W., Washington, D.C. 20006

Institute of Food Technologists
221 North LaSalle Street, Chicago, Ill. 60601

Source: New York Life Insurance Company booklet.

Sources of information on careers in media and communications

National Association of Trade and Technical Schools
2021 L Street, N.W., Washington, D.C. 20036

Printing Industries of America, Inc.
1730 North Lynn Street, Arlington, Va. 22209

National Association of Printers and Lithographers, Inc.
570 Seventh Avenue, New York, N.Y. 10018

American Newspapers Publishers Association
11600 Sunrise Valley Drive, Reston, Va. 22091

Education Council of the Graphic Arts Industry
4615 Forbes Avenue, Pittsburgh, Pa. 15213

National Art Education Association
National Education Association
1916 Association Drive, Reston, Va. 22091

Photographic Art and Science Foundation
111 Stratford, Des Plaines, Ill. 60016

National Association of Broadcasters
1771 N Street, N.W., Washington, D.C. 20036

Corporation for Public Broadcasting
1111 16th Street, N.W., Washington, D.C. 20036

Federal Communications Commission
1919 M Street, N.W., Washington, D.C. 20554

Also see *Lovejoy's Career and Vocational School Guide.*

Additional sources of helpful career information

American Institute of Architects
1735 New York Avenue, N.W., Washington, D.C. 20006

American Society of Civil Engineers
345 East 47th Street, New York, N.Y. 10017

American Society of Heating, Refrigerating and
   Air-Conditioning Engineers
345 East 47th Street, New York, N.Y. 10017

American Society of Sanitary Engineering
   960 Illuminating Building, Cleveland, Ohio 44113

Associated General Contractors of America
1957 E Street, N.W., Washington, D.C. 20006

National Association of Home Builders of the U.S.
15th & M Streets, N.W., Washington, D.C. 20005

National Society of Professional Engineers
2029 K Street, N.W., Washington, D.C. 20006

Society of American Registered Architects
Suite 1710, 180 North Michigan Ave., Chicago, Ill. 60601

Superintendent of Documents
U.S. Government Printing Office, Washington, D.C. 20402

U.S. Department of Labor
3rd Street & Constitution Ave., N.W., Washington, D.C. 20210

AFL-CIO National Headquarters
815 16th Street, N.W., Washington, D.C. 20006

National Association of Women in Construction
2800 West Lancaster Avenue, Fort Worth, Texas 76107

Sources of information on careers in transportation

American Trucking Associations, Inc.
1616 P Street, N.W., Washington, D.C. 20036

Association of American Railroads
1920 L Street, N.W., Washington, D.C. 20036

National Maritime Union of America
36 Seventh Avenue, New York, N.Y. 10011

International Organization of Masters, Mates and Pilots
39 Broadway, New York, N.Y. 10006

Personnel Operations Division
Federal Aviation Administration
800 Independence Avenue, S.W., Washington, D.C. 20591

The American Trucking Associations, Inc., publishes a *Directory of Transportation Education in U.S. Colleges and Universities,* which lists transportation programs ranging from a single course to entire departments at more than 600 colleges, universities, and junior colleges. Available free from address above.

Also, automobile companies, airlines, railroads, bus companies, and local transit companies publish career and educational material. Inquire at your local dealer or ticket office.

Sources of information on careers in recreation

To begin looking into job opportunities and study offerings in the fields of recreation, you can write to the following for brochures and booklets if your guidance counselor doesn't already have them:

National Recreation Park Association
1601 North Kent Street, Arlington, Va. 22209

National Therapeutic Recreation Society
1601 North Kent Street, Arlington, Va. 22209

National Industrial Recreation Association
20 North Wacker Drive, Chicago, Ill. 60606

No matter what aspect of hospitality or recreation career interests you most, you will need a good knowledge of the basic subjects taught in your school. Your academic work, whatever your level of education, will be the foundation upon which your career is built. The better prepared you are in basic subjects like English and math, the more likely it is that you will advance quickly in your job.

In Canada, see your local Canada Employment Centre. The address and phone number are listed in the telephone directory. Career literature also is available from Information Canada, Ottawa, Ontario K1A 0S9. Specific questions on careers may be directed to: Director, Occupational and Career Analysis and Development Branch, Employment and Immigration Commission, 305 Rideau Street, Ottawa, Ontario K1A 0J9.

Sources of information about careers in the natural resources

American Fisheries Society
5410 Grosvenur Lane, Bethesda, Md. 20014

American Forest Institute
1619 Massachusetts Ave., N.W., Washington, D.C. 20036

American Geological Institute
5205 Leesburg Pike, Falls Church, Va. 22041

American Institute of Biological Sciences
1401 Wilson Boulevard, Arlington, Va. 22209

American Institute of Planners
1776 Massachusetts Ave., N.W., Washington, D.C. 20036

American Meteorological Society
45 Beacon Street, Boston, Mass. 02108

American Ornithologists' Union
National Museum of Natural History
Smithsonian Institution, Washington, D.C. 20560

American Society of Agronomy
677 South Segoe Road, Madison, Wis. 53711

American Society of Landscape Architects
1750 Old Meadow Road, McLean, Va. 22101

American Society of Range Management
2120 South Birch Street, Denver, Colo. 80222

Marine Technology Society
1730 M Street, N.W., Washington, D.C. 20036

National Environmental Health Association
1600 Pennsylvania,
Denver, Colo. 80203

National Recreation and Park Association
1601 N. Kent St., Arlington, Va. 22209

National Sanitation Foundation
Attn: Educational Division
NSF Building, 3475 Plymouth Rd., Ann Arbor, Mich. 48106

National Wildlife Federation
1412 16th St., N.W., Washington, D.C. 20036

The Nature Conservancy
1800 North Kent Street, Arlington, Va. 22209

Society of American Foresters
5400 Grosvenur Lane, Washington, D.C. 20014

Soil Conservation Society of America
7515 N.E. Ankeny Road, Ankeny, Iowa 50021

U.S. Environmental Protection Agency
401 M Street, S.W., Washington, D.C. 20460

Water Pollution Control Federaion
2626 Pennsylvania Avenue, Washington, D.C. 20037

Where to learn more about the arts

The groups listed below are only a few of the many sources of information about arts careers. They may be a helpful starting point.

Actors' Equity Association
165 West 46th Street, New York, N.Y. 10036

American Association for Health, Physical Education, and Recreation
  Dance Division
1201 Sixteenth Street, N.W., Washington, D.C. 20036

TABLE A–1 *(continued)*

American Council on Education for Journalism
School of Journalism
University of Missouri, Columbia, Mo. 65201

American Crafts Council
44 West 53rd Street, New York, N.Y. 10019

American Federation of Arts
41 East 65th Street, New York, N.Y. 10021

American Federation of Television and Radio Artists
1350 Avenue of the Americas, New York, N.Y. 10019

American Institute of Graphic Arts
1059 Third Avenue, New York, N.Y. 10021

Associated Councils of the Arts
1564 Broadway, New York, N.Y. 10036

Council of American Artists Societies
112 East 19th Street, New York, N.Y. 10003

John F. Kennedy Center for the Performing Arts
2700 F Street, N.W., Washington, D.C. 20037

Magazine Publishers Association
575 Lexington Avenue, New York, N.Y. 10022

National Academy of Design
1083 Fifth Avenue, New York, N.Y. 10028

National Art Education Association
1916 Association Drive, Reston, Va. 22091

National Association of Broadcasters
1771 N Street, N.W., Washington, D.C. 20036

The Newspaper Fund
P. O. Box 300, Princeton, N.J. 08540

Public Relations Society of America
845 Third Avenue, New York, N.Y. 10022

Screen Actors Guild
7750 Sunset Boulevard, Hollywood, Calif. 90046

Television Information Office
845 Fifth Avenue, New York, N.Y. 10022

Writers Guild of America
1212 Avenue of the Americas, New York, N.Y. 10036

General information

U.S. Department of Labor, Bureau of Labor Statistics, Washington, D.C. 20212 publishes the *Occupational Outlook Handbook,* a listing and description of more than 800 jobs and careers, pay, working conditions, and education or training needed. $6.25, or at your library.

The same agency publishes free of charge the following leaflets:

Jobs for Which a High School Education Is Generally Required
Jobs for Which Junior College, Technical Institute, or Other Specialized
   Training Is Usually Required
Jobs for Which Apprenticeships Are Available
Jobs for Which a High School Education is Preferred but Not Essential

The publications listed in Table A–2 can be helpful. They may be available at your career center.

Occupational Outlook Handbook (yearly editions), Superintendent of Documents, U.S. Government Printing Office, Washington, D.C. 20402, $8. Lists up-to-date information on job duties, employment outlook, educational requirements, and earnings for 300 occupations and 35 industry.

Occupational Outlook for College Graduates (yearly editions), same source as above, $4.50. Lists same information for 100 occupations that require some college credits.

College Placement Annual, College Placement Council, Inc., P.O. Box 2263, Bethlehem, Pa. 18001, $5. Lists career opening information on approximately 1,000 employers

The books listed in Table A–3 provide valuable information on various types of careers or on the job search and career planning processes. You may be able to find some of these in the library or career center.

TABLE A–3
Career information bibliography

Richard Nelson Bolles. *What Color Is Your Parachute?* Berkeley: Ten Speed Press, 1977. ($4.95)

David Campbell. *If You Don't Know Where You're Going, You'll Probably End Up Elsewhere.* Niles, Ill.: Angus Communications, 1974. ($1.95)

James E. Hawkins. *The Uncle Sam Connection: An Insider's Guide to Federal Employment.* Chicago: Follet Publishing Co., 1978. ($4.95)

Tom Jackson. *Guerrilla Tactics in the Job Market.* New York: Bantam Books, 1978. ($2.50)

Richard Lathrop. *Career Analysis Guidelines.* Berkeley: Ten Speed Press, 1977. ($5.95)

Kathy Matthews. *On Your Own: 99 Alternatives to a 9-to-5 Job.* New York: Vintage Books, 1977. ($3.95)

Guy Moore. *The Career Game.* New York: National Institute of Career Planning, 1976. ($10.00; Ballantine paperback, $5.95)

Barbara A. Pletcher. *Saleswoman: A Guide to Career Success.* Homewood, Ill.: Dow Jones-Irwin, 1978. ($9.95; Pocket Books paperback, $2.75)

John Shingleton and Robert Bao. *College to Career.* New York: McGraw-Hill, 1977. ($5.95)

Studs Terkel. *Working.* New York: Avon Books, 1975. ($2.50)

The changing employment picture

We have purposely avoided listing specific jobs, since that information is available in a more up-to-date form in some of the sources we have suggested. But you should keep in mind that the picture is always changing. In addition to that, you will continue to change. Most people make at least three different career shifts during their working life. We hope that you will use your skills and talents in a productive manner.

26 HOT JOBS

According to labor forecasters, these are the jobs with the best employment prospects for college graduates in the late 1970s and early 1980s:

Accountant
Chemical engineer
Chemist/food scientist
Computer programmer
Dentist
Dietician
Electrical engineer
Geologist
Health services administrator
Industrial engineer
Insurance actuary
Landscape architect
Manager trainee
Occupational therapist
Osteopathic physician
Personnel executive
Petroleum engineer
Pharmacist
Physical therapist
Public relations executive
Registered nurse
Social worker
Statistician
Urban planner
Veterinarian

INDEX

* Bold face type indicates page on which definition of the entry can be found.

This book has been set VideoComp in 10 and 9 point Vermilion, leaded 2 points. Part numbers are set in 48 point Vermilion Bold, part titles and subtitles in 36 and 24 point Vermilion Bold. Chapter numbers and titles are set in 24 point Vermilion Bold. The size of the type page is 37 by 48 picas.